PIONEER

OF

INNER SPACE

Fitz Hugh Ludlow New York

(SCHAFFER LIBRARY, UNION COLLEGE)

COLLECTED WORKS OF
FITZ HUGH LUDLOW

VOLUME 7

PIONEER

OF

INNER SPACE :

THE LIFE OF
FITZ HUGH LUDLOW,
WITH COLLECTED LETTERS
AND POETRY

BY DONALD P. DULCHINOS

EDITED BY
DONALD P. DULCHINOS
STEPHEN CRIMI

COLLECTED WORKS OF FITZ HUGH LUDLOW
VOLUME 7
PIONEER OF INNER SPACE: THE LIFE OF FITZ HUGH LUDLOW
BY DONALD P. DULCHINOS
WITH COLLECTED LETTERS AND POETRY

EDITED BY DONALD P. DULCHINOS AND STEPHEN CRIMI

LOGOSOPHIA, LLC
90 Oteen Church Road
Asheville, NC 28805
www.logosophiabooks.com
logosophiabooks@gmail.com

Library of Congress-in-Publication Data
Dulchinos, Donald P.
Collected Works of Fitz Hugh Ludlow, Volume 7: Pioneer of Inner Space: The Life of Fitz Hugh Ludlow with Collected Letters and Poetry

ISBN 978-0-9966394-9-1
Distributed by Small Press Distribution
Non-Fiction

Cover design by Jack E. Taylor
Interior layout and design by Susan Yost

INTRODUCTION TO
LOGOSOPHIA EDITION

FITZ HUGH LUDLOW burst on the literary scene in 1857 with the unlikely best seller *The Hasheesh Eater*. Written when he was just 20 years old, the book swept Ludlow into a career as a prolific novelist, short story author, arts critic, travel writer, journalist and editor. His friends and colleagues ranged from Walt Whitman to Brigham Young to Mark Twain. The material published in Ludlow's Collected Works displays a depth of observation, a breadth of erudition and an appetite for extreme experience applied to the emerging modern American nation.

Pioneer of Inner Space began with the discovery by its author that Fitz Hugh Ludlow wrote a lot more than *The Hasheesh Eater*. But starting a biography of a famous drug user in the Just Say No decade was daunting. As he wrote:

> The 1980s were sobering for the Union graduate. The backlash at what seemed an innocuous dalliance with marijuana was enormous in the "Just Say No" decade. Early in that decade, the graduate returned to visit Union, and found the school had instituted an annual event called Fitz Hugh Ludlow Day. One of its early themes was to have fun without drinking; it coincided with the raising of the drinking age from 18 to 21. Most of the Union students (with the exception of the Kappa Alpha members) had little acquaintance with or interest in Ludlow. Some of them were members of SADD, Students

Against Drunk Driving, a stance unthinkable to hell-raisers of earlier times. The ebb and flow of social attitudes toward altered states of consciousness seemed destined to continue, and perhaps *The Hasheesh Eater* is a barometer of these.

Indeed, the author now resides in Colorado, where cannabis is now completely legal, and it is no accident that our compilation of Ludlow's collected works coincides with yet another turn in social attitudes.

Academic attitudes have changed somewhat as well. As pure literature, academics have not found further interest in *The Hasheesh Eater*. But some trends in academia have led to more recent interest. The first new edition of *The Hasheesh Eater* since 1989 came out from Rutgers University Press in 2006, edited by and with extremely informative annotations from Stephen Rachman at Michigan State University. This edition was presented as "A Volume in the Subterranean Lives: Chronicles of Alternative America Series." And so, some portion of a new generation of English professors has emerged with more sympathy to the outlook.

Along those lines, a recent popular history called *Rebel Souls, Walt Whitman and America's First Bohemians,* by Justin Martin, featured Ludlow among the many denizens of Pfaff's restaurant, citing *Pioneer of Inner Space*, but was equally unable to identify any specific Ludlow writings in the Bohemians' home journal, *The Saturday Press*. Online, Lehigh University created a web site called *The Vault at Pfaff's*, with biographical facts on Ludlow and the other Bohemians, and links to some Ludlow transcripts that are available online. And perhaps most poetic and most gratifying, Harvard's Houghton Library, named after the publisher of Ludlow's *The Heart of the Continent*, is now home to the collections of the Fitz Hugh Ludlow Memorial Library, "the world's largest private collection of material documenting altered stated of mind".

As a popular matter, there have been no other new editions of *The Hasheesh Eater*, possibly due to the advent of digital, print-on-demand publishers who have raided the public domain. A scan of Amazon.com will yield offers of a Kindle edition, a compendium of the book with others and called a "Substance Abuse Six-Pack," and print-on-demand offers from companies like *Theophania Press* or *Forgotten Books*.

Only two new major sets of Ludlow writing were finally found by the author thanks to the ongoing digitization of 19th century books, newspapers and magazines. The first source being the HathiTrust research project, which is an amazing resource. The second source is the result of the net-enabled proliferation of genealogy research outfits.

The first new discovery is a series of papers describing life and habits among the men's clubs of New York, "Evenings at the Club" in the *New York Commercial Advertiser*. These certainly provide interesting perspectives on the upper crust of mid-century New York City, coming from a hustling journalist who would finally be invited to join the Century Club after his triumphant appearances in the *Atlantic Monthly* in 1865.

The second is a series of three short stories in *Harper's Weekly* newspaper, Ludlow's first fiction publication. These stories are less biographical and somewhat more derivative of other light fiction of the time. So again, nothing that changes our views of Ludlow's writing or career.

The last somewhat surprising discovery is a Ludlow poem called "Socrates Snooks", a humorous item that only survives in an anthology called *The Best Loved Poems of the American*

People, edited by Hazel Felleman of the *New York Times* in 1936 and more or less in print to the present day. There is no source for its original publication in that anthology, and the author has found no other reference in all the research for the biography or the collected works.

The poems of Ludlow are included in this volume. Many of them are unpublished, clustered around his college years and ranging from humorous to somewhat sententious. Perhaps only "Too Late", written in his declining years, is deeply felt and holds up well.

This volume also reproduces all of Ludlow's surviving letters in their entirety. Ludlow's personal papers have never surfaced. Consequently, many of the suggestions in letters that he wrote are missing the context of ongoing conversations between Ludlow and his major and minor literary friends and acquaintances.

After almost twenty years, and with assistance from the Internet, the author expected more in the nature of discoveries of biographical facts that had eluded him in the pre-digital research of the 1980's and 1990's. But the essential arc of Ludlow's life as described in *Pioneer of Inner Space* is intact. None of the intriguing questions—what was the great trauma of his sister Helen's broken engagement? what moral crime did Lizzie Stoddard accuse Ludlow of?—have been answered.

There are mildly interesting notes and ads in various digitized newspapers for Ludlow's lecture career following the Western trip with Bierstadt, and "celebrity" observations of his being at the Elmira Water Cure, or taking time off and "rusticating on Fire Island." (A selection of these clippings is included in this volume as Appendix 2.)

One significant new finding was that Bierstadt was the one who nominated Ludlow to the Century Club, his entry into full respectability in New York society. (There also came information that Ludlow himself nominated an old Union College KA brother, Warring Wilkinson for membership. Wilkinson taught for many years at the NY Institution for the Deaf and Dumb, which partly explains the plot of Ludlow's story "The Music Essence". Wilkinson soon after founded the California Institution for the Deaf, Dumb and Blind, which he led until 1909.)

Finding Bierstadt's nomination only makes his betrayal a little more poignant. In the aftermath of Ludlow's divorce and his ex-wife's remarriage to Bierstadt, Ludlow was relieved of his Century Club membership (but not Bierstadt!).

And finally, another new discovery sheds further light on the Ludlow/Bierstadt scandals. This finding was newspaper reports of Ludlow's testimony in the McFarland murder trial, the so-called Murder by Gaslight. Daniel McFarland, whose wife left him, murdered Albert Richardson, an editor at the *New York Tribune*. Richardson was set to marry the woman, who may or may not have been divorced by then. McFarland and his wife were acquaintances of Ludlow, who testified among other things that McFarland had been mentally unbalanced prior to the shooting, and so might be innocent by reason of insanity. The prosecution then put Fitz Hugh's reputation on trial. As the *Newark Courier* reported,

Domestic infelicities are about as common ills as flesh is heir to. In the McFarland trial, Fitz Hugh Ludlow, an author of some note, was placed upon the stand, and certain questions pertaining to conjugal propriety were submitted for his elucidation. At the close, Judge Davis asked that Witness if he was a married man, and received an affirmative answer. He then stated his intention of showing that Mr. Ludlow, while married, eloped with another woman to Kansas, and various other interesting particulars of his matrimonial irregularities; but the court interposed and forbade it. The fact that Ludlow's former wife procured a divorce from him and subsequently married Bierstadt the artist, shows one of two things; that either that gentleman was guilty of some criminal conduct justifying a divorce, or else that his family position is a counterpart of McFarland's. Hence, should the latter be the case, will not the acquittal of McFarland justify Ludlow in shooting Bierstadt at sight? Things are getting very decidedly mixed in and around this trial.

Elsewhere, this case and Ludlow's testimony led to the *Hudson Star* characterizing both Ludlow and first wife Rosalie as holding to "The Monstrous Doctrine of Free Love." Recalling that this was the era of transcendentalists and other experimental communities suggesting extra-marital affairs were acceptable, it's interesting to speculate how the Mormons with multiple wives could have led to Ludlow and Bierstadt to conclude there would be no problem with adultery. But when Ludlow was caught out, Bierstadt may have been delighted to pick up the pieces. Could he even have talked Ludlow into making the first move?

From this story then, we may expect that further digging into the digitized files of the 19th century may yet lead to other insights and revelations into the life of an already complex and intriguing man of letters, Fitz Hugh Ludlow.

CONTENTS

I.

LOST AND FOUND

AT Union College in Schenectady, New York, in 1975, a 19-year-old undergraduate majoring in economics developed a strong interest in recreational drugs and their effect on the mind—an interest common to students in the 1970s, albeit one already becoming more scarce. The undergraduate joined an organization known as the Kappa Alpha Society, the first Greek letter social fraternity in the country. Learning something of its history as part of the initiation requirement, he was introduced to an alumnus of the organization, Fitz Hugh Ludlow, class of 1856 at Union. Ludlow was still honored by the school as the author of the college alma mater, and of a peculiar book called *The Hasheesh Eater*, published in 1857. Reading the book, the undergraduate was delighted to find it a fully detailed rendering of the twenty-year-old author's experiences, over a hundred years before, with the drug hashish, then legal and part of the primitive pharmacopoeia of the day. The ornate prose of the book reflected a breadth of classical learning, but the student was equally struck by the Kappa Alpha members' emphasis on Ludlow's ties to Mark Twain. They asserted that Twain would publish nothing without Ludlow's review and approval. The undergraduate joined Kappa Alpha, and eventually graduated Union.

After graduation, the student found a copy of *The Hasheesh Eater* recently published by an organization called the

Fitz Hugh Ludlow Memorial Library. This was even more intriguing. The book contained a significant amount of biographical material, quotes about Ludlow including a paean from Twain, and details of a varied and intriguing career after the publication of the best-selling *The Hasheesh Eater*. A year later, the Union graduate came across a short story by Ludlow in a turn-of-the-century anthology in the Denver Public Library.

These discoveries sparked the graduate to compile Ludlow's bibliography, a list which eventually grew to number some 130 items. Ludlow's career lasted only thirteen years before his death in 1870, a death attributed by some to opium addiction. The bibliography reflected a varied literary career as short-story writer, journalist, music and drama critic, lay science-writer, playwright and travel raconteur. His bread and butter was romance, formulaic stories and novels that were nevertheless sprinkled with dry wit and topical commentary. A childlike whimsy seemed to bubble underneath the erudition, and surfaced in poems, drawings, and even a dramatic adaptation of Cinderella used to raise money for the Civil War wounded—his various writings had evidently secured him recognition among New York's high society.

Many of Ludlow's short stories were published in the satiric journals of the Bohemian subculture that was just emerging, such as *Vanity Fair* and the *Saturday Press*. Walt Whitman was a famous fellow-reveler in the Pfaff's Restaurant coterie of fugitive journalists and ne'er-do-wells in pre-Civil War New York City. And yet this dissolute company served as an odd counterpoint to Ludlow's most compelling stories, meditations that turned on religious themes, a preoccupation inherited from his Abolitionist preacher father. Even the hashish journeys were interpreted in a Christian (as well as Transcendentalist) context.

The search unearthed another full-length book, *The Heart of the Continent*. As a travel writer, Ludlow explored the far reaches of America, Florida in the South and California to the West. His first-hand reports of the Western frontier were used by both the Smithsonian Institution and the Wells Fargo Company to further their interests in Manifest Destiny. Ludlow's stagecoach trip across the Great Divide appeared to be the watershed of his life in many ways. The Civil War had interrupted his slowly maturing fiction-writing career, and his turn toward descriptive and scientific writing derailed the further crafting of his natural storytelling gifts. Further, his partner on the Western trip, painter Albert Bierstadt, not only turned great canvases of Rocky Mountain splendor into a millionaire's lifestyle, but contended shortly thereafter for the love of Ludlow's own wife. *The Heart of the Continent*, not published until months before the author's death, returned to print as one of a series of books of Americana in 1971, a hundred years after its first publication. It remains a comprehensive contemporary view of the American West at the very beginning of its exploitation. But like *The Hasheesh Eater*, it fell into obscurity with the author's death.

Ludlow's place in history, or lack thereof, puzzled the Union graduate. *The Hasheesh Eater* was published in the 1850s, the decade of *Moby Dick*, *The Scarlet Letter*, *Uncle Tom's Cabin*, *Walden*, and *Leaves of Grass*, "one of the most revitalizing periods of genius in American literature."[1] *The Hasheesh Eater* was almost as revolutionary in its own right. The young graduate thought that there clearly existed a substantial enough body of work to warrant a larger footnote in the history of literature. Yet it became apparent from his research that academia had paid scant attention to Ludlow. A professor at Union had assembled a short pamphlet on his life, filled with biographical misinformation and a dim view of Ludlow's importance and propriety, perhaps not surprising in the staid 1950s. Three students had completed theses on Ludlow over the past 65 years, and only one of these attempted any real analysis. Yet even in this meager consideration came one critical tribute to *The Hasheesh Eater*, from Cornell professor Morris Bishop: "This is a considerable literary achievement."[2]

And so the investigation continued. The investigation included a visit to Michael Horowitz, an antiquarian bookseller and scholar of drug literature (also father of actress Winona Ryder, and friend of Timothy Leary, Winona's godfather.) Horowitz himself had come across *The Hasheesh Eater* in his bookselling rounds in the early 1960s, and was astonished to find a full-length treatment of drug use of that age, and one that was not a diatribe against use of the drug. The Beatniks had discovered Ludlow, reprinting *The Hasheesh Eater* in a broadside in 1960 alongside the works of Kerouac, Ginsberg and Jean-Paul Sartre, and passed on the knowledge to the Hippie generation, through publication of the book by Beat icon City Lights Books. Horowitz ultimately founded the Fitz Hugh Ludlow Memorial Press, and published the book himself.

Excerpts and analyses of *The Hasheesh Eater* appeared in half a dozen books on the Sixties' drug scene, as well as in the *Berkeley Barb*, the dean of the underground newspapers. Timothy Leary himself provided a sort of benediction, while living in exile in Switzerland after a prison escape. Reflecting upon other famous exiles to Switzerland, he placed himself in "the alchemic-shaman tradition of Paracelsus, Ludlow and William James."[3] (Ludlow died in Switzerland.)

Tracing Ludlow back further in time, the Union grad found that *The Hasheesh Eater*, after four editions prior to the Civil War, disappeared for forty years until a reprinting by a British publisher in 1903, with illustrations by Aubrey Beardsley. That edition caught the attention of two great eccentrics of the early twentieth century, Aleister Crowley and H.P. Lovecraft.

Crowley was a self-styled adept in the occult arts, a member of the Golden Dawn group that once claimed poet W.B. Yeats for a member. Crowley's search for ceremonial magic techniques had led him to yoga and other Eastern practices. He was familiar with tales of hashish use when he came upon Ludlow's work. He reprinted large portions of it in his journal, *The Equinox*, and recommended its usefulness as a textbook. "The fact, never witnessed by me before, of a mind in that state being able to give its phenomena to another and philosophise about them calmly, afforded me the means of a most clear investigation."[4]

H.P. Lovecraft, the writer of supernatural fiction, was once queried as to whether he'd read Ludlow's *The Hasheesh Eater*. He replied: "I possess it upon mine own shelves, and would not part with it for any inducement whatever." He went on to say that he had "frequently reread those phantasmagoria of exotic colour, which proved more of a stimulant to my own fancy than any vegetable alkaloid ever grown and distilled."[5]

Ludlow and his best-seller surfaced again in 1937, during the anti-marijuana crusade of Harry Anslinger, commissioner of the Federal Bureau of Narcotics. (Incidentally, *marijuana* was the name given to the plant by yellow journalists of the era to feed on racist fears—it was more commonly known as hemp.) Dr. Robert Walton of the University of Mississippi, at the request of the government, produced a sober analysis of the drug and included a lengthy discussion of *The Hasheesh Eater*, commending it as a sophisticated medical case history.[6] Dr. Walton's conclusions about the dangers of pot were mixed (and even the AMA testified against criminalizing hemp) but Anslinger was uninterested in scientific debate, and led a campaign of misinformation and hysteria (immortalized in the film *Reefer Madness*) which resulted in marijuana being made illegal in 1938.

Walton's attention to Ludlow as medical commentator was perceptive. Ludlow had published the first serious essay on opium addiction in America, and then helped edit a book, *The Opium Habit*, that contained Ludlow's suggested regimen for treating opium addiction, a regimen derived from his own entanglement with the drug and informed by his years of struggle with alcoholism. *The Opium Habit* returned to print in 1981 as one of the Arno Press' "Addiction in America" series, anticipating the recovery movement of the 1980s. Moreover, Ludlow's serial-magazine novel *The Household Angel* pioneered a view of alcohol as something other than a moral failing. Alas, *The Household Angel* was never published in book form. These two books lay forgotten for a hundred years, predictably perhaps, in view of twentieth-century American views of drugs. It was apparently easier to treat such ideas as simply taboo until the effects of abuse became too great to ignore.

Ludlow's opium essay and follow-up book were influential with opium users and brought him an enormous volume of correspondence. He understood them in part because he understood the attraction, and was able to bring to bear a keen analytical mind and a sympathetic heart to plans for treatment. He died before putting such plans in place, and in an ironic turn of events was embroiled in the scheme of a snake oil salesman peddling an opium "cure."

The 1980s were sobering for the Union graduate. The backlash at what seemed an innocuous dalliance with marijuana was enormous in the "Just Say No" decade. Early in that decade, the graduate returned to visit Union, and found the school had instituted an annual event called Fitz Hugh Ludlow Day. One of its early themes was to have fun without drinking; it coincided with the raising of the drinking age from 18 to 21. Most of the Union students (with the exception of the Kappa Alpha members) had little acquaintance with or interest in Ludlow. Some of them were members of SADD, Students Against Drunk Driving, a stance unthinkable to hellraisers of earlier times. The ebb and flow of social attitudes toward altered states of consciousness seemed destined to continue, and perhaps *The Hasheesh Eater* is a barometer of these.

The curators of the Fitz Hugh Ludlow Memorial Libr*y, in storage since the '60s, have recently held discussions with the Albert Hofmann Foundation, one of a number of drug policy and consciousness study organizations that sprang up in seeming defiance of the War on Drugs, to find a new home for its collections. *The Hasheesh Eater* saw print once more in 1989, and was serialized in 1992 in a new magazine, *Psychedelic Illuminations*.

And as it appeared to him that Ludlow's place in American history will never permanently fade into obscurity, the Union graduate, class of 1978, thought it fitting to compile a biography, in hopes of shedding a little light on an unusual, but apparently very durable and very American man of letters, Fitz Hugh Ludlow.

1 Michael Horowitz, ed., *The Hasheesh Eater*, Fitz Hugh Ludlow Memorial Library Press, San Francisco, 1975, p. iv.

2 Morris Bishop, "Fitzhugh Ludlow," in Fitz Hugh Ludlow, Union Worthies Number Eight, Schenectady, NY: Union College, 1953, p. 17.

3 Quoted in *The Hasheesh Eater*, San Francisco: Level Press, 1975.

4 Crowley, Aleister, "The Psychology of Hashish," *The Equinox*, Volume I, No. 4, September, 1910, p. 241.

5 *H.P. Lovecraft: Selected Letters*, Ed. by August Derleth and Donald Wandrei, Sauk City, WI: Arkham House, 1965, p. 118, 206.

6 Robert Walton, *Marihuana: America's New Drug Problem*, Philadelphia: Lippincott, 1938.

LUDLOW FAMILY TREE

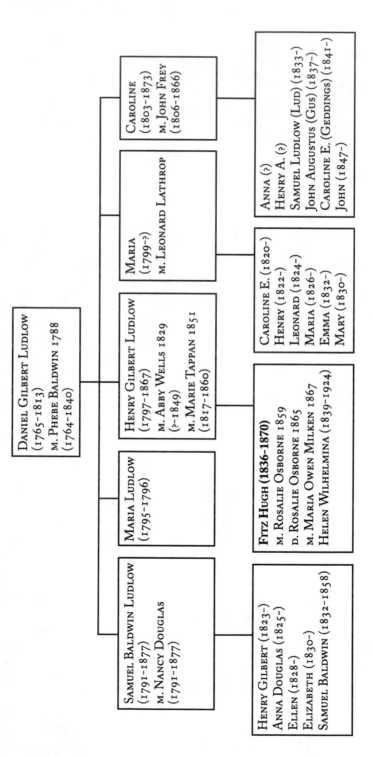

DANIEL GILBERT LUDLOW
(1765–1813)
M. PHEBE BALDWIN 1788
(1764–1840)

SAMUEL BALDWIN LUDLOW
(1791–1877)
M. NANCY DOUGLAS
(1791–1877)

MARIA LUDLOW
(1795–1796)

HENRY GILBERT LUDLOW
(1797–1867)
M. ABBY WELLS 1829
(?–1849)
M. MARIE TAPPAN 1851
(1817–1860)

MARIA
(1799–?)
M. LEONARD LATHROP

CAROLINE
(1803–1873)
M. JOHN FREY
(1806–1866)

HENRY GILBERT (1823–)
ANNA DOUGLAS (1825–)
ELLEN (1828–)
ELIZABETH (1830–)
SAMUEL BALDWIN (1832–1858)

FITZ HUGH (1836–1870)
M. ROSALIE OSBORNE 1859
D. ROSALIE OSBORNE 1865
M. MARIA OWEN MILKEN 1867
HELEN WILHELMINA (1839–1924)

CAROLINE E. (1820–)
HENRY (1822–)
LEONARD (1824–)
MARIA (1826–)
EMMA (1832–)
MARY (1830–)

ANNA (?)
HENRY A. (?)
SAMUEL LUDLOW (LUD) (1833–)
JOHN AUGUSTUS (GUS) (1837–)
CAROLINE E. (GEDDINGS) (1841–)
JOHN (1847–)

II.

THE ROOTS OF ECSTASY

FITZ HUGH LUDLOW's grandfather was Daniel Gilbert Ludlow, born in 1765. Daniel was married to Phoebe Baldwin (b. 1864), whose surname would later grace several generations of the Ludlow family. In addition to farming, Daniel ran a saddler's shop, and later a country store, in the village of Kinderhook, along the Hudson River in upstate New York, about twenty miles south of Albany. Daniel was highly respected in Kinderhook, acquiring the partly honorary titles of Postmaster and Judge.

Daniel and Phoebe were "people eminent for their Christian excellence."[1] Their son recollected his mother as a "very devoted woman, and Christian." But Daniel, "like everyone else in those days, was accustomed to drink freely of spiritous liquors—no one thought of total abstinence as a virtue, and no one practiced it."[2] This directly contradicts a later description of Daniel as "a pioneer of the Temperance movement, who by his counsel and example anticipated the organized effort of reform by nearly a quarter of a century."[3] If both of these are true descriptions, then the lifelong conflict in Fitz Hugh Ludlow between devout, and even aggressive Christianity and his "habits of stimulus" had its roots two generations and some fifty years before his birth.

Daniel and Phoebe Ludlow's second son, Henry Gilbert, was born in 1797. Thirty-nine years later, Henry's wife would give birth to Fitz Hugh Ludlow. Phoebe's brother

11

Samuel Baldwin was a man of more formal learning, "one of the most accomplished scholars of his day," according to one report.[4] Baldwin took a hand in the early education of young Henry, although the "Little Judge" was often criticized as "gay, airy and thoughtless."[5] Fitz Hugh's sister would say, in later years, "Between father and son there were many points of resemblance."[6]

After Daniel Ludlow's death, and despite doubts about "his diligence and love of learning," Henry became a student in the law office of his older brother Samuel.[7] Through Samuel's efforts, Henry was admitted to study at Princeton. But the watershed event in Henry G. Ludlow's life came in April 1820. He described it in a remarkable letter to an old friend, Mr. William Niles of South Hadley, Massachusetts, on June 24:

> I am extremely fortunate in having it in my power to communicate to you the pleasing intelligence that I have made a public profession of Religion, after having experienced a very great change of heart—You can hardly believe it, but so it is, your old friend who was one of the most giddy and vile sinners you ever knew has been arrested in mid career and plucked as he verily believes...from the burning—At Nassau there has been a very great revival under the labours of the Rev. Asahel Nettleton, a man famous for revivals wherever he goes. More than 100—about 116 in the village and the next adjoining town of Schodack have within the last 8 or 9 weeks become hopeful converts—Among them myself and Mr. Mason... You have always wished that such a change in me might take place—If any one wanted it I did. Five weeks ago today I left Lebanon for this place [Nassau] having a desire to experience a change. I found Mr. Mason in some distress and immediately joined with him in an address to the throne of grace. We continued in prayer all of Thursday night and pretty much

all of Friday. On Friday evening I for the first time discovered the coldness of my heart and wept bitterly. Mr. Nettleton prayed with me. I determined to give my eyes no sleep until I found rest in Christ. The great adversary of Saul however lulled me to rest and I slept soundly that night. The sun rose and I awoke alarmed at my hardness—went to see Mason and found that he had experienced no relief—I came to the conclusion that I had better return to New Lebanon, believing that there was no blessing in store for me. At the table Mr. N. and others were conversing upon the case of a young acquaintance of mine who that morning after a night of distress had found relief. The Spirit brought it home to my heart and I arose from my half finished meal, went to my chamber, threw myself to the floor and determined to wrestle with Jacob until I prevailed like Israel. The Lord blessed the resolution and I remained in this position under considerable distress until 1 P.M. when God in his mercy gave me relief—Oh my dear Mr. N. what joy was in that moment—I arose a new creature in Christ and continue to love him yet—Never did I know before what it was to be happy...

I have only room to say that I have sold all to follow Christ— And in a few weeks expect to take my departure from Princeton to prepare for the ministry.[8]

Henry immediately became active in the revival work, possibly allied with Dr. Nettleton, in Coxsackie, N.Y. By August, he had moved to Newark, New Jersey and wrote a long letter to his soon-to-be sister-in-law Nancy Douglass, back in New Lebanon, describing the strange circumstances and bizarre behavior of his first three months as a Christian:

My dear sister Nancy may accuse me of inattention to my engagements and neglect of my friends with some degree of propriety but did she know the state of my mind which like a shipwrecked mariner is tossing upon the wide ocean of uncertainty and at times despair she would no doubt forgive me…At times I am almost deranged…My eyes assumed the terrific appearance of a maniac. My whole frame was at times convulsed and I resembled rather the inhabitant of a Bedlam than a being whose intellectual faculties are in operation. In conformity with the wishes of my dear mother and the advice of our family physician I started last Friday for this place.

The humbling circumstances of my late disappointed hopes in conjunction with the belief that I am still the object of God's indignation conspire to derange my intellect and ruin my health. I came here to study preparatory to my entering upon the ministry. Think then how I must feel after I have disposed of all to follow Christ to find myself still a rebel against the majesty of Heaven…How long I shall stay here is uncertain. There is such a deadness here in matters of religion that I am fearful of its consequences as it respects myself.[9]

Henry had been caught up in what some historians call the Second Great Awakening, a wave of religious excitement that spawned dozens of new sects, ranging from the Shakers to the Mormons, and which left upstate New York with the sobriquet, the Burnt District.[10] While Henry was not alone in his experience, he was unusual in the intensity of his conversion, as revealed in this letter. Convulsions wrack the faithful even at modern-day revivals, but for them to continue long after the revivals indicates at the very least an enormously excitable temperament. Such extraordinary sensitivity, not to mention suggestibility, were surely passed on to his son Fitz Hugh, at least potentially. And in Henry's latter-day sermons, his impressionable son must have been at least subconsciously convinced of his own special destiny as a vessel of, if not God, at least some supernatural force.

Henry entered the Princeton Theological Seminary in 1821. Soon after, he told his mother, "it does appear as though He does not intend that I ever shall go through a long course of study preparatory to my entering upon the duties of the ministry."[11] He then described his revival work in Wilmington, Delaware (where he had gone for relaxation) and the saving of sixty or so souls. Henry did finish at Princeton in early 1824, but his early successes almost led him to destroy his ministerial career before it began. In 1826, Henry was preaching in New York City, at the Broome Street Presbyterian Church, while its regular pastor was in Europe. The time had arrived for his ordination into the priesthood but, as a product of first-hand divine intervention, he was disturbed with some of the doctrine contained in the Confession of Faith.

On the day of his ordination, "just before meeting, I went into my closet to dedicate myself anew to God, when my conscience was again aroused and with such power that I could not resist it." When the hour came, in front of a large congregation and many friends, the pastor put the question to Henry of whether he subscribed to the Confession of Faith. Henry paused and said, "I cannot subscribe unconditionally. I agree with it in all fundamental points and those essential to salvation, but there are some minor ones with which I disagree." The old pastor was flabbergasted, halted all further proceedings, and dismissed the congregation in an uproar. Meanwhile, Henry sat down "in a sweet calm of conscious integrity."

After some difficult negotiations, Henry was finally accepted and "set apart to the office of an Evangelist" on September 26, 1826, in a church in Hartford, Connecticut.

"What shall I render to the Lord who has counted me faithful putting me into the ministry? My soul, body, & spirit." As if to confirm his direction, Henry there met the woman who was to become his wife, Abby W. Welles, a relative of President Woolsey of Yale. In April of 1826, Henry became pastor of the Presbyterian Church on Spring St. in New York City. In late fall of 1829, Henry married Abby.

A year later, "Our prospects of *increase* are brightening daily." Abby became pregnant, and "if God spare my dear wife I hope to make you [Henry's mother] another fine present before many months. She enjoys fine health and is much better than she has ever been since our marriage." The fear of God was not a perfunctory inclusion. The same letter relates the horrors of an outbreak of scarlet fever in the city, and Henry's somewhat impoverished congregation was hard hit. He sadly tells of his mentor, Reverend Dr. Samuel Cox, burying three children in one week (ages 5, 3, and 2), two of them buried in one grave. "The influenza has been very general and very fatal." Six months later, tragedy struck home. Abby, weakened by cholera, gave birth to a son who died almost immediately. Abby herself was in danger, but survived. Henry's grief was mixed with zealotry.

> Thus, dear mother, has the cloud passed over and sunshine throws its radiance around us. Our little Son was a fine boy and parental love desires his society. But good has done right and acted in love by taking him away. We were altogether unprepared to receive such a blessing if he had been spared. Our sins too needed the blow which has been inflicted. If God in mercy accompanies it with the influence of his Spirit we shall doubtless find that his mercy was greater in taking than in giving...I have long needed His afflicting rod and anything short of unmingled damnation is pure rich mercy.[12]

Henry and Abby then spent two months in Brooklyn Heights, a pastoral spot as likely to escape the plague as any "in the midst of this valley of the shadow of death." As people began to return to the city at the end of August, Henry attempted to find meaning in the suffering. He hoped that people would turn to Christ in response to the tragedy, and hoped it would not cause people to "act like the Pharaoh and harden their hearts when the thunderings and lightnings cease." At the same time, Henry also took a positively savage view that "A vast deal [*sic*] of moral filth has been swept away—Probably 2,500 drunkards and debauchers of every class and both sexes have been removed…The cause of temperance will doubtless receive a mighty impulse. If men can now proceed in the murderous traffick of vending ardent spirits, the world will call them murderers. Doubtless the children of these wretches will be more carefully educated than if their parents had lived…the cholera has been the result of wisdom and love…few useful lives have been taken." Even allowing for his paternal grief, this attitude probably did not mellow appreciably by the time he had to account for the stimulant-using habits of his son, Fitz Hugh.

After these personal trials, the Reverend Henry Ludlow took a prominent role in a national drama. Along with temperance, the movement for the abolition of slavery was gaining increasing support in the U.S. In New York, Henry Ludlow was part of a group, including industrialists Lewis and Arthur Tappan and Dr. Cox, which spoke out for abolition (a group "only less stellar than that led by William Lloyd Garrison in Boston.")[13] Henry had first been a supporter of the so-called American Colonization Society, whose aim was to restore the slaves to their homeland by sending them to Liberia. Immediate abolition, however, gained strength as Tappan, Ludlow and the rest linked the urban, industrial, antislavery movement to the rural, revivalist, Presbyterian orthodoxy. They then tried to ally themselves with the much-larger benevolent societies, and led a boycott of the Colonization Society. This outraged a wealthy philanthropist member of the Colonization Society, Gerrit Smith, who was to become important to Henry Ludlow and his family very soon afterward.

REV. HENRY G. LUDLOW, CIRCA 1830.

Tension and enthusiasm raced side by side through New York, and through Henry Ludlow, in 1833 and 1834. The British parliament formally abolished slavery in August, 1833. In December, Garrison and the Tappans united to form the National Anti-Slavery Society. On May 10, 1834, Henry Ludlow opened a New York meeting of the Anti-Slavery Society with a prayer, after which several men, including Dr. Cox, spoke and "appeared to be glowing with zeal for the holy cause to which they are devoted."[14] *The Liberator* newspaper reported the following minutes:

> Mr. Robert Purvis moved that a subscription and collection now be taken up in aid of the Anti-Slavery Society.
> Rev. Henry G. Ludlow seconded the resolution. He did it with the more satisfaction because he believed this meeting to be the funeral of colonization. He had formerly thought he was doing God service when aiding to expatriate the colored people and send them to the darkness of Africa to get light. But he now saw his error, and hoped to live to counteract it.
> The subscription and collection amounted to $2,360.[15]

Throughout the month of June, anti-abolitionist feelings were stirred up by rumors circulated in the press, notably the *New York Courier*.[16] William Green, Vice President of the Anti-Slavery Society, was alleged to have invited black men to his home in order to introduce them to his spinster daughters.[17] Reverend Dr. Cox had supposedly called Jesus Christ a black man from the pulpit. Another version of the story had him remark that Jesus, being born in an "Oriental" land, was probably of "swarthy complexion, who, if living in this country, might not be received into good society."[18] In either case, Cox denied saying it a week later. Henry was not overlooked. He was accused of officiating at the marriage of a white woman and a black man and encouraging such unions. Anti-abolitionist feeling may have been due to more than just bigotry and ignorance. The cholera epidemic of a year past had left a scar of fear on the populace, and high unemployment raised added fears of new competition for jobs, were slaves to be freed. The intermarriage issue was an appeal to the worst instincts of an already wounded city.

The storm broke on the 58th anniversary of American independence. A traditional parade on the Fourth celebrated New York State Emancipation Day, and was known for drinking and rowdiness on the part of free Blacks. Lewis Tappan and other embarrassed liberals of the time opened the Chatham St. Chapel (a large theatre converted to a church for the transient population of New York) for a "special Negro service" of commemoration. The proceedings began with "a fervent and peculiarly appropriate and feeling prayer by Reverend H.G. Ludlow of this city."[19] Henry's prayer was followed by the singing of a hymn written by poet John Greenleaf Whittier, and a reading of the Declaration of Independence. Then the mob arrived. Several orators were shouted down, over the calls of Dr. Cox for silence. Prayer books were thrown from the balconies, but a squad of police arrived to prevent further disruption.

Mobs continued to form and rumors to fly for the next several days. On Wednesday the seventh, a group of African Americans met at the Chatham St. Chapel. A white mob gathered there, then moved on the home of Lewis Tappan, threatening his family before being dispersed. The next night, a mob broke into the homes of Tappan and Dr. Cox, demolishing and burning furniture. Friday the 12th was bedlam. *The Liberator* reported as follows:

An immense crowd gathered at the Presbyterian Church in Spring St. of which Mr. Ludlow is pastor, and very deliberately prepared them-selves for a regular attack upon this edifice. A barricade of carts and wagons was placed across the street, in order to prevent the military and authorities from interfering with the designs of the multitude, who commenced a fire of stones and missiles at the church. By such means the doors and windows were broken, and the crowd made a rush for the interior. The building was instantly filled to overflowing, the organ pulpit and pews demolished, and the infuriated mob were in the act of tearing down the galleries when a troop of cavalry arrived and put an end to these proceedings. The mob then passed up Laurens St. to the house of the pastor, the Reverend Mr. Ludlow, whose family had retired. Here they broke in the windows and the doors, and did all the injury they thought proper, and left the grounds.

The extent of the damage which was done to the church is beyond calculation.

When asked the reason for the attacks, one rioter replied, "Why, Dr. Cox says our Saviour is a nigger, and ___ me if I don't think his church ought to be torn down."[20] Two black churches and some twenty houses were partly destroyed that night.

In following days, crowds collected near Henry's church, but were dispersed. No services were held by Henry that Sunday, and many black families had left town. Henry was shaken by this violent test of his faith. He removed Abby from the city, and then wrote a letter to the *Journal of Commerce* on July 25, published on August 9:

Gentlemen—Will you be so kind as to insert this communication in your paper? I regret very much the necessity of appearing in this manner before the public, but circumstances seem to render it unavoidable...

I perceive on perusing some of our newspapers, and have also been informed by my friends, that the rumor is abroad and credited too, that I have either in private or openly advanced the Amalgamation of the White and the Black people. And have given practical proof of my faith by marrying a white to a black. I wish to disabuse the community of the impressions made by these reports.

1. I did in my pulpit, no longer ago than on the Sabbath evening previous to the late excitement in New York, openly, and in the presence of a large congregation of our fellow citizens, oppose the doctrine of Amalgamation. I told them that my object was to prevent it. This is still my wish—and I neither desire nor expect it.

2. I have never been present at the marriage of a White to a Colored person, nor have I ever officiated as a minister on such an occasion, nor do I wish to do so.

As some of the public presses have been misinformed on the subject, and circulated these reports, I ask them, as an injured individual, to give equal publicity to this denial.

I wish also, while thus presenting myself before the public, to acknowledge my faults. In reviewing the history of the last few weeks, and inquiring into the occasions of the unhappy divisions existing between the Anti-Slavery and Colonization Societies, I feel that I am not guiltless. I owe it to that society as well as the public to say, that I went to the meeting of the Anti-Slavery Society in May, without any expectation of being called upon to speak. The resolution I seconded was put into my hand but a moment before I arose, and I uttered what I did under strong excitement. It was a perfectly impromptu, undigested and intemperate effusion, and I believe generally as much regretted by the Anti-Slavery as the Colonization Society. As soon as I had time to reflect, I repented of it, and confessed my fault wherever I had the opportunity. I number among the members of that institution some of the dearest friends and kindest benefactors I have on earth, whose funeral I should attend with as sincere sorrow as any Colonizationist would feel. Differing as I did from them, I ought not to have used language calculated to irritate but to sooth. I hope they will accept this public acknowledgement as the sincere confession of one who loves them still—of one who wishes to have no conflict with men, but with principles.

– H.G. LUDLOW

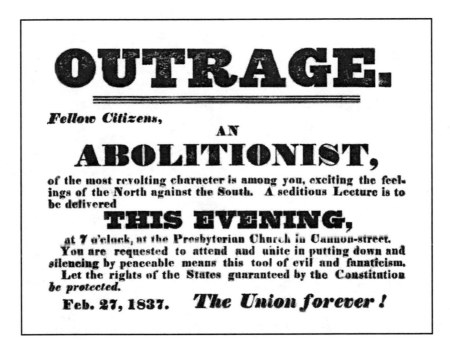

POSTER FROM THE HEIGHT OF THE ANTI-ABOLITIONIST MOVEMENT.

While this letter may reveal a wavering of conviction, neither Ludlow nor the rest were long deterred from their crusade. The following year found the ladies of Henry's church sponsoring a series of abolitionist meetings. Tappan led a group in ambitious publishing plans, including a series of four journals aimed at different audiences. One of these was a pamphlet entitled "Slavery in America," and contained a negative description of the Colonization Society, with an introduction by Cox. For his trouble, Cox, along with William Lloyd Garrison, was hung in effigy in 1835, although the violence of 1834 was never again approached.

This time of ferment was the environment in which Henry and Abby once again attempted to have a baby. Early in 1836, frail Abby Ludlow once more became pregnant. On September 11, 1836, Fitz Hugh Ludlow was born.

Fitz Hugh's christening was itself a product of Henry's zeal. His namesake was Fitzhugh Smith, the son of Gerrit Smith, a philanthropist and reformer, and indeed the same Gerrit Smith of the Colonization Society who was outraged by Henry Ludlow and other abolitionist "radicals" in 1832. Smith was drifting away from the Colonization Society by 1835, and after some appeals to his vanity he joined the upper New York State Anti-Slavery Society in November.[21] Smith's son Fitzhugh died at the age of 11 in July of 1836, and Gerrit Smith attempted to withdraw in grief from abolitionist activities. "The truth is my afflictions have unmanned me and I have not religion enough to rise up and go about my maker's business."[22] Indeed, he decided not to attend the first anniversary meeting of the New York State Anti-Slavery Society in October. Then he changed his mind, a reversal attributed to two emotional letters written by Smith's friends. Also in that interim, Henry Ludlow named his newborn son after Fitzhugh Smith, in September.

It was eminently rational and good in Henry's mind to treat the christening of his own son as another act in the crusade of righteousness. It was not the first or the last time ideology would take precedence over his personal life. The separation into two names (Fitz Hugh) is unexplained, unless by Henry's lack of a personal relationship with Gerrit Smith's family, which makes the christening all the more astonishing.[23]

The infant Fitz Hugh Ludlow soon grew to be a comfort to his troubled father. Henry wrote to his brother Samuel:

> This morning [October 27, 1837] we have been not a little amused by the trying efforts of our little son, not 13 m 15 d old, to run along. He made his first experiment last eve. and now with tottering step crosses the room. He is a sweet child and is improving in every way…when he is threatened with dangerous disease, as he was a day or two since with the croup…he is strongly entrenched in the core of our heart. He is better but still coughs a good deal.

But the boy was resilient. His sister later reported that when he was two, he "would climb upon the breakfast table and eat Cayenne pepper from the castor!"[24]

Fitz Hugh was something of a catalyst for his father's career, for in 1837 Henry took a new position as pastor of the Church Street Church of New Haven. Henry's welcome, however, was rather cold. On a visit to Hartford one day in October of 1837, Henry was mobbed and beaten for his abolitionist views in the town of Meriden, 17 miles north of New Haven. Henry continued nonetheless to travel in devotion to the cause throughout Fitz Hugh's infancy and early childhood. If anything, his abolitionist efforts were stepped up in New Haven. He continued to correspond with the New York abolitionists and became involved in the *Amistad* case.

A shipload of some 500 slaves mutinied, led by one of their number called Cinque.[25] They spared their slavemaster's life so he could navigate them back to Africa. The slaveholder attempted to steer them instead to a Southern slave state, and they ended up off the coast of Long Island Sound. There they were taken into custody by the Navy, and the slaves were charged with piracy, and incarcerated in the Ludlow's new home town, New Haven. Lewis Tappan, upon hearing of the case, arrived in New Haven to take up the cause. Tappan, Ludlow and others hired Yale divinity students to attempt to convert the "pagans." Stress upon religious training helped make the case a respectable cause for the involvement and support of the general public. Two lawyers responded to the cause, Theodore Sedgewick, of New York, and Roger Sherman Baldwin, of New Haven, the latter a recruit of Henry's, possibly related to his mother's family. The trial drew national interest, and as one observer put it, "The South is watching with deepest solicitude to see what disposal a Federal Court holding its session in a free State, will make of self-liberated black men who have asserted their rights Bunker-Hill fashion."[26]

The judge threw out the piracy and murder charges on the grounds of lacking jurisdiction over crimes committed against foreigners at sea. However, the prisoners remained in New Haven until the decision whether the slaveholders from Cuba could claim their property. Meanwhile, the slaveholders were countercharged with false imprisonment and placed in jail. The Africans' cause was supported by "gentlemen" who saw it as a safe cause, especially since the Africans had never officially become slaves and thus subject to the tolerance of the Federal government at the time. A letter of encouragement from John Quincy Adams appeared in the *Liberator*, alongside a letter from Henry commending the efforts of Sedgewick and Baldwin. Finally, the prisoners were absolved and ordered to be sent back to

Africa. Tappan and the rest delivered the news to the freed Africans, and Henry was there to offer up a prayer of thanks, which was translated into the Africans' native dialect. Tappan reported later that the Africans "followed him audibly, and with apparent devoutness."[27]

The year 1840 was a milestone for Henry in two other ways. His mother Phoebe died at age 76, and the Ludlow home became a way station on the Underground Railroad.[28] Young Fitz Hugh, at age four, met the first passenger, Isidore Smith. Henry immediately baptized him as "John Peterson" to protect his identity, and little Fitz Hugh held the bowl which served as a font. He later wrote "To this day I feel a sort of semi-accountability for John Peterson." John Peterson's painful history was impressed upon Fitz Hugh in a way words could not when the man stripped off his shirt. "All down his back were welts in which my father might lay his finger; and one gash healed with a scar into which I could put my small, boyish fist. The former were made by the whip and branding irons of a Virginia plantation—the latter by the teeth of his blood hounds. When I saw that black back I cried." John Peterson stayed with the Ludlow family several weeks before confiding that his wife and children had been left behind. He went back for them, and six months later returned with the family—and a horse stolen from a slaveholder's stable to boot.

Although Henry's public life went well, his private life was insecure. He writes in February of 1842, while introducing one of his pastoral students to a new congregation, that his wife Abby's health "is very infirm; and I fear never will be much better. She coughs incessantly and has a constant pain in her breast." Despite her infirmity, Abby was able to

bear a second child, Helen Wilhelmina, born to the Lud-
lows in 1839. Three years later, "Helen talks a great deal, and
quite sensibly."

Abby's poor health led Henry to hire a housekeeper, who
Fitz Hugh remembered as Polly Leet, the "first woman who
carried Puritanism into the kitchen."[29] "While she stayed
with us, Polly Leet and your then-infant correspondent, con-
tinued in a state of truceless war." The woman would protest
about making apple pie and other "luxuries" and was incensed
whenever Fitz Hugh attempted to enter the kitchen. In fact,
she was "so turbulent to me on occasion of my entering her
domain…that when I dreamt of the she bears who tore those
poor little babies for grumpy, evil-dispositioned old Elisha,
the biggest one always looked like Polly Leet with fur on."
Fitz Hugh relates at least one instance of childhood hijinks,
when he told Polly the wind had blown the laundry off the
clothesline, and used the diversion to swipe some sliced apples
that were slated for pie-making. Despite their uneasy coexis-
tence, Fitz Hugh remembered being nonetheless sad to see
her go when the time came for her to leave.

Six-year-old Fitz Hugh had already learned to read
"almost without help," and his father considered him
"a bright boy." The young Fitz Hugh was called upon to
entertain friends of his father by standing on a chair and
reciting poems. In fact, Henry was already holding theo-
logical discussions with the precocious Fitz Hugh. "I have
been talking to him of the love of Christ, and he evidently
felt the strong pressure of its obligations to love him. I told
him he might if he wished kneel and consecrate himself to
God, and he did it with a fullness and appropriateness of
expression, and an apparent sincerity of feeling that would

have surprised you and put to shame many an old professor in my church." The proud father reflected happily a moment before appending, "Still, I do not say or think he is a Christian." Henry's religious zeal and residual guilt over the death of his first son no doubt contributed to his intense scrutiny of Fitz Hugh's progress.

Henry's activism over the years had brought him some degree of fame, and if they took some toll on his family and attention to his children, they also alienated some of his parishioners. In February of 1842, he submitted his resignation from the Church St. Church in New Haven. In a formal statement, he denied any ill feelings, unhappiness or feelings of failure (noting that indeed the church had grown under his leadership) but that he did not wish to be "an obstacle in the way of your prosperity. It has been said that if I were out of the way, persons of influence would come to your aid." Apparently, Henry's abolitionism was too radical for some wealthy members of the community. In a letter, Henry confided somewhat bitterly that the church was in debt some $12,000, and "they hoped when they called me here that the *rich* would come in and help pay their debt." Henry closed this missive with an assurance that he had placed his faith in the Lord to see him through. However, as a practical matter, he asked in his resignation letter for payment of his salary through the next four months, and a letter of recommendation. The letter that was shortly forthcoming gushed with praise and included, at Henry's reminder, the fact that under his 4-year, 9-month tenure some 350 new members had joined the church.

Within a month, Henry was offered a position with the Presbyterian Church of Poughkeepsie, New York, at a salary of $1,200. His fame evidently had brought him many inquiries, and he felt Poughkeepsie's not only generous but from a congregation more advanced than New Haven's in "intelligence and property." He also allowed as how the climate would be "exactly suited to Abby's lungs." At the time, she had been confined to her room for several weeks.

The next seven years of Fitz Hugh's young life are largely undocumented, although he included several sketches of these years in his later short stories. He recollected making kites out of old *Commercial Advertiser* newspapers (considerably larger than present-day newspapers) attached to frames with thick flour paste.[30] He recalled less-pleasurable times in Sunday School, being told "there was a place for bad boys in the world to come—and with my head against the red-hot stove I could not doubt it."[31] One reminisce describes a boarding school which was populated by many children of Southerners:

> Aesthetically it was a good school. We wore kid gloves when we went to meeting, and sat in a gallery like a sort of steamer over the boiler, in which deacons and other large good people were stewing through long, hot Sunday afternoons. If we went to sleep, or ate cloves not to go to sleep, we were punched in the back with a real gold-headed cane. The cane we felt proud of, because it had been presented by the boys, and it was a perpetual compliment to us to see that cane go down the street with our principal after it; but nothing could have exceeded our mortification at being punched with it in full sight of the girls' school gallery opposite, we having our kid gloves on at the time, and in some instances coats with tails, like men.
>
> Among the large crowd of young Southerners sent to this school, I began preaching emancipation in my pinafore. Mounted upon a window-seat in an alcove of the great play-hall, I passed recess after recess in haranguing a multitude upon the subject of

Freedom, with as little success as most apostles, and with only less than their crown of martyrdom, because, though small boys are more malicious than men, they cannot hit so hard.

On one occasion, brought to bay by a sophism, I answered unwisely...A little Southerner turned on me fiercely and said, "Would you marry a nigger?"

Resolved to die by my premises, I gave a great gulp and said "Yes!"

Of course one general shout of derision ascended from the throng. Nothing but the ringing of the bell prevented me from accepting on the spot the challenge to a fist-fight of a boy whom [General Robert E.] Lee has since cashiered from his colonelcy for selling the commissions in his regiment.[32]

In *The Hasheesh Eater*, Fitz Hugh wrote this remembrance of childhood along the Hudson River:

A feeble childhood soon exhausted...superfluous activities, and into books, ill health and musing I settled down when I should have been playing cricket, hunting, or riding. The younger thirst for adventure was quenched by rapid degrees as I found it possible to ascend Chimborazo with Humboldt lying on a sofa, or chase harte-beests with Cumming over muffins and coffee. The only exceptions to this state of imaginative indolence were the hours spent in rowing or sailing upon the most glorious river of the world, and the consciousness that the Hudson rolled at my own door only contributed to settle the conviction that there was no need of going abroad to find beauties in which the soul might wrap itself as in a garment of delight. Even at these seasons exercise was not so much the aim as musing. Many a time, with the handles of my sculls thrust under the side-girders, and the blades turned full to the wind, have I sat and drifted for hours through mountain-shadows, and past glimpses of light that flooded the woody gorges, with a sense of dreamy ecstasy which all the novelties of a new world could never have supplied.

Gradually the Hudson came to supply all my spiritual wants. Were I sad, I found sympathy in the almost human murmurs of his waters, as, stretched upon the edge of some rocky headland, I heard them go beating into the narrow caves beneath me, and return sighing, as if defrauded of a hiding-place and a home. Were I merry, the white caps danced and laughed about my prancing boat, and the wind whistled rollicking glees against my stays. In weariness, I leaped into the stream; his cool hand upbore and caressed me till I returned braced for thought, and renewed as by a plunge into El Dorado. In the Hudson I found a wealth which satisfied all wishes, and my supreme hope was that on his banks I might pass all my life.[33]

Fitz Hugh's sister Helen added a few reminiscences:

His taste for literature showed itself from the time when, before he had learned to write, he printed little books of imaginary travel and history, copiously illustrated with sketches of his own. His favorite plays were imaginative, and like some other children of genius, he possessed a kingdom peopled by the creations of his fancy, though his little sister and himself were its only visible rulers and subjects. He was passionately alive to everything that thrilled his poetic sense, and fearless in gratifying it. When a mere child he was missed from the house during a violent thunder storm, and was at last discovered sitting on a fence in the drenching rain, "to watch the lighting." From his eleventh year he was in the habit of writing little poems which sometimes found their way into the newspapers and were always attributed to a maturer hand. At school he was a brilliant scholar, excelling in everything but mathematics for which he seems to have inherited from his father a hearty aversion. He was a favorite with teachers as well as the classmates whose leader he was in many a daring boyish exploit. In one of these, he swam across the Hudson at Poughkeepsie, before his parents knew that he had ever attempted a stroke.[34]

But ill health alternated with physical endurance in child-hood, and would throughout his later life. Fitz Hugh began wearing spectacles, and inviting teasing, at age twelve.

Fitz Hugh's childhood friends mostly are lost to history, although cousins Baldwin Ludlow, son of Uncle Samuel, and Ludlow "Lud" Frey, son of Henry's sister Carolyn, were frequent companions, often following the lead of their more adventurous and creative cousin.[35] Cousin Lud called Fitz Hugh "the smartest and most learned boy I ever saw. He has read all the Latin and Greek that was ever heard of…and he has the greatest stock of general and miscellaneous knowl-edge that was ever seen in a boy his size."[36]

Abby Ludlow's lifelong health problems finally killed her in the winter of 1849, when she was in her early 40's and Fitz Hugh was 13. Among those sending condolences was Samuel F. B. Morse, who had invented the telegraph just five years earlier, and who was a member of Henry's church at Poughkeepsie:

> It is in an hour like this my dear pastor, that God's grace shows its efficiency, and I cannot doubt that your heart, though bleeding and crushed, experiences the healing and sustaining and consoling influences of the blessed religion you have so long and so often and so effectively administered to others…
> My prayers are for you, and yours—
> Most affectionately, your friend, Sam. F. B. Morse

There is no direct word on the effect of his mother's death on Fitz Hugh, but she clearly was unable to provide constant attention through his formative years. Fitz Hugh had inherit-ed little from his mother but a tendency to ill health. Henry's attention to Fitz Hugh during this time seems to have been concentrated on academic and religious training (along with an occasional "whipping"), and the precocious Fitz Hugh was a ready pupil. An 1847 letter from Henry related that Fitz Hugh was currently working on the seventh book of Virgil, and also noted "I found a few weeks ago the following poetical effusion which I think pretty good for a little boy of ten:

> The Voice of the Holy Spirit
> How often in the depths of night
> When all around is in repose
> And e'en the Zephyr quiet lies
> Upon the bosom of the rose.
> I hear a soft and still small voice
> Pouring its accents on my ear
> Pleading so softly with my heart
> That I cannot but stop & hear
> And thus thro' many a silent night
> And many a solemn midnight hour
> I hear that voice come to my heart
> With all its holy gentle power.[37]

Henry's bereavement was short-lived. Abby's death was followed by a remarkable courtship between the 53-year-old widower and a 33-year-old woman named Marie A. Tappen of New Haven. The first surviving letter of the courtship is dated August 5, 1850, and began "And now my dear M., I wish I could tell you in what a singular state of mind I am." It continued:

> I am perfectly satisfied that the course you have adopted and so resolutely adhered to, of postponing your final decision until you had more light, is right and worthy of the noble girl whose judgment and conscience stood their ground so firmly against the powerful current of our mutual affection. I shall

if the result is in harmony with my wishes, value more highly the boon which a God of mercy shall bestow upon me, in yourself, or if in dissonance, bow with a sweeter grace to a fiat which the almost audible voice of the Almighty shall utter.

...I am not staying away to discipline my heart...but simply and only because the feelings of your dear Sister as well as our mutual sense of the proper seem to forbid it. It seems right too that until the great question is settled I should not address myself to the most powerful passion of the human soul and thereby warp the reason in the pursuit of duty.[38]

The offer of marriage only twenty months after Abby's death, assuming a courtship of some duration, indicates Henry took as brief a bereavement as possible. A letter written by Marie the same day sorrowfully contended there are "reasons that forbid our union that I cannot alter...as long as this is my conviction I must act accordingly...I have one favor to ask—may I retain your letter? I shall love to read it & in after years it will be an evidence that I once had your heart."[39] However, Henry's letter, containing a long explanation of how he understood her feelings and would abide by her decision, arrived before Marie could mail hers. She unsealed the envelope and added the following:

You ask for my confidence & friendship. You have it, yes, if I may, I will be your dearest earthly friend, your guide and counsellor in all those matters which perhaps as a lady I can more truly & justly apprehend. I will be all this until another with a stronger & higher claim take from me my office, or if the future should not reveal such an event, & the untoward circumstances which now control my conduct should change, & your wishes continue what they now are, I will then stand by your side at the Holy Altar, & before God & man pledge myself to love honor & obey you through life.

Before long, the "untoward circumstances" changed, and the couple agreed to marry in March of the following year. Henry seemed to find comfort, reassurance and approval from her, and she noted the irony. "Is it strange that I should feel proud knowing as I do the extent of my influence over a man for whom I have always felt a friendship & who is my senior by 20 years?…I am not an angel mon ami, but a woman, a frail imperfect woman as liable to wrongdoing as any other of our fallen race."[40]

That last identification of her enculturation brought her thoughts to young Fitz Hugh, who was now a student at the Poughkeepsie Collegiate School. "And as to your 'darling boy' whose character has interested me long aside from any interest I might feel in him for his father's sake it will give me pleasure to be as far as circumstances and the answering response in his own heart will allow all you could desire. I will take him by the hand & gently lead him on into those paths characterized by *virtue uprightness* & *noble deeds*, trusting that his father's God & mine will bless the undertaking & likewise lead him to tread the *paths of holiness*." Marie certainly had the finest and most eloquent of intentions, but there was clearly something in the boy which led her and Henry to feel he would need more than the average teenager's share of reining in. The adolescent Fitz Hugh was no doubt confused about the prospects of a new mother so soon after losing Abby, and not a little angry.

In fact, from the fall of 1850 until the March 18 wedding, the main point of concern appeared to be young Fitz Hugh, now 14 years old. The Poughkeepsie Collegiate School and Fitz Hugh were apparently not getting along (Fitz Hugh called a teacher at Poughkeepsie "the most confounded fool that I ever saw,")[41] and Henry temporarily bundled him off to Burr Seminary in Vermont. Fitz Hugh had bounced around several other schools, including one in Oswego, where his Aunt Caroline Frey lived. Fitz Hugh said charitably of Oswego, "the streets are as dull & desolate as the avenues of a graveyard."[42]

Henry mentioned several times in letters to Marie that he had not heard from Fitz Hugh in several days. Just after Christmas, 1850, Fitz Hugh wrote directly to Marie, which she found quite uplifting:

> I cannot find words my dearest friend to convey to you my precise feelings whilst reading Fitz Hugh's letter especially that part in which he pours out his feelings in regard to me. The tears gushed to my eyes & I felt like saying God bless *my* dear boy. I trust God will bless him & sanctify his talents & make him an honored instrument to promote His glory.[43]

Marie's feelings were in turn a comfort to Henry:

> I cannot tell you how much I calculate upon the power of [your] voice in my family. Marie—my Fitz Hugh—*our* Fitz Hugh will I think be subdued by it, and his hitherto fretted, irritated, impulsive spirit will learn to bend its neck to the yoke when with accents of love and your own soft & gentle hand light on him. Forget all the past, my Marie. Remember that he was *then* a little heedless boy—a sickly turbulent passionate reckless child. Forget and forgive for my sake. He will repay your culture—and if he lives he will live to bless you. My brother in a late letter...says he is improving finally and laying aside his unpleasant peculiarities.[44]

Fitz Hugh had achieved quite a reputation for himself at the ripe old age of fourteen. He was known to his friends in

Poughkeepsie as "Fishhook."[45] A neighbor related a story of the Reverend Ludlow interrupting his service to "reprimand those who were causing a commotion in the gallery, sometimes pin-pointing the disciplinary remarks with the words, 'Fitz Hugh, I mean you.' "[46] All this fuss was raised about such a cherub as could write the following letter to his father about Marie:

> I am glad that you feel satisfied with my feelings upon the subject of our having a friend once more to watch over us & bless us with her presence. Your extract from her letter to you made me feel still more that she was the only person to whom I could give such respect and love as I ought. My heart's warmest wishes are for her welfare & I pray that God may grant her his richest blessings and me the power to render her home with us agreeable. My heart is most deeply in the undertaking. May I also have strength to cause her never to repent the day that led her footsteps to my hearthstone. I could not refrain from writing when I read the outpourings of a heart which gave to my father the interests of a wife & to my dear little Sister and myself the interest of a mother. Does Helen know the step that has been taken? I know that if she does she cannot but hail it with the deepest joy.

So went the engagement of Henry and Marie, alternating between continual reassurances to each other of their love and the rightness of their marriage, and of their ability to deal with the demon Fitz Hugh:

> I think F. is truly susceptible to kindness and who is not? His education has been very bad in this respect and I mourn in bitterness of spirit that myself have miserably blended love and firmness in my management of him—I cannot tell you Marie, the agony I feel and have felt in view of the impatience—

passion—severity which I have manifested toward him. Oh! if I could only recall the past and begin again! But my regrets are unavailing—and I can only weep tears of blood over my unfaithfulness not to say cruelty in his government…can it be that God has been preparing you by all your education and all your discipline in the church of affliction to save my noble but wayward, heedless boy.

Marie replied (1/20/51):

I feel quite sanguine my dear & perhaps it is best that I do with regard to my influence over him. I know he is wild & wayward & destitute of religious principle but I know that he has noble qualities which can be acted upon if I can really get his heart with God's blessing…I know that God answereth prayers & that there have been many prayers put up in [his] behalf by that father who…desires above all that [he] should become the follower of Christ.[47]

Henry (1/29/51):

I have written to F. just what you wished me to and intend the very first opportunity I can get to converse with Mr. Carpenter. I have not however decided which of your two plans is best, but think that the one which gets him at work on a farm is. If he is to acquire physical stamina, it is now. He is growing rapidly and needs physical far more than mental development. The only thing I regret is that he will for the coming year be deprived of the charm of your society habitually—still if he returns at the close of it to his home, sobered by toil and better able to appreciate his home, it may be best for him to go. I know from past experience he will do nothing useful in the way of work unless compelled to… It is true from my more intimate acquaintance with his constitutional temperament—his early feebleness—his unhappy education—I have more pity for him than a stranger could have and can make allowances when another would not.[48]

Little Helen Ludlow, meanwhile seemed oblivious to F's flaws. In a letter to Marie, she says "I can never repay your kindness in consenting to become my mother, but I will endeavor to make you happy...Papa had a letter from brother, a short time ago. He is very well but I think rather homesick. I wish for the time when we shall all be together. I am afraid that we shall lose some months of his society next summer. His Uncle Mr. Frey invited him to spend some time with him next summer, but I do not know whether my father has decided to let him go or not...Brother in his letter sends much love to his 'Mother elect.' "[49]

Fitz Hugh also wrote to his cousin Lud, who was staying with Henry while Fitz Hugh was at Lud's family residence: "he says he has grown an inch since he left home and he has grown so fat that when he goes to laugh he has to unbutton his waist-coat as a preliminary."[50] A whimsical sense of humor was also evident in drawings of "some of his oddities" that he sent to a cousin.[51]

Henry (1/31/51):

You may rest assured that my feelings toward [Fitz Hugh] will be graduated by his feelings & conduct towards you—I read his letter rather hastily and did not note the mark of disrespect to you which it contained—I must say however my dear that I had not the least ideas it was so intended as disrespect. I have always known his feeling towards you—and from my heart believe that it is truly what he expresses in a former letter with which you were so much pleased—I say this not in justification of his impertinence—but merely in palliation. My heart is very sorrowful in the view of it—and I could weep tears of blood over my wayward—hot headed—impulsive boy—on your account as well as his. My hope is that under your gentle hand he may be moulded to fairer proportions—and especially—as I know what God has done for his father, who at his age was a far less hopeful boy.[52]

The next day, Henry added:

...and I am greatly mistaken if our dear F's explanation has not greatly modified your view of his character. Dear Marie, you may depend upon it, F. is often 'more sinned against than sinning' imperfect as he is—Few understand that Boy—and early education has made him something of an Ishmael whose 'hand was against every man and every man against him'—All that he wants for the future is a long gentle hand like Marie's and I promise you that you will lead him with a cord more delicate than 'the spider's most attenuated web'—He has never had since he was born such an experiment made—I do think Marie that you will yet derive your choicest comfort from his society—and should you survive me & he too, will find him your stay and staff.[53]

Fitz Hugh had arrived at the Frey's in Palatine by February 11 on his way back from school. A note from Aunt Nancy [Ludlow] in Palatine offers, "I have only time for a word. But I wish to say I am much gratified at the course you have been taking with F...a wholesome impression has I trust been made, but whether it will be abiding, or will in the end work savingly I of course cannot know, but let us hope the best dear Br. After doing all you think it duty to do, you ought to hope & wait quietly upon God if possible—but in the meantime do not spare your son—truth will not kill or hurt him whatever he may think—He must be probed and made to know his own case."[54]

That wonderful piece of composition alluded to by Henry was not exactly a comfort to his "Mother elect." In fact, Henry says, "As I have heard no more from F. I was almost sorry after I heard of your indisposition that I had troubled you with that letter from him…but hope it will not unduly excite you."[55] And a day later, "You have read my letter from our boy & no doubt prayed earnestly for his soul."[56] Finally, on February 19, the prodigal son returned home:

> Fitz Hugh has returned, and with a dreadful cough…His general health seems good and he has grown considerably—I have had no opportunity of learning the state of his mind as he retired to his bed-room and he was much excited by the circumstances of his return to his father's house. Probably no serious change has taken place and soon will come the tug of war.[57]

In a postscript on the 20th,

> Fitz Hugh's cough is not quite as severe as it was last night. He coughed incessantly till almost midnight. Poor boy! He seems purposed to be a better boy than he has been—but alas can the Ethiopian change his skin or the leopard his spots without a Divine interposition…I am now at a loss to know what im-mediate disposition to make of him—Oh for wisdom. Have you any dear M—any light—I might get a place perhaps in a store—but then the temptation to falsehood and dishonesty in selling are too many and too strong for a boy not remarkable for a truthful spirit—I think it may be best to put him in one of our Farm Schools and have him go through a thorough course of English studies which he never has been—We will then have him at home during the out of school hours.

But Fitz Hugh was glad to be home in Poughkeepsie after the Oswego graveyard, "if you may judge by the way he carried on; he danced, and jumped, and sung, in fact he made such a racket that I told him the neighbors would know for certain that there had been a new arrival."[58] The next day Henry had a long chat with Fitz Hugh and Helen about the impending wedding, set for March 18. He assured Marie that they both feel "pleasantly and properly" toward her.[59] A week later, Fitz Hugh was reported to be studying Geometry six hours a day. "It comes hard for him, but I think he means to persevere."[60] Marie in turn is delighted to "hear that F. is pursuing his studies at home. I trust he will be able to reap the benefits of such a course which he must if entered with good will and a determination to persevere." Time with his cousin Lud was also calming. "Fitz Hugh and I have fine times together now. We have taken a great many walks about the country lately—he is about as odd a genius as I ever saw."[61] Fitz Hugh also told Lud "he would like to ram [Oswego] down into a big cannon and shoot it out of the Universe."

Two final weeks were dedicated to wedding preparations, as Marie finished dressmaking and sewing for her new home—"you may imagine me as arrayed for the bridal hour."[62] After a final exchange on the propriety of looking to God and Christ to guide them, Henry left for New York City (the wedding site) a weekend early "to consult Dr. Green in reference to F's throat, which troubles him again."[63]

The wedding evidently proceeded with a minimum of controversy, although outside the immediate family there had been gossip of the age difference between Henry and Marie, as well as other hard feelings. Fitz Hugh however appears to have acquitted himself honorably, or at least quietly, at the wedding on March 18, 1851.

Around this time, Fitz Hugh made his published literary debut in the *College Hill Mercury*, a student publication of the Poughkeepsie Collegiate School. As noted earlier, Fitz Hugh had displayed a creative literary bent, and a sharp wit, at a young age. The *College Hill Mercury* was edited by students appointed monthly, who sought to obtain paid subscriptions from alumni and others sufficient to pay for its publication. Fitz Hugh occasionally served as editor. Fitz Hugh's poem in the fifth issue of the magazine, dated December 30, 1850, was entitled "Truth on His Travels":

> Truth, tired of lying hidden,
> In volumes old and musty,
> To rise from the dust forbidden,
> In the brain of Doctor Rusty;
> Determined no longer to lie in check,
> Chained down by an old opinion,
> Which for numberless years had galled his neck,
> And made him the sage's minion.[64]

The poem proceeded to make apparently wry references to a couple of the School's instructors, and was a whimsical treatment of the sadness felt by any young idealist when the world clouds his vision of goodness and light. Overall, it was a pleasant enough piece of work from a fourteen-year-old youth. If it seems a bit early for disillusionment, the stance was possibly an imitation of adult readings, although Fitz Hugh was after all, quite precocious.

Fitz Hugh returned to Burr Seminary in April of 1851, as Henry gave up on his punitive Farm School idea, but did not return him to College Hill. Fitz Hugh finished the term in July, and his statement of disbursement included not only items like shoes and summer hats, but one dollar for "damage of water-pipe repaired."[65] In 1852, Fitz Hugh spent time at yet another academy, in Bloomfield, New Jersey. Also around this time, Fitz Hugh confessed a surprising, but perhaps inevitable, commitment to the Church. The previous year, "I hated to hear anything about Christ or any part of the subject of religion, but now it would please me very much if I could converse with you (Henry)." Fitz Hugh helped organize a series of prayer meetings in Poughkeepsie, saying "the more I see exhibited of human nature & its utter depravity, the more I feel that he alone can strengthen & uphold us."[66]

Sister Helen, meanwhile, entered school and began studying music. Henry was apparently busy as ever, traveling to Bridgeport, Connecticut for extended business trips, during which Fitz Hugh and Helen stayed with family in Poughkeepsie. Henry even traveled to Chicago at this time, colliding with a cholera epidemic there. Henry was also still converting the masses, mentioning a woman in 1853 whose conversion was "like Elizabeth Morse." This was Samuel F.B. Morse's daughter, and Mr. Morse was appreciative:

My dear Pastor
Trust in God, and never for a moment give way to any despondency in regard to your means of support. As long as my purse holds out, while the pirates leave anything in it you shall never want. Who, away from my own immediate family, has a better claim to its contents than he who so faithfully administers to us the bread of life.

You will oblige me by receiving the enclosed for back salary for the last year as my individual subscription for the same sum per annum hereafter.[67]

All in all, Henry had not exactly been exercising a constant oversight in Fitz Hugh's upbringing. Religious ferment was still strong in New York, and its commingling with streams of social reform kept Henry a peripatetic parent through much of Fitz Hugh's childhood and adolescence. Henry's itinerant ways, combined with a sickly mother, left a child prodigy to form his own set of values. Still, Henry appeared to at least have brought Fitz Hugh around to an interest in the Church. Whether Henry's brand of Presbyterian Christianity had taken hold remained to be seen.

Henry also earned enough to keep Fitz Hugh in school and still be able to afford luxuries like service from the new Poughkeepsie Gas Light Co. Henry had a decided interest in science and technology, reflected also in his approach to health care for the children. A letter from around this time noted "Helen is decidedly taller—our homeopathy cured her." Fitz Hugh soon would demonstrate similar interests in medicine of a different kind.

1 "A Disciple Whom Jesus Loved," *The Evangelist*, (n.d.), in Ludlow-Frey papers at New York State Historical Association Library in Cooperstown, NY (hereafter NYSHA Library).
2 "Dear Father's Recollections of Life," sketch by Helen Ludlow, in papers at NYSHA Library.
3 "A Disciple Whom Jesus Loved," op cit.
4 Ibid.
5 Daniel Ludlow to Samuel Baldwin, 1812, NYSHA Library.
6 Helen Ludlow, sketch written "a few years after his death," 1873-75 (?), now in Schaffer Library, Union College, p. 1.
7 Samuel Baldwin to Phoebe Ludlow, April 4, 1814, NYSHA Library.
8 Samuel Baldwin to Phoebe Ludlow, April 4, 1814, NYSHA Library.
9 Henry Ludlow to Nancy Douglass, August 26, 1820, NYSHA Library.
10 Henry Ludlow to Nancy Douglass, August 26, 1820, NYSHA Library.

11 Henry Ludlow to Nancy Douglass, August 26, 1820, NYSHA Library.

12 Henry Ludlow to Nancy Douglass, August 26, 1820, NYSHA Library.

13 Allan Nevins, *The Evening Post: A Century of Journalism*, New York: 1922, p. 145.

14 *The Liberator*, May 17, 1834, p. 78.

15 Ibid.

16 Nevins (1922), p.146.

17 Bertram Wyatt-Brown, *Lewis Tappan and the Evangelical War Against Slavery*, New York: Atheneum, 1971, p. 116.

18 Oliver Johnson, *William Lloyd Garrison and his Times*, 1881, reprint Miami: Mnemosyne Publishing Co., 1969, p. 162.

19 Wyatt Brown (1971) p. 117.

20 *William Lloyd Garrison and His Times*, p. 162.

21 Smith later became an Abolitionist candidate for President, and later formed a Prohibitionist Party in 1869.

22 Ibid.

23 It is not even certain that Henry was personally close to Smith. Harlow's thoroughly researched biography of Smith omits any mention of Henry, and no letters of Smith's are to or from Ludlow. However, there are no other Fitzhughs or Fitz Hughs among Henry's or Abby's friends or family.

24 Helen Ludlow, n.d., letter in Shaffer Library, Union College.

25 From whom Patty Hearst's abductor, leader of the Symbionese Liberation Army, got his code name.

26 Wyatt-Brown (1971) p. 208.

27 Ibid., p. 210.

28 Fitz Hugh Ludlow, "If Massa Put Guns into Our Han's" in *The Atlantic Monthly*, April, 1865, p. 505.

29 Fitz Hugh Ludlow, "Goodbye Article" in *The Golden Era*, November 22, 1863.

30 Fitz Hugh Ludlow, "The Prisoners of Portland" in *The Golden Era*, June 19, 1864.

31 Fitz Hugh Ludlow, "Little Briggs and I," *Northern Lights*, January, 1867.

32 Fitz Hugh Ludlow, "Little Briggs and I," *Northern Lights*, January, 1867.

33 Fitz Hugh Ludlow, *The Hasheesh Eater*, New York: Harper and Brothers, p. 63.

34 Helen Ludlow, 1873-75, p. 2.

35 A letter from Ludlow Frey to Caroline Frey, March 10, 1851, NYSHA Library, tells of Fitz Hugh leading him along a railroad track and across a rail bridge, stopping to speak with a "half-witted boy" fishing off the bridge.

36 S. Ludlow Frey to Caroline Frey, April 2, 1851, NYSHA Library.
37 Henry Ludlow to John and Caroline Frey, March 24, 1847, NYSHA Library.
38 Henry Ludlow to Marie Tappen, August 5, 1850, NYSHA Library.
39 Marie Tappen to Henry Ludlow, August 5, 1850, NYSHA Library.
40 Marie Tappen to Henry Ludlow, August 12, 1850, NYSHA Library.
41 Fitz Hugh Ludlow to S. Ludlow Frey, January 13, 1850, NYSHA Library.
42 Ibid.
43 Marie Tappen to Henry Ludlow, January ?, 1851, NYSHA Library.
44 Henry Ludlow to Marie Tappen, December 30, 1850, NYSHA Library.
45 Paul Hasbrouck to Carl Niemeyer, March 1, 1953, NYSHA Library.
46 Ibid.
47 Marie Tappen to Henry Ludlow, January 20, 1851, NYSHA Library.
48 Henry Ludlow to Marie Tappen, January 29, 1851, NYSHA Library.
49 Helen Ludlow to Marie Tappen, January 29, 1851, NYSHA Library.
50 Helen Ludlow to Marie Tappen, January 29, 1851, NYSHA Library.
51 S. Ludlow Frey to Carrie Frey, February 26, 1851, NYSHA Library.
52 S. Ludlow Frey to Carrie Frey, February 26, 1851, NYSHA Library.
53 Henry Ludlow to Marie Tappen, February 1, 1851, NYSHA Library.
54 Nancy Douglass to Henry Ludlow, February 14, 1851, NYSHA Library.
55 Henry Ludlow to Marie Tappen, February 15, 1851, NYSHA Library.
56 Henry Ludlow to Marie Tappen, February 16, 1851, NYSHA Library.
57 Henry Ludlow to Marie Tappen, February 19, 1851, NYSHA Library.
58 S. Ludlow Frey to Carrie Frey, February 26, 1851, New York City Public Library (hereafter NYCPL).
59 Henry Ludlow to Marie Tappen, February 22, 1851, NYSHA Library.
60 Henry Ludlow to Marie Tappen, March 5, 1851, NYSHA Library.
61 S. Ludlow Frey to ?, n.d., NYSHA Library.
62 Marie Tappen to Henry Ludlow, March, 1851, NYSHA Library.
63 Henry Ludlow to Marie Tappen, March, 1851, NYSHA Library.
64 Fitz Hugh was apparently at Burr Seminary at the time this was published, although he may have submitted it earlier.
65 Statement now among Ludlow Papers at New York City Public Library.
66 Fitz Hugh Ludlow to S. Ludlow Frey, April 15, 1852, NYCPL.
67 Samuel F.B. Morse to Henry Ludlow, March 8, 1853, NYCPL. Morse was at this time undergoing legal battles over his telegraph patent.

III.

TEENAGER ON DRUGS

In 1853, Fitz Hugh was seventeen, studying both at home and at the Seminary. His creativity continued to flower, as shown in a surviving pictographic letter, but far more dramatic elements of his personality were about to emerge. Sometime in 1853, Fitz Hugh made the acquaintance of a Mr. Anderson, the Poughkeepsie apothecary.

PICTOGRAPHIC LETTER WRITTEN WHEN FITZ HUGH WAS 17,
AT THE BEGINNING OF HIS PHARMACEUTICAL EXPLORATIONS.
(COURTESY OF THE NEW YORK PUBLIC LIBRARY)

The basics of medical science were in place in 1853, but medical treatment still yielded intermittent success. Drug prescriptions for various ailments were largely at the snake-oil stage, and no drugs were illegal. Morphine, chloroform, and a range of others were regularly used for relief of pain and various other symptoms, but cures were still often a matter of waiting and praying. Young Fitz Hugh, already with a history of frailty and ill health, was no doubt early administered one or another of these agents. His curiosity, if not his health, was nurtured by these treatments. But it is his friendship with Anderson that opened the door to active experimentation with a variety of drugs, not for cure but for exploration, and leading to his ultimate place in history.

Four years later Fitz Hugh would write of his early days in Wonderland: "About the shop of my friend Anderson the apothecary there always existed a peculiar fascination, which early marked it out as my favorite lounging-place."[1] And Fitz Hugh was no passive observer here. The seventeen-year-old evidently had gained the patronage of Anderson for the pursuit of a course in medical literature. Anderson was less aware of Fitz Hugh's personal experiments:

> Here especially, with a disregard to my own safety...have I made upon myself the trial of the effects of every strange drug and chemical which the laboratory could produce. Now with the chloroform bottle beneath my nose have I set myself careering upon the wings of a thrilling and accelerating life, until I had just enough power remaining to restore the liquid to its place upon the shelf, and sink back into the enjoyment of the delicious apathy which lasted through the few succeeding moments. Now ether was substituted for chloroform, and the difference of their phenomena noted, and some other exhilarant, in the form of an

opiate or stimulant, was the instrument of my experiments, until I had run through the whole gamut of queer agents within my reach.

In all these experiences research and not indulgence was my object, so that I never became the victim of any habit in the prosecution of my headlong investigations. When the circuit of all the accessible tests was completed, I ceased experimenting, and sat down like a pharmaceutical Alexander, with no more drug worlds to conquer.[2]

TILDEN & COMPANY, NEW LEBANON NY,
PURVEYOR OF HASHISH EXTRACT.

It was the winter of 1854, and Henry was in New York City visiting an old friend living on Wall Street. Marie wrote to him that she missed him, and that "the children are well and try to please you."[3] She later implores him to send her a figurative heart, and to make that heart "large enough to cover poor Fitz Hugh, poor boy he needs a large one I know." But there is no mention of Fitz Hugh's pharmacological explorations. Perhaps they were kept successfully from the family, or perhaps they were overshadowed by his continued general rudeness and superciliousness. It is worth noting that Fitz Hugh's anti-social behavior preceded his drug use.

One morning in the spring of 1854, Fitz Hugh strolled into Anderson's for his daily visit. Among the apothecary's new acquisitions was *Cannabis Indica*, which he described as "a preparation of the East Indian hemp, a powerful agent in cases of lock-jaw."[4] In Fitz Hugh's words, "On the strength of this introduction, I took down the little archer, and, removing his outer verdant coat, began the further prosecution of his acquaintance." Thus began one of the most unusual friendships of the 19th century.

What Fitz Hugh met was an olive-brown extract, the consistency of pitch, and a "decidedly aromatic odor." He was about to taste a pinch when the doctor cried out, "Hold on! do you want to kill yourself? That stuff is deadly poison." "Indeed!" replied the startled adventurer. "No, I can not say that I have any settled determination of that kind".[5] Replacing the vial, Fitz Hugh repaired to the doctor's library and consulted a standard reference of the day, Johnston's *Chemistry of Common Life*. There, along with the layman's explanations of why flowers smell good, was a series of chapters entitled "The Narcotics We Indulge In." Skipping past the chapters on tobacco, the hop and its substitutes, and the poppy, Fitz Hugh came to Chapter XVIII, Indian Hemp.

The entry begins with commonplace knowledge. "Our common European hemp (Cannabis sativa) so extensively cultivated for its fibre, is the same plant with the Indian hemp (Cannabis Indica) which from the remotest times has been celebrated among Eastern nations for its narcotic virtues." Indeed, hemp was an early export of the American colonies in the 18th century. It was used to make canvas (the same root word as "cannabis"), rope for ships' rigging, for making paper, and for other uses. George Washington himself cultivated the plant, as we know from his diaries. (Those same diaries, incidentally, note the procedure of separating the male from the female plants, which marijuana enthusiasts point out is a common technique for increasing the psychoactive potency of the plant, and a technique unnecessary for other uses.)[6]

Johnston's book goes on to further relate that "In the sap of this plant—there exists a peculiar resinous substance, in which the esteemed narcotic virtue resides...the resin is collected...by pressing the resinous plant on coarse cloths, and afterwards scraping the resin from these." Johnston also mentions the other products of the hemp plant, including the dried plants known as "gunjah" (which we most commonly refer to in the late 20th century as marijuana). Fitz Hugh then read with interest a capsule summary of the extent of the use of hemp, ranging from reference to its use by the Greek historian Herodotus through its mention in Lane's translation of the Arabian Nights. An account of the effects of hemp were the most interesting passages in Johnston's book. Small doses were said to induce an increase of appetite and "great mental cheerfulness." Larger doses, however, were more remarkable. In the East, "they find themselves almost transported to the scene of the numberless marvels which the Prophet has collected in his paradise."

Fitz Hugh decided to add hashish to the list of his for-
mer experiments. He proceeded to sneak a ten-grain chunk
(about ⅔ of a gram) and swallowed it "without a tremor
as to the danger of the result." However, the dose proved
too small to bring about any effect at all. Prudently allowing
several days to pass, he snuck another chunk, this time of fif-
teen grains, but again felt nothing. Twice more he repeated
the experiment with no success.

One evening, having become fairly sure that he was
immune to the influence of hashish, he took a two-gram
dose after tea, and went to visit a close friend. After several
hours of pleasant conversation and music, Fitz Hugh was
prepared to abandon the experiment until, at last, the drug
announced its presence:

> Ha! what means this sudden thrill? A shock, as of some un-
> imagined vital force, shoots without warning through my
> entire frame, leaping to my fingers' ends, piercing my brain,
> startling me till I almost sprang from my chair...I could not
> doubt it. I was in the power of the hasheesh influence. My first
> emotion was one of uncontrollable terror—a sense of getting
> something which I had not bargained for. That moment I
> would have given all I had or hoped to have to be as I was
> three hours before.[7]

Fitz Hugh knew that this was only the beginning. He
thought prophetically, looking at his friends, that he "had
entered upon a tremendous life which they could not share. If
the disembodied ever return to hover over the hearth-stone
which once had a seat for them, they look upon their friends
as I then looked upon mine."[8] The rest of the evening was a
turmoil of new sensations, but Fitz Hugh almost imme-
diately became aware that no-one of his friends suspected

his internal state. He answered questions, laughed at jokes, and tapped his foot to music, but each response carried with it vastly greater import than he could express. When addressed in conversation, it seemed to him that the time between the first words of a sentence and its last were so great that it should be impossible to remember what question had been asked. His sense of space had also expanded, so that he felt the three feet between his armchair and the table around which they sat was "an infinity of space."

In the midst of these perceptions, Fitz Hugh felt as if a portion of himself were sitting and calmly observing his intoxicated self, and this double warned him to leave before he could no longer conceal his agitated state. After what seemed an eternity, he was able to make his goodbyes and escape to the streets of Poughkeepsie. Once again, his sense of distance left him, and he felt "doomed to pass through a merciless stretch of space." The walk home became an epic journey:

> I dwelt in a marvelous inner world. I existed by turns in different places and various states of being. Now I swept my gondola through the moon-lit lagoons of Venice. Now Alp on Alp towered above my view, and the glory of the coming sun flashed purple light upon the topmost icy pinnacle. Now in the primeval silence of some unexplored tropical forest I spread my feathery leaves, a giant fen, and swayed and nodded in the spice-gales over a river whose wavers at once sent up clouds of music and perfume. My soul changed to a vegetable essence, thrilled with a strange and unimagined ecstasy. The palace of Al Haroun could not have bought me back to humanity.[9]

But before he got home, he encountered his first full-blown hallucination, a vision of a man with a face of "ferocious wickedness." This phantom attempted to detain him, saying "You shall bear my burden for me." Fitz Hugh fled at full speed and finally reached his home. Although the familiar surroundings dampened his state of mind, he found that new effects kept appearing. He began to feel acutely aware of his own bodily functions, believing he could feel the very blood rushing through his veins. His heartbeat seized his consciousness, and he felt that it had accelerated to a dangerous degree. After a flash of fear that he was close to a seizure, he took out his watch in order to take his own pulse.

He found that this concentrated action was easily accomplished, and actually brought his perception back to its natural state. His pulse proved to be quite normal. No sooner did he feel relieved than the hallucination was back in full force. He tried washing his face in cold water and reasoning with himself, but the feeling remained.

Fitz Hugh had walked into this new country utterly without a guide. The effects of the drug were virtually unknown in this country, and even Fitz Hugh's extensive pharmacological readings had not left him equipped for rationally assessing the situation. Even opium had been explicated by De Quincey and others, but hashish was a different animal. Not a narcotic or anesthetic, it was a substance with effects of a wholly different order, and Fitz Hugh had no basis for comparison. Finally, with a presence of mind unusual in a teenager, Fitz Hugh decided to leave the house and go to a doctor.

When he arrived, he rang the bell and then immediately forgot the name of his family physician. While trying to remember, he kept ringing the bell, as he had the impression he was waiting a small eternity. When the servant threw open the door, she was out of breath and expecting at least a few gaping wounds. Fitz Hugh was shown in to see Doctor H., who had just finished a long operation.

"I am about to reveal to you," said Fitz Hugh, after locking the door behind the servant, much to the puzzlement of the Doctor, "something which I would not for my life allow to come to other ears...I have been taking hasheesh—Cannabis Indica, and I fear that I am going to die." After a brief inspection, the doctor said, "Nothing the matter with you; go home and go to bed." Fitz Hugh was stunned at this medical indifference. "But—is there—no—danger of—apoplexy?" "Bah," replied Doctor H. eloquently.[10]

Fitz Hugh slowly moved to leave, when the Doctor stopped him and said he would give him a sedative to carry if he absolutely felt the need. "Call my servant." Fitz Hugh stepped outside and called, and then lapsed into a reverie which seemed to last, once again, for an eternity. When he stirred from this meditation, he asked the Doctor if he should call the servant again. "Why you have just this moment called her." "Doctor" he solemnly replied. "I will not believe you are deceiving me, but to me it appears as if sufficient time has elapsed since then for all the Pyramids to have crumbled back to dust." "Ha-ha you are very funny tonight," said Doctor H. "I will send her for something which will comfort you on that score, and re-establish the Pyramids in your confidence."[11]

As she fetched the sedative, Fitz Hugh decided to compare the time with outside events. Looking at his watch, he noted the minute. Putting it away, he drifted again into a series of hallucinations. First he was imprisoned by a gnome, then the Doctor's house was adrift in a vast ocean, and finally a huge army filed past. When he looked again at his watch, only thirty seconds had passed. "My God, I am in Eternity!"

> In the presence of that first sublime revelation of the soul's own time, and her capacity for an infinite life, I stood trembling with breathless awe. Till I die, that moment of unveiling will stand in clear relief from all the rest of my existence.[12]

This is Fitz Hugh's first interpretation of his experience, and it is fittingly religious in nature. Other philosophies would be called up to order his inner worlds, in particular the Transcendental philosophy of Emerson, but always Christian theology was close at hand.

Sleeping powder in hand, Fitz Hugh returned home, and threw himself into bed. But if only it were that easy. "The moment I closed my eyes a vision of celestial glory burst upon me." Relieved of outside sensory data, Fitz Hugh's youthfully vivid imagination was given free rein by the hashish influence. Natural scenes and architectural wonders appeared with spotless clarity. A crystal stream whose waters "discoursed notes of music which tinkled on the ear like the tones of some exquisite bell-glass;" a Parthenon far more perfect and worshipful than any the ancient Greeks could have conceived; a "congress of crones" presided over by a witch knit out of purple yarn; an enormous cavern whose roof was hidden by clouds; and then emergence into a horizonless sea.

> Through all the infinitudes around me I looked out and met no boundaries of space. The whole atmosphere was one measureless suffusion of golden motes, which throbbed continually in cadence, and showered radiance and harmony at the same time... now bathed in my ethereal travel by the rivers of the rainbow,

which, side by side, coursed through the valleys of heaven; now dwelling for a season in the environment of unbroken sunlight, yet bearing it like the eagle with undazzled eye; now crowned with a coronal of prismatic beads of dew. Through whatever region or circumstances I passed, one characteristic of the vision remained unchanged: peace—every-where godlike peace, the sum of all conceivable desires satisfied.[13]

His visions ended with the sight of himself laying down to sleep, and when he did awaken it was morning—"actual morning and not some hasheesh hallucination."[14]

This first experience of Fitz Hugh's may surprise some readers who have heard of or experienced the milder sensations that come of smoking marijuana or hashish. Many researchers have noted the variability of the effects of these substances, and taking the drug orally tends to intensify the experience. As with many of the hallucinogens, the mindset of the user determines to a large degree the experience.[15] As will be seen, Fitz Hugh's prodigious literary appetite, the strong religious impressions made by his father, and his native imagination combined to evoke a myriad of sensations, emotions and activities while under the influence of hashish.[16]

Fitz Hugh rose carefully the morning after his first experiment, testing to see if there had been any lingering ill effects. But he found no pain, no sluggishness or hangover, and no physical weariness or mental depression. What did remain, however, was the memory of the evening's adventure. "[D]uring the whole day I could not rid myself of the feeling that I was separated from the preceding one by an immeasurable lapse of time. In fact, I never got wholly rid of it."[17]

A few days later, he confessed the story of that evening to the lady of the house where he had first fallen under the hashish spell. Claiming to be "satisfied with my one successful experiment," he did not plan to continue using the drug. He professed to truly believe this statement when he made it, but even the characterization of the journey as "successful" belied his cautious intentions:

> Had the first experiment been followed by depression, I had probably never repeated it. For days I was even unusually strong; all the forces of life were in a state of pleasurable activity, but the memory of the wondrous glories which I had beheld wooed me continually like an irresistible sorceress.[18]

But Fitz Hugh sensed the knowing nods of his audience, who judged that he had merely underestimated the lure of narcotics:

> Censure me not harshly, ye who have never known what fascination there is in the ecstasy of beauty; there are baser attractions than those which invited me…I yielded to no sensual gratification. The motives for the hasheesh-indulgence were of the most exalted ideal nature, for of this nature are all its ecstasies and its revelations…I yielded moreover, without realizing to what. Within a circle of one hundred miles radius there was not a living soul who knew or could warn me of my danger.[19]

A little more than a week after his plunge into the world of hashish, Fitz Hugh rolled twenty grains of hashish into a pill and swallowed it, saying "here is the final test for the sake of science." On this day, he ate the pellet just after lunch, and then napped for several hours. He awoke late in the afternoon, still untouched by any dreams and visions.

His friend Dan came by, whom he described as "one of those choice spirits whom you are always glad to have beside you, whatever may be your feeling." Dan's flexibility would soon enough be tested. The two set off for a stroll through the suburbs of Poughkeepsie, continuing on to a road running south "which in many respects affords one of the most delightful walks which can be imagined." As the sun began to set, the two traveled "arm-in-arm, so filled and overcome with the beauty of the view that we read each other's feelings and went silently."[20] (It may be noted that several people had to this point been taken into Fitz Hugh's confidence, including a family physician who may have had every reason to go directly to Reverend Henry with a friendly warning. Still, there is no indication that Henry received any such information, at least not from family letters. Henry had certainly not withheld his other feelings from such letters.)

Half a mile out of town, "without the smallest premonition, I was smitten by the hasheesh thrill as by a thunderbolt." Fitz Hugh recognized the sensation unmistakably, and later described it, sparing no hyperbole: "the nearest resemblance to the feeling is that contained in our idea of the instantaneous separation of soul and body."[21]

Once again, space began to expand, so that the hill over which the road ahead disappeared "came to be perceived as the boundary of the continent itself." Any fear he might have felt at the return of the strangeness was banished by the intense pleasure caused by the sunset. Nor could he keep the joy within. "I cast off all restraint; I leaped into the air; I clapped my hands and shouted for joy."[22]

"My dear friend," declaimed Fitz Hugh, "we are about to realize all our youthful dreams of travel. Together you and I

will wander on foot at our will through strange and beau-
teous countries; our life spreads before us henceforward
unoccupied by cares…we shall travel together, linked soul to
soul, and gaining exstasy by impartition. At night we shall lay
ourselves down to sleep on the banks of primeval Asian riv-
ers, and Bulbul shall sing us to sleep with his most delicious
madrigals. When the first auroral tinges are glassed back
from the peaks of Himmaleh [Himalaya], we will arise, and
bathing ourselves in rock o'ershadowed fountains, will start
again upon our immortal way. On! On!" What could Dan
say? "I will go with delight," agreed the poet. And on they
went through the hasheesh-extended "perpetual sunset."[23]

Finally the pair of intrepid travelers reached the top of the
hill, and Fitz Hugh was so transported by the panorama
that stretched before them that "my ecstasy became so
great that I seemed to cast off all shackles of flesh. The lover
of beauty who should, for the first time, drink in the richness
of this exalted view through the channels of the soul which
are ordinarily opened, might well burst forth into singing
were not reverence the stronger feeling."[24] The visionary
poet William Blake had conceived a similar metaphor a
hundred years earlier, the "doors of perception," through
which, were they opened, "everything would appear to man
as it is, infinite."[25]

Fitz Hugh's intoxication exceeded even his romanticism
when he cried out, "Why need we in our journey, touch
the earth at all? Let us sweep through the air above this
expanse of beauty and read it like the birds." But when he
realized that Dan was without his means of flight, he con-
sented to merely stroll with an "airy tread" along with Dan.
"Now we went singing, and I question whether Mozart

ever rejoiced in his own musical creations as I did in that symphony we sang together. The tune and the words were extemporaneous…and I heard delicious echoes back from the dome of heaven." And further: "I lived in what we sang: our music seemed a wondrous epic, whose pages we illustrated, not with pictures, but with living notes."[26]

These intense episodes alternated with bouts of giggling, until the two reached the outskirts of town. Here, Fitz Hugh found again that part of him remained rational and aloof while the rest of him was at play. He had sense enough to lead Dan into a side street where they might avoid too many chance conversations. As it was now completely dark, they sat on a bench and turned their attention to the full moon. Fitz Hugh stared at the now intensified brightness of the lunar orb, until the hashish once again brought forth visions, this time of "myriads of shining ones from the realm of Faery, who plunged into the translucent lake of ether as into a sea, and swam to the moon and ascended its gleaming beach."[27] They returned home, where Fitz Hugh drank some water, or rather a liquid which "danced and sparkled like some liquid metempsychosis of amber." Evidently his parents were away, and he spent the rest of the evening in a state of "unutterable calm…I looked at the stars and felt kindred with them; I spoke to them and they answered me. I dwelt in an inner communion with heaven."[28]

The summer passed with a handful of further experiments. Apparently, these were accomplished without his being discovered. By then, Henry had decided to send young Fitz Hugh to Princeton, where Henry had studied theology, and Henry's Uncle Sam Baldwin had studied the law before him. There was a little trepidation on Henry's part, for one condition of Fitz Hugh's entrance to college life was a ledger kept by him of the spending of $111, "Received from my father up to September 6th, 1854." It is a record of his journey to Princeton, and setting up house-keeping there, and is illustrative of contemporary life for Fitz Hugh.[29]

Taking a carriage to the river from Poughkeepsie, Fitz Hugh boarded the steamboat Alida, which for 75 cents took him and his baggage (handled by a deckhand for 6 and ¼ cents) to New York City. Paying 37 cents more to get his baggage from the dock to the Jersey Ferry, he stored it for 12 cents while having dinner (45 cents). Fitz Hugh bought a copy of the works of the Roman historian Tacitus, gave 3 cents to a "poor blind man," and boarded the ferry. The stage to Princeton was $1.20, with an extra quarter for the stage from the depot to the college. After a 38-cent supper, Fitz Hugh picked up a *New York Times* and retired for the evening.

The next morning after breakfast (also 38 cents), he commenced settling in. He paid Mrs. Sekenek $2.50 for one week's board, and went shopping to furnish his room, shared with one other man. A bureau bookcase ($4), a table ($2) a settee ($3) and a looking glass ($1.25 for Fitz Hugh's share) were the first acquisitions (moved by a servant for 50 cents). A bed ($2.19) was delivered, and shelving was acquired for 81 cents.

Fitz Hugh was not entirely dependent on servants, helping wallpaper the room (which cost 92 cents), varnish the furniture ("being a defaced red, when bought") and paint the door of the room. Other accoutrements purchased in the next two weeks were shaving mug, bowl and pitcher

($1.25), a broom (12 and ½ cents), oil cloth (21 cents), a key and lock (18 and ¾ cents) and a lamp (18 and ¾ cents).

Adjusting to his new setting was not without some distress. After a supplemental $25 arrived in early October, Fitz Hugh noted the purchase of medicine for diarrhea and a bottle of bed-bug poison, "both to remedy evils which afflicted me greatly." Later, he noted two bottles of wine, "taken when sick at beginning of term." It is not clear if he became sick before or after acquiring said bottles. An additional entry for "Druggists Do." [*sic*]—$1.00—suggests that Fitz Hugh was developing new pharmaceutical contacts.

One should hasten to add that Fitz Hugh noted 50 cents for "collections in Church" at the end of his ledger. It is not clear whether he forgot to mention his three or four Sundays at church and rounded off his charitable contributions which he could not remember, or whether he simply forgot to attend church without his father stirring about on Sunday preparing to go to work.

On the academic side, Fitz Hugh picked up a notebook "for taking rough drafts of lecture and pencil" at 37 and ½ cents. He subscribed to the College Literary Monthly for two dollars. Near the end of September, he paid his college tuition and board bill for the session, a total of $71.83. Books were $7.03. Except for Tacitus, we have no record of the object of his studies at Princeton, although he did belong to the Cliosophic Society, a debating fellowship. His stay at Princeton was short, however, as Nassau Hall, his dormitory, burned down in March, 1855. (Goodbye furniture, goodbye wallpaper.) This led to his "dismission" from the College of New Jersey (as Princeton was still known).

FITZ HUGH LUDLOW FROM HIS COLLEGE DAYS. HE WEARS
HIS KAPPA ALPHA SOCIETY KEY IN THE FIRST IMAGE.
(COURTESY OF SCHAFFER LIBRARY, UNION COLLEGE)

1 *The Hasheesh Eater*, p. 15.

2 *The Hasheesh Eater*, p. 16.

3 Marie Ludlow to Henry Ludlow, January 17, 1854, January 24 1854, NYSHA Library.

4 Indica is derived from the Cannabis Sativa plant, but was the name given to medical preparations in the nineteenth century. It is not a different species.

5 *The Hasheesh Eater*, p. 18.

6 Jack Herer, *The Emperor Wears No Clothes*, Van Nuys, CA: HEMP Publishing, 1991, p. 2.

7 Jack Herer, *The Emperor Wears No Clothes*, Van Nuys, CA: HEMP Publishing, 1991, p. 2.

8 Jack Herer, *The Emperor Wears No Clothes*, Van Nuys, CA: HEMP Publishing, 1991, p. 2.

9 Ibid., p. 24.

10 Ibid., p. 30.

11 Ibid., p. 34.

12 Ibid., p. 33.

13 Ibid., p. 41.

14 Ibid.

15 See for example Norman Zinberg, *Drug, Set and Setting*, New Haven: Yale University Press, 1984. Incidentally, the term "hallucinogen" is a widely-used term but somewhat misleading. It has connotations of unreality, where many experience what they call "heightened" reality. "Entheogen" is a word coined by mycologist R. Gordon Wasson as a substitute for hallucinogen. See Wasson, *Persephone's Quest*, New Haven: Yale University Press, 1986. Hallucinogen is used here as a convention.

16 Some of the visions related here, taken from his writings, may have been embroidered in the telling or imbued with more structure than they had during their occurrence. They are presented as an accurate reflection of his subjective experiences and memory of them.

17 *The Hasheesh Eater*, p. 43.

18 Ibid., p. 45.

19 Ibid., p.46.

20 Ibid., p 49.

21 Ibid., p. 50.

22 Ibid., p. 51.

23 Ibid., p. 52.

24 Ibid., p. 55.

25 Blake, *The Marriage of Heaven and Hell*. Aldous Huxley later used the quote as the title of the account of his introduction to mescaline, *The Doors of Perception*, finding the metaphor as accurate as Fitz Hugh had a century earlier.

26 *The Hasheesh Eater*, p. 56.

27 Ibid., p. 59.

28 Ibid., p. 60.

29 The ledger is now among the Ludlow-Frey papers, NYSHA Library.

IV.

HIGHER EDUCATION

FITZ HUGH entered Union College in Schenectady, New York in the spring of 1855, becoming a member of the junior class. (College curricula were not "accredited," so there were no recognized intercollegiate standards or minimum number of courses required for a college degree.) Union College, although not widely known today, was a rival to Harvard in its early years. Harvard's trademark crimson school colors are the result of a compromise with Union during the intercollegiate crew championships between Union and Harvard in 1875. (Both were contending for red, and Union came away with the subtler garnet.) Union was the first college chartered under the U.S. Constitution. As late as 1829, only Harvard and Yale enrolled more students. So the transfer from Princeton was not a demotion in any sense for Fitz Hugh.

However, Union had achieved a singular reputation, owing to the eccentric genius who had served as president of the college for over fifty years, the redoubtable Eliphalet Nott. President Nott had pioneered at Union just ten years earlier a combination of the liberal arts with a scientific/engineering curriculum that was unique at the time. At least, the program was as scientific as possible for one including a course entitled "Electricity Et Cetera." Further, the name Union reflected the progressive outlook inherent in the school since its founding. The name signified the union of German, English and Dutch Americans, as well as persons of many different religious faiths, who were united in their pursuit of higher education. While Union in the mid-nineteenth century was still very respectable academically, it was known by this time primarily for "the Doctor's" stern hand with gifted but wayward youth. Indeed, Union was known among intercollegiate wags as Botany Bay (after the famous prison). Nott would have a considerable effect on the young hashish eater.

ELIPHALET NOTT (1773-1866), PRESIDENT OF UNION COLLEGE FROM 1804-1866. ENGRAVED IN 1833 FROM AN 1820 PAINTING BY EZRA AMES. AN 1880 PHOTO OF THE SIXTEEN-SIDED NOTT MEMORIAL, WHICH STILL IS THE CENTER OF THE UNION CAMPUS. (GREMS DOLITTLE PHOTOGRAPHIC COLLECTION)

Fitz Hugh's "dismission" from Princeton was due to fire rather than delinquency. Nevertheless, Reverend Henry Ludlow was happy to see his son under the wing of a personality as forceful as Nott's. If only Henry, the staunch Abolitionist, had been aware of an address Nott had delivered to the Colonization Society on the slavery question in 1829, he may have been less sanguine. Calculating that by the end of the century there would be twenty-four million slaves in the U.S., Nott opined:

> Twenty four million! And is the republic so soon to embosom such an appalling amount of ignorant, vicious, degraded and brutal population. What a drawback from our strength! What a hindrance to our growth! What an impediment to the fulfillment of our destiny! Could our worst enemies, or the worst enemies of republics, wish us a severer reproach, or a heavier judgement?[1]

College in this era was a much more formal institution than it is today, or even than it was fifty years ago. All Union students (all men, incidentally, as Union remained until 1973) were expected to attend a chapel service every morning. The idea of a young man away from the steadying influences of his family was thought to be a little strange, possibly dangerous, and probably immoral. Dr. Nott himself once sermonized on the subject:

> the natural place for a young man is with his parents and friends; separated from these he was apt to become slovenish, boorish, and reckless. This would be seen with those who went into the army, or assembled in factories or colleges.[2]

This thought reflects a social transition in progress. In America in the mid-19th century, there was a rapidly growing middle class of professionals and merchants. Besides the familiar doctors and priests (like the Reverend Henry), there was a growing number of scientists and engineers appearing on the horizon. Fitz Hugh was one of the first of a generation attending college, not as the son of nobility or wealthy landowners, but as the leading edge of the great middle class. Fitz Hugh remarked on it later:

> It is in the American college, with its freedom from fictitious distinctions, its rejection of all odious badges which set genealogy and money over mind and heart; its unrestrained intercourse between congenial souls, and its groupings of congenialities by society bonds, that the most perfect development of the social and individual man takes place.[3]

Fitz Hugh seemed to bear out Nott's opinion of young men's delinquency, as much by his absences from class, for which he was fined $1.12 (compared to a semester's tuition charge of $19.00) as by his hashish indulgence. The latter, as we have seen, had happened anyway even under the careful nose of the Reverend Henry himself. President Nott also showed no evidence of having been aware of his prize student's mind-altering pursuits. A fellow student remembers Fitz Hugh this way:

> Ludlow, at that period, was about twenty years of age, slender, of medium height, light as to eyes, hair and complexion. He was regarded as somewhat "queer" by the other students, among whom he was not very popular.
>
> He was reticent, and hilarious and talkative at intervals; he was a confirmed punster. He came into a room one day, where some students were chatting. He carried a stiff silk hat in one hand and smoothed its nap with the other. "Say, fellows, what kind of a hat is this?" he asked. Beaver, silk and other materials were mentioned. "Wrong, all of you. Don't you see it's felt?" as he continued to rub its surface.[4]

The recollections of another fellow student:

Fitz Hugh Ludlow, when in college, was intensely homely, with a very large mouth, and he wore spectacles, which was an unusual thing at that time. He was one of the brightest men I ever knew, a remarkable conversationalist, full of wit and humor, with a wonderful flow of language. It was our habit to sit on the terrace in front of the college and sing after supper.

He was genial and generous but had no sense of "meum" and "tuum." He did not hesitate to appropriate anyone's clothes, yet he would have willingly loaned his own clothes but he never had any to loan. He was modest, yet self-confident and with his buoyant temperament and brilliant wit made many friends and, I think, no enemies.[5]

A Poughkeepsie acquaintance also had remarked on Fitz Hugh's "wonderful powers of conversation (which were) a pleasing fascination."[6]

Fitz Hugh lived on the college campus, with roommate Robert Camps. They lived at the South College, the main residential hall on campus. The school was nestled in the heart of Schenectady, population 8,000, and insulated by wooded areas on the north and a terrace wall on the south, on which students used to sit and overlook the grazing lands of the Mohawk River valley.

Among the courses Fitz Hugh attended, when he did attend, were Astronomy, Optics, classical Greek, and the less classical Analytic Mechanics and Electricity Et Cetera. He received grades of 4 (out of 5) in the first three, but only a 2 and a 3 in the scientific courses. He was reported by a classmate to have come out of his final mechanics exam, thrown his textbook high into the air, and shouted "Whoop, la!

good-bye Jack."[7] Indeed, his lesser achievement in science was reflected in his choice of courses. Among the available curriculum Fitz Hugh left untouched were botany, chemistry, geometry and calculus. Through his father's training, Fitz Hugh was already conversant in Latin and Greek.

Fitz Hugh was not at Union long before he found a preparation of hashish available from a local chemist. This preparation was sold under the name of Tilden's Extract. The laboratory of Tilden and Company in New Lebanon, New York, also operating from New York City, sold both solid and liquid preparations of hashish. (Similar extracts were also produced by such modern pharmaceutical giants as Eli Lilly, Parke-Davis, and Squibb.)[8] They described its medical qualities as:

> Phrenic, anaesthetic, anti-spasmodic and hypnotic. Unlike opium, it does not constipate the bowels, lessen the appetite, create nausea, produce dryness of the tongue, check pulmonary secretions or produce headache. Used with success in hysteria, chorea, gout, neuralgia, acute and sub-acute rheumatism, tetanus, hydrophobia and the like.[9]

The chemist told Fitz Hugh that this was a weaker batch of the drug than that which his pharmacist in Poughkeepsie had obtained. Fitz Hugh therefore decided to take about fifty grains (more than three grams) to compensate for the lesser strength, compared to the thirty grains which had been his previous maximum. Unfortunately, pharmaceutical science was still in its infancy.

Fitz Hugh took his first dose at Union at eight o'clock one spring evening. After waiting until midnight without any effects, he concluded that the preparation was even weaker than the chemist had represented. He decided to call it a night, and went to bed. Fitz Hugh awoke suddenly in the middle of the night to find himself "in a realm of the most perfect clarity of view, yet terrible with an infinitude of demoniac shadows." Worse still, beyond his bed he saw a funeral bier. Upon the bier was a corpse, "distorted with the pangs of assassination." Candles burned at the head and foot of the corpse.[10]

Fitz Hugh crawled as far away from the bier as he could, and then found to his horror that the walls of the room were closing in, and the ceiling was coming down. (Fitz Hugh had read Poe, and perhaps this vision, or the telling of it, was colored by "The Pit and The Pendulum.") Helpless, he was being forced nearer and nearer the corpse. Finally, "I fell into the fearful embrace of death." The ceiling pressed him closer upon the corpse until the whole room went black.

When he 'awoke,' the corpse was gone. But Fitz Hugh had taken its place on the bier! As he lay there, new visions appeared. Next to him, a fiend made of white hot iron, a "ferrous incarnation of all imaginations of malice...dazzling with the glory of the nether penetralia." A second demon appeared, then more demons. They began a "chant of the most terrific blasphemy...so fearful that no human thought has ever conceived of it...I still remember the meaning of the song they sang...far be it from me even to suggest its nature, lest it should seem to perpetuate in any degree such profanity as beyond the abodes of the lost no lips are capable of uttering." Suddenly one of the demons thrust a fiery pitchfork into Fitz Hugh's side, and hurled him into a flaming cradle that appeared from nowhere. The cradle had bars which caged him. "Let us sing him," said one of the fiends to the other, "the lullaby of Hell." And so they did, in an apocalyptic dirge that seemed to last an eternity. Finally, they vanished.[11]

Fitz Hugh was left with a tremendous thirst. He somehow found himself in a European village, standing before a vast fountain which was "sculptured in mockery of water, yet dry as the ashes of a furnace." He ran from house to house in the village, crying "water water, water!...a hand seized my arm...and gradually I became aware that my roommate was standing before me with a lighted lamp." Fitz Hugh entreated him, "Water! water, Robert! For the love of heaven, water!" Camps fetched some, but no mere glass for the fevered Fitz Hugh. "I snatched the pitcher, and drank a Niagara of refreshment with every draught."[12]

The combination of the refreshing drink and the lighted lamp banished all further terrors. What had been iron was now transmuted into silver and gold. A crystal gate appeared, and Fitz Hugh passed through into a valley carpeted with roses. He found himself leading a great army, and people lined his path honoring him as their liberator. Their paeans of tribute rose to a crescendo, and then faded to leave him in his room once more. Yet now, abruptly, he "plainly discovered" that his soul had left his body:

> I was that soul utterly divorced from the corporeal nature, disjoined, clarified, purified. From the air in which I hovered I looked down upon my former receptacle. Animal life, with all its processes, still continued to go on...I do not remember, in the course of the whole experience I have had of hasheesh, a more singular emotion than I felt at that moment. The spirit discerned itself as possessed of all the human capacities, intellect, susceptibility, and will—saw itself complete in every respect; yet, like a grand motor, it had abandoned the machine

which it once energized, and in perfect independence stood apart...Through the walls of the room I was able to pass and repass, and through the ceiling to behold the stars unobscured.

This was neither hallucination nor dream...A voice of command called on me to return into the body, saying in the midst of my exultation over what I thought was my final disenfranchisement from the corporeal, "the time is not yet." I returned and again felt the animal nature joined to me by its mysterious threads of conduction. Once more soul and body were one.[13]

At this, Fitz Hugh's lesson in both the transcendence and treachery of hashish ended. It is worth noting that so-called "out-of-body experiences" have been widely reported throughout history. They are reported by a range of individuals even today, some more or less reliable than others. Although there is no accepted scientific proof of such states, the subjective experiences have been associated with near-death situations as well as experiences induced by psychedelic drugs such as LSD.

The next morning Fitz Hugh awoke totally refreshed, but the memory of the demonic visitation was still quite vivid. Indeed, although he felt he had done no psychological harm to himself, he did have the feeling that he was much older in some sense than he had been the day before. Overall, Fitz Hugh decided that day to "experiment with the drug of sorcery no more." It is interesting that his first negative experience with the drug came at Union, a place where as some noted he was not immediately popular and was under some pressure to succeed. This experience was also the result of something like an "overdose."

The imagination which fed the fires of hallucination had been many years in development. Fitz Hugh's childhood illnesses allowed for considerable reading about various and distant places. His physical weakness, combined with a precocious intellect, encouraged a rich fantasy life to compensate. His creative gifts emerged in his prep school literary endeavors, and also in a reputation among family and friends as a storyteller. A surviving letter written from Union to the child of a family friend in Woodcliff, N.Y., sheds light on this aspect of his personality. The letter is carefully and plainly printed, in consideration of a child who would be unable to read his usual stylish penmanship. The printing and the simple phrasing demonstrate an ease in communicating with children.

My Dear Pet Alice.
Did you ever see anybody at your house with a pair of spectacles on his eyes, whose name sounded like "Cousin Fitz Hugh?" How would you like to have a letter from him? I ask you this because I am Cousin Fitz Hugh, and though I am more than one hundred miles away from your sweet home, I think of you very often and am sitting down now to converse with you on paper. Very often do Mr. Camps and I think about you. I live now in the same house with him and we have the same room. This house is called a College, and there are a great many men living in it and learning lessons every day. They learn a great number of things, such as how to read books with very funny letters and strange hard words, in a language called Greek. It is harder than French but it is the language in which the blessed Bible was written at first by those good men who put on paper the things that the Lord told them. Would you like to see the Greek ABC? Ask Gerty if she does not think it queer. Here it is.

$$\text{A B Γ Δ E Z H Θ I K Λ M N Ξ}$$
$$\text{Σ T Ψ Φ X Ψ Ω}$$

A good many of the students, as they call those who study here like Mr. Camps and me, learn more bad than good. They drink rum, and fight, and sometimes tease the teacher very much. Once they took a poor old horse into the house and carried him up stairs and made him look out of the window to make his owner angry. But some are very good men. I like this place very much, although I have to study so hard that I have had no time to write to you before.

I want to see you and Gerty and Lulu very much, but I am afraid it will be several months before I can. You must kiss them both a great many times and give yourself at least a dozen every day for me.

With much love to my darling Alice, her cousin Fitz Hugh bids her a most affectionate

Good Bye.[14]

This letter illustrates a love of children perhaps surprising for a rebellious teenager. The letter also raises several questions. Did Fitz Hugh consider himself one of the men at college doing more bad than good? Was rum worse in his eyes than hashish? And if he was studying so hard, how did he find time for his drug habit? For indeed Fitz Hugh's explorations were about to become a habit. Although he had sworn off the hashish after witnessing his own face on the coffin, time gradually erased the horrors of that night:

Whenever I recalled my last night of vision, it was only to dwell with tenderness upon the roses of my valley, and exult in the echo of the paeans which had glorified my march. So beautiful did such memories make the inner world, that I wearied of the outer till it became utterly distasteful, like a heavy tragedy seen for the fortieth time. I tried in vain to detect in the landscapes that ever welling freshness of life which hasheesh unveils: trees were meaningless wood, the clouds a vapory sham. I thirsted for insight, adventure, strange surprises, and mystical discoveries. I took hashish again.[15]

It was a pleasant spring afternoon, the kind that were particularly appreciated after the long, mostly overcast Schenectady winter, and which made concentrating on one's studies particularly difficult. Fitz Hugh took a dose just after lunch, and was sitting down to tea at four when "the thrill smote me." Miss McIlvaine, the boarding house matron, was refilling his teacup with the liquid "that cheers but does not inebriate" when her serving arm appeared to travel an extraordinary distance to reach him. The wallpaper became alive with satyrs, Chinese mandarins appeared in the corner of the room, and Fitz Hugh knew it was time to leave. Sam Newbury, one of his new friends at Union, followed him out of the room thinking he was ill. "The look of wild delight with which I greeted him would have revealed my secret even had I not spontaneously imparted it to him."

> I besought him to go with me, painting in the most glowing tints the treasures which such a gigantic tour as I had laid out would add to his acquaintance with the grand Kosmos. He consented to become my compagnon de voyage for a few hundred miles, at any rate.[16]

They set off to walk across a field in the center of the campus, stretching about two hundred yards. This modest meadow grew and transformed before the entranced Fitz Hugh into "a tremendous Asiatic plateau thronged with innumerable Tartars." Fitz Hugh remarked on the tribes of origin of his imagined hordes. It so happened that

Newbury was "a man unexcelled by any of his age that I have ever met for the breadth of his historic, geographical, and political knowledge." Newbury, though solicitous, was not so sympathetic as Fitz Hugh's previous guides. He couldn't let an historical inaccuracy pass unchallenged, even if its source was sheer hallucination. To Sam, Fitz Hugh's flight of fancy might at least be internally consistent. "It is impossible," said Sam, "that the tribe of which you speak should occupy this territory through whose boundaries you inform me we are traveling." Fitz Hugh's feelings were proportionately sensitive. "Alas! my friend, I see you do not sympathize with me. Let us travel apart."

Newbury was taken aback but conscientiously followed his wayward friend and soon had appeased Fitz Hugh's expanded pride. After a long but pleasant journey, the pair reached their dormitory. Newbury was not so intrigued or worried by Fitz Hugh's state of mind that he did not ask to be excused from further adventure. Fitz Hugh, in a more lucid state that came upon him as often as twice an hour during his hashish sojourns, asked Newbury to convey him to another friend, Sid Norton. Norton was appraised of Fitz Hugh's condition, and agreed to take over the duty of chaperone. These two set off from dorm out the back way where a "very large domain of woods and fields extends to the east."

> Our way skirted the banks of a little stream, which, tinkling over its rocky bed, makes music through all those shades from boundary to boundary. Coming to a convenient place, we crossed it on broad stepping-stones a pebble's throw from a low waterfall, which, higher up the bed, was now swollen by recent rains. An instantaneous dart of exultation shot through me. Could it be possible?
> "The Nile! The Nile! the eternal Nile!"[17]

Turning to Norton, he continued, "Companion of my journey, see you yonder cataract? (Remember this stream is about ten feet wide, and this cataract may have been as much as two feet high.) Above it lie the sources. Out of that gleaming chasm which you behold toward the east, this mystery-veiled river has poured his floods since God first awakened the years."

THE HANS GROOT KILL RUNS THROUGH THE UNION COLLEGE CAMPUS. UNDER THE INFLUENCE OF HASHISH, LUDLOW EXPERIENCED HIMSELF CROSSING "THE ETERNAL NILE!"

Leaving the cradle of civilization, the pair passed by two students reciting Shakespeare to each other. As Sid steered him clear of the unwitting students, Fitz Hugh overheard one say "with this farewell, I'm on my way to Padua." With these simple words, Fitz Hugh was transported from

Africa to Italy. In fact, he would later note that by picturing some exotic locale prior to eating the hashish, he could program himself to visit that place while under the influence. This suggestibility was operative during the experience as well. It might be noted that, years later, Dr. Timothy Leary, Dr. Norman Zinberg and other researchers in psychedelic drugs elucidated the doctrine of "set and setting" as a way to guide drug induced states of consciousness for therapeutic reasons.[18]

While strolling through a broad piazza, surrounded by works of Art, Fitz Hugh was once again elevated to the feeling of immense pride in his own superhuman powers. Moreover:

> I was invested with a grand mission to humanity, and slowly it dawned upon me that I was the Christ, come in the power and radiance of his millennial descent, and bearing to the world the restoration of perfect peace. I spoke, and it was done: with a single sentence I regenerated the Creation.[19]

This mission accomplished, Fitz Hugh fortunately passed out of this identity as the hashish influence began to wane. Returning to the college, a more humble but equally fanciful phenomenon presented itself. As he joined a group of his friends, he saw their faces take on the appearance of objects symbolizing their personality. One friend was a noted whist player, and his face changed to a fan-like display of playing cards. Another, known for his studious habits, became "a book-case bristling with encyclopaedias." Fitz Hugh was so amused by the latter that he couldn't help trying to pluck out one volume, and found himself pulling the man's nose.

After these frolics, Fitz Hugh attempted to retire for the night. However, awakening a short time later, he found that his hashish indulgence had taken on a new character. Whereas he had previously woken refreshed and without a mental or physical hangover, he now found that he was still hallucinating. He watched his body undergo a number of strange transformations, into a sawmill, a bottle of soda water tickled by his own effervescence, and then into a bottle of Eau de Cologne. From there, he became a hippopotamus and ambled over to the next room. Studying there was Ed, a friend of Fitz Hugh's renowned for "wasting the midnight burning-fluid."

"Tidings" cried Fitz Hugh, "tidings from the interior of Africa." With a "look of astonishment and half terror, for he had never seen me in the hasheesh state before, the lover of books opened unto me and I passed in." The hippopotamus began to speak of his homeland, but Ed pleaded preoccupation, and the hippo turned to leave:

> I opened the door to leave his room for the sake of finding a more respectful auditor, when Lo! to my shame, I had altogether mistaken my species, for I was the tallest giraffe that ever dallied amorously with a palm-bud. Abasing my exalted head to suit the dimensions of the door, I passed out and was again restored to human semblance.[20]

This day's hashish journey restored Fitz Hugh's faith in the general positive nature of the drug, as opposed to his previous "bad trip." Further, the experience began a new phase in Fitz Hugh's hasheesh life, for he found that the effect of continued use blurred the boundaries between trials. Instead of individual experiences, each trip now became tangent to the next, so that the whole was a continuous band, "one unbroken yet checkered dream."

The spring passed this way, and though Fitz Hugh may have claimed a continuous altered state of consciousness, he was able to retain the outer appearances of his personality. Here is another letter to his little friend Alice Crosby:

My Dear Pet Alice.
Though I live in a place that has that great big hard name that you see above at the top of my letter, I have not grown strange and crooked like that name, but I am the same that I always was, and I love you my little darling, just as much as ever. I think of you very often, and want very much to be out at our dear Woodcliff again, with you on one knee, and Gerty on the other, and Lulu climbing up upon my head while I tell you stories just as fast as the mill inside of my head can make them. If our lives are spared so that we may meet again in about 3 weeks, I will have plenty of very nice things to tell you, and we may hope for many a pleasant hour together.

But while I am talking of so many other things I must not forget to tell my dear little Alice how much I thank her for picking strawberries to send me. They were very beautiful, and so large and fat that I wonder what you give them to eat. The man at whose house I get my meals is very stingy, and has only given us strawberries for tea once this summer, and then they were so small that I guess they must have been the grand-sons of yours if they belonged to the same family at all. One of your strawberries could have taken one of those we had in his arms like a baby just as this picture shows.

I thank you very much for thinking of me my dear Alice so much as to pick this pretty present for me, for I have no little girls here to love me, and to know that you care for me when I am far away is a very sweet thought.

You must pray for your precious sisters every day, my dear, so that they with you may make your father and mother as happy as heart can wish, and at the same time please our dear Father who is in Heaven.

Give our darling Gerty and Lulu my heart full of love. Tell them that I often think of them and want to see them very much. Kiss them and the baby for me many times.

And now darling, I must say Good Bye. It is quite late and my bed is crying "come Alice's cousin, come old fellow, or you will be too late for prayers tomorrow morning." So I answer "I'll be there in one minute, Bed, after I have sent a great, great deal of love, and a kiss in this ring [here there is a circle drawn, within it the words "kiss this for me"] to Alice from her cousin Fitz Hugh."[21]

(COURTESY OF SCHAFFER LIBRARY, UNION COLLEGE)

This letter raises an interesting point. Fitz Hugh's hashish habit was in full swing, yet we see no evidence of it unless one feels the last three paragraphs of this letter are too sac-charine for a normal mind. Prolonged hashish use apparently had no detrimental effect on Fitz Hugh's capacity to carry on a "normal" life.

Fitz Hugh visited briefly with his family in the late sum-mer, presenting his sister Helen with a poem on her 16th birthday. It contained one poignant stanza:

> She is not here who gave thee birth
> Her foot grew silent in thy spring,
> But if the saints may look on earth
> She watches o'er thy blossoming.[22]

Helen was now a student at Abbott's Collegiate Ins-titute for Young Ladies. The curriculum here was not as progressive (or masculine) as that of Union College. Helen studied music, painting, bookkeeping, writing, and most importantly, French phrases and French geography. This was no doubt in preparation for accompanying her future, educated, husband into Good Society.

Fitz Hugh was soon back in Schenectady for the fall semester. He summed up his eventful nineteenth year in a letter to his cousin Samuel Ludlow Frey, or 'Lud,' including thoughts on Christian theology tinged by his transpersonal experiences with hashish.[23]

> My Dear Lud,
> I must indeed in view of your three letters hitherto unanswered own my conduct uncousinly & unworthy a good correspondent. Since I last saw you I have been through many changes of place & circumstance & after losing my health, trying to find it on a farm & failing, traveling, teaching, entering Princeton, being burned out & losing all

my small possessions, I at last find myself in Union, within a year of my graduation. Two weeks from today will find me if living a senior, and the roll of a few short succeeding months will bring me to the gate of real life, & thrust me out from these preparatory cloisters forever, into the world, the dusty, mighty, toilsome world. When you pray, ask for me that I may be nerved for struggle with its opposing forces, for might to stand up to its responsibilities.

I have heard & indeed with no small pain, that you are all going to leave your quiet valley with its varying lights & shades, its old memories, its peaceful streams, its wild woods & days that have poured out for you hitherto a mingled cup of joy & sorrow, & turning your back on the rising sun are about to seek a far off home, many a league away in Western woods...But be you not desponding, dear Lud, Stoutheart be strong! Our earthly migrations are but the exchange of one poor shadow for another; the substance is above.

"We look not at the things which are seen but the things which are not seen, for the things which are seen are temporal, but the things which are not seen are eternal." I know you have the Christian's hope dear cousin, therefore be strong. May your home in the west be very happy.

Papa & I talk of spending part of August in the Adirondacks, enjoying the wild sports of that solitary region. He needs it very much, having performed most arduous labor in a very precious Revival of God's work in our Church this past winter & spring which I think numbers about 50 converted, & the interest is still unabated. If we do camp out there this summer on our way back, we will if possible come & make you a visit. Give my heart full of love to darling Aunt Caroline, Carry who never sends any to me in her letters, to Helen, naughty girl that she is, Gus, Johnnie & your Father if they are at home. Don't pay me in my own coin but write shortly.

Your sincerely affectionate cousin, F.H. Ludlow[24]

NORTH COLLEGE AT UNION, BUILT IN 1814, WHERE
LUDLOW RESIDED DURING HIS HASHISH ADVENTURES.
(SCHENECTADY COUNTY HISTORICAL SOCIETY)

1 John R. Bodo, *The Protestant Clergy and Public Issues*, Princeton: Princeton University Press, 1954, p. 126.
2 Carl Niemeyer, "Fitz Hugh Ludlow and Union College," *Fitz Hugh Ludlow, Union Worthies Number Eight*, Schenectady: Union College, 1953, p. 7.
3 *The Hasheesh Eater*, p. 155.
4 J.R. Tryon, *Union Alumni Monthly*, 1906, p. 17.
5 Francis Bangs Wilkie, Personal Reminiscences of Thirty-Five Years of Journalism, Chapter IV, reprinted in *Union Alumni Monthly*, November 1937.
6 *Poughkeepsie News*, January 12, 1871.
7 "The Song to Old Union," *Concordiensis*, Volume XIX, January 29, 1896, p. 1.
8 Herer (1991), p. 2.
9 From an ad reproduced in Fitz Hugh Ludlow, *The Hasheesh Eater*, San Francisco: Level Press, 1975, p. 201.
10 *The Hasheesh Eater*, p. 67.
11 *The Hasheesh Eater*, p. 67.

12 Ibid., p. 72.

13 Ibid., p. 75.

14 Fitz Hugh Ludlow to Alice Crosby, n.d., now in collections of Schaffer Library, Union College, Schenectady, NY (hereafter Schaffer Library).

15 *The Hasheesh Eater*, p. 85.

16 Ibid., p. 89.

17 Ibid., p. 89.

18 See for example Zinberg (1984).

19 *The Hasheesh Eater*, p. 96.

20 Ibid., p. 100.

21 Fitz Hugh Ludlow to Alice Crosby, July 7th, 1855, Schaffer Library.

22 Fitz Hugh Ludlow, "To my Sister on her Sixteenth Birthday" in manuscript book now at Schaffer Library.

23 LSD researcher and psychologist Stanislav Grof classed some LSD experiences as "transpersonal," postulating individual consciousness going beyond the spatial or temporal boundaries of the physical body. See Stanislav Grof, *Beyond the Brain*, Albany: State University of New York Press, 1985.

24 Fitz Hugh Ludlow to S. Ludlow Frey, July 11, 1855, NYCPL.

V

"LET THE GRECIAN DREAM"

WILLIAM C. GIVENS, *UNION COLLEGE, SCHENECTADY, N. YORK*, AFTER A PRE-
SUMED LOST DRAWING OF THE SCHOOL'S ARCHITECT, JOSEPH RAMÉE.
(COURTESY OF THE UNION COLLEGE PERMANENT COLLECTION)

FITZ HUGH was not elected to Phi Beta Kappa, unlike many
of his close friends. Although he ranked in the middle of his
class in grades, he was awarded a scholarship, called a "char-
ity grant," in each of his three senior semesters worth $10 a
term. (Tuition and board amounted to $70 per term.)

Several Union professors influenced Fitz Hugh. Captain
Isaac Wilbur Jackson, a Union alumnus, was a long-time
math teacher. In addition, he was an avid horticulturist,
and developed the land in back of North College into what
would later be known as Jackson's Gardens, still there and
impressive today. This was the land of Fitz Hugh's Egyptian
adventure, and doubtless several others as well. Jackson was
also one of the founding members of the Kappa Alpha Soci-
ety at Union, a literary secret society considered to be the
first social fraternity in the American college system. (Union
calls herself the "Mother of Fraternities.") This fact was to
benefit Fitz Hugh before he left Union.

Another influential figure on campus was Laurens Perseus Hickok, vice president of the college and professor of mental and moral philosophy.[1] Hickok, also a Union graduate, had moved through a number of pastoral positions before teaching, and returned to Union in 1852. Hickok, as vice president, had expected to succeed to the presidency as soon as Dr. Nott retired, but the ascension would take another ten years, until Nott finally died in 1866. Hickok was considered something of a radical in his time, being acquainted with the German philosophers before they were well known in America. His magnum opus was *Rational Psychology* (published by Union in 1854), an attempt to, as one historian put it, "translate the 'old time religion' into a rational system of knowledge."[2] This philosophical predilection is reflected in Ludlow's thoughts on the hashish experience. One critic has gone so far as to proclaim that "*Rational Psychology*...is, in fact, Fitz Hugh Ludlow's philosophy."[3] This is not surprising, as Fitz Hugh was thoroughly grounded in "the old time religion," and his ready absorption of modern ideas impelled him to reconcile the two, much as Hickok had. Whether or not *Rational Psychology* was Fitz Hugh's metaphysical bible, it seems clear that Hickok's approach did shape the young Fitz Hugh in lasting ways.

Other professors were of lesser influence, although one Jonathan Pearson, known to students as Pinky and serving as college treasurer, remained in touch with Fitz Hugh in later years.

But the true talents of Fitz Hugh Ludlow were not accurately prefigured in the standard collegiate curriculum, nor in the innovative scientific programs. Fitz Hugh earned his highest grades, and foreshadowed his future reputation, in a course unique to Union. It was called "Kames," and was taught by the good doctor himself, Eliphalet Nott. Nott's main textbook was *Elements of Criticism*, written by Lord Kames of Scotland, a friend of Benjamin Franklin. The book presented a theory of aesthetics supposedly based on Newtonian physics. At Union, the book was only a departure for the personal theories and opinions of Eliphalet Nott. One critic has remarked that the Kames course substituted inquiry for authority, certainly an adventurous notion at a time when the classics were still the core curriculum in many schools.[4]

LAURENS PERSEUS HICKOK (1798-1888) ABOUT THE TIME
HE WOULD HAVE TAUGHT FITZ HUGH LUDLOW.

One of the essential assignments in the course was the "declaiming of one's own compositions before the class." It was here that the fantasist and storyteller Fitz Hugh was

sure to shine. As one commentator has said, "it is probable
that the high marks in 'Kames' and Fitz Hugh's scholarship
grants were reflective of Fitz Hugh's literary and oratorical
gifts."[5] Fitz Hugh sharpened his natural skills through prac-
tice, accompanying friends to a local church (to which they
had a key) for the purpose of critiquing each other's ora-
tions. Several years later, Nott would say of Fitz Hugh, "…
he was considered here a young man of very decided talents,
and unimpeachable character. Having completed his college
course, he left the institution esteemed alike by his companions
and his instructors, as well as distinguished by literary hon-
ors."[6] In less formal settings, Fitz Hugh was also recognized
for these abilities. A classmate, and for one term roommate,
J.R. Tryon (later to become surgeon and Rear Admiral in the
U.S. Navy) remembered Fitz Hugh as a "brilliant talent" with
a "keen sense of humor." Tryon's reminiscence also described
the Fitz Hugh Ludlow of 1856: "In appearance, he was above
the medium height, slight in figure, with regular features, fair
complexion, brown hair and blue eyes. He was nearsighted
and wore glasses. His countenance always beamed with intel-
ligence." Of Fitz Hugh's character, Tryon said generously,
"Fitz Hugh Ludlow as I remember him in College Days was
conspicuous for his uniform good nature, affectionate dispo-
sition, unbounded enthusiasm, marked generosity, congenial
companionship, simplicity and courage. These qualities, com-
bined with other noble traits of character constituted the
genius revered by his Alma Mater."[7]

The following letter to cousin Ludlow Frey reveals that
Fitz Hugh's talents for declaiming had reached outside the
Union campus, and also offers us one of his earliest, albeit
sarcastic, discussions of the subject of temperance:

My Dear Lud,

I was so busy all vacation, reading & writing about 10 hours a day & have been so busy ever since I came back this term that I have not been able to relieve myself of my indebtedness to you for your last letter, nor to Gus thanking him for bringing me my book from Poughkeepsie. I now take the opportunity which a few hours leisure gives me to do both.

And now I will tell you when under certain conditions you may expect to see me. Uncle John when I was at your house offered me an invitation to lecture at Canojoharie, or told me he would get me one. Was this jocular or will he really keep his word? I may be out on the Western rail-road in your direction in a short time to lecture at one or two other places, and if your father would like to have me stop at Canojoharie for the same purpose, I will do so if we arrange upon the day. The lecture I will give, if I do speak there, is "The Peculiarities of Genius." I would like to have you write me very soon even though it be but a few lines, saying whether the good people of your place would like a lecture from me & if so, what time would be best suited to your wishes. I shall then be able to make the arrangements dovetail together.

I suppose you are now like all the United States buried in snow up to your neck. It is said that some people belonging to a church not far from Schenectady have to climb in at the belfry windows on account of a drift which has covered their house of worship but I hardly think this credible as we have yet had no snows near college which reached above the second story windows. A mining company has however been incorporated for the purpose of sinking perpendicular shafts down to a cabbage garden snowed 50 feet under in this vicinity in order to supply sauer-kraut materials to the Dorp [Schenectady] Dutchmen, several of whose families have perished from a deprivation of their accustomed food and an indulgence in a new article of diet which they have endeavored to substitute for sauer-kraut called potatoes. The sufferings of the Dutch families around here is beyond conception.

One of them in my district whom I called upon as visitor of the poor of Schenectady told me one of the most affecting stories of destitution I have ever heard. He said that during one whole week in the course of the present winter he and his whole family had subsisted upon nothing but beef-steak & bread & for several days had been limited to 20 glasses of lager per diem.

They had received no assistance from charity whatever except that on one occasion a benevolent in the neighborhood had sent them in a dish of coleslaw when they did not know where to look for the morrows cabbage-stalk. I gave the man a large red cabbage which he hugged frantically for joy, at the same time bedewing my feet with tears. I put him down in my visitors book for further relief & offered him some temperance tracts which he accepted gratefully saying that they were the very things to light his meerschaum with. Thus the glorious cause of temperance & humanity is flourishing among us, and I hope that the legislature will enact as our society has petitioned, a law for the suppression of vice and immorality against the drinking of tea & coffee & the use of tight boots which people our jails & prisons & send so many victims to an untimely grave.

Much love to all the Palatiniers, & believe me ever your very affectionate cousin

Fitz Hugh Ludlow[8]

Winter in Schenectady was a long and dreary siege. Students were expected to be in chapel every morning at six for services and a Nott lecture in the dark. Even one of the Good Doctor's inventions, a coal burning stove, was small comfort. But Nott felt that the discipline was essential for his "slovenish, boorish, and reckless" college men.

In the winter of 1856, Fitz Hugh formally solidified his bonds with several of his slovenish friends and hashish chaperones by being initiated into the Kappa Alpha Society.

This is the same Kappa Alpha begun by Professor Jackson and eight other students in 1825. That group had revolved around a charismatic character named John Hart Hunter. A twentieth-century guide to college fraternities, *Baird's Manual*, said of K.A.: "the founders possessed an aptitude for their task amounting to genius. They stamped upon their Society a character which it has never lost." A later K.A. yearbook described itself with a nod to its founding fathers: "The high standard they set still marks K.A. and inspires its members. Our ideals are exemplified in beautiful secret observances, from which we derive a special enjoyment. Our outwardly visible attributes are respected by the college world. Solicitous of our unique repute, we wish to remain not in the commonly accepted sense a fraternity, but a Society."[9] While Kappa Alpha did and does conduct a secret initiation, it does not include the kind of "hazing" for which fraternities in general are infamous. Rather there are certain philosophical discussions and extensive personal preparation that is undertaken.[10]

Whatever the secret activities of the Society, in the outward manifestations Fitz Hugh was exemplary. As Tryon later put it, "as a Kappa Alpha in College he was most loyal and enthusiastic and prominent in poetry and song, and the society cherishes his memory with a fidelity undiminished during the many years that have passed since he immortalized it by his presence."[11] "Immortalize" might be excessive, but K.A. is still very active on the Union campus, and the current members of the Society are well acquainted with Fitz Hugh and his legacy.

Other attributes of K.A. included literary endeavor and that old college favorite, unadulterated hedonism. Phi Beta

Kappa was the first secret society in college history, but K.A. was the first "social fraternity," and its members in 1856 upheld that tradition as well. Fitz Hugh characterized K.A. shortly after graduation as "the closest circle of earthly fellowship wherein I have known what it is for heart to be knit with heart."[12]

With a sympathetic crew of literate and adventurous friends, Fitz Hugh continued his hashish journeys with deeper and more thorough indulgence. As he became more involved, Fitz Hugh sought to widen the scope of his experiment and began to initiate his friends. He did not think that he was endangering them in any way, and still called his activities "research." The roster includes:

WILLIAM N.

We know nothing about William except his name, and the fact that his reaction to hashish was the closest Fitz Hugh had seen to the stereotype of the marijuana user with which we are familiar today. That is, William sat in a chair in a stupor, eyes half closed, totally introverted.

ROBERT BARNUM

"One of my friends in college was a man to whom it would have been physically, spiritually, and morally impossible ever to have borne any other name than Bob."[13] Bob was impulsive, enthusiastic, excitable and fond of queer researches and romantic ventures, i.e., a perfect candidate for hashish studies. Bob began with two grams after dinner, and hours later was dancing wildly across the room with loud peals of laughter. Before long however, Bob was worried, wondering "what will become of me?" Fitz Hugh recognized the fear just as he had recognized the joy. "Trust me, however singularly you may feel, you have not the slightest cause for fear. I have been where you are now, and, upon my honor, guarantee you an unharmed return. No evil will result to you; abandon yourself to the full force of your feelings with perfect confidence that you are in no danger." One hundred years later, this would be known as "going with the flow."[14]

Outdoors, Bob was enveloped in a Middle Eastern dream. Fitz Hugh noticed that many of his friends had visions of Oriental scenes just as he had. He attributed this to the drug's association with its use among Eastern peoples. Again, the modern phrase would be "set and setting," where the person's mindset or preconceptions would invariably shape the effects of the drugs upon the mind. Fitz Hugh went further in his writings, saying that Eastern people's "inscrutable" personalities are the result of their indulgence, the way the English are shaped by beer, and Americans by tobacco.

Returning to Bob, that worthy was bathing in silvery moonlight, which unexpectedly turned to a shower of soot that nearly buried him. Fitz Hugh found that the power of suggestion from outside was ineffectual at bringing Bob to a more pleasant state, and Bob demanded to be taken to a doctor. The school doctor, who had no acquaintance whatever with hashish, told poor Bob that he was "foolish to have made the experiment…might die…would give him a powder…ahem." Fitz Hugh followed the phlegmatic physician into the next room and somehow persuaded the man that the most important thing he could do was reassure Bob that he was in no danger. This was done, and Bob settled down.

Bob went to sleep with Fitz Hugh nearby as sentinel, and had magical dreams. The next morning, and for several days, Bob felt a continuing state of delight, although without hallucinations. The challenge accepted and met, Bob never took hashish again.

FRED WEAD

Wead was one of Fitz Hugh's classmates who had more than a brief fling with the seductive cannabis indica. For several months, Wead traveled by Fitz Hugh's side. His personality seemed predisposed to calling forth music during these occasions. He would have Fitz Hugh sing or hum a melody, and would sometimes see grand castles arising out of the air as the songs notes rose, and then crumble as the notes descended. On one occasion, Fred and Fitz Hugh visited a musician friend and asked him to regale them. Fred hallucinated a grand cathedral, and then a funeral procession entered bearing the body of Mendelssohn. The pianist identified the piece as Mendelssohn's Funeral March. Fred swore that he had never heard it before, and Fitz Hugh added the event to his catalogue of the possibly transpersonal.

DANIEL MANN

This is the same Dan from Poughkeepsie that accompanied Fitz Hugh on some of his early flights. Dan was now president of Kappa Alpha, and characterized by Fitz Hugh as "the Coryphaeus of witty circles. The light of all our festivals, he was still imaginative in higher spheres, and as worthily held the rostrum and the bard's chair as his place by the genial fireside."[15] As Dan was a poet and musician, Fitz Hugh predicted that the effect of hasheesh upon his sensitive nature would be delightful. However, Dan took the hashish at a time when he was in what Fitz Hugh called a state of "morbid excitability." (Without further elaboration, one might conclude that this was around the time of final exams.) Dan felt the initial "thrill" that Fitz Hugh often described, but it was so intense as to be painful. They went to a room where Dan could lie down. When he did, "of a sudden all space expanded marvelously, and into the broad area where he reclined marched a multitude of bands from all directions, discoursing music upon all sorts of instruments, and each band playing a different march on a different key, yet all, by some scientific arrangement, preserving perfect harmony with each other, and most exquisitely keeping time. As the symphony increased in volume, so also did it heighten in pitch, until at last the needle-points of sound seemed to concentrate in a demon music-box of incredible upper register which whirled the apex of its scream through the dome of his head, inside of which it was playing." Despite some musical and visual pleasures, the experience was more on the unpleasant side for Dan, and its effects persisted for months, including weaker thrills, and a "hashish tint" to his dreams.

As a result of his various friends' experiences, Fitz Hugh concluded that personality type seemed to correspond in general to the effect of hashish. Extreme personalities, the "sanguine" or the "bilious," sustained the most powerful changes, while "lymphatic" ones generally felt little or no influence, save perhaps for vertigo or nausea. And what were the long term effects on his friends? A quick glimpse of their futures may reveal outcomes which will more slowly unfold in this story of Fitz Hugh's life.

Sid Norton became a chemistry professor at Ohio State University, perhaps carrying out more objective studies of pharmacological agents. After helping Dan Mann to start a chapter of Kappa Alpha at the University of Virginia, Sam Newbury had scarcely begun a law career when he was called to the service on the side of the Union. He rose to the rank of Captain, and then tragically fell in battle at Petersburg, Virginia in the summer of 1864. Fred Wead died a Colonel in the same year at Cold Harbor. Ed Bartlett, who "wasted the midnight burning fluid," survived the War as the clergyman at the side of William Tecumseh Sherman on his "march to the sea." The man known as "Bob" moved to the frontier, becoming a manufacturer in St. Louis, the embarkation point for the Wild West. Several of Fitz Hugh's other brothers in Kappa Alpha became doctors or lawyers, and the crew also included a teacher of the deaf and blind, a rear admiral in the U.S. Navy, and the first president of Smith College, Laurenus Clark Seelye. Indeed, none of them seemed to suffer any career-inhibiting, long-term effects from their collegiate hashish explorations. But Fitz Hugh took the indulgence much further than any of them.

One day late in the fall of 1855, Fitz Hugh was at the dinner table when he was "seized by the hand of the hasheesh genie."[16] Pulled outdoors, he was caught up in the revels of a band of the worshippers of Bacchus, the god of wine. (The ancient Greeks formed secret mystery religions around the worship of Dionysus.) "Together with the troops of Bacchantes I leaped madly among the clusters; I cried Evoe Bacche with the loudest. I drank the blood of grapes like nectar; I reeled under the possession of the divine afflatus. Around me in endless mazes circled beauteous shapes of men and women; with hands enclasped we danced and sang, and the Maenad houris overshadowed me with their luxuriant disheveled hair."

This intoxication soon passed, and as he emerged from the campus gardens there came an unexpected supplication. "Kill thyself! kill thyself! Thou shalt be immortal, thou shalt behold the hidden things of God." Swept up just as suddenly as by Bacchus, Fitz Hugh drew his jack knife, opened the blade and raised it to his throat. The blow of an invisible hand struck the knife from his grasp, and the suicidal urgings ceased. In the silence, Fitz Hugh raised his eyes to the darkening skies. An "angel of midnight blackness floated" in the sky above, poised to strike the poor mortal down. But then, "across the firmament a chariot came like lightning; its wheels were rainbow-suns that rolled in tremendous music; no charioteer was there, but in his place flashed the glory of an intense brightness." At its approach, the angel of death fled, and another dramatic pageant had played itself out in the head of Fitz Hugh Ludlow.

On yet another occasion, the theatrical element became manifest in his hashish dreams. Fitz Hugh found himself on a stage, performing as a victorious soldier before a vast audience. But as he held forth, he "saw a strange and dreadful look of suspicion overshadowing every face of the thousands in my audience."[17] Soon he realized "they know my secret!…at that instant, one maddening chorus broke from the whole theatre: "Hasheesh! hasheesh! he has eaten hasheesh!" This is the proverbial drug users paranoia, here given epic proportions in Fitz Hugh's fantasy. Fitz Hugh apparently drew no suspicion from his apothecary sources for the large quantities he purchased, or he had made new pharmacist friends from whom to "borrow" supplies. But his religious upbringing left resi-dues of guilt in an otherwise rebellious, intellectual soul. In the unguarded thrall of a hasheesh hallucination, this pent-up remorse took vivid and sometimes nightmarish forms.

As the frequency of his consumption increased, the habit took on more complex forms and behaviors. After especially pleasant journeys, he began to take additional doses before the effects of the first trip faded. Alas, this strategy did not prove effective. One day Fitz Hugh luxuriated in ancient Greece and Rome, raising his hand to touch an angel on the dome at St. Peter's Basilica; "a mighty stretch of arm indeed; yet to the hasheesh-eater, all things are possible." Although ten grains had produced a pleasant morning, he decided to take five more in order to prolong the euphoria. As he sat among some friends doing some writing, he found his thoughts flowing more easily onto paper. Before long, he couldn't keep up with the flow of ideas and leapt to his feet. A "fever boiled in my blood, and every heart-beat was the stroke of a colossal engine."[18] He could no longer contain himself and fled the room.

It was "Bob" who recognized the problem, owing to his own experiences, and chased him. They passed outdoors, but a procession of hellish scenes rolled past. Here, "a sister mourned bitterly for a brother who was about to descend into Hell!" There, burned "the serpentine fires of an infinite furnace...From the abysses of my soul a cry of torture went up for discords which I had caused in the grand harmony of universal law." All this Fitz Hugh suffered in silence. After a while, Bob thought a suggestive reference might set off an interesting fantasy, but he did not choose well. "See the Styx" he offered. "My God" cried Fitz Hugh, "am I again journeying toward the Infernal? Yes, it must be so; for even this man, who has learned nothing of my past torture, knows and tells me this is one of the rivers of Hell!" Whoops, thought Bob. "This is not the Styx at all," said he, "but only a small stream which runs through Schenectady."[19]

After an extended calming talk, Bob coaxed Fitz Hugh into a restaurant for a glass of wine. But infernal visions continued until Fitz Hugh spied a crucifix upon the far wall of the restaurant. It was only when this image spoke to the frantic Fitz Hugh, "by the breath of the Spirit thine iniquities are borne utterly away," that the nightmare effects of the attempt to extend euphoria finally passed away.

But the realization that hashish was more a habit than an experiment had finally dawned on Fitz Hugh. "It may be that the fact of its ascendency gradually dawned upon me; but, at any rate, whenever the suspicion became definite, I dismissed it by so varying the manner of the enjoyment as to persuade myself that it was experimental still."[20]

With this approach in mind, Fitz Hugh joined a college field trip down the Hudson River by steamboat to see an opera. Both the water voyage and the sublime music would be new phenomenon come under the lens of cannabis indica. On the ship, Fitz Hugh joined his fellow travellers in a smorgasbord, defined as "five hundred Americans of us had, for the incredible space of fifteen minutes, been fiercely elbowing each other in insane haste to secure that grand national end, indigestion." After dinner, cigars were lit and the young men sung for an hour or three a series of college songs: "There is Music in the Air" and "Co-ca-che-lunk" were two that stood out in his memory. These he felt were, in their place, as satisfying as the most exalted of operas.[21]

The boat reached New York City the next morning. Fitz Hugh had been born in Gotham, but that was not enough to prepare him for the effects of a morning dose of the Muse. Hashish intensified the mad rush of the crowds of the city. Although a city of only one million in 1856, New York was a truly intimidating place after bucolic Schenectady. Not only the number, but the faces of the people were horrific. All seemed either diabolic or despairing, bent on securing some financial conquest or resigned to hopelessness of their situation. Unable to stand walking the mean streets, Fitz Hugh boarded an omnibus carriage. This only allowed him time for paranoia among his fellow passengers, as he "distinctly heard them use the word 'hasheesh.'" Reaching a friend's house, he pleaded exhaustion and tried to sleep. He finally rested, but "began to be aware that I should never again, in the hasheesh state, be secure in the certainty of unclouded visions. The cup had been so often mingled, that its savor of bitterness would never wholly pass away."[22]

But for now the opera awaited, and Fitz Hugh ate another solid chunk of hashish. As he concentrated on the music, he discovered a new example of the heightening of sensory experience which resulted from hashish:

> Seated side by side in the middle of the orchestra played two violinists. That they were playing the same part was evident from their perfect uniformity in bowing their bows, through the whole piece, rose and fell simultaneously, keeping exactly parallel. A chorus of wind and stringed instruments pealed on both sides of them and the symphony was as perfect as possible; yet, amid all that harmonious blending, I was able to detect which note came from one violin and which from the other as distinctly as if the violinists had been playing at the distance of a hundred feet apart, and with no other instruments discoursing near them.[23]

Before further analyzing this phenomenon, Fitz Hugh was drifted on to a whimsical fantasy, that he had himself lost all human proportions and become that obelisk in Central Park, Cleopatra's Needle. This silliness ended any scientific exploration that night, and the opera went on in a haze of fantasy and slapstick distraction.

The tales related thus far have also underreported another characteristic that is part of the mythos concerning marijuana and its derivatives, that of "the giggles." In Fitz Hugh's case, the tendency toward laughter was filtered through two of his strongest attributes, his classical education and his deep love of puns. "For hours I walked aching with laughter in this land of Paronomasia, where the whole Dictionary had arrayed itself in strophe and antistrophe, and was dancing a ludicrous chorus of quirk and quibble...Rarely did the music of a deeper wit intermingle with the rattling fantasies of the pun-country; never was anything but the broad laugh heard there, and the very atmosphere was crazy with oxygen."[24]

This potentially annoying habit found its way into his writing as well. For Fitz Hugh had continued to develop his creative talents along with the academic and the psychoactive. One of his pastimes was to pen poems, sometimes to set to music and sometimes not. Following is one of the latter, solely and completely dedicated to the art of Paronomasia. Fitz Hugh even helped the uninitiated by underlining the puns:

BENNY HAVENS

There was a jolly fellow, who lived about the town,
He disapproved of toddy, and so—he *put it down*;
He attended public dinners for fun and freedom's sake,
And like a second Polycarp went smiling to the *steak*.[25]

His vests were irreproachable, his trowsers of the kind
Adown whose steep declivities hound rushes after hind;
They were a speaking pattern, all the tailors would agree,
But, O, alas! they were too *tight* to speak coherently.
Up half a dozen pairs of stairs our hero went to bed
With nothing but the angels and the rafters o'er his head,
And so although he loved to be when brandy vapor curled
There never was a man who lived *so much above the world.*
No board of all the roof was known a meeting e'er to hold
And so the room was nothing but a trap for catching cold
There was a door; the carpenter had left the lock behind
It must have slipped him as he had no *Locke* upon the mind.
Our hero's uncle used to dye to keep himself alive
He kept a shop in Hemstead Row at number 35
But when as every dyer must he felt his colors fail
Before he kicked the bucket he turned a little *pale.*
He called his nephew to his side & with a mournful mien
Said "I feel blue to leave you (You musn't think it green)
I've not gained much by dying but I leave you all my pelf
It may assist you, if you ever want to dye yourself."
His spirit fled and left the youth to woe and rolling collars
As dolorous as any man who has a heap of dollars
But "oh" said he "let others dye, they're fool enough I trow
For though the colors may be fast, the trade is very slow."[26]

As spring approached after a long and brutal Schenectady winter, Fitz Hugh's literary side bloomed and flourished. His poems and songs were celebrated by both his close friends and the student body in general. Francis Wilkie, editor of the student magazine *New Era*, asked Fitz Hugh to contribute. He responded with an appropriately academic/philosophic piece grandly entitled, "Hymn for the Soul of Man." Here are the opening and closing verses:

We are not things of yesterday;
Our souls' ancestral rivers run
From fountains of antiquity
That gushed ere God lit up the sun.
Across the solitudes of Time,
No more by mortal footsteps trod,
Where the dead nations sleep sublime,
Come whispers of our source in God.

Arise to deeds of great intent,
O man! and with thy valiant hands
Rear heaven-high a monument
Whose shadows shall reach other lands
The glories of a noble strife
Survive the pulses of endeavor
The echoes of a mighty life
Ring through time's corridors forever.[27]

Hashish had taken Fitz Hugh to heaven and hell, and his personal experience with transcendence informed the verses that for others might have been academic exercises. But Fitz Hugh's heart did not normally rest in such a solemn place, not in this pastoral collegiate fantasyland. Life was not meant for brooding. The everyday Fitz Hugh was to be found in happy intellectual communion with his friends in Kappa Alpha and the allegorical elevation of everyday life. Typical was the following address to the Society at one of their winter literary meetings:

The much to be lamented self sequestration of our honored secretary is a grammatical ellipse which no common noun like yr humble servant can hope to supply, nor should he desire as is common in most ellipses of these kinds. His idiopsythic cerebral material do not adapt him to the function of a reverboraciously megalogical allocutor and in his pro tempore supposititious officiation he would supplicate yr congruency while he postulated your auscultation to a locutration characterized by logistic paucity and intensified sententiousness. In the rhetorical tradition of this scheme, megalogy gives out. He will there-fore discourse upon the subject in microphonistic platitudinousness.

First we speak of the Sigs [Sigma Phi, the second Greek letter social fraternity founded at Union]. They have lately had an initiation, but as is the case of the man who couldn't pay his stakes at the horse race, we see in this no change for the better. Unlike salvation, they may now be found indeed without money but certainly not with-out price. Their new pledge is a young man whose life is one gratuitously prolonged imprecation...Mr. Weed still continues to sing. He does not believe in hiding his talents in a napkin, and in deference to the napkin's feelings we agree with him.

In the Philomathean (debating society) yr humble servant is happy to say we are still in the ascendent. In the new Battle of Hastings on Saturday we came off with palms of victory, though the chicks of the other party went away with flying colors. But any further talk of them would be not only of no further use but an illustration of the aphorism out of nothing nothing can come.[28]

In slightly less formal (and polysyllabic) surroundings, Fitz Hugh could also be counted on for a song or poem to celebrate the eternal rites of passage of college students and young people everywhere. He noted that in honor of the 21st birthdays of Sid Norton and Dan Mann in January of 1856, "we had supper at Slater's, on the night of the 10th and the morning of the 11th in celebration of the occasion."[29] Although Union practiced a curfew at the time, Fitz Hugh and company were not averse to burning the kerosene lamp at both ends. This became a habit that would last Fitz Hugh most of his life. An address to his fellow Kaps was inspired by the debauch celebrated that evening:

> The restaurated introcession of calorificated diurnal periods is causational of cerebral hebetude and muscular flaccidity. Judging analogically from that Jarinaceolidginous preparation denominated bread and butter, we might conclude our chunk of calories spread over the big slice of a summer day would be a pretty attenuated lamina. Strange as it may appear this is not the case.
>
> But it is one of our multiplicity of beatitudes that the incandescent ventral organ possesses in refrigerant imbibition a fire engine for the extinction of its combustion. For let us not be oblivious of the esophagus, that glorious old railway to the fabulary depot down whose track have passed so many immigrant trains of bivalves and fat capons all presented with a free pass by the magnanimous sons of Kappa Alpha. Often may its track be sprinkled during this season and let us all vote whether Whig or Democrat for the improvement of at least one canal, the alimentary.[30]

Yet another evening of carousing was capped by a poem, this one to a friend leaving for Kentucky upon graduation:

> Again in this good old College
> I sit as in days of old,
> When I shook the tree of knowledge
> And it rained down pippins of gold.
> And though I coined none of those pippins
> To the shape of a Phi Beta key,
> Yet their fragrance is none the poorer
> In the hoards of memory.[31]

And another, a "song written for the conjoint birthday occasion of my leal and loved brethren in the bonds of KA,

Sid Norton and Dan Mann":

> Let the voice of song ring glad and long
> And the Stars smile on our meeting
> For right good cheer befits us here
> In our brotherly birthday greeting;
> And may all the sum of the years to come
> Be as warm with joy's bright ember,
> And as free from care to the much loved pair
> Whose birth our songs remember.[32]

Nor was it only fraternal friends that were showered with words of love:

TO A RED HEADED GIRL

All thy curls are winding stairs,
Where my passion nobly dares
To mount higher, still and higher,
Though the staircase be on fire.[33]

While at Union, Fitz Hugh wrote a number of Valentine poems which have survived in manuscript. These were addressed to Miss Fanny B., Miss Louisa B., Jenny Taylor of Washington D.C., Laura N***, and several others, all in 1856. Louisa B. is probably Louisa Burritt, evidently a family friend, and the woman to whom "Hymn for the Soul of Man" was dedicated. Another poem, entitled "My Gentler Memories," painted a tribute to household harmony and is dedicated to the Burritt family.[34]

Although by no means stinting in his attention to the fairer sex, as far as is known there were no special female objects of Fitz Hugh's affection at this time. Union was all-male, as were most colleges at this time, and upstate New

York was still a puritanical place. There were options available to gentlemen of this era, but such things of course were not mentioned in polite correspondence. However, one of Fitz Hugh's surviving poems is the strangely titled "To a young Lady, Possessor of a one-eyed dog". Unlike the genteel valentines mentioned above, where a girl's glance was likened to a "dart from Cupid's quiver," this one has an earthier tone:

> I want an all consuming love
> to meet the rapturous flame of mine,
> no love that waits for time to prove
> the root of my heart's passion-vine;
> the only love that I can hear
> is that which in abandonment
> finds all in me and naught elsewhere
> and knows not the word "repent."[35]

Fitz Hugh's affection, in less passionate form, is also reflected in other gifts. In consideration for the generations of Kaps to come, Fitz Hugh once presented to the younger brother of Earl Stimson, a fellow member of K.A., a copy of *Mark Hurdlestone, or Two Brothers,* written by Mrs. Moodle, a popular light novelist. He inscribed the book, "To my dear little Friend Dan Stimson, From F.H. Ludlow, KA, Union, May 1856."[36]

As Fitz Hugh's college career approached its culmination, celebration was mixed with the mundane pursuit of assuring one's graduation. The final extant presentation of Fitz Hugh to Kappa Alpha includes the following:

> Due to the absence of our secretary, you this evening ocularly apprehend the idiosyncratic apparition of a novitiate profer-

ring to yr advertance a presentation. He is implenified with
the realization of his impotence to be adequately suppositious
to your absent brethren, therefore humilistidly supplicates yr
benign consideration for any of his aberrations.

When last we met ___ was constrained to be absent by a gla-
diatoralistic encounter with the demon calculus. It felicitates us
to have the potency to certify that calculus got the worst of it.[37]

Along with literary frolics, hashish was an integral part
of Fitz Hugh's final days at Union. The effects of hashish
had evolved to yet another, and perhaps inevitable stage. Fitz
Hugh now faced "the appearance of Deity upon the stage of
my visionary life, now sublimely grand in very person, and
now through the intermediation of some messenger or sign,
yet always menacing, wrathful, or avenging, in whatever
form or manner the visitation might be made."[38] One such
heavenly vision was interrupted by sudden jolts of panic and
terror as Fitz Hugh felt some awful presence approach, and
then speak. "Thou hast lifted thyself above humanity to peer
into the speechless secrets before thy time; and thou shalt be
smitten—smitten—smitten."

These visions were shaped by Fitz Hugh's religious train-
ing under the Reverend Henry Ludlow, redolent with an
evangelist's fire and brimstone. Their emotional force tem-
pered his early inclination to take them lightly, and Fitz
Hugh began to wrestle with imposing some meaning on
these visions of heaven and hell as they alternated with
increasing frequency.

The penultimate of the visions of this latter stage of Fitz
Hugh's hashish habit came when he heard a disembodied
voice weeping. When he called for the reason, the voice
answered "the Mighty One, who was of old held supreme,

hath discovered that his supremacy is void. Fate blind Fate, that hath no ear for thy yearnings, sits mover of the spring of all things, and He to whom thou prayest is a discrowned king." Fitz Hugh had hallucinated the ultimate blasphemy against his father and his society, the death of God. (Nietzsche was at this time 12 years old.) "In my own spirit there sounded an echo to the celestial groaning, and with tearless horror I went straying through the rayless abyss of accident, a tortured creature without a goal."[39] This fundamental existential dilemma was to reoccur again and again in Fitz Hugh's fortunes and failures. On this night, however, Fitz Hugh found salvation. The disembodied voice reaffirmed the existence of God, and Fitz Hugh shouted with joy.

There were few mortals to hear his rejoicing, for it was now four o'clock in the morning. But Fitz Hugh needed companionship, and so went to the door of his cousin, Baldwin Ludlow. Baldwin, the son of Uncle Samuel Baldwin Ludlow, had enrolled at Union in 1856. Baldwin had also joined Kappa Alpha, and was once more accompanying his cousin in his wanderings, now fueled not just by adolescent energy but recreational drug use as well. Fitz Hugh pounded on Baldwin's door, shouting "Baldwin! it is necessary that I should speak with you":

> It was at first very difficult for me to persuade him how intensely I was suffering, for my habit of self control subdued even my face. At last we were in the open air, and I walked clinging to Baldwin's arm.[40]

Fitz Hugh then proceeded to find himself in an Egyptian city, but an Egypt razed by the wrath of God. And Fitz Hugh saw his own heart buried under that long-dead city, too far for the resurrecting hand of even God to reach. After failing to communicate his horror to Baldwin, Fitz Hugh lifted his face from his cousin's side, where he'd hidden it. Now the transformation had occurred yet again, and a vision of pastoral peace was presented by the predawn Union campus. He believed this scene to be located in ancient Troy. (Troy, New York, incidentally, is a city bordering Schenectady.)

> A warrior still living came into my view...he stood silently gazing upon the dead at the gates of the besieged city. The hasheesh voice spoke to me, "This is Achilles standing over the slain Patroclus."[41]

That this tableau should be witnessed in the company of Baldwin was a sad and spooky irony indeed, for one of these cousins and friends would be dead within two years. Cousin Baldwin was quite pleased to be at Union. In May, he wrote that "I called...upon Drs. Nott and Hickok, and then the following day passed a very respectable examination and was admitted as I desired, 3 term Soph. [*sic*]...I found the faculty here much more thorough than I had supposed, both in examination and ordinary recitations. The college is splendidly located, and in all that concerns me here just to my tastes. I have a fine airy room, second story, fronting the Mohawk, board about a mile from the college at a Temperance, Sedgewick's, House—fare excellent...Fitz is here enjoying his last term tremendously; laughing, charming and aquaviting at a great rate."[42]

The long night with Baldwin had ended with sunrise, and with the hashish eater in a tranquil mood. As Fitz Hugh observed, "ecstasy had always the last word, and, on returning to the natural state, I remembered great tortures to be sure, but only as the unnecessary adjuncts to a happiness which I fondly persuaded myself was the legitimate effect of the drug...After this, therefore, I took hasheesh many times; nay, more, life became with me one prolonged state of hasheesh exaltation."[43]

After experiences of particular fear or panic, Fitz Hugh would beg Divine Intervention, promising "save me, and I will never take hasheesh again." But the spirit voices chided him, reminding him how often he had made that vow. "On returning to the natural state I always recollected having made the promise, but regarded it as the act of an unphilosophic fear in irresponsible circumstances and moved by a suffering which it was perfectly possible to prevent by sufficient attention to general health and spirits as elements materially modifying the effect of the drug."[44]

Taken at face value, Fitz Hugh's words reflect his ability to return to his hashish memories in the sober light of day and assess which of his visions were fantasy and which were genuine insight. In this case, he acknowledged that even he had been indulging too much. At the peak of his habit, Fitz Hugh would take as much as an eighth of an ounce, almost four grams at a time. He resolved now to cut that in half to under two grams in a single day. Of course, resumption even at this lower level was sufficient for new ecstasies and agonies.

And hashish was not the only vegetative inspiration available to the college man of 1856. That more favored intoxicant of the New World, tobacco, helped inspire Fitz Hugh to write the following ditty, describing a favorite leisure activity of the college senior.

TERRACE SONG

Ye Union boys whose pipes are lit
come forth in merry throng,
upon the terrace let us sit
and cheer our hearts with song.
ol' Prex [Nott] can have his easy chair
the Czar may have his throne,
their cushions may get worse for wear
but not our seat of stone!

Thou grand ol' seat of stone,
thou jolly old seat of stone;
then here's to thee right merrily
thou grand old seat of stone.

'Twas here the old alumni sat
in the balmy nights of yore,
and many a voice was joined in chat
whose music rings no more,
From many a lip the spirals curled
and when they rolled away,
the smoker went into the world
and came no more for ay!

Thou grand ol' seat of stone,
thou jolly old seat of stone;
the changing year still finds thee here
thou grand old seat of stone.

The capstone of Fitz Hugh's collegiate compositional career came at the end of his senior year. Eliphalet Nott summoned Fitz Hugh to his office and requested that he turn his talents to a commencement ode. A youth spent with the classics, adolescence at the side of hashish, and newfound (if intermittent) maturity and contentedness discovered at

Union, combined in the writing of the poem which would become the Union College Alma Mater.

ODE TO UNION

Let the Grecian dream of his sacred stream
and sing of the brave adorning
that Phoebus weaves from his laurel leaves
at the golden gates of morning
But the brook that bounds through old Union's grounds
gleams bright as the Delphic waters
And a prize as fair as a god may wear
is a "dip" from our alma mater.
Then here's to thee the brave and free
old Union smiling o'er us
And for many a day, as thy walls grow gray,
may they ring with thy children's chorus.

According to classmate Henry Raymond, Fitz Hugh took about 45 minutes to compose the lyric. This poem, set to the air "Sparking and Bright" (an old traditional drinking song) was sung at the commencement exercises of 1856, and has been sung at every Union graduation ever since.

Fitz Hugh's more serious finale, "Commencement Poem," was included in the commencement program for 1856. It is fortunate for generations of Union students that it also is not recited at each commencement. It is a long and sententious thing, and the closing stanzas conveys the general sense of it.

God brings again the light, shall He
uplift the sun forgetting thee?
Down from the spirit's inner walls
the horror of great darkness falls;
At once the veil of doubt and sense
glides off, for what he hopes to see

Becomes the real, so for hence
he knows his immortality.

Fitz Hugh received his degree in June 1856, and faced the
world outside of sheltered academia and the long embrace
of hashish.

1 The discussion of Hickok is based in part on Leonard Jenkin, "The
   Golden Wrong: A Life of Fitz Hugh Ludlow, with an Examination of
   his Writings," Columbia University dissertation, 1972. Jenkin in turn
   references the *Dictionary of American Biography*, Vol. V., New York, 1932.
2 Joseph Blau, *Men and Movements in American Philosophy*, New York:
   Prentice-Hall, 1952, quoted in Jenkin (1972).
3 Jenkin (1972), p. 84.
4 Carl Niemeyer (1953), p. 6.
5 Ibid.
6 Eliphalet Nott to Mrs. Amos Osborne, January 3, 1859, in Hendrichs
   (1973).
7 J.R. Tryon to DeWitt Clinton, n.d., Schaffer Library.
8 Fitz Hugh Ludlow to S. Ludlow Frey, January 28, 1856, NYCPL.
9 *Kappa Alpha Record*, Ithaca, NY: The Executive Council of the Kappa
   Alpha Society, 1960, p. xi.
10 There is mention of Masonic observances in the building of the Society's
   first lodge. See *Kappa Alpha Record* (1960) p. 3.
11 J.R. Tryon to DeWitt Clinton, n.d., Schaffer Library.
12 *The Hasheesh Eater*, p. 312.
13 Ibid., p. 103.
14 Incidentally, it anticipates the practice of psychedelic therapists in later
   years who themselves took psychoactive substances before using them
   with patients in order to better guide their therapeutic progress. See for
   example Peter Stafford and Bonnie Golightly, eds., *LSD: The Problem
   Solving Psychedelic*, 1967, p. 219.
15 *The Hasheesh Eater*, p. 120.
16 Ibid., p. 123.
17 Ibid., p. 128.
18 Ibid.
19 Ibid., p. 143.

20 Ibid., p. 153.

21 Ibid., p. 154.

22 Ibid., p. 161.

23 Ibid., p. 162.

24 Ibid., p. 167.

25 Polycarp was a Christian martyr who was noted for smiling through his sentencing and death by burning at the stake.

26 Fitz Hugh Ludlow, "Benny Havens," in manuscript in several copies, Schaffer Library, Union College.

27 Fitz Hugh Ludlow, "Hymn for the Soul of Man," *The New Era*, reprinted in *Union Alumni Monthly*, November, 1937.

28 This and other selections are from the archives of the Kappa Alpha Society, C.C., and are used with the permission of the Executive Council of the Kappa Alpha Society.

29 "Union Worthies," 1953, p 9.

30 Kappa Alpha Archives, op cit.

31 Manuscript book at Schaffer Library, Union College.

32 Ibid.

33 Ibid.

34 Ibid.

35 Ibid.

36 Inscribed book now In archives of the Kappa Alpha Society, C.C. Stimson would later become a Kap as well, and on the Union Campus today the gate to Captain Jackson's garden is dedicated to Stimson's memory, "whose attachment to KA makes it especially appropriate that his name should be associated with the observance of its centennial (in 1925.)" The gate is inscribed with the verse, "Climb high, climb far, your goal the sky, your aim the star." *Kappa Alpha Record*, p. 4.

37 Archives of the Kappa Alpha Society, C.C.

38 *The Hasheesh Eater*, p. 188.

39 Ibid., p. 190.

40 Ibid., p. 192.

41 Ibid., p. 194.

42 S. Baldwin Ludlow to S. Ludlow Frey, May 16, 1856, NYCPL.

43 *The Hasheesh Eater*, p. 196.

44 Ibid., p. 208.

VI.

WRITING *THE HASHEESH EATER*

FITZ HUGH graduated from Union in July of 1856. Though planning to pursue some kind of professional career, Fitz Hugh's first thought was of leisure activity. He traveled to Niagara Falls for a short stay. Upon arrival at the Falls, he discovered that he had left behind his hashish supply. He searched the area only to find that "the most concentrated cannabine preparation (available in the area) is the jib-stay of a fore-and-after."[1] Fitz Hugh discovered in its place that the use of tobacco eased the "horrors of abandonment." "Making use of this knowledge, I smoked incessantly when out of the immediate presence of the waters—never could I bring myself, however needy, to puff in the face of Niagara." Indeed, Fitz Hugh was so moved by the natural wonder that he penned a poem, which begins:

> Niagara! I am not one who seeks
> To lift his voice above thine awful hymn;
> Mine be it to keep silence where God speaks
> Nor with my praise to make his glory dim.[2]

Returning to Poughkeepsie, Fitz Hugh returned to hashish and pondered his future. Unable to face withdrawal cold turkey, he sought to reduce his dose to ten or fifteen grains. These were enough to bring forth visions behind his closed eyes, but the world remained untransformed and the urge for full indulgence was constant.

Fitz Hugh acknowledged that he now had an unhealthy relationship with the drug.

One day while visiting the local bookseller, he leafed through the current issue of *Putnam's Monthly Magazine*. His slightly altered mind was stunned when he came across an article entitled "The Hasheesh Eater." It described episodes of hashish intoxication in Damascus, Syria and in Connecticut. The article was written as a memoir of a man who had been under the drug's influence in Damascus for several years, and had been forced to quit by a long illness. The anonymous author had visions and dreams much like Fitz Hugh's, including imagery inspired by the tales of the Arabian Nights, although these were given more substantiality by the author's residence in Arab lands. Other effects included the swift changes from one fantasy to the next, and the expansion of space and time as often experienced by Fitz Hugh. In fact, Fitz Hugh's reaction was "this man has been in my own soul."[3] If this were not enough, the punch line was the ending: "Since then I have taken no other hasheesh than such as that." The author had successfully abandoned hashish!

Fitz Hugh inquired in writing of the editors as to the identity of the author. They told him in confidence that the author was none other than Bayard Taylor, a very popular writer, especially known for his travelogues of far off places, which he sometimes visited as diplomatic representative of the United States. Fitz Hugh wrote Taylor, asking for counsel as to the best way to escape his addiction. Taylor replied, in a letter described by Fitz Hugh:

> My anxiety could not have made it more full than it was of information and assistance; my gratitude could not have exaggerated the value of its sympathy and encouragement...

It strengthened my resolution, it opened for me a cheering sky of hope, it pointed me to expedients for insuring success, it mitigated the sufferings of the present. It is, and ever will be, treasured among the most precious archives of my life.[4]

According to biographical studies, Taylor's experiences with hashish were limited to a few experiments, and it is doubtful that Taylor was ever an "addict." As a minute observer of local customs in books such as *The Land of the Saracen,* he may very well have become familiar with native patterns of hashish usage, and have known that it was perfectly feasible for Fitz Hugh to give up his habitual usage; he may also have known, as is known today, that hashish is not physically addictive. Fitz Hugh was at this time very much a product of fundamentalist morals, and his guilt over hashish use had less to do with scientific analysis of its effects as with the expectations of society that he feel bad about using any stimulant.

Fitz Hugh did not immediately give up using hashish as a result of Taylor's letter. But Fitz Hugh listened carefully to the elder explorer, and some of Taylor's ideas are echoed in Fitz Hugh's later writings.[5] In any case, the letter was cheering to Fitz Hugh not only for its comments on hashish, but for the literary relationship that had been established.

This momentous contact took place as Fitz Hugh was casting about for something to do with his collegiate training. He planned to "defer the prosecution of more immediate professional studies" and find some type of employment that would support him while leaving a "reasonable amount of leisure for private reading." Fitz Hugh registered at Union to be notified of any teaching positions which often were addressed there, hoping to teach Greek and Latin, "the arts of address," and literature. One offer came in from a small town which he identified only as "situated somewhere between the Hudson and Fort Laramie, in a village glorified with some name of Epic valor, mighty in the appanage of ten dwelling-houses and a post office." Although the town was not able to offer a great salary they could promise that it was a promising opportunity to "establish himself as a moral centre in the community." Fitz Hugh declined the position, thus losing "the priceless opportunity of radiating circular waves of an unctuous excellence, through it is impossible to tell how large an area of uninhabited timber-region."[6]

BAYARD TAYLOR BY THOMAS HICKS, 1855.
(NATIONAL PORTRAIT GALLERY, SMITHSONIAN INSTITUTION)

Fitz Hugh soon accepted a more remunerative position as a teacher of classics at Watertown Academy, a college preparatory school in Watertown, N.Y., a small town in upstate New York, not far from the mouth of the St. Lawrence River on Lake Ontario. As he packed, Fitz Hugh had hopes that his new life would eliminate any temptation to return to the thrall of hashish. He was to be teaching the ancient and the English classics, subjects "congenial to long-consolidated tastes."

Upon arrival, Fitz Hugh was associated with a teacher who was also new to the academy, but who was an experienced teacher. Grateful for his teaching savvy, Fitz Hugh found that his personality was less than congenial. However, he was gratified to discover a "large and well-selected library...In a good library how swiftly time melts away." Fitz Hugh's initial hopes were encouraged; "quiet, books, and a regular life should create in me a new stimulus and energy." It was not long however, before reality intervened.

> Long after the last noisy foot had pattered down the front steps of the school building did my table groan with incorrigible exercises which demanded correction, on leaf of which, laid upon the grave of any worthy—Molière for instance— who spoke the language which it assassinated, would have brought up as deep a groan from the depths below as when the mandrake is uprooted.[7]

Fitz Hugh began to work late hours to keep up, unable to sleep well if he left any work for the morrow. The late hours, the hard work and a lack of physical exercise all contributed to a state of mind that was not primed to resist the siren call of his former mistress. Indeed, as he found himself listening to music with closed eyes, visual echoes of his hashish visions slowly rose from memory. Fitz Hugh began to miss his former companion, and to withdraw from the social life of Watertown. Before long, he found himself struggling with two temptations. "One of these was self-destruction, the other return to hasheesh…Either of them ultimately led in the same direction."

But standing in the path of the young man's demise was Dr. William V. Rosa, also a graduate of Union College (circa 1812). Rosa had studied medicine in Philadelphia, and then in Paris. Rosa and his wife were prominent in the community by virtue of his occupation, and were, like the Ludlow family, good Presbyterians, at least on the surface. But Fitz Hugh was drawn by the more esoteric knowledge Rosa pursued in his medical theories, that the spirit which energized the body was as important a focus of treatment as the mechanism itself. Fitz Hugh felt his own experiments, enabling the direct perception of that spirit, corroborated Rosa's theories.

Fitz Hugh began to get control of his workload. "As the mountain of exercises and compositions grew gradually more and more level with the plane of my table, and the evening wore on toward night, I was wont to soliloquize, 'One hour more and I will go to see the Doctor.'"[8] In Rosa's company, Fitz Hugh felt himself freed of the restrictions of his schoolteacher persona, once more becoming the neurological explorer. One of the first effects of this friendship was to encourage Fitz Hugh to again commune with his poetic muse. Possibly through an introduction by Bayard Taylor, Fitz Hugh was published for the first time in a national magazine, *The Knickerbocker,* in October of 1856. The poem was entitled "A La Dame A Voile Noire" (To the Lady of the Night Wind), and was bylined, "by a new contributor".

> As Night the rosy bosomed hills enfolding
> Softens their tracery in his weird embrace,
> So, more ethereal grew the matchless moulding
> Of thy pure, earnest, spiritual face,
> Most pensive maid, Beneath the shade
> Of that strange veil of melancholy lace.
> Art thou an abbess gliding from the chancel
> Where Eloisa poured her soul and prayed,
> Unshrouded and revivified to cancel
> Some debt of Christian charity unpaid
> In years agone,
> When the mid-night tone
> Of Death's cold angel made thy heart afraid?
> Perchance thou'rt but a type of Death's own essence,
> Unearthly beauty whose dark borderings
> Turn men's hearts chill with horror at his presence,
> And make them slaves who timely shall be kings,
> But if a heavenly gale
> Lifts up the veil,
> Straightway they're ravished with Death's inner things.
> Perhaps thou art a beautiful temptation,
> Some mystic bodiment of deadly sin,
> Like her who in the veil of consecration,
> Mixed with the orisons of the Capuchin,
> Him nightly wooing
> To his undoing,
> Till to his lost soul Satan entered in,
> Thou art too beautiful: I'll look no longer
> For be thou woman, fantasy, or sprite,
> A spell is sinking over me that's stronger
> Than silence in the watches of the night,
> For good or evil,
> From saint or devil,
> I dare not lift my eyes to read aright.[9]

Despite a typical form and style, this is no typical love poem. The hashish influence seems evident, particularly in the anthropomorphosized entities of Night and Death. There is also a touch of Poe, an influence which would become more evident in some of Fitz Hugh's later work.

Fitz Hugh also wrote a longer poem while in Watertown, entitled "Hymn to our Intercessor," which was never published and seems to be an exorcism of a long winter more than anything.

> I am not yet quite used to be aware that
> all my labor and my hope had birth
> Only to freeze me with the coffined stare
> of void and soulless earth.[10]

Dr. Rosa turned out to be a sympathetic support for Fitz Hugh in the latter's attempt to abandon his hashish dependency. Rosa's investigation of the mental side of the human organism had given him a perspective which proved essential to Fitz Hugh's recovery. What Fitz Hugh seemed to need from hashish was its ability to allow him to commune with the inner spirit that energized the material world. This inner spirit was tangible for Fitz Hugh under the influence, and without the drug the world was nothing but an empty shell. As he put it, "I had known the living spirit of nature; in its husks I no longer found any nourishment." In his writing, Fitz Hugh was conscious that his habit of imbuing natural things with a spirit would be regarded as blasphemous. But what he viewed as his proof of the transcendence of spirit was simply a characteristic of Creation, and not necessarily inconsistent with Christian theology.

Fitz Hugh and Dr. Rosa began a practice of speaking in parables to try out new ideas upon the other. Dr. Rosa one day held forth on two "particles" of electricity who lived in a bar of iron. One of the particles had traveled around, and gained the perspective to see that indeed they lived within a substance called iron. The other particle, which had stayed home and built a place for itself in the community, dismissed the traveller for trying to convince him that there existed this thing which was not evident to the senses. Indeed, the traveling particle was labeled by the pillar of the community with the ultimate insult, "visionary." This allegory of Fitz Hugh's hashish journeys is plain.

As the autumn passed and winter set in, Fitz Hugh found that while the desire for hashish had dwindled, he was still susceptible to the "demon houri." There were certain times when the longing was more powerful than others. One of these was a simple clear and sunny day. "That beauty which filled the heart of every other living thing with gladness, only spoke of other suns more wondrous rolling through other heavens of a more matchless dye."[11]

As a means of combatting these longings, Fitz Hugh employed a number of weapons. As mentioned, one was tobacco, although he found that once he had built his dependence on smoking, any deprivation of the sotweed would call up corresponding sensations of cannabine withdrawal. Another more whimsical method was to blow soap bubbles. These bubbles recreated in a harmless but real way the colors of his hasheesh tinged world. "I could have consumed hours in watching the sliding, the rich intermingling, the changes by origination, and the changes by reaction of those matchless hues, or hues at least so matchless in the real world that to find their parallel we must leave the glories of a waking life and go floating through the firmament of some iridescent dream."[12]

One final method, which Fitz Hugh deemed most effective of them all, was recommended by Bayard Taylor. This was, whenever the longing came upon him, to set down in words the experience of some previous hashish dream. This practice he began on a regular basis, and it soon had the fringe benefit of producing an article, which was published in *Putnam's Magazine,* perhaps through Taylor's influence or perhaps welcomed by the sensation that Taylor's earlier article had caused. The article was entitled "The Apocalypse of Hasheesh," and appeared in *Putnam's* December, 1856 issue without a byline, as did most works in *Putnam's.*[13]

It was not a story or reminisce like Taylor's earlier article, but an essay, taking as its theme the philosophical, if not religious, implications of hashish intoxication. The theme was encapsulated in this sentence: "The value of this experience to me consists in its having thrown open my gaze to many of those sublime avenues in the spiritual life, at whose gates the soul in its ordinary state is forever blindly groping." The article also harkened to Fitz Hugh's hallucinations of himself as Christ, along with other features of his visions (e.g. the expansion of space and time).

The latter part of the essay, which occupied five pages of the magazine, dealt largely with Fitz Hugh's hypothesis that the Greek philosopher Pythagoras utilized hashish as a teaching tool, and as a part of the ritual initiation into his secret society. Fitz Hugh's classical education acquainted him with the thought of Pythagoras, and his membership in the Kappa Alpha Society at Union broadened that acquaintance. (The

K.A. initiatory process requires some study of Pythagoras.) Fitz Hugh emphasized that hashish heightened one's native intuition, and intuition was a characteristic that Pythagoras prized above the logic championed by Thales and the other early Greek philosophers.

The essay closed with several observations. One was the belief that hashish gave one an experience "which the untrammeled immortal soul could alone endure." The second point was a warning, that hashish was not a toy, and that the visions revealed were best left in the province of the soul, for the individual to experience when that soul was freed of its mortal body. Fitz Hugh closed with a reference to the Bayard Taylor piece in the September *Putnam's*, claiming that since reading it he had "shut the book of hasheesh experience."

Fitz Hugh spent Christmas in Watertown, several hundred miles from his family and friends in Poughkeepsie. He did remember them, though, as one surviving gift reveals. It is a copy of Hawthorne's *House of the Seven Gables* (published in 1851), and is inscribed with a poem to the book's recipient, little Mary Roosevelt, who was mentioned in one of the letters to young Alice Crosby written from Union:

> When the drop-light with its gas
> sheds cheer on parlor tables
> Till they shine like polished glass
> Have I seen the dark-eaved House of the Seven Gables
> With her cheek upon her hand
> Shadowed from the marble gleams,
> Drawn through Hawthorne's mystic land
> The young girl seemed half-reading, half in dreams.
> The Old Man heard again
> The stories of his father
> Conversations with the men

Who burned witches & drawled psalms with Cotton Mather
    The mother dropped a stitch,
    From her lap fell down her knitting,
    As she burned the page on which
The ruffled ghosts of Pyncheon House were flitting.
    The boy pored on dissembling
    The fear with which he read.
    And then lay all night trembling
    While cold fingers plucked the quilt about his head.
    And perhaps you are too young
    To read of ghostly trial
    For the sun of life hath flung
But very little shadow on your dial
    Yet take this witchly present
    And in reading it remember (Not only on the present
    Twenty-fifth day of the chilly month December,
    But until Time shall end)
    Him, who, little young Miss Mary
    Will ever be your friend
Though like the Pyncheons' fortune his may vary.
I've sung my jingle & got to the end
And just left room for the name of your friend

    Fitz Hugh Ludlow K A
    Watertown, N.Y. Dec. 25, 1856[14]

Fitz Hugh, even in this spontaneous sketch, easily mixed admiration for the book with his affection for the little girl and her family.

Fitz Hugh spent the holidays with Dr. Rosa, and the time spent gave Rosa an opportunity to expound upon the doctrines of Emmanuel Swedenborg, with a persuasive effect on Fitz Hugh. According to a friend of Fitz Hugh's, "The doctrine concerning the Lord which he [Fitz Hugh] found unfolded there met all the demands of his nature...Swedenborg's conception of the Divine Humanity, or glorification of Jesus, he [Fitz Hugh] used to say, he did not think to be true; or merely believe to be true; he knew it to be true, for it solved the entire problem of theology, life and death!"[15]

Emmanuel Swedenborg (1688-1772) was the son of a Swedish bishop. He became a Baron at age 31 and entered the House of Nobles. In the meantime, he virtually founded the science of crystallography, wrote numerous scientific papers, and "mastered the known natural science of his day."[16] Swedenborg then began the study of yoga-like exercises, as well as the philosophy of the mind. His explorations culminated in 1744, when he claimed to be conversing with angels and spirits. Swedenborg proceeded to publish over 200 books on the spirit world, describing in detail its architecture, science, and even foods and sports. He was not, however, locked up as a madman. In fact, he was a respected finance minister, who would conduct business meetings interspersed with short chats with angels invisible to his business guests.

Swedenborg's mystical books were strewn with his own theological interpretations of the scripture. The Church of the New Jerusalem was founded to preserve his religious teachings (the father and brother of poet/mystic William Blake were both members), and it was these doctrines which Fitz Hugh seemed to take to heart. One of its chief conceptions was that "the divine is in the heart of every man. Man was posited to have a twofold nature; the internal man is truly in heaven—the earthly life is only a simulated life." Fitz Hugh's musings in "The Apocalypse of Hasheesh" are in total agreement.

If this were not enough, Swedenborg had influenced Ralph Waldo Emerson and the Transcendentalists, of whom

Fitz Hugh said "I was suckled at the breast of Transcendentalism."[17] And finally, a number of Masonic lodges were founded on the teachings of Swedenborg. Although there is no direct evidence that Fitz Hugh was a Mason, the Kappa Alpha Society is attributed some Masonic links.[18]

Dr. Rosa encouraged other non-traditional interpretations of the mysteries of life, for example, lending Fitz Hugh a book on yogic trances. Fitz Hugh's later acquaintances like Mark Twain would comment on Fitz Hugh's knowledge of "astrology, necromancy, and other black arts."[19] Fitz Hugh's mystical preoccupations surfaced in a poem he wrote to a friend, Miss Sessions, on New Year's, 1857, in thanks for a letter opener she gave him as a gift:

> To the eye of the shallow proser,
> This seems but a paper-knife;
> But look with me, and behold it
> A symbol of human life.
> How skilfully was it fashioned
> From rainbowed mother-of-pearl!
> Its handle how cunningly carven
> In delicate twist and curl!
> Yet hark! for its inner spirit
> Discourseth in lower tone,
> Lessons of graver meaning,
> That the thoughtful may hear alone.
> The union of soul and body
> Is a cunningly-shapen knife,
> Daily cutting the pages
> Of the mystical Book of Life.

But Fitz Hugh's dalliance with Swedenborg and other outré topics was no more a topic of discussion with his father than his hashish use. In a letter from Reverend Henry to Fitz Hugh's aunt, he says "We hear from F now and then. He is working very hard and the discipline will I trust be healthful." However, the winter in Watertown proved quite the opposite. The teaching load eventually proved more debilitating than "hasheesh had been at its most nerve-wracking stages." It was clear by late that winter that some kind of rest and treatment was necessary. "The former was easily attained by closing my connection with the educational 'Knight of the Rueful Countenance'—a connection which all the while had not been chemical, like that of an acid with a base, but mechanical, like that of a force with a lever."[20]

The "treatment" of his hashish habit was more problematic. He had to return home to Poughkeepsie, where his father was anything but pleased with Fitz Hugh's retreat from the world of work. Fitz Hugh first resorted to opium, which he had sampled in his early days at the apothecary shop. He found that opium merely served to recall all the worst aspects of the hasheesh experience, that "I was only exchanging one bitter cup for another." At the advice of a physician, Fitz Hugh then tried alcohol as an interim relief. "A very short trial of their effect having convinced me that their stimulus was as dangerous as opium, I abandoned this also as a means of relief."[21]

This left only one solution to his problems. Fitz Hugh picked up his pen and began to write the entire story of his hashish journey, in autobiographical form, as a means of achieving a prolonged focus on a project, but one which required less effort (or less distasteful effort) than teaching. This narrative, taking the reader from Fitz Hugh's first forays into Anderson's pharmacopeia to his resignation from Watertown, became a 365-page manuscript. The writing took only four months. The manuscript was submitted, virtually without revision, to Harper Brothers publishers, then one of the major publishing houses in the U.S. The lack of revision had become Fitz Hugh's custom in writing, and although the shortcomings of the approach became apparent in some of his later projects, he had a remarkable facility for composing mentally before setting pen to foolscap. In *The Hasheesh Eater*, the concentrated effort and emotional closeness to the material gave coherence to the whole.

The editor of *Harper's Monthly Magazine*, George William Curtis, had seen Fitz Hugh's piece in *Putnam's*, and later would note that he was "prepossessed by the article." Indeed, he was so prepossessed that Fletcher Harper and his brothers entered into a contract to publish Fitz Hugh's manuscript on July 1, 1857:

> Fitz Hugh Ludlow being the author and Proprietor of a book entitled "The Apocalypse of Hasheesh" grants and guarantees to Harper & Brothers the exclusive right to publish the same during the term of copyright.
>
> Harper & Brothers agree to stereotype and publish said work, in good style, and at their own expense, and in consideration of the right herein granted, agree to pay said Ludlow, or his legal representatives, semi-annually, in the months of February and August, by notes at four months, Ten per cent, on their trade list prices for each and every copy of said work sold by them over and above the sale of one thousand.

This was quite an achievement for a man not yet twenty-one-years old. It was especially reassuring to have reached this deal at a time when America was undergoing an economic downturn.[22] Two days after signing the contract, Fitz Hugh delivered the manuscript along with the following note:

Messr. Harper & Brothers,
Dear Sirs, I enclose to you all my book, paragraphed, chaptered, prefaced & appendixed. It is now ready for the composer.

As an appointment calls me for the next two weeks into Vermont please direct the proof-sheets that are to be corrected within that time thus, Fitz Hugh Ludlow, Arlington, Bennington Co. Vt. They will reach me in one day from New York. When I leave Vt. I will inform you by note from there, giving my next direction.

May I trouble you to mention to Doctor Palmer when he calls at your office, that the enclosed packet directed to him, awaits him with you. You will thus oblige

Yours very Respt'ly, Fitz Hugh Ludlow[23]

An article by Doctor Palmer, a physician familiar with hashish, was included as an appendix to Fitz Hugh's manuscript.[24] As to the "appointment" in Vermont, the following letter to cousin Samuel Ludlow Frey clarifies that point:

My Dear Lud,
If I have seemed neglectful either of your letter or its very kind invitation, it has been only in seeming. I have been very little at home for the last four months. Either in New York on business or in Vermont & Schenectady for relaxation, I have been as much occupied as any decent man should be.[25] I have had about fifty letters to answer this last week, the first week indeed that I could call my own for a long time. I am sorry now that I have time to be obliged to say that it is physically impossible for me to get to your dear home or to Oswego at all this summer. The combination of proof-sheets for my forthcoming book would keep me near New York even had I the spondulicks[26] to get away, which I am not so imaginative a person as to believe I have, just at present. I have therefore magnanimously put funds into the hands of my family & have said "Go, be happy" at the same time staying

at home myself to pass the period of their absence in a sylvan retreat known as Mr. Poorman's place.

You must come and see me instead. My home from next September until I make my name, fortune, or way in the world, somehow or other will be in New York. Where to find me I will write you particularly and shall claim you as my guest most jealously whenever you will consent to come down to that little village.[27]

1 *The Hasheesh Eater*, p. 221.
2 The full poem appears in *The Hasheesh Eater*, p. 225.
3 *The Hasheesh Eater*, p. 229.
4 Fitz Hugh does not identify the author by name in *The Hasheesh Eater*. Taylor's biographers also do not attribute the story in *Putnam's Monthly* to him, and at least one commentator attributed it to Fitz Hugh himself. If the author was not Taylor, Fitz Hugh nevertheless was shortly thereafter put in touch with Taylor in the New York literary scene. They shared the same Victorian/confessional approach to such sensitive subject matter, and Fitz Hugh might have been influenced in that direction by Taylor when it came time to write *The Hasheesh Eater*.
5 See for example the discussion of Taylor in J.T. Crane, *The Arts of Intoxication*, p. 96-7.
6 *The Hasheesh Eater*, p. 234.
7 Ibid., p. 237.
8 Ibid., p. 252.
9 Fitz Hugh Ludlow, "A La Dame A Voile Noire," *The Knickerbocker*, October, 1856, p. 204.
10 Manuscript book now at Schaffer Library, Union College.
11 *The Hasheesh Eater*, p. 257.
12 Ibid., p. 263.
13 Fitz Hugh Ludlow, "The Apocalypse of Hasheesh," *Putnam's Monthly Magazine*, December, 1856, p. 625.
14 Now in Schaffer Library, Union College.
15 Frank Carpenter, "In Memoriam. Fitz Hugh Ludlow as he was Known by a Friend," *New York Evening Mail*, December 24, 1870.
16 Jeffrey Mishlove, *The Roots of Consciousness*, New York: Random House and The Bookworks, 1975, p. 55.
17 Emerson's landmark essay "Nature" was attacked by some critics as simply

a presentation of Swedenborg's metaphysical philosophy. See James F. Lawrence, "The Swedenborgian Church," in *Gnosis*, Vol. 1, No. 12, p. 57.

18 *History of Kappa Alpha*, Kappa Alpha Executive Council, 1975, p. 2.

19 Franklin Walker, *San Francisco's Literary Frontier*.

20 *The Hasheesh Eater*, p. 283.

21 Ibid.

22 Wyatt-Brown (1971), p. 229.

23 Fitz Hugh Ludlow to Messrs. Harper and Brothers, July 3, 1856, Henry Ransom Humanities Research Center, The University of Texas at Austin (hereafter Ransom).

24 The Dr. John Palmer mentioned in the letter was the first city physician of San Francisco, arriving there in 1849 at the start of the gold rush. From there he sailed across the Pacific to work for the British East India Company during one of the opium wars. There he became acquainted with the use of opium and hashish. Fitz Hugh added as an appendix an article by Palmer from the *New York Tribune* on "Hasheesh in Hydrophobia." Palmer's article noted the seminal contributions of W.B. O'Shaughnessy, a surgeon who worked in India and introduced cannabis to the attention of the West in 1839.

25 In his book *The Heart of the Continent*, Fitz Hugh fondly remembers Love's Tavern on the stage road in Bennington, VT.

26 Slang for cash money.

27 Fitz Hugh Ludlow to S. Ludlow Frey, August 3, 1857, NYCPL.

VII

THE

HASHEESH EATER:

BEING PASSAGES FROM THE

LIFE OF A PYTHAGOREAN.

"Weave a circle round him thrice,
And close your eyes with holy dread,
For he on honey-dew hath fed,
And drunk the milk of Paradise."
KUBLA KHAN.

NEW YORK:
HARPER & BROTHERS, PUBLISHERS,
FRANKLIN SQUARE.
1857.

TITLE PAGE FROM THE FIRST EDITION OF *THE HASHEESH EATER*.

"I SUPPOSE you know that Fitz Hugh's book is at last out. I shall read it if I can find time," wrote Fitz Hugh's Cousin Carrie (Frey) Geddes to her brother Ludlow Frey in December of 1857.[1]

The Hasheesh Eater was published by Harper Brothers in New York City in November of 1857. It retailed for a dollar. (Novels at the time sold for 50 cents, special items like reference books for $1.50.) The book was published simultaneously by Sampson Low and Son in London under an arrangement with Harper Brothers, a joint venture often undertaken by the two publishers.

The book was published anonymously, at whose request it is not known. (Buried deep in the book is one reference to the author as Mr. Fitz-Gerald, probably undeciphered by even readers who knew Fitz Hugh.) The book is subtitled, "being passages from the Life of a Pythagorean," and the preface is signed "The Hasheesh Eater, the Son of Pythagoras." The change in title from "Apocalypse of Hasheesh" seems an obvious attempt to recall DeQuincey's *Opium Eater*.

The Hasheesh Eater took the form of autobiography, with Fitz Hugh tracing his hashish adventures in chronological order as he passed through college and his first teaching job. (Much of this story has been recounted in previous chapters.) The narrative was periodically broken up by chapter length commentaries on the lessons of his experience. Chapter VI, "The Mysteries of the Life Sign Gemini," contained his conclusions that hashish revealed the true existence of a soul separate from the body, and he offered the story of an Indian fakir's trance state as a separate confirmation of the truth of this idea.

In another commentary, "The Book of Symbols,"[2] Fitz Hugh attributed to the hashish state the ability to penetrate to the world of "ideal forms." He carped that the English translation of St. Paul, "which it is not lawful for a man to utter," should be "which it is impossible to utter to man." (The translational quibble was not presumptuous given Fitz Hugh's reading of the Bible in the early Greek version.) Moreover, "Though far from believing that my own ecstasy has claim to such inspiration as an apostle's, the states are still analogous in this respect—they both share the nature of disembodiment, and the soul, in both, beholds realities of greater or less significance, such as may never be apprehended again out of the light of eternity."

In Chapter XXIV, Fitz Hugh argued the hashish visionary should not be discounted because others have falsely claimed visionary states. "Who is to say that at that season of exaltation I did not know things as they are more truly than ever in the ordinary state? Let us not assert that the half-careless and uninterested way in which we generally look on nature is the normal mode of the soul's power of vision."[3] Another chapter summarized his view that Pythagoras knew hashish, as Fitz Hugh in beholding the universe under the influence "became conscious of a numerical order which ran through it." Fitz Hugh also took the time in this chapter to respond to a "modern critic" who thought Pythagoras was a fraud.

The book closed with two essays. "Labyrinths and Guiding Threads" summed up the experiences, and consulted the philosophers for their confirmation of and insight into his ideas.[4] Hume's philosophical approach was valid, argued Fitz Hugh, but his reputation as an infidel was unjust. Fitz Hugh thought the modern-day Transcendentalists had preserved Hume's rigor of thought while admitting to the existence of the divine. Fitz Hugh's Union professor, Hickok, was mentioned as the only real metaphysician of America, perhaps the greatest now living anywhere, but as being sadly unknown to ninety percent of contemporaries, who preferred "such books as read themselves to us while we lie half asleep on a sofa."[5]

Fitz Hugh then attempted, inspired by some of the characteristics of the hashish state, to scientifically prove the essential unity of all phenomenon. All senses are reducible to the idea of Force, and all forces act under one single central law. This idea grew directly out of the synesthetic experiences of the hashish intoxication. Fitz Hugh in later years returned to such "unified field" concepts. (See Chapter 18.) This essay's conclusion was deferential to the Creative Spirit, and admitted that of the ethereal world revealed by hashish, "we have no right to succeed to the inheritance til we come of age."[6] Baudelaire held a similar pious view of hashish, that "this acuteness of thought, this enthusiasm of the senses and the spirit must have appeared to man through the ages as the first blessing."[7]

In a last essay, "Ideal Men and their Stimulants", Fitz Hugh addressed the attraction of hashish and other substances for gifted personalities.[8] As different people perceive the world differently, and have their own tastes in music and aesthetics generally, so we must be "kinder in our judgement of the man who runs to narcotics and other stimulants for relief." The essay became a defense of Coleridge, and developed a psychological profile of that worthy explaining why opium was his inevitable recourse.[9] Poetically, Fitz Hugh would later follow a similar path.

The Hasheesh Eater was the lead book review in the November issue of *Harper's Monthly* (although only two of the eight books reviewed that month were published by Harper Brothers). The review, which coincidentally preceded a review of *Lectures on Temperance* by Eliphalet Nott, reads as follows:

> The intensely interesting "Confessions of an Opium Eater" appear to have suggested the plan of this remarkable volume. Unequal to De Quincey in literary culture and in the craft of book-making, the author of this work compares favorably with him in the passion for philosophical reflection, in the frankness of his personal revelations, and in preternatural brilliancy of fancy. In point of compact and orderly method in the narration of his story, he has a decided advantage over De Quincey. The comparative merits of hasheesh and opium as a stimulant to the intellect and the source of wild, imaginative dreams, may be learned from a comparison of the two volumes. But let no one be tempted to verify the accuracy of the representations in either case by personal experience. The use of such drugs of enchantment is one of the most fatal of all diabolic illusions. If any of our readers are ignorant of the deadly herb whose infernal power is here recorded, let them know that hasheesh is the juice of the Indian hemp, the southern branch of the same family which, in northern climes, grows almost totally to fibre, producing materials for mats and cordage. Under a tropical sun the plant loses its fibrous texture, and secretes profusely an opaque and greenish resin. This has been used for ages in the East as a narcotic and stimulant, and at this day forms a habitual indulgence with all classes of society in India, Persia, and Turkey. The effects which it produces, both physical and intellectual, are of the most extraordinary character. The experience of the author in its use is here frankly and fully related, in a narrative which is equally rich in psychological illustration and in imaginative vision.[10]

The review is notable in that the bulk of it is taken up not with a review of the writing or the content, but in simply introducing the reader to a subject about which the reviewer presumes the reader knows nothing. It illustrates the fact that hashish, and most drugs, were unknown to the general public in America at the time. Like De Quincey's book before him, Fitz Hugh's work held the interest of readers by the exotic nature of the subject more than anything else.

This review, in one of the "taste-making" magazines of the time, sparked the book's popularity. *The Hasheesh Eater* was not, however, reviewed by *The Atlantic Monthly*, the Boston-based journal, perhaps because Boston publisher Ticknor and Fields looked dimly upon the book of a competing publisher. But other reviews followed which fed the flame of fame. A more narrow audience found the book through a review in *The Christian Examiner*, a monthly general interest journal with a religious emphasis:

> Nothing more shows the poverty of our systematic Psychologies, and the hopelessness of an exhaustive analysis of the soul, than those volumes which show its wayward rioting when released from the healthy limits of its activity. "The Hasheesh-Eater" will remind every reader of De Quincey's "Confessions"; yet the two are as independent as two works of such a nature could well be. We have a narrative, written with a good deal of genius and literary power, of an experience less pathetic, but, if possible, even more gigantesque and strange. The Hasheesh-Eater is an American college-student, apparently, who, with a passion like Hahnemann's for experimenting in drugs, falls at last upon the pale-green gum of the Indian hemp. Its specific effect in dissolving "the flaming bounds of place and time" we have not time to trace through the very curious details he has given. The most interesting point suggested is the key which this narrative gives to the peculiar

fancy and imagery of the "Arabian Nights", and other Asiatic tales, as well as to the myths related of Pythagoras...Like De Quincey, the writer is faithful to make his book a terrible warning, even while it dwells on the terrible fascination of the drug. It is "the fruit of that forbidden tree" of knowledge. If we understand his argument, he claims that hasheesh unveils to the mind a real world of being, not unreal "subjective states." "It is as much cause for thanksgiving," he says, "as for aspiration to something clearer, that we now 'see through a glass darkly.' Let us not repine, for there is a reason in these half-opaque and tinged panes. A sun as consuming as he is wondrously glorious is shining just outside."[11]

This reviewer seems at a loss in interpreting Fitz Hugh's borderline blasphemous musings. It was too much to acknowledge that a plant secretion might yield a glimpse of the divine. It was easier to see the book as an object lesson warning against such hedonistic adventures. This had the effect of course of recommending an otherwise lurid read as a lesson in good Christian behavior.

Another, more secular review appeared in *The Knicker-bocker*, publishers of Fitz Hugh's first poem.

Can our readers recall that not far 'Backward in the abysm of Time,' when Lord Byron's 'terrible melancholy' raised up a host of simulators of the same, with wide down-turned shirt collars and lustrous up-turned eyes: Byronic in every thing, except features, mind, knowledge, GENIUS? "Very well, then" as Mr. Bunsby would say, do they also remember, that since De Quincey wrote his 'Confessions of an English Opium-Eater,' many weak-minded aspirants to the fame which accrued from that successful work, have imitated the author in so far as to excite their entire thimble-full of brains with the 'smoking mud,' (under which name High Commissioner Lin denounced the drug) and afterward published their 'Confessions'? This

'Hasheesh-Eater' is of the highest order of the great 'Opium-Eater's simulators. The small tribe before him have not followed De Quincey in writing a book: no; their brains could not hold out, under spiritual pressure, sufficiently long: so they content themselves with single papers, or short serials, in some popular journal or magazine. The 'Hasheesh-Eater', on the contrary, is evidently a man of talent and his reveries and experiences suffice to fill a book without the 'forcing process.' Everybody knows what opium is, but everybody may not know that Hasheesh is the resin of a peculiar sort of hemp, called 'Cannabis Indica,' which in southern climates loses its fibrous texture, and secretes this powerful narcotic drug. How the narrator came to eat Hasheesh; what were its effects; what fascination it exerted over his fancy; what dreams he dreamed; what joys and pains he felt; and in what manner he relinquished the use of this soul-exciting, soul-subduing drug, forms the subject-matter of the volume under notice. Its descriptions are somewhat fascinating: and we should not be at all surprised to find the 'Hasheesh of commerce' quoted before long in the mercantile prices-current of our commercial daily journals. The 'Yan-ne-kees' always want to 'try things,' from a new mechanical-power, a new patent-medicine, or a new drug, to a new religion.[12]

One might call this a jadedly enthusiastic review, notable again for its presumption of the reader's ignorance of hash-ish, and familiarity with De Quincey.

In a British review of *The Hasheesh Eater*, published in the *Saturday Review* of February 13, 1858, after the obligatory explanation of what exactly hashish is, the reviewer also noted that Fitz Hugh:

...attributes the vast powers of imagination displayed in Oriental fiction, and especially in the Arabian Nights, to the use of hasheesh...our Transatlantic Pythagorean out Hafizes Hafiz in his Orientalism, and shames Sheherazade with the amount of local colour introduced in his visions. If this were the case with all temperaments, hasheesh might be a boon to those whose circumstances have prevented them from acquiring a knowledge of the land where the cypress and myrtle are, as is stated, typical of the manners and customs of the inhabitants. But unfortunately it is not every one who, by swallowing a bolus, can behold "the minarets wave on the plain of Stamboul"—to quote the lusciously descriptive words of Bon Gaultier. Frequently the results of a dose are anything but Eastern in character. For example, one "Bob," a friend of the author's who is induced to take twenty-five grains of the drug, has a vision which savours of Bermondsey rather than Bagdad, as it comes in the questionable shape of a shower of soot falling on him; and, on one occasion, the author himself having suffered the unpythagorean metempsychosis involved in being a soda-water bottle, implores the gods that he may be elevated "to some more spiritual essence." Upon which, he says—

"My neck grew longer; my head was night-capped with snowy kid; ethereal odors of delight streamed through my brain; and, exultant with apotheosis, I beheld my patent of nobility stamped on my crystal breast, in these golden characters: Eau de Cologne."

No doubt by this time the reader begins to "take" as Mr. Ollapod would say—to perceive the real drift of the Hasheesh-Eater—viz., that it is a solemn jeu d'esprit, a grave burlesque, intended to ridicule transcendentalists and visionaries of the Coleridge and De Quincey school. The effect is very much increased by the skillful way in which the author provokes, and at the same time deprecates, the charge of having copied from the *Confessions of an English Opium Eater.*

Generally speaking, his experiences are of a far less soothing type, and his descriptions of them read uncommonly like the rhapsodies of one labouring under a combination of nightmare and delerium tremens. Here, as we take it, lies the joke, if joke there be, or at least the moral purpose. Anxious to deter his fellow-creatures from committing excesses on hasheesh, what better mode could the author adopt than to point out that the results are, in the first place, unpleasant and absurd, and secondly, may be just as well attained by what the doctors would call exhibiting pork chops, and throwing in brandy-and-water freely afterwards?

There will always be a number of young enthusiasts ready to adopt anything, from a creed to a medicine, that may be sufficiently outre, especially if they think parents and guardians and steady-going people generally object to it. Some time ago, they used to turn their shirt collars down and loathe mankind, in the Byronic fashion—now they turn them up, and adore medievalism, to show they are not mere materialists. Hasheesh is the very thing for these young persons,—there is so much about the Soul, and Essences, and the Arcana of Spiritualism, and Boodh, and Seeva, and other Grand Mysteries of Ancient Philosophy, to be said in connexion with it. It is no great matter, perhaps, but if it was any object to our Pythagorean to prevent them from fuddling what brains they have on hasheesh pills, in the hope of spiritualizing themselves, he would have done better in refraining from mentioning the subject at all. He can write well, and has plenty of imagination of his own, without having recourse to stimulants; and on any other field he would have been just as entertaining, and probably much more useful.[13]

Apart from the almost unbearable stuffiness of the reviewer, there are two important points raised. The first is the contention that this is a burlesque of some sort played on the Transcendentalists. Fitz Hugh states in the book that he "suckled at the breast of the Transcendentalists." While it is true that Fitz Hugh held very little to be sacred, there is nothing in that brief mention to suggest that they were being set up as targets. But this part of the Saturday Reviewer's focus raises a larger issue, namely how accurately *The Hasheesh Eater* reflects the real experiences of Fitz Hugh.

As a case in point, the episode of giraffes and perfume bottles strikes an odd note in the symphonic whole of the book. The pendulum swings from heaven to hell and back, rarely slowed enough in the middle ground for that portion to be illuminated. More frequent occurrence of whimsical visions might be expected given the imagination displayed in Fitz Hugh's letters, poems and stories. Nevertheless, it may be that the extremes of the vision were what Fitz Hugh needed to exorcise in ending his habit, or simply made for a better dramatic narrative. Certainly Baudelaire, Gautier, Dumas and others of the French Le Club des Haschischins (whom Fitz Hugh never cites) reported enough similar dreams and visions to corroborate the extremes of his story. And alcohol, despite the *Saturday Review's* opinion, is unlikely to have inspired such transcendental visions as Fitz Hugh related.

The moral point of the Saturday Reviewer, that impressionable young minds might be unwisely drawn to experiment themselves, is actually borne out by the evidence. John Hay, who became Abraham Lincoln's personal assistant, a close friend of the Lincoln family, and later Secretary of State under Theodore Roosevelt, was one of these young men. A classmate of Hay's at Brown University recalls:

> On one occasion, at least his enthusiasm for literature was carried to excess. 'The Hasheesh-Eater' had recently appeared; and Johnny must needs experiment with hasheesh a little, and see if it was such a marvelous stimulant to imagination as Fitz Hugh Ludlow affirmed. 'The night when Johnny Hay took hasheesh' marked an epoch for the dwellers in Hope College.[14]

A professor at the college remembers "how he had been routed out of bed very late one night to minister to the very sick boys who had participated in the adventure."[15] Hay did not dismiss the experience lightly. He later wrote in a letter describing Brown, "where I used to haunt the rooms of the Atheneum, made holy by the presence of the royal dead; where I used to pay furtive visits to Forbes' forbidden mysteries (peace to his ashes), where I used to eat Hasheesh and dream dreams. My life will not be utterly desolate while memory is left me, and while I may recall the free pleasures of the student-time."[16]

Comparisons of *The Hasheesh Eater* to De Quincey, which were then ubiquitous, seem relevant only in that both treated the effects of a mind-altering stimulus on the writer. In De Quincey's *Confessions*, opium played only a small part relative to the other concerns and events narrated from De Quincey's life. It was clear that De Quincey was the easy comparison for reviewers, as well as a selling point for the book, but the confusion of a mild psychedelic substance like hashish with a true narcotic like opium is something that has persisted even to the present day. Contemporary scientists agree that hashish, unlike opium, is largely not an addictive drug, despite Fitz Hugh's professed continued fascination.[17]

It may also be true that Fitz Hugh's admitted "debt" to De Quincey resulted in a little "imitative handwringing" appearing in the book despite Fitz Hugh's first-hand knowledge of the difference in effect between hashish and opium. A later critic thought that the guilt over the indulgence "may be the result of Ludlow's paranoia, or really engendered by his society's strictures against any form of intoxication… Poughkeepsie is always just a small American town, where neighbors might peek from behind the curtains at Reverend Ludlow's self-conscious son passing by."[18]

While *The Hasheesh Eater* was a sensation, and inspired some emulation, it never attained the status of a classic, despite the favorable contemporary comparisons with De Quincey. It went out of print during the Civil War, and remained unavailable until 1903. It may be that the strong Puritan strain in this country, which continued building until Prohibition in 1920, prevented the book from being accorded any recognition but that of a footnote among respectable folk. After Fitz Hugh's death, the book was relegated to the status of curiosity. Only Professor Morris Bishop of Cornell, among modern critics, was moved to write of the book, "This is a considerable literary achievement."[19]

In the short term, Fitz Hugh became famous. His identity as author of the book was known to his family. But his family relations, never idyllic, were the first to show the effects of the onset of fame. Cousin Carrie told her brother Ludlow, "How glad I am that I board here and not at Uncle's [Reverend Henry]. I know I should be homesick all the time, and it is awful when Fitz is at home. I should think they would be sorry when he comes and glad when he goes away. He is all the time disputing and he contradicts his Father every word he says; he's so impudent that I think Uncle would turn him out of the house."[20] The full extent of Fitz Hugh's hashish adventures, not to mention his embrace of Swedenborg, was now fully known to Henry. The glow of the publishing triumph left Fitz Hugh more confident than ever in challenging his father.

Henry fought back in his own way. Cousin Carrie—who wrote in February, "I have commenced Fitz's book, but when I have time to finish it is another thing"—was preoccupied at the time with a personal religious crisis resolved by her conversion by Reverend Henry Ludlow.[21] "Little did I realize when I left home that I was coming here to find my Savior."[22] The Reverend Henry performed his pastoral duties well that year, also converting Samuel Morse's daughter Sarah.

The father-son battle was soon eclipsed by a sadder occurrence. In January of 1858, Fitz Hugh's cousin Baldwin died suddenly. "Baldwin's death is indeed a terrible blow to the family," remarked Carrie in a letter to her brother.[23] It must have been an acute loss to Fitz Hugh. Baldwin was his classmate at Union, fellow K.A. member, a hashish companion, and one of his closest friends from childhood. He was very like the brother Fitz Hugh never had. A close friend and confidant from childhood was no longer available as a friend or stabilizing influence.

By early 1858, Fitz Hugh had moved to New York City. Through a family connection, he had been accepted as an assistant and student of a New York City lawyer by the name of William Curtis Noyes. Noyes had, as a young man, studied the law under Judge Samuel B. Ludlow, Fitz Hugh's uncle. Judge Ludlow had predicted that his young student would "take, at an early day, a prominent rank at the Bar."[24] Noyes had been a district attorney in Oneida county, and then moved to New York City, where his major achievement was to formalize the New York State Criminal Code. Noyes agreed to take on the young Ludlow as a student and assistant in his busy Wall Street firm. But Fitz Hugh was still eager to enter the literary field, and he soon was writing anxiously to Fletcher Harper, the youngest of the four brothers who published his book.

Fletcher Harper, Esq. Dear Sir,
Not having by me our contract for the Hasheesh Eater, nor
fully remembering its terms, as to time, I ask your kindness
to inform me whether I am right sir in thinking that the first
payment fell due yesterday Jan 1st. If so, and you find it quite
convenient to let me have the note of your house for percent-
age on the books sold, which I believe is at four months, I shall
feel very much obliged to you as, like most young authors I
am not superabundantly provided with funds just now. If I
mistake the terms of the contract [he had] will you have the
goodness to let me know it by a line addressed to me here—if
I do not, to enclose the note to my order, to the same place,
since business at the office will probably prevent my calling
personally for a few days to come.
    Yours very truly, Fitz Hugh Ludlow[25]

George William Curtis, transcendentalist associate of
Ralph Waldo Emerson and editor of *Harper's Monthly*,
described his meeting with Fitz Hugh soon after Fitz's
arrival in New York:

a slight, bright-eyed, alert young man, who seemed scarcely
more than a boy, called one morning upon the Easy Chair
[Curtis' name for his editorial musings], and with a frank, win-
ning manner said that he was Mr. Ludlow, the author of the
Putnam paper upon "Hasheesh," and that he had come to town
to read law, and open an office, and try his luck in literature.
    The Easy Chair, prepossessed by the article and by
some acquaintance with Mr. Ludlow's father—an excellent
clergyman, of Poughkeepsie—and attracted by the sweet
way and sparkling talk of the young man, asked him a great
many questions, and answered a great many upon the general
subject of literature as a profession. How necessarily doubtful
it was, even precarious; how full of peculiar temptations for
men of certain temperament, which the Easy Chair was sure

it recognized in the young man; how totally incompatible the unreserved devotion and industry essential to the chance of success in it was with the similar industry and devotion necessary to professional advancement—all this, with a great deal of detail, the Easy Chair stated to the young man, who had already tasted the sweetness of a first triumph, and who listened with smiling eyes of incredulity to the tale.

Some little while afterward Ludlow said that he had opened an office, and with a merry laugh, declared that while awaiting real cases he wrote imaginary ones, and in default of lawful fees, was content with literary, which were not wanting; for he had an airy grace of style in writing which well reproduced the sparkling and child-like candor of his social manner.[26]

GEORGE WILLIAM CURTIS (1824-1892),
ABOUT THE TIME HE MET LUDLOW.
(LIBRARY OF CONGRESS, BRADY-HANDY PHOTOGRAPH COLLECTION)

Helen Ludlow later described his physical appearance as a young adult:

> In person Mr. Ludlow was somewhat above the medium height, and of slight but well proportioned frame, his step elastic and his motions full of nervous life. His dark blue eyes were full of gentleness in quiet, and beaming with light when he was roused to enthusiasm or mirth. His complexion was fair and delicate, his hair a soft brown of that silky quality that expresses a corresponding fineness of organization.[27]

A magazine editor later described him as "slender but sinewy," with an "expressive" mouth and "his entire face as beautiful as that of a woman."[28]

Later in the winter of 1858, Fitz Hugh received his first royalty payment from Harper. The book was selling briskly, enough for a second printing to be ordered later in the year. Although sales data do not survive, this could mean sales of anywhere from 3,000 to 6,000.[29] At the terms of Fitz Hugh's contract, this would mean he had earned around $200-$500. Comparing this to a decent annual income of $1,200-$1,500, it is clear that Fitz Hugh was not exactly striking it rich. But for a young man just out of college, with no family and no debts, it was a welcome windfall.

Around this time, *Graham's Illustrated Magazine* published an excerpt from *The Hasheesh Eater*, which they entitled "The Wild Land of Dreams," and gave this introduction:

> Those desirous of reading one of the most extraordinary, fantastic and beautifully-delirious books ever written, should get "The Hasheesh Eater" recently published by Messrs. Harpers of New York. We should prefer not instituting a comparison between it and the Opium Eater by De Quincey, but the press

has generally done so, and we take the liberty of giving our own views as follows. Inferior as a polished writer and trained metaphysician to De Quincey, the Hasheesh Eater excels his prototype in wild gorgeous imagery in exhausting the phantasmagoria of bewildering beauty, and above all, setting forth that oriental spirit and gorgeous primaeval symbolism, without which no opium or hasheesh eating, be it literal or spiritual—come it in the form of pills or aesthetic studies—can ever be perfect. We give the following, not as a fair specimen of the book, (which it is not), but as one best suited to our typographic limit. [There followed an extract from Chapter III.][30]

And as reviewers had suggested, several journalists took up that sincerest form of flattery. A contemporary *New York World* newspaper article related a *World* reporter's experiment with hashish. Coincidentally, like Fitz Hugh he experiences a hallucination of the Nile River, and declares "For me, henceforth, Time is but a word. The hashish eater is immortal."[31] The "immortal" Fitz Hugh Ludlow did not take long to find a milieu in New York suited to his disposition.

"We were all very merry at Pfaff's," sang Thomas Bailey Aldrich.[32] Pfaff's Restaurant was located in the basement of a building at 647 Broadway, near Bleecker Street. It was run by a German immigrant named Charles Pfaff, and served, as a news-paper ad had it: "the best Viands, Lager Bier, Coffee, Tea, Wines, Liquors, Havana Cigars, in Short, the Best of Everything!" Charles Pfaff was also known as the best judge of wine in New York.[33]

One day in 1856, a well traveled, middle-aged writer named Henry Clapp went into Pfaff's with a new acquaintance, Fitz James O'Brien, the son of a wealthy Irish family who had gambled away his personal fortune in Europe and come to America to make his way by his wits. Clapp decided that the Pfaff's ads were no mere hyperbole. Pfaff also specialized in coffee, on which Clapp "chiefly subsisted" along with tobacco. Clapp had been a journalist and an abolitionist in New England, and once helped translate the writings of the French socialist Fourier.[34]

Clapp brought his friends to Pfaff's as a regular gathering place, a coterie of journalists, poets, storytellers and rascals who conspired on a weekly newspaper called the *Saturday Press*. The *Press* was conceived by Clapp as a direct challenge to the literary establishment of the day, which at that time was centered in Boston. In old New England, the brahmins of Boston, Oliver Wendell Holmes, James Russell Lowell and their circle considered themselves the voice of literary America. Clapp thought that Gotham, the center of commerce, was a truer home for the true American. It was a place to thumb one's nose at the staid New England scions. "The thought of Boston made me ugly as sin," said Clapp, and his paper, begun in October of 1858, was to reflect that disdain. For example, in one "news" item appeared the following: "Dr. O.W. Holmes in Boston made another attempt to prove Boston to be the "Hub of Creation"...no city in the world was ever more celebrated for the ease with which, on the slightest pretense, it can get up a hubbub."[35] Fitz Hugh must have been similarly outraged at a typical observation of Holmes':

> A pun is prima facie an insult to the person you are talking with...[a] little trick may upset a freight train of conversation for the sake of a battered witticism.[36]

But Clapp's *Saturday Press* was more than just a reaction to Bostonian stuffiness. William Dean Howells would write:

It would not be easy to say just why the Bohemian group represented New York literature to my imagination, for I certainly associated other names with its best work, but perhaps it was because I had written for the 'Saturday Press' myself, and had my pride in it, and perhaps it was because that paper really embodied the new literary life of the city. It was clever, and full of the wit that tries its teeth upon everything. It attacked all literary shams but its own, and it made itself felt and feared. The young writers throughout the country were ambitious to be seen in it, and they gave their best to it; they gave literally, for the 'Saturday Press' never paid in anything but hopes of paying, vaguer even than promises. It is not too much to say that it was very nearly as well for one to be accepted by the 'Press' as to be accepted by the Atlantic Monthly, the main organ of the Boston literary establishment, and for the time there was no other literary comparison. To be in it was to be in the company of Fitz James O'Brien, Fitz Hugh Ludlow, Mr. Aldrich, Mr. Stedman, and whoever else was liveliest in prose or loveliest in verse at that day in New York.[37]

Although Fitz Hugh would later contribute to the Saturday Press, it was in Pfaff's that he first found a familiar home. This cellar, also known as Pfaff's "Cave," had a low ceiling and stone walls. "The beer barrels and hogsheads were ranged about; and indeed it was all quite medieval and gypsy-like and picturesque."[38] The basement was unusually large and opened out into a cavelike space directly under Broadway's sidewalk; hence its habitués also called themselves the Cave Dwellers. In this space was a table around which could fit around thirty chairs, and it was reserved nightly for their use.

Here, Fitz Hugh joined other young writers, artists and actors in carousing and in cultivating a literate criticism of "New England respectability and New York boorishness… The retold story and the repeated bon mot were rigorously barred, but the new good thing was sure of applause."[39] And "sometimes we were serious enough, especially when it came to settling the score at two o'clock in the morning."[40]

DIFFERING PERSPECTIVES OF THE GOINGS-ON AT THE BOHEMIAN WATERING HOLE PFAFF'S: TOP, PFAFF'S "AS THEY WERE SAID TO BE BY A KNIGHT OF THE ROUNDTABLE"; BELOW, "BOHEMIANS AS THEY ARE DESCRIBED BY ONE OF THEIR OWN NUMBER". *NEW YORK ILLUSTRATED NEWS*, FEBRUARY 6TH, 1864. (IMAGE COURTESY OF THE VAULT AT PFAFF'S)

The Bohemian label had been appropriated by Clapp from Frenchman Murger's *Bohemian Life*. One contemporary defined a bohemian as "a man with literary or artistic tastes, and an incurable proclivity to debt."[41] Whenever the paper was in trouble Clapp would take in new business partners. According to writer Edmund Clarence Stedman, "when he [Clapp] got what he called 'fresh blood,' he used to divide it up among the boys."[42] On the other hand, sometime assistant editor Thomas Bailey Aldrich related to a friend that Clapp had trouble sleeping in the morning, while Aldrich often slept off hangovers until 9 A.M. Since, in fine Bohemian fashion, no one kept the books, whoever was in the office took the advertising money as it came in. Due purely to sleep habits, Clapp confiscated the receipts and Aldrich suffered.[43] Charles Pfaff himself was sympathetic to the Bohemian cash flow problems. He would give his customers plenty of credit and they would pay their bills when they could. Fitz Hugh was soon a needy beneficiary of this largesse, already scrambling for money despite his best seller.

Pfaff's stimulated public comment, and curiosity seekers came to observe. A number of youthful malcontents, feeling that Pfaff's crowd represented what they were looking for, moved into the neighborhood, taking rooms in adjacent boardinghouses. Fitz Hugh lived among them on Clinton Place, on the stagecoach line, at $5 rent per week. Fitz Hugh once described some of his neighbors who were Cuban nationalists. When the Cubans meet:

> One word in every six is *Libertad*. When it isn't *Libertad* it's very likely to be *Despotismo*. And if it isn't Libertad or Despotismo, the chances are fair of its being *Muerta*. Liberty,

Despotism and Death! the most magnificent things having been done about them on paper, there is a thunder of bravos.[44]

The mixture of literary rebels and wild bachelors alarmed the public, editorials denounced them, and in general the Bohemians met what is now a predictable reaction to such outsiders.[45] When humorist Artemus Ward first appeared at Pfaff's with a friend he said to the friend, "Don't be afraid, they won't hurt you. These are Bohemians. A Bohemian is an *educated* hoss-thief."[46] Fitz Hugh once told a story of his New York perambulations that serves to counterpoint the outcry. He once strolled around town with two friends dressed alike in a "charmingly odd" fashion in order to get a reaction. Alas, "Nobody looked at us, nobody was in the least astonished at us."[47] This was New York City, even in 1858.

On the literary side, Pfaffians had several characteristics. Some of them disliked Emerson because he had referred to their idol, Edgar Allan Poe, as "the jingle-man."[48] Fitz Hugh would later write several stories in Poe's style, including "The Yellow Cat" and "The Phial of Dread." Fitz Hugh the hashish dreamer found a kindred literary soul in the late Baltimorean, his own debt to Emerson notwithstanding.

Editor Clapp's own writing appeared in several places, such as a book called *Husband vs. Wife*, which was a collection of doggerel about the usual clichés of the war between the sexes. This sort of hack writing was what sustained the array of contributors to the *Saturday Press*, for, as Howells had noted, the pay was scarce. Fitz Hugh was one of the few young rebels who had been published in the major magazines, such as *Putnam's* and the *Knickerbocker*. Fitz Hugh first appeared in the Saturday Press in 1858.[49]

The angry young men had gathered around Clapp, whom they called "The Oldest Man"—he was 46 in 1858.[50] Clapp was small and slight of stature,[51] and in a lighter mood, he was a witty friend. When Artemus Ward (Charles Farrar Browne) got an offer from California to do some lecturing, for which he was becoming known, the telegram came asking, "what will you take for forty nights?" Before Browne could say anything, Clapp cried out "Brandy and soda, answer them."[52] But in his more common, cynical moods, no one was safe from Clapp's verbal lance. Horace Greeley, who had at times employed the otherwise destitute Clapp, was referred to as "a self made man who worshipped his Creator."

Competing writer Henry T. "aimed at nothing and always hit the mark precisely."[53] A prominent clergyman was "waiting for a vacancy in the Trinity." In *The Saturday Press*, he was just as irreverent. Under the byline of Figaro, Clapp wrote:

> Reverend Henry Ward Beecher recently purchased 27 acres in Westchester County for $13,000. It is said that Mr. Beecher's income is larger than that of any other Minister of Christ in the country, being at least $15,000…It is encouraging to know that Christianity has at last, got a "where to lay its head."[54]

Such outrageous disdain for respectability was nectar to Fitz Hugh. He had fought his adolescent battles with the Reverend Henry, and to find a whole group of like-minded young men was as exhilarating as finding his fellow hashish-eater in *Putnam's Magazine*. Moreover, the social criticism was embedded in an after-hours lifestyle at Pfaff's for which Fitz Hugh had been well trained at the Kappa Alpha gatherings at college.

But there were more than schoolboys at Pfaff's. If Henry Clapp was the king of Bohemia, then its queen was Ada Clare. Her given name of Jane McElheney had disappeared with her escape from the South. She moved to New York to become an occasional writer and actress. Clare achieved notoriety after a love affair with one of the first great American composers and performers, Louis Gottschalk. The tryst ended with Ada the mother of a baby boy (which she went to Paris to deliver).[55] In 1855 and 1856, while Gottschalk played a series of concerts which brought comparisons to Liszt and Chopin, she would invite him to social events at her salon, matter-of-factly refer to Gottschalk's paternity, but never seek to rekindle the flame.[56] She was blond and beautiful and witty as any man at Pfaff's. Critic William Winter said "she was a great beauty and poor old Clapp was hopelessly in love with her."[57] She wore her hair scandalously short, but despite her tarnished reputation she was very much of a den mother to the group. She organized literary contests and passed the hat for group celebrations.[58] Ada defined the Bohemian as "not, like the creature of society, a victim of rules and customs; he steps over them all with an easy, graceful, joyous unconsciousness, guided by the principles of good taste and feeling. Above all others essentially, the Bohemian must not be narrow-minded; if he be so, he is degraded back to the position of a mere worldling."[59]

Fitz Hugh passed the test quite easily, borne by the shocking nature of his book, and confirmed by his verbal agility. Years later, Fitz Hugh would cultivate a friendship with Gottschalk, and Miss Ada Clare was an uncommon acquaintance about whom they would reminisce, delicately, for reasons unique to each.

"QUEEN OF BOHEMIA" ADA CLARE (1836-1874),
ACTRESS AND PFAFFIAN. (EPHEMERAL NEW YORK)

Another even more spectacular belle of Bohemia was Adah Menken. She moved to New York from New Orleans to try her hand, and the rest of her shapely body, at the stage. After a brief, failed, marriage to a challenger to the world boxing championship, Menken achieved fame and notoriety as the lead in a popular play called "The Mazeppa," the climax of which had her clad in just a body stocking and strapped to a horse which charged up a ramp and offstage. She was one of several actresses who, seemingly as a prerequisite to the trade, wrote poetry, perhaps to verify their ability to be sensitive to the emotional requirements of the roles they played.[60] She came to Pfaff's late in 1859, partly to cultivate the drama critics who frequented the place.[61] She became close friends with the other notorious woman, Ada Clare. Fitz Hugh would also re-unite with Menken in years to come, in a different land, and with tragic consequences for him.

ACTRESS AND POET ADAH ISAACS MENKEN (1835-1868).
(HARVARD THEATER COLLECTION)

The most famous of all the Pfaffians was Walt Whitman. The groundbreaking *Leaves of Grass* had just been published, and many people were outraged about this man who sang about himself and lust and other indelicate subjects. Clapp was convinced he had found the great voice of all that he believed in. Clapp defended Whitman in several reviews in *The Saturday Press,* and published portions of the poet's work, at a time when *The Atlantic Monthly* and others would not.[62]

Whitman wore a slouch hat and "eccentric garb of rough blue and gray," red shirt open at the neck, and had long, flowing, hair.[63] He would ride during the day beside drivers on Broadway stagecoaches, enjoying the company of the ordinary man. But at night, he went to Pfaff's "to see, talk little, and absorb."[64] "It was Whitman's imposing personality and unconventional attire that made him the most noticeable figure of the whole group," wrote a contemporary. "I heard him describe many times events and incidents of Pfaff's... [He] was a frequent visitor to Pfaff's, and during the hours when the brightest lights of Bohemia were guests. His Bohemia, with his enjoyment of life and nature, was all the time; and while, from his slow speech and a lack of expression of humor or wit, he must have seemed a dull companion at Pfaff's, he enjoyed the company and associations greatly... His free and easy appearance, his open shirt and swaggery walk, naturally attracted people to him."[65]

Whitman later reminisced about Pfaff's—"the food was well cooked, German method, and cheap; the ale (beer was but coming in then) good, and other liquid refreshments healthy. There was no formality—Bohemia sat around in groups...a portion of that Bohemia did not recognize another portion of visitors as Bohemians. It took hard work and merit to have full membership. The top lights recognized themselves, and made a bit of an inside clique or cabal...What wit, humor, repartee, word wars, and sometimes bad blood!"[66] The latter may refer to one incident where Whitman physically attacked George Arnold when the latter raised a toast to the Confederacy. "I think there was as good talk around that table as took place anywhere in the world," said Whitman. Whitman began but never finished a poem entitled "The Two Vaults":

The vault at Pfaffs where the drinkers and laughers meet to
    eat and drink and carouse,
While on the walk immediately overhead, pass the myriad
    feet of Broadway,
As the dead in their graves, are underfoot hidden
And the living pass over them, reckoning not of them,…
Laugh on Laughers!
Drink on Drinkers!
Bandy the Jest! Toss the theme from one to another![67]

One night celebrating Clapp's birthday, they were hoisting beers, and the lot fell to Whitman to offer the toast. By that time the group was soused, and Whitman drew himself together dramatically to gesture to Clapp and opine, "that's…the feller!"[68]

Another Pfaff's pioneer, Fitz James O'Brien, was in many ways the archetypal Bohemian. O'Brien would battle destitution in a number of ways. He was equipped with a bunch of pass-keys to the lodgings of his fellow Bohemians, and slept in the bed that was most convenient at the time he felt the need of slumber. (The keys of course had been collected from each friend when, after being invited to spend the night, he borrowed the key and didn't return it.) *Saturday Press* editor William Winter once put him up for two nights, during which he slept only four hours. But he had written a narrative poem in that time which made him enough money to be on his own a while.

O'Brien, like Fitz Hugh, published in *Harper's* and other major magazines. His "The Diamond Lens" and "The Wondersmith" "revived the fashion of the weird short story" in the tradition of Poe, the Bohemian patron saint.[69] As an example of the Pfaffian cross-pollination, Fitz Hugh followed

O'Brien in writing Poe-influenced tales, such as "The Phial of Dread." Another Pfaffian, Charles Gardette, published a poem called "The Fire-Fiend" as an actual lost manuscript of Poe, successfully deceiving a number of critics. O'Brien's "The Wondersmith" grew out of anecdote by Clapp about a man with a glass eye, which O'Brien turned into a tale of an orb that retained and replayed the scenes that had once passed before it.

WALT WHITMAN AT PFAFF'S BEER CELLAR IN 1857.
(LIBRARY OF CONGRESS)

And if cross-pollination wasn't enough, the Bohemians would simply write about each other (as Jack Kerouac among others would become famous doing in latter-day Bohemian contexts.) Fitz Hugh quoted O'Brien as "an Irish friend of mine" in one of his earliest short stories,[70] and O'Brien included a hashish eater in one of his stories. Clapp published a story linking O'Brien to a certain Lord Inchiquin, so he was called by friends Baron Inchiquin (or as Aldrich would put it, Baron Lynchpin).[71] Hence the following letter, the result of O'Brien's affair with actress Jenny Danforth, the estranged wife of a naval officer:

> Mon Cher Baron
> Adieu! I leave to-day but to return Tuesday...Remember me while I am away. Come when I return. I will not say I shall pray for you nightly but I shall certes think of you much. I am in earnest about the matter we have spoken of. I think of you *ce soir* at your Club dinner. Drink me silently. Be good. Let the festive cup alone.
> Ever faithfully, yours, Jenny[72]

This is one of the few references to a drinking problem on the part of a Pfaffian, but more than a few observers noted that very few of the Pfaffians lived to a ripe old age. Fitz Hugh's later bouts of drinking in hard times may very well date from his Pfaffian lifestyle. But the especial value of the companionship was the ready availability of cogent and brutally honest literary feedback. Winter once remarked that:

> Candor of judgement, indeed, was the inveterate custom of that Bohemian group. Unmerciful chaff pursued the perpetrator of any piece of writing that impressed those persons as trite, conventional, artificial, laboriously solemn, or insincere:

and they never spared each other from the barb of ridicule. It was a salutary experience for young writers, because it habituated them to the custom not only of speaking the truth, as they understood it, but of hearing the truth, as others understood it, about their own productions. "I greatly like your poem of 'Orgia'," said O'Brien to me, "and I like it all the more because I did not think you could write anything so good."

Some literary acquaintances of Fitz Hugh's didn't like it at Pfaff's. Bayard Taylor, for example, Fitz Hugh's hashish godfather, found young men unimpressed by his world travels and never returned.[73] However, Taylor did write a semi-autobiographical novel, *John Godfrey's Fortunes*, set in a familiar-sounding basement tavern called The Ichneumon. There were also *Atlantic Monthly* protegés like William Dean Howells, who despite words of praise for Pfaffians, was routed in his only contact. He met the crowd in August 1860, and reported:

> I went to the office of the Saturday Press with much the same sort of feeling I had in going to the office of the Atlantic Monthly in Boston, but I came away with a very different feeling. I had found there a bitterness against Boston as great as the bitterness against respectability, and as Boston was then rapidly becoming my second country, I could not join in the scorn thought of her and said of her by the Bohemians... when their chief [Clapp] asked me how I got on with Hawthorne, and I began to say that he was very shy and I was rather shy, and the king of Bohemia took his pipe out to break in upon me with "Oh, a couple of shysters!" and the rest laughed, I was abashed all they could have wished...That very night I went to the beer-cellar, once very far up Broadway, where I was given to know that the Bohemian nights were smoked and quaffed away...

As I neither drank beer nor smoked, my part in the carousal was limited to a German pancake, which I found they had very good at Pfaff's, and to listening to the whirling words of my commensals, at the long board spread for the Bohemians in a cavernous space under the pavement. There were writers for the Saturday Press and for Vanity Fair (a hopefully comic paper of that day), and some of the artists who drew for the illustrated periodicals. Nothing of their talk remains with me, but the impression remains that it was not so good talk as I had heard in Boston. [Contrast to Whitman's opinion above.] At one moment of the orgy, which went but slowly for an orgy, we were joined by some belated Bohemians whom the others made a great clamor over; I was given to understand they were just recovered from a fearful debauch; their locks were still damp from the wet towels used to restore them, and their eyes were very frenzied. I was presented to these types, who neither said nor did anything worthy of their awful appearance, but dropped into seats at the table, and ate of the supper with an appetite that seemed poor. I stayed hoping vainly for worse things till eleven o'clock, and then I rose and took my leave of a literary condition that had distinctly disappointed me.[74]

Winter later gave the Pfaffian judgement of Howells: "They thought him a prig." After all, he left the place well before midnight.

Some other writers who were bona fide Pfaffians would remain close to Fitz Hugh in later years and other settings. These included Edmund Clarence Stedman and Thomas Bailey Aldrich, like him a young bachelor with some early successes. These two along with Fitz Hugh began to frequent a literary salon hosted by Richard Henry Stoddard and his wife Elizabeth, known as "Lizzie and Dick," in a boarding house on Tenth Street. People there were somewhat less irreverent, and said things like "what a holy gift is this

Poetry," and sought "that spirit of art and beauty which men call Poetry."[75] Fitz Hugh sympathized with these romantic types in his more sedate moments. Stedman was a child of privilege overcoming a checkered past, having been expelled from Yale in 1851, and briefly lived at the Fourieristic Unitary Home in New York in 1856.[76] He had become friendly with Bayard Taylor, through whom he met Fitz Hugh.

The formation of the Tenth St. Salon was fortuitous for Fitz Hugh, as the Pfaffian lifestyle had begun to take its toll on him. Tobacco and alcohol were *de rigueur* at Pfaff's. More than one of his fellow revelers sought out the Pythagorean for an initiation into the delights and debauchs of hashish, and he found it hard to refuse their appeals.

Income from *The Hasheesh Eater* was holding steady. The book had been successful enough to warrant a second edition. However, Fitz Hugh's party expenses mounted, and there were to be no more legal fees. Although he passed the bar examination in 1859, he had already fallen out with Mr. Noyes, who by this time would probably have liked to write a penalty for general depravity into the New York Criminal Code. Despite Fitz Hugh's intellectual capacity for the job, his interests were clearly elsewhere, and he soon left Noyes' firm to become a full time freelance writer. His sister later traced this decision to a general breakdown in his health:

> During this illness, his plans of life were changed; he felt that while doing his best to please his friends, he had proved the possibility of living by his pen, and that he might make his mark in the profession of his choice, while that of the law had become increasingly distasteful to him. This conviction settled, he acted upon it with his usual promptness of decision.[77]

Fitz Hugh was determined to make his living at writing, his first love, but his infrequent payments from the *Saturday Press* weren't a living wage. He turned to the bastion of New York literary respectability, namely *Harper's Monthly Magazine*. Charles Nordhoff, the editor at the time, knew Fitz Hugh from *The Hasheesh Eater*, and Fletcher Harper's recommendation was sufficient for Nordhoff to seek his work. Nordhoff and Fitz Hugh reached an agreement in mid-1858 for him to provide some items for *Harper's Monthly*. However, Fitz Hugh was still in the thick of the New York nightlife. He sought, and with Fletcher Harper's approval, received the substantial advance of $60 for services yet to be rendered. Then he disappeared from view of the concerned *Harper's* editors until October, 1858. In that time, however, profound changes were to occur in the young Bohemian's life.

1 Caroline Geddings to S. Ludlow Frey, December 20, 1857, NYSHA Library.
2 *The Hasheesh Eater*, p. 146.
3 Ibid., p. 269.
4 Ibid., p. 269.
5 Ibid., p. 305.
6 Ibid., p. 329.
7 Baudelaire.
8 *The Hasheesh Eater*, p. 330.
9 This thesis is the subject of a book by Linda Schierse Leonard, *Witness to the Fire: Creativity and the Veil of Addiction*, Boston: Shambhala, 1989.
10 *Harper's Monthly*, November, 1857, p. 834.
11 *Christian Examiner*, January 1858, p. 147.
12 *The Knickerbocker*, February, 1858, p. 197.
13 *The Saturday Review*, February 13, 1858, p. 166.
14 William Thayer, *John Hay*, New York: AMS Press, 1972, p. 47.
15 Tyler Dennett, *John Hay: From Poetry to Politics*, New York: Dodd, Mead & Company, 1933, p. 22.

16 John Hay, *A Poet in Exile; Early Letters of John Hay*, Boston and New York: Houghton Mifflin Company, 1910, p. 23.

17 John Hay, *A Poet in Exile; Early Letters of John Hay*, Boston and New York: Houghton Mifflin Company, 1910, p. 23.

18 Andrew C. Kimmens, *Tales of Hashish*, New York: William Morrow and Company, Inc., 1977, p. 173.

19 Morris Bishop, "Fitz Hugh Ludlow," in *Fitz Hugh Ludlow*, 1953, p. 17.

20 Carrie Geddings to S. Ludlow Frey, November 30, 1857, NYSHA Library.

21 Carrie Geddings to S. Ludlow Frey, February 11, 1857, NYSHA Library.

22 Carrie Geddings to S. Ludlow Frey, March 21, 1857, NYSHA Library.

23 Carrie Geddings to S. Ludlow Frey, January 21, 1858, NYSHA Library.

24 *A Baccalaureate Discourse delivered July 16 before the Class of 1865 by Samuel W. Fisher*, President of Hamilton College, Utica, N.Y.: 1866, p. 25.

25 Fitz Hugh Ludlow to Fletcher Harper, Jan. 2, 1858, Ransom.

26 *Harper's Monthly*, December, 1870, p. 139.

27 Helen Ludlow, 1873-75(?), p. 9.

28 *Harper's Bazar*, 1870, p. 723.

29 The best-selling authors like Dickens had print runs of 7,500 to 15,000 for each edition of their books. *Uncle Tom's Cabin*, probably the best-seller of the decade, sold over 100,000 copies in numerous editions.

30 Fitz Hugh Ludlow, "The Wild Land of Dreams," *Graham's Illustrated Magazine*, 1858, p. 150.

31 Clipping of undated article, found in first edition of *The Hasheesh Eater* at New York City Public Library.

32 Thomas Bailey Aldrich, "At the Cafe'" in *Vanity Fair*, Volume 1, Number 1, 1860.

33 Gay Wilson Allen, *The Solitary Singer*, New York: Macmillan, 1955, p. 228.

34 Rufus Wilson, *New York in Literature*, Elmira, NY: Primavera Press, 1947. Clapp had made a pilgrimage to Paris. One story went that in France he met Alexandre Dumas (pere) and suggested that they write a play together. Dumas said "Monsieur, you cannot find in Scripture or elsewhere an instance for hitching the ox and the ass together." Clapp immediately replied "Monsieur, by what authority do you call me an ox?" Clapp also met Horace Greeley in France, promised him a series of articles for the *New York Tribune*, got a cash advance, but never delivered the articles. On his return to New York in debt, he managed to somehow placate Greeley and eventually did write some pieces for the Tribune.

35 *Saturday Press*, May 28, 1859, in response to one of Holmes's papers from *The Atlantic Monthly*, later collected in *The Autocrat of the Breakfast Table*, Boston, New York: Houghton Mifflin and Company, 1886.

36 Ibid.

37 William Dean Howells, *Literary Friends and Acquaintances*, New York: Harper and Brothers, 1902, p. 70.

38 Charles T. Congdon, *Reminiscences of a Journalist*, Boston: J.R. Osgood, 1880, p. 338; Emily Hahn, *Romantic Rebels*, Boston: Houghton Mifflin, 1967, p. 20-33; Rufus Wilson, *New York Old and New*, Philadelphia: J.B. Lippincott Company, 1902.

39 Ferris Greenslet, *Thomas Bailey Aldrich*, Boston: Houghton Mifflin & Co., 1928, p. 45.

40 Congdon (1880), p. 338.

41 Ibid.

42 Laura Stedman and George Gould, *The Life and Letters of Edmund Clarence Stedman*, New York: Moffat, Yard & Company, 1910, p. 208.

43 J.C. Derby, *Fifty Years Among Authors, Books and Publishers*, p. 232.

44 Fitz Hugh Ludlow, *The Primpenny Family*, *Vanity Fair*, January 19, 1861, p. 25.

45 Hahn (1967), p. 28.

46 William Winter, *Old Friends*, Freeport, NY: Books for Libraries Press, 1971, p. 89.

47 Fitz Hugh Ludlow, "A Goodbye Article," *The Golden Era*, November 11, 1863.

48 James L. Ford, *Forty Odd Years in the Literary Shop*, New York: 1921, p. 62.

49 A surviving set of the *Saturday Press* has not been located.

50 Hahn (1967), p. 28.

51 Ibid.

52 Stedman and Gould (1910), p. 208.

53 Mark Anthony De Wolfe Howe, *Memories of a Hostess*, Boston: The Atlantic Monthly Press, 1922, p. 184.

54 *Saturday Press*, May 28, 1859.

55 Allen (1955), p. 229.

56 Howard Breslin, *Concert Grand*, New York: Dodd, Mead & Company, 1963, p. 186.

57 Rufus Rockwell Wilson (1947), p. 65.

58 Hahn (1967), p. 26.

59 Ibid.

60 Hahn (1967), p. 23.

61 Allen (1955), p. 262.
62 For example, the *Christian Examiner* paper in November, 1856, referred to *Leaves of Grass* as "impious and obscene...a work that teems with abominations."
63 Wilson (1902), p. 141; Winter (1971), p. 64.
64 Wilson (1902), p. 141; Winter (1971), p. 64.
65 Thomas Donaldson, *Walt Whitman the Man*, New York: Francis P. Harper, 1896, p.202.
66 Ibid., p. 208.
67 Walt Whitman, "The Two Vaults," unfinished poem in Gay Allen Wilson, *The Solitary Singer*, New York: New York University Press, 1967, p. 270.
68 Winter (1971), p. 91.
69 Ibid., p. 67.
70 Fitz Hugh Ludlow, "Our Queer Papa," *Harper's Monthly*, November 1858.
71 Francis Wolle, *Fitz James O'Brien; A Literary Bohemian of the Eighteen Fifties*, Boulder, CO: University of Colorado Studies, 1944, p. 63.
72 Wolle (1944), p. 63.
73 Bohemians would have appreciated Humboldt, who said of him "that of all men he had ever known Taylor had traveled the farthest and had seen the least." Albert Smyth, *Bayard Taylor*, Detroit: 1970, p. 95.
74 William Dean Howells, *Literary Friends and Acquaintances*, New York and London: Harper & Brothers, 1902, p. 72-73.
75 Samuels (1966), p. 35.
76 Edwin Cady, *The Road to Realism*, Syracuse: Syracuse University Press, 1956, p. 122.
77 Helen Ludlow, 1873-75, p. 4.

VIII.

REGULAR HABITS

FITZ HUGH had fully embraced the New York City social scene as a notorious author and night warrior. But both ends of the candle were fast approaching each other, and before the deal with *Harper's* magazine could save him, Fitz Hugh went down in flames. His health, precarious since birth, gave out before his ego gratification or his money. His twenty-second New York winter, combined with the nonstop lifestyle and substance abuse, led to a bout of pneumonia accompanied by continuous headaches. Being prohibited by his doctor from any strenuous activity, including that of writing, Fitz Hugh left the city sometime in the early spring, to visit a resort in the Catskill Mountains. He described it in a story as "Old Babyland":

> Old Babyland is a nook among the mountains, far, far up on the very top of Sullivan County, where fashion cometh not, but home-happiness goeth with you—where nature has never been dethroned, and civilization sits from June to September at her feet, drinking in her eloquent music, learning her wise, sweet lessons with a joyful meekness. To the wide piazzas of the Mansion House, close by the singing ripples and the thickets of laurel-rose, among the highland birches, and beeches, and evergreens, solaced by the birds and the echoes of Kaw-na-ong-ga, "The lake that ever is silver-white."[1]

There, Fitz Hugh recovered from the rigors of work and play in a pastoral setting, alongside the families of the rich and the famous. One day the children of the resort decided to have a "no-grown-ups" picnic. It is reflective of the whimsical side of Fitz Hugh's personality, coming to the fore in this idyllic setting, that the children invited Fitz Hugh as the token adult, because of his ability to tell "mouse stories." So they set off one morning with the requisite supply of bread and cookies. When they got to the site, they ate lunch and then turned to Fitz Hugh for the afternoon's entertainment. Fitz Hugh responded with an amusing tallish tale, after which the children had many questions about whether the tail that had been cut off by the trap ever grew out again. In the midst of the discussion, another adult was spotted and ordered to leave, but she pleaded to stay. Rosalie Osborn was eighteen, and Fitz Hugh described her thus:

> Her form, the freshly blossomed woman; her height, five feet; her complexion, marble struck through with rose flush...Her hair, dark, waving, glossy brown, drooped low behind. Eyes of the same dye, large, long lashed, and thoughtful. Her nose just aquiline enough not to be Grecian; her mouth, rose-buds that kissed each other.[2]

A relationship developed. Fitz Hugh was charming and whimsical enough to be loved by the child in Rosalie, but sophisticated and learned enough to attract the woman in her. His learning, which he was happy to display in a pedantic manner that she demurely encouraged, was attractive as a base for future financial prospects. His exotic life and early success were exciting enough to attract the strong-willed daughter of a domineering father.

ROSALIE OSBORN (1841-1893), MARRIED FITZ HUGH LUDLOW IN
1859. PAINTING BY THOMAS BUCHANAN READ, C. 1863. (COLLECTION
OF MRS. ORVILLE DEFOREST EDWARDS, DOBBS FERRY, NEW YORK)

Rosalie's father, Amos Osborn, was the son of the first
man to build a distillery in the small town of Waterville

in upstate New York. This gave the family a great deal of wealth and attendant social standing in Waterville. Osborn sold the distillery eleven years later and bought three farms. His further ambition led him to sail on a clipper ship to Australia in 1855 on a trade mission of sorts. He returned with the beginnings of a herd of Australian sheep which he introduced to America. Amos Osborn was described none-too-gently by Fitz Hugh as "Our Queer Papa," in a story by that name:

> The father of Elsie Landon was a mighty queer old gentleman. One of those men whose constitution is so mixed with antagonist elements that you wonder how they ever manage to get a unanimous vote of their faculties upon any action of life. He was rich, very rich; such people often are; but how they succeed in business is a problem. His manner was as vacillating as this:…Elsie's improprieties he frequently treated by saying, "Horrible! really I seem to be in a bad dream! Well I shall have to confine you to your room; go, reflect. Why, bless me! here are the horses at the door. Elsie, wouldn't you like to ride around the lake my love?"[3]

The courtship of Rosalie presented major barriers, as Fitz Hugh put it:

> I loved her as child—I loved her as woman—and that love was all the broader and deeper for attaching itself to all the multitudinous lights and shades of her nature in both aspects. But then, the old gentleman was worth—nobody knew how much, and I;—nobody knew how little. Simply a good-looking gentleman with brains, who had published.[4]

And Fitz Hugh had one thing more, a father who was a not altogether quiet and respectable minister of the

Lord. After seventeen years in Poughkeepsie, the Reverend Henry had become restless again. His specialty was in building congregations, not in maintaining them. As the day-to-day business of running a mature parish became more intractable, Henry would leave town more frequently on missions of revival. As Fitz Hugh was wooing the fair Rosalie, Henry went to Oswego to visit his brother Samuel, who was currently serving as the secretary of the Northwestern Insurance Company. By the middle of the month, Uncle Samuel had arranged for Henry to move to Oswego to become the pastor of the Congregational Church, of which Samuel was one of the founders. This activity may have kept Henry and Amos Osborn from meeting until after the engagement of their children.

Fitz Hugh had gone to Old Babyland because he'd met young people of privilege in New York. His father was never of that class, and had only gotten Fitz Hugh through Princeton by alumni ties and through Union by scholarships. When Fitz Hugh dropped the law as a profession, Henry could help no more. But Fitz Hugh's early literary success and skill at borrowing money had gained him entrée to a place that was one of a circuit of resorts frequented by the "invalids of opulence and elegance."[5] The circuit included the famous Saratoga Springs, Ballston Spa (near Schenectady), and the Great White Sulphur Springs. All these were reputed to have healing powers, but mostly they were, as Fitz Hugh had described, places where nature has never been dethroned. (Incidentally, Fitz Hugh took an interest in the sources and chemistry of the springs he visited, and would maintain this interest in his later travels.)

The courtship of Rosalie was brief. Old Man Osborn was scandalized by the frequent rendezvous which Fitz Hugh and Rosalie orchestrated around the more formal events of Babyland. There seemed no respectable way out but to have a marriage take place.

Fitz Hugh celebrated the prospective engagement with an autobiographical short story published in the November, 1858 *Harper's Monthly*, thereby finally meeting his obligations to Fletcher Harper and Charles Nordhoff. The story, "Our Queer Papa; A Case of Organic Affection," offered elopement as the answer to the lovers' dilemma. It then tracked the anger of Osborn, followed by their eventual reconciliation through the literary device of a beneficent stranger, in the person of an organ-grinder who turns out to be Papa (hence the organic affection of the title, showing Fitz Hugh's long-cultivated punning compulsion in full bloom.) The plot development was surrounded by flowery sentiment that was popular at the time. In contradistinction from his satirical forays in the *Saturday Press*, Fitz Hugh showed that he had absorbed the stylistic lessons of the sentimental novels of his day (such as the novel he had given as a gift to young Danny Stimson while at Union College).

This story was immediately followed by another even more saccharine tale, "The Loan of a Lyre," which appeared in *Harper's Monthly* in December, 1858. The plot was a prototype for what would later be found in countless television situation comedies. The famous poet Meliboeus Barcarole receives a letter from an ardent female devotee who informs him that she will be coming to stay with him, the lonely romantic, whose poems say his door is always open for a kindred soul. Of course, Barcarole is happily married and forty years old, but he arranges for his nephew to impersonate him, and the ensuing play-acting results, of course, in young love. Even the girl's evil father, the Wall Street magnate "Cottin Bayles, Sr.," who attends "Leviathan Anniversary Meetings of Brobdignagian Societies," cannot stop them.

It is touches like the latter, a snide rejoinder to the respectable Century Club in New York City (which denied membership to the successful but a tad too-disreputable young author) which are the saving graces today of a story which otherwise has not aged very gracefully. At the time, however, *Harper's* was still in the sway of what a later critic called "The Feminine Fifties." The light and airy sketches of happy romance are the ancestors of the Harlequin romances of today, and just as formulaic and predestined in their conclusions. Fitz Hugh did what he could within the framework, weaving in philosophical musings and autobiographical material that distinguish his work from most of his contemporaries.

Fitz Hugh's dry wit and playful language also differentiated his stories. In "The Loan of a Lyre," a plan of deception shapes up so well that "I was one universal chuckle at the promise of his success." His nephew had "conquered the disadvantages of wealth" and had "risen from the most extreme opulence to a very honorable position among the intellectual men of society." And Barcarole's hair was groomed so that "every curl was conscientiously educated into symmetry with the best adipoise secretion of Canadian bears."

The story also contained an autobiographical reflection on fame that had come so early to Fitz Hugh:

...laying claim, I fancy, to something like a transatlantic reputation, having been reviewed in the Atheneum as the author of "Another mass of American stuff"...It is pleasant to be famous. I like to have men poke one another in the ribs, when they see me on a railroad car, and say, "There he is—that's *Barcarole!*" I am fond of being called on to write sonnets for great occasions.

Then came the down side of fame, which in the story had to do with the poet Barcarole's "wondrously lifelike and graphic" poems, but was a thinly-veiled appeal to Fitz Hugh's own family and acquaintances to reconsider *The Hasheesh Eater*:

...it never could be understood by the general reader how I was not in earnest in every thing I wrote...I am not "A Deserted Soul"; yet, if I choose, can not I write "The Battle-cry" of that unfortunate being without disagreeably identifying myself with him?

This appeal was primarily aimed at the one most dubious, Queer Papa Osborn himself, who assumed *The Hasheesh Eater* was as debauched as advertised in his book. (Little did he know!) Fitz Hugh brought "The Loan of a Lyre" to the Osborn homestead in December of 1858, just before joining his own family for Christmas. Rosalie for her part was building bridges to the rest of the Ludlow family with the help of the Reverend Henry himself:

To him whom I hope, some day, to call my dear Father, I write—and firstly a few lines in explanation of my delay in replying to his much prized letter.

Fitz Hugh is probably at Oswego by this time, gladdening you all by his presence, and, in return, taking much pleasure with the dear ones at home.

He will tell you, doubtless, that I have been suffering from severe colds which have utterly incapacitated me for mental exercise. I have only written to him letters which were he not lenient and partial would have seemed dull and insipid.

I received your most welcome letter last evening. Thank you for your kind and thoughtful suggestions: it gives me great happiness to find that you think of me with so much tenderness and affection. My heart, also is full of love for yourself, Mrs. Ludlow, and dear Helen.

As to my medical treatment—Dr. Foster suggests that I use stimulating baths to produce action upon the surface, thus counteracting mucous initiation, which course I am now pursuing with benefit. If this improvement should not continue, I must act upon your advice trying Allopathy.

May God grant me restoration and the capacity commensurate with my desire, of being useful to those who love me. May He aid me in realizing those bright imaginings and joyful hopes with which you have so lovingly visited me. I could say much upon this and kindred topics but a neuralgic headache and the closing mail oblige me to close this brief missive. I hope soon to write to my darling Helen. Please accept the kindest regards of my parents for yourself and family—my own warmest love for you all. I must not omit to mention my joy at Mrs. Ludlow's convalescence. Yours most affectionately,

Rosalie H. Osborn[6]

But if Rosalie and the Reverend Henry had hit it off, old Amos was still unconvinced. He instructed his wife to check the references of the young man. And she went right to the estimable President of Union College himself, Eliphalet Nott. Nott responded:

Madam:
Yours of December 29 is at hand, and I hasten to say in reply

that Mr. Ludlow is personally known to me chiefly as a pupil while prosecuting his studies in Union College.

During that period he was considered here a young man of very decided talents, and unimpeachable character. Having completed his college course, he left the institution esteemed alike by his companions and his instructors, as well as distinguished by literary honors.

Feeling, however, a deep interest in his welfare, I have frequently enquired after him, and been gratified to learn that the stand taken by him in New York was such as to justify, in his friends, the hope that he was destined to make a distinguished professional, or literary man.

In that hope, I myself have sympathized, and most cordially wish him and your daughter, should their destinies be united, every blessing.

> Very respectfully yours,
> Eliphalet Nott

P.S. If it is desired to attain more particular information as to Mr. Ludlow's present standing and prospects, that information must be sought in New York where he resides, and has, it is believed, resided for a great part of the time since he left Union College.[7]

Elsewhere, Fitz Hugh was mending other fences. After visiting Waterville and Oswego, he relocated to the Clifton Water Cure in Ontario County, far up in Northwestern New York State. This was a resort that grew up around the sulphur springs in Clifton, renowned for their curative properties. Here Fitz Hugh spent time in hot baths and otherwise recovering from the excesses of New York nightlife, long anticipating the Betty Ford Clinic celebrity recoveries of a later age. While convalescing, Fitz Hugh wrote to Fletcher Harper:

Fletcher Harper Esq.:

Very Dear Sir,

I have for weeks been wishing very much to write to you, and this on many accounts, but, for pressing reasons which will now appear, have not done so until now, when I am able at the same time to offer you the congratulations of the New Year.

A few weeks ago I had occasion for sixty dollars. I wrote to our friend Nordhoff to trouble himself with his wonted kindness to ask that an advance to that extent might be made me—and you were so good as to direct that it should be done as I asked. Whereupon the cheque was forwarded.

At the time I wrote Nordhoff, I told him that I should have several articles for him ready by Christmas Day. I as fully expected to fulfill my promise, to the letter. I had hardly made it however, before the nervous ailment, of which I am now, thank God nearly cured, resulted in a congested state of the brain, which had lasted up to a week ago with continual pain and part of the time much danger. I was restricted by my physicians to the very slightest mental effort with which my affairs could be carried on—reduced to the very minimum of letter-writing, even to nearest relatives. Brain fever—or congestion of an active type was apprehended for me, and threats were made both by the Doctors & the disease that I should never be able, very likely, to use my head (all-necessary as it is to me) again, if I used it now.

Let this account to yourself and my friend Nordhoff for the non-fulfillment of my engagement and my silence, heretofore, as to the reasons.

I write so particularly all the facts of the case, because I am peculiarly anxious to have my integrity & good-faith stand well with you as a House—with you as a man. I know no better time of the year than this, when we are all exchanging felicitations with each other, to speak of the light of most sincere friendship and respect in which I regard you. Long before I knew you I had been thrown somewhat among enemies of your firm. An especial clique there was (more sectarian than anything else) that never spoke of yourself and your co-partners to me otherwise than with strong hostility, and the consequence was, that until through the kindness of our friend Mr. Curtis I was introduced to you, I had never possessed any opportunity of coming unbiased to my own conclusions in regard to a set of men upon whom it is necessary, for their great prominence in the world of Books & Commerce, to come to some conclusion of one kind or another. Permit me to express to you, my dear Sir, the sincere & very great pleasure with which I have in my own person been disproving every slander which ever came to my ears. As a simple rendition of justice between man and man, let me own to you how growing has been my feeling of warm personal regard to you for all the unusual generosity you have shown in the maintenance of all our relations. Unusual, I say, because it is indeed rare to find any appreciation of each other among men beyond the mere even balance of money-justice. To you, my dear Sir—with pleasure I acknowledge it—I owe almost every encouragement I have received in the progress thus far of a literary career. The debt is far from a heavy one to me. I love to assure you that I am conscious of it. I am but twenty-two years old now—I have had somewhat of illness & of bad habits in stimulus-using to fight on my way up into a more successful and untiring career. The Water Cure and my will has utterly conquered my habits of stimulus—not even tobacco do I touch now—and my health is fast becoming thoroughly resettled. Be assured that when I again return to hard work as an author, I shall recollect (I never forget such things) your kindness to a young writer, and will endeavor to prove more substantially the friendship of

    Fitz Hugh Ludlow

My best remembrances to Nordhoff, I hope to send him the Mss. I promised—this month.[8]

Despite this confession, *Harper's* saw no work of Fitz Hugh's for another eight months. Any of Fitz Hugh's personality quirks or health problems may have contributed to this lapse, but the travail of getting married was mainly responsible.

The recommendation of Nott may have been one of the keys to unlocking Amos Osborn's hardened heart, although Nott's health was then starting to fail and his guarantee of Fitz Hugh's character was less than foolproof. There was likely some checking into the character of the Reverend Henry as well. The allopathy advice to Rosalie might have seemed a little too closely related to faith healing or other *declassé* pursuits. In this regard, Henry's friendship with Samuel Morse may have been salutary. This friendship had continued in Henry's first year in Oswego, as demonstrated by a note Morse added to a letter from his wife to Henry in May, 1859:

> In the midst of a thousand interruptions, my dear pastor, I can only add my sincere love to you and yours. I reiterate my dear wife's command to you and your wife to come right here when you come this way.[9]

All the reference checking and water curing finally had the happy effect of sealing the marriage of Fitz Hugh and Rosalie. Henry addressed them as "my children" in a letter in April, and offered some words of advice which showed that he was quite pleased with the prospect:

> Remember that Rose is my daughter...All that we can all do to make for her a home in our bosom shall be done...We cherish pleasing hope that this union will be a mutual blessing. Our dear Rose will I know with most conscientious economy and prudence conform to providential circumstances and keep you my son within the limits of your income. If I am indebted to my dear wife for anything it is that she at once upon our

marriage kept our Books and made me what I had never been before, an honest man…Your happiness will depend upon the most rigid economy, the most punctilious payment of what you owe, when you owe.[10]

Henry also chided Fitz Hugh about not inviting his stepmother's parents to the nuptials. Fitz Hugh had never accepted Marie as his new mother, and was not likely at this point to offer her any extra consideration, even though she was at this time in poor health, that Ludlow family trait.

Other details were taken care of as the wedding approached. Fitz Hugh became better acquainted with his in-laws-to-be. A month before the wedding, he was comfortable enough to give Rosalie's sister Mary an autographed copy of a first edition of *The Hasheesh Eater*, inscribed "To Mary C. Osborn, From her loving brother, Fitz Hugh Ludlow."[11]

The big day came on June 15, 1859. All that survives to mark it is a notice in the *Waterville Times:*

> MARRIED.—In this village, at Grace Church on Wednesday morning, 15th inst., by Rev. Mr. Wittingham, Mr. Fitz Hugh Ludlow, of New York and Miss Rosalie Harper Osborn, daughter of Amos O. Osborn, of this village.[12]

The honeymoon lasted for months, in travels throughout New York State including Syracuse and Binghamton. Reverend Henry wrote them plaintively in September, as they had visited everyone but him.

> You must be dutiful children and let me hear from you as often as you can…You must not forget that I am really growing old and that you will not have me a great many years to bless you or be blessed by you.

I greatly rejoice in your mutual love and happiness and feel a very rich and incalculable blessing from God that He has given such a wife to my son & such a daughter and sister to us. You cannot my dear Boy esteem, love, cherish her too highly— and I am glad to see that you lack words to express the wealth of your affection & esteem for her—Proverbs 31, 10-31.[13]

It is difficult to imagine Fitz Hugh at a loss for words at any time. In the fall, Fitz Hugh returned to New York City with his new bride, and promptly set to work again as the famous author. His first effort showed the Pfaffian influence and indicated that his Bohemian days were not so far behind him. "The Phial of Dread: By An Analytic Chemist," appearing in the November, 1859 issue of *Harper's Monthly,* was an attempt to emulate that Pfaffian hero, Edgar Allan Poe. The attempt was quite compelling.

The story opens with a man on the run from some unspeakable tragedy. The reason is kept shrouded, but is wrapped up in a phial of strange green liquid which "murders me like slow lightning." He feels compelled to bury the phial of dread under the floorboards of the boarding house where he hides. The atmosphere of terror builds through skillful touches of plot (the boarding house owner's son died but one week before, and the man must sleep in his bed) and outré style ("I moved away by palpitating like a sea-jelly rather than with feet like a man").

After a series of apparitions involving a young girl with blood pouring from her heart and entrapped in the phial itself, the mystery is revealed, as he is forced to serve as a channel for her to tell the awful story. The girl had been left in his charge, but unknown to him was suicidal. She had gone with him to his chemist's laboratory, and after passing by hemp ("too slow, uncertain, painful") and morphine ("too much commonness, ostentation in that") she plunged a knife into her heart and died immediately. The chemist, however, is also caught up in the madness, and instead of notifying the authorities, he immediately chopped up her body, placed the remains in a fiery apparatus and distilled her very life-essence and "poured all my life from the receiver into the phial...I am with him now—shut up in this liquid life of hell." In the climax, as the girl's father bursts upon him with the police, he smashes the phial. The girl's essence pours out "a violent vapor...with a strangling grave odor which pervaded my very brain" and finally ascends to the heavens, leaving the man to tell the tale from the Bloomingdale Insane Asylum.

This wild story may have been less than reassuring to Amos Osborn, but it was a bold tale for an otherwise tame *Harper's Monthly*, and it won Fitz Hugh a new reputation as a storyteller. The story may have been born of his old (or renewed?) hasheesh dreams, but the writing marked a major improvement over his first two tales of light domestic comedy. But Fitz Hugh returned to that saleable genre in the next month's *Harper's Monthly* with a story entitled "Regular Habits."[14] This story marked his arrival as an author with staying power. It was his first to be published in *Harper's* under a byline, an honor accorded in the magazines only to such literary talents as Dickens and Thackeray.

"Regular Habits" was another variation on the courtship of a maiden, but here that ostensible plot was secondary to a battle of wills between Dr. Benjamin Brightyse, a pompous domestic tyrant who believed that "regular habits" such as rising precisely at 5:30 A.M. to the sound of a gong were prerequisites to a happy and productive life, and Horace Lyle, a precocious college graduate ("Union College, A.M., K.A."—a tribute to Fitz Hugh's beloved alma mater and literary society) who argues that one may have regular habits without puritan restrictions. Hence, Lyle smokes tobacco (a bad habit in Brightyse's book) but only after each and every meal, and drinks a rum punch according to a precisely consistent recipe (namely "Jamaica, one half pint; water, at 190 degrees Fahrenheit, two gills; the juice and half the peel of one orange, and one ounce of sacch. alb."). In sum, the story allows Fitz Hugh to defend a hedonistic lifestyle as productive of professional success, creativity, and true happiness.

Again, an otherwise light sketch is encrusted with little gems: Brightyse allowed for daylight savings time "as an unwilling concession to the frailties of the laggard sun." The story also allowed for Fitz Hugh to comment on topical issues. One of these was evolution, about which the Doctor believed that six days meant six days, whereas Lyle (i.e., Fitz Hugh) believed that "Trilobites Longifrons" must have had "personal motives of his own and his Creator's for going into the stone where he was found a million years after." Fitz Hugh had just discovered Darwin, and would be a life-long proselytizer for the doctrine of evolution. Further, the story allowed Fitz Hugh to offer a short rationale for why he had abandoned the law as a profession:

> Then I read an article in the Law Magazine, with the dulcet title of "The Inchoate Equities of Minor Cestuique-trust, when the Malversation of the Ancestor has worked Estoppel of the plea of Nultiel record in Law" and wondered how the d__l any body could ever be an attorney.

Lyle teaches the children topics from nature to the music of Pythagoras himself, and the story concludes with Lyle marrying the pretty daughter.

The mixture of the cliché and the clever was making a name for Fitz Hugh as one of the most popular of new authors. The byline augured a bright career in literature, and, with his beautiful wife beside him and his "habits of stimulus" behind him, there seemed ample reason for a socialite to reminisce years later: "he held the town in his slender right hand."[15]

1   Helen Ludlow, 1873-75, p. 4.
2   Ibid., p. 790.
3   Ludlow, "Our Queer Papa," p. 789.
4   Ibid.
5   Federal Writer's Project, *New York, A Guide to the Empire State*, New York: 1940.
6   Rosalie Osborn to Henry Ludlow, December 17, 1858, NYSHA Library.
7   Eliphalet Nott to Mrs. Amos Osborn, January 3, 1859, courtesy Mrs. Joyce Randall Edwards.
8   Fitz Hugh Ludlow to Fletcher Harper, January, 1859, reprinted in J. Henry Harper, *The House of Harper*, New York: Harper and Brothers, 1912, p. 149.
9   Samuel F. B. Morse to Henry Ludlow, May 28, 1859, NYSHA Library.
10 Samuel F. B. Morse to Henry Ludlow, May 28, 1859, NYSHA Library.
11 Inscribed copy of *The Hasheesh Eater*, formerly in Fitz Hugh Ludlow Memorial Library.
12 *Waterville Times*, June 18, 1859, p. 3.
13 Henry Ludlow to Fitz Hugh and Rosalie Ludlow, September 22, 1859, NYSHA Library.
14 Fitz Hugh Ludlow, "Regular Habits," *Harper's Monthly*, December, 1859, p. 72.
15 Mary Elizabeth Sherwood, *A Transplanted Rose*, New York: Harper & Brothers, 1882.

IX.

THE NOVELIST

THE Harper brothers published a companion periodical, *Harper's Weekly*, and in 1860, they turned to the hot new talent in fiction, Fitz Hugh Ludlow, to write the lead story for their first issue of 1860. The *Weekly* serialized Fitz Hugh's first novel, entitled, less than thrillingly, *The New Partner in Clingham & Co., Bankers.*[1] Fitz Hugh's appearance was prominently advertised, described as the "author of 'The Hasheesh Eater,' etc. etc." On the second page, the story was headlined a "Serial Story of American Life." *The New Partner* was illustrated by Harper's staff artist John McLenan. (Among Harper's other illustrators was Winslow Homer.) Other serials running in the Weekly that year were by Wilkie Collins, George William Curtis (now Fitz Hugh's editor at *Harper's Monthly*) and the most popular of all serial writers, Charles Dickens, whose *The Uncommercial Traveler* ran concurrently with *The New Partner*.

The novel eventually ran fourteen weeks and reached a total of around 43,000 words. Fitz Hugh was simultaneously writing other stories and articles, and his practice was to write one installment of the novel at a time, and another when the next deadline came near. This approach led to uneven writing, descending into cliché when he dwelt on love interests and family values, and displaying creativity when he added elements of suspense or, as in the pivotal chapter of this story, drunken revelry.

The skeleton of *The New Partner* is melodrama, but humor is the main concern. The story concerns a bank in the small town of Cheswick which is going to the dogs, as described in the first chapter "Under the Dog-Star, A Sirius Chapter," or as Fitz Hugh puts it, a bank which undergoes a "dreadful abandonment to canine clemency." Money is missing, the various clerks and bookkeepers have taken to drinking and gambling at all hours, and Mr. Green the manager seems not to have any control. A new clerk arrives, ostensibly to replace one of the clerks, but he is really the youngest partner in the parent bank and is making an undercover investigation. The villain is found out by a ruse during a drunken party to be Mr. Green, who eats strychnine rather than go to prison. The heroine is a light-headed beauty, devoted to her father, who falls in love with the hero on the strength of a chance meeting. She marries the hero at the end, and thus becomes the New Partner, satisfying Fitz Hugh's paranomasian compulsion. The unrelenting saccharine of the dénouement is an effective satire of the genre which had already become Fitz Hugh's bread and butter:

> Took in the New Partner, finally, with great thanksgivings audible from the lips of each, and greater ones, inaudible, from the mingled soul of them both, to Him who had so opened their doors to the Angel-daughter Faith, that blessing them for their welcome she made within them a dearer home for her sister Love, wherein both dwelt, twin angels, unshakably, eternally.

It is hard to judge *The New Partner* as a first novel, because it is so light in its approach, but it did hint at Fitz Hugh's ability to sustain a narrative. Moreover, it contained Fitz Hugh's first extended treatment of altered consciousness since *The Hasheesh Eater*, with alcohol the more prosaic subject of examination. The description of the night of whist and whiskey punch which is the lynchpin of the novel included the following passages:

> [T]he first bookkeeper, McDowlas, (whom we have not mentioned before, and perhaps shall not mention again, because he never did anything worth mention; not even to get drunk with a comical originality, but rather stupidly and incapably so).
>
> Song followed song; applause became more and more excessive; and the large tin-pail [full of whisky punch] whose centripetal attraction kept the ring around it in hilarious revolution, got lower and lower.
>
> "Guess it won't hurt him," curtly answered Mr. Todds. "If he's been drunk before, he's used to it; if he hasn't, why he'll do it better next time. That's my philosophy. If a man can't be a brick sometimes, what's he live for?"

Fitz Hugh, whose name was now associated with *The Hasheesh Eater*, apparently no longer felt compelled to leaven the account of revelry with the moralizing and guilt found in *The Hasheesh Eater*. As in "Regular Habits," Fitz Hugh's Bohemian past was still reflected in his work, and seemed the greater inspiration for *The New Partner*'s better passages.

And again as in "Regular Habits," Fitz Hugh had settled by this time into a more staid lifestyle befitting a newly respectable author. He had also grown a set of "English whiskers," a beard slightly curled and "a shade more golden" than his auburn hair.[2]

The house of Richard Henry Stoddard and his wife Elizabeth at 181 E. 13th St. had become the site of weekly Saturday evening receptions. According to Edmund Clarence Stedman, "Habitués were Thomas Bailey Aldrich, Mr. & Mrs. Thomas Hicks [Hicks had once painted Henry Abbott in Syria, smoking a hookah][3], Mr. & Mrs. Fitz Hugh Ludlow, James Lorimer Graham and Wilston Barstow (Mrs. Stoddard's brother.)"[4] These poets were known later as The Genteel Circle, and theirs was a delicate passion for poetry and the literary life. The group had its beginnings with Richard Henry Stoddard and Bayard Taylor's friendship in the 1850s. By 1860, Stoddard was married and settled, and Taylor had already traveled extensively. Stedman was a younger writer who worked at the *New York Tribune*, where he met Taylor. Taylor introduced him to Stoddard and later to Fitz Hugh.

This group had created a minor literary movement, and Stoddard's poems in 1855 were later said by Stedman to be "among the first to initiate the movement here in poetry for poetry's sake."[5] Whitman, however, mercilessly argued the other side—"Do you call those genteel little creatures American poets? Do you term that perpetual, pistareen, paste-pot work, American...verse?"[6] Not to be intimidated, or shamed, Stedman's first poems were collected at Stoddard's urging and published in 1860.[7] Taylor and Stoddard were also acquainted with the quintessential Pfaffian Fitz James O'Brien. Taylor and O'Brien discussed poetry with a fervor which Stoddard envied.

RICHARD DREW STODDARD (1825-1903) AND ELIZABETH DREW
STODDARD (1822-1902). (INTERNET ARCHIVE)

One day a poetry contest was proposed by Taylor—"We'll each write down a title, and putting them together draw one and write to it, and see what the result will be, and who will finish first...The test lay between O'Brien and Taylor, sometimes a dead heat, but oftener than not O'Brien ahead with a second or two to spare. It was rare sport while it lasted and it lasted there and elsewhere until the breaking out of our great Civil War destroyed our relish for, and enjoyment of, such mimic warfare."[8]

As Stedman and Fitz Hugh and the rest married or moved to somewhat more respectable jobs, they were often ridiculed (if jealously) by their still-Bohemian friends. Stedman noted that when, after joining the staff of the Tribune, he published a satirical poem "The Prince's Ball" in *Vanity Fair*, "all the old Bohemian crowd, my assailants, are making friends again." He found this ironic, for the poem was written for money. "The urgent need of money and, ergo, of popular American reputation or notoriety, makes us prostitute our Art…they tell me it saved the paper."[9] Stedman would later describe his friends, the ones that were a step beyond Pfaff's but perhaps not ready for the august Century Club (Stedman was destined for the Century Club because he was university educated [Yale], unlike Aldrich, Stoddard and Taylor):

> There was not much of a literary market at that time. Newspaper salaries were very low. There were few magazines, and scarcely any but Harper's and The Atlantic paid much of anything. New York itself was not literary and looked with distrust, if not contempt, upon working writers. These people were mostly from the country. They had scarcely any acquaintances in the city outside of their profession. You can easily see that they were thrown back upon themselves and made the most of that artistic, happy-go-lucky bonhomie and comradeship.[10]

The Stoddard's new house was the main locale for Saturday evening receptions. There were also frequent artists receptions at the Studio Building on Tenth Street (the studio of Emanuel Leutze, painter of "Washington Crossing the Delaware"), where Fitz Hugh would meet two men with a strong influence on his life. One was the premier Shakespearean actor in the country, Edwin Booth, whose brother John Wilkes would soon eclipse Edwin's fame with his own infamy. The other was painter Albert Bierstadt, who had just stepped from the shadows of Frederick Church and the rest of the Hudson River school by traveling to the West and painting enormous (and enormously popular) canvases of the natural splendor of the Rocky Mountains.[11] Stoddard's salon also included, at various times, writer and folklorist Charles Leland, painter Launt Thompson, Thomas Bailey Aldrich and later his wife, Lilian Woodman. Another commentator described these people as the Bayard Taylor circle. "It was composed almost exclusively of poets, artists, and actors Lacking a sympathetic popular audience, they formed a mutual admiration society in which they upheld the ideals of the old generation as they understood them."[12] Taylor was "the tall, stalwart figure; the symmetrical head, with its crown of dark, slightly grizzled, curling hair; the aquiline, bearded face; the dark eyes, glowing with kindly light."[13] A reminiscence by Mrs. Thomas Bailey Aldrich gives a feel for the refined evening events. Then Lillian Woodman, she describes an evening at the Stoddards':

> After them, Fitz Hugh Ludlow, a writer of good stories, and a smoker of hasheesh—seeing visions. Mrs. Ludlow's picture had a charm all its own of youth and beauty; brown hair, brown eyes, slight figure, tartan plaid dress—greens and blues in happy mixture, with a final touch of the blue snood

that bound her hair, with just a curl or two escaping. Launt Thompson, a sculptor—Mr. Aldrich, a poet.

Soon after…the habitues of Mrs. Stoddard's salon were invited to the Booths' for an evening; and to the two young friends was given the pleasant task of assisting Mrs. Booth in receiving the distinguished guests. It would be useless to describe the tumult of excitement this invitation brought. To gaze from afar on the celestial beings who wrote books had been their highest aspiration. But to touch the hand that had penned words that burn was beyond all imagining.[14]

Young Lillian asked to be introduced to Aldrich, "an alert, slender young man, with clear, steady gray-blue eyes, and crisp golden hair: let us imagine his witty, winsome manner."[15] But when he was brought she felt his mind was elsewhere. "It was so palpable that he did not want to come; it was so obvious that he did want to go. Once or twice he spoke across the room to Mrs. Ludlow, for that was the Dulcinea who had entangled him in the meshes of her brown hair."[16]

At the end of this dinner, painter Albert Bierstadt "who at that time was probably the most talked-of artist in New York," invited everyone to his studio in two weeks. On this occasion, Lillian dressed her prettiest, and when Aldrich entered his "look of quick surprise was not without a certain triumph to one whose ears had so lately been attuned to the refrain of the old melody 'Phillada flouts me, flouts me.' On this evening Mrs. Ludlow was without her cavalier."[17]

This reminiscence reveals hints of the character of the Ludlow marriage. The beautiful Rosalie was decorous, and did not discourage attention. Fitz Hugh was charming, and carried the attraction of early, though vaguely disreputable, literary fame. The Ludlow family influence on Aldrich is also reflected in a poem entitled "Has-cheesh" [*sic*]:

> Stricken with dreams, I wandered through the night;
> the heavens leaned down to me with splendid fires;
> The south-wind breathing upon unseen lyres
> Made music as I went...
> Then I heard the roll
> of unseen oceans clashing at the Pole a terror seized upon me...
> Fanged, warty monsters, with their lips and eyes
> Hung with slimy leeches sucking hungrily.
> Away vile drug! I will avoid thy spell,
> Honey of Paradise, black dew of Hell![18]

YOUNG THOMAS BAILEY ALDRICH (1836-1907).
(HOUGHTON LIBRARY, HARVARD)

Elsewhere in the great Gotham, Fitz Hugh stayed in contact with some of his old Kappa Alpha cronies, who met regularly in New York City along with members from other collegiate chapters (at Cornell, Williams, Hobart, Princeton, and the University of Virginia). An item in the *New York Evening Post* noted a meeting in which "the old songs were sung, the memories of old times revived and with some of the impressive ceremonies of the society at an hour short of the only break that the association has ever experienced—the break of day—the assembly adjourned, to meet again in one year at a similar entertainment."[19]

Fitz Hugh and Rosalie also periodically met family obligations, dining with New York City friends of the Reverend Henry from his early abolitionist days. Fitz Hugh had also overcome initial suspicions among Rosalie's family and friends from Waterville. One of them, the editor of the local *Waterville Times*, prevailed upon Fitz Hugh during a visit to write a story for the paper. Fitz Hugh dashed off a quick sketch entitled "The Ransom of a Heritage," which appeared in three parts in the *Times* between February and March. "The Ransom of a Heritage" was quite thin in plot and style, and was plainly written as a favor without a great deal of forethought or effort. The *Waterville* editor introduced the story this way:

> We commence today an admirably told story by Fitz Hugh Ludlow, Esq. which was published in Harper's Monthly [it was not—*ed.*], that best of Magazines. We are in expectation of being able to lay before our readers one or more letters from the same charming writer, descriptive of southern life and scenery.[20]

The "letters descriptive of southern life and scenery"

mentioned in the *Waterville Times* were vaguely promised because the Ludlows had begun to prepare to winter in Florida.[21] Fitz Hugh and Rosalie had met in a health spa of the north, and now sought further rehabilitation in the deep south. Rosalie had been in poor health for much of the first year of their marriage. Fitz Hugh's heavy writing schedule at the end of 1859, (which resulted in "The Phial of Dread," "Regular Habits," *The New Partner*, "Little Brother," and "The Ransom of a Heritage") was compounded by some final legal work for Noyes. The work, combined with the emotional toll of Marie's illness on Henry and the rest of the family, and of Fitz Hugh's social obligations with the Osborn family, resulted in "the receipt for getting ill":

> Take twenty four hours of the ordinary capacity and put into it forty eight hours of steady application to business...the latter may be obtained at any of our metropolitan counting houses or law offices. Add to taste an infusion of bitter mental anxiety, and four hours sleep...Let the mixture be made boiling hot, and then put in all the nerves or brains you may find convenient. Just before the preparation boils over, pour in any powerful combination of stimulants: Brandy Smash or Laudanum cocktail is very good for the purpose, in the proportion of three to every 24 hours.[22]

So Fitz Hugh was ill again, despite a less manic but apparently not ascetic lifestyle. A number of remedies, including patent medicines, water cures, sermons, and cigars, all proved wanting. Further, after this process, Fitz Hugh was "so visibly dilated that my friends began to contemplate the approaching necessity of carrying me around in a pail—or putting me in a bottle like beer, with my name on a label—only the inscription would hardly have been Byas *Stout*."[23]

A friend invited Fitz Hugh and Rosalie to go with him to Florida when he returned there in the fall. "In three weeks from the date of that offer, I was en route for the land of Ponce de Leon, seeking like him, the receipt for getting well—the Fountain of Youth." They set off in December 1859 on the steamer *Montgomery* for "the land of flowers, turtles, and alligators." But the exotic tour for rehabilitation had an undercurrent of uneasiness, as abolitionist John Brown had just been hanged for the Harper's Ferry raid.

On the way down the coast, the ship steamed into a storm that raged for twenty-four hours, and drove all but six passengers cowering or vomiting to their state-rooms. Fitz Hugh allowed modestly that he was one of the six, assisting the afflicted, (one of whom "was a perfect statue of the God of Sea-sickness, done in streaky marble") delivering food and water, etc., without sleeping the whole night. And "but for the fact that sea-sick people have very short memories— that half dozen of us would have had as many statues erected to us in the most durable kind of sea biscuit on the principal square of Savannah."[24] The Ludlows stopped over in Savannah, Georgia, "where the oranges as yet sell for the Boreal price of three cents apiece—pine apples [*sic*] ask a shilling for themselves" and there are "perambulatory roses—beautiful young girls, talking blithely in that honied Southern tone of theirs."

The *Montgomery* arrived in Jacksonville, Florida, a town of 3,000 at the time. Fitz Hugh's first impression was of the variety of nationalities and states represented. Here a Virginian, there a Cockney or a "natty little Frenchman," and the cosmopolitan New Yorker, a shrewd businessman who looks as if "when he has finished with Florida, there is no telling but he may embark in a partnership with George Francis Train to build a railroad to the moon."[25]

1858   MONTGOMERY   H.B. CROMWELL & C⁰   HEYL/50

STEAMSHIP MONTGOMERY, WHICH WAS THE USS MONTGOMERY DUR-
ING THE CIVIL WAR. (U.S. NAVAL HISTORICAL CENTER PHOTOGRAPH)

His second impression was more sobering, that the largest representation herein "this genial Winter summer morning belongs not to the living nationalities of the world—but to the dead." Florida was already known as a refuge for the aging as well as young victims of consumption and other diseases. Fitz Hugh and Rosalie had both suffered youthful afflictions and were themselves at one end of the spectrum of the ill in Florida. "They are a sight which well eyes never get use to. Whether they be men crumbling away out of Life's golden prime like these on the verandah, or fair girls burning up in a wierd [*sic*] cruel fire ere the young peach-down on their cheeks has been kissed by lips of love."

Fitz Hugh set about to explore the Jacksonville environs, and to do so he had purchased in the north a small rowboat which he christened the *Lady Rose*. "Her first crew consisted of the lady after whom she was called—and who had some time previously signed articles to accompany a writer

upon a certain other voyage immortalized in four pictures
of the late Thomas Cole [marriage]; a northern gentleman
weak in the pulmonary but strong in the muscular region,
spending the Winter at the South for the development of
both these departments; and lastly the public's humble ser-
vant...The terrestrial Lady Rose (as opposed to the aquatic)
pulls a pair of sculls with all the skill and endurance which
could be asked of the Lady Rose's Captain. (When I say
"Lady Rose" now, I mean the boat. I know my self and the
position of a married gentleman too intimately to shock my
lady readers by pretending that I am Captain in any other
sense.)...I frequently assume the tiller ropes—and come out
in the character of the invalid...or the cruel husband...usu-
ally the Lady receives cheers—and I, mere withering looks of
indignation."[26]

Rosalie wrote to Fitz Hugh's stepmother in February, 1860
from Jacksonville, Florida, describing their winter there, and
illuminating Rosalie's view of her husband.

My Dear Mother,
I suppose you have all recieved [sic] our family letter and
have learned of our well-being and well-doing from that
so I will merely say in this letter that we are usually well and
employing our-selves as we always do—Fitz Hugh writing
and making himself generally useful to all the house and par-
ticularly useful to me—while I am learning some new songs,
reading your new books, commencing a few letters and trying
very hard to be industrious in my mending and health-getting.
All goes on as usual I believe, but there is change enough
to make life very agreeable and worth living for.

Now, in this house, we have some of the loveliest and some
of the most disagreeable people I ever met; I quite enjoy the
mixture; it is amusing as well as profitable to watch the mingling

of opposites. Oh, it is terrific and grand to get Mr. Hart (the elder F.F.G.) Judge Pierson (the man of irascible temperament and sounding periods), Mr. Shumway (the Black Republican [Northerners in favor of an end to slavery], sarcastic Philadelphian), Mr. Dew (the younger F.F.G. who in perfect mildness is opposed politically, philosophically and religiously to the good and imitable Father-in-law Mr. Hart), and last but not least Fitz Hugh, whose moderation and sublime indifference on the "Goose-question" is most annoying to the two hot-headed fireeaters [Southerners in favor of secession rather than any compromise] who strive continually to engage him in discussions. It is grand I say to hear these five in a controversy. It makes no difference what subject is started—they all disagree and we are bound to have a word-fight on all occasions.

When it comes to politics we have fine times. Mr. Hart roars like a revolutionary cannon, beats the poor table with his fat, red fist until the dishes dance and with his other hand hurls thunder bolts on all the world in general but particularly on Southern *democrats*—he himself is a whig—who truckle to the North. Judge Pierson who is a democrat and has fought *duels!* rises on such occasions, with carving knife in hand and vows vengeance on Mr. Hart and everybody who dares to disagree with him. He is a Fire-Eater, a Disunionist, and much to his own satisfaction, an Ex-Judge of the Supreme Court!

Mr. Dew worships Buchanan and Wise as much as Mr. Hart hates them, has promised however to vote for Mr. Ludlow when he is nominated for the Presidency.

Mr. Shumway—in these discussions—"gets mad" to use his own expression—but his voice is too weak to enable him to argue so he can only mutter his favorite expletive "by George" and leave Mr. Ludlow to defend, as well as he can, the interests of the North. Fitz Hugh does this by laughingly parrying their thrusts and occasionally giving sharp retorts. He has already made a compact with Judge Pierson to the effect that when the Union is dissolved they shall provide one another with sugar-cane and ice.

Yes, this is an amusing household and equalled in its argumentative tendencies by no family except the Ludlows and they are as fond of discussions as you are of flowers. Notwithstanding our disagreements we are as loving a household as one could well find. (My right arm and shoulder are aching, with such long continued use, so much that I cannot for the present go on but I hope to finish this letter before night.)

Mar. 1, 1860

I am really ashamed, my dear Mother, to recommence this letter at so late a date—not so very late either for it is the first of the month—but I have very good excuses which you being an invalid will appreciate. My write (right) arm and shoulder have been very lame and my wrist has been smitten with neuralgia too—it is only just well enough now to use—so this letter as well as many other things, has been neglected.

It is a charming day, like all of our weather here in this sunny land of fruit and flowers—I am expecting Mr. Ludlow every moment to take me out rowing—how much I should enjoy it if you and Father and Helen were to sail with us. You, with your love of the beautiful could never admire sufficiently this lovely river of lakes—the Eilaka as the Indians called it—the scenery is not grand like that on the Hudson but there is a quiet, dream-like tropical beauty about it that always charms me. The sunsets on the river and in this climate are perfectly gorgeous—throughout the whole day the atmosphere is tinged with rosiness but at night the whole heaven and earth are flooded with glory. Our moonlight and starlight too are beyond anything I ever saw at the North—I do not enjoy them so much although they be so glorious for the reason I suppose that I am no longer a romantic maiden.

But Mr. Ludlow has come and I must close this long rambling letter. I wish I might expect to hear from you but I know from my own experience how impossible it must be for you to write. I hope this will find you unusually well. I will write to Father and Helen next. With a great deal of love from Fitz Hugh and myself to you all I remain your aff. daughter R.O. Ludlow[27]

As Rosalie noted, it was impossible for Northerners to vacation in the South without the slavery issue arising. But Fitz Hugh was puzzled that Southerners talked of slavery before their own slaves, even at one dinner claiming that they would arm their slaves and let them loose on the North. At that, one of the old Black waiters called Fitz Hugh aside.

"Massa! Do dem Abolitionists raly mean to come and help us?" the old man asked.

"Don't talk about such things, Cæsar" counseled Fitz Hugh. "No, they can't come. They couldn't help you if they would."

"Well Massa—I jis tell ye what! I'd like to see 'em put guns into our hands—and set us ahead to do the fightin'. *Dey'd find out who we'd fight for.* Dey durs'nt put de guns into our hands! *No! They durs'nt!*"[28]

Fitz Hugh's inquisitive nature and obvious sympathies led to another encounter with the local slave population. Back at the guest hotel, one of the black servants, Wesley by name, had been acting violently, and the other servants determined that he should "get religion." Fitz Hugh's later-published account put a primly Protestant distaste in his judgement of their ceremony, but it is a fascinating glimpse of the syncretistic interpretation of Christianity by African slaves that would later grow into the strong African American churches of the twentieth century.

Aunt Rose walks up and down in a space left clear by the group in the kitchen, holding Wesley by the hand. As she goes she sings,

Way down in the lonesome valley,
Jesus he come bimeby

The others catch up the last vowel sound and prolong it indefinitely, with voices of strange, wild sweetness.

Bimeby-yyyy-eyey

Then comes a chorus in which all the negroes join—

What you wants little brother is to git religion,
Jesus he come bimeby-y-y-eyey-y

Then Aunt Rose—still walking with Wesley, who gibbers on her and the others of the meeting with questioning wonder— breaks into a fresh verse:

I've got an old mother in the lonesome valley

the rest joining her in the same refrain as before.

Then follow prayers by different negroes—so earnest, so sincere—yet at the same time so wildly incongruous and ignorant, that it would seem like holding up to ridicule things sacred to us all, did I venture to quote from them.

Another exquisitely sweet chant follows—with as little connected meaning in its words as the first one. But it is evidently intended as a description of heaven. These are all the lines I can recall:

Early in the mornin' an nuffin' to do
But jump in the chariot and ride right along—
No more mornin' horns for me,
No more drivers' calls

Chorus

> Oh yah, Oh no no no nooooooo.
> But early in de mornin' and nuffin' to do
> But jump in de chariot and ride right along.

Another prayer followed. Then another chant in the minor—sweet voiced as before—yet painfully melancholy. It ran thus—

> What shall poor sinners do
> When de moon turn into blood

At this stage, I felt almost like crying—so wrought were my physical feelings. Wesley yielded to that feeling—and a shout instantly ran through the room—"He's got it! he's got it!"

When I left—they had set the poor creature on a table—and were listening with rapture to some utterly incoherent mutterings and screams which they had forced out of him as the relation of his religious experience.

The next morning, Dan [one of the servants] told me they had kept the meeting up all night. "We got so happy," said he, "we most like to stomp the floor troo."[29]

Fitz Hugh's published response to all this was that it refuted the school of thought that rationalized slavery as the white man's attempt to bring Christian salvation to the Negro. The ritual he described was a sad parody borne of the slimmest understanding of European Christian rituals. Yet Fitz Hugh confessed in the above recounting that he himself had been entranced by the power and sincerity of the bastardized ritual. As a veteran of one unauthorized religious approach, the transcendence arising from hashish use, he privately must have sympathized with this other, unorthodox method of communion with the divine.

Despite some quibbles, such as describing the atmosphere in the Everglades as "oxygen 21%, nitrogen 79%, mosquitoes 65%," Fitz Hugh ultimately waxed lovingly over the sum of his Florida impressions:

> I was more enamored of it than of any wild country I ever saw. During the weeks at the ranch and Enterprise, I penetrated every lagoon which my boat would ascend—found my way through every dense wood and glen where there was a way—shot birds on the marshes where the water was waist deep, and alligators everywhere. I found no ill result of any of these expeditions save one—sunstroke after a long rowing trip.
>
> I became more and more attached to Florida with every day. I parted from it at last, as one tears himself away from a beautiful capricious girl for whom he has endured some hardships and many more petty annoyances—but whom he will remember forever, as one of the loveliest dreams of a lifetime.[30]

The trip cost over $700, not cheap for a man who may have earned around $1,500-$2,000 for his writing that entire year. The publishing arrangement with the *Commercial Advertiser* may have covered a portion, and the *Montgomery's* steamship line may have also contributed in return for some free advertising.

Meanwhile in the North, Fitz Hugh's *New Partner* serial in *Harper's Weekly* was well-received, and he placed yet another story in *Harper's Monthly*, entitled "Little Brother." It ran in three parts between February and April, contemporaneously with *The New Partner* (and with "Ransom of a Heritage").[31]

"Little Brother" was less a melodrama than a humorous sketch of a memorable rogue/child named Augustus Jones, Jr. It has a plot equally as thin as "Ransom," but the interplay of language and subject is delightful, if now a bit dated. The story meanders toward its conclusion because it is so much fun to pause and remark on the various characters and places and ideas encountered along the way. For example, young Kate Smith sends a message to a suitor that she'll see him "directly," by which she means a half hour or so:

> "Directly" is an idea of such wonderful elasticity that, in the seventh sphere of the spiritual world, where Mrs. Hatch informs us that we shall be clothed with ideas in lieu of matter, it will probably answer to the India rubber of this present gross life, and be manufactured into all sorts of ethereal overshoes, belting shoulder-straps, water proof coats, and stretchable arrangements whatsoever, by some Horace Day of that stage of existence.[32] "Directly" with the soldier and sailor, means as long as it takes to turn on their heels; with the waiter at the eating-house where I lunch, it means as soon as the fat man in the next box has ceased to be hungry, thirsty, and morning-paper-ivorous.

Kate's suitor is a rogue disguising himself as a gentleman in order to marry Kate and gain access to her father's stockbroking fortune. He explains to Kate how he spent all morning devoting himself to good society by practicing everything from minuets to billiards. She thanks him "on behalf of our whole sex!" Then Smith, Senior joins their conversation, but:

> If I should record the conversation it would not assist the progress of this story. How could it assist the progress of any thing to bring together three people, two of whom suppose Panama to be a manufactory for large durable hats, and the remaining one of whom tells said two that Panama has gone up to 117, as if it were a piece of information calculated to

excite the liveliest emotions of pleasure, but left them ignorant whether Panama had floated to that degree of latitude, or now numbered so many souls of population, or what.

Augustus is forever annoying his older sister with various pranks. Their mother tells the sister that he would outgrow it. "Then, why wasn't he sent away somewhere till he did? Or put somewhere—a large barrel, for instance, with the head knocked out to give him air, as they do with young tomatoes and pie-plants till they arrive at an age when they can come to the table?" Augustus' reply to why he was so naughty was the result of much considered research in books that had been read to him: "all the good children in books die!"

Along the way, Fitz Hugh also tossed in a bouquet for an old family friend, as a wandering Augustus is located via the city's telegraph network:

> Wonderful, beneficent, omnipotent telegraph! What marvel that mothers kiss thee? And though the graceless, ungrateful tribe of intellectual prigs, and the hair-splitters of the Supreme Court who back them, harass with endless patent cases the silver hairs of our noble, thrice-beloved Morse—does not every click of his offspring's electric tongue that brings home a wandering child throb a sweet note of reward in the great philosopher's throat?

Fitz Hugh sprinkled the tale with features from his life—a young doctor who resides at Fitz Hugh's bachelor address on Clinton Street, a description of some of the neighborhoods of New York City, a humorous recounting of various ethnic dialects ("I'll be dommed if ye aren't after finding it's a divilish sarious matter," says the Irish cop, and "You may pe sure of dat, mit all yer kid kloves and de colt vatch-shain!"

adds the German), a free plug for his publishers (the family took on vacation "four *Harper's Magazines* for the current month, that no one might be tantalized by witnessing the perusal of such an interesting periodical when he or she had it not") and the observation that:

> a man's true self is such a deep down substratum, so overlain by successive layers of constitutional caution, educational reserve, handsome physique, elegant manners, tailor-skill, and innumerable deceptive conventional circumstances, that it is hard for any one, however world-sharpened, to penetrate the crust and get at the basis of the human geological system.

Inevitably, according to the formula, the handsome young doctor exposes the masquerade of the would-be suitor and saves Kate with the assistance of the Little Brother, who, of course, then becomes everyone's darling. Formula or not, this story characterized the graceful touch Fitz Hugh brought to his writing and the great affection he brought to his observations of the people around him.

The year 1860 also saw the publication of the third edition of *The Hasheesh Eater*. It followed promptly on the heels of the second edition, as its popularity showed only slight signs of slowing. In fact, Fitz Hugh's success in the fictional world brought curious readers to his most famous work. *The New Partner* had been bylined as written by the author of *The Hasheesh Eater*, as the Harper Brothers were quite adept at cross promotion and keeping their star in prominent view. In fact, Harpers' magazines were started as a way of promoting their book line.[33] It is curious, however, that the Harpers did not choose to publish *The New Partner* in book form. That was their practice with some of the serials, for example with Dickens and George William Curtis. *Partner* was not deathless literature, but neither was that a Harper's requirement. Fitz Hugh began to bristle at such treatment.

The Ludlows returned from Florida in May, 1860. Needing money to replenish their accounts, Fitz Hugh responded with a new genre story. "The Century Plant" appeared with byline, but no mention of *The Hasheesh Eater*, in *Harper's Monthly* in June 1860. Sales of *The Hasheesh Eater* were still brisk, though, and the Harpers perked up an otherwise lackluster *Monthly* with Fitz Hugh's presence. The Harpers felt no luxury to split the story into three parts even though it was as long as "Little Brother."

"The Century Plant" runs along romantic lines, where a bitter old sea captain (possibly inspired by the Ludlows' sea journey to Florida) is given charge of his beautiful orphaned niece who falls in love with one of the Captain's ex-sailors who is now a painter. The Captain forbids marriage until his aloe, the Century Plant (because it lives to that age) blossoms again, as it has not since his beloved was forced to marry another twenty years ago. True love, and the fortuitous discovery of the now-widowed beloved in Brazil by the artist who had been hired to teach painting to the girl, was the impetus for the obligatory happy ending, which in this case offers not one but two weddings.

Again notwithstanding the formula plot, there are several stylistic and biographical passages that flavor this story. The captain's bitterness is well drawn: "he deigned only a cold, black bow to Lyon—like a tall storm-cloud nodding over a main-truck." On the lighter side, when Amber professes her love, it is worth more to the young painter than all the praise for his art combined with a "carte blanche on the Bank of the Inexhaustible Bowels of Golconda." In the course of the story, Fitz Hugh flatters his wife: "Indeed this is the case with me when I am absent from my little wife even for two days—I think of so much gladness and welcome that I finally have to leave it to be expressed a few years hence, when we are more spiritual. And we confidently expect, as soon as we arrive in the Good Country, to find several thousand of those here unspeakable conversations waiting for us to enjoy, with the words we could not get at in this world all ready for us!" He also praises some of his artist friends—"Church, Rossiter, Tait, Richards, Dix, Kensett, Heine, and the others who make an American school for America."

Around this time, a letter from Cousin Carrie Geddings to her brother mentions that "Fitz Hugh and his wife are expected in a few weeks," but in an addendum writes that since she had written the first part of the letter, she "learned that Fitz is not coming here, he has taken the *Editorship* of a new paper in N.Y. called The Methodist, something that has been started by the Harpers."[34] (She also adds that "Rosa is coming here to stay as long as she can be separated from her *husband*, which I imagine will not be so long.")

However, by the time *The Methodist* (which actually was not connected with the Harpers) began publication in July, the editors were Reverends Crooks and McClintock. The journal aimed at being more of a popular journal than other Methodist publications, in order to compete with the organs of other denominations. It was certainly logical for them to have sought a mainstream secular author such as Fitz Hugh to edit, but they somehow overlooked the fact that Fitz Hugh was the son of a *Presbyterian* preacher.

The publisher's decision to seek elsewhere for an editor may have also been on more than mere sectarian grounds. The August 11 issue of *The Methodist* contained criticism of Fitz Hugh's old crony Walt Whitman, saying that while in Rabelais "wit redeems obscenity," *Leaves of Grass* is "nothing but filth and trash—no gleam either of poetry or prose." The September issue carried a sermon by the Reverend J. T. Crane, whose later book, *The Arts of Intoxication,* related that a nameless "student of Union College, New York became addicted to the poison, and, after his escape from the enemy, recorded his experience in a volume entitled 'The Hasheesh Eater'. He corroborates all that has been quoted from Mr. Taylor and Dr. Livingstone. The hemp intoxicant is a hateful poison." Not only wasn't Fitz Hugh the proper flavor of Christianity, he had led a life that, if not outside the mainstream of Christendom, certainly was close enough to the line to contraindicate his editorial shepherdship.

Fitz Hugh responded to the whole affair with a meditation on the evils of sectarian religious squabbling, overlaid on his Harper's boy-meets-girl formula. The story was entitled "The Cruise of the Two Deacons," and ran from July through September in *Harper's Monthly.* A girl and a boy who attend two slightly different branches of Congregational Puritanism (the Old Meeting and the New Meeting) in the town of Muskeogue (one of "the other Long Island places that end with ogue") fall in love. Their respective fathers are the leading deacons in the opposing churches, and so their marriage is quite impossible.

But unlike Fitz's previous love stories, this little romance is decidedly an after-thought to his real concern with satirizing unfounded religious intolerance. The two competing sects are characterized as being similar in this way: "Sound faith, sound doctrine, and another kind, indigenous to polemic theology, sound bastings of all who varied from a certain reading of the Catechism." After a few paragraphs of examples, Fitz Hugh highlights several individuals who entertain thoughts that perhaps the other Meeting isn't so bad, these thoughts being the product of hard labor, the time when "the operation of the mind is mostly pure, common-sense logic, free from the party-feeling which ferments in idle moments like beer when the barrel stands still." The mother of the boy in the story is "one of those good people who, having been all their lives accustomed to look at so much of the truth as is bounded by the rim of their spectacles, are taken aback when the little outside edge first presents itself." The children themselves resolve the theological contradictions on their own, in part through being jointly appalled by a third group of believers:

> I was quite scared to hear father read what those folks were up to; they didn't care for one day more'n another, and the women wore short hair and trowsers, and the men lived on greens and never cut their finger-nails, and laughed at Poll [sic—for the Apostle Paul] and all the 'Postles, sayin they were behind the age; and they all got drunk and went off to Indiana, and were divorced from their wives, and they called themselves by some long wicked name that Father had to look twice through his specs to get the notion of...it was Tran-scen-den-tal-ists.

But the gradual reconciliation of mother and children is secondary to the fathers, deacons number one and two, who by accident are chartered to crew the same fishing expedition by three weekenders from New York City (who knew that the "natural products of Muskeogue are certain excellent salt codfish and Puritan Congregationalists.") The two deacons gradually become embroiled in a theological argument over predestination (one for, one against) in front of the three businessmen. After the deacons reach the impasse of calling each other names ("Calvinist and Arminian!" and "Emmonsite!", respectively), one of the businessmen quite matter of factly concludes that "You're both right. As Deacon Allen says, a man can turn round and be good any time he likes...And as Deacon Townsend says, Heaven will do it all up for him whenever it is done; so he can just hand the matter right over, and dance and fiddle till getting good happens to him." The two deacons were thunderstruck. "Could this really be the light in which men calling themselves Christians were looked at in their differences by men of the world?" The two deacons are brought to harmony through the plot device of a storm which wrecks their boat and forces them onto a makeshift raft together. They pray for forgiveness from God and each other, and are consequently saved to see their children married in a ceremony jointly officiated by the personnel of both meetings.

Fitz Hugh reached a new level of sophistication in this story. The real-world difficulties he had encountered, a lifetime's exposure to a professional preacher-father, and his transcendental experiences with hasheesh, had inspired the most serious piece of writing than he had attempted since *The Hasheesh Eater* itself. The pacing of the story is more accomplished, and the gathering storm and the growing doctrinal uncertainty are nicely counterpointed. The action of the storm itself is sure handed, with Fitz Hugh showing a

flair for dramatic tension that he had displayed only occa-
sionally in past tales, for example in "The Phial of Dread."
Only a hasty formulaic conclusion, perhaps dictated by edi-
torial space limitations, marred this fine fictional effort.
Although the story did not serve to resurrect the offer of
editorship, neither did *The Methodist* seem to harbor any ill
will toward Fitz Hugh, noting approvingly in a review of
other periodicals that Ludlow was appearing in the Sep-
tember issue of *Harper's Monthly*.[35]

The growing maturity of Fitz Hugh's fiction was also
attracting the attention of other publishers. Just as Fitz
Hugh was poised to raise his literary career to a higher level,
yet another tragedy struck. His stepmother Marie, the
invalid addressed in Rosalie's letter from Florida, died on
June 25, 1860. Fitz Hugh rushed to Oswego, and Rosalie
followed behind, as the following letter of June 28 indicates.

> My Dear Father
> I have been hesitating to write all the week since Fitz Hugh
> went not knowing definitely when I could go to Oswego...I
> wished to go on with Fitz Hugh so as to comfort your poor
> afflicted hearts as well as I was able, but I could not arrange
> it so I will be all I can to you now though.
> In great haste for the stage leaves soon,
> > Your affectionate daughter,
> > Rosalie O. Ludlow
> > Much love to darling Helen.[36]

"The Two Deacons" continued to run through the Sep-
tember issue of *Harper's*, but Fitz Hugh's pen was inactive.
Although he had been a combative teenager when his father
first decided to remarry, time may have mellowed those vio-
lent feelings toward his stepmother. Marie was his mother

during the hasheesh years of college, and nursed him more than once through his intermittent health breakdowns. And Fitz Hugh certainly felt sorry for his now-aging father, left alone but for his now-adult daughter Helen. Still, a poignant entry in Helen's diary in February of the following year, just six months after Marie's death, is probably the most telling indication of the lingering detachment of the stepchildren:

> February 27—12th anniversary of Mama's [i.e. Abby Welles Ludlow] death

Fitz Hugh and Rosa appear to have spent the rest of the summer in Oswego, Waterville, and elsewhere in upstate New York. When they returned to New York in the fall, Fitz Hugh attacked the literary world with high energy. He sold another story to *Harper's*, a sure source of income at the time. In fact, Fitz Hugh's stories appeared in eight of the twelve issues of *Harper's* that year. "My Velvet Shoes" appeared in *Harper's Monthly* in October of 1860. Far from signaling the arrival of Fitz Hugh as a mature author, it was nothing if not a quick sketch for the "spondulicks." A poor but honest bookkeeper and his thrifty wife assist an even-poorer immigrant family to find financial and romantic happiness (for their beautiful—of course—daughter). The story is almost redeemed by the Ludlow wit—for instance, a catalog of available women's wear includes "Smith's Adjustible Bustle, Podridge's Blistered Steel Nonpareil, and Tompkins's Grand Back-Action Self-Supporting Tape-Woven Elastic." There is also "the recent rain which as yet the Controller has been unable to reach with a notice prohibiting further disbursement." But these nuggets are unfortunately outnumbered by clichéd advice to husbands, such as "Why don't men praise their wives more? It doesn't hurt Mrs. Lambswool at all—it always does her good," as well as the incredible observation, "what would woman be without man's genius to adore? what would man's genius be without woman to adore it?" Still, an item in the October 27 Methodist illustrates the demands of the audience of the era—"Among the other articles, we would particularize the fine story of 'My Velvet Shoes.' It is racy, pathetic, humorous, and of the best moral. All husbands should read it."

While the business deal with *The Methodist* may have fallen through, it did remind Fitz Hugh that there were other markets for his writing besides *Harper's*. Except for his work for the now defunct *Saturday Press* (which he had renounced to appease the Harpers), and single pieces in *Putnam's*, *The Knickerbocker*, and the *Waterville Times*, Fitz Hugh had only published in Harper's publications.

This exclusive arrangement ended when Fitz Hugh reached an agreement with the *New York Commercial Advertiser* for a series of descriptive articles about his voyage to Florida. These were published in the first column of the front page of each weekly edition of the newspaper between October 19, 1860 and January 22, 1861, a total of 24 columns. The series was entitled "Due South, or, Florida Sketches." The series was an obvious fit for the *Commercial Advertiser*, which was a primary advertising vehicle for all manner of shipping. The deal may very well have been made earlier, and saved for the following winter vacation season.

This arrangement gave Fitz Hugh the opportunity to explore a different kind of writing. His easy style and strong descriptive powers lent themselves to this brand of travel writing. Fitz Hugh began the series by giving the prospective traveler packing instructions (ranging from "a very small library consisting principally of light literature," to "a stout bowie knife—for employment on beasts, not men.") Tales from their boat voyage and observations of people and scenery along the way occupied much of the articles. After identifying and elucidating the healthful effects of the climate, Fitz Hugh found them outweighed by Florida's culinary travesties. "Barbarism is easy in the Tropics:"

> Topmost of culinary blasphemies!—they have fried a venison steak! And fried too, in *Swine's fat!* No matter that the variety of edibles is unending—every esculent quadruped from the bear to the squirrel...Wild turkeys are a drug—But as you are a cooking animal, Florida has you by the weakest wrist. Fish, flesh, fowl and vegetable—there is no difference. You might open your mouth and shut your eyes, and sole sensation would be—*Hog.*

After diversions about the economic life of Florida, and some description of natural history, Fitz Hugh launched into a lecture after his father's heart about the "abcess to the whole South," slavery. It was Fitz Hugh's contention that, although the South would contend in Congress or a battlefield to uphold its institutions, every Southerner felt "a bitter sting next to his vitals" every night in bed. If a Northerner would merely be friendly instead of challenging, the Southerner would ask him how he might be "rid of it without an operation that might cost him his life."

On January 10, 1861, Florida seceded from the Union, and Fitz Hugh's last letter appeared in the *Commercial Advertiser* on January 22, 1861. It is not known if this was the last of his letters, or if his editor had cut him short due to the sudden obsolescence of southern travelogues for northern readers.

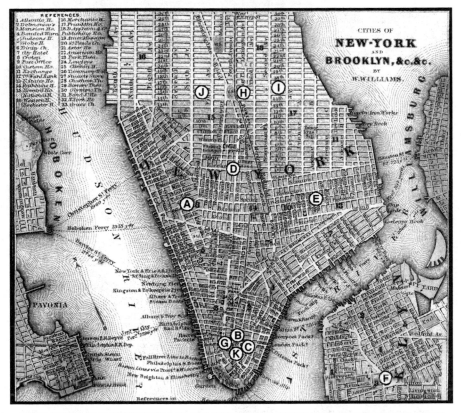

THE POINTS HIGHLIGHTED ON THIS MAP DEPICT LOCATIONS IN NEW
YORK CITY RELATED TO THE LIFE OF FITZ HUGH AND HIS FAMILY (A-K).

A *246 Spring St.*
Reverend Henry Ludlow's
Presbyterian Church, 1834

B *50 Wall St.*
Office of William Curtis Noyes,
Place of employment for Ludlow, 1858-59

C *55 Wall St.*
Custom House New York
Place of employment for Ludlow, 1862

D *647 Broadway Pfaff's Beer Cellar*
Frequented by Ludlow and his literary
companions, 1858-60

E *99 Clinton St. (now Street)*
Fitz Hugh and Rosalie Ludlow
residence, 1858-59

F *Brooklyn*
Fitz Hugh and Rosalie Ludlow residence,
1859-62

G *41 Nassau St.*
The Evening Post
Place of Employment for FHL, 1862

H *42 East 15th St.*
(now at 7 West 43rd St.) Century Club

I *1 Livingston Place, Stuyvesant Square*
FHL and Rosalie Ludlow residence, 1862-65
FHL Residence, 1866-1868

J *18 West 14th St.*
FHL and Maria Ludlow residence, 1869-70

K *Delmonico's Restaurant, 2 William St.*

Nevertheless, this series in the *Commercial Advertiser* yielded Fitz Hugh continued visibility and popularity, and demonstrated a broader range of style and subject matter for which he was suited. Consequently, his marketability among other publishers continued to widen. *The Methodist* in November 1860 reported the startup of a new publication, *Vanity Fair*, and "among the contributors to *Vanity Fair* are Fitz James O'Brien, Frank Warden, Fitz Hugh Ludlow, Aldrich, Prof. Lowell, Chas. Leland." Here Fitz Hugh published his second novel, *The Primpenny Family*, which began in January of 1861. The novel reached its climax, along with the drama of secession, as the guns of Fort Sumter fired in April, 1861.

1 Fitz Hugh Ludlow, *The New Partner in Clingham & Co., Bankers Harper's Weekly*, January-April, 1860. *The Weekly* would go on to greater fame when in 1862 it began publishing the cartoons of Thomas Nast, whose political jabs helped to destroy the power of Tammany Hall.
2 Helen Ludlow to Leander Hall, June 1, 1876. Fitz Hugh later wrote in *The Heart of the Continent* (1870) of the "epithet, 'clean-shaven', which is distinctive of no class of sensible men at the present day." p. 340.
3 The painting is now in the National Gallery of Art.
4 Stedman and Gould (1910), p. 204.
5 Robert Scholnick, *Edmund Clarence Stedman*, Boston: Twayne Publishers, 1977, p. 24.
6 Richard Maurice Bucke, editor, *Collected Works of Whitman*.
7 Scholnick (1977), p. 25.
8 Richard Henry Stoddard, Prologue in Bayard Taylor, *The Echo Club and Other Literary Diversions*, New York, 1872, p. xvii.
9 Stedman and Gould (1910), p. 218.
10 Ibid., p. 209.
11 Ibid., p. 214.
12 Samuels (1966), p. 102.
13 Winter (1971), p. 179.
14 Mrs. Lillian Woodman Aldrich, *Crowding Memories*, Boston and New York: Houghton Mifflin Company, 1920, p. 18.

15 Ibid., p. 19.

16 Ibid., p. 20.

17 Ibid., p. 24.

18 Thomas Bailey Aldrich, "Hascheesh," in *The Poems of Thomas Bailey Aldrich*, Boston: Houghton, Mifflin and Co., 1887, p. 30.

19 *New York Evening Post*, January 7, 1861, p. 2.

20 *Waterville Times*, February 11, 1860, (n.p.).

21 The *Waterville Times* never received those letters, as Fitz Hugh would make other, more lucrative arrangements for their publication. Rosalie would later briefly serve as New York City correspondent to the Times.

22 "Due South," *New York Commercial Advertiser*, October 20, 1861, p. 1.

23 Ibid.

24 "Due South," No. IV, p.1.

25 Train was a Wall Street financier.

26 "Due South," No. XV, p. 1.

27 Rosalie Ludlow to Marie Ludlow, February 28, March 1, 1860.

28 "Due South," November 10, 1860, p. 1.

29 "Due South," November 19, 1860, p. 1.

30 "Due South," January 22, 1861, p. 1.

31 Fitz Hugh Ludlow, "Little Brother," *Harper's Monthly*, February-April, 1860.

32 Horace Day was a vendor of rubber goods, a luxury item at the time. Mrs. Hatch was evidently an occultist known to New Yorkers.

33 J. Henry Harper, *The House of Harper*, New York and London: Harper & Brothers, 1912, p. 23.

34 Carrie Geddings to S. Ludlow Frey, June 23, 1860.

35 *The Methodist*, July 28, 1860, p. 3. The magazine also noted that *Harper's* circulation at that time was 150,000.

36 Rosalie Ludlow to Henry Ludlow, June 28, 1860.

X.

THE WAR BETWEEN THE
STATES OF CONSCIOUSNESS

ABRAHAM LINCOLN was elected president of the United States in November 1860, as reported in the *New York Commercial Advertiser* alongside Fitz Hugh's installment number XI of "Due South." The political passions that had frequently risen to the surface of Fitz Hugh's escapist travelogue had been ignited by the end of his series. Fitz Hugh recognized, like much of the country, that something had changed irrevocably, and yet the instinct remained to continue on with familiar patterns of life. And so he did, until events forced him to adapt.

Florida seceded twelve days before the last installment of "Due South" and five days after the start of Fitz Hugh's new novel in the debut issue of *Vanity Fair*. As noted earlier, Fitz Hugh had made a reputation sufficient for other publishers to seek him out. Fitz Hugh would place writing in four different periodicals and with two book publishers in 1861. He would sell only one story to *Harper's* that whole year, after averaging a story every three months with the Brothers since 1858. It may be that Harper's felt Fitz Hugh was getting overexposed in their pages. The fourth edition of *The Hasheesh Eater* was published late in 1861, but it would not sell enough to warrant another edition. Fitz Hugh's tale of depravity had been surpassed by the more real horror of the Civil War, and other distractions and titillations were now in order.

In a way, *The Primpenny Family* was a farewell to Fitz Hugh's early adulthood, a full-length treatment of the innocent years before bitter strife aged all his circle overnight. Stedman took a job as a war correspondent, Whitman became a nurse who saw firsthand the bloody results of the war, and O'Brien went off to be a soldier, as suited his reckless manner. *Vanity Fair* enabled Fitz Hugh to rekindle some of the old Bohemian spirit while still maintaining his new mantle of respectability. Moreover, his old cronies were now in a position to pay him for his work. *Vanity Fair* (named after the Thackeray novel) was started by Frank Wood and other graduates of Pfaff's literary university, and was modeled after England's famous *Punch*. As such, it was a collegial place for Fitz Hugh to put his new novel. The new paper was characterized by *Harper's Monthly*:

> This is the first really clever comic and satirical journal we have had in America, and really clever it is. It is both sharp and good-tempered, and not afraid to say that its soul is its own—which shows that it has a soul. Our readers will be glad to know where they can find native fun that has something better in it than mere *patois*.[1]

"The staff of Vanity Fair met on Fridays in the editorial rooms at 1133 Nassau Street, and drank, and smoked, and discussed the next issue."[2] Charles Leland became editor of *Vanity Fair* in 1861, assisted by Charles Farrar Browne, a.k.a. Artemus Ward. Browne had been making a name as a humorous lecturer in Cleveland. He made contact with New York in early 1860 and was engaged to write for *Vanity Fair* under his performing name, "Artemus Ward."[3] Leland was an occasional visitor to Pfaff's, but up until now relatively unacquainted with Fitz Hugh. However, a friend of Leland sent him a long letter filled with praise of Fitz Hugh Ludlow, "formerly a very peculiar young pedagogue at Watertown and Poughkeepsie, and now author of 'The Hasheesh Eater.' "[4] At the time of his friendship with Fitz Hugh, Leland was acquainted with voodoo and other syncretic practices of slaves in America. Leland later wrote books about gypsies and witches. The two shared a certain fascination with these fringes of American life, and Leland invited Fitz Hugh to contribute a serial to the paper. Thus, *The Primpenny Family* was born.

The Primpenny Family, under Fitz Hugh's byline, began in the January 5, 1861 issue of *Vanity Fair*, and ended in the April 13 edition, fourteen weekly chapters and forty thousand words later. Fitz Hugh was once again obliged, having agreed to supply the serial, to write a chapter a week. He was able to produce the requisite quantity of words, but the deadline precluded any coherent thematic structure apart from what could be supplied on the fly. He even refers to the problems of serial writing in a direct aside to the reader at the beginning of Chapter V:

> For the last three chapters we have been in a basement in Bleecker Street. At the rate we are getting on, this biography of a highly respectable private family will outlast the annals of the public Government, and our young friends who began it with so much cheerfulness about the time of their debut in society will sleep with their fathers before they get to the middle of the first third, previously, however, assembling their grandchildren around them to leave valedictory directions about erecting a house for the preservation of the back numbers, and injunctions to see Mr. Primpenny through if it takes ten more generations. The fact is that the grandeur of

the theme originally stretched itself into Infinity before the biographer's mind, and in attempting to daguerrotype this impression upon the pages of VANITY FAIR, he forgot that two per week of those pleasant surfaces were an inadequate number for the purpose...At any rate, (I mean the rate we have been going) some of us will be called off by other engagements before Mr. Primpenny comes to a conclusion at the commencement of the 22nd century A.D.

We must therefore be concise hereafter. This porpoise of a biographer who has been accustomed heretofore to flounder hugely through the mighty sheets of the daily and the monthly, must henceforth condense his bulk into that delicate animalcule which can disport itself in a drop of VANITY's exquisitely pungent and aromatic vinegar.

The biography tells of Isaiah Primpenny, who made a fortune in coal scuttles (the buckets in which coal for residential stoves was carried) and his son Stuyvesant, who not only doesn't want to take over the family business, but also dismisses three respectable professions in the first page, much as Fitz Hugh did in his early adulthood:

DOCTORS
I believe there are people who love to see legs taken off—who prefer a good case of delirium tremens to a dinner at Delmonicos...He's the kind of man that has the divine right to be a doctor. I haven't. I'm too infernally lazy. And I haven't the faith.

CLERGY
There are two kinds of clergymen. One's the regular saleable pattern, which has been put up in packages with a well-known trade-mark on 'em, like your coal-scuttles, for the last two hundred years. I've been down to the factory. I've seen how they're made...They take a mild young countryman for the raw article. He must be soft, untempered stuff, without any

unmalleable mixture in his ore, like ideas of his own for instance...Then they melt him down...impregnated through and through with theological notions of the proper blue and blistered color...chill 'em in a bath of ice water, which gives 'em the temper they call 'impregnable orthodox firmness.'

But there's another...The square outspoken man...who says Look here, I'm showing you tough old five-barred gates to climb over, and I'm going to climb over them myself. Every sort of people from the rich to the poor, from the churchman to the fellow who never goes to church, has been putting these gates across your way for the last six thousand years. Jump them I tell you.

Now—I *won't* be the first parson—and to state it frankly, I *ain't able* to be the second!

LAWYERS
I had rather crawl into the coal-scuttles than through that opening! There's too much humbug about it! Too much creeping through other men's dirty sewers, under the pretense that because they are other men's it don't nasty your own white pantaloons at all. If I could be WILLIAM CURTIS NOYES at a leap, I'd do it, though how he has got to where he is and still kept the pure, honorable, noble man that he is, I don't know! There must be some way—but I'm not acquainted with it.

The reference to Noyes confirms that it is the author speaking of his own life's decisions in these passages. Most important is the second type of clergyman, by which Fitz Hugh certainly meant his own father. This bordered on a humble admission that he was not the man his father was, were it not embedded in a carefree context of literary success that enabled a lighter-hearted view of life.

Appearing in *Vanity Fair* rather than *Harper's* gave Fitz Hugh considerably more leeway than the genre formulae he had adroitly followed before. Here, the dissolute young man is the hero rather than the villain of the piece, the fainting ladies are of no particular romantic interest to him ("a gallantry which sent such a strange thrill to her heart as she had not felt since the day she tried the galvanic battery in the Philosophy class at boarding-school"), and drunkenness is rampant not as part of a temperance lecture but as a source of humor and plot twists throughout the story. Also, men of action are seen not as suitable bridegrooms but simply full of hot air. The evening of drunkenness recounted in *The New Partner* is here expanded. The men toasted Miss McCrowder, as "The Pocahontas of a degenerate age," and Mr. Muffles tipsily recalls the kindness of Miss M. during the past week, when

> I looked sad. Know I looked sad. Strangers around me suspected melancholy news. Lost near relation. Something of that kind. No such thing. Under a cloud. You know what cloud, Primpenny. Cloud financial description. Very bad cloud, financial. Miss McCrowder looked at me. Asked me to have cup of tea. Miss M pours tea. Thought do my headache good. Didn't have headache. But said take tea. Miss McCrowder gave me cup. Own fair hands. Didn't put any hot water in it. Stronger than usual. Mark of sympathy. Haven't forgot little kindness. Heroic woman Miss McCrowder. 'Nother tumbler punch.

Mr. Muffles is asked to refrain from further drinking and go read the paper. "Good idea. Do it directly. Not taken too much punch yourself? Seem excited. Talk brilliantly, but fast. Come along too. Read Express." This little dialect of drunkenness demonstrates not only a fine ear for dialogue but a deep understanding of the promise and reality of action while intoxicated—the result of close observation and long experience:

Mr. Primpenny on the other hand became under the effects of punch, a winged steed. He increased with every tumbler in a sense of gigantic power which made him eventually quite dramatic. He was wont to think that if he could stay at the third tumbler, he would conquer the world in one year, or with the greatest ease become the poet of the nineteenth century.

The Hasheesh Eater reared his decadent head in references to brandy-and-laudanum cocktails, and to "innumerable see-gars and Pythagorean meditation." Fitz Hugh even worked in a visit to Pfaff's itself, where Mr. McCrowder did not find the address directory he was looking for, but did find "some very nice Philadelphia bottled ale, which was the next best thing."

Fitz Hugh wrapped up the story in the April 13 issue with a dénoument that was brisk and businesslike. Each character's fate is concluded in a sentence, and both Stuyvesant and Muffles get married and have a child, so that "neither of these estimable couples is doing what I must now do with deep regret…Put an end to the Primpenny family."

At the same time he started *The Primpenny Family*, Fitz Hugh had also placed a short story, entitled "The Taxidermist," in the pages of his first professional publisher, the *Knickerbocker*. The *Knickerbocker* had briefly gone out of business in 1859. It had been revived by James R. Gilmore, and was publishing work at this time by Fitz Hugh's cronies Stoddard, O'Brien and Aldrich. This was an interesting nexus to contrast with the authors published around the time of Fitz Hugh's first appearance in the *Knickerbocker* just four years earlier, when the magazine featured an earlier generation—Harper's editor George William Curtis, Fitz Hugh's medical consultant Dr. J. W. Palmer (who wrote the afterward to *The Hasheesh Eater*) and even old Henry Clapp. "The Taxidermist" was more in the mode of Fitz Hugh's *Harper's* stories, but with a return to the thematic influences of Poe that marked "The Phial of Dread." It is a tale of love that endures through reincarnation. A young man falls in love with a homely spinster (Fitz Hugh takes a full page to describe her "unearthly homeliness," another departure from his genre formula) who dies before they can speak their love. Before she dies, she renames his taxidermy "bird-resurrection" and has an out of body experience: "I had the power of being outside of myself, of looking down on myself, and I was—very beautiful." The woman is resurrected as a bird which is killed by a cruel man, then as an organ-grinder's monkey that dies at the hand of its unsavory master, and finally as an eighteen-year-old girl who is possessed by the spinster, and whom the taxidermist subsequently marries.

The story is so conventionally narrated that the supernatural touches are quite arresting, in contrast to "The Phial of Dread" where Poe's sometime frantic style was invoked as well as his outré plotting. Here, Fitz Hugh had fused the best of the suspense and romance genres, and this story seems to continue the growth of a mature voice heralded by the thoughtful "The Cruise of the Two Deacons" and the satirical The Primpenny Family.

The Primpenny Family ended abruptly, due to the latest tragedy to strike the Ludlow family. On April 1, 1861, Rosalie's mother died. Rosalie, only twenty years old at the time, was devastated. Of frail health to begin with, the emotional trauma only added to her troubles. Fitz Hugh cut short *The Primpenny Family* to help with family matters in Waterville.

JANUARY 5, 1861.]   VANITY FAIR.

THE
PRIMPENNY FAMILY.

BY FITZ-HUGH LUDLOW.

CHAPTER I.

ISAIAH PRIMPENNY, Esq., had made a fortune in coal-scuttles. You may have noticed the singular fact in natural history that when a man has made his fortune in coal-scuttles, it becomes inconceivable to him why every other member of the human family does not rush into coal-scuttles immediately.

STUYVESANT PRIMPENNY—ISAIAH's son—found a fortune already made, and did not stop to inquire how it was done. In the abstract he had no objection to coal-scuttles. They were undoubtedly very respectable. But he had just as lief that they were hearth-rugs, or general provisions, or drugs, or sewing machines. The fortune was made. He did not care what had done it. Accordingly, when ISAIAH PRIMPENNY proposed to him to continue the coal-scuttles in his own name, he steadfastly refused to have anything to do with them.

ISAIAH presented the case from all its most alluring points of view. There never was such a brilliant opening for any young man. STUYVESANT replied that it was an opening he didn't wish to crawl into. "But just to look at it soberly," insisted ISAIAH, "You will have the benefit of all your father's long business acquaintance." "Which consists principally," interposed STUYVESANT "of the most precious old muffs who ever talked hardware at a dinner party!" "But they are the solid men of New York." "Not half as solid as Old Red Sandstone in the Park." "Don't exasperate me by your trifling, STUYVESANT! I have been in hopes that you were going to make a respectable man of yourself. That you would build up an honorable name in society, and go out of the world leaving it better than when you came into it." "And finally lie in the most eligible spot in Greenwood with a monument over me presenting to tourists through that delightful locality the following inscription : 'After contributing munificently to the wants of the age in the form of something like five hundred thousand coal-scuttles, this Benefactor of Mankind fell a victim to his benevolence, being bored to death at the early age of thirty-five years. The instruments which caused his demise may still be seen in every variety of elegant pattern at No. — Greenwich-street, where liberal discounts will be made to the trade. The good die young.'"

"Sir!" said the Father of the PRIMPENNYS, "You are jesting with me. I am in earnest! And I tell you that you do not know which side your bread is buttered on!"

"My dear Governor," replied STUYVESANT, leaning back in his luxurious arm-chair, "I have now reached the ripe age of twenty-five years, and thus far, in all my extended travels, I have never found any difficulty in discovering the buttered side of that succulent you mention. Indeed, it has so invariably turned up buttered that I am led to suspect that it is buttered on both sides."

"Yes sir! and that is the trouble with you! I have brought you up too easily! I erred on the side of parental tenderness. I wished to spare you the hardships which embittered my earlier youth, and I have made you a voluptuary. I should have put you in the work-shop at fourteen years, thrust a hammer and a solder-iron into your hand, and told you to earn your bread as I did!"

"Under these circumstances I should have run away," replied STUYVESANT calmly.

"You would, would you? Where would you have run to, I'd like to know, my young rascal?"

"I should have taken to street begging. I should have seated myself on the Hospital steps, with a large placard on my breast, stating that this was the deserted child of ISAIAH PRIMPENNY, Merchant of No. — Greenwich Street. I should have procured the insertion of a paragraph in the Herald, headed "Destitution in High-life—Shameful Abandonment of offspring by a prominent Fifth Avenue Hardware dealer. And you would have been glad enough to come after me and bring me home, where I should have revelled in luxury as before."

"You are a rascal!" exclaimed ISAIAH PRIMPENNY, but in a tone considerably softened by those words, "High life" and "Fifth Avenue," which always had a remarkable effect on him, when coupled with his name, as being a sort of popular tribute to his hardly attained position in society.

"You are a rascal! If you had tried that sort of thing, I should have flogged you soundly I would have given you luxury when you got home! But STUYVESANT, I am not joking with you—though you may think you make me smile. It is time for you to do something. You are determined, I see, to disappoint my fondest expectations, to abandon your old father in the business by which he has reared his family to its present position. Now what will you do? Will you be a merchant in any other line if I give you capital and find you a partner?"

"Sink the shop! I hate shop of all kinds!"

"Will you study a profession, then? You can get admitted to the New York bar, with eight months' study, and I am able to throw cases into your hands."

"I had rather crawl into the coal-scuttles than through that opening! There's too much humbug about it! Too much creeping through other men's dirty sewers, under the pretence that because they are other mens', is don't nasty your own white pantaloons at all. If I could be WILLIAM CURTIS NOYSALL a leap, I'd do it, though how he was got to where he is and still kept the pure, honorable, noble man that he is, I don't know! There must be some way—but I'm not acquainted with it. No, I don't care to be a lawyer."

"What do you think of being a doctor, then—or a clergyman?"

"Well—as to the doctor, Governor, just look at it a minute. I believe there are people who love to see legs taken off—who prefer a good case of delirium tremens to a dinner at DELMONICO's. They are fond of epilepsy - they dote on dissections—and if they aren't called up at three o'clock in the morning to go and see a man who's fallen off a six-story building, they don't enjoy their sleep one bit afterwards. Now such people are born to be doctors. When they hear the night-bell, they don't say 'damn it!' and go to sleep remembering to give orders to have the wire cut in the morning. They believe in medicine, they do. They give a blue-pill for pain in the toe; and, by Gemini! they've got the science to trace it all the way down from the throat, through the membranes, and clear to the tip end of the system, where it belongs. There's PIPES, for instance! I used to know him when he walked Bellevue. Hanged if he couldn't see the bill bulge out all the way down, till it got to the right place! He's the kind of man that-has the divine right to be a doctor. I haven't. I'm too infernally lazy. And I haven't the faith."

"But how about the clergyman? You've been well brought up. All you've got to do is to stop using those expletives. You mustn't say internal for instance—not out of the pulpit you know."

"Well Governor—you're an elder in one of the up-town churches —but I'll tell you frankly what I think of that business, meaning no offence to anybody. There are two kinds of clergymen. One's the regular saleable pattern, which has been put up in packages with a well-known tradesmark on 'em, like your coal-scuttles, for the last two hundred years. I've been down to the factory. I've seen how they're made. I know every grind of the machine. And this is the way they do things. They take a mild young countryman for the raw article. He must be soft, untempered stuff, without any unmalleable mixture in his ore, like ideas of his own for instance. Then they melt him down with half a hundred lots just like him. Then they pour out the molten metal into casts, all of them precisely alike. Then they burn the casts over in an oven with the charcoal of a dozen old doctors, until they're impregnated through and through with theological notions of the proper blue and blistered color. Then they draw 'em out, and chill 'em in a bath of ice water, which gives 'em the temper they call ' impregnable orthodox firmness.' Then they stick 'em into the handle-known as a diploma—put the factory stamp on them, wrap them in packages, and cram a year offer the lot to cut the bread of life for the adversary, according as either side of their double-edge is wanted, for select country congregations. These ministers—to drop the cutlery comparison—are always provided in the seminary with

Irving, a lesser known author who promptly included three of his own stories. The book was published by H. Dexter & Co., and was mostly ignored.

Two months after Mrs. Osborn's passing, Fitz Hugh's first *Harper's* story in eight months, "Thrown Together" appeared in the June 1861 issue of the *Monthly*. It would be his only piece of fiction until the end of the year. This was another of Fitz Hugh's quick hack pieces, with a plot to appeal to the more empty-headed of lady readers ("Women, like babies, know a great deal more than we men are apt to give them credit for"), and a small ration of Fitz Hugh's humorous touches. The action, such as it is, takes place on the same steamship *Montgomery* that Fitz Hugh and Rosa took to Florida. There is a storm at sea, and like Fitz Hugh in "Due South," the main character here is one of few not to become seasick. And there is one reference to an old acquaintance: "He understood her now—as the riotous Walt Whitman would say, he 'included' her."

One curious inclusion is a pet red squirrel (red squirrel?) named Beppo. Beppo was also the name of the organ-grinder's monkey in "The Taxidermist." No primary evidence describes a Ludlow family pet, but this coincidence does suggest it. After two years of marriage and no children as yet, perhaps Fitz Hugh and Rosalie had acquired an animal to fill up the house in Brooklyn (though probably not a marmoset or a red squirrel).

As Fitz Hugh became settled in New York, as settled as he ever would be, family relations visited periodically. About this time, the upheavals of the Civil War brought Fitz Hugh's cousin Henry Frey to New York to seek his fortunes. Fitz Hugh played the part of the sophisticated, city cousin from whom Henry sought advice on how to get a job at the New York City Customs House, then the largest government revenue producer in the country. Henry wrote to his father that he had seen Fitz Hugh, who "told me there was a new man up for the place and if he should turn out to be the man he—Fitz Hugh—could get me a place sure."[5] The "new man" was Hiram Barney, who was indeed appointed Collector of the port of New York in March 1861 by President Lincoln. Fitz Hugh was acquainted with Barney through literary connections, such as Edmund Clarence Stedman, as well as through his original Manhattan mentor, William Curtis Noyes. Henry Frey sought Noyes' help, as well as urging his father to encourage friends to write letters of recommendation, and to "emphasize that I'm a good Republican." However, despite the efforts of both Fitz Hugh and Noyes, Henry Frey was unable to secure a position at the Customs House. Cousin Ludlow Frey (or "Lud"—Henry's younger brother) complained to his mother about Henry's fate, and identified a likely reason for that fate. It was "shameful to keep time-serving Democrats in office and to disappoint Republicans who have helped elect the present Administration...Barney is a Democrat."[6] In May, Henry gave up and joined the army, which "pays 108.50/ month."[7] Meanwhile, Henry's youngest brother Gus, drilling twice a week with a militia unit in Oswego, wrote to Lud that "we are no doubt living in a very important period of the World's History—a period to be remembered from its record of blood."[8]

In the immediate family, Fitz Hugh's sister Helen had just turned twenty-one and completed her education at the Springler Institute, the predecessor of Vassar College. From Reverend Henry's home in Oswego, she occasionally visited

Fitz Hugh and Rosa. Early in 1861, Helen suffered an unrequited love affair that is described in a fragmented way in her diary.[9] She prays for guidance for the times "when I find earthly love in danger of superseding heavenly." Later in January, she is "alone all day with my sad sad thoughts. Oh *what* shall I do?" In February there is a letter from her suitor, "bless him," but in March another letter causes her to write "love like a shadow flies." April 2, there is "hardly time to think," as this is the day after Rosa's mother died. May 13 is heavily underlined with a cross and bible citation, and, on May 27, Helen notes that she "lost this book until today, of which I am very glad." In the aftermath, Helen fled to Brooklyn with Fitz Hugh and Rosa to see their new house, which is "very pretty indeed."

Helen spent the summer in Fitz Hugh's social circle, which revolved around the Genteel Circle. Helen's diary also paints the social picture that first summer of the war, before any of the Northerners really had been touched by the violence. In June she heard Henry Ward Beecher, the prominent abolitionist, speak, and wrote him a fan letter. "I hope Father will let me send it."[10]. In July, there is a party with several people, including "F H Ludlow—the Author." Helen revered her brother, even when times were unsettled. In August, she and the Reverend Henry traveled to see the new Vassar College, and then to Schenectady, where "Dr. Nott gave me his blessing...charming time." She also met Professor E.L. Youmans, who later founded *Popular Science* magazine—later still she received Professor and Mrs. Youmans for tea—"delightful people."

However, several references indicate that Helen's sister in law was at times emotionally distraught. On August

23—"Rosa expected"; on August 28—"Rose *came*. She thinks there is no hope." There is no elaboration on this cryptic entry, although it is a foreshadowing of unsettled times to come.

On July 21, 1861, the Battle of Bull Run ended the romantic notions of New Yorkers concerning the distant war. The Confederates routed the Union forces, and only a lack of further planning prevented their marching straight to Washington; a good thing, considering that the capital's socialites had traveled to the battle scene with the notion of viewing the carnage as a sporting event.[11] Walt Whitman described in a newspaper account the beaten Northern army straggling through the streets of Washington after the battle. Fitz Hugh's friend, Edmund Clarence Stedman, had been named war correspondent for the *New York World*. His dispatch from the Bull Run battle was instrumental in awakening New Yorkers and others in the North to the hard, bloody, reality of the war. The New York literati were in close touch. "Sted" wrote C.B. Conant, "we're all proud of you. Ludlow just cried when he read of your brave thing with the flag." (Stedman, 27 at the time, had in the midst of the battle grabbed the standard of the Massachusetts Fifth and rallied some of the men.)

As the conflict deepened, Fitz Hugh took an editorial position at the *New York Evening Post*.[12] This move acknowledged that even he, preeminent among the Pfaffians for not to this point having had to take on administrative tasks to put food on the table, was now facing a dearth of publishers. Despite a quick start, Fitz Hugh would earn only $600-$700 from his writing in all of 1861. In fact, Fitz Hugh had even written his one-time professor at Union, Jonathan

("Pinky") Pearson, in search of a teaching job. Union turned him down, and Fitz Hugh complained to Pearson:

> I have hardly ever seen the time, even when my prospects in a worldly view were most flattering, when I would not have abandoned them to return to the pleasantest home of my life...I should have been very glad if Union had ever appeared to care for my connection with her as much as I did.[13]

A newspaper job, though becoming common among the literati, was not attractive to Fitz Hugh. Indeed, he had even satirized the many New York daily and weekly papers in this passage from *The Primpenny Family*:

> This newspaper flourished amazingly. It did a tremendous business in advertising its own men, and was the organ of politics, morality, intellect, and fifty dozen other things to them, their families, and several of their intimate friends. It did its literary business of course just as all the papers do. Likewise its news. It paid for things by measure. For instance, Pluffy, Senior Editor, would say in the morning to Duffy, one of the staff—"Write two feet of Missionary Intelligence for tomorrow, will you?" Then turning to Cuffy, senior political Editor, he would add, "And you one yard of Glorious Union, if you please." Bye-and-bye, as the day wore on, and energetic business people in New York had roused themselves and committed a few shocking crimes or killed themselves by a variety of interesting accidents, Casualty Reporter Stuffy came running in with a beaming countenance to bring five inches of murder. If it was an Alderman, then they let Stuffy put on an extra inch, which told in his pocket. If there was a rail-road accident, that was more or less fate for Stuffy. Only they were pretty strict on Stuffy, because he liked to dilate. They were careful to insist on his minding the graduated scale. "Remember Stuffy, they would say, that brakeman is only 25

cents worth. If it had been a conductor, you should have had half a dollar for him, and when you smash us the president of the road—egad! you shall have five dollars."

The Editorials were taken care of by a very efficient corps, who from laudable motives of economy always kept a good deal of the matter which they should use every day ready set up so that it could go into blanks which they left in their copy.

This excellent plan enabled him to write as follows: "Our ____ Cotemporary, the Daily Slammer is a ____. The article which appeared yesterday in his columns is characterized by his usual ____ and more than his usual ____. We can only say in the words of the poet: ____ ____ ____ ____."

This, when it came out in the next morning's Poker, read as follows: "Our *disgusting* Cotemporary, the Daily Slammer, is a *fool*. The article which appeared yesterday in his columns is characterized by his usual *stupidity*, and more than his usual *malignity*. We can only say in the words of the Poet: 'Truth crushed to earth shall rise again.'"

By these means the Daily Poker flourished greatly.

No Ludlow bylines appeared in the *Evening Post*, but two letters written on the *Post*'s letterhead give some idea of his duties. In August, Fitz Hugh answered some editorial correspondence to an acquaintance:

My Dear Mr. Hubbard,
The gentleman referred to as having taken such interest in the Fire Loavres [elite corps of the Union Army] is Prosper M. Wetmore. I communicate his name in confidence to yourself and any of the artists it may be necessary to report the disbursement to under the same obligation as to outsiders, for the reason that Mr. Wetmore does not like to be brought publicly forward in connection with certain reforms of a corps somewhat demoralized, in which he has been prime mover.

He of course is a safe steward for the beneficience of the artists. Strange also by the way, isn't it? This war has made a general bouleversement of all our relations. Art always used to be the steward and bursar of a generous Commerce—Commerce, now in the shape of the old moneyed man, P.M.W. is (if you like) about to return the favor by distributing the acquisitions of a generous art.

My wife is now spending a few days at General Morris's. I shall write to her this afternoon enclosing your kind remembrances. Were she here she would cordially join in his, your friend, Fitz Hugh Ludlow.[14]

In September, Fitz Hugh wrote to Stedman, who was traveling back and forth between New York and Washington.

My Beloved Stedman,
You are a man of letters—and love me just as much as if I should write you a thousand apologies for not writing. Me voila! Here is all that is left of Ludlow. [Here is a comical line drawing of Fitz Hugh buried up to his spectacles in "Reviews," Notices," "Communi-cations" and books of Philosophy.]

I write this to beg that you will expedite as far as possible in all that relates to his conference with the powers that be—my friend Mr. Hamilton.

He is coming on immediately. You know him already and, as far as convenient, I am sure, will put him in communication with those powers he needs to engage.

I saw your wife one day week before last in going down to Long Branch—she looks well—better than ever before.

Mr. Hamilton will need nothing of course but to introduce himself to you.

Love from Rose (who is now up the river, after Long Branch and Saratoga) and from your companion in bonds and faithful friend,
Ludlow[15]

The Evening Post was edited by William Cullen Bryant, then sixty-eight-years old, known to earlier and later generations as a poet, and assisted by his son-in-law, Parke Godwin. It had a circulation of around 30,000, small compared to Greeley's *Tribune* or the *Times*, but was profitable owing to its being "the organ for the most exclusive and expensive advertising."[16] The paper was only eight pages long, laid out in broadsheets an inch or two wider than modern newspapers, with a total of eleven columns. Page one was less than half news, with the last seven columns taken up by lists of cargo coming into the port, commercial insurance agents advertisements, and other ads. Only the first page had major headlines, with most items being grouped under categories like architectural improvements, city intelligence, and music and the drama. One of Fitz Hugh's jobs was evidently collecting and organizing the daily crush of such notices.

A large part of the back of the paper was taken up by various legal notices and other types of announcements, including Dividend Notices, Election Notices (for corporate directors), and Special Notices (which ranged from government issue of war bonds to a notice for a meeting of the American Bible Society). The bulk of the hard news was, of course, war news, ranging from reports of military action to the introduction of a bill in Congress prohibiting the sale of liquor to soldiers of the Union army. In one issue, there was a statement in favor of emancipating the slaves, signed by Bryant, William Curtis Noyes, and other New York luminaries.

As indicated by the letter to Hubbard, Fitz Hugh was also writing some arts reviews, one of which was entitled "An Evening with a Necromancer," about the magician

Herrmann. The column on Music and the Drama also included "operatic gossip." Another letter sheds some light on his life as a critic.

> Thursday A.M.
> My Dear Coffin,
> I enclose with pleasure a check for Mrs. Barry Gray and yourself to Linda [Kellogg] on Friday (tomorrow) night. If you wish one for Brooklyn (Sat; Traviata) say so and I will get that too.
>
> I shall send you some more opera gossip, critical & historical, either this P.M. or tomorrow morning—and the biographical notice of Parke Godwin at the same time. I will be much obliged to you (should you see him) if you will tell Henderson so that he may save me a couple of columns.
>
> Very truly your friend,
> Fitz Hugh Ludlow[17]

Editor Bryant required that his newspaper be described as a "Democratic-Republican newspaper"; this at a time when "there came to be very quickly a large swarming out of Republican newspaper offices into Consulates, government clerkships, and other places under the new administration [of Lincoln]."[18] Fitz Hugh himself, who had quickly tired of the low, if steady, wages and the many duties, became part of that swarming. Stedman could have been part of that crowd, having written a campaign song for Lincoln.[19] Instead, Stedman had removed his family to Washington as war correspondent for the *World*, and wrote to Fitz Hugh to recommend he seek to replace a mutual friend Edward House at the New York City Custom House, the crown jewel of political patronage in the country. Lincoln's ascendence to the presidency had brought many men of literature to seek government service. Herman Melville was among those seeking consulates; William Dean Howells was appointed to the embassy in Venice.

Fitz Hugh got the Custom House job, and Rosa wrote to Stedman a quite emotional letter. "It was so kind and brotherly of you to think of Fitz's taking House's place, and still more thoughtful to write him about it. There's something about you, Stedman, that one doesn't find in every man—something that I like and respect amazingly."[20] Rosa at this time was still in bad health, and as Fitz Hugh mentioned in both letters above, she was traveling quite a bit. Helen's diary notes on October 3, "Rose ill—poor child," and October 12, "letter from Rose—hopes of going to NY." Fitz Hugh's job involved reviewing the manifests of ships arriving in New York harbor and assessing their value for payment of the appropriate duty. The New York Custom House was the center of not only revenue but controversy at this time. Payoffs for false appraisals of arriving shipments (leading to lower duties) were common. The U.S. House of Representatives investigated the Custom House, and in March 1863 Barney testified as follows:

> [O]wing to the war and unprecedented state of affairs occasioned by it, I have been charged with very many new duties... entirely foreign to the ordinary functions and powers of collectors of the revenue...including, upon suspicion, to seize and detain vessels and property for violation of revenue laws.[21]

The House concluded that "Many frauds have been exposed, the government relieved from many unconscionable contracts, and millions of dollars saved to the treasury. Yet it is a matter of regret that punishment has not been meted out to the basest class of transgressors…pretending loyalty to the flag, who feast and fatten on the misfortunes of the nation."

Fitz Hugh's work was deadly drudgery, and the pay only adequate, at around $3 per day.[22] Helen later recalled that he earned $1,100 from the Custom House that year, and said he took the job because of the "depression."[23] Indeed, in 1862, Fitz Hugh would earn less than $300 from writing, less than even his Bohemian days. Fitz Hugh had company at the Custom House, as many other literary types worked there, including Stoddard (who had been recommended by Nathaniel Hawthorne, and been there since 1853) and Aldrich.[24] On some days, they relieved the boredom with letters on literary topics treated in the magazines. On others, they indulged in literary sport, an example of which has been preserved on Custom House letterhead, namely a contest in translation of an Italian love poem:

Italian 1.
Dall uno del mio cuore
Lorse mia sol prece
Che l'idol mio ammiuri
Che io l'ammiori, e muoria

Aldrich 1.
Out from the depths of my heart
Has arisen this single cry
Let me behold my beloved
Let me behold her & die

Ludlow 1.
From the bottom of my heart
There broke one single cry
Let me look on my idol
Look on him & die!

Italian 2.
Alfin, com'alma peccatrice
Alle porte del ciel io giungo
Nonper entrar cogli eletti
O! Friammai…soltanto per mouor!

Aldrich 1.
At last, like a sinful soul
At the portals of Heaven & lie
Never to walk with the blest
Ah never! Only to die.

Ludlow 2.
Then I come to the gates of heaven
A soul all sinful & lonely
Not with the Elect to enter
Ah never! to die! to die only![25]

As Fitz Hugh continued to read and occasionally con-tribute to the magazines (as much as a full time job would allow), he corresponded with other writers. In November, he wrote to Charles Leland concerning a literary produc-tion with political overtones:

My Dear Leland,
I have a favor to ask of you. Will you give me the name of the writer of those wonderful sketches of travel through the Cotton States which have appeared in the Knickerbocker? I am pretty sure from internal evidences that you yourself have done a good deal towards cutting the rough diamond of adventure disclosed therein—and the songs are very much more like what C.G.L. knows the negro feels than what that sable brother would be able to say for himself. But Gilmore [publisher of the Continental Monthly] told me that the trav-eller and his adventures are real—and having an extra-cerebral

status somewhere, I wish to know where that is. Will you do me the kindness to tell me by return mail?

I will tell you in perfect secrecy why I want the information. That man, whoever he is, knows something about the conspiracy to dissolve the Union, which, if ventilated, would put a number of our now white-washed political rascals in their true position before the people. To do this is the duty of every man who loves his country, and especially at this juncture loves New York.

...Your leaders on the hard war-nut which is to be cracked have given the Knickerbocker a prestige it never had before, and are the admiration of all your friends. You see an issue which is plainly impracticable to the present half-wisdom of the country, but which, as sure as God lives on Earth as well as in the Heavens, will be forced upon the heart of the great people before its prodigally poured blood can congeal into a cement for eternal empire. Your lyrics on the subjects of the war and freedom I consider the best things you ever did. There is the Thor-hammering in them blending into a grand anvil chorus with the sweep of Braga's lute.

Before I close let me say one thing. You have a friend here (soi-disant—I call him sycophant) who is no friend of mine. You and I have always been friends. Let no word of his ever make us otherwise. I mention no names—paper is not a good medium for unpleasant facts. I prefer air—which I will use when we meet. Please reply immediately—and let no one make you dream for a moment that I am other than always your sincere friend, Fitz Hugh Ludlow[26]

This investigation into the "conspiracy to dissolve the Union" may have contributed to Hiram Barney's crusade to clean up the Custom House, although there is no published acknowledgement of Fitz Hugh's role in the ensuing House investigation. As the year came to an end and the War grew in magnitude, Fitz Hugh's regular hours at the Custom

House began to leave a little room for fictional endeavors. He produced three stories in the next four months.

"The Music Essence" appeared on New Year's Eve in the *New York Commercial Advertiser*, which had published the "Due South" series the previous year. The story was the lead item of the special holiday supplement, and featured a large type byline and the legend "WRITTEN EXPRESSLY FOR THE COMMERCIAL ADVERTISER."

The story's central thematic concern with music grew out of his exposure to the New York music scene as reviewer and "operatic gossip" columnist with the *Evening Post*. Indeed, contemporary performers like D'Angri and Carl Formes, whom Fitz Hugh had praised in reviews, were called upon here to flesh out the story. In it, a young man falls in love with a beautiful deaf mute. He believes she is so sensitive that if he can translate music so it may be apprehended through a sense other than hearing, she will derive more pleasure from it than the most sensitive ear. He does this through an invention that converts sound into color, which he christens the *kaleidophone*. "The Music Essence" represents a further development in Fitz Hugh's style. The story seems clearly a vehicle to present his musings into the nature of music itself. The narrative bogs down at one point as Fitz Hugh expounds on the subject:

> Music in its pure scientific aspect is quite independent of sound—uses sound only as its ordinary normal expression— and by all the more delicate intellects—the poets especially— is constantly translated according to a system of analogies, into other than audible forms…All music it seemed to me, finally resolves itself into a science of tensions, and one nerve as well as another may convey the relations of tension, provided

that we attain the means best calculated to awake their plea through the sense.

Fitz Hugh's hashish experience may have informed these musings. One of the more well documented effects of hashish and cannabis in general is an increased sensitivity to and appreciation of music (cf. Fitz Hugh's visit to the opera in *The Hasheesh Eater*, described in Chapter 5). In more extreme drug experiences, synesthesia has been reported, and Fitz Hugh's personal experiences may even have been the genesis of the kaleidophone.

The story is also a departure in plot resolution. Again, with the freedom from formula afforded by the setting of this story in the *New York Commercial Advertiser* (i.e., not *Harper's*), Fitz Hugh is not obligated to include a happy ending. Indeed, after his beloved deaf mute undergoes an operation to restore her hearing, he finds her sensitive nature is overcome by a world in which there is "too much *noise*. I do not hear enough *music*." She eventually wastes away and dies, now "among the music of the Angels!" but leaving the narrator alone in tragedy.

The ending is well foreshadowed by the departure in style. Fitz Hugh not only begins the story with a short, vague description of an earlier tragedy in which the narrator narrowly avoids jail, but also refrains from virtually all puns, humorous asides and other wordplay that had been his trademark up to this time.

Encouraged by the success of "The Music Essence," Fitz Hugh wrote two more stories in quick succession. "A Drawn Game," a more conventional piece for the February issue of *Harper's Monthly*, was only his second appearance there in two years. In part, it is another exorcism of his father and his desire for Fitz Hugh to be a minister, or at least a professional man. The goal of the main character here is to be an engineer on the new Western railroads (the first sign of Fitz Hugh's burgeoning interest in the exotic Wild West) and not the preacher he became to satisfy his father. The story is an almost effortless genre production, interesting only for the tinge of the supernatural in the lynchpin of the story, a dream chess match for the soul of the narrator.

The supernatural takes the primary position, however, in his next story, "A Strange Acquaintance of Mine." It appeared in the March 1, 1862 edition of the *New York Leader*, yet another of the daily New York newspapers. These papers were new markets for stories, and Fitz Hugh's friends such as Aldrich, Stedman, and Ada Clare were published there. The *Leader* and other similar papers did not pay well and certainly were not considered literary showcases at the level of the *Atlantic Monthly*, or even *Harper's Monthly*. However, they did tend to favor sensationalism. Fitz Hugh's weird stories were welcome relief from the steady stream of depressing war news.

"A Strange Acquaintance of Mine" is narrated by a doctor at Bellevue Hospital, who dedicated himself "to the study of hidden causes. If any nexus existed between the physical disturbances and the mental and moral condition of my patients, I swore to find it out, and would bring my treatment to bear on that middle field, that mysterious bridge uniting mind and body." This doctor recalls Fitz Hugh's old mentor, Dr. Rosa of Watertown. In the story, this attitude earned the narrator the sobriquet of "The Crazy Doctor" from the more mainstream doctors who were still insecure about the tentative successes of their profession in the mid-19th century. The story is about one of the Crazy Doctor's patients, one Cosmo Smagrito, suffering from unexplained seizures. Smagrito is a survivor of the yellow fever epidemic of New Orleans, and relates a story within the story which makes up the bulk of this piece, entitled "The Yellow Cat." It is this tale which is thoroughly steeped in mysticism and brings forth hashish-tinged visions in the course of Fitz Hugh's prose:

> Perhaps I had slept too little of late—but I felt a strange wakefulness—a new power and penetration of eyesight which I could not understand. The air was like a hot lead vapor, but yellow—a sort of stationary, unrippled smoke. Yet I could see through it as clearly as through high mountain atmosphere, and things really a great way off looked large and plain. Besides, though the air was still, there were things in it that moved; crawling blue streaks, like small worms of vivified steel wire.
>
> The full moon was just rising through a spectral fog. Its mournful globe of blood seemed rather to infect than clear the air, which grew yellower and fuller of ghastly livid streaks with every step I took towards home.

The Yellow Fever is devastating New Orleans, the well-to-do have abandoned town, but Cosmo and his wife have sworn to comfort the sick until the plague reaches their street. One night, Cosmo watches a friend die, and on his way out notices a yellow cat which follows him out, and then stops at the first house on his street. The next day, a girl in that first house dies, and after two reoccurrences, the cat is understood to be the harbinger of death. This realization occurs to Cosmo in a waking dream:

The door slowly opened, and with noiseless, tiger-tread, a spectral cat glided out...After the cat came first the little one who was already dead...(then) every man, woman and child in all St. Felix Street issued from the belonging houses in saffron robes of burial...They mounted into the hearse whose capacity seemed inexhaustible. It held them all, and when the street was swept of every life save my own, the spectral cat sat down on a black board in front, and purred to a skeleton driver who sat beside him. That terrible anatomy, for a cirrup, uttered a shriek to the horses, spectral as the cat, who champed and frothed a yellow vapor before him—and then the whole vision drove away, lessening into nothing, toward that cemetery where our dead seemed to reek above the earth in an open day held by commonality with mortals.

Cosmo then attacks the cat and, in a stirring battle that would have made Poe proud (Fitz Hugh even includes an aside for the reader not to think this is some fictional "phantasy of Poe"), kills the beast from hell and ends the epidemic.

Fitz Hugh uses Italian language and translation extensively in the story—perhaps he had just learned the language (see the translation contest with Aldrich described previously), or had begun to practice it in his trips to the opera. The story also includes a black servant named Caesar (introduced in "Due South"), and describes a character "as one in a magnetic dream" (a reference to Mesmer and the infant science of hypnosis). Fitz Hugh's writing now seemed to reflect a growing desire to synthesize the classical Western tradition and progressive ideas belonging to the modern industrial age, while attempting to somehow drown out the awful realities of the war.

And the shooting War Between the States dragged on. While in early 1862 the North appeared in control, a few months later the Army of the Potomac was thrashed by Robert E. Lee. By May, Stonewall Jackson was threatening Washington D.C. Stedman wrote to Stoddard in February 1862, that "the old circle of friends has been pretty much broken up by the war...I should be quite happy if you two [Dick and Liz] were here...And if Ludlow could come too, Washington would not meet with the fate of Sodom for want of three virtuous men and pipe smokers. Fitz Hugh sends me his last story [probably "A Strange Acquaintance of Mine"]. He has talent enough for anything, and a heart as noble as native sunshine can make it." In April, he again wrote to Stoddard, "You don't know how much I yearn for New York—to see you, and the Ludlows, and the dear Old Bay...my love to Aldrich despite his impudences." And again in September, this time to Aldrich—"Do you ever see the Ludlows? And how do you pass your life generally?"

But if Stedman was merely lonely, others of the old circle had fared much worse. The mercurial Fitz James O'Brien had obtained a commission on General Lander's staff, a commission originally sought by Aldrich. After a brief but evidently effective stint, O'Brien was wounded on February 16. Civil War-era surgical techniques then took their toll. He scrawled a letter to a friend—"All my shoulder bone and a portion of my upper arm have been taken away. I nearly died. My breath ceased, heart ceased to beat, pulse stopped. However, I got through. I am not yet out of danger from the operation, but a worse disease has set in. I have got tetanus, or lock-jaw. There is a chance of my getting out of it, that's all. In case I don't...you and Frank Wood should be my literary executioners, because after I'm dead I may turn out a bigger man than when living."[27] This bit of cynical gallows humor was to be expected, and O'Brien would have been pleased at the response to the news of his death from complications. Henry Clapp quipped coldly, "O'Brien was shot in Aldrich's shoulder."[28]

In March, Rosalie was ill again, and Fitz Hugh wrote to his sister asking her to come to N.Y. and help with the nursing. On the 13th, Helen told her diary "Rose looked very sick," and on the 15th, "Rose restless but better—Fitz Hugh over in the City." On the 16th, Rose was much better, but on the 17th "Fitz did not come back til late. Rose nervous. Went to look for him at Carpenter's. Not there. Bilious Attack—Ah! Poor Fitz!" Helen gave no elaboration here, and we don't know if Fitz Hugh was in the City for business or pleasure with Rose sick back in Brooklyn. In any case, Fitz Hugh was always prone to fits of temper, and the pressures of war and economic recession were growing.

On the 18th, Helen noted in her diary "Carpenter called. I like him!" Frank Carpenter was a painter and part of the circle delineated above, and would become one of Fitz Hugh's closest friends. Carpenter invited Helen to an artists reception which included Bierstadt and Prentice Mulford. Helen related with embarrassment the next day that "Mulford *did* think I was *deaf. Stupid!*"

But after this interlude, more trouble surfaced. On the 21st, a letter had arrived from a Mrs. Lee, and "Rose frightened and good cause. I went over to see about it. Oh Shame!—What will the end be—F. wrote a quick note to her. Invited there tomorrow." But the next day they could not go on account of rain.

Things settled down again, and Helen "went with Carpenter and his wife to see Dickens." Charles Dickens was the

most popular lecturer in the U.S., dramatizing his own sto-
ries with different voices for each character. Another month
went by with Helen back in the New York social whirl, now
meeting "literary types Rouse, Dana, Conant," now men of
science like Agassiz and Youmans, now opera stars like Kel-
logg and Brignoli, who had been the subject of Fitz Hugh's
operatic gossip in the Post. "We are at Uncle Henry's and
he and Helen are in N.Y." wrote Fitz Hugh's Aunt Caroline
Frey to Cousin Lud in April.[29]

On April 29, a Mr. Knowlton came to follow up on the
Mrs. Lee problem. Apparently, Fitz Hugh and Rosa could
no longer afford their house in Brooklyn, and they would
have to leave the following Thursday. May 1 was moving
day, and on May 2 Helen asks "shall I ever forget these last
three days?" The Ludlows ended up in an apartment at No.
1 Livingston Place in Manhattan.

The relocation took its toll, and Fitz Hugh as well as Rosa
was now suffering. Helen notes in mid-June that she visited
them at the Clifton Water Cure (a health resort), with "Rose
much better, Fitz too." Rosa was well enough by July to join
with Helen in writing to Fitz Hugh's childhood friend Dan-
iel Mann a ditty entitled Machine Poetry.

> R Our dear friend Dan
> H Thou loyal Mann
> R How much we wish to see you.
> H We sadly miss
> R Thy kindly kiss
> H Oh tell us Dan where be you?[30]

Through the turmoil of the spring, Fitz Hugh remained
at the Custom House.

LUDLOW'S FRIEND, PAINTER FRANCIS BICKNELL CARPENTER
(1830-1900), WHOSE PORTRAIT OF FITZ HUGH LUDLOW GRACES
THE COVERS OF THE *COLLECTED WORKS*. (LIBRARY OF CONGRESS
PRINTS AND PHOTOGRAPHS DIVISION)

His domestic and financial difficulties are not mentioned
in the following letter, and his acquaintance with Henry

Ward Beecher, probably through his father's abolitionist work, is the spark for this letter. It is especially interesting to see that Fitz Hugh is now quite easily referring to the Custom House in the editorial we voice. (And the letter was written on Custom House letterhead.)

My dear Leland,

Mr. Beecher this morning asked me if I knew Kirk of the Southern experiences—because he wishes to put him in correspondence with a Baltimore lady who had become very much interested in his book. I said no—but that you did. He then requested me to enclose the within letter to you, begging you to forward it to Kirk and have him answer its inquiries, if he will, to the direction given—then return it to me for Mr. Beecher who wishes to keep it a sample of the good seed which may spring up in thorny places. May I burden you with this good office? It will be such both to H.W.B. [Hiram Barney] & myself as well as the lady. I wish I could write more at length to thank you for your course on the great issues but am awfully driven—People who think the commerce of the U.S. is going to the bad had better note that we are doing a larger business at the Custom House than has been transacted for six or seven years—and on Saturday (26th) cleared the largest number of vessels to Europe that ever left this port on one day within our history.

Please remember about having Kirk return the letter to me. Beecher asked that particularly.

I dine with Dick Stoddard this P.M. Lizzie has been very sick but is better now and goes with Dick to spend a week at the [painter Jervis] McEntees' farm house in a day or two. All your friends are well. My wife is out of town (Would I were with her!) or would invite in kind remembrances to Mrs. Leland & God bless you to you with your friend,

Most faithfully,
Fitz Hugh Ludlow[31]

By this time it may be apparent to the reader that all was not sweetness and light with the young Ludlow couple. In each of the last three letters, Rosa had been out of town. It may be that Fitz Hugh was more likely to write letters without his wife around, but combined with Helen's chronicle of her illness (and Rosa's own letter from Florida in 1860) it begins to look as if Rosa was becoming somewhat of an emotional burden to Fitz Hugh as well as a social asset. Their financial difficulties also seem to indicate that there was no Osborn money flowing in, except to finance Rosa's frequent trips up the Hudson to Saratoga Springs and to Waterville.

In the summer of 1862, Fitz Hugh's friend Frank Carpenter was at the White House to paint the President. Lincoln told him at one point that the Union "must change our tactics or lose the war."[32] Lincoln had recently rebuked Fremont and another General for issuing emancipation proclamations while Lincoln was trying to negotiate with border states for compensated gradual abolition. In August, Greeley published "The Prayer of the Twenty Million" which accused Lincoln of being too soft on the slavery question. On September 23, Lincoln issued the Emancipation Proclamation, the thirty year dream of Reverend Henry Ludlow and the long time abolitionists.

Still at the Custom House, Fitz Hugh found it hard to be inspired by that turn of events. Like all his peers he continually sought supplemental income, and after almost eight months without publishing, a new offer came along. The *Home Journal*, a weekly newspaper edited by veteran New York writer N. P. Willis, hired Fitz Hugh to write a regular column of drama and music criticism. Willis was an old friend of Bayard Taylor from the 1840's, when they both knew young William Cullen Bryant and others of an earlier generation of New York writers. The *Home Journal* was the lightest of magazines, not unlike a *People* magazine redeemed by a small amount of intelligent writing. The paper unabashedly covered society news, fashion news from France, and news of the arts. Willis had endured criticism that the *Home Journal* was too superficial, and replied that since the millennium had not come, some one had to provide the light touch, else "gayeties would then go undescribed, novelties unsketched, the bubble of the moment unseized, foreign eccentricities and humors untranslated, lovely women unportrayed."[33] Willis contributed commentary on the War, entitled "Lookings-On at the War," surely as frothy a title as one could use in writing a column about war. The *Home Journal* also published the poems of all of the Genteel Circle, including Taylor, Stoddard, Aldrich and O'Brien. At the turn of the century, the *Home Journal* would metamorphosize into *Town and Country* magazine.

On October 11, 1862, Fitz Hugh's "Masks and Music" made its debut in the *Home Journal* with an epigraph from *Midsummer Night's Dream*, "Say what abridgement have you for this evening? What mask? What musick? How shall we beguile the lazy time if not with some delight?", and also with these words:

> The time that needs beguiling most is the evening of a day which has been spent in powerful sensations. In ordinary seasons we pass by a natural transition from a desk in the counting-room to a doze in the arm-chair. But who can leap at once from bulletin to bed? How strangely feel the cool sheets of the housewife's press after those flaming ones which issue from the Evening

Post's! Thought flies on wildly like a light cavalry skirmisher unwilling to be overtaken by the sluggish infantry of sleep. And when, overpowered at last, we yield to slumber the citadel key of the brain, each dream that rushes in to occupy the place is but an exaggerated newsboy, screaming tenth editions.

The Theory of Transposition
In times of great excitement the popular mind must be let down gradually from day to night through a judicious twilight of sensations. Much needless wonder is expressed at the present bountiful array and flattering success of evening entertainments. Their reason lies in their necessity. Good music, good acting, just now take their place as the modulation of our life's descent from key to key.

Notwithstanding the above essay, the economic troubles of the previous few years were finally beginning to end, stimulated by the economic boost of the war effort. Fitz Hugh was still busy at the Customs House, but evidently was able to find time to attend performances and write his reviews. After four installments, "Masks and Music" was so well received that Fitz Hugh's byline was added. (His sister recalled that the column was "much talked about.")

"Masks and Music" was devoted to opera, drama and classical concerts. The opera was Fitz Hugh's main concern, with commentary not only on the performances but on the very existence of the institution itself in New York City. His second installment began "What's the matter with the Academy of Music?" He claimed the right to ask about any public institution (e.g. "my Orphan Asylum—mine, because I put something in its anniversary plate, and because in this up-and-down world my descendents may lodge there some day.") In the absence of any opera productions, he states "We do not believe the trite reproach that an opera-house is as yet in advance of our civilization." When the opera season is finally announced, Fitz Hugh wonders "what will be the effect on those starveling habitues of Fourteenth Street who for the last twelve-month have been wandering hollow eyed, sunken cheeked...glowering savagely on organ grinders, and not to be trusted in the same room with a melodeon?"

Fitz Hugh thought opera the pinnacle of artistic creation. He claimed that Beethoven "saw prophetically that Opera should be the highest musical development of the next era." Fitz Hugh's favorite librettist at the time was Giacomo Meyerbeer, "Shakespeare's nearest approximation for lyric purpose." When criticizing performers, Fitz Hugh found special fault with opera singers who couldn't act as well as sing, because opera was the ultimate test of a performer. Fitz Hugh wrote approvingly of one tenor, "He does not regard the opera as a concert with higher salaries." Laura Kellogg was in Fitz Hugh's opinion the finest opera singer, as confirmed by her ability to command great salaries in Europe. She was only in New York for two weeks during the time he wrote the column. In addition to the greats, Fitz Hugh would find time to give a good word to the competent, such as the productions of the Deutsche Opera. And of one certain performer, "We wished to make a good deal of her—just as Nature has done. It would hardly be fair to state that she is the largest prima donna on any stage, were it not possible to assert that she is one of the best." Later he semi-retracts, "Lorini did such splendid justice to her part in 'Ernani' that we regretted having ever made any reference to her size, and felt like sending her a table of avoirdupois weight with carte blanche to make any alteration she pleased in the relation of pounds to tons."

Apart from opera, Fitz Hugh often reviewed concerts of classical music. There was one dominant American performer and composer at the time, and he was Louis Moreau Gottschalk. A later critic called him "the first American to manifest a marked genius for playing the piano and for composing piano music…the peer of Franz Liszt."[34] Fitz Hugh commented, somewhat esoterically, that "we believe that his Rosicrucian alchemy is equal to the task of creating a splendid fantasia tomorrow from the suggestions of a mere old-fashioned stew taken today at Downing's [restaurant]." Gottschalk had had an affair with Pfaffian Ada Clare in the mid-1850s, resulting in a child out of wedlock. He left her and traveled for five years, returning in 1861 to discover she had been Queen of Bohemia, where Fitz Hugh had known her well.

Fitz Hugh's reviews were the beginning of friendship with Gottschalk himself. The pianist was moved to write to Fitz Hugh, and the February 14 column of "Masks and Music" includes a letter from Gottschalk to "my dear L.", agreeing with Fitz Hugh that while Beethoven was great, not everything he wrote was of the same caliber. Gottschalk had spent time compiling Voodoun music in and around New Orleans, and he and Fitz Hugh may have compared notes about African American spirituality.[35] After one show, Fitz Hugh and Rosa were invited backstage, and Rosa later recounted that Gottschalk "averred that he perceived music through every sense."[36] This recalls *The Hasheesh Eater*, and the story "The Music Essence." Artists in many media, from music to painting, found Fitz Hugh a sympathetic ear. Consequently, Fitz Hugh's friendship obscured impartiality—"we have attended every concert since his [Gottschalk's] return" from Boston. And Fitz Hugh's Bohemian blood still simmered at the thought of the capital of respectability:

> Gottschalk has returned from Boston, having scaled that classic peak with great success and frozen himself by sitting down thereon much less than might be expected...Music herself suffers there from a chronic influenza. Beethoven on the brain, complicated with an inflammatory affection which doctors would call Mozartitis—these seem its principal symptoms. To please the peak's taste, you must be stone-cold dead to a degree which New Yorkers cannot imagine.

As with opera, Fitz Hugh also went beyond the music itself and wrote a short piece in an adjoining column in December on the new Chickering piano, "almost an orchestra of itself," praise echoed the next week by Gottschalk himself in a letter to the *Home Journal*.

"Masks and Music" also spent considerable column inches on drama. One subject for Fitz Hugh's exposition stood out above all others, namely Edwin Booth. "This finale of Iago is the most powerful piece of acting we ever beheld on the stage." The whole fourth installment of "Masks and Music" was devoted to Booth. "An evening spent with such an actor as Edwin Booth is the quintessence of intellectual activity. The three hours during which he is coming and going on the stage, have concentrated in them the results of a wider, deeper, intenser, mental life than is compressed into any other exhibition of Genius." Further, "[h]e has reached more of the soul of Shakespeare, both in reading and in action, than any actor of our generation has attained." Fitz Hugh answered critics who were less than totally enthralled by Booth—they are the same people, he sneered, who say "Niagara is one hundred and sixty five feet high, but not so broad as we might wish. Niagara is a grand feature of natural scenery, but we have heard less noisy cataracts." Although he worshipped Booth, Fitz Hugh was critical of many dramatists.

One play was adapted from a novel that was so convoluted that Fitz Hugh "can forgive the present dramatist for failing to make of it a play which is orderly and interesting." In this critique, Fitz Hugh identified the predicament of the era's American theatre, the "era of…Edwin Booth, when our theatre was notable chiefly for its actors" as opposed to the development of American playwrights.[37]

As with Gottschalk, Fitz Hugh's reviews were a vehicle of deepening friendship with Booth. Their closeness is attested to by an exasperated Booth, "Please take good care of [these books]; I vowed never to lend another book, my library has been so scattered by this means. Fitz Hugh Ludlow and other friends raised Cain with my books."[38] Elsewhere, Booth had noted that Ludlow, in a review, "thinks I am a splendid savage."[39] In a way, Fitz Hugh had found replacements for his old friends, scattered by the war. His role as critic had brought him as well into a nicer society than the old Bohemians.

Fitz Hugh also was disconnected from the Ludlow family, who were still perambulating much like other families in these times of the steadily worsening war. Cousin Henry had gone to board at his Uncle's, the Reverend Henry, in Oswego, and taken a position with the insurance company there.[40] Cousin Carrie Geddings had gone to New Orleans, a part of the deep south little touched by the War. At Lake

Couchartrain, she noted "trees festooned with this South-ern Moss such you know as Fitz and Rose brought from Florida," and the "blackest darkeys I ever saw."[41] And young Cousin Lud had gone to visit Fitz Hugh in New York, where he underscored Fitz Hugh's financial predicament, "I don't think I should like to live in N.Y. unless I were rich."[42] Then young Lud added this political commentary: "one thing I am in favor of, an unlimited dictatorship. As long as we have a hydra headed government antagonistic in views we are certain of no success. If we would preserve our constitution there must be unity of action and this we can only have by making one man the ruler and director of all things."[43] This was not an uncommon sentiment at the time.[44]

The New Year turned with the Ludlows' life in its usual unsettled state. Cousin Gus visited, noting "Uncle and Helen, I think, will go to N.Y. this week. I was quite surprised to find them here. Uncle is blue enough, and it is enough to make a well man sick to be in the same house with him. The trunk of clothes came to hand safely, but I have not as yet got any word from N.Y., nor heard a word from Fitz about it."[45] In one letter, Gus gave as a return address "Fitz Hugh Boarding House—No. 1 Livingston Place, New York."[46] The Osborn family, in contrast, did not visit—Rosalie was more likely to see them in Waterville or at Saratoga. Carrie Geddings arrived from her southern tour in February, and wrote to her mother on Custom House stationary, that she was staying. "I thought Rose would be the best one to go shopping with me. I gave my card to the servant and in a moment heard some one running in the hall and Fitz Hugh rushed into the room. I was never more surprised than to see Lud here. Rose was not up yet, but got up right away and went out with me. She said 'if you were only going to stay long enough I would make your bonnet for you.' Fitz went to see his landlady and found that we could stay here, so then I concluded to stay until Tuesday, and we got the material for my bonnet and Rose commenced it yesterday."[47]

The old Genteel Circle still kept in tenuous contact. In a letter to Stoddard, Stedman remarked on Mrs. Stoddard's last story in *Harper's*, that "I received her message through Mrs. Ludlow, who with real kindness writes me once in a while all the news of my friends."[48] Fitz Hugh's continuing employment at the Custom House was noted somewhat jealously by his occasional editor Charles Leland. "I have a great mind to apply for a Custom House place myself...I must see Simon to find out what Custom House offices are within my narrow capacity. I'm not sure that I should decline being tide-waiter. I want work so badly *Dieu sait* that office begging is my last resort, and that I have tried hard enough to get something else to do. I certainly deserve as much as Clark (a previous Knickerbocker editor), Stoddard, Ludlow, or any other of the literati there—and Lincoln knows it."[49]

However, by this time Fitz Hugh was tiring of the routine, and the general weary and crazy feeling in New York. On February 14, 1863, the last installment of *Masks and Music* appeared. Although it ran on page one for the first time since its debut, there was no hint of its discontinuing. Perhaps Fitz Hugh felt some presentiment that New York was going to be unpleasant for some time to come.

In March, Mary Booth, Edwin's wife, died suddenly. Booth had a drinking problem—Mrs. Stoddard wrote "Mr. Booth has lost all restraint and hold on himself. Last night there was grave question of ringing down the curtain before the performance was half over. Aldrich and Thompson would take turns watching him. He was drunk when the news came of Mary's illness, and she was dead before he returned to her from a performance." Booth wrote "My heart is crushed, dryed [sic] up, and desolate."[50] Booth reported soon after that "Ludlow has written me such a long beautiful letter, full of hope, inspiring words and consolation. I wish I could write as well as he."[51]

On a less personal but equally deadly note, a national draft law was passed by Congress that spring. The law exempting from service those who paid into the federal treasury the sum of $300 (the better part of a year's wages for laborers, the same laborers for whose jobs the freed slaves would likely compete). Fitz Hugh may have made such a payment, although he was also likely to have been excused for general poor health.

The draft began on July 11, and on the 13th a mob wrecked the Provost-marshal's office, raided a "colored" orphan asylum, and then attacked another enrolling office. The riots began in a district filled with Irish laborers (Democrats) who were looked down on by other northerners. Fitz Hugh himself had satirized them in stories. The so-called Know Nothing party had risen up partly in reaction to swelling numbers of Irish (fleeing the potato famine of 1848), German, French, Italian, and other non-English immigrants.

The mob also attempted to sack and burn the offices of the *New York Tribune* (Greeley was among the staunchest of abolitionists), and then began chasing and lynching blacks in the streets. The state militia was called in and the riot quelled, but not before as many as 1,000 people had died.[52]

Fitz Hugh saw blood in the water, and looked for an escape route. Like his father some 30 years earlier, he preferred not to engage too closely on behalf of principle, and so planned to leave New York.

(BRITISH LIBRARY)

1 *Harper's Monthly*, April 1860, p. 511.
2 Albert H. Smith, *Bayard Taylor*, Boston and New York: Houghton Mifflin and Company, 1896, p. 137-138.
3 Don Carlos Seitz, *Artemus Ward*, New York and London: Harper & Brothers, 1919, p. 68.

4 Elizabeth Pennell, *Charles Godfrey Leland*, Freeport, NY: Books for Libraries Press, 1970, p. 255. Leland in 1880 called *The Hasheesh Eater* "a book forgotten but of great vogue within my memory."

5 Henry Frey to John Frey, February 28, 1861, NYSHA Library.

6 S. Ludlow Frey to Caroline Frey, June 13, 1861, NYSHA Library.

7 Henry Frey to John Frey, May 17, 1861, NYSHA Library.

8 Augustus Frey to S. Ludlow Frey, 1861, NYSHA Library.

9 This diary is now among the Ludlow-Frey papers, NYSHA Library.

10 Reverend Henry was still as outspoken as ever. One of his particular targets was his parishioner Samuel Morse, who was in a peculiar position with regard to slavery, as he believed it to be a divine institution while also believing that secession was totally unacceptable. Morse sent Henry at one point in May ten closely written pages replying to a letter of Henry's, noting "the tone of your letter calls for extraordinary drafts on Christian charity...conscience in this matter has moved some Christians quite as strongly to view Abolitionism as a sin of the deepest dye, as it has other Christian minds to view Slavery as a sin, and so to condemn slaveholders to excommunication, and simply for being slaveholders." Samuel F. B. Morse to Henry Ludlow, May 13, 1861, NYSHA Library.

11 Bruce Catton, *The Coming Fury*, New York: Doubleday, 1961, p. 434.

12 Forerunner to the infamous *New York Post*.

13 Quoted in Niemeyer (1953), p. 11.

14 Fitz Hugh Ludlow to Mr. Hubbard, August 13, 1861.

15 Fitz Hugh Ludlow to Edmund Clarence Stedman, September 15, 1861.

16 Charles Henry Brown, *William Cullen Bryant*, New York: Scribner, 1971, p. 369.

17 Letter found in a copy of *The Hasheesh Eater* at the Library of Congress. Coffin could be Charles Carleton Coffin (1823-1896).

18 Charles Nordhoff, *Reminiscences of Some Editors I Have Known*, San Diego, CA: The Tuesday Club, 1900, p. 8.

19 Stedman and Gould (1910), p. 214.

20 Ibid., p. 253.

21 Dorman P. Eaton. *The Spoils System and Civil Service Reform in the Custom-House and the Post Office*, New York: G.P. Putnam & Sons, 1882, p. 22. Eaton noted that Collector Hiram Barney's predecessor, Mr. Schell, was an "intensely Democratic partisan from Tammany Hall." Barney, a Republican lawyer, removed 525 out of 702 officials, and "brought in a better class of men than he found...But he could not withstand the system."

22 Richmond C. Beatty, *Bayard Taylor, Poet Laureate of the Gilded Age*, Norman, OK: 1936, p. 250.

23 Helen Ludlow to Leander Hall, June 1, 1876, Schaffer Library.

24 Otis Skinner, *The Last Tragedian*, New York: Dodd, Mead & Company, 1939, p. 119.

25 Manuscript now in Houghton Library, Harvard University.

26 Fitz Hugh Ludlow to Charles Leland, November 27, 1861, Fitz Hugh Ludlow Collection. Clifton Waller Barrett Library Special Collections, University of Virginia Library (hereafter UVA).

27 Harper (1912), p. 183.

28 Edward Hingston, *The Genial Showman*, London: J.C. Hotten, 1871, p. 99. Clapp had long since suspended publication of the *Saturday Press*.

29 Caroline Frey to S. Ludlow Frey, April 29, 1862, NYSHA Library.

30 Helen Ludlow and Rosalie Ludlow, July 22, 1862, from Helen's diary, NYSHA Library.

31 Fitz Hugh Ludlow to Charles Leland, July 28, 1862, Historical Society of Pennsylvania.

32 Edward Carpenter, *Six Months at the White House*, Watkins Glen, NY: Century House, 1961, p. 8.

33 Cortland Auser, *Nathaniel P. Willis*, New York: Twayne Publishers, 1969, p. 128-9.

34 Vernon Loggins, *Where the World Ends: the Life of Louis Moreau Gottschalk*, Baton Rouge: Louisiana State University Press, 1958, p. xi.

35 Robert Tallant, *Voodoo in New Orleans*, p. 20; see also Fitz Hugh's experience in Florida, Chapter 9.

36 Gordon Hendricks, *Albert Bierstadt, Painter of the American West*, New York: Harrison House/Harry S. Abrams, Inc. (1973), 1988, p. 181.

37 Harold Clurman, *Lies Like Truth: Theatre Reviews and Essays*, New York: Macmillan, 1958.

38 Letter from Edwin Booth to William Winter, June 28, 1878, printed in Daniel J. Watermeier, editor, *Between Actor and Critic*, Princeton, NJ: Princeton University Press, 1971, p. 115.

39 Eleanor Ruggles, *Prince of Players: Edwin Booth*, New York: Norton, 1953, p. 127.

40 Henry Frey to John Frey, November 4, 1862, NYSHA Library.

41 Carrie Geddings to Caroline Frey, November 25, 1862, NYSHA Library.

42 Carrie Geddings to Caroline Frey, November 25, 1862, NYSHA Library.

43 S. Ludlow Frey to Caroline Frey, February 22, 1863, NYSHA Library.

44 Bruce Catton, *Terrible Swift Sword*, New York: Doubleday, 1963.

45 Gus Frey to Caroline Frey, February 13, 1863, NYSHA Library.

46 Gus Frey to Caroline Frey, March 9, 1863, NYSHA Library.

47 Carrie Geddings to Caroline Frey, February 8, 1863, NYSHA Library.

48 Edmund Clarence Stedman to Richard Henry Stoddard, January, 1863; printed in Stedman and Gould (1910), p. 308.

49 Charles Leland to Mrs. Charles Leland, January 13, 1863, in Elizabeth Robins Pennell, *Charles Godfrey Leland*, Boston: Houghton, Mifflin and Co., 1906.

50 Edwina Booth Grossman, *Edwin Booth: Recollections by his Daughter*, Freeport NY: Books for Libraries Press, 1894, 1970, p. 141.

51 Edwin Booth to Richard Henry Stoddard, in Otis Skinner, *The Last Tragedian*, New York: Dodd, Mead, 1939, p. 92.

52 Wilson (1902), p. 383.

XI.

THE OVERLAND STAGECOACH

"Go west young man, and grow up with the country," wrote Horace Greeley in the *New York Tribune* in 1851. The westward movement had begun in earnest in the 1830's as the early generations of colonists began to feel crowded. The Gold Rush erupted in the 1850's, setting the stage for a sea change in American culture that was only briefly slowed by the lack of information flow back to the East.

Fitz Hugh was an Easterner by birth and mindset. His travel experience had been confined to the eastern seaboard, albeit as far south as exotic Florida. His writing did not reference the western frontier as the defining characteristic of the country. He did not see, as Whitman had, some "frontiersman striding out of the wilderness to lead the country." The test of the country in Fitz Hugh's view was to establish the cultural life of America to be as distinct and independent from England and the rest of Europe as was its political life. But this independence was incremental, and would evolve organically from its European roots.

The Civil War had dashed these hopes against the rocks of internecine conflict. Fitz Hugh, like other intellectuals of his generation, were seeking new answers in the face of this great confusion. It was in this frame of mind that Fitz Hugh looked to the West. It was a new physical frontier, with an attraction similar to the spiritual frontiers opened by hashish. And it was a new cultural frontier, with inspiring perspectives on the eternal verities that were sure to fertilize Fitz Hugh's thoughts as the breathtaking Rocky Mountains had begun to inspire artists.

The western frontier had been romanticized in the East not only by poets like Whitman but artists as well. The most notable was painter Albert Bierstadt, one of the Hudson School of landscape painters. Bierstadt's trip to the West in 1859 had given him a whole new land in which to apply his techniques. Inspired by a Bayard Taylor lecture, he had accompanied a military expedition surveying a rail route through Wyoming to the Pacific, and spent half that year on that trip or along the Oregon trail.[1] Bierstadt's paintings, such as "Rocky Mountains—Lander's Peak," had captured the fancy of the patrons who visited the studios at the Tenth St. studio where Bierstadt and the others entertained. It was there, and among the Genteel Circle, that a friendship developed between the painter and Fitz Hugh. Soon, Fitz Hugh was calling attention to Bierstadt in reviews. For example, in May of 1863, Fitz Hugh described "Mountain Brook" in glowing terms in the *Evening Post*, possessing "nearly the same degree of excellence as his marvelous 'Light and Shadow' in last year's [National] Academy [of Design]" [a painting Ludlow had also glowingly reviewed in the *Post*].[2] Fitz Hugh also delivered a speech at the opening of the April show at the National Academy of Design which praised Bierstadt's work.

Bierstadt's growing reputation convinced a number of patrons to finance another western trip for the artist. Bierstadt offered Fitz Hugh the role of literary accompanist to chronicle the trip and whet the appetite of prospective art buyers with tales of the works in progress. Fitz Hugh convinced Godwin of the *Evening Post* to publish his commentary on the trip, and signed onto the expedition.

Rosalie however, was not a part of the plans. The West was no place for a lady, and Fitz Hugh was so caught up in the excitement that he did not really consider that Rosalie would do anything but faithfully wait for his return. Surely, their financial needs demanded action, and the publishing business had lagged during wartime. Yet the previous year's domestic unease was still hovering between them. In this context, it's interesting to note a contemporary description of the couple at an artists reception in March:

> ...not far distant, with his beautiful wife at his side, Fitz Hugh Ludlow, the author of 'The Hasheesh Eater', a work of unrivaled eloquence and genius; his dark eyes have a somewhat remote and dreamy expression as if he were still haunted by the remembrance of its perilous glooms and glories.[3]

Although the transportation arrangements were largely Bierstadt's, Fitz Hugh needed to raise some money in advance of the trip. He arranged for a story to be published in *Harper's*, his first there in over a year and a half, and submitted "The Battle and Triumph of Dr. Susan." The story would not appear until July, when Fitz Hugh was in Salt Lake City. Although the story appeared destined by its origins as a revenue producer to be one of Fitz Hugh's lesser genre efforts, "Susan" actually assumed a place in the steady progression of Fitz Hugh's storytelling craftsmanship, owing to the personal nature of its kernel.

It is the story of two women competing for one man, and one of these is Dr. Susan, physician at a familiar Ludlowian setting, a Water-cure. Dr. Susan is very competent and self possessed, and further, masculine in manner. In physical stature, "[s]he encroached on the region of the lesser virile longitudes" and her heroes ranged from Joan of Arc to Sappho. "She was a masculine soul—run by a freak into the feminine mould...when she dies she will become a strong-winged man-angel, not a golden-voiced woman one—finding at last her right place in the array of Being." The competition for the narrator's affection was nurse Helen Talfourd, a more typical Ludlowian heroine of demure beauty. Naturally, the narrator falls in love with her rather than Dr. Susan, although the good doctor has taken an equal romantic interest in her patient.

The story contained brief mystical touches, "...for days I had been vacillating on this side of the gate which lets men in from the Hither to the Farther Mysteries", and poetic flourishes, "an odor as of a whole almanac of Monday mornings condensed into one blissful moment by some hydraulic press." The story included several passages comprised entirely of dialogue, Fitz Hugh's first attempt at drama, inspired by his critical writings on theatre. When Helen later falls ill and only Dr. Susan can save her, Dr. Susan is at first unable to bring herself to save her rival, but finally gives in and does the right thing. Although the ending was Harper's happy for Mr. and Mrs. Narrator, Dr. Susan remains a lonely, tragic figure. In this, she appeared to be modeled after none other than Helen Ludlow, Fitz Hugh's sister who had so recently suffered romantic trauma. Dr. Susan faces her own loss by saying "I shall be useful, I shall be famous perhaps. There is something in these to live for." The narrator (and Fitz Hugh) adds his consolation, "in The Everlasting Life, give her to find that Twin-Soul which the world that is hath not for her!"

The other major autobiographical element in the story is Fitz Hugh speaking as the voice of the valetudinarian.[4] Fitz Hugh, with three trips to the water cure by this time, had this in common with the narrator who "staggered under the ninety five pounds of which the typhus fever had left me residual legatee." Fitz Hugh noted that "In hydropathic institutions, cure of anything more serious than a tooth-ache takes at the least several years," and he even articulated a typology of the water cure baths: 1) Nervous-complaint tubs; 2) Tubs containing Obstructions of the Biliary Ducts; and 3) Rheumatic and Gouty tubs. The patients of each spoke in a characteristic dialect. In one passage Fitz Hugh appeared to address his wife: "It is very hard for a man to become accustomed to the truth that a woman may regard him with veneration for other qualities than physical prowess." One of Fitz Hugh's motives for his journey to the West may well have been to prove to Rosalie that she had not married some chronically ill bookworm, but a more robust adventurer. Rosalie's admiration for men of action in their circle, like Stedman and Bierstadt himself, added some jealous energy to Fitz Hugh's proposed trip.

At any rate, the trip was the talk of their friends and family. Edwin Booth, recovering from the death of his wife, wrote "How I would rejoice if I could take the trip that Ludlow is to start on next May."[5] Cousin Gus, more pragmatically, thought "if I could get out of the army, I could then get the place [Fitz Hugh] now holds in the Customs House."[6] *The Evening Post* of May 12 announced:

Bierstadt, the artist, has departed on his journey to the 'far West'. He is accompanied by Fitz Hugh Ludlow, who, it is understood, will make copious notes of the tour, which, on his return, will be published in book form. Mr. William Hill, of Providence, and Horatio E. Durfee, of New Bedford, also accompany the artist. The party will go directly from here to San Francisco, stopping only for brief periods here and there, on their route, to make sketches and notes of the scenery and the people. While in the Yo Semite Valley they will be joined by two artist friends of Bierstadt—Messrs. Perry and Williams of San Francisco—and after a sojourn in the valley of two or three weeks, the entire party will proceed to the later-named city...They propose to be absent from six to eight months, so that it will probably be Christmas before they get back to New York.

Coincidentally, ten days later, another stagecoach set out with more pecuniary goals. "The party consists of William G. Fargo of the American Express Company; D. N. Barney, president of the United States Express Company, and of the company known as Wells, Fargo & Co.; B. P. Cheeney, managing director at Boston of Wells Fargo & Co; and Ben Halladay, of the Overland Stage Company...The purposes of the expedition are to look after and advance the great and growing interests of the several companies in California, and to enjoy the scenery and incidents of such a trip."[7] Perhaps not so coincidentally, Halladay had made special arrangements for Bierstadt and Fitz Hugh to travel via the Overland Mail Stagecoach. The "growing interests" of the company lay in the expanding exploitation of the Western territories. Bierstadt's paintings, like Greeley's editorials, represented terrific free advertising for the lands made accessible by the conveyances of Halladay and the others. Greeley himself had ridden on the first Overland Stage to Denver in 1859.[8]

HALLIDAY'S OVERLAND STAGE OFFICE IN DENVER IN THE 1860S.
(LIBRARY OF CONGRESS)

On a more scholarly note, the recently formed Smithsonian Institution had contacted Fitz Hugh and Bierstadt to request their assistance in mapping the western territory. The party took with them materials to help with this topographical contribution. The party also benefited from Fitz Hugh's marriage ties to Colonel William Osborne, Rosalie's cousin, and then President of the Platte County railroad between St. Joseph, Missouri and Atchison, Kansas Territory, the end of the line at the time.[9] Osborne provided them free transportation to Atchison, where the stagecoach journey would begin. Rosalie had prevailed upon Fitz Hugh to accompany him as far as the train (and civilization) reached, and so joined the party as they set out. The first leg of the journey took the travelers by train to Philadelphia, where Bierstadt was among several New York artists whose work was on display at the Academy of Art there. The Pennsylvania Central railroad then carried the crew through Pittsburgh and on to Ohio. They stopped in Cincinatti, visiting painter Thomas Buchanan Read, who was so taken with Rosalie's beauty that he offered to paint her portrait. The party then procured transport from the Ohio and Mississippi Railroad to St. Louis. Here they spent four days preparing for the journey. Supplies were acquired that had been neglected in New York, ranging "from blankets to black tea, from bowie-knives to blow-pipes."[10] While in St. Louis, the party visited with Robert Barnum, Fitz Hugh's old Kappa Alpha brother, now a businessman in the city. Barnum imparted one bit of wisdom and warning: "many people become insane crossing to California overland."[11]

Fitz Hugh took the opportunity to send off the first of his series of reports, entitled "Letters from Sundown," which appeared in the *Evening Post* on May 26. "In the dressing-gown and slippers of civilized life, I look through my window across the Missouri to a land which is the front-yard of barbarism."[12] The Mississippi River lived up to its Big Muddy billing, as Fitz Hugh remarked on the hotel plumbing where "the faucets apparently ran nothing but hot and cold mud. Iced mud was presented to slake the thirst."[13]

The Civil War was not a constant fact of life here. "Despite the bitter feeling between the large secession element of St. Louis and the much larger Union population, business is thriving, and among the loyal classes society is gay." But the War was not entirely without impact. A presidential edict banning rebel sympathizers was put into effect in Northern territories, and some fifty men had been imprisoned in

St. Louis. Fitz Hugh had apparently obtained a letter of introduction from Schuyler Colfax, then speaker of the House of Representatives, which gained him admittance to the Fort where the rebel sympathizers were held, and one of them told him "d__d if this isn't the best thing Abe could do for the Confederacy. It's only recruiting for Jeff. Davis, that's all." In neighboring St. Joseph, Fitz Hugh described the jailed sympathizers as being now "among the people whose brothers they helped the most hellish set of ruffians ever collected to hack, slit and disembowel…They will wake up some night before long with a noose round their necks."[14]

Fitz Hugh bid a sad but not tearful farewell to Rosalie as the expedition boarded the Platte County railroad from St. Joseph to Atchison in the Kansas territory and the beginning of the Overland Stage route. On May 31, Rosalie boarded a steamer to Omaha from St. Louis, and wrote to her father and sister:

> I should have advised you long ere this of Fitz's movements after leaving St. Louis but I myself was in suspense until just before I came on board this boat en route for Omaha with a pleasure party of St. Josephians. I am taking the first opportunity I have had since hearing from Fitz. I had hoped to hear from you while at Cousin William's but I daresay I shall find a letter for me at St. Louis.

She continued on June 2:

> I have just arrived by Steamer and find to my great sorrow not one letter from anybody. I wish you would write to the widow and afflicted next to hearing from Fitz—whom I am beginning to think about as one forever lost to me it is so long since I have heard from him. I should like to have

communicated with his Father and sister. I enclose to you the only letter which I have received from him. When we were here before Fitz and I together wrote you both a long letter. Have you ever received it?

But I am feeling very unhappy this morning—a broken night's rest on the boat and no letters this morning make me nearer the blues than I have been since Fitz left.

Well, I hope I shall hear from Fitz and from you soon. Perhaps you are sick or have written to Chicago where I am going in a week or ten days to the care of James A. Smith, Chicago, Illinois. But goodbye until I feel better.[15]

But Fitz Hugh was indeed embarked on a new life, unlike any he'd known before. The day of their arrival in Atchison, "we were invited to a hanging."[16]

Lynch, C. J., was to sit that afternoon upon a couple of bush-whackers. His is a most impartial tribunal, which to avoid giving offense, acquits nobody...The sentence being deter-mined...he was lifted to the wagon, the rope was adjusted, the wagon driven away, and there, a horrid fruit of man's hate-ful passions, he hung, uncovered to all vengeful eyes...As the poor wretch swung there, now past injuring them, and to all noble natures an object of pity, if only for the first time, the men cracked their brutal jokes, and women laughed at them... Women in the dress of ladies leaned across the tea-table and asked, "Have you been to the hanging?" with as much sang-froid as a New Yorker might say, "Have you seen Faust?"

On June 5, Fitz Hugh sent along the second "Letter from Sundown," this one originating from the Comstock ranch in Nebraska. Comstock was a sixty-year-old widower, who lived on a ranch with several of his children and grandchildren. The house-hold was run by his two daughters, "who for skillful housewifery, sterling common sense, and native refinement, are surpassed by few women whom I ever met at the East. It was a perpetual surprise to me to hear girls whose whole life had been spent on the Plains or in the backwoods, talk of Longfellow and Bryant, Dickens and Thackeray, Scott and Cooper, when they came in from the milking."[17] Needless to say, the exotic literary man Fitz Hugh was as welcome to their eyes as they to his aesthetic, and temporarily bachelor, eye.

The men soon embarked on a buffalo hunt to provide Bierstadt his first subjects of local color. Fitz Hugh was full participant in the hunt by his own account:

> There is a magnificent bull eighty yards before me, and to the left. I whirl my carbine round from my back, and take what I consider good aim for a shot behind the fore-shoulder. But I am green to the work—my horse's gallop throws up my piece—my ball whistles over—and my first bison has another lease on the prairies.[18]

Meanwhile, one of the veterans of the Comstock ranch had wounded a bison and called Bierstadt to make a sketch of a live bull. Fitz Hugh observed, "I seemed to see Prometheus on his rock...It was the first time I had seen moral grandeur in a brute."[19] After a rest, one of the Comstock people expressed a wish to get at the cows of the herd, which entailed some flanking maneuvers on horseback. In the course of these, Fitz Hugh was separated by the buffalo stampede. "I was entirely separated from my companions. The ground was in splendid order for running; my horse had acquired his 'second wind', and his enthusiasm fully equalled my own. I never knew the ecstasy of the mad gallop until now...I looked over my shoulder: there in plain sight was another herd, tearing down on our rear…For nearly a mile in width stretched a line of angry faces, a rolling surf of wind-blown hair, a row of quivering lanterns, burning reddish-brown… It was death to turn back. I should be trampled and gored to death." The herd ahead divided into two columns to pass around a low butte. "Quick as lightning this providential move of theirs suggested the means of my salvation. I made for the mound, reached its summit, and to [his horse's] great disgust, though he was fearfully short-breathed, and trickling with rivulets of sweat, halted him instantly to await the rear column." Two rifle shots to the center of the herd served to split the stampede into two columns which passed on either side. "I was safe; I had such a view of buffaloes as I never could have expected, never would enjoy again."[20] This was indeed the kind of stirring adventure for which Fitz Hugh had been hoping. At dinner that night, "There was a dreamy quiet over the whole twilight landscape, and I sat in it smoking my pipe, with a sense of perfect rest."[21]

In addition to the thrill of the hunt, Fitz Hugh spent large amounts of time filling his fieldbook with descriptions of the surrounding geology, soil and plant life, a self-described "amateur scientist". Some of the sights "staggered me in my own preconceived view, and that of many geologists, regarding the igneous origin of the harder conglomerates."[22] Fitz Hugh was no trained scientist, but would admit no limit to the eclectic range of his intellect. Later in the trip, he theorized that the frequent tornadoes of the Plains are born by forcing condensed air that is heated over the Plains during the day and then forced through canyons in the mountains, where they were "concentrating themselves and acquiring a vertical motion."[23] These statements were not quite as naive in their time as they sound today, and Fitz Hugh was a careful observer, if not a professional scientist. He took notes on a multitude of other topics:

> [A fresh killed antelope was served without condiments,] nor would sauce of any piquant kind have been anything but an unwarrantable intrusion on the inmost Eleusinian mysteries of gourmanderie.[24]
>
> Above us was the great pure dome of a heaven so free from all taint of earthly smoke that the stars seemed to have been let down like cressets leagues closer to our heads than in the city, and burned in diamond points without veil or trembling.[25]
>
> The simplest saying of any man who has lived like these pioneers much away from his kind takes the form of an aphorism. He has not been where he could give away the sap of his reflection before it crystallized.[26]

ALBERT BIERSTADT, *THE BUFFALO TRAIL*, 1867.
(MUSEUM OF FINE ARTS, BOSTON)

And as for the raunchier campfire stories, Fitz Hugh would only say, "O, if one could only print the good things which musn't be printed, what a book that would be."[27] After the buffalo hunt, it was back to the stagecoach. Fitz Hugh found his favorite box seat next to the driver unoccupied, "thus avoiding the dreadful grudge which is created in the minds of a stageful of insides, by newcomers entering at an inhuman hour, with a proposition to re-sort their heads and legs."[28] Their drivers were all of a mold after the legendary William Trotter, subject of countless tall tales. For example, their first driver told Fitz Hugh that "When I fust came out from Ameriky (and that's the universal phrase for getting west of the Missouri River) I found lots o' bad liquor here. It 'curred to me that ef I pitched right in, I might help him to drink it all up shortly. But after tryin' that on a matter o' three years, I found they had kept a gainin' on me and that the folk had a dam sight more of it than I supposed. They kept a bringin' and a bringin' it on—and finally, when I began to see the turkeys a walkin' round with little green hats on, I reckoned it was time to quit."[29]

Fitz Hugh found that "the happiest hours of the trip were those which I spent on the box. This was a place where legs were stretchable and faculties wide awake."[30] Indeed, Fitz Hugh rode there, for twenty-four hour stretches, through changes in drivers, until exhaustion forced him into the coach for a crowded, fitful sleep. There he dreamt of desperately pursuing a comfortable sleeping place all the way to the Congress where he was thwarted by members of the "Anti-Sleep Party" who carried him off and he awoke "jolted down upon the floor of the stage."[31]

From the driver in Nebraska, Fitz Hugh found that all western emigrants were called pilgrims. This term, with its religious connotations, even applied to a gentleman who "drove bulls with a black snake, swore blood-curdlingly and chewed literal pounds of plug tobacco…After that shock to pre-conceived opinions I should not have been staggered if a turn of the road had brought me on a prophet playing penny-poker or an apostle shooting prairie-hens."[32] Among these pilgrims were a "very picturesque party of Germans going to Oregon." Fitz Hugh's eye began to wander in earnest: "I never saw so many bright and comely faces in an emigrant train. One real little beauty, who showed the typical German blonde through all her tan, peered out of one great canvas wagon cover, like a baby under the bonnet of the Shaker giantess, and coqueted for a moment with us from a pair of wicked-innocent blue eyes, drawing back, when the driver stared at her, in nicely simulated confusion."[33]

Fitz Hugh's stage continued across Kansas, and reached the Platte River where the North and South forks of the Platte met. (Fitz Hugh called the Platte "the shallow politician among streams.")[34] The stage then followed the South Platte another 274 miles to Denver, a total of 650 miles from their starting point in Atchison. Fitz Hugh describes his first view of the Rocky Mountains:

> To see what they looked, and know what they were, was like a sudden revelation of the truth, that the spiritual is the only real and substantial; that the eternal things of the universe are they which afar off seem dim and faint.[35]

The Bierstadt-Ludlow party reached Denver around June 10, 1863. They were greeted by Governor Evans, the first Governor of the territory, who immediately offered them use of his personal horses and carriage to explore the surrounding area. The travelers decided to spend several days in and around Denver before heading on to Salt Lake City. Specifically, Bierstadt was interested in visiting the Pikes Peak region, and the spectacular Garden of the Gods rock formations near Colorado Springs. Fitz Hugh suggested they also survey Central City, a mountain town that was the center of mining activity in the Colorado territory. Mr. John Pierce, the "surveyor-general" of the territory, and Chief Justice Hall officiated as "sage, philosopher and friend" to the party as they traveled south to Colorado Springs. A later book asserts that the name "Colorado Springs" was first used by the famous traveler and writer, Fitz-Hugh Ludlowe [*sic*], who visited the region in '67.[36]

Bierstadt was busily occupied with color sketches of the Garden while Fitz Hugh roamed among the formations "weathered into all manner of curious profiles, here simulating a griffin, here a Goddess of Liberty, here an eagle, and a dolphin supporting a shield after the old heraldic style, and everywhere some strange likeness which needs no vivid imagination to decipher its meaning."[37] Other formations became "idols, gypsies about their camp-fire, witches, or mummies in their coffins." "The Wonders of Colorado" appeared in the July 24 and 25 editions of the *Evening Post*, still under the general title "Letters from Sundown; The Artists' Western Expedition," and carrying only the initials F.H.L. at the end. Also in this edition of the *Post* was a review of the August edition of *Harper's Monthly*, including an excerpt from its feature story, "The Battle and Triumph of Doctor Susan."

After Colorado Springs, William Byers, editor of the *Rocky Mountain News*, took Bierstadt to an area that is now the city of Idaho Springs.[38] Byers later recounted several

Bierstadt anecdotes.[39] At one mountain vista, Bierstadt was immediately taken and said "I must get a study in colors; it will take me fifteen minutes." He then proceeded to work silently until finished. When done, Bierstadt packed up his materials and said "There, was I more than fifteen minutes?" to which Byers replied "Yes, you were at work forty-five minutes by the watch!" Byers also described a fishing session in a stream where the fish were so easy to catch that Bierstadt abandoned his hook and "caught them with his naked hand. Sometimes he would touch the fish with the ends of this fingers and rub it back and forth very gently for quite a little time before seizing it. The fish appeared to enjoy the sensation and would lean up against his fingers. I called it 'tickling them out of the water.' In this way he caught, in a few minutes, I think, eighteen."

Fitz Hugh, along with Messrs. Perry and Williams visited Central City, the "settlement which has been built up by the mining interest of Colorado." Although the city was teeming with miners and visitors, the Easterners managed to get accomodations and spent the first evening at the Central City "Opera House" where he was surprised to see some genuinely good acting. He had been prepared to see poor, and noted that "My devotion for the histrionic art brushes two extremes—best of all I love splendid acting, next best do I love the abominably poor sort."[40]

Several days later, editor Byers took Fitz Hugh and Bierstadt seventy miles west of Denver into the mountains, where Bierstadt made several color studies of a mountain of "over 15,000 feet, or considerably taller than Mont Blanc...The blue of the sky was so intense that if Bierstadt paints it up to its exact truth, no dweller in the plains will believe him."[41] (Ironically, Bierstadt's paintings later came to be criticized as exaggerating the dramatic beauty of the mountains.) Fitz Hugh wrote about that mountain the following tribute to one who apparently was not constantly on his mind, but who was on Bierstadt's:

> That glorious roseate mountain stood nameless among the peaks in its virgin vail of snow; so Bierstadt, by right of first portrayal, baptized it after one far away from our sides, but very near and dear to our hearts—a gentle nature who had followed us clear to the verge of our Overland wanderings at Atchison, and parted from us bravely lest she should make our purpose fainter by seeming moved. Henceforth, that shining peak is MONTE ROSA.[42]

PAINTER ALBERT BIERSTADT (1830-1902), FITZ HUGH LUDLOW'S
ERSTWHILE FRIEND AND LATER ROMANTIC RIVAL.

Rosalie Ludlow had long since retraced her steps back east from St. Louis, and was not entirely depressed. She had enough spirit left on the way to accept the invitation of Thomas Buchanan Read in Cincinatti to pose for a portrait.[43] Rosa did not need a husband to be assured of sufficient attention.

While Bierstadt sketched, Fitz Hugh made two descents into the gold mines of Colorado (Bobtail Lode and Gregory Lode), one by means of a bucket. Fitz Hugh reported that this, "as a first experience of getting let down a hole two hundred and twenty five feet deep at the end of a vibrating rope, was somewhat appalling."[44] Fitz Hugh reported in detail on the methods of mining, the geological character of the gold found in the region, and the history of the Colorado gold rush, in the July 30 *Evening Post*, in an installment of "Letters From Sundown (No. IV)" entitled "The Colorado Gold Mines." By this time, the "Letters" were carrying Fitz Hugh's full byline.

On June 23, after a two week stay in the Denver area, Fitz Hugh, Bierstadt and the rest returned to the Overland Stage for the trip to Salt Lake City. Through a friend of theirs in New York, the artist, author and physician Dr. Fessenden N. Otis, the party had letters of introduction along the Stage line from Otis' brother, the Overland Road superintendent. However, these letters did not greatly ease the harsh conditions of the trip. Fitz Hugh later offered a "recipe" for recreating the stagecoach experience:

> Procure a stout Irishman—two pair of anvils—a pine plank six inches wide—a very salt ham—one hundred pounds of Babbitt's baking soda—three muskets—and a large variety of rubbish, such as canteens, old boxes, and carpet bags stuffed

with brickbats. Convey these into a room as nearly air-tight as possible and heated by a large register from a patent furnace. Lay the plank across two chairs, and stretch between the chairs a strap of the hardest raw-hide you can procure. Sit down on the plank, contract your chest to its smallest dimensions, shut your knees together; then have the anvils symmetrically arranged on each side of you, so that one pair compresses your shoulders and another your knees. Should this compression, as may well happen, fail to give you an adequate idea of the original, a few wooden wedges may be judiciously driven in between the anvils and your person. When you are securely keyed into position, order the attendant to insert the heaviest of the carpet-bags between your legs. If he be at all skillful he will be able with but slight difficulty to arrange it so that a corner of one of the bricks with which it is stuffed rests accurately against your ankle-bone. He will then distribute the canteens and other rubbish about your feet and legs, tangling, if possible the strings and handles, but leaving uncovered a single toe upon which he will set the butt of the heaviest musket. The others are to be held across your lap. These preliminaries settled, you will have a nice idea of the Overland Stage stopping at a station. You now wish to attain its sensation in a state of motion through the alkali ruts. For this purpose, order your Irishman (whom you have previously, of course, provided with the stoutest purchaseable pair of cowhide boots) to kick you with the utmost violence, at intervals never more than three minutes apart, but always irregular that you may be totally unprepared for the shock. Between kicks, your attendant will from time to time throw onto your face a handful of the Babbitt's Saleratus—in the way of giving you an approach to the notion of the Overland atmosphere. A person with the requisite self control may in addition greatly increase the liveliness of his conceptions by refraining entirely from the use of water for twelve hours at a time, and then drinking nearly a quart of swamp-drainings seasoned with brimstone, table salt and potash. Three times during the day he will request his attendant to warm over the register a slice of ham two inches thick, which he will proceed to eat when the fat is partially melted. It is desirable that he should sleep between kicks, in order that his head may drop and strike upon one of the anvils, but all experimenters have not the fortitude to complete the vraisemblance of the trip by this felicitous addition...A faithful adherence to the above method for seven days and nights will give the domestic traveler an experience as nearly resembling the original as he can hope for.[45]

The party took seven days to make the trip to Salt Lake City. The Overland Route took them north from Denver to Virginia Dale, and then across what is now southern Wyoming. They crossed the Laramie plains south of Elk Mountain, and descended to the Platte river, which they crossed by ferryboat at a point southeast of what is now Rawlins, Wyoming. Here, the Duck Lake Station of the Overland Stage, was the halfway point of the journey between the Missouri River and the California terminus of the stagecoach line. They were 983 miles out from Atchison and 272 miles from Salt Lake City, with 930 miles to go to the Pacific Coast.

Along the way, they passed such notable landmarks as "The Dirty Woman's Ranch" and "the Wind River Range, and Lander's peak, its monarch, so that I could make the long desired comparison of Nature's reality with Bierstadt's famous portrait of it."[46] They also passed bands of Arapahoe and Shoshone Indians, the latter notable as one of few that were friendly toward the white settlers. Fitz Hugh's impressions along this leg of the journey were colored by literary and cultural allusions. He compared a driver who drove at a breakneck speed in a blinding storm to "Quintus

Curtius at $50 a month."[47] He also tasted mineral water which "reminded me strongly of a very favorite foreign water, the Vichy." Fitz Hugh noted that their route took them "over a country so demoniacally wild that Gustave Dore should have seen its vast basaltic cliffs, its heaped up mass of trap rock seeming the foundations of some colossal city long since dead, its strange precipices carven into ghastly profiles—before he drew the horrid solitudes through which he sent his wandering Jew."[48] Fitz Hugh took copious notes for the naturalists in his audience, although most of these detailed observations did not make their way into the *Post* articles.[49] Fitz Hugh studied the geology of the area, such as "fossil beds which fill the heart of the geologist with delight," although with limited time he could only identify Ostracidae and an Inoceramus.[50] Messrs. Otis and Halladay had instructed their drivers to halt upon the request of the Ludlow/Bierstadt party for half hour periods of specimen gathering. Most of these were wrapped in bags of India rubber cloth brought from the east for the purpose.

Halladay had indeed done a great deal for the expedition, and Fitz Hugh was ever mindful of their debt and proselytized for the stage line at several opportunities in his published travelogues. He offered the opinion that a steady intercommunication was necessary to keep the Pacific States from forming a separate union in the future.[51] Fitz Hugh also commended the tight management of Halladay. He mentions seeing him at a reception at Dodsworth's in New York City just before the artists had departed. Then a station keeper near the Platte River told him that Halladay had just visited the day before Fitz Hugh's party arrived. (Remember also that Halladay had been traveling with

FITZ HUGH LUDLOW AROUND THE TIME OF HIS OVERLAND STAGE
JOURNEY. (SCHAFFER LIBRARY, UNION COLLEGE)

William Fargo in a party that had left New York ten days after Fitz Hugh.) "The indomitable energy required of the man...could keep in steady running order a daily freight and passenger line across the entire Continent. [Halladay] was forever dropping into cabins under the snow-peaks and adobes sweltering on the sand of the desert; making the master's eye felt by the very horses."[52] Referring to the beneficial aspects of mountain air in treating tuberculosis, Fitz Hugh supported the long discussed Pacific Railroad as the way to make this health spot accessible to sufferers in the rest of the country. This testimonial was perhaps for the benefit of Rosalie's uncle William Osborne, who may have entertained notions of expanding his Platte County railroad from Atchison to points further west.

In early August, the travelers crossed the Great Divide through Bridger Pass. "There is something indescribably sublime, a conception of universality, in that sense of standing on the water-shed of a hemisphere...having made our triumphal passage from the Atlantic to the Pacific slope of the Continent through Bridger's pass, [we] came down by way of Fort Bridger to Salt Lake City."

1 *Denver Post*, May 17, 1987, p. 2F.
2 *The New York Evening Post*, May 16, 1863, p. 1. In the same article, Fitz Hugh praises a portrait by his friend Frank Carpenter of none other than the Reverend Henry G. Ludlow—"those who remember the original will recognize this copy as one of the happiest possible successes in portraiture."
3 Unidentified clipping cited in Hendricks (1973), p. 135.
4 The condition of being an invalid.
5 Skinner (1939), p. 92.
6 Gus Frey to Caroline Frey, March 9, 1863, NYSHA Library.
7 *New York Evening Post*, May 22, 1863, p. 2.

8 Federal Writers Project, *Colorado*, p. 81, claimed that one purpose of the trip was to produce material for railroad brochures—this book, however, is generally unreliable.

9 The Osborn family apparently used both spellings, Osborn and Osborne—some references to Rosalie and her father use the latter, most do not.

10 Fitz Hugh Ludlow, "Letters from Sundown," *New York Evening Post*, May 26, 1863, p. 1.

11 Fitz Hugh Ludlow, *The Golden Era*, "Reminiscences of an Overlander," February, 1864.

12 "Letters from Sundown," May 26, 1863, p. 1.

13 Ibid.

14 All quotes in this paragraph, Ibid., p. 1, 2.

15 Rosalie Ludlow to Amos Osborne and Mary Osborn, May 31, 1863, NYSHA Library.

16 Fitz Hugh Ludlow, *The Heart of the Continent*, New York and London: Hurd and Houghton, 1870. The book was a compilation of diary notes and reports published contemporaneously with the trip. Quotes included here are considered an accurate account of Fitz Hugh's experiences and feelings during the trip.

17 *Heart of the Continent*, p. 29.

18 "Letters from Sundown," June 5, 1863, p. 1.

19 *Heart of the Continent*, p. 68.

20 Ibid., p. 72-75.

21 Ibid., p. 89.

22 Ibid., p. 97.

23 Ibid., p. 170.

24 Ibid., p. 50.

25 Ibid., p. 57.

26 Ibid., p. 58.

27 Ibid., p. 60.

28 Ibid., p. 106.

29 "Reminiscences of an Overlander," February 21, 1864, p. 1.

30 Ibid.

31 Ibid.

32 Ibid.

33 *Heart of the Continent*, p. 111.

34 "Letters from Sundown," July 24, 1863, p. 1.

35 *Heart of the Continent*, p. 131.

36 Manly Dayton Ormes, *The Book of Colorado Springs*, Colorado Springs, CO: Dentan Printing Company, 1933, p. 3.

37 *Heart of the Continent*, p. 148.

38 William Newton Byers, "Bierstadt's Visit to Colorado," *Magazine of Western History*, January 1890, p. 237.

39 Fitz Hugh did not in published travel writings describe Bierstadt or any of his fellow travellers.

40 "Letters from Sundown," July 30, 1863, p. 1.

41 "Reminiscences of an Overlander," February 28, 1864, p. 1.

42 Ibid.

43 Reproduced in Gordon Hendricks, *Albert Bierstadt*, New York: Harrison House/Harry Abrams Inc., 1988, p. 114.

44 "Letters from Sundown," July 30, 1863, p. 1.

45 "Reminiscences of an Overlander," January 31, 1864, p. 5.

46 "Reminiscences of an Overlander," March 6, 1864, p. 1.

47 *Heart of the Continent*, p. 273. Fitz Hugh compared his disregard for his own personal safety to Quintus Curtius in *The Hasheesh Eater*.

48 "Reminiscences of an Overlander," March 6, 1864, p. 1.

49 "Reminiscences of an Overlander," March 6, 1864, p. 1.

50 *Heart of the Continent*, p. 269.

51 Ibid., p. 219.

52 Ibid., p. 249.

XII.

AMONG THE MORMONS

"Never been in Utah afore, I reckon?" said the driver half interrogatively.

"No nearer than the Wind River Mountains."

"They don't have many o'them fellows there?"

"What fellows?"

"Why, these here Mormons," said with a slighting tone.

"You don't seem to like them much, judging from your tone," opined Fitz Hugh. "That's unfortunate, seeing you have to drive thirty or forty miles every day in their country. But you jest use them well, and go your own way quietly, you'll never get anything but good treatment from them. If you're a new hand here, as I should judge you are, take an old traveler's advice, and always think half a dozen times before you speak once. If you should happen to be overheard talking about Mormons in such a tone by that tall young man with the bushy eyebrows who sat opposite me at breakfast, you'd be spotted at once, and it might make no end of trouble for you all along the road. You know whom I mean—that brown-complexioned young Mormon: what's his name?"

The driver, lulled by this speech, blurted out "Cowperthwaite! Well—why—why—how did you know he was a Mormon?"

"D'ye remember how the girl knew her father? Jest as easy! How do I know you are one? The same way."

"Well, that's so! No use o' concealin' on it as I know. I ain't ashamed o't,—you bet! But d—d if you aint a queer 'un? You beat my time, anyhow. Wall, I'm glad to see you're so friendly."[1]

Thus did Fitz Hugh and company make their first contact with Mormonism a safe one. For, as Fitz Hugh pointed out, "nothing happens along the great avenues to Salt Lake, of which Brigham Young does not get the earliest advices... The secret police system of France was never more efficient than Brigham Young's...The 'one-man power' system is hastening towards its final extinction, but its last days are its greatest. It dies giving birth to two of its grandest exemplars in a single age—Louis Napoleon and Brigham Young."[2]

The group spent a night at Fort Bridger, garrisoned by detachments from Nebraska, Kansas, and Colorado regiments. They left the next day, much to Fitz Hugh's disappointment as there was an Indian powwow scheduled to take place that day, which "would have supplied much valuable genre material."[3] Three soldiers were detailed to escort the stage from the Fort to Salt Lake City, as Indian massacres were an occasional hazard. Fitz Hugh and the others, however, were less than pleased with the extra crowd, and "our intellects, prevented by long cramping and distortion of their fleshly receptacle, lacked the equanimity for a just striking of the balance between death by scalping and the same disaster more slowly effected by squeezing."[4] The rest of the trip passed safely, and gradual indications of the past presence of the Great Salt Lake became evident in the scenery. Not long after these, signs of the Mormon occupation appeared in the form of green fields:

> With a delight no words can paint, no heart can feel save that of a traveller who for a thousand miles has seen the earth beneath his feet an almost unbroken ashen gray, or burnt brown, did we look out upon a boundless scope of living green—green grass, green grain- fields, green gardens.[5]

And not long after that came the encounter that confirmed the identity of the tenders of the field. At one of the first farmhouses, Fitz Hugh sought to purchase some fresh milk. A matronly woman greeted him and escorted him to the dairy closet of a house full of babies and two young women.

"Those are very pretty babies," offered Fitz Hugh politely.

"Yes I think so," she replied, "but you must allow for a grandmother's partiality."

"These young ladies are your daughters, then?"

"They are my daughters-in-law, sir."

"So you have both your sons and their wives with you? Indeed you are to be envied, with such a delightful home about you in other respects."

"These babies, sir, "answered the woman gravely, "are the children of my *son*, now abroad on the Lord's business—my son, Mr. Kimball, after whom this place is called. These young ladies are his wives and I am the first wife of one you have often ere this heard of in the States—Heber Kimball, second President, and next to our prophet Brigham Young in the government of Utah." Fitz Hugh was stunned:

> I, a cosmopolitan, a man of the world, liberal to other people's habits and opinions to a degree which had often subjected me to censure among strictarians in the Eastern States, blushed to my very temples, and had to retire into the privacy of my tipped milk-bowl to screen the struggle by which I restored my moral equipoise...I had been thinking about Mormon peculiarities all day long; yet the first apparition to my senses of that which had absorbed my intellect, took me entirely aback![6]

Fitz Hugh pondered further,

> How could those pretty young women sit and look at each other's babies...see, each in the opposite infant, the plain ap-ostolic seal stamped on its little countenance,—yet rock away

so cheerfully...besister each other...What strange unsexing operation must their souls have gone through to keep them from frenzy—murder—suicide? I afterward put this question to their father-in-law, Heber the first, and his terse, all-conclusive explanation was, "Triumph o' grace."[7]

Fitz Hugh's "poor monogamic brain" kept wondering as the party traversed the final thirty miles into Salt Lake City. The party moved into the Salt Lake Hotel, "the only one frequented by Gentiles," located on the main street. Their arrival into Salt Lake City came only 16 years after the Mormons themselves had arrived. It was then that Brigham Young went up to a mountain and an angel appeared unto him from God and "the martyred prophet", Mormon founder Joseph Smith, telling him that this was the promised land. Now there were 17,000 people in the city, with a total of 80,000 Mormons living in the territory.

Not long after their arrival on July 1, Fitz Hugh, Bierstadt, and three other members of the party were invited to attend the Fourth of July ball. Although the Mormons did not consider themselves part of the United States, having undergone continuous persecution for their unorthodox beliefs, they celebrated the holiday as a sort of secular summer party. Since the Mormons celebrate Sabbath on Saturday, they had moved the ball to the evening of July 3, with festivities to begin at 4 P.M. After a night's rest, Fitz Hugh and Bierstadt were greeted the morning of the third by Heber Kimball, Brigham Young's right hand man. Kimball welcomed them as fellow New Yorkers. Fitz Hugh knew Ontario County, where Joseph Smith claimed to have dug up tablets of scripture on which the church was based, from taking a water cure at Clifton. Kimball diplomatically did not chide Fitz Hugh for not taking the spiritual opportunity of visiting the birthplace of Mormonism, and took them around the city on a leisurely tour. Among the sites were Brigham Young's two houses, located across the street from "the temple whose magnificent foundations are now rising in colossal blocks of bird's eye granite." In and around the city, "the traveller finds much to expand his mind." During the tour, Kimball had cause to reference several of his wives, including German, Danish, and Irish women. Fitz Hugh thought that after this recitation, Heber's first wife, would by this time be regarded by Heber as "a forgotten fossil in the Lower Silurian strata of his connubial life." But Heber even surprised him here, by saying "Yes! that is my first wife, and the best woman God ever made!"[8]

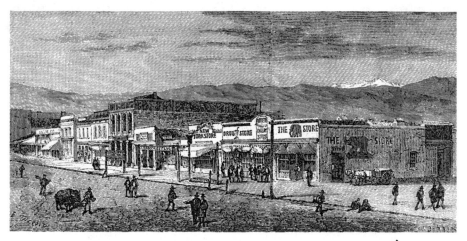

MAIN STREET, SALT LAKE CITY AT THE TIME OF LUDLOW'S AND BIERSTADT'S VISIT.

After these initial observances of polygamy, Fitz Hugh was quite curious to see what manner of preachers the Mormons were, Fitz Hugh himself having been born into the profession. Heber was his first subject: "I have heard men who could misquote Scripture to suit their purpose, and talk a long time without saying anything; but in both these particulars Heber Kimball far surpassed the loftiest efforts within my previous experience."

HEBER C. AND VILATE KIMBALL AND FAMILY.

Seven women shall take a hold o' one man! There! What d'ye think o' that? Shall! Shall take a hold on him! That don't mean they shan't, does it? No! God's word means what it says, and therefore means no otherwise—not in no way, shape, nor manner. Not in no Way, for He saith, 'I am the Way, and the truth, and the life.' Not in no shape, for 'a man beholdeth his nat'r'l shape in a glass.' Nor in no manner, for 'he straightway forgetteth what manner of man he was.' Seven women shall catch a hold on him. And ef they shall, then they will! For everything shall come to pass and not one good word shall fall to the ground. You who try to explain away the Scriptur' would make it fig'rative. But don't come to ME with none o' yer spiritooalizers! Not one good word shall fall. Therefore seven shall not fall. And ef seven shall catch a hold on him,—and as I jist proved, seven will catch a hold on him,—then seven ought; and in the latter-day glory, seven, yea, as our Lord said un-tew Peter, 'Verily I say un-tew you, not seven but seventy times seven,' these seventy times seven shall catch a hold and cleave. Blessed day! For the end shall be even as the beginning, and seventy-fold more abundantly. Come over into my garden.

Fitz Hugh concluded "This invitation always wound up the homily...if there ever could be any hope of our conversion, it was just about the time we stood in Brother Heber's fine orchard...having sound doctrine poked down our throats, with gooseberries as big as plums, to take the taste out of our mouths, like jam after castor oil."[9] Fitz Hugh, Bierstadt and the other artists were the only Gentiles invited by President Young to attend the ball with around 3,000 latter day saints. "Under these circumstances I felt like the three-thousandth homeopathic dilution of monogamy."[10] Fitz Hugh upon arrival sought out Young to thank him for the flattering exception made to the Gentiles. Flattery, however, likely had little to do with their invitation. "Brigham had become decidedly wary of writing men," wrote a later commentator, "having met many who came with honeyed words and departed to spit brimstone. When gentlemen of the press appeared, the Prophet put on his clean shirt and his best company manners, then detailed Porter [Rockwell, the "enforcer" of Mormondom] to observe the wanderings of the scribes about the Holy City and to guide their footsteps away from certain apostates and Gentiles who knew too much."[11]

Fitz Hugh approached the great man standing in a balcony of the theatre, "looking down on the dancers with an air of mingled hearty kindness and feudal ownership."[12] Brigham Young as Fitz Hugh saw him was a man about five foot ten, bordering on the portly, and appearing to be in his forties, although actually he was almost seventy years old:

His hair is a rich curly chestnut, formerly worn long, in supposed imitation of the apostolic coiffure, but now cut in our practical Eastern fashion, as accords with the man of business, whose metier he has added to apostleship with the growing temporal prosperity of Zion…Like any Eastern party-goer, he is habited in the 'customary suit of solemn black,' and looks very distinguished in this dress, though his daily homespun detracts nothing from the feeling, when in his presence, that you are beholding a most remarkable man.

Brigham's manners astonish any one who knows that his only education was a few quarters of such common school experience as could be had in Ontario County, Central New York, during the early part of the century.[13]

Brigham began their conversation at the theatre by telling Fitz Hugh that he was late; it was after nine o'clock. Fitz Hugh replied that "this was the time we usually set about dressing for an evening party in Boston or New York." "Yes," offered Brigham, "you find us an old-fashioned people; we are trying to return to the healthy habits of patriarchal times." "Need you go back so far as that for your parallel? It strikes me that we might have found four-o'clock balls among the *early* Christians." This is surely Fitz Hugh at his most un-self-conscious. Two sentences into a conversation with Brigham Young and already out with a pun. Brigham smiled at this, "without that offensive affectation of some great men, the air of taking another's joke under their gracious patronage, and went on to remark that there were, unfortunately, multitudinous differences between the Mormons and Americans at the East, besides the hours they kept."[14]

"You find us trying to live peaceably," said Young. "A sojourn with people thus minded must be a great relief to you, who come from a land where brother hath lifted hand against brother, and you hear the confused noise of the warrior perpetually ringing in your ears." Fitz Hugh thought that "despite the courtly deference and Scriptural dignity of this speech, I detected in it a latent crow over that 'perished Union' which was the favorite theme of every saint I met in Utah." Fitz Hugh hastened to assure the President that "I have no desire for relief from sympathy with my country's struggle for honor and existence." "Ah!" replied President Young in a voice slightly tinged with sarcasm. "You differ greatly, then, from the multitude of your countrymen, who since the draft began to be talked of, have passed through Salt Lake, flying westward from the crime of their brothers' blood." Fitz Hugh, having himself of course fled the war in a way, was hardly equipped to fully debate the President, even if that were not impolitic. Still, Young was benevolent enough not to further press his advantage.[15]

After a conversation about the Indians, in which Young denounced the military policy of the Government, averring that one bale of blankets and ten pounds of beads would go farther to protect the mails from stoppage and emigrants from massacre than a regiment of soldiers, he tactfully changed the subject to the beauty of the Opera House. This building, Fitz Hugh acknowledged, was the equal of any in America save perhaps New York, Boston and Philadelphia. Fitz Hugh talked to the President a while longer on similar, smaller topics, until Brigham was called away by some young girls to join in a contradance. The visiting author "was much impressed by the aristocratic grace with which he went through his figures." As for Fitz Hugh, he excused himself from several dance invitations to take notes of his impressions of the dress and demeanor of Utah's "good society," which he knew would be of prime interest to a high percentage of his readers back east. Fitz Hugh may have been having sensualist thoughts after this long separation from Rosalie, but the whole Mormon social system seemed so much a paradise for gentlemen rogues as to render him unable to follow up with any active flirtation. He retired after a full night of taking notes on the appearance of the Mormon ladies in their finery.[16]

BRIGHAM YOUNG AND 22 OF HIS 55 WIVES. (LIBRARY OF CONGRESS)

On the next day, the Sabbath, Fitz Hugh attended Mormon services, escorted by one of Brigham's son-in-laws, Mr. Clawson. Services in the summer took place not in the Tabernacle, but in an outdoor bower. One hymn, "O California" (Nevada was then part of California territory, another home to early Mormon settlements) was "sung to an adaptation of the ancient Negro favorite, 'Oh Susannah.'" After the hymn, Heber addressed the crowd on the subject of the federal troops under Colonel Connor, who he felt were an insult to the Mormons. Nor was he subtle. "The devouring flames of the Lord should roast them till the flesh sizzled on their bone, and they should cry out for Death to come; but Death wouldn't have nothin' to do with their lousy carcasses, any more'n you or I, brethren and sisters, would touch a lump o' cowyard manure when we'd just washed our hands to go to meetin'."[17] After this uplifting oration, Heber was followed by George Smith, cousin of the Prophet and Revelator Joseph Smith. Smith gave a short lecture, touching briefly on the sect's early persecution, but mostly being humorous and hopeful and altogether the good cop to Heber's bad cop routine. Fitz Hugh was also thinking that Smith easily and justifiably might have waxed more wrathful given Mormon history. Fitz Hugh was well aware of the early history of Mormon persecution in Ohio and Missouri, culminating in 1845 when a mob attacked a jail where Joseph Smith was being held and murdered him. The Sabbath service was for the most part as sober and secular as any Presbyterian meeting. This was something of a surprise to Fitz Hugh, who had had a friend who witnessed a Saint speaking in tongues in Nephi, Utah in 1857.[18] As Mormonism began with divine visitations to Joseph Smith in the 1820's, and with the living Prophet Brigham Young having heard the instructions of the Lord in leading the saints to Utah, first hand religious experiences were still oral history to the Mormons. Fitz Hugh remarked that "The supernatural is used with infrequency... and is used as an instrument of control by Brigham" as the possessor of divine revelation.[19] Spirituality also was the reason for polygamy. Brigham Young himself had, according to best estimates, seventy wives, plus a hundred more who married him to ensure their later life in heaven with him. In this prodigious achievement, Fitz Hugh called him The Great Marrier (though not to his face, nor even while in the same territory.)[20] Fitz Hugh, despite being taken aback by his first encounter with the merry wives of Mormondom, was still clearly tolerant of the social features of Utah. He acknowledged in later writings that "social moralities are manufactured; artificial, not natural."[21] Fitz Hugh was convinced that the Mormons were polygamists not out of lust, but belief, actually being closer to Puritan than not.

However, there were other aspects of Mormonism that Fitz Hugh found more offensive than polygamy. "I came to a different conclusion than I had in the East...I regard them not as hypocrites but as fanatics, [because] a dozen wives is but small compensation for being slave of a system which cuts your throat if you rebel, and fleeces you of all you possess if you don't." Fitz Hugh noted that upon conversion, a Mormon must give all "surplus" wealth (as determined by Brigham) directly to church. Thereafter, the Church demanded an annual tithe of 10% of income or farm production. Further, the earlier comparison of Young to Napoleon was not offhand. He noted that "Brigham Omni potent" was the final arbiter of marriages, and that while for bad matches divorce is very easy to obtain in Utah, only Brigham Young can grant it.[22]

In a tale that brought home the horror of the whole sexual/political system, Fitz Hugh re-told the story of a young man whose sweetheart was forced to marry an old Saint.[23] After some intrigue, the young lovers dallied while the old man was in Europe. Unfortunately, one of the older wives saw and the Mormons abducted the young man and castrated him (as Fitz Hugh was forced to put it for editorial purposes, "that vengeance which was inflicted on Abelard by the uncles of Eloise...robbed him of manhood's self.")[24]

"If the Mormon lives for the glory of the Engine, when his life ceases to glorify the Engine it must terminate," wrote

Fitz Hugh. Thus entered Porter Rockwell, the Destroying Angel. He was the leader of the Danites, the assassins of the Church, who were by this time legendary for their skill and ferocity in killing the enemies of Zion. Fitz Hugh looked forward to meeting Rockwell. Speaking of destroying angels, "Having always felt the most vivid interest in supernatural characters of that species, I was familiar with most of them from the biblical examples of those who smote Egypt, Sodom, and Sennacherib." On the day after the Ball, Porter Rockwell called on Bierstadt and Fitz Hugh with a large stagecoach, and took them out riding to the Hot Springs. There, Fitz Hugh added to his store of knowledge of the Mineral and Hot Springs of the World ("Salt Lake City,—128 degrees F., copious evaporations, spring-fed pools support algae.") Rockwell joked about his deadly reputation, as when Fitz Hugh suggested that they could not stay any longer in Salt Lake City because the Mormons had "a reputation for stopping people who showed such taste to take a permanent residence." Rockwell answered that the travelers would not be able to get past his door on the west side of the city without being forced to share his dinner table. "Bless yer soul, but we're savage! Once drew a sassige on a Yankee Gentile myself—crammed it right down his throat with scalding hot gravy and pancakes. We Mormons torture 'em awful."[25]

But there was no joking around reality. In an article published in the East six months later, Fitz Hugh reported that "Porter Rockwell has slain his forty men. This is historical. His probable private victims amount to as many more."[26] This report grew in the telling to 150 in various later news articles. Two years later, a New York Tribune writer visited Utah and had "considerable difficulty in convincing Rockwell that it had been Ludlow, and not himself, who had charged him with the many killings. 'If ye had said it,' said the Destroying Angel, 'I'd've made it a hundred an' fifty-one.'"[27]

Fitz Hugh later confirmed two killings in 1866 which had led General William Tecumseh Sherman to threaten Utah with an invasion now that the South had been subdued.[28] However, at the time of Fitz Hugh's visit, the Civil War continued, and the federal government could not pay much attention to the Mormon problem. Fitz Hugh had noticed that although the U.S. government still claimed authority here, it was not an absolute authority. Even if a Mormon was brought to trial in a U.S. court, the jury would still be all Mormons, and the verdict certain to reflect the needs and beliefs of the Saints. Colonel Conner, sent by U.S. to safeguard its interests in Utah, was outmanned. Although he had an alliance of sorts with Porter Rockwell against the Indians, the Mormons were still the law of the land in the Utah of the settlers and emigrants. As Fitz Hugh wrote, "Fanatics are always desperate...And til the Mormons are feared as such, the laws of the Nation will be as much a dead letter in Utah as they are in South Carolina."[29]

Ultimately, Fitz Hugh was convinced that "Mormonism *is* Brigham Young...I once asked Brigham if Dr. Bernhisel (an acquaintance of Bierstadt's from his 1859 trip) would be likely to get to Congress again. 'No,' he replied with perfect certainty; 'we shall send _____ as our Delegate.'" Prior to election day, Brigham would send that name to the Deseret News, and "a counter nomination is utterly unheard of; and on election day _____ would be Delegate as surely as the sun rose." Brigham's power was absolute in Fitz Hugh's view not only because Brigham chose to wield it but because Mormondom would perish without it. "The instant he crumbles, Mormondom and Mormonism will fall to pieces at once, irrevocably."[30]

PORTER ROCKWELL WANTED POSTER.

Fitz Hugh's analysis of the Mormons was frank, but the Mormons had attempted to purchase a more flattering portrait. Apparently, more than a few writers had taken money to write favorably of the church, and Fitz Hugh received the same offer. He declined, but probably not without weighing the always precarious balance of his personal finances.

Before leaving the Mormons, the following diatribe, comparing the Mormons to another religious minority, sheds light on a less pleasant aspect of Fitz Hugh's personality:

> You cannot talk with one of their strongest men, like Young or Kimball, for an hour without seeing that their national model is the Jewish people…in spite of their being like the Jews, shameless polygamists, assassins, bigots, inquisitors, delighters in massacre, extortioners and zealots, they claim to do all these things under the sanction and by the order of God Almighty— in fact to be "His chosen people." They are an attempt to revive the Israelitish Civilization in the 19th Century.[31]

The bigotry in this passage strikes a false note in an otherwise harmoniously kind man. Elsewhere in his travel notes, Fitz Hugh had described a restaurant near Colorado Springs which he uncharitably thought "indicated our approach toward Mexican boundaries and Mexican manners. The latter fact was abundantly attested by the slovenliness with which the house was managed, the discomfort of its rooms, and the melancholy recklessness of its table."[32] Another target of vitriol were Indians they later encountered in California who "reached the ugliness of aboriginal specimens which we have encountered" in Utah. "Sometimes a strange incongruous romance, like moonlight on a puddle, lights up these mongrel liaisons, and infuses into them a burlesque of sentiment."[33]

Fitz Hugh's racism certainly echoes the "conventional wisdom" of the age—Benjamin Franklin once referred to "the design of Providence to extirpate these savages [Indians] in order to make room for the cultivators of the earth."[34] To be sure, prejudice against the non-WASP, and condescension toward the Negro, was prevalent in his time. But Fitz Hugh had shown through his close attention to the unconventional a more tolerant soul than passages like the above would suggest. There is some question whether some of this material was editorial in nature, perhaps solicited or embellished by Fitz Hugh's various editors. Whatever part of Fitz Hugh was responsible for these lapses also surfaced in some of his more trite short stories. Fitz Hugh was by profession a writer of light prose, and one of the rules of light prose is to never challenge the preconceptions of your readers. Nevertheless, Fitz Hugh managed to often rise above stereotypes. He described another encounter with "the most prosperous Indian tribe" they had yet seen, "[F]ar above the average brutality of the Diggers…and not afraid to look one in the eye."[35]

The remainder of Fitz Hugh's sojourn in Utah consisted of exploring the Great Salt Lake, or as Fitz Hugh called it, The Dead Sea, on July 5. The group stayed at the Black Rock Ranch, undressed there, and proceeded to the beach, which was "very disagreeable, consisting of flinty rock fragments, sharp as a razor, from one to eighteen inches long, and all seeming to lie edge and point upward." Once in, Fitz Hugh found the water exhilarating. He felt "none of the acidity and burning with which the lake affects some skins—only a pleasant pungent sense of being in pickle, such as a self-conscious gherkin might experience in Cross & Blackwell's aristocratic bath of condiments." The buoyancy combined with this feeling so that "a more delightful gamboling-place cannot be imagined." "After coming out from a ridiculous attempt to dive, which resulted very much as it would if the lake had been an India-rubber air-bed, I was unable to laugh or give facial expression to any emotion whatever until I had scrubbed my features with fresh water and towel—so had the salt crystallized on me, rigidly and instantaneously," or "as an old Mormon had called it, to 'Lotswificate' me." This was partly because "I had been a Nazarene ever since leaving New York, [with] long hair and full beard."[36]

Messrs. Hill and Durfee preceded Fitz Hugh and Bierstadt out of town on another stage and on July 6, the writer and artist embarked on the last leg of the journey. On their way out of town, they stopped for dinner at Porter Rockwell's house. Rockwell kept up the second stage station out of town, and insisted on having the artists for dinner, prepared by "two Mistresses Rockwell in concert."[37] After this repast, the two continued West.

Although they thought they had a two man stage, when they reached Fort Crittendon, a number of soldiers crowded in. Fitz Hugh and Bierstadt barely had time to complain, for just beyond the Fort the stage was attacked by a small band of Indians. In a furious attack, the Indians shot and killed the driver with an arrow, and also killed one of the soldiers. In the midst of the battle, one of the soldiers grabbed the reins and turned the stage back to the Fort, leaving the Indians behind. Fitz Hugh, ever mindful and never squeamish, retrieved "the arrow which gave the driver his death wound."[38] Thereafter, the stage carried uncomplaining as many soldiers as possible. They set out the next day amidst rumors that there had been a bloody attack several stations up the line. "With this subject for reflection we traveled moodily all day—scarcely speaking to each other and the desert growing more savage." The alkali plains of Nevada were raw (it was July) and the trail was frequently scarred with ruts which jolted the passengers out of whatever sleep they could steal. After a nerve and bone rattling leg of the journey, their arrival at Canon Station verified the awful rumors.

> Under a heavy cloud of black, clinging smoke, lay the charred beams and smouldering rafters of the house—while a little further off, the ruins of great trusses of hay were still steaming above the conflagration of the stables. On that further pile lay the mangled remains of all the stage stud—ten or a dozen fine animals who had perished with their halters unloosed; and nearer by, among the burning planks of the house, were stretched the bones of six horribly mutilated men, the flesh still partly adhering to them, and the whole mass rapidly becoming undistinguishable, roasting into our nostrils with the smell of mingled man and beast-hood, a loathsome holocaust to the Demon of Primeval Innocence.[39]

This episode might have been the ultimate influence on Fitz Hugh's negative judgment of the Indians. Fitz Hugh described the grim resumption of the trip, "we toiled on fifteen or twenty miles further, expecting every moment to be surrounded by the devils who had murdered our poor countrymen and destroyed the station." The party rode "with our rifles in our hands, their muzzles sticking out of the windows…I had a Ballard's rifle, which in buffalo or antelope hunting had never failed me. It fired seven times in one minute, with perfect accuracy. Bierstadt's double-barrelled musket, loaded with buck-shot, was in his hands; and across our knees lay our loaded six-shooters." Rumors of slaughter at the next stop, Antelope Station, proved false. In two more agonizing days, they had reached Ruby Valley, finally out of Goshute territory, and actually into the California Territory (now Nevada.)[40] Wasting no time, the stage plunged back into the desert. In four more days of overcrowding, during which a fellow passenger, a man from Illinois, became delirious from exhaustion and had to be held in the stage by force, they had covered the 250 miles to Virginia City. Fitz Hugh and Bierstadt spent a day (July 14) in Virginia City, which was still in throes of gold rush fever, and explored the "exhaustlessly rich" Ophir Shaft gold mine. Then they spent two days at Lake Tahoe (changed from Lake Bigler after that namesake had become a Copperhead) "where the glorious air and scenery additionally benefitted me." Finally, "I risked my life down the slope of the Sierra with one of those reckless drivers…and finally got to San Francisco via Folsom and Sacramento…but with a constitution so frightfully undermined by the Overland Journey that I never expect to recover fully from it as long as I live."[41] This was an astute prophecy.

As Fitz Hugh spent time in Utah and the desert, his "Letters from Sundown" had not only made it back to New York for publication in the *Evening Post*, but had also traveled in the pages of that paper back out West to California by steamer and across Panama. Because the Eastern papers were a rarity west of the Mississippi, many Western publishers reprinted various portions of those Eastern papers. On August 2, a San Francisco weekly paper called *The Golden Era* carried a reprint from the June 5 *Evening Post*. *The Golden Era* was published by Joseph Lawrence, who had gathered about him a stable of young writers. One of these writers was an ex-steamboat captain who called himself Mark Twain.

1   *Heart of the Continent*, p. 279-280. Conversations like this were probably somewhat dramatized by Fitz Hugh, but are repeated here as indicative of subjects discussed, and of speaking mannerisms of which Fitz Hugh was a keen observer.

2   Ibid., p. 286.

3   Ibid., p. 296.

4   Ibid., p. 299.

5   Ibid., p. 302

6   Ibid., p. 308-309.

7   Ibid., p. 312.

8   "Among the Mormons," *Atlantic Monthly*, April, 1864, p. 484.

9   *Heart of the Continent*, p. 347.

10 *Heart of the Continent*, p. 347.

11 Charles Kelly, *Holy Murder; the Story of Porter Rockwell*, New York: Minton, Balch, 1934, p. 223.

12 *Heart of the Continent*, p.366.

13 Ibid., p. 367.

14 Ibid., p. 369.

15 "Among the Mormons," p. 488-489.

16 *Heart of the Continent*, p. 374-375.

17 Ibid., p. 508-512.

18 Ibid., p. 532.

19 Ibid., p. 531.

20 "Reminiscences of an Overlander," March 20, 1864, p. 3.

21 First quote from *Heart of the Continent*, p. 333; second quote from "Among the Mormons" in *The Atlantic Monthly*, April, 1864.

22 *Heart of the Continent*, p. 534-541.

23 The young man's name was given as Polypeith, a Latin conglomeration of Fitz Hugh's which translates as "many apes". This is the same root as Pithecanthropus, Java Man, the discovery of which was an early confirmation of the theories of Darwin, one of Fitz Hugh's heroes at the time. Thus, this is a hidden joke of Fitz Hugh's.

24 *Heart of the Continent*, p. 542-552.

25 Ibid., p. 353-354.

26 "Among the Mormons," p. 452.

27 Albert Richardson, *Beyond the Mississippi*, Hartford, CT: American Publishing Company, 1867.

28 Kelly (1934), p. 230.

29 "Reminiscences of an Overlander," March 27, 1864, p. 1.

30 *Heart of the Continent*, p. 565-567.

31 "Reminiscences of an Overlander," March 27, 1864, p. 1.
32 *Heart of the Continent*, p. 172.
33 Ibid., p.456.
34 Frank Waters, *The Book of the Hopi*, New York: Penguin, 1963, p. 278.
35 *Heart of the Continent*, p. 459.
36 Ibid., p. 397-404.
37 "Reminiscences of an Overlander," March 29, 1864, p. 1.
38 "Reminiscences of an Overlander," April 17, 1864, p. 1.
39 Ibid.
40 Colonel Connor of the U.S. Army continued skirmishing with the natives until the autumn of 1863, and made peace with the Indians. Connor informed the Overland Mail Company the following October that "all routes of travel through Utah terri- tory...may now be used with safety." Robert M. Utley, *Frontiersmen in Blue: The Army of the Pacific*, 1861-1865, New York: 1967, p. 225.
41 "Reminiscences of an Overlander," April 17, 1864, p. 1.

XIII.

THE HASHEESH INFANT
AND THE WASHOE GIANT

THE San Francisco *Daily Alta California* newspaper on Sunday, July 19, carried a short item:

> DISTINGUISHED ARRIVALS—By the overland mail route, Fitzhugh [*sic*] Ludlow, author of "The Hasheesh Eater," and the painter, Albert Bierstadt, arrived here on Friday evening last.

The travelers moved into the Occidental Hotel, the finest in the city. After the grueling overland journey, Fitz Hugh waxed poetic in his notes upon arrival.[1] "Lewis Leland is not merely a watchful, thoughtful host; and this charming little breakfast in the small room is no ordinary, vulgar morning meal. The hotel is a palace of magic; Leland is the powerful sorcerer; Michael, breaking my eggs there, is his benevolent genie; this breakfast is the result of divination, the instantaneous product of a wish, and I might change my order to edible birds'-nests, reindeer cutlets, or peacocks tongues by simply turning my napkin over and crying 'Ho'; and I am the young Persian prince who during the night was brought here by sorcery three thousand miles through the air on a—what? I was just going to say 'a carpet':—and that woke me out of my dream! For the Overland Stage is no carpet!"[2]

San Francisco itself Fitz Hugh found to be wonderful. "It ignores the meteorological laws which govern the rest of the world." Everyone in S.F. was "kind and helpful" and Fitz Hugh had trouble only with a local express-company, the Californian Express Company, of which he would later say "we should by this time have acquired sufficient familiarity with extortion from the Company's officials."[3] Meanwhile, the local literary paper, *The Golden Era* also announced the visitors:

> MR. BIERSTADT, the distinguished New York artist, whose painting of a western scene on the Platte river has been one of the chief attractions of this year's Exhibition of the National Academy of Design, arrived in this city on 17th instant, accompanied by Mr. Fitz Hugh Ludlow. They made the overland trip leisurely, taking time to obtain sketches of the grand and exquisite scenery en route.[4]

The same issue noted two other Eastern refugees who were due in town, Artemus Ward—"the incomparable showman is to arrive this month," and "Mrs. Adah Isaacs Menken is on her way westward. She steamed from Gotham the 1st of July. Prepare for Mazeppa. The Opera House will *scene* her." (Ward's appearance and first lecture did not take place until November, while Menken began performing in August.) The travellers soon were part of the local gossip. A column written by Charles Henry Webb, West Coast correspondent for the *New York Times* and alumnus of Pfaff's, entitled "Things," was a catchall of goings on about the town. Writing under the pseudonym Inigo, Webb wrote his column in the form of a letter to local celebrities. "Things" had this to say concerning the Mazeppa the first week after Bierstadt and Fitz Hugh had arrived:

Were you ever at the Melodeon? If you have visited that place of amusement don't be ashamed to own it, for I was there myself the other night. To my surprise all the best people were there. My friends, the distinguished "Overlanders" were there—one of them is writing a book about it, the other has sketched it for an oil painting...(The Melodeon) contributes to morality. Had I a son (I'd) take him and if he did not become disgusted with everything he saw and heard there, I should expect to see him in Congress some day.[5]

CHARLES HENRY WEBB, "INIGO" (1834-1905).

It was Inigo who nicknamed Fitz Hugh the Hasheesh Infant. After having read *The Hasheesh Eater*, all the western writers expected an aging, dissolute, world weary man, and instead found a bespectacled and erudite young man eager for new sensations. Not long after arrival, a local prize fight had the town talking, and Inigo wrote in his column a challenge to Mark Twain, the "Washoe Giant" and Fitz Hugh, the Hasheesh Infant, for a journalistic battle. The column, as was Inigo's custom, degenerated into puns, ending "Inigo is bent on giving Ludlow Fitz, and rending apostolic Mark in Twain." A kindred soul!

MARK TWAIN IN 1866, ABOUT THE TIME HE MET LUDLOW.

Sam Clemens had only just become "Mark Twain" in February.[6] Twain had recently come to San Francisco from the gold rush town of Virginia City, in Washoe territory, now part of Nevada. He already had a reputation as a humorist from his stint on the Virginia City Territorial Enterprise, in which he had written about a petrified man found thumbing his nose at the coroner, and where he had labeled a reporter at a rival paper Rice the Unreliable.[7]

The travellers stayed only two weeks in San Francisco before Bierstadt urged Fitz Hugh on to new adventures. Though Fitz Hugh had found fertile new literary fields to explore, Bierstadt impressed upon him his duty (and appetite for new experiences) and they headed off to Yosemite. They were joined on this mini-expedition by Virgil Williams, a friend of Bierstadt's from his days in Rome, and Enoch Wood Perry, with whom Bierstadt had studied in Dusseldorf.[8] These were added to the original party of Fitz Hugh, Bierstadt, Hill and Durfee, along with "a highly scientific metallurgist and physicist generally, Dr. John Hewston of San Francisco."

They were also to have been joined by the head of the First Unitarian Church, Reverend Thomas Starr King, the man known as "the moral center of California." King in fact was credited by many with keeping California in the Union during the Civil War.[9] (Fitz Hugh had seen King lecture once just before he went off to Union College.)[10] King was forced to cancel, telling the party "on the eve of our setting out, that work for the nation must detain him in San Francisco, after all." This work included raising money for the Sanitary Commission, a predecessor to the Red Cross. He was said to have raised about one quarter of the $4,800,000 raised during the war.[11] Fitz Hugh was intrigued by King's work for the Commission and would later become involved in the Commission's work in New York. This was partly due to the friendship of Starr King with Jessie Fremont, wife of then Senator John Fremont, the famous explorer who had blazed the first trail through the Rocky Mountains. Ms. Fremont was also a patroness of Bret Harte (then a fledgling writer and one of the Golden Era crowd), and she met Fitz Hugh at formal gatherings in San Francisco.

The Yosemite party set out around August 1, at which time the *Alta* commented, "They will have a jolly time of it."[12] Fitz Hugh described it himself as "No Saratoga affair, this!" The party brought the oldest clothes they owned, high knee-cap boots, and were "armed with Ballard rifles, shot-guns, and Colt's revolvers which had come with us across the continent." They also bought hardy saddle horses at about $70 apiece, "but the New York market could not have furnished us with such horses for one hundred and fifty dollars." Fitz Hugh observed that everyone in California was an accomplished rider, despite the new "street-railroads." They took a steamer across the bay into Stockton, and then took four leisurely days to cover 100 miles across three small rivers to Mariposa, on the eastern edge of "the great Yo-Semite." There they picked up a hired hand and a young boy to assist them into the wilderness. The boy, at fifteen years, "was one of the keenest speculators in fire-arms I ever saw; could swap horses or play poker with anybody."

Two days into the 50 miles to the Yosemite Valley, they spent an afternoon "visiting the Big Trees." Fitz Hugh mounted one of the fallen giants and "ascertained its diameter as thirty-four feet—its circumference one hundred and two feet plus a fraction." Fitz Hugh later noted that "Estimates, grounded on the well known principle of yearly cortical increase, indisputably throw back the birth of these largest giants as far as 1200 B.C. Thus their tender saplings were running up just as the gates of Troy were tumbling down, and some of them had fulfilled the lifetime of the late Hartford Charter-Oak when Solomon called his master-masons to refreshment from the building of the Temple." There is still an inscription on Register Rock near Vernal Falls, "Camped here August 21 1863 A Bierstadt Virgil Williams E. Perry Fitz Hugh Ludlow."[13]

After a third day of travel, the party stood on Inspiration Point, and "[n]ever were words so beggared for an abridged translation of any Scripture of Nature." They faced the "tremendous precipice which stood smiling, not frowning at us, in all the serene radiance of a snow-white granite Boodh." Fitz Hugh was moved by this natural beauty in ways he hadn't been since Niagara Falls during his hashish days:

> I never could call a Yo-Semite crag inorganic, as I used to speak of everything not strictly animal or vegetal. In the presence of the Great South Dome that utterance became blasphemous. Not living was it? Who knew but the debris at its foot was merely the cast-off sweat and exuviae of a stonelife's great work-day? Who knew but the vital changes which were going on within its gritty cellular tissue were only imperceptible to us because silent and vastly secular?[14]

Fitz Hugh and company met up with some of the local native Americans, one of whom told them the legends of the mountain Tis-sa-ack, and Fitz Hugh allowed that "Sometimes these Indian traditions, being translated according to the doctrine of correspondences, are of great use to the scientific man." Pohono Falls were said to be named after an evil spirit, and "this tradition is scientifically accounted for in the fact that many Indians have been carried over the fall by the tremendous current both of wind and water forever rushing."

Their first night in Yosemite proper was spent on the banks of the Merced River, in a green meadow, ringed by woods. They named the camp "Camp Rosalie, after a dear absent friend of mine and Bierstadt's." How dear we cannot say, but Rosalie was quite removed. No steamer-delivered letter awaited the overlanders in San Francisco, nor was Rosalie steadily informed of the Overlanders progress.[15] Other Eastern friends were on their minds, as in the case of calling the hunting of botanical and entomological specimens "Agassizing", after the eminent Harvard botanist who could not find them a scientific companion for the trip. In camping:

> During our whole stay in the Valley, most of us made it our practice to rise with the dawn, and, immediately after a bath in the ice-cold Merced, take a breakfast which might sometimes fail in the game department, but was an invariable success, considered as slapjacks and coffee.[16]

After several weeks in this location, the party moved about five miles up the valley, and then dispatched their hired man to fetch more supplies. After seven days and no sign of him, Fitz Hugh had to set out "to save the party from starvation." Fitz Hugh eventually tracked down the pack animals, which the man had sold after losing the provisions money at poker and disappearing into the wild West. After Fitz Hugh's return, they moved to a third and last camp behind the South Dome.

From there led a trail for three miles, beyond which they had to move on by foot. After a grueling climb, they came to the base of "yo-wi-ye" or Nevada Fall. This was as far as they could advance, "standing in a cul-de-sac of Nature's grandest labyrinth...eight hundred feet above us, could we climb there, we should find the snow peaks." While they had hoped to reach those peaks, they "endured all these pains only to learn still deeper Life's saddest lesson,—'Climb forever, and there is still an Inaccessible.'" Humbled and exhausted, the party backtracked their way to San Francisco.

ALBERT BIERSTADT, *MERCED RIVER, YOSEMITE VALLEY*, 1866.
(METROPOLITAN MUSEUM OF ART)

The thriving metropolis had not stood still. Adah Menken had arrived in town in early August, and Mazeppa (the play in which she appeared apparently nude—see Chapter 7) was up and running by the 26th. Inigo reviewed the play on the 30th: "I don't know whether you have been to see 'Mazeppa'. If not, you are a rare exception to everyone else in San Francisco, and a few in San Jose and San Mateo."[17] Inigo noted that another critic had called her the "best actress in her line that the continent afforded," and opined that "her line is not a clothes line." Inigo reported a week later that he had been back to see Adah several times, "principally to see whether or not there is anything improper in the play, for several of my friends assure me that there is."

Menken was accompanied in her travels by her second husband, former Pfaffian Robert Henry Newell, who wrote under the pun name Orpheus C. Kerr. Although his writing was accepted into *The Golden Era*, the western writers found him in person somewhat boring, and he paled beside the larger than life Adah. She received $500 a night for sixty nights at Maguire's Opera House.[18] The normal price of admission was raised a considerable 50 cents exclusively for her appearance. As mentioned in Chapter 7, Adah was as intent on her literary reputation as her dramatic one. She used her stardom to attract the leading local literati, and had discussed her writing in intimate sessions with Twain and others. Bret Harte was fascinated by her, as was Charles Warren Stoddard, who wrote that "Every curve of her limbs was as a line in a Persian love song. She was a vision of celestial harmony made manifest in the flesh."[19]

Menken wrote an essay defending Walt Whitman for the *Golden Era*, and her own free verse was published there. "Colonel" Joe Lawrence, who became editor of the *Golden Era* in 1859, had instituted a policy of getting not only the best local writers but also soliciting contributions from visitors to the West during their stays. Lawrence made sure that Menken's written work, such as a poem entitled "Working and Waiting," made its way into *The Golden Era*.[20] In that same issue, "Fitz Hugh Ludlow" appeared as the headline to the following paragraph:

"On Good Living," an admirable paper from the pen of Fitz Hugh Ludlow, one of the most popular and best approved of American Literati, is published in another column. He wrote "The Hasheesh Eater" and found himself famous. As the author of several successful novels, a constant contributor to leading magazines of the country, and one of the editorial corps of the New York Evening Post, Fitz Hugh Ludlow has ably sustained the reputation founded and established by his first work. He has lately "staged it" over the plains, and his "reminiscences of an Overlander," a series of entertaining sketches, embracing the scenery, incidents, observations and adventures of trans-continental tourist, will be published in the GOLDEN ERA, to which journal Mr. Ludlow is engaged to contribute regularly during his sojourn in California.

"On Good Living" appeared with Fitz Hugh's byline, identifying him as "Author of The Hasheesh Eater, The New Partner in Clingham & Co., Little Brother, Cruise of the Two Deacons, Regular Habits, Little Good for Nothing, The New Soul of John Markham, Battle and Triumph of Dr. Susan, Etc."[21] The article, rather than a polishing of his travel notes, was an extemporaneous sermon with a simple theme:

The truely spiritual man is he who lives well...
  Whether good living ruins the soul or not, (as affirmed by the stoics) bad living enfeebles it...Had [the stoic] dined with the effeminate person who he despised, he had carried to the

sanctuary (church on Sunday) an ethereal subtlety of perception, and elasticity of nerve, a vigilance of the moral faculties, which had not only brought him home possessor of the theological truths he is now dead to, but had forever shaken his belief in the debasing influence of sweetbreads with mushrooms, stewed terrapin, and venison haunch with currant jelly.

I have seen men whose banquets had reached this acme of spirituality—the dishes before them were called what you please upon the bill of fare, but to their glorious minds a transubstantiation had taken place which made all of the steamy savors from beneath the covers whispers of music, thoughts of bliss rather than smells and when the covers were lifted off, fed them not on brawn and fat and vegetable tissue, but on all the great things of Art and History!...I hasten to explain what I mean, lest the above paragraph should mark me for a transcendentalist...

I am a strong believer in the doctrine that what a man likes won't hurt him.

And, as he had said before, Fitz Hugh found that, in regard to cooking in the territories, he condemned a country which could "comprise all depths of gastronomic degradation in this one formula: Fries its steaks!...The missionary is sadly needed...to smash those false Gods, the frying pans." Had the martyr St. Lawrence fallen into the hands of the heathen, "they would have fried him in a pan with some of the cold grease of yesterday's Christian."

It was this kind of irreverence cheek-by-jowl with classical East Coast learning that won over Twain and the others, and from then on there was nothing but appreciation for a peer in one sense, and respect for a model of prestigious literary success in another. Fitz Hugh often joined the loungers in Joe Lawrence's office, with Lawrence being that favorite thing of Fitz Hugh's, "an inveterate pipe-smoker."[22]

Also appearing in the *Era* of the 13th was a notice "The N.Y. Evening Post publishes a letter from Fitz Hugh Ludlow on his Overland trip, in which he writes concerning the drama at Central City, Pike's Peak mines" [see Chapter 11]. This was apparently the last Ludlow "Letter from Sundown" to appear in the *Post*. Presumably Lawrence's *Golden Era* had matched the *Post*'s price [Twain reported payment of $50/month for 4 articles][23], and Fitz Hugh considered his debt for travel expenses covered by the Post paid in full. The *Daily Alta California* took note of *The Golden Era*'s new vibrancy with a short note on September 20. "As a literary paper it has no equal on the Atlantic side, and certainly deserves the extensive patronage it is receiving. Fitz Hugh Ludlow, of Hasheesh fame, Bret Harte, "Mark Twain," "Inigo," "Orpheus C. Kerr" and a host of other celebrities contribute to its columns."

Yet another ex-Pfaffian arrival that summer was Ada Clare, who was shortly quoted by Inigo as remarking "that as long as men prefer a small foot in a woman to a kind heart, and an hourglass figure to a tender soul, women will continue to torture their feet and squeeze their ribs out of place, and their hearts and souls will remain what they too often are, shallow pools, withered and dried up or filled with stagnant and bitter waters."[24] Clare wrote occasional columns for the *Era* as well, and renewed her acquaintance with Fitz Hugh and Bierstadt. In the September 20 *Era*, both the East and West were represented. "How to Cure a Cold" by Mark Twain (he tried warm salt water and "threw up my immortal soul") appeared alongside "On Marrying Men" by Fitz Hugh Ludlow. The latter was Fitz Hugh's commentary on the scarcity of the fairer sex in the West, a fact testified to more tangibly by the lusty reception of Adah Menken at Maguire's Opera House:

> If I had not for years been a Benedict, wearing upon my coun-
> tenance the sedate stamp of chronic matrimony, I should look
> forth to a misspent life of Bachelordom the moment I decided
> to set my permanent picket peg in San Francisco. For, to my
> eyes, the harvest of bachelors truly is plenteous, and the labo-
> rers are few, I should go back to mother Earth a shock of corn
> fully ripe, without even having felt the sweet laceration of a
> feminine scythe.

Fitz Hugh then catalogued several types of Marrying Men, ranging from the "desperately eager Marrying Man, who takes such pains to make himself attractive that his flurried breath is as a steam whistle warning careful mamas off the track the moment he comes through" to the "easy, unconscious Marrying Man, who is always slipping into some good matrimonial thing before he knows it; who not being rich, has heiresses thrown at his head." The latter may have been a reference to himself, but Rosalie surely would have been put off by the tone of this article if she ever saw it. She could also not be happy to learn that Fitz Hugh's visit to San Francisco coincided with women of loose mor-als like Ada Clare and Adah Menken. Nevertheless, Fitz Hugh's humorous commentary fit right in with the Gol-den Era circle. Twain's "The Lick House Ball," a satire of San Francisco's social life ran in the following week's issue, with descriptions of socialites wearing an "elegant goffered flounce...with a frontispiece formed of a magnificent cau-liflower imbedded in potatoes. Thus attired Miss B. looked good enough to eat." More significantly, "M'Liss" by Bret

Harte appeared in this issue, marking the debut of this important American writer.

The Overlanders stayed in the city less than two weeks this time, between the 10th and 20th of September. Then they set off for Oregon and the Columbia River. The *Golden Era* published a short article called "Bierstadt in the Yo-Semite" on September 27, noting that Bierstadt has gone to Oregon, but had left his portfolio of sketches in color, which the writer then proceeds to describe. "Mr. Bierstadt's reputation is continental and independent of the praise or blame of this shelving strip along the Pacific...But that Californians may learn to appreciate the genius of the painter, and through it the glory of their own State, we call attention to some of the peculiar charms of these sketches." Not long after, Inigo himself wrote on the same subject in the *Era*. However, he could only pay serious tribute briefly before he noted "I do not intend to give him any orders for pictures, as he has his time for three years to come spoken for, and will not undertake to touch anything sooner. Besides the prices which he obtains for a picture three feet square are so enormous that I could not safely order of him anything more extensive than a neat little landscape, say one inch by two."[25] And at least one paper, the *San Francisco Evening Bulletin*, paused from praise long enough to report that Bierstadt's name was one of 794 drawn in his New York City neighborhood of 5,680 eligible men for the draft.[26]

Original Overlander compatriots William Hill and Horatio Durfee had by this time "become sated with travel" and had gone back to New York via steamer. Fitz Hugh and Bierstadt took their respective notebooks and color boxes and boarded the Sacramento River steamer, which took them in three days to Tehama, a small settlement where the river became too shallow for navigation. This leisurely float was one of "pure sensuous delight in the fact of life and motion under such a spotless sky and in an air that was such breathable elixir."[27] Fitz Hugh, as always, demonstrated a fine grasp of life's peak experiences.

In Tehama they returned to horseback and were only slightly disturbed at the sight of horsemen in the distance who they took for Indians ("we felt our scalps begin to detach themselves slightly from the cranium") but who turned out to be cavalry. After one night with a family (six children under the age of twelve—"it is a duty to visit the afflicted"), and a third night at Dog Creek, the riders were within sight of their initial goal, Mount Shasta. Fitz Hugh noted that the price of everything was a dollar; bed for a night, a horse's forage, and breakfast, no matter how bad the food. One more day of riding, with a stop at Soda Springs where Fitz Hugh "took a draught of the most delicious mineral-water I ever drank" (and Fitz Hugh knew his spring water) and they reached Sisson's Ranch in the Strawberry Valley, in the shadow of Shasta. Sisson had a wife and baby daughter, and "the presence of this mother and child in a wilderness which otherwise howled chiefly with rough sporadic men and equally rough ubiquitous bears, was a perpetual delight to us, so far from our domestic communications."

The Overlanders spent a week here. Bierstadt, "the most indefatigable explorer of every party we were in together," came away with "a score of Shasta studies taken under every possible variety of position, sky, and time of day." Fitz Hugh meanwhile explored the area and sketched his impressions. In another day, they covered the distance to Yreka, a mining town already gone bust with the discovery of gold further east, and now "devoted principally to stables, gambling-shops, and liquor dens...swarming with Chinese of ill odor and worse repute." In another day's journey, they climbed the Siskiyou mountains and left California for Oregon.

It was here that Fitz Hugh's frail constitution again let him down. The overland journey, as he had written, had "frightfully undermined his constitution." Despite this, he had plunged almost immediately back into the epic journey by going to Yosemite, and then after a week spent resting by writing several articles and cavorting with the Pfaffians of the West, rushed northward to complete the itinerary set so ambitiously six months earlier. In the mountains of Oregon, with only the more robust Bierstadt beside him, Fitz Hugh's body finally gave out. They had struggled on horseback for about a week along the foothills of the Cascade Range past the Rogue River, Grave Creek, and the Umpqua River. Fitz Hugh collapsed, coughing and feverish, in an area known as Long Tom Country about thirty miles south of Salem near the Callapooia River. He fell from the saddle with "a violent attack of pneumonia, which came near terminating my earthly with my Oregon pilgrimage." Bierstadt dragged him to the nearest home, a rural cabin miles from any doctor. There, Fitz Hugh weathered the worst of the illness, "saved by the indefatigable nursing of the best friend I ever traveled with—and the impossibility of sending for any doctor in the region."[28] This actually was the onset of tuberculosis in Fitz Hugh, whose lungs had never been healthy.[29]

The invalid and his nurse spent five days at the house, with a man named Cartwright, and were charged sixty dollars (about what their Occidental Hotel rooms cost) plus board and attendance "to a man who ate nothing and was not waited on." Fitz Hugh had Bierstadt make an entry in his journal "in stopping with anybody in the Long-Tom Country, make a special contract for maternal tenderness, as it will invariably be included in the bill." After this expensive stay, Fitz Hugh was well enough to be loaded onto a straw bed in a wagon. "During the period I jolted on the straw, I diversified the intervals between pulmonary spasms with a sick glance at the pages of Bulwer's "Devereux" and Lever's "Day's Ride."These books, not being the Bible, aroused the interest of the driver.

"D'ye think it's exackly the way for an immortal creatur' to be spendin' his time, to read them novels?" Despite his illness, the son of the preacher could not resist engaging the outmanned enemy. "Why is it particularly out of the way for an immortal creature?" "Because his higher interests don't give him no time for sich follies." "How can an immortal creature be pressed for time?" "Wal, you' find out some day," sputtered the driver, and recovered by snarling at his horse "G'lang Jennie."

As they continued along the Willamette River, they were struck by the beauty of the Cascades, particularly the "incandescense" of Mount St. Helen's:

> When we first looked, we thought St. Helen's an illusion—an aurora, or a purer kind of cloud. Presently we detected the luminous chromatic border—a band of refracted light with a predominant orange—tint, which outlines the higher snow-peaks seen at long range,—traced it down, and grasped the entire conception of the mighty cone.

Thus, one more sight of transcendent beauty united the two kindred souls, after one had nearly lost his life, in communion with the wonders of the continent. "No man of enthusiasm, who reflects what this whole sight must have been, will wonder that my friend and I clasped each other's hands before it, and thanked God we had lived to this day."

By October 20, they had reached Portland, and put up at the Dennison House. There they met Messrs. Ainsworth and Thompson, of the Oregon Steamship Company, who offered the Overlanders a tour of the Columbia River. Despite his weakened condition, Fitz Hugh accepted and off they went again. The captain of the first steamer they boarded prior to the tour refused to let Bierstadt or Fitz Hugh pay for their ticket because he had seen Bierstadt sketching and Fitz Hugh writing, and would take no money from artists.

The Columbia River tour was anticlimactic. Fitz Hugh dutifully noted the character of the rock formations along the shore (basalt) and noted that St. Helen's was a volcanic cone and had been seen to smoke within the last twelve years. But there were few of the dramatic views that Bierstadt sought as subjects, and the river even reminded Fitz Hugh of the Hudson River back home. Further, Fitz Hugh was moved to remark upon "one of the characteristic surprises of American scenery everywhere. You cannot isolate yourself from the national civilization...the same enterprise which makes itself felt in New York and Boston starts up for your astonishment out of all the fastnesses of the continent...In our journey through the wildest parts of this country, we were perpetually finding patent washing-machines among the chaparral—canned fruit in the desert."

They steamed as far east as The Dalles, where the Columbia rushed through high cliffs and out of the mountains.

There, Bierstadt sketched Mount Hood and Fitz Hugh worked on his books and maps until swept up by a social party which invited him, "under the brevet title of Professor, to the house of a popular citizen, who, I was assured, would be glad to see me...this is not the way people form acquaintances in New York; but if I had wanted that, why not have stayed there?" After four days, they declined the Steamship Company's extended invitation to push on to or up the Snake River, in favor of returning to Portland to meet the California steamer, the "Pacific", which they intended to catch back to San Francisco on October 30. Unfortunately, by the time they returned the rains had set in, and they became, in Fitz Hugh's depressed words, "The Prisoners of Portland." The steamer was overdue, and the weather was so wet that they were confined to their hotel, "pale and trembling upon the verge of writing serial stories for the [N.Y.] Ledger."

Fitz Hugh would sit in his room and smoke his meerschaum (just the thing for his rheumy lungs) and ask every visitor upon their entry to his room, "Any news from the steamer?...I don't know why it is that I always begin conversation with the question...unless it be that each new arrival is so much wetter than the previous one, that I feel instinctively this gentleman may possibly have just swam up from Astoria and heard something about the Pacific before he left." To pass the time, Fitz Hugh started The Society for the Propagation of Culinary Christianity, primarily to combat the curse of fried pork. Bierstadt, despite being the only other member, modestly declined the offer of the presidency of the Society, and so that duty devolved upon Fitz Hugh himself. Finally, the steamer arrived on

November 3, and Culinary Christians sailed for San Francisco on November 5.

In their absence, *The Golden Era* published "On Care that Killed the Cat," written by Fitz Hugh prior to their departure for Oregon, along with the following introduction: "A brilliant article, 'On Care that Killed the Cat,' written expressly for the Golden Era by the distinguished author Fitz Hugh Ludlow, will be found in our columns." Even Bierstadt had found time amidst the traveling and sketching to design a new masthead for *The Golden Era* during his stay.[30] "On 'Care' That 'Killed the Cat'" was an idiosyncratic piece taking as a starting point a proverb (familiar to Fitz Hugh at least) "Hang care! Care killed the cat," by which was meant basically "Don't worry, be happy." This essay had its pithy moments, but was clearly an off the cuff special for his new friends at the *Era*.

On November 8, Fitz Hugh began to take his literary leave of the city with the first of several essays giving his opinion of San Francisco. The essay was entitled "Plain Talks—No. 1, How It Strikes One." He warned the reader beforehand that he is about to undertake a "frank expose" of how he found San Francisco. By this time, he and Bierstadt had built up so much good will that Fitz Hugh felt secure in treating the irreverent westerners in the same way they treated each other. He also noted parenthetically that he was writing said expose in the shadow of Mount Shasta, "400 miles away from Public Opinion" and "the only vehicle of transfer to that isolated place being Wells & Fargo's Express. I should hate to have any Opinion, of me at least, reach me by that conveyance, since that Grand Incorporated Society of Extortion would charge it so much for the ride, that by the time it obtained its destination it would be a very *Poor Opinion* of me indeed." Having stated his intentions and sealed them with a pun, Fitz Hugh enumerated the following impressions, good and bad:

> The candid visitor must regret that the grading of San Francisco seems to have been done by a Giant armed with a fish slice and a coal-scoop under the influence of Delirium Tremens.

He critiqued an Episcopal church for its architecture:

> Suppose not that the architect of the church mentioned had a lot of eminent ecclesiastical heads out of which he was making a variety of godly lemonade in a parochial squeezer; or a quantity of dicephalic Christian currants from which he was extracting the genuine juice of orthodoxy for a jelly to comfort the faithful—and a few hard Episcopal heads had squirted unmashed with great agony through the holes of the squeezer or burst the muslin of the jelly-bag to appear with an expression of martyrdom in a hard Jammy spurt outside—then you will get some ideas of the way those architectural adornments appear to a candid visitor.

He further was disappointed in the physical appearance of Maguire's theater:

> The whole resources of the house seem to have been lavished on the act-drop; and after dressing those extraordinary nymphs, buying French corsets to bring their waists to the true wasp model, setting them on their toes in a position which would have maddened with jealousy Humpty Dumpty's unsuccessful doctors, and furnishing the proper trimmings of palatial architecture, garden scenery and cavaliers—the management appear to have had nothing left for upholstery

to the seats, fresh paint, neat carpentry, or even soap, mops and brooms. San Francisco's principal theatre at least ought to be clean.

However, the goings on within the Maguire were quite to Fitz Hugh's liking:

Adah Isaacs Menken is a townswoman of mine—yet I sincerely acknowledge that no foreign nursery of the Graces has ever furnished to our stage a more exquisitely beautiful woman with a face more electrically obedient to the emotions of deep heartfelt gladness, and pathos as deep. She has comic appreciation and power, but her forte lies in passages of feeling where she can use those tender, earnest eyes of hers, and that lovely pleading mouth. She possesses physical charms to a very unusual extent, and her intellectual means for interpreting that serious register of passion which commits and absorbs the whole nature of the woman feeling it, are fully equal to the sculpturesque delicacy of her face and figure.

This paean surely excited the lovely Adah. Six months and three thousand miles from home, did Fitz Hugh write it as an instrument of seduction? This is a distinct possibility. They surely reminisced together of the Pfaffian days, but whether things went further no one knows. But Fitz Hugh's eye for beauty had been vigorously exercised since leaving Rosalie in Atchison, Kansas. Also in this article, Fitz Hugh distributed literary bouquets:

Among the many brilliant, sensible, witty and pathetic original things which I find in the Era, none ever interest me more by the beauty of their style, the unique depth and sweetness of their thought than the contributions of your "Bret"—Mr. Harte of San Francisco.

In reference to Harte's review of Bierstadt, Fitz Hugh wrote "I never saw any critique on painting more admirable than this of Bret's, for its beauty both of feeling and expression."

Fitz Hugh and Bierstadt were scheduled to leave on the Panama steamer on November 23. The Overlanders made the rounds of farewell parties, and at one on November 16, Fitz Hugh wrote the following poem in the autograph book of Charles Warren Stoddard:

I will not wish thy life a tinted bubble
　　Floating forever on an unvexed sea
I will not prophesy thee skies whose trouble
　　Like sun-smit morning clouds shall quickly flee;
Life hath great triumphs in its darkest seasons
　　For him who bids black heavens shed rains of peace,
And he who bears the facts & waits the reasons
　　Finds dew upon his solitary fleece.
Oh be it thine through life's still varying tissue
　　To see God's presence like a golden strand
Brighten it ever till the web shall issue
　　Out of the loom into the Weaver's hand;
May God in kindness grant thee little sorrow
　　But be earth's changeful seasons what they may,
Look through the gates of the Eternal Morrow
　　For there awaits thee an unclouded day.

In the course of several visits, the travelers had spent time looking at Watkins' photographs of Yosemite "in Starr King's drawing-room [where] we had gazed on them by the hour."[31] Reverend Starr King described their visits:

We have had a delightful time here with Bierstadt & Fitz Hugh Ludlow, the "Hasheesh Eater." They visited us several times, staying till after midnight & talking under the inspiration of tea. Bierstadt painted a charming sketch of Mt. Shasta—our Mt. Blanc—for Julia, but by accident carried it away with him. He will send it back, doubtless, from New York.[32]

REV. THOMAS STARR KING (1824-1864)
WITH HIS WIFE JULIA WIGGINS.

Fitz Hugh in turn later related that "Starr King [told] with great gusto the story of a New England official, a small, unusually small in the respect of avoirdupois, but great in soul, who, on being threatened with personal violence by the malcontent whom he was sent to arrest, replied, "Shake me? Shake me? When you shake me, you shake the State of Massachusetts!"[33]

From King's vestibule of heaven, Fitz Hugh also ranged across to the doorsteps of hell. San Francisco's large Chinese population, immigrants meeting the demand for labor on the Western railroads, had brought with them the custom of opium smoking.[34] Opium dens, called "hongs," were common in San Francisco. Saloons on Kearny Street, including one known as "The Morgue," were havens for addicts as well as tourists. A pharmacy on Grant Street was known to have been open all night to meet the demand.[35] Opium dens were not outlawed by the city until 1875.

Fitz Hugh had tasted opium in the form of laudanum (an extract) at Anderson's apothecary in 1856. It seemed logical to visit a den to investigate the smoking of the substance, and he managed to find his way there in the whirlwind final week on the west coast. Mark Twain, who had seven years earlier investigated the importation of cocaine from Brazil as a potential get rich quick scheme, may have been one of Fitz Hugh's guides.[36] Fitz Hugh later wrote the following as part of his impressions:

> I shall never forget till my dying day that awful Chinese face which actually made me rein my horse at the door of the opium hong where it appeared, after a night's debauch, at six o'clock one morning when I was riding in the outskirts of a Pacific city. It spoke of such a nameless horror in its owner's soul that I made the sign for a pipe and proposed, in "pigeon English," to furnish the necessary coin. The Chinaman sank down on the steps of the hong, like a man hearing medicine proposed to him when he was gangrened from head to

foot, and made a gesture, palms downward, toward the ground, as one who said, "It has done its last for me—I am paying the matured bills of penalty." The man had exhausted all that opium could give him; and now, flattery past, the strong one kept his goods in peace.[37]

SCENE TYPICAL OF A LATE 19TH CENTURY SAN FRANCISCO OPIUM DEN.
(LIBRARY OF CONGRESS)

One other aspect of Fitz Hugh's personality emerged in proximity to the *Golden Era* crew. Darwin's book *The Origin of Species* had appeared just four years earlier in 1859. Fitz Hugh carried it with him to California, much taken with its arguments. The book was still far from accepted. Bierstadt's advisor, Louis Agassiz, Harvard Professor of Natural History, was opposed to Darwinians' attempt to "belittle the Creative work, or say that He first scattered the seeds of life in meager or stinted measure."[38] As an old rebel from the Boston stuffed shirt crowd, Fitz Hugh unsurprisingly opposed Agassiz of the Saturday Club and threw in with the brave new world. No doubt the perception of the book's blasphemies against establishment theology was also attractive. The *Golden Era* crew were delighted to find the Hasheesh Infant to be an enthusiastic proselytizer for Darwin. Inigo wrote a column entitled "The Bohemians in Court," in which a *Golden Era* contributor was brought into Police Court for striking a man. The defense called Fitz Hugh to the stand:

> better known by the soubriquet of the "Hasheesh Infant," wearing a grey flannel shirt and dragoon boots and bearing a huge book under his arm—Darwin's Origin of Species... Ludlow, being a lecturer by profession, was placed on the stand to lead off. It is true that he was absent when the little affair happened, but from this fact it was logically argued that he would be less trammeled by facts; and his being a well known contributor to Harper's established the supposition that he had a lively imagination and that from his testimony the others would learn what to say.
>
> He did all that was expected of him and more. Taking off his spectacles, and looking mildly but firmly at the Judge, he informed him that the prosecuting witness was a villain of the deepest dye. He had dreamed of such monsters in visions superinduced by Hasheesh, but had never met one before in real life...As for the defendant, he had known him, it might be for years and it might be forever. He was a Bohemian by nature and by profession. He had written worse things than he had ever done, but that was a matter with which critics had to do, and not courts. If the court pleased, he would read ten or a dozen pages from Darwin to illustrate what he meant.
>
> The Court declined—"Who was Darwin?"
>
> At a sign from a sturdy policeman, Ludlow left the stand muttering something about, Hang care, care killed a cat.[39]

Fitz Hugh wrote a "Goodbye Article" which appeared in the *Era* on November 22. He continued his Plain Talk there, launching into a digression starting "you see, I hate the Indians…I fully believe that the only treaty with them…must be written in blood…with that only style whose characters an Indian can read—the scalping knife." His witnessing of the aftermath of the massacre in Utah had permanently overwhelmed any sympathy he might have cultivated for the more "noble" Native Americans he met during his trip. But always returning to the light touch:

> Another reason why I take away such delightful memories of San Francisco, is the fact that I had all the strawberries I wanted there clear into the latter days of September…Both Bierstadt and I love that fruit with a tender human love—only to be explained by the doctrine of Metempsychosis on the ground that in our earlier stage of development we ourselves were male plants of the Alpine variety, and an avalanche having untimely nipped us before our marriage with a pair of lovely maiden strawberries to whom we were passionately attached, we now go seeking our beloved by a blind instinct through bushels of fruit.

He praised the Reverend Starr King at length for the power and beauty of his sermons, but Fitz Hugh's fondest thoughts of the West were reserved for the writers of *The Golden Era*. Inigo (Webb) he included as a Californian although noting the *Era* had "stolen him and the gleaming scalpel of his unerring pen from a bright Metropolitan career." Fitz Hugh also warned Webb about the latter's attempts to speculate in silver mines with his writing earnings, fearing that his ventures would bring "not one but a hundred eagles perpetually over his liver (if he carries his purse in his right hand breast pocket.)" Fitz Hugh added further praise of Bret Harte, noting "Both Harper's and the Atlantic would, I am sure, welcome him with enthusiasm."

Fitz Hugh's strongest words were for "that Irresistable Washoe Giant, Mark Twain" who "takes quite a unique position. He makes me laugh more than any Californian since poor [George] Derby died. He imitates nobody. He is a school by himself. With him and the highly idiomatic De Quille [William Wright] you will certainly have a comic literature of your own before long, needing no importations from our side of the desert." Twain took the encouragement to heart. Twain wrote to his mother in January, 1864:

> And if Fitz Hugh Ludlow (author of The Hasheesh Eater) comes your way, treat him well. He published a high encomium upon Mark Twain (the same being eminently just and truthful, I beseech you to believe) in a San Francisco paper. Artemus Ward said that when my gorgeous talents were publicly acknowledged by such high authority I ought to appreciate them myself, leave sage-brush obscurity and journey to New York with him, as he wanted me to do. But I preferred not to burst upon the New York public too suddenly and brilliantly, so I concluded to remain here.[40]

While Fitz Hugh stayed among the Californians, Twain "humbly submitted his work" to Fitz Hugh for advice and correction.[41] Fitz Hugh was not the first or last to be accorded that honor (Bret Harte, Artemus Ward and William Dean Howells were others), but it was a measure of Twain's respect for his intelligence and ability. Years later, a copy of The Hasheesh Eater surfaced which was inscribed "From the Library of Samuel L. Clemens."[42]

The *Era* in turn bid farewell to its guests in an editorial on the 22nd. After a tribute to Bierstadt's genius, they launch into a paean to Fitz Hugh:

> "The immortals," says Schiller, "never appear alone." With Bierstadt goes his friend and fellow traveler, Fitz Hugh Ludlow, who will make a book of his overland journey hither. Those who have read "The Hasheesh Eater," a book of precocious genius, written in his twenty-first year, reaching far into that mysterious realm where, but a few years before, De Quincey had "sounded his dim, perilous way," will believe that the work is in no unworthy hands. Those later readers of the "Little Brother," "The New Partner in Clingham & Co.," where this power is sustained and carried through the subtle details of social life with incomparable grace of fancy, and a spiritual power over the essence of language peculiar to this man alone, will need no further endorsement. But we apprehend his success here will not be based upon these works solely…We shall look for his book with pleasant anticipation. It will be the ripened fruit higher up on the vine whose graceful tendrils have lately chanced to wreathe and adorn the columns of this paper.

Critic Franklin Walker summed up the journey thus:

> During his four months' visit he influenced the isolated community of San Francisco writers in a subtle, pervasive way, entangling himself in the web and woof of Western literary tradition. He was a voice of encouragement from the outside world.[43]

Fitz Hugh and Bierstadt left on the Pacific Mail Steamship Company's *Constitution*, on November 23.[44] Starr King was there to see them off. "I could not bear to have you go away without one more good-bye," he told them. And off went the steamer bound for Panama. The Captain and ship's doctor allowed Fitz Hugh the use of their desks and libraries, and when the boat hit the Panama Bay, two weeks later, Fitz Hugh penned a letter (which was not published in the *Era* until January), describing his boat trip thus far. "We encountered the usual blow in the Gulf of Tehuantepec—a locality which seems to have been set off by Providence as a sort of Kinder-Garten for the obstreperous children of Aeolus and Neptune, where all the year round they squall to their heart's content."

The second installment of "How It Strikes One," under the title "Plain Talks No. 2," was written after the party had taken the express boat to Panama City, crossed Panama, and steamed on into Cuba for coal and cargo. In this one, the candid observer had somewhat lower estimations of the California art world than he did for its literature. He did, however, praise Bierstadt's friends Perry and Williams for their future potential, while lamenting their need to earn money by portrait painting. This article closed with the following:

> I have found so much cordial hospitality—so much genuine and hearty patriotism—such good feeling—and such an admirable substratum, in heart and intellect, for the success of a first-class civilization in respect to Art, Literature, Ethics and Religion, that I should most disingenuously end my "Plain Talk" about California, did I not say that next to my own beloved New York, the city of my nativity and residence, I love that which has so generously received and entertained me—San Francisco.

In Havana, "I find great abuses," but the only one he shared with readers was the absence of coins of low denomination, which required that the consumer "must buy a whole bunch of bananas in order to get the refreshment he needs from one." The stay in Cuba was brief, and the steamer arrived in New York on December 17, 1863.[45]

1 Later published in *The Golden Era*, January 31, 1864, p. 5.

2 Ibid.

3 Fitz Hugh Ludlow, "On Horseback into Oregon," *The Atlantic Monthly*, July 1864, p. 77.

4 *The Golden Era*, July 19, 1863, p. 8.

5 Inigo, "Things," *The Golden Era*, July 26, 1863, p. 5.

6 Franklin Walker, *The Washoe Giant in San Francisco*, San Francisco: Folcroft Library Editions, 1973, p. 8.

7 Ibid., p. 8

8 Hendricks (1973), p. 129.

9 William Simonds, *Starr King in California*, San Francisco, P. Elder and Company, p. 48.

10 Richard Frothingham, *A Tribute to Starr King*, Boston, Ticknor and Fields, 1865, p. 227.

11 Alvin Harlow, *Bret Harte of the Old West*, New York, J. Messner, Inc., 1943, p. 212.

12 *Auction*, May 1970, quoting the *San Francisco Daily Alta*, August 1, 1863. Hendricks says the *Alta* was quoting a Stockton paper.

13 Arkelian, Marjorie, *The Kahn Collection of Nineteenth Century Paintings by Artists in California*, Oakland: The Oakland Museum, 1975, n.p.

14 Fitz Hugh Ludlow, "Seven Weeks in the Great Yo-Semite," *The Atlantic Monthly*, June, 1864, p. 739.

15 There is no existing correspondence.

16 Fitz Hugh Ludlow, "Seven Weeks in the Great Yo-Semite," *The Atlantic Monthly*, June, 1864, p. 739.

17 *The Golden Era*, August 30, 1863, p. 4.

18 Bernard Falk, *The Naked Lady*, London: Hutchinson, 1952, p. 68.

19 Falk (1934), p. 71.

20 *The Golden Era*, September 13, 1863.

21 "Little Good for Nothing" and "The New Soul of John Markham" are stories mentioned in a later reminisce by Helen Ludlow, but have not been unearthed by the research for this book.

22 Charles Warren Stoddard, *Exits and Entrances*, Freeport NY: Books for Libraries Press, 1969, p. 243.

23 Albert Bigelow Paine, *Mark Twain: a Biography*, New York: Gabriel Wells, 1923, p. 100.

24 *The Golden Era*, August 30, 1863, p. 6.

25 *The Golden Era*, October, 1863.

26 Hendricks (1973), p. 130. The same source reports that National Archives records show he had paid his $300 exemption to be excused from service. There was no similar mention of Fitz Hugh.

27 Fitz Hugh Ludlow, "On Horseback into Oregon," *The Atlantic Monthly*, July, 1864, p. 75.

28 Fitz Hugh Ludlow, "On the Columbia River," *The Atlantic Monthly*, December, 1864, p. 703.

29 According to a later writer, "it seems probable that the first episode in 1863 was the primary tuberculosis infection. The 'pneumonia' and 'pulmonary spasms' following an arduous journey would be ideal descriptions of the usual setting for such an illness. People often had either mild or occasionally severe primary infections…which partially healed themselves. The organisms remained in the body, however, and if the circumstances arose, repropagated and caused a secondary infection picture." Dr. Sandor Burstein to Peter Vogel, February 20, 1974, now in the Fitz Hugh Ludlow Memorial Library.

30 *The Golden Era*, January 17, 1864, p. 4; "Bierstadt furnished us pictures, engraving the design which figures in the title-head of our paper."

31 Fitz Hugh Ludlow, "Seven Weeks in the Great Yo-Semite," *Atlantic Monthly*, June, 1864, p. 740.

32 Thomas Starr King to Sarah, December 2, 1863.

33 *Heart of the Continent*, p. 329-330.

34 The Chinese Opium Wars, where the British essentially introduced the habit to China at gunpoint, had only just ended. Many of the Chinese had been transported to America in a manner not much better than the African slave trade, whence comes the term "Shanghaied". See Jack Beeching, *The Chinese Opium Wars*, New York: Harcourt Brace and Jovanovich, 1975.

35 *San Francisco Examiner*, October 15, 1878.

36 Samuel Clemens to Henry Clemens, August 5, 1856, printed in Albert Paine, editor, *Letters of Mark Twain, Vol. 1*, New York, 1917, p. 34.

37 Fitz Hugh Ludlow, "What Shall They Do to Be Saved?" in *The Opium Habit*, New York: Harper & Brothers, 1868, p. 263.

38 James Austin, *Fields of the Atlantic Monthly*, San Marino, CA, 1953, p. 165. As Agassiz wrote in *The Atlantic Monthly* on most scientific topics,

Darwinism was slow to gain popular acceptance.

39 Inigo, "Things," *The Golden Era*, November 22, 1863, p. 1.
40 Cited in Fitz Hugh Ludlow, *The Hasheesh Eater*, 1975, p. 213.
41 Van Wyck Brooks, *The Times of Melville and Whitman*, p. 285.
42 Sold by Sarah Clemens Samosoud in 1951; record of Fitz Hugh Ludlow Memorial Library.
43 Walker (1973), p. 166.
44 Hendricks (1973), p. 134.
45 Ibid.

XIV.

HIGH SOCIETY

Fitz Hugh was exhausted when he boarded the steamer in San Francisco. The three week cruise, on a 300 foot paddle wheel luxury vessel, served as an admirable recuperative regime. With two such ships sandwiched around the trans-isthmus railroad across Panama, the entire journey took about three weeks. By the time he returned to New York, he was ready to tell the world of his journeys. *The Round Table* magazine noted a reception on February 13 at the Tenth St. studio, where "Mr. Bierstadt's studio was very interesting, containing as it did the fruits of his Western tour."[1]

Rosalie was there to greet Fitz Hugh, but the seven month absence had been emotionally trying. If she wasn't worried over Fitz Hugh's life being at risk, she may very well have worried for his uxorial soul in the heart of decadent Salt Lake City, not to mention the thought of the "tender pleading mouth" of Adah Menken. Rosalie herself was not entirely without temptation. Cousin Carrie Frey Geddings wrote to her mother on January 24, 1864, that "Flo Clark [a friend]…rather raves over Rosa, her beauty &c&c. but I think she has acted rather absurd for a married lady this winter from all accounts. I have but little respect for a married *flirt*."[2]

It was also clear even before Fitz Hugh had left that the young couple were not especially fertile. They had been married four years when he headed West, time enough in that era for the average couple to be blessed with issue. Although she may have blamed herself, might not her "one forever lost to me" have had something to do with this situation? Nor was Fitz Hugh completely recovered from the Oregon collapse. Cousin Gus reported to his sister that "F. is in a very bad way, suffering from neuralgia."[3]

Nevertheless, Fitz Hugh was soon hard at work on further transcription of his notes from the West. By January 31, 1864, the first of a new series of "Reminiscences of an Overlander" picked up where "Letters from Sundown" left off. The new series was published in Fitz Hugh's recent literary haunt, *The Golden Era*. On February 21, 1864, an installment entitled "From the Missouri to the Rocky Mountains" appeared. It was more a commentary on the grueling style of Overland travel than a description of the territory.

Fitz Hugh's writing during the Western trip had earned perhaps $600-$700 over the last half of 1863, but travel expenses ate up a great deal of that. Early in 1864, he had added another marketable skill to his repertoire by initiating a lecture tour. *The Golden Era* of February 19 reported that "Fitz Hugh Ludlow recently delivered a lecture called 'Across the Continent' at Dodsworth's Hall, New York. It describes his overland journey from the Atlantic to the Pacific Coast."[4] Lectures in the U.S. at this time often featured such luminaries as Henry Ward Beecher, but "Artemus Ward" and others of Fitz Hugh's acquaintance had broadened the field. Fitz Hugh, who was known widely through his writings, was able to attract interest in personal appearances. And Fitz Hugh was a seasoned performer, known for "declaiming his compositions" since his time with Dr. Nott at Union College.

Lecturing was a pleasant occupation, but not especially lucrative. While the *Era* was paying enough to steal Fitz Hugh's transcontinental tales from the *Evening Post*, Fitz Hugh in need of serious funds went to his old reliable publisher, *Harper's Monthly*. He quickly penned and published "John Heathburn's Title" in the February and March numbers of the *Monthly*. In many ways typical of his *Harper's* work in structure and style, "Heathburn" was much more important in another way. This story reintroduced hashish, and substance abuse, as important elements in Fitz Hugh's writing.

John Heathburn is the "pure and noble" male hero of the story, but his half brother George Solero is an alcoholic and a laudanum addict. The narrator, an old school chum of the two brothers, is a recent graduate of medical school who is called by John to come to Norfolk, Virginia to help treat George. George had become such a drunkard that he burned down the house of the family's Negro servants because the eldest of those had prevented him from drinking. "I roasted the black devil that let me roast with hell inside me, and wouldn't give me a drop to cool my tongue!"

When first told the problem, the narrator asked if sedatives had been administered. "Yes," replied John, "we got a doctor up from town, who gave him a dose of Indian Hemp—'Cannabis', I believe he called it—but it only made him wilder, and, if possible, put him into greater agony." "Of course!" replied the narrator, "It is a drug whose effects after those of liquor are most fearful. I remember its nearly proving fatal in the hospital once; but excuse me, go on."

"The fact is" continued John Heathburn, "we didn't dare to give him opium, which is the only other adequate sedative that seems to be known. It was tried once before, when he was suffering from the after-effects of a debauch, and though it relieved him at the time, his knowledge of its effects made him substitute it after that for liquor, as I shall tell you; and he was tending to the still worse hell if possible of that awful narcotic, when a supper, arranged by his friends, turned him to liquor again. But I have my suspicions that he has been alternating the two ever since." In fact, after a period of apparent sobriety, a local doctor informed George's father that George had been buying laudanum steadily for five months. The narrator then agrees to take the case of George Solero, as "these cases have been my peculiar study; indeed the subject is a specialty to which I hope to devote my medical life." Fitz Hugh himself may have treated his pulmonary spasms in Oregon with opium. Between that and his acquaintance with opium smoking in the hongs of San Francisco and his reading of De Quincey, it appears that Fitz Hugh shared much in common with the narrator of this story. He wrote:

> [O]pium is a giant. It controls men for damnable evil—sometimes for temporary good, long years after the nervous system, which narcotics require as their basis for operation, has been utterly destroyed for all other purposes…[the task of the doctor is to make his patient] feel that the Evil within him, and so far as he can see encircling him externally also like a globe of adamant, is still penetrable, vanquishable by the Good of another stronger soul still further outside. In fine, must be forced to see the incredible truth that, in this Universe with whose horrible realities he has become intimately acquainted, the Good is still the only all-powerful, all-whelming Principle; that it alone, but it certainly, shall bring his and every other Evil under.

This passage is prophetic in its invocation of a major theme of modern-day twelve-step substance-abuse recovery programs. The first break in the case comes when George tells the narrator "that I was the first man who ever knew what he had seen and where he had been…After this I arose and took my medicine chest from my trunk. In it lay a box of the solid extract of Cannabis Indica—the Indian Hemp or Hasheesh of the East—then little known to the practice, and now too little known in its highest office of controlling bad mental symptoms, but which I had already used with great success in cases of the most terrible delirium among those feeless patients whom I had treated in New York." The narrator's treatment of rest made possible by a daily dose of hashish disguised with myrrh flavoring, combined with close scrutiny of George's daily regimen of exercise, nourishment and occupation, led to a successful cure within four months.

This episode occupies only one of eight chapters in this picaresque novelet, the last half of which is devoted to the requisite love story. One passage is of biographical interest: "Upon men who have sinned and suffered as he did the influence of any intense mental stimulus, I have found, often acts similarly to a resumption of the physical indulgence [in opium]." And while it contained personal elements, "John Heathburn's Title" also reflected the growing use of opium in the U.S., in part a result of the treatment of wounded soldiers from the Civil War. Further, the story's portrayal of opium as medicine signals the onset of the era of patent medicines.[5] Beyond the drug related observations, several passages in this story reflect a maturing prose style:

In an upper room of one of the great hotels of New York, late at night, a young man sat alone. The fire in his grate had died down to dull cinders; yet he kept his chair silent and motionless, not knowing that the air grew chill. Light seemed as little a matter of care to him as heat—the jet of the one burner by the pier was turned so low that the room was lonelier for it, and walls were draped in long funereal shadows of the man and the things around him.

The city outside of him was lying in its first sleep. The hand of the giant Work had fallen by his side like a tired child; no longer pushing to and fro along the roaring streets the carriages, and carts, the beasts and hurried, wearied men who did his pleasure.

On February 28 and March 6, "Reminiscences of an Overlander" continued in the *Golden Era* with an installment called "Denver to Salt Lake: Both Inclusive." This segment picked up where "Letters from Sundown" left off, describing the Overlanders in and around Denver and the Pikes Peak region. Some of the commentary overlaps the Post letters with slight differences. On March 20, the *Era* published "First Impressions of Mormondom," and on March 27 some further sketches of Brigham Young, Heber Kimball, and a tribute to fearless Indian killer General Conner. On April 17, the final installment of "Reminiscences of an Overlander," Salt Lake to San Francisco, made its appearance. But this was not simply because the journey had ended. Rather, Fitz Hugh had negotiated a far more prestigious showcase.

The Atlantic Monthly, long the epitome of everything the Bohemian Fitz Hugh hated about Boston, had followed the Overlanders' journey with great interest. Although others had journeyed West before, Fitz Hugh was a respected journalist and author (at least by New York standards) and the journey was still a novel subject. More important, the *Atlantic* thus far had published little about the great frontier. The April, 1864 issue of *The Atlantic Monthly* saw Fitz Hugh's debut in the premier showcase of literary America with a piece entitled "Among the Mormons." This sketch covered material similar to the last *Era* pieces, but was a little less blunt (Mormons are not accused of being, "like the Jews, shameless polygamists, assassins, bigots" etc.) and, well, a little more respectable.

The *Atlantic* also brought out Fitz Hugh the pedagogue, dilating in academic detail on rock formations of the Cathedral Buttes. He was also at his most delicate describing (and sniffing at) Mormon social mores. And at his most graphic, he closes the 16 page essay with a concise description of the Indian massacre which his party discovered in the Utah desert, with "six men, their brains dashed out, their faces mutilated beyond recognition, their limbs hewn off   a frightful holocaust steaming up into our faces."

Fitz Hugh's debut in the *Atlantic* was a success. As Bayard Taylor would later write to Stedman, "I see yr. name among the stars of the Atlantic. Rejoice my friend! Boston hath accepted you! But in all gravity, this is a good thing because the Atlantic is accepted by the populace as the representative magazine of American literature."[6] The *Atlantic*'s editor, James Fields, commissioned another piece on the westward journey, covering the travellers' stay in Yosemite. It seemed that the trip West had indeed rescued a moribund career and had sent Fitz Hugh on his way toward a prominent place in American letters and life. Fitz Hugh was also no doubt aware that most of what was published in the *Atlantic* was published in book form sooner or later. Having seen several novels and numerous short stories ignored by the Harpers book publishing arm, he was ready to seek new pastures. Further, government spending on the war effort had stimulated the economy and brought it out of the doldrums of the pre-War years, so that there was more of a market for his writing, and books and magazines generally.

As if to confirm his ascension to the literary aristocracy, Fitz Hugh was called upon to contribute to the largest of all charitable efforts in support of the Union Civil War armies. This was the Sanitary Commission, the forerunner to what eventually became the Red Cross.[7] The Sanitary Commission had been raising money to help treat or comfort the Civil War's mounting casualties. One newly popular method was through the staging of carnivals or fairs to raise money, and New York City's civic leaders began planning a "Sanitary Fair" for the spring of 1864. On the planning committee were such friends and acquaintances of Fitz Hugh as Fletcher Harper, Charles Nordhoff, and Henry Ward Beecher, not to mention prominent socialites Mrs. John Jacob Astor, Mrs. Alexander Hamilton Jr. and Mrs. William H. Van Buren.

Jessie Fremont, wife of Senator (and Major General) John Fremont, was also active in this effort, partly at the urgings of her minister, Thomas Starr King. Jessie was one of the first ladies of California, daughter of Senator Thomas Hart Benton, and wife of the famous explorer, military man, and Republican party candidate for president in 1856.[8] Jessie did much relief work, and also was a patroness to the likes of Starr King and writer Bret Harte. King called her "a strong friend of mine—my own admirer in the universe,"[9] and Harte called her his "fairy god-mother" after she procured for him a government appointment.[10]

John Fremont was an ardent abolitionist, and in the course of his command of Union armies in Missouri, had issued a proclamation freeing slaves in the area. This proclamation had irritated Lincoln by being premature and too expansive, but ultimately Fremont proved to be an ineffective leader against Confederate armies under Stonewall Jackson. (This at a time when the Union army had begun invading the heart of the south.) The commands of Fremont and two other major generals were subsumed under General Pope by Lincoln and his strategists, and Fremont resigned rather than serve as less than commander in chief. After a stay in California, Fremont soon began to explore another run at the presidency in the 1864 election. In May, he was nominated as candidate by a third party calling itself the party of Radical Democracy.

Jessie Fremont, meanwhile, had contacted socialites in New York about involving their families in the Sanitary Fair, and someone hit upon the idea of a play starring the children of the wealthy. Reverend King recommended his recent acquaintance, Fitz Hugh Ludlow, to choose the play. (Fitz Hugh's involvement may have come as early as January, judging by a reference in "John's Heathburn's Title" to "the fascinating woman of wealth and society, leaving all that is universally held dearest by her class, to expend a queenly life on the care of sick soldiers.") The result was Fitz Hugh's adaptation of the fairy tale Cinderella into a musical play. Fitz Hugh was delighted by the chore. He had never lost his touch for spinning a tale for the young ones, and dove happily into the writing of the script and songs.

Ironically, before the Fair commenced, Thomas Starr King caught pneumonia and died. Fitz Hugh was greatly affected by the death of the man whom he had admired in the past, and had been fortunate enough to meet. In the midst of his occupation with the Cinderella production, Fitz Hugh conceived and took on the additional task of producing a memorial tribute to King. He solicited contributions from the likes of John Greenleaf Whittier, and acquired several letters written by King. The core of the volume was a long poem Fitz Hugh wrote himself, entitled "Abest: Surrexit."

> And we who scarce can see through tears
> Carve on the arch he would not wait
> From heaven to see: "Stand, tell the years
> We lost him—but he saved the State."

This is probably the worst single piece of writing Fitz Hugh ever produced. For 41 stanzas covering seven pages, Fitz Hugh displayed an utter lack of coherent theme and a repeated willingness to descend into cliché or banality, e.g. "But ever through God's open door, see the full triumph of the Right," and "I am not beneath the pall! Good must be the goal of all." There is not a single noteworthy idea or turn of the phrase in the whole poem, unless it is the bizarre reference to God as "Man's Almighty Lover." The failed effort understandably resulted from the workload, but was not a good omen for a high level of future productivity.

The entire volume, with an introduction by Fitz Hugh, was entitled *In Memoriam, Thomas Starr King*, and was published "For the Benefit of the Sanitary Commission" and sold at the Fair, "at the table of Mrs. Fremont, in the Arms and Trophies Department."[11] Fitz Hugh's introduction was at least coherent, with acknowledgements of King's role in keeping California in the Union, in supporting the

Sanitary Commission, and his support "for the investiture of the Chinaman with such civic rights as belong to industry (and) his life-long efforts to strike off the fetters of the slave and give the Negro a standing on the floor of manhood." The introduction was signed by Fitz Hugh "on behalf of the New York Friends of Thomas Starr King," and Fitz Hugh also mentioned that "what we have written is the nucleus for a Memorial to Starr King which shall embrace a biographical sketch, such extracts from his letters as may be published without any intrusion on sacred privacies...Our duties once performed to the Sanitary Fair, we shall begin the collection and editing of our material." *The Round Table* magazine reported these further plans as well on April 30, but the project was never completed. *The New York Times* reviewed the pamphlet on April 21:

> IN MEMORIAM—THOMAS STARR KING
> A beautifully executed pamphlet being the above title has just made its appearance on the book table of the Fair. Its issue has been unavoidably delayed, but nevertheless its exquisite tributes to the memory of a divine held dear in the hearts of many of our citizens will find for it a large sale during the last days of the fair.

And the Sanitary Fair souvenir program "Spirit of the Fair" contained the polite notice "At Mrs. Fremont's table, in the Arms and Trophies room, is to be found the Memorial Tribute, in clear and tender stanzas, to the late Thomas Starr King, by Fitz Hugh Ludlow."

Fortunately, Fitz Hugh had devoted time, effort and more graceful love to his adaptation of Cinderella. This is a virtual masterpiece of whimsy. It took Fitz Hugh only a page to get in his first pun in, and the play is sprinkled with them. The Prince and other members of royalty all speak in verse, as in a Shakespearean play. Even the staging was elaborate. When the pumpkin and mice are turned into horse and carriage, ponies were led onstage, like a nursery school version of Mazeppa. The script also called for a chorus and orchestra, and the playlet included a song from the Opera of Mother Goose, several movements from Gungl's Venus-Reigen, the Soldier's Chorus from Faust, and the following sung by the fairy Godmother to the air of "Io te voglio ben' assajo:"

> Oh! what a life the fairy leads!
> Now on the sunbeam going,
> And now in the ground beneath the seeds,
> She keeps the flowers a-growing;
> Now to the deep sea-floor she dives
> To tend the birth of pearls;
> And now she watches over the lives
> Of good little boys and girls.

The finished script was published in New York by J. A. Gray and Green printers just prior to the start of the Fair. Proceeds from the performance were earmarked for the Fund for Soldiers' Orphans. Fitz Hugh used a printed copy as his rehearsal copy, and continued to make last minute changes up until showtime.[12] Some of these changes include the excision of several lines which seem aimed at the adults in the audience. In one, the queen says "you're nervous, dear" but Fitz Hugh edited out the follow-up "Take some of Mrs. Winslow's Soothing Syrup. Children cry for it—see advertisement," not only as an adult spoof of commercialism, but perhaps because that Soothing Syrup was one of many patent medicines of the time which included opium as an ingredient.[13] Also edited is a passage where the Prince says "I'm hit in the very heart!" and the queen responds "Tell your papa; And with his father we will go to war." Although a few adult jokes remained, such as Dromio asking when helping ladies try on the slipper—"Would you like to take chloroform?" most such subtleties were removed in favor of telling the story to and for the children. Dromio seeks the Prince's mystery girl with the couplet:

> For His Highness has vowed by the Moon and Big Dipper
> To marry the lady who puts on the slipper.

The play ends with Cinderella forgiving her haughty step-sisters, saying "Our charity is like an omnibus, There's always room for just two more."

The Fair began with a parade and festivities on April 4. In attendance were Union Generals McLellan, McDowell and Burnside. Performances in the "Children's Department" were postponed due to inclement weather and the unfinished state of the room. The *Times* described the play as follows:

> One of the prettiest devices to swell the receipts of the Metropolitan Fair, while it gives innocent pleasure to thousands of children, is a representation of the story of "Cinderella, or the Little Glass Slipper" acted wholly by children from five to thirteen years of age. Mr. Wheatley has kindly offered the use of Niblo's Garden for the purpose and Mr. Fitz Hugh Ludlow has lent his skillful pen to put the story into proper shape, while the labor of getting up the performance, and the expense of putting a host of children into "court dress," has

been cheerfully assumed by Mrs. Gen. Fremont. The result will be a fairy-like spectacle…A son of Gen. Fremont plays the part of Prince, while a son of Prof. Morse is the herald—a fit office for the inventor of the world-speaking telegraph.

The review in the *Times* on April 17 read:

The little fairies had a grand time at Niblo's Gardens on Sat. evening and their performance of "Cinderella, or the Little Glass Slipper" was very successful. The house was filled to its utmost and many went away unable to gain admission. The dresses, some of which were furnished by the children's parents, and the rest by Mrs. Gen. Fremont, were very rich and appropriate; the scenery was very handsome and the little people performed their parts admirably. Bouquets were thrown them in great profusion, and the applause was frequent and hearty. The receipts were $2,842—a very handsome gift from fairy-land.

Elsewhere at the fair, Bierstadt's "Rocky Mountains, Lander's Peak", was on display directly across the room from Fredric Church's "Heart of the Andes" (and just down the hall from Leutze's "Washington Crossing the Delaware"). This placement signified Bierstadt's arrival as an equal to Church, and his painting would sell the next year for $25,000, then the highest price ever paid for an American painting.[14] In an auction for the benefit of the Fair, Bierstadt's smaller painting "Valley of the Yosemite" sold for $1,600. Bierstadt had also enhanced the marketing of his work by setting up an Indian Department at the Fair, with artifacts and live Indian "performances." The New York Fair ultimately brought in a total of $1 million for relief efforts.[15]

8   CINDERELLA.

[A flash of lightning, a clap of thunder, rattling wheels
heard without, and the orchestra plays the first, second
movements and Da Capo, of Gungl's Venus-Reigen,
pianissimo.

CIN. [*Hurrying to throw off her finery*] O dear! What
shall I do? There's a thunder-storm; the girls have come
back. I shall be killed! Dear! dear! dear!

[FAIRY GODMOTHER *again from behind the scenes*]
WOULD you like to be at the party?

[CINDERELLA *sinks fainting with fear on the nearest
sofa*] I'm frightened to death. O dear, *dear* me! Why
did I come here?

[The back scenes slide apart—orchestra playing "Donna
e mobile," *crescendo* from *pianissimo.* FAIRY GOD-
MOTHER discovered standing somewhat above the
stage—rose-lights thrown upward against her face and
bust—in a hoop of lace and flowers.

FAIRY G. M. Cinderella! Cinderella!

CIN. [*Trembling, with her face still hidden in the sofa-
cushion.*] Ye-ye-ye-yes, ma'am! Oh! don't punish me!
I'll never do it again!

FAIRY G. M. Cinderella! Cinderella!

CIN. [*half rising.*] That isn't the voice of one of my
Haughty Sisters. Who called?

[She rises entirely—turns—sees the Fairy—and stands
in dumb astonishment. The Fairy skips down from her
frame—comes tripping into the boudoir—and the back
scenes close behind her.

FAIRY G. M. [*Singing—Air,* Donna e Mobile.]
What! don't you know me?
Sleeping below me,

LUDLOW'S OWN LINER NOTES FOR HIS VERSION OF "CINDERELLA".

The Fremont connection also led, briefly, to another lit-
erary market for Fitz Hugh. General Fremont and the
Radical Democracy group had begun a publication called
The New Nation. Fremont's presidential platform included a
constitutional amendment abolishing slavery, confiscation

and redistribution of all lands held by Rebels, and in general gave voice to the concerns of Republican radicals. The party also advocated civil rights such as voting for freed slaves, which more conservative Republicans still found a little too progressive. However, the party never was more than a fringe third party, and by September, the Republicans had prevailed upon Fremont to drop out of the race in the interests of party unity, enabling Lincoln to be reelected.[16]

The New Nation (which a California wag said in view of Fremont's radical racial views "must be a miscege-nation") began in the Spring of 1864, and to leaven the political tracts its editors sought some literary input.[17] Fitz Hugh contributed a sketch entitled "The Spring Openings—A Comparison." This sketch was a cross between *Golden Era* satire and *Harper's Monthly* civility, comparing the introduction of the new Spring fashion styles to the flowering of plants in nature. Fitz Hugh says that Nature "has meditated deeply on constitutional fitnesses, studied her own features, and suited her costume to them, until the wood wanderer comes back from Nature's spring opening to Madame Fen-Follet's with a sense of pain and anti-climax, which reaches deeper than the Aesthetic...We accept the Parisian fashions, but the grace to wear them wisely seems untranslatable. We bow down to successive dynasties of color; to-day humbling ourselves under the tyranny of universal mauve, to-morrow becoming the slaves of cafe au lait." Further, "The woman who buys an ugly Cashmere because it costs ten times as much as a handsome Paisley may not know it, but she is taking a reverse step toward barbarism." Fitz Hugh soon, however, "severed his connection with The New Nation" for reasons unknown.[18]

After the Sanitary Fair, Fitz Hugh continued to mine his Western travel notes. In June, Fitz Hugh's next travel article appeared in the *Atlantic Monthly*, entitled "Seven Weeks in the Great Yo-Semite." After an introduction on some of the delights of San Francisco, Fitz Hugh produced some of his most poetic work in describing the splendors of Yo-Semite.[19] Fitz Hugh followed this piece with the next installment of the trip, "On Horseback Into Oregon," appearing in the *Atlantic* in July. This article covered the trip from Sacramento up to the California/Oregon border, closing with a tribute to Mount Shasta, only a little less enthusiastic than the Yo-Semite paean. In it he also sprinkled the travelogue with topical references, such as comparing a bird opening and closing its wings to a pupil of Dr. Dio Lewis, a New Yorker who had devised an exercise regime which was an early type of aerobics routine.

The travel articles were quite well received, and Editor Fields had his eye on Fitz Hugh to continue contributing to the *Atlantic* on a number of fronts. One project was to provide commentary on New York City, which, even though Bostonians still considered it crassly commercial and literarily inferior, at least could not be ignored.

In the midst of his New York article research, Fitz Hugh reverted to his old paper of record for the overland journey, *The Golden Era*, for a transcript of his stay in Portland. "The Prisoners of Portland" appeared in the *Era* on June 12 and June 19. Subtitled "an Historical Novel of the Present, Past and Future; In Two Short (May Its Readers Echo "Too Short!") Books—and No Chapters Whatsoever; Doleful, Damp and Dramatic," these pieces were probably a relief from his serious *Atlantic* essays. In the *Era*, Fitz Hugh was once again the free spirit, and he polished up a narrative probably written originally as a complete essay, as opposed to the rougher notes of his other travel writings. In the *Era*, Fitz Hugh could be rained on "to a degree which washes all the sterner carnal affections out of everybody but Horace Day, the great India Rubber man."[20]

The *Golden Era* was still reminiscing about the Overlanders long after they left for home. In January of 1864, the *Era* included a column "introducing" the *Era* to prospective readers in Asia and Africa. In bragging about contributors, they say "Fitz Hugh Ludlow, Orpheus C. Kerr, Artemus Ward, and Albert Bierstadt arrived in California. We purchased their pens and pencils before they had been an hour in the country." The *Era* also reported on February 14 that "Perry, the artist, has finished some very good pictures from studies of the Yosemite Valley, which he took in company with Bierstadt and Ludlow last summer."

After sending off "The Prisoners of Portland," Fitz Hugh wrote to Editor Fields:

> My Dear Mr. Fields,
> Excuse the great haste which makes me rush at once into business by saying that if you can get along without the "Greatness of New York" Article until November I can furnish you with two more Articles of travel between now and October. One of them will give a running sketch of the entire ride which one may be prophetically seen to take on the Pacific R.R. and furnish some idea of the status which would prevail through the shorter axis of our continent were the enterprise now completed. Another would treat generally of the Columbia River and its scenery & science.

If these be satisfactory please let me know. I intend to bring my book out during the winter. The engravers and I are hard at work on it now.

In great haste but Truly Your Friend, Fitz Hugh Ludlow[21]

Snubbing the Harpers, Fitz Hugh had contracted with Hurd and Houghton (now Houghton Mifflin after the addition of George Mifflin in 1872) to collect his travel writings from the *Atlantic*, *The Golden Era*, and the *New York Evening Post* into one epic work in two planned volumes.[22] Hurd and Houghton was viewed as a more serious house than Harper. The *Boston Evening Transcript* reported "Hurd and Houghton bid fair to do for New York what Ticknor & Fields have done for Boston...having raised the style of printing and caused the publishers and reading community to recognize its claims and capabilities as a fine art, as well as a special economy."[23] *The Golden Era* added on October 30 that "Fitz Hugh Ludlow's book...is to be illustrated from drawings made by Bierstadt who was accompanied by Mr. Ludlow on his tour of the Pacific Coast." Some of Bierstadt's sketches were being converted into woodcuts for Fitz Hugh's book. Bierstadt meanwhile was finishing some paintings, such as Mount Hood from the Oregon trip, and the *Evening Post* reported that he "is painting two pictures, to order, for ten thousand dollars each."[24]

In September, Fitz Hugh wrote a summation of his journey to the West in the form of a prophecy of the final route of the transcontinental railroad, entitled "Through Tickets to San Francisco." It appeared in the *Atlantic* in November. Fitz Hugh wrote, "the initial fulfillment of a promise which America has made to herself and all the other nations shall be completely fulfilled only when an iron highway stretches across her entire breadth, from the Atlantic to the Pacific Ocean." He had no doubt this would occur after the war when "no entangling alliances with a dead-weight social system bias our plain judgement." While "there is no doubt that the ideal principle of democratic progress demands the absolute non-interference of Government in all enterprises whose benefit accrues to a part of its citizens, or which can be stimulated into life by the spontaneous operation of popular interest," the Pacific Railroad "concerns the entire population of the United States." Fitz Hugh gave examples of how the railroad would stimulate, e.g., the iron from mines in Missouri to San Franciscan implement manufacturers. Another part of his justification for the railroad was that it would replace "the ordeal of the steamer" trip. Fitz Hugh spared no hyperbole in extolling the comfort of the high speed trip. "We seat ourselves in comfortable armchairs...the gentlemen may smoke, if the ladies like it. [E]very through-train being obligated by statute to carry a first-class physician and surgeon[,] we all enjoy a sense of security and independence, which is like occupying a well-provisioned Gibraltar on wheels." Fitz Hugh worked in a little transcendental touch by appreciating that there would be no troublesome resetting of watches in every station, Dayton time, Cincinnati time, etc., "whether, indeed, all time be not a pure subjective notion, and any o'clock at all a mere popular delusion."

The proposal of a rail route gave Fitz Hugh the opportunity to summarize and parade his knowledge of the terrain, and he adorned the travelogue with occurrences on an imaginary trip that occupied most of the article. The train passes a buffalo herd, where hunters can disembark long enough to kill tonight's steak dinner, although Fitz Hugh sniffed at "pseudo-hunters, who will bang away with their rifles at the defenceless herd, until the ground flows with useless blood, and somebody suggests to them that they might as well call it sportsmanship to fire into a farmer's cow-yard, resting over the top rail." The fictional train encounters a thunderstorm on the Plains, where "we shall witness in one hour more atmospheric perturbation than has occurred within our whole previous experience on the Atlantic slope." And near Denver, the travellers witness "the grand snow-peak of Mount Rosalie," the first reference to Mrs. Ludlow in Fitz Hugh's writing since his return.

Many factions were vying for the route of the transcontinental railroad, and Fitz Hugh was prescient in his prediction of a route which was eventually very close to the actual route, choosing for instance Denver instead of Cheyenne, Wyoming as one of the way stations.[25] At the end, Fitz Hugh simply asked, "Is not all this worth doing in reality?" The reality occurred twelve years later with the completion of the transcontinental railroad. After Fitz Hugh's article appeared, Speaker of the House of Representatives Schuyler Colfax made a trip to the west to examine the route for the proposed Pacific railway, beginning the serious work of implementing the dream.[26] Colfax was accompanied by Samuel Bowles, editor of the Springfield [Massachusetts] *Republican*, who would publish a book on the trip the next year, influenced by Fitz Hugh's literary trailblazing.

The prophecy was followed in December in the *Atlantic* by "On the Columbia River." The trip through Oregon had taken place with Fitz Hugh's usual keen observational powers considerably impaired by the pulmonary attacks. After a brief description of his recuperative trials, the narrative describes the sailing and steaming up the Columbia River as far east as the Dalles. Fitz Hugh closed the final chapter of his reminisce by writing "it was still among the memories of a lifetime to have seen the Columbia in its Cataracts and its Dalles."

Fitz Hugh's work in the *Atlantic*, and his work on the Sanitary Fair, signaled his arrival in high society. Formal recognition came when Fitz Hugh was nominated to the Century Club, the foremost men's club in the City. Fitz Hugh's early mentor Bayard Taylor had been elected to the Century Club in 1851, and family friends like Samuel Morse and William Curtis Noyes were also members. Also in his "pledge class" were Edmund Stedman, Richard Stoddard, and Parke Godwin, William Cullen Bryant's son-in-law and assistant editor of the *New York Evening Post* (Bryant was one of the charter members). Their nominations were held up briefly in an attempt by Southern sympathizers to blackball Godwin for the *Evening Post*'s anti-Rebellion stance. The blackball attempt failed, and Fitz Hugh and the rest were elected on November 12.[27]

Other Ludlow friends and acquaintances in the Club included Bierstadt, E.L. Youmans, Edwin Booth, and poet and businessman Edward Stansbury, a son of one of the old families that summered in the spas of Long Branch where Fitz Hugh and Rosalie had spent time. Later members in Fitz Hugh's time would include artists Frederick Church and Winslow Homer, and Fitz Hugh's young Union College friend Daniel McMartin Stimson (see Chapter 5). Fitz Hugh attended one Century Club banquet in celebration of Shakespeare's birthday, where each menu item was accompanied by an appropriate aphorism from the Bard. Another Century Club event honored Fitz Hugh's former editor William Cullen Bryant on his 70th birthday. Poems were written in Bryant's honor by Longfellow, Whittier, Lowell and Oliver Wendell Holmes, as well as by such lesser lights as Stoddard and Stansbury. A book of sketches by Bierstadt, Church, Hicks, McEntee and others was also presented. It was the social event of the season. Fitz Hugh had come a long way from the Bohemian disdain of the literary establishment. Perhaps he felt only a twinge when Mark Twain later visited the Club and wrote of his awe of the intellectual firepower there arrayed—"I averaged the heads and they went 3 sizes larger than the style of heads I have been accustomed to."[28]

After the Bryant festival, Rosalie caught pneumonia. Although there is no extant evidence of her activities during Fitz Hugh's eventful 1864, Rosalie probably assisted at the Sanitary Fair and was otherwise occupied. For a change, it was Fitz Hugh doing the nursing, and he stayed home at No. 1 Livingston Place, on Stuyvesant Square, writing letters like the following to Edward Stansbury:

My Dear Ed'ard which his other name was Stansbury,
I am again in search of you with money! You are a rare & wonderful man. Hundred dollar bills which flee some folk chase you. [here Fitz Hugh had drawn a comical picture of a 100 dollar bill with arms and legs chasing a man with a long beard and walking stick] You are a male Danae—but an unconscious one. Gold pours in on you but you know it not. I came to see you yesterday—and you were out. It is terrible my Ed'ard, to be out when the Gods call. Be always at home to Fortune—Tomorrow may I smile on you to the extent of $100?

If you will, please be so kind as to send up Joseph for the am't tomorrow about 1 P.M. I would go down today—but Rose is very ill with pneumonia, both the Doctor and I are more alarmed about her than ever before—and I dare not leave her for an instant. I am very anxious indeed. I was up with her almost the entire night. I am pretty well fagged out—but you & I thank God have good constitutions and have made them tough for suffering by bearing all the panic & responsibilities possible in this life.

God bless you my dear boy. Love to yours & you from me and mine & believe me one of your best friends, Ludlow[29]

109 E. 15TH STREET, WHERE THE CENTURY CLUB MET.
(COURTESY OF CENTURY ASSOCIATION ARCHIVES FOUNDATION)

Fitz Hugh also borrowed $240 from Edwin Booth during the year, but was finally catching up with his finances.[30]

Five pieces in the *Atlantic*, a *Harper's* two part story, nine travelogues in the *Golden Era*, plus pieces in the *New Nation* provided at least a little comfort zone. Fitz Hugh may have earned $1,500-$2,000, more than any year since 1860, the height of his post-Hasheesh Eater fame. Nurturing his newfound respectability, Fitz Hugh wrote to *Atlantic* editor James T. Fields about his still-in-progress article on New York City:

> My Dear Mr. Fields,
> I have not heard from you since I forwarded the Mss. of the N.Y. article but am sure I should have done so had you not received it. If there be time I wish to make the following addendum in a foot- note on the last page of the article.
> "In addition to the obligations elsewhere recognized, an acknowledgement is due to the well known archaeologist and statist of New York, Mr. Valentine, who furnished for the purpose of this article the latest edition of his Manual in advance of its general publication, to the much increased convenience of the writer."
> Believe me in great haste but very truly yours, FHL
> P.S. My wife has been so ill with pneumonia ever since the Bryant Festival that she has not been able to put the cap-stone on an excellent review of Emily Chester. My constant press of work & natural anxiety for her have kept me from finishing & publishing it—but I will in a few days.[31]

This letter contains several corrections over crossed out areas, as well as a P.S., both of which do not appear in *any* of Fitz Hugh's extant manuscripts. Fitz Hugh wrote almost everything in one draft, "having always in mind exactly what he wanted to say."[32] This indicates the depth of his distress at this time. It is also interesting to note that Rosalie's own literary aspirations (recall her stint as New York correspondent for the *Waterville Times*) had been revived, perhaps by Fitz Hugh's long absence.

A full year had passed since Fitz Hugh's return from the West. His professional life was at its peak of prestige and energy, but his wife's illness was the first foreshadowing of hard times ahead. When Rose failed to recover, Fitz Hugh arranged to bring her upstate to Aunt Carrie Frey's house in Palatine Bridge. Aunt Carrie's daughter was puzzled by this move:

> I was sorry to hear of Rose sickness and that poor Fitz was so down again. But why in the name of sense don't he go home with his wife! That's what I should like to know. I should think he would want to be with her, but if not there why not to his own father's house? I don't envy you at all having him with you. It will do for a while but for a "regular diet" I should object. I think you are all very good to take him.[33]

Inexplicably, Fitz Hugh chose this time to begin a lecture tour. Fitz Hugh was a popular speaker, but New York was crowded with the likes of talents like Charles Dickens and Artemus Ward. This led Fitz Hugh to explore such locations as Philadelphia and Cincinnati, where he had made contacts on his way out west. His first lecture topic, borrowed from the pages of *The Golden Era*, was "Good Living." This is a subject on which Fitz Hugh continued to expound in 1864, whether in the *New Nation* where he "deplores making expense rather than art the measure of good living," or in the *Atlantic* where he praises the proposed Pacific railroad's kitchen "which makes us quite independent of that black art known as Western cookery." Fitz Hugh wrote to E.R. Perkins of Philadelphia about his proposed lecture appearance:

I should much prefer to lecture for you a little later in the
season if I am to go to you on any other night than Dec. 22nd.
What do you say to the 29th of Dec.? I wish to stay a little
longer in Buffalo, upon business apart from lectures, than I
could if I lectured there and before you on successive nights.
If you can make no other arrangement than the 22nd, I will
come to you then, but another night, say Dec. 29 or Jan. 6th,
would better suit.

Yours very truly, Fitz Hugh Ludlow[34]

Another complicating factor in Fitz Hugh's life was the
growing strain between Fitz Hugh and his young peers in the
literary business. Stedman noted in a letter that the *Atlantic*
was prejudiced against N.Y. writers, and that he could no
longer send his writings there.[35] He must have been very
jealous of Fitz Hugh's success. The Genteel Circle of Sted-
man, Stoddard, Taylor and Aldrich had begun to gather
again after the war had scattered them, but Fitz Hugh and
Rosalie were only briefly a regular part of these gatherings.[36]
Before long, Fitz Hugh faced a bitter falling out with the
Circle, and particularly Dick and Lizzie Stoddard, described
in the following letter to Stedman in December. The letter is
written from Aunt Carrie's Palatine Bridge home.

My Dear Stedman,
If it did not involve a joke (and Christ knows how little I feel
like that) I would quote an old saw brought over from aboli-
tion times & say "You have acted like a man and a brother."

If you see Stoddard remind him of the fact that I loved his
little Millie as no one not his own parent could do...Remind
him that when many friends forsook him because of hard
feeling they had for things said at his house, I, though I had
hard things said to me, stuck by him and Elizabeth—always
would have done so—had I not received the final insult a

man ever stands from a woman and one for which he would leave ripped up his dearest friend among men had he been hanged for it next day.

Remind him that when I was all alone among the waves of calumny and popular indignation—when my friends like those of Jesus "forsook me & fled"—that I came up to kneel beside my sick wife and take her to my broken heart and there found his wife waiting not only to insult me in my agony but to go down and talk ill of me to one of the few friends who dared to come to me.

Remind him that all my life I have sought to do him and his wife good—acting like an own brother in the criticism of both their works; asking all manner of kindness for even their faults where my influence was of any avail.

Remind him how one of the very best friends he ever had in the world now owes his widowhood & utter desolation in life to—call it a mistake—on the part of Elizabeth—and how the only apology which has ever been made for what to the lowest wretch the world would call cruelty—at least the only apology on the side of the house which the [illegible] law disinherited, has been the grossest insults and most insane threats ever made by privileged woman to patient, chivalric man.

Remind him that my whole career is proof enough that I neither wish to injure him nor his family and then ask him to come to me not like a second in a duel but an old friend to whom facts may have been represented—or at least to a man ready to do justice to the wife whom he is perfectly right, noble, and honorable in wishing to protect. If he wishes fight—if Barstow [Lizzie's brother] wishes it—let either of them say so. I am not in the ordinary sense a duellist—but in extreme cases, where people cannot settle the matter peacefully, I am a fighting man and will gladly accept a challenge from any man who thinks himself aggrieved and will not give me even a chance to know for what I must apologize.

I have written to Dick merely asking him what he wishes me to apologize for. If he will tell me—or if he be unwilling to entrust such a delicate matter to paper, if he will send at our own divided expense a special messenger—you e.g. if you will be so good—to tell me personally; Stedman, do you believe that I am a man of such false pride, so mean, so cowardly, as not to be willing to repair any wrong I may have done in heat ever to the uttermost?

But I cannot—& by the Eternal God I will not, deny words that I do not know—endorse any human beings' character in general terms—or crouch to the twin boy from out of my own mother's womb in humility for our utterly indefined and nameless wrong.

Let not a man whom I have loved—whom I still love (in spite of our latest inter-communication) so much as Stoddard, utterly shut up all door of compromise. I told him—I now tell you (and you have traveled East I believe [here is drawn a triangle with the letter G in it])[37] Stedman, before God I tell you as if I were on my death bed (as I well nigh have been) that I stand ready to do all

"that doth become a man
Who dares do more is none."[38]

Mrs. S. has more grievously insulted me than any male creature ever did—any female since I played "oats pease beans" with choleric little girls in the street—and if I held the extreme code of honor I should seek R.H.S. or W.B. and demand satisfaction of them for the behavior of one for whom they stand responsible. Far enough am I from that. If I were buried under a mountain of frog scum by any woman I would understand too well how little control any man has over any woman's actions to hold her husband, brother, lover accountable.

I stand all alone in the waves. I am however a rock—and assure you "Nec flatu nec fluctu movear." At the same time the littlest naked child may stand on me & be safe.

Tell Stoddard and his wife for me that though they may ruin me by their reports even as one of them (whom I would have defended with my own heart had she not turned on me in my distress) has tried to do to the very friend who offered my weary body an asylum. Tell them that the furthest thing from my wish is to hurt their names, reputations—prospects in any way.

For both their sakes, Rose's, yours and mine, let them not bring a broken hearted and desperate man to bay. Self Defence is the last, the uncontrollable—the automatic principle of human nature. I stand through the result of long unhappiness and public abuse in a place where life is so little dear to me that to hazard it on a cast of my honor's die would be no bravery whatever.

To you I say "I am sick but strong." If you are the man you say—bid the Stoddards act kindly and wisely. For their sake for your sake, for Rose's, for that of all who, false or true, have ever proferred me love & fealty—I will do the same. Until the 16th address me here—after that to Buffalo, N.Y.

Yours, both friend and [illegible], Ludlow[39]

This extraordinary letter is the most personal writing of Fitz Hugh that is extant—he even curses in print for the first time. It is hard to divine what awful series of events of "unhappiness and public abuse" had occurred to bring him to such a state. What had driven his friends away? What insult could Elizabeth Barstow Stoddard have delivered to elicit such a reaction? Was it an accusation of impotence? Was it an accusation of infidelity?

Stedman noted in a letter that he had invited Stoddard and others to join him on Christmas, but Fitz Hugh was not invited, whether because he was out of town or because Stedman now stood against Fitz Hugh as well. However, Ludlow was not the only one to have run afoul of Lizzie. Bayard Taylor wrote to Stoddard a few months later that "Liz ignored Marie Taylor's letter of apology...where no such insult was given—where no person of healthy common sense could see an insult."[40] A year later, Taylor would write Aldrich that "[Stoddard] has a hard burden to bear and is not—never will be I fear—his natural self... she is hopelessly diseased, mentally and morally, and he, absorbed dreamy, unpractical as he is, does not—in fact cannot see her condition."[41]

In any event, while his wife and one of his best friends were rocking his new-found stability, Fitz Hugh's family was not making things any easier. A letter from Carrie Geddings on Christmas, 1864 makes mention of a Helen breaking off her engagement. It is not clear if this is Fitz Hugh's sister, but Helen would have been 25 by this time, nearly a spinster by the standards of the times.[42] Cousin Carrie offered further commentary after getting a Christmas letter from her mother:

> I think Helen [Fitz Hugh's sister] is treating you decidedly mean, and I should not hesitate to tell her so either, this making a convenience of you, and then keeping you entirely in the dark about the whole affair. What did Fitz want to come for anyway, I should think New York was large enough for him to hide in if he wanted to get away from his wife. I don't pity him one bit. Uncle and Helen I do feel very sorry for, but I don't think Helen treats you as she should. I would not keep Fitz in the house without knowing why he came. I think *you ought to insist upon knowing.*[43]

Money was still a problem, although the November letter to Stansbury indicates that Fitz Hugh was starting to gain on financial problems. However, as one commentator has noted, when short of money Ludlow "tried everything to get it—even, according to Osborne family tradition, selling his wife's jewels."[44] Despite family and friends' distress,

Fitz Hugh followed through on his lecture commitments, but he traveled without his wife.

Cousin Carrie kept a running commentary on Fitz Hugh going into the new year. Her venom increased along with her volume. On January 1, she wrote to her mother:

> You did not say how you heard about F. but I suppose from Helen. I am indignant at her that she should have brought him to Palatine, one could expect no more of such a beast as he is. But I should think she would have more consideration for you all. It can't be that she sympathises with him, I am sorry for Helen and Uncle, but it is no more than might have been expected long ago of him. I wonder what more has happened that took Uncle H. to New York again. I would not bother myself with it if I was in his place.
>
> F. has sunk too low to be treated with any consideration any more. I have got through owning him for a relative. What an everlasting liar Fitz is. I don't believe he saw any one from home who knew me, and if he did he lies about his telling him that he often rode horseback with me for I was on a horse but twice all last summer and the only young man I ever rode with was Capt. Nichols now on Gen. Sherman's staff so he probably did not see him.[45]

Carrie and others in the family were now suspicious of Fitz Hugh, traveling extensively despite his ill wife. Fitz Hugh's father the Reverend Henry had also returned from New York City, through heavy snow in upstate New York, to once more lecture his wayward son. Henry may have noted with satisfaction the passage of the 13th amendment, presaging at last the end of the war, but as the trials of the Union subsided, those of the Ludlow family grew.

In the midst of his now controversial travels, Fitz Hugh finished his article on New York City. "The American Metropolis" appeared in the January 1865 edition of *The Atlantic Monthly*. This was an encyclopedic description of New York City in 16 pages. It began with the 1864 population estimate of one million, noted the consumption of 189 million pounds of beef and 304,000 barrels of whiskey entering New York in the last year, and ended with prophetic speculation about the annexation of Brooklyn, and not so prophetic manifest destiny concerning Hoboken and Jersey City.

This article was, for all its statistics, Fitz Hugh's paean of love to the greatest city in the world. Stuyvesant Park, next to which Fitz Hugh lived for many years after the war, was "one of the loveliest and most elegant pleasure-grounds open to the New York public, surrounded by one of the best-settled portions of the city, in every sense of the word." And the tolerant cosmopolitan New York still held a place in his bohemian heart with its "multitudinous varieties of temperament, race, character. [The New Yorker] avoids grooves, for he knows that New York will not tolerate grooviness." And further:

> we believe that New York is destined to be the permanent emporium not only of this country but of the entire world—and likewise the political capital of the nation. Had the White House (or, pray Heaven! some comelier structure) stood on Washington Heights, and the Capitol been erected at Fanwood, there would never have been a Proslavery Rebellion.

Fitz Hugh called on friends such as Mr. Ogden, First Auditor of the New York Custom-House, and Solon Robinson, agricultural editor of the *New York Tribune*, for various facts and figures. Another friend, Dr. Alanson Jones, President of the Board of Surgeons attached to the Metropolitan

Police Commission, told Fitz Hugh that the "large majority of deaths, and cases of disease, occur in that city among the recent foreign immigrants—and that the same source furnishes the vast proportion of inmates of our hospitals, almshouses, asylums, and other institutions of charity." The city also provided for the people transportation: "She victimizes them with nearly two thousand licensed hackmen… she offers for her guests' luxurious accommodation at least a score of hotels, where good living [that favorite theme of Fitz Hugh's] is made as much the subject of high art as in the Hotel du Louvre." The closing line in Fitz Hugh's hymn to Gotham is, "the future has a stature for her which shall lift her up where she can see and summon all the nations."

Editor Fields of the *Atlantic* was pleased with Fitz Hugh's thoroughness and readability on such an analytic article.[46] He proceeded to solicit articles from Fitz Hugh on more challenging topics. One of the subjects was physical science, which had heretofore fallen through the cracks in the *Atlantic* between the natural history topics covered by Professor Agassiz and biology as covered by Asa Gray. Fitz Hugh's eye for physical details were evident from the travel pieces, and his attention to developments in science was reflected in his writing (such as a reference in "The Prisoners of Portland" to Babbage's calculating machine, the precursor to the modern computer). Fitz Hugh was glad to take on the assignment, not only for the prestige but for the money, up to $50 per article.[47]

In January, Fitz Hugh began work on an article to be titled "Correlation and Persistence of Forces," a topic that was equivalent to the unified field theory of a later time. On the 31st, Fitz Hugh wrote to Professor Joseph Henry, the first director of the twenty-year-old Smithsonian Institute in Washington D.C. Professor Henry had been appointed in 1846, and had written to none other than Union College President Eliphalet Nott of his doubts when he was first appointed to head the Smithsonian.[48] Nott may have introduced Fitz Hugh and Professor Henry, which led to Henry's contacting Fitz Hugh and Bierstadt about help in the mapping of the western territory back in 1863.

> Professor Henry
> Dear Sir,
> In my Atlantic article on Correlation & Persistence, I wish very much to obtain your researches in that field that I may give at least a popular account of them, supposing they be, as I have thought might prove the case, too highly mathematical for transcription in form.
> At a time when all the scientific men of the country are regretting both your & their own loss in the burning of your papers, I feel hesitation in troubling you upon this matter but should think my article incomplete could you not oblige in this respect,
>> yours very truly, Fitz Hugh Ludlow[49]

The letter refers to the fire that had swept through Professor Henry's offices at the Smithsonian only a week before. Apart from his poor timing, Fitz Hugh neglected the fact that Professor Henry had published very little on physics, with his recent work dealing with meteorology.[50]

In the process of researching this article, Fitz Hugh contacted another family friend, Professor E.L. Youmans of Boston. Youmans had been part of the New York crowd at the Tenth Street studio in 1862, where Fitz Hugh's sister Helen had also met Youmans and his wife. Youmans was, like Fitz Hugh, a proselytizer for Darwin, and just as important "I smoke!—praise be to God for tobacco!"[51] Youmans in 1853 had written a book called *Alcohol and the Constitution of Man* on the chemical history and properties of demon rum. A later article in 1875 discussed the psychoactive Siberian mushroom, known now as Amanita muscaria (said by some to be the divine "soma" of the Hindu Vedas), to which Fitz Hugh had made passing reference in *The Hasheesh Eater*. Youmans was clearly a kindred soul.

Youmans, a professor at Antioch College, was the editor in 1864 of a book entitled *The Correlation and Conservation of Forces*, which included essays by Faraday and others. This became one of Fitz Hugh's main sources for the article in progress. Later, Youmans would go on to found the *Popular Science Monthly* magazine in 1872, inspired by Fitz Hugh and others of his "journalistic relations" in New York, to bring the discoveries of science to a popular audience.[52] Fitz Hugh gathered as much material as he could, and began the crafting of the article. However, it took considerably greater effort than his accustomed light fictions, and progress was slow.

Fitz Hugh's relationship with the prestigious *Atlantic* was all the more ironic now that the *Saturday Press* had resumed publication under "Figaro" himself, Henry Clapp. Artemus Ward and Ada Clare were writing for it, and the paper even reprinted stories by Fitz James O'Brien and Lizzie Stoddard.[53] Ada Clare presented a defense of Bohemians' love of things "above and beyond convention," and Clapp threw in a dig that "Bierstadt will have to quit painting his mammoth paintings due to the high cost of canvas." Fitz Hugh did not publish in the new *Saturday Press*, perhaps feeling that it would be a step backwards, or a foolish attempt to recapture lost youth. However, just as Clapp had seen the future where no one else had by defending Walt Whitman eight years earlier, he now repeated the scoop with Whitman's prose counterpart as forerunner of the modern American writing style.

SCIENCE WRITER AND EDITOR EDWARD LIVINGSTON YOUMANS
(1821-1887).

Mark Twain had finally taken the advice of Ludlow and Artemus Ward and appeared in an Eastern magazine when the *Saturday Press* published "Jim Smiley and His Jumping Frog" (now known as "The Celebrated Jumping Frog of Calaveras County") in the November 18, 1865 issue. The

San Francisco *Daily Alta* said "Mark Twain's story in the Saturday Press of November 18th, called 'Jim Smiley and His Jumping Frog' has set all New York in a roar, and he may be said to have made his mark. I have been asked fifty times about it and its author, and the papers are copying it far and near."[54] Several other pieces by Twain appeared in the *Press* in 1866, and he relocated to New York. Twain began spending time with Bohemians Charles Henry Webb (who'd gone broke in San Francisco when investments didn't pan out, much as Fitz Hugh had warned) and Edward House (who Fitz Hugh had replaced at Custom House in 1861, and who had been a Civil War correspondent for the *Tribune*)[55] Twain and Fitz Hugh may have had incidental contact (Twain did visit the Century Club) but no records of it are extant.

Regardless of the stirrings of new Bohemianism, Fitz Hugh had made the pages of the *Atlantic* and was taking full advantage of this most remunerative of opportunities. Fields accepted a short critical review from Fitz Hugh, his first return to his critical pen since the end of "Masks and Music" in the *Home Journal* four years earlier. In the February 1865 *Atlantic Monthly*, Fitz Hugh's review of sculptor Harriet Hosmer's "Zenobia" appeared.

> We hold that it has been left for America to complete the aesthetic, as well as the social and political emancipation of the world.

Hosmer's statue of Zenobia (queen of a land conquered by the Romans) was a classical subject, but Fitz Hugh noted that Hosmer had not "made her Zenobia a Greek woman." Rather, the features were American, and Fitz Hugh proclaimed this typical of how America influenced Art, "the opening of its doors into the open air of aesthetic catholicity." (Incidentally, Rosalie's review of Emily Chester, mentioned in Fitz Hugh's letter of November 11 to Fields, never appeared.)

Fitz Hugh's career progressed on other fronts as well. "The Loan of a Lyre" was reprinted in *The Treasure Trove Series* published in New York. This was only the second of Fitz Hugh's stories to be anthologized, after "The Taxidermist" in 1861's *Tales of the Time*. Fitz Hugh's lecture tour also proceeded apace. He followed his December trips to Buffalo and Philadelphia with engagements in Ohio, Kansas and Missouri later in the winter. In a letter from New York to William F. Phillips of Cincinnati on March 2, Fitz Hugh remarked on his growing popularity on the road:

> I have twice past [*sic*] through Cincinnati since your note of Feb. 14th was written, but not having given orders to forward my mails, only knew of it on my arrival home three days ago.
>
> I shall be happy to address yourself and the "many citizens" whose flattering invitation you proffer, some evening during the last week in this month when I shall again go west via Cincinnati. The "Good Living" lecture I have recast into a magazine article—a form more suitable to its presentation— and am now giving only "Across the Continent"—a running description of the original scenes & people between the Missouri & the Pacific. I need not say it is no rechauffe of matter previously published.
>
> Should this lecture meet your views, I will inform you definitely of the exact time I should like to be with you, as soon as the railroad business on which my movements to a degree depend is arranged beyond peradventure.
>
> Hoping to hear from you as early as convenient I remain,
>   Truly yours,
>   Fitz Hugh Ludlow[56]

During these trips, however, Fitz Hugh was disseminating more than his vast and recondite knowledge.

1 *Round Table*, February 13, 1864.
2 Hendricks (1973), p. 116.
3 Gus Frey to Carrie Geddings, January 8, 1864, NYSHA Library.
4 As late as January 22, 1865, Fitz Hugh was listed as a contributor to *The Golden Era*.
5 Further, in New York at the time laughing-gas exhibitions were very popular. Men and women would go up on stage and breath gas, and generally stagger around appearing drunk. Such performances were cheered by the audience. *Round Table*, March 26, 1864.
6 Bayard Taylor to Edmund Clarence Stedman, October 31, 1866, in Stedman and Gould (1910).
7 In fact, the Geneva convention of 1863 was the first where the use of the symbolic Red Cross was agreed to as a universal badge of neutrality. *American Journal of International Law*, July, 1910, p. 547.
8 Catton (1961), p. 474.
9 Thomas Starr King to Sarah King, December 2, 1864.
10 Alice Eyre, *The Famous Fremonts*, Santa Ana, CA: Fine Arts Press, 1948, p. 282.
11 *Round Table*, April 30, 1864, p. 314.
12 Fitz Hugh Ludlow, *Cinderella*, New York: J. A. Green, 1863; copy in New York Public Library.
13 Howard Shaffer and Milton Earl, *Classic Contributions in the Addictions*, New York: Brunner/Mazel, 1981, p. 10.
14 Hendricks (1973), p. 154.
15 Reported in the *Sanitary Fair Bulletin*, May 15, 1864.
16 Bruce Catton, *Never Call Retreat*, New York: Doubleday, 1864, p. 372.
17 *The Californian*, May 28, 1864.
18 The original cite is unavailable. The sketch was later reprinted in the debut issue of *The Californian*, May 28, 1864, under the title "Finding A Sensible Tongue in Trees".
19 Some of the quotes from this article may be found in Chapter 13.
20 Horace Day was a New York merchant specializing in rubber goods, and a great favorite of Fitz Hugh's—see footnote 32 in Chapter 9.
21 Fitz Hugh Ludlow to James Fields, 1864, Houghton Library, Harvard University, MS Am1294.

22 Helen Ludlow later wrote that the work was planned as 2 volumes to be a "minute survey of the Pacific Railroad and regions tributary to it." Helen Ludlow to Leander Hall, June 1, 1876, Schaffer Library. The preface to *Heart of the Continent* also refers to this intent.

23 Ellen Ballou, *The Building of the House: Houghton Mifflin's Formative Years*, Boston: Houghton Mifflin, 1970, p. 115.

24 *The Golden Era*, August 21, 1864, September 4, 1864.

25 This article gave the proposed route, one of few such attempts since surveyor/civil engineer Edwin Johnson wrote a book in 1854 which was the first proposal for a transcontinental railroad. Johnson's route was also similar to the actual route. See Edwin F. Johnson, *Railroad to the Pacific*, New York: Railroad Journal Job Printing Office, 1854.

26 William Newton Byers, *Encyclopedia of Biography of Colorado*, Chicago: The Century Publishing and Engraving Company, 1901, p. 96.

27 *The Century, 1847-1946*, New York: The Century Association, 1947, p. 390. A signed copy of the Century Club constitution is among the Ludlow-Frey papers, Cooperstown, NY, with "1 Livingston Place" written on it.

28 *The Century*, 1847-1946 (1947), p. 27.

29 Fitz Hugh Ludlow to Edward Stansbury, November 10, 1864.

30 Friend Frank Carpenter wrote "Improvident Ludlow may have been, and unmindful of the punctualities which govern business life and men, but when he borrowed money it was more than likely that it was for others' use rather than for his own. He often forgot to be just before being generous, but this seemed the defect of his organization." *New York Evening Mail*, December 24, 1870.

31 Fitz Hugh Ludlow to James Fields, November 11, 1864, UVA.

32 Frank Carpenter (1870). The one exception is a P.S. attached to a drunken scrawl of June 24, 1867 to J. R. Gilmore—see page 205.

33 Carrie Geddings to Caroline Frey, December 20, 1864, NYSHA Library.

34 Fitz Hugh Ludlow to E.R. Perkins, November 9, 1864, Historical Society of Pennsylvania.

35 Stedman and Gould (1910), p. 343.

36 Stedman and Gould (1910), pp. 330, 336, 347.

37 This may be a Masonic reference.

38 *MacBeth*, Act 1, Scene 7.

39 Fitz Hugh Ludlow to Edmund Clarence Stedman, December, 1864, Edmund Clarence Stedman Papers, Rare Book and Manuscript Library, Columbia University.

40 Fitz Hugh Ludlow to Edmund Clarence Stedman, December, 1864, Edmund Clarence Stedman Papers, Rare Book and Manuscript Library,

Columbia University.

41 Bayard Taylor to Thomas Bailey Aldrich, March 16, 1866.

42 Fitz Hugh had one cousin, Anna Frey, who was known as "Helen".

43 Carrie Geddings to Caroline Frey, December 30, 1865, NYSHA Library.

44 Hendricks (1973), p. 115; probably from Mrs. Orville DeForest Edwards.

45 Carrie Geddings to Caroline Frey, January 1, 1865.

46 Fields included verbatim in this article the footnote Fitz Hugh had belatedly provided in his letter of November 11, 1864.

47 His friend Edmund Clarence Stedman was getting $50 an article from the *Atlantic*, and Fitz Hugh must have been getting close to that range. Edmund Clarence Stedman to Bayard Taylor, May 28, 1866, in Stedman and Gould (1910).

48 Thomas Coulson, *Joseph Henry: His Life and Work*, Princeton: Princeton University Press, 1950, p. 182.

49 Fitz Hugh Ludlow to Joseph Henry, January 31, 1865, Huntington Library, San Marino, CA.

50 J. G. Crowther, *Famous Men of Science*, New York: W. W. Norton & Co. Inc., 1937, p. 162. Henry's research on electromagnetism prior to moving to the Smithsonian was contemporary with Faraday. Indeed, Henry's researches in electromagnetism were part of the inspiration for the invention of the telegraph by none other than Ludlow family friend, Samuel F. B. Morse.

51 John Fiske, *Edward Livingston Youmans, Interpreter of Science for the People*, New York, D. Appleton and Company, 1894, p. 202.

52 Fiske (1894), p. 147.

53 *Saturday Press*, August 5, 26, September 16, December 23, 1865.

54 Paine (1923), p. 278.

55 Justin Kaplan, *Mr. Clemens and Mark Twain*, New York: Simon and Schuster, 1966, p. 25.

56 Fitz Hugh Ludlow to William F. Phillips, March 2, 1865, Albert Whelpley Collection, Cincinnati Historical Society, Cincinnati Museum Center.

XV.

THE PYTHAGOREAN LOVE TRIANGLE

FITZ HUGH and Rosalie had not resolved the domestic troubles that arose from his western trip, and neither had discouraged the attentions of others. Cousin Carrie had hinted at these troubles in her letter of January 1, and Fitz Hugh's squabble with Lizzie Stoddard also seems to point to problems.

On one of his lecture trips, Fitz Hugh met the mysterious Mrs. Ives. Uncle Samuel's daughter Ellen Ludlow filed the following report on March 30:

Anna gave me your [Aunt Caroline Frey] little private [note] inquiring about Fitz Hugh, I respond in a P.S. so that you may tear it off if you don't wish everybody to see it.

Several weeks ago he decamped from New York with his new lady, privately, & after a while, a relative of Rose saw, in a hotel register at St Joseph's, Missouri, this entry, viz. "Fitzhugh [*sic*] Ludlow, wife & servants." After this, he was seen by one who knew him at Leavenworth, in Kansas. The next we hear of him is again in New York & we learn that he left his affinity in Kansas.

Her own mother, we are advised, advanced the money for the expenses of her journey & temporary residence in Kansas, where she is doubtless to obtain a divorce from her husband, Mr. Ives. About the same time, the petition of Rose for her divorce will doubtless be granted. After this, what the next scene in the drama will be needs no ghost to tell. There will be a new wedding some time & somewhere, & you & I will have no invitation to it. The uncle of the new lady says that she will remain with Fitz as long as he can furnish her an abundant supply of money. When that fails, she will desert him for someone else. He occasionally writes to his father, maintaining his great dignity & the propriety of his proceedings & pouring curses upon the head of poor Rose. He still figures in the last Atlantic & says he is writing twenty pages per day for his forthcoming book.

The whole thing is a great mystery as well as a most fearful tragedy.[1]

Fitz Hugh and Rosalie's six-year history of flirtation and transgression had finally culminated in separation. Rosalie walked out on Fitz Hugh sometime in the winter. He remained in the apartment on Stuyvesant Square, from which to base his lecturing forays to the west as well as continuing to write. Despite his professional successes, the unraveling of his marriage took an emotional toll. Fitz Hugh really did not think that his indiscretions would filter back to the East, nor did he think through Rosalie's potential reaction when the stories did hit home. At best, he was thoughtless. At worst, he had abandoned Rosalie on her sickbed, weary of her constant illnesses and resort recoveries.

Rosalie was young and starry eyed when she married the handsome mysterious Hasheesh Eater. She was reassured by the apparent financial success of publication at an early age, and the promise of further glory was intoxicating. But Rosalie never let family ties loosen very much. (Indeed it was a relative of hers, perhaps Colonel Osborne of the Platte County railroad, who first discovered Fitz Hugh and Mrs. Ives.) Fitz Hugh had struggled throughout the war years, and never achieved the wealth Rosalie knew in her childhood. Neither had the trip to the West been transformed into a best seller to revive his fame, although there had been momentum in that direction with the *Atlantic* articles.

Rosalie had not been a demure and submissive wife during his absence. She was the most attractive of all the wives of Fitz Hugh's literary contemporaries, and Mrs. Thomas Aldrich had noted her magnetism among the other young writers as early as 1860. In 1862, Rose had written Edmund Clarence Stedman that "there is something about you one likes and respects amazingly." Judgmental Cousin Carrie called her "a married flirt."

ROSALIE AT A COSTUME BALL WHEN MARRIED TO BIERSTADT.
(COURTESY OF THE BROOKLYN MUSEUM)

Another factor was the lack of children. The couple had been married six years without producing a child. Fitz Hugh's delight in children argues that he certainly was willing to be a father. Rosalie also expressed sadness on the subject.[2] It was not clear whether one or the other was biologically unable to reproduce, but when Fitz Hugh's behavior gave her the option, Rose was emotionally ready to move.

After Rose left, Fitz Hugh gradually became aware that there were professional ramifications as well. The refined literary circles of the *Atlantic Monthly* preferred a more stable air of authority in its writers. In April, Fitz Hugh published " 'If Massa Put Guns Into Our Han's' " in the *Atlantic*. But soon after, his separation from Rosalie became widely known, and it shortly became clear that Fitz Hugh's work was no longer welcome there.[3]

The timing of "Massa" was ironic, coming as Fitz Hugh's married life reached a milestone. The essay served as a summation of a life immersed in abolitionism, and was in part a response to the last ditch threats of some in the South to arm their slaves in defense of their masters:

> The record of any one American who has grown up in the nurture of Abolitionism has but little value by itself considered; but as a representative experience, capable of explaining all enthusiasms for liberty which have created "fanatics" and martyrs in our time, let me recall how I myself came to hate Slavery.

Fitz Hugh recounted in the article the use of his home as a station on the underground railroad, an incident at his boarding school, and then his trip to Florida with Rosalie in 1860.[4] In the *Atlantic*, Fitz Hugh was free to include a more adult theme than was permitted in the *Commercial Advertiser* travelogues that were published as "Due South" four years earlier:

> The most open relations of concubinage existed between white chevaliers and black servants in the town of Jacksonville. I was not surprised at the fact, but was surprised at its openness.

Fitz Hugh concluded that "it is very amusing to hear the Southerners talk of arming their slaves." He recounted the forced separation of a slave from his wife and child, and another servant who saw his daughter "sold away into the horrors of concubinage to one of the wickedest men on the river." The latter told Fitz Hugh:

> if de Massas only do put guns into our han's, oh, dey'll find out which side we'll turn 'em on!

Fitz Hugh's essay was rendered moot by the surrender of Lee at the end of March, an announcement that came probably while the April issue of the *Atlantic* was arriving at newstands. The coming end of the war may have been a factor in Rosalie's decision to leave him, and the triumphs of the nation were intermingled with Fitz Hugh's private tragedy. Cousin Carrie wrote to her mother on April 9, "the war is ended. Glory! Glory! Glory! Glory!," but then continued:

> I don't wonder that poor Uncle is almost killed. It must be terrible for him & Helen. They have always been so proud of [Fitz Hugh's] talent and genius, or H has, and now to have him sunk so low in crime I expect to hear of him out with the Mormons the next thing with that woman. I think he is crazy

and I hope he is—it won't be quite so bad then if he is not ac-
countable for what he does. He is a pretty fellow to be cursing
poor Rose. Whatever she may have done is no excuse for him,
and if he had done as he should she never would have been
so fond of the attentions of other men. I don't entirely excuse
her, but I will stand up for her against him. I have no patience
with him.[5]

Fitz Hugh, who throughout the winter had been feeling
the effects of a full lecture and writing schedule, was look-
ing for respite. Rosalie's exit only put further strains on him,
though he still had not abandoned hopes of reconciliation.
The physical science article he had been working on was
no longer welcome at the *Atlantic*, and its complexity was
beyond *Harper's* or the other lighter journals, and so there
was also no money coming in from writing. Fitz Hugh's
lecture touring had also petered out. While they may have
paid as much as $100 per appearance, after traveling expenses
and the strain of traveling by stage and steamer, the effort
simply was not worth it. Moreover, his affair with Mrs. Ives
came to an end, perhaps, if the Ludlow family characteri-
zation was right, because he was short of cash and no longer
attractive, even compared to the alternatives in Kansas.

Speaking to Mr. Ogden of the Customs House dur-
ing the writing of "The American Metropolis" piece gave
Fitz Hugh the idea to approach the Republican admin-
istration for a sinecure. He wrote to Hiram Barney, who was
the Collector at the Customs House during Fitz Hugh's
employment there. He wrote the letter from the Trinity
building on a blue Monday morning sometime in March.
Incredibly, Fitz Hugh invoked Rosa as a reason why Barney
should help him.

My Dear Mr. Barney,

I last night came to the conclusion that I would apply to the present administration for a consulate in some one of the Mediterranean ports. My health is failing under the pressure of an amount of work which while necessary to earn my bread will soon put me beyond the need of any. I am now getting letters of recommendation to the President from all my New York and country friends. Will you give me one? If you feel willing to confer this service you may perhaps save me from leaving the world before I have attained the place I am struggling towards among the literary men of my country, dragged back by the terrible double weights of poverty and sickness. I love literature dearly—it is my chosen work—but just now I must have bread, and easier than I now get it.

I don't know how much weight it would have with Mr. Lincoln to tell him that I am a young literary man of some promise (if you think so)—but past administrations have shown a willingness to do the honor to literature of selecting some of their representatives from that class which was quite surprising when we consider how few other creditable things they were willing to do. If you are willing to write for me—it may be best to speak of my literary status—you are the judge of its expediency.

I am a staunch Republican—have been so through defeat and victory. I have the promise of considerable influence among my other friends in the party—but particularly wish yours also—both because I have always felt you were a very kind and warmly interested friend of mine—and because if I either break down or die in my present state my poor wife will be left without a farthing—and every atom of additional influence has a chance of averting that likelihood. Should you feel it is in your heart to give me a recommendatory letter to Mr. Lincoln—please leave it here with one of your clerks and I will call tomorrow noon for it. And with many sincere thanks I shall be as ever, Your true friend, Fitz Hugh Ludlow[6]

This is a sad letter, pathetic in its reference to Rosalie and to himself as a man of some literary "promise," ignoring his appearance in the radical Fremont's *New Nation*, and exaggerating Fitz Hugh's influential friends. Indeed, Fitz Hugh had only one other real contact with Lincoln, his friend the painter Frank Carpenter. Carpenter had been to the White House in February 1864, and stayed six months to paint "the scene commemorative of the first reading in cabinet and council of the Emancipation Proclamation."[7] Carpenter also painted several portraits of Lincoln and the Lincoln family. Carpenter was called "the Gilbert Stuart of his era" for painting celebrities, and had mingled with the Tenth Street studio crowd five years earlier.

But Fitz Hugh had a darker connection to Lincoln as well, through Fitz Hugh's friend the actor Edwin Booth. Edwin had in March of 1865 completed a 100-night run of Hamlet, and had been honored on March 22 with a medal (by Tiffany) to commemorate the feat. Although the performances were hailed as a "wonder of the age," Booth had grown tired of the role and after the medal was conferred, he moved quickly to a new play in Boston. He had been there only a week when the news came that Lee had surrendered. And in only two weeks more, Edwin was playing a new role when news came that his brother John Wilkes Booth had murdered the President on April 14.[8] Fitz Hugh's appeals to Lincoln for employment were now moot. It must have been around this time that Fitz Hugh wrote to Frank Carpenter the following:

> I sometimes lose all faith in the existence of any being who takes the slightest interest in at least our earthly welfare, and sink down into a darkness of heart like that of Egypt. Where

is the right hand—the outstretched arm—where He who clothes the lilies and will much more clothe us—where any merciful, loving Lord at all?[9]

Fitz Hugh's family situation continued to deteriorate. Cousin Carrie wrote on April 16 about Lincoln's assassination, noting the stores were closed and residences draped in black. "Rebels richly deserve their fate, for Retaliation and Extermination will now be the requirement of our Armies."[10] On April 21, Carrie returned to the subject of Fitz Hugh's indiscretions. "I wonder how Mrs. Treadway knew about Fitz, but I suppose every one knows it though I would not wonder to see the whole thing in the papers. Poor Uncle and Helen, I think of them very often, how terribly mortifying it must be to them, how far greater a sorrow than his death ever could have been."[11] In an April 30 letter, she continued, "I am more than ever mad and disgusted with Fitz. Can it be possible that he has so little feeling for his father and sister as to go to Oswego. I think too that if Rose ever lives with him after all this she deserves no pity. I hope Uncle will go to New York. I think it would be much better for him."[12]

Henry may very well have rejoiced at the end of the Civil War and the final realization of his lifelong dream of abolition. He must at the same time have viewed with some pride Fitz Hugh's tribute to the roots of the crusade in the *Atlantic*. However, it appeared there were to be no further moves to new churches and new conversions. In May, upset by his son's sins against holy matrimony, and citing his failing health and deteriorating eyesight, Reverend Henry submitted his resignation to the church in Oswego. He almost immediately regretted his decision, which was quickly accepted by his flock, and agonized that he might have had more left to give to the Lord's work. And as Uncle Samuel put it:

His case, however, would not have been so distressing, if he could have indulged the least hope for his prodigal son. Notwithstanding Helen's hope, all the reform about him is that he don't in fact live with his second wife—& the only reason for this is that she has got sick of him. In other respects, I see no change whatever. Liquor & hasheesh & he are still intimate, & his life is just as irregular as it can be. He sits up frequently all night writing his hack, & sleeps all day. I think he couldn't write at all without his stimulants.

His whole history in detail is familiar to the citizens here, so that he is a town talk & shunned on all hands by respectable ladies & gentlemen. In short, he is just what he was, & no better. I should not be surprised if under his general dissipations & irregularities, his life should wind up at any time—& at any rate, that his brain should lose its entire power. This is the great irony in the soul of his father, so that is it's a marvel to me that he can preach, or do anything else. He told me the other day that you could not take F. into your family, for which he didn't blame you in the least, knowing that his presence with you must destroy all your domestic quiet & comfort. He said that you would be willing to take Helen, but she seems to be blindly bound to stick to him in all places & under all circumstances.

My opinion is that if she must be with him, they had better go unto some remote retirement & not remain in such a wide awake gossiping city as this, where she must of necessity suffer many mortifications & slights, as F. does not hesitate to crowd himself upon ladies society wherever he can—But I need say no more & what I have said, I commit to the privacy of your own family.[13]

As Fitz Hugh wandered through upstate New York, he continued to rework his various travel writings into book form, as he had since October of 1864. Material from "Letters from Sundown" in the *New York Evening Post* had to be revised, as did "Reminiscences of an Overlander" from *The Golden Era*. There was also an immense amount of diary material which had not yet been turned into any product at all. The first half of the book contained a mixture of revisions of previous articles and new journal extracts. All of this material amounted to four chapters of the rewrite. Fitz Hugh then wrote up entirely new material of the trip from Denver to Salt Lake, and called it "Into the Rocky Mountains." Chapter Six contained more of the same, and was called "The Approach to Salt Lake." This set the stage for some extended coverage of the Mormons. Fitz Hugh prepared a descriptive chapter on the Mormons, another sixty pages entitled "Utah's Life Principle and Destiny" detailing Mormon social, political and theological organization and practice, and another on "The Dead Sea," some ninety pages total. A fourth chapter on the Mormons, including verbatim material from the *Atlantic* article "Among the Mormons," was called "The New Jerusalem." The last three chapters of the book were ultimately taken almost verbatim from the text of three of his *Atlantic* articles, "Seven Weeks in the Great Yo-Semite," "On Horseback into Oregon," and "On the Columbia River." Left out entirely were "Through Tickets to San Francisco" and "The Prisoners of Portland," which were not in fitting with the frontier theme. Most of this revision took at least two years, from October 1864 until August of 1866.

However, publication was further delayed by bad luck. Fitz Hugh had reached tentative agreement with Hurd and Houghton to publish his manuscript, but as revisions dragged on they began to get nervous. Another book was reported in preparation based on the 1865 Western trip of Speaker of the House of Representatives Schuyler Colfax with newspaper editor Samuel Bowles. Fitz Hugh had obtained a letter from Colfax prior to his western journey in 1863 that allowed them to visit cavalry outposts (see Chapter 11). He had evidently met Colfax in transit during Fitz Hugh's lecture tour of 1865, and wrote the following:

My Dear Mr. Colfax,

Immediately after I met you last, (on the Erie Road as you will recollect) I went home, and was instantly taken seriously ill. I have never been nearer death than then. Indeed at the time I saw you, nothing but the determination to discharge to the very conclusion a responsibility which in the face of all manner of malignity, slander and opposition I had borne for several months, kept me up long enough to get home and lie down for what I & my few staunch friends supposed was my last illness. That responsibility honorably demitted I should have been very willing to die, for adversity had revealed to me depths of human baseness and ingratitude, yawning right under the supposed solid ground I trod in my sunnier time, which made me shudder at the thought of living any longer on this earth. A wonderful constitution carried me through however, and although I have been too feeble to do anything like the previously accustomed daily work of my life for the last six months, I am now, thanks to noble friends who have (as a strange exception to the general rule) clung all the closer to me when I needed their love, and to the Water cure treatment at this place, getting well rapidly.

I make this statement not because I think it can be of any interest to you to be troubled by the recital of my private affairs but because I wish to rid myself of the imputation of discourtesy and negligence which might otherwise rest upon me in view of my not having complied with your request by sending you that book of Gilpin's. You had set out on your journey before I could lift myself from my bed to a chair and I did not know where to direct to you short of Denver, while I also knew that without trouble or pecuniary loss you could get as many of Gilpin's books at the Territorial library there as you desired. Please accept my apology for the apparent neglect to obey your wishes has troubled me much ever since I was well enough to think of this world's matters again.

I have a favor to ask of you. My illness has retarded the completion of my book of travels. My publishers are getting very much alarmed because they say that your book will entirely supersede mine.

I am sure I should gladly yield the palm to you, but for my publishers' sake, I should be glad to tell them (if it is so) that though our track was the same that the point of view in which we look at the subject is different. I don't suppose we should really interfere. I believe that your book is to be of particular interest to the statesman, statistician, emigrant and commercial man while mine is devoted principally to Scenery with Bierstadt's illustrations, to botany, Geology, Science in general, Adventure, hunting, Anecdote & the usual chatty matter of the tourist.

If I could say to Hurd & Houghton that the interference does not exist it would make it much easier for them & me to cultivate equanimity during the remaining few weeks necessary to get the book to press.

Forgive my troubling you—drop me a line if you will be so kind—tell me how to direct Gilpin's book to you now—and believe me

Very Truly Yrs., Fitz Hugh Ludlow[14]

Fitz Hugh published nothing between April and the end of the year. He seems to have taken instead to drinking and smoking, and possibly a return to hashish as well. As for the latter, it was no doubt yielding very little in the way of the exalted dreams of his college years. It appears that alcohol was the dominant drug at this time, causing Fitz Hugh to vent his anger at family members and probably allowing some hashish- tinged blasphemies to escape as well. This funk may have had something to do with the *Atlantic* cutting him off as well. Consequently, Fitz Hugh also was not selling any writing, and so income had dropped to a trickle. It is difficult to say how out-of-control Fitz Hugh was at this time, but the Ludlow family, as always, was ready to analyze him, try his legal case, and judge him as well.

While Fitz Hugh continued his literary, geographical and inebriatory peregrinations, the Reverend Henry in June had returned to New York City, still regretting his decision to retire. But he had gone to work for the American Missionary Association, whose treasurer was his long time friend Lewis Tappan. Samuel wrote of Henry again in June:

> [H]e has another dreadful, crushing burden to carry, in his miserable, profligate F.—He is still here, he & Helen boarding at the new Welland: he shows no symptoms of reform yet, and is about as bad as bad can be. It may appear strange to some that we cannot give them quarters in our big castle: but the sacrifice of house & all home comforts to disorder & uproar, day & night, is more than reasonably can be required of us, unless, by it, we could hope to recover the fellow from his abandonment. Br. H. realizes this, and does not blame you, or us, for declining to harbour him. Helen we could take very easily: but they cannot be separated. She is determined to stick close to him, altho' her efforts to restrain him are not successful.[15]

Uncle Samuel had invited Fitz Hugh to stay at his home but:

Fitz Hugh remained with us a week, when we found that it was a burden of labour & cure, which we could not carry. Wife had as much outdoor farmwork as she could attend to—Anna had her usual headaches…everything was cast on poor Ellen pressing her above measure. So we were driven to the painful necessity of suggesting that they find a boarding place & they went last Mon. to the New Willard House— board incl. fuel & lights for both $21—How long they will remain there, or in town, will depend on the future arrangements of Brother H.—I pity Br. exceedingly, for what the poor miserable wicked F. will do, no one can tell—& what his father will, or can, do is just as difficult to say.[16]

Upon hearing of Uncle Samuel's involuntary hosting, Carrie wrote on the 14th "I don't see how they can let Fitz stay at Wildwood. I wouldn't have him in my house."[17] A week later, she continued, "I shall lose all sympathy for Uncle & Helen if they continue to make so much of that rascal. It looks to me much like encouraging him on what he has done. It's a likely story that Rose has *led him on* to do what he has. But of course she gets the blame. I don't think I would let the fear of offending Uncle Henry keep me awake many nights. I think you are the ones to be offended if one proposes to you such a thing as taking that drunken rascal into the house again. But he always has a peculiar way of telling a person their duty."[18]

Cousin Anna jumped into the gossip on June 5:

You ask me what I think of F.H. I cannot say that I believe there is any radical change in him. He is a strange being—I cannot understand him. I think that he sometimes takes stimulants & sometimes does not. We have heard of excesses in drinking, but I cannot tell you how much is true. Helen & I talk of him but I don't wish to ask her too close questions.

She has thought him mending in his habits—I don't know what she feels now. I was there today. He seemed perfectly himself, was writing in his book.

As to Rose, I don't know what to think. They will probably never be united again. She seems to have wavered much, but the last I hear there was no prospect of an arrangement. F. contends that the wrong is hers.

You will regard all of this as confidential inside yr. family. I hope it is not wrong to say this much. I pity the strange misguided man & seek not to judge him. I fear that all his stimulants will injure his mind.[19]

Cousin Carrie's commentary resumed on July 20 when she heard news of Rosalie's travels. "Where has Rose been visiting? You left out the name of the place. I think it would look much better for her to stay at home quietly."[20] Rosalie was evidently unconcerned about appearances, even though divorce proceedings were not yet underway. Separation was allowed to continue without resolution for some time, and it was probably assumed that the wronged wife would wait at home for her wayward husband to return in contrition. Rosalie clearly was having none of that.

On August 5, Carrie was still advising the family on how to deal with the situation. "I don't think Helen is doing herself any good by sticking to that scamp so—for I don't believe one word about Fitz having given up drinking. They may believe it but I don't."[21] In September, Reverend Henry wrote to Caroline Frey:

Helen is here taking care of her Brother at a Water cure, corner of 14th St. and 6th Avenue. The Dr., a scientific man, says he will cure him in a month if he will follow his directions. I have no confidence in anything but the grace & power of the Almighty. F. seems to be very anxious to abandon all stimulants & get well. But can the Ethiopian &c &c [i.e. can a Black person change the color of his skin.] Pray for him my dear sister. Helen is well and a most noble girl & clings with the patience of hope and has staked her all upon the issue. Her gentleness is wonderful & she is the only one who possesses any influence over him. I fear he will be so unwilling to obey rules that they will get tired and dismiss him from the Cure. You know his self-sufficiency.

As yet among all your afflictions you know nothing like mine. The Lord grant you never may.[22]

Uncle Samuel wrote to his sister on September 9:

H.G.'s removal to NY has not been for his profit, either in body or mind...Add to this his crushing sorrow w/ poor Fitz & he has about as much of a load as he can carry...Some time ago Fitz left Katovah where they were boarding for a Brooklyn Water Cure which did not meet their expectations on trial, when they removed to another of a German doctor's in NY where they now are. F. I believe is improving some, though it is quite uncertain whether he will ever recover his strength or his deliverance from his own consequences—alcohol, hasheesh and tobacco. Helen still clings to him hoping but his father hopes for no betterment in his case short of regenerating power.[23]

Cousin Anna wrote to her aunt on September 28:

HG preaching has grown perfectly wearisome & unbearable...full of severe extreme views...he has seemed to feel worse about [leaving Oswego] than he has about Fitz Hugh although I don't really suppose he does. F. is supposed to be doing pretty well at least Helen thinks he is. I fear though that she is deceived. I think she shows great strength of faith

& also great love for Fitz. She has grown old in her loving devotion to him. Thought her very much changed before she left.[24]

Cousin Anna wrote to her aunt again in December, "I hardly know what to say about Uncle & Helen's coming. I had hoped Helen would come because she would be so much company for you but Uncle…won't be so agreeable. Still as you say I hardly see how you can refuse. Is he doing nothing now? Oh dear I wish they had a home somewhere."[25] Uncle Samuel also tried to help during the holidays, but wrote to his sister the day after Christmas that "HG in deep melancholy…often made merry with this class of sufferers, not now able to lift a finger for his own healing or deliverance."[26] Caroline wrote to her husband John Frey early in 1866 that "Helen at Catskills, HG *believes* Fitz was with her."[27] Uncle Samuel replied to Caroline in turn on the 8th of January, "I learn from Br. H. that he is now at N. Haven with his friend Miss Davenport…Hillhouse Ave. for a season—how long I don't know & Helen with him—poor fellow [have written him many letters] to divert his mind from the dark channels in which it runs."[28]

Cousin Carrie returned to comment on Fitz Hugh after a four month hiatus: "I am glad on the whole that Uncle H. and Helen have decided not to come…Is Uncle in no business at all now? What has become of that society? Poor Helen…has a hard lot. I wish she could be happily married. Did she say nothing of Fitz? They have him to thank for all their trouble. I don't know of anything too bad for him."[29] And in mid- winter, Uncle Samuel was still worried about his Brother Henry's health. "Helen says he is out of doors a great deal with his old New Haven friends…You cannot know exactly the state of a hypochondriac man."[30] But he evidently recovered soon after, as Carrie wrote her mother on February 11th, "I am so glad to hear Uncle H. is better. I wonder what has become of F. & Rose." Later the same day Carrie had "good news from Henry. Fitz he says is doing well—writing again for Harper's 'The International' and 'Gray Jockey' in Jan & Feb numbers are written by him."[31] By March 5, Samuel reported that "Br. H. on ascending grade…he did not feel bound to provide for such a scape grace as Fitz."[32]

And indeed, Fitz Hugh emerged from eight months of sickness and mania to find once more literary harbor in *Harper's Monthly*. The Harpers, seeking to recover their pre-war profitability, probably took Fitz Hugh back without questioning his brief apostasy with *The Atlantic*. In January, 1866, the first installment of "An International Affair" appeared. This piece is notable as Fitz Hugh's first short story to draw from his Western experiences.

The main character in the story is the narrator's horse, named Cholooke, after "the greatest of the Great Yo-Semite falls, in California." Despite the thematic source in the Western journey, Fitz Hugh for the first time set a story in a foreign country (Ireland) where he had never been. Cholooke was a horse that bucked so violently as to produce "in the most hermetically sealed countenance what refined doctors nowa-days call 'nasal hemorrhagia.'" The beast also would deliver a sudden blow "delivered backward with the hardest part of the skull." Even after broken of these habits, Cholooke on occasion balked, "a Gibraltar in horse-flesh." Fitz Hugh's wordplay and sense of humor, even after eight months of tribulations and inebriations, seemed intact. Fitz

Hugh spent several pages of this story demonstrating his knowledge of horsemanship, e.g. how to hook spurs in the cloth meshes of the saddle so as to avoid the shock as the bucking animal strikes the ground. After this lecture in the story, the narrator then says "I shall have been followed thus far by horsemen. If any other readers have accompanied them I will make the rest of the way as interesting, in other technical respects, as I know how."

The human characters include Mr. Von Haarlem, the narrator, his Irish friend, Mr. Fitz Patrick, and Fitz Patrick's daughter Daisy, who was of course "the very perfection of womanhood." The foil was Algernon Maurice Sidney Trevannion, captain of a company in Her Majesty's Guards, whose "intellect always ignited with a damp fuse." Fitz Hugh characterized English ethnocentrism and ignorance of geography: "In this respect none but the Chinaman can be his parallel; and I am not sure but the Chinaman would by this time have abdicated in his favor, had he not drugged that pagan off the track of enlightenment by cramming opium down his throat at the point of the bayonet." Dramatic tension after a fashion was introduced when Trevannion challenged Von Haarlem to a duel because of the American's general impertinence. The narrator notes he would have chosen for the duel "my own familiar and favorite weapon, the breech-loading Ballard rifle at 100 yards," Fitz Hugh's choice on the buffalo hunt in 1863.

Part 2 of "An International Affair" wasted no time ladling out formula, as the narrator described Daisy's " 'lovingness,' if you will forgive me for setting up a branch mint of the vernacular, to supply deficits in the coinage of Webster." Fitz Hugh inserted several paragraphs in small print beginning

"Private and Confidential: to be read only by people who have been in love" and ending with "The apathetic public may begin to read again." And further:

> Then I knew how much I loved her, and felt how completely my happiness was merged in hers—how I loved her, had been loving her, loved her at first sight.

It is also difficult to judge how this ready sentiment flowed out of Fitz Hugh's tumultuous love life. It may be that as a professional he had a ready reservoir that came automatically to hand. In the midst of the story, the narrator recalled memories of those dear to him. "I saw my white-haired father sitting on the veranda of the parsonage at home, and my little brown-haired sister Nellie reading the morning paper to him as he and she sat at the wicker lunch-table under the grape-trellis, rich with promises to pay, maturing in October." This was no doubt a tender tribute to Reverend Henry and Sister Helen, recuperating in New Haven while Fitz Hugh attempted to rebuild his career.

The very next issue of *Harper's* carried another equine story also modeled on Fitz Hugh's Western journey, "The Gray Jockey; A Rocky Mountain Camp-Fire Story." The story was loosely structured as a tale told around the campfire (perhaps influenced by Twain during his journey) and was notable for Fitz Hugh's first real villain in many years, one Lemuel Lonehand. "If he was part Hindoo he surely came of the Brahmin caste, for a subtler being never walked on two legs…he was an adventurer, living solely on the success of his bets at races and the green cloth…Lonehand's style of cunning was artistic and conscientious…he took the same religious care of his joints and surfaces in tinkering up a tenpenny treachery and an unpardonable sin." In terms of autobiography, one of the storyteller's asides was "Women are the making of creation; 'ay and the marring too' do I hear you say, Ben Turner on the bearskin yonder?" Fitz Hugh also played back and forth between California inside jokes "let him think, as we say in California, 'that he was playing me for a Chinaman'" and New York inside jokes "kept him a candidate for Doctor Peet and One hundred and Fifty-second Street."

"An International Affair" and "Gray Jockey" fit effortlessly into the formula of *Harper's*, and were enhanced for that purpose by the flavor of the Overland journey. However, between non-fiction, lectures and now stories, Fitz Hugh had begun to reach the bottom of the raw material accumulated in the Western trip. As if to underscore the exhaustion of the material, detractors appeared to nibble away at Fitz Hugh's position of authority.

In January, *Across the Continent* appeared, written by Samuel Bowles, the editor of the *Springfield* (Massachusetts) *Republican*, and to whose travel companion Schuyler Colfax Fitz Hugh had appealed several months earlier. Bowles had written a travelogue as a series of letters to the *Republican*, much as Fitz Hugh had conceived for the *Evening Post*. Bowles simply published the letters as is in book form, printed and published by the *Republican* as well.[33] Bowles even noted in his introduction that "Fitzhugh [*sic*] Ludlow created wider interest by his brilliant but few and disconnected papers in the 'Atlantic Monthly' on special themes in the journey."[34] Bowles' book was popular, eventually selling 15,000 copies, and Cousin Carrie of all people wrote about it in a February 25 letter. After having noted that she was loving Bowles' book, she wrote:

he gives Fitz a dab every chance he gets—speaks of him in one place as "author of the largely imaginative articles in the Atlantic Monthly" and again in speaking of the SF climate he says there is nothing like it either here on the Pacific Coast or elsewhere, "so far as Bayard Taylor has traveled or Fitz Hugh Ludlow imagined in Hasheesh."[35]

Elsewhere, Bowles describes the rock sculpting wind, or "Wind augers Mr. Fitzhugh Ludlow called them, I believe; but some of his stories as to their performances are purely imaginative, and only excite ridicule among the mountaineers."[36] Bowles sniffs that Ludlow told of Porter Rockwell being a murderer "at the same time that he acknowledges being his guest, and availing himself of his courtesies to see the country."[37] Cousin Carrie on March 18th admitted that "We were quite interested in those two stories of Fitz—they are both good but particularly the International Affair I think. I hope Fitz is *really* doing well, did Rose ever get her divorce do you know?"[38] Rose had not yet acted, but Fitz Hugh was absorbing punishment in other ways. It must have been distressing for Bowles' book to come out while Fitz Hugh was still compiling his own. Even worse, Bowles had duplicated or stolen the title of his book from Fitz Hugh's lecture title, and forced Fitz Hugh to think about another name for his own book on the trip. Worse, Bowles' book caused Hurd and Houghton to further postpone publishing plans, despite Fitz Hugh's earlier plea to Colfax.

The travail of literary work occupied Fitz Hugh in March and April, and there was plenty more on his mind. Post-war America was still unsettled, as the April newspapers reported on the impeachment of President Johnson. But this event paled in significance for Fitz Hugh beside another legal action that occurred the next month. A notice appeared in the *Waterville Times* on May 10, 1866, and read as follows:

> DIVORCED—At the last term of N.Y. Supreme Court, a divorce was granted against Fitz Hugh Ludlow, the well known writer, on the petition of his wife, Rosalie H. Ludlow, daughter of Mr. A.O. Osborn of this village. The defendant was charged by the plaintiff with adultery with a Mrs. Ives. Both in New York City and in the West.

They had been separated a little over a year when the divorce was granted. Fitz Hugh had spent the first eight months of that year destitute, drunk and homeless, before recovering his equilibrium. We do not know Fitz Hugh's immediate response to the divorce, but Cousin Carrie is predictably the first to offer comment on May 20. "I saw almost the same notice of Fitz's & Rose's divorce that you sent me in one of our daily papers here. It is a disgraceful thing and my heart aches for poor Uncle H & Helen."[39] Fitz Hugh's fragile momentum was derailed, and he did not publish anything for several months after the divorce. Indeed, the only word that summer came in July that "Fitz in N.Y. and 'far from well'."[40] And Fitz Hugh would get worse before getting better. On November 22, 1866, just six months after the divorce, the *Waterville Times* reported:

> MARRIED—In Waterville, on the 21st inst., by Rev. Dr. Meachum, rector of Grace Church, Albert Bierstadt of Rosalie Harper, eldest daughter of Amos O. Osborn, Esq.

How deep the knife had been plunged! Had Bierstadt, his closest friend, been carrying on with Rosalie even before the western trip? Was Rosalie not only a flirt but a gold digger as well? Or was she simply seeking a man who better fit her family's standards of financial security?

Fitz Hugh had often paid only passing attention to his wife. She was occasionally mentioned in articles, but never by name. By contrast, Bierstadt had caused their Yosemite campground to be named Camp Rosalie, and had named a whole mountain after her in one of his paintings. This was an affair that had old and deep roots.

On October 11, the *New York Evening Post* reported that Bierstadt's "The Rocky Mountains" had been sold to James McHenry, a major partner in the Atlantic & Great Western Railway, for $25,000. "Storm in the Rocky Mountains, Mount Rosalie" sold for $20,000 (more than Fitz Hugh made in ten years of writing!) Yet even as Bierstadt attained financial security, critical comment began to turn against him. The *Round Table* magazine on October 14 noted that they had been assured "that Mr. Bierstadt's pictures are utterly unreliable... gross caricatures of nature...He is a third rate painter." And *Watson's Weekly Art Journal* had also criticized "Storm in the Rocky Mountains" by calculating, based on the height given for the hills in the foreground, that for Mount Rosalie to be visible it would have to be ten thousand miles high. "Impossible," concluded the journal. (These critiques are ironically reminiscent of Samuel Bowles' jibes at Fitz Hugh.)

But no matter. Bierstadt was, for the moment, eminently successful and wealthy.[41] Bierstadt had built an estate called Malkasten in Irvington-on-Hudson, N.Y., beginning in October 1865. He moved Rosalie there and wrote to a friend in December 1866, "My only regret is that I did not know my wife when I was twelve years old, and could have married her then. I am the happiest man living."[42]

Cousin Carrie, so often prone to take Rosalie's side in the long-running dispute with Fitz Hugh, wrote on December 17, "I always had a high opinion of Bierstadt from what I had heard of him until now. I think this marriage a very strange affair. She will enjoy her wealth I suppose but I don't envy them their happiness."[43]

No letters survive to tell directly of Fitz Hugh's feelings. But as he searched for expression of his pain and anger, the revisions to the notes of the western trip became the target of his bitter feelings. Every mention of Bierstadt's name was systematically found and deleted.[44] In Chapter 3, Fitz Hugh changed Bierstadt's name to "our artist" or "other overlander." Fitz Hugh cut out of Chapter 4 a description of Bierstadt's tour of the Garden of the Gods with *Rocky Mountain News* editor Byers. Fitz Hugh also completely excised the narration of the naming of Mount Rosalie, which in the February 28, 1864 *Era* had read as follows:

> Bierstadt, by right of first portrayal, baptized it after one far away from our sides, but very near and dear to our hearts—a gentle nature who had followed us clear to the verge of our Overland wanderings at Atchison, and parted from us bravely lest she should make our purpose fainter by seeming moved. Henceforth that shining peak is MONTE ROSA.

By the time Fitz Hugh reached the final three chapters, which were eventually published virtually verbatim from the *Atlantic* articles, Rosalie's and Bierstadt's betrayal was clearly tearing him apart. Five references by name to Bierstadt in the "On Horseback to Oregon" article had been altered to "artist companion" or simply to remove his name altogether. In "On the Columbia River," a reference to Fitz Hugh's being saved from pneumonia "by the indefatigable nursing of the best friend I ever traveled with" was changed to "the indefatigable nursing of the friend I traveled with." But the worst was saved for Rosalie. In "Seven Weeks in the Great Yo-Semite" in the *Atlantic* published in June 1864, there is a passage:

> Here we pitched our first Yo-Semite Camp,—calling it "Camp Rosalie," after a dear absent friend of mine and Bierstadt's.

In the book, the passage was savagely rewritten as:

> Here we pitched our first Yo-Semite camp,—calling it "Camp Rattlesnake," after a pestilent little beast of that tribe which insinuated itself into my blankets, but was disposed of by my artist comrade before it had inflicted its fatal wound upon me.

1 Ellen Ludlow to Caroline Frey, March 30, 1865, NYSHA Library.
2 See "Epilogue".
3 As noted earlier, Stedman who had found the *Atlantic* no longer welcomed New York writers at about the same time.
4 All recounted in earlier chapters.
5 Caroline Geddings to Caroline Frey, April 9, 1865, NYSHA Library.
6 Fitz Hugh Ludlow to Hiram Barney, (n.d.), Huntington Library.
7 Carpenter (1961), p. 8. Carpenter had painted a portrait of the Reverend Henry Ludlow in 1863, as noted in Chapter 11.
8 Richard Lockridge, *Darling of Misfortune*, New York and London: The Century Company, 1932, p. 143-145.
9 Frank Carpenter (1870).
10 Carrie Geddings to Caroline Frey, April 16, 1865, NYSHA Library.
11 Carrie Geddings to Caroline Frey, April 21, 1865, NYSHA Library.
12 Carrie Geddings to Caroline Frey, April 30, 1865, NYSHA Library. At least one historian thought that Fitz Hugh returned to Kansas for Mrs. Ives and brought her back East, and even up to Oswego. See Hendricks (1973), p. 167. However, this seems improbable.
13 Samuel Baldwin Ludlow to Caroline Frey, May 30 1865, NYSHA Library.

14 Fitz Hugh Ludlow to Schuyler Colfax, September 6, 1865, Fitz Hugh Ludlow Memorial Library.

15 Samuel Baldwin Ludlow to Caroline Frey, June 12, 1865, NYSHA Library.

16 Samuel B. Ludlow to Dr. C., June 11, 1865, NYSHA Library.

17 Carrie Geddings to Caroline Frey, May 14, 1865, NYSHA Library.

18 Carrie Geddings to Caroline Frey, May 21, 1865, NYSHA Library.

19 Anna Ludlow to Caroline Frey, June 5, 1865, NYSHA Library.

20 Carrie Geddings to Caroline Frey, July 20, 1865, NYSHA Library.

21 Carrie Geddings to Caroline Frey, August 5, 1865, NYSHA Library.

22 Henry Ludlow to Caroline Frey, September 1, 1865, NYSHA Library.

23 Samuel B. Ludlow to Caroline Frey, September 9, 1865, NYSHA Library.

24 Anna Ludlow to Caroline Frey, September 28, 1865, NYSHA Library.

25 Anna Ludlow to Caroline Frey, December 7, 1865, NYSHA Library.

26 Samuel B. Ludlow to Caroline Frey, December 26, 1865, NYSHA Library.

27 Caroline Frey to John Frey, January, 1866, NYSHA Library.

28 Samuel B. Ludlow to Caroline Frey, January 8, 1866, NYSHA Library.

29 Carrie Geddings to Caroline Frey, January 21, 1866, NYSHA Library.

30 Samuel B. Ludlow to Caroline Frey, February 3, 1866, NYSHA Library.

31 Carrie Geddings to Caroline Frey, February 11, 1865, NYSI IA Library.

32 Samuel B. Ludlow to Caroline Frey, March 5, 1865, NYSHA Library.

33 *Round Table*, January 20, 1866, p. 36.

34 Samuel Bowles, *Across the Continent*, Springfield, Mass: Samuel Bowles & Co., 1865, p. iv.

35 Caroline Geddings to Caroline Frey, February 25, 1866, NYSHA Library.

36 Bowles (1865), p. 75.

37 Ibid., p. 129.

38 Caroline Geddings to Caroline Frey, March 18, 1866, NYSHA Library.

39 Carrie Geddings to Caroline Frey, May 20, 1866, NYSHA Library.

40 Samuel B. Ludlow to Caroline Frey, July 14, 1866, NYSHA Library.

41 Bierstadt today is considered a model of the combination of artistic talent and aptitude for self-promotion. See *Albert Bierstadt, Art & Enterprise*, National Gallery of Art, November, 1991.

42 Hendricks (1973), p. 172.

43 Carrie Geddings to Caroline Frey, December 17, 1866, NYSHA Library.

44 Based on inspection of articles from *The Golden Era* and the *Atlantic* that were otherwise incorporated intact into the book.

XVI.

SECOND CHANCES

FITZ HUGH published nothing for several months after the divorce. Much of the pain went into the editing of his Western book, which remained unpublished.

Fitz Hugh's father had returned to New York City in mid-1865, working for old friend Lewis Tappan at the American Missionary Association, and Fitz Hugh must have slunk back to his father in defeat. Henry was by now too tired to fight or to reform his prodigal son. It remained for Fitz Hugh to recover as best he could, with Helen there to nurse his fragile physical health. But there comes a time when a man must face his demons and fight with whatever weapons lay at hand. Fitz Hugh picked up pen and wrote another story for *Harper's Monthly*.

"A Result of 'The Lambeth Casual'" appeared in *Harper's* in September, 1866. In it, Fitz Hugh parades his acquaintance with New York's elite, beginning the story with dinner at Delmonico's, the preeminent symbol of evening elegance in New York City. Later imprisoned, the narrator relates that "A high hat which I wore, being of white felt, led me at first to be mistaken for Mr. Greeley; but a gentleman who was in for stealing cabbages, and afterward acquitted on the ground of having a mania for vegetables, corrected the mistake of the audience, saying that he knew the philosopher well, and had often sat in convention with him." After some amusing highjinks, the story ends with the obligatory connubial dénouement.

This story was the kickoff to the most productive writing period of Fitz Hugh's life since before the War. In the short term, the lightweight "Lambeth" story gave him the money to attack a more pleasant prospect, the completion of his article on the unification of forces, begun with a letter to Professor Henry of the Smithsonian almost a year earlier.

Fitz Hugh titled the essay "E Pluribus Unum." Unable to place it in the *Atlantic* as originally planned, Fitz Hugh sold the piece to a recently founded New York periodical, *The Galaxy*, in November, 1866. Editors of *The Galaxy* conceived it as a New York competitor with the Boston magazines, and so set out to pay authors competitively with the *Atlantic*. Payment was $8 per page, resulting in about a $70 payment to Fitz Hugh.[1] Although the payment may have been adequate, Fitz Hugh was not given a byline, the only article in that issue without one. Moreover, *The Galaxy*, not aiming at quite so lofty an audience as the *Atlantic*, shortened the piece considerably from Fitz Hugh's manuscript. As a friend later noted, "This article, as he wrote it, was too long for the purpose of The Galaxy, and it was cut down and changed somewhat in form in its publication, which annoyed [Fitz Hugh] very much, as any interference with his manuscript always did."[2] The alteration may have included the insertion of a phrase introducing the article as a "brief popular talk." In more Fitz-like prose, "every reader whose education enables him to enjoy the other portions of this periodical will finish the article with the feeling of having had opened to him a new field for his thought as limitless and as noble as those trodden by the feet of Milton."

The article was primarily a summary of a book, *The Correlation of Forces*, edited by his old friend Professor Youmans.

That book contained essays by Faraday and other notables, mostly European. Americans were nevertheless instructed to take pride because publisher jealousy in Europe prevented such a compilation, and because Youmans' introduction showed conclusively that Benjamin Thompson, an American, "was the first philosopher who expressed absolute convictions upon the subject of correlated or translated forces." All of which extended to another field—Fitz Hugh's critical notions that America would complete the artistic as well as political emancipation of the world. Fitz Hugh also briefly acknowledged Professor Henry (who never did respond to Fitz Hugh's badly-timed request for information). "The profound researches and reasonings of Professor Henry are known to every expert in the higher mathematics of physical philosophy."

The complexity of the subject matter, and the state of the art are reflected by Fitz Hugh's summary of Mayer's essay, to wit, the heat of the sun cannot be explained by chemistry or by friction of rotation, and so Mayer "proceeds to explain it by the perpetual fall into the sun of comets, asteroids, meteorites and other wandering masses of cosmical matter." Laughable today, this theorizing actually was consistent with the thinking of such contemporary luminaries as Lord Kelvin. Fitz Hugh was a reporter here, not a scientist. He concluded with the following:

> Here, let us part from our subject as from the newly opened door of some vast temple, conceive that we have only looked, not entered in...grander knowledge and delights remain for those of us who may hereafter enter the temple and those who shall enter it after us. Of such it may be the privilege to correlate soul and body; the builder and the built; the

creative genius and the matter which it shapes; the mind's world of perception and the physical world of touch. Though the highest mind in vain be sought along the ladder of logic, it may yet be given us to develop some conclusive law which shall explain the relations of all existence, for the thought of the age tends toward a belief in the primal unity of being.

Despite what was apparently only a dim understanding of physics, Fitz Hugh was proud of this article, and saw it as contributing to his more serious reputation even if the *Atlantic* had once more spurned him. Youmans was said to have pronounced it "the ablest and most brilliant popular treatise on the subject" he had ever read.[3]

In the fall, one of Fitz Hugh's old friends, J.R. Gilmore, approached him for help in starting up a new literary journal to be based in the *The Atlantic Monthly*'s backyard, Boston, and to be called *Northern Lights*. Gilmore had entered the magazine field in 1861 by publishing the *Continental Monthly*, which was edited by Fitz Hugh's old friend Charles Leland. Gilmore had published a collection of sketches called *Among the Pines* that were admired by Lincoln, and he had interviewed the President in 1863. Popular author Julia Ward Howe was recruited as editor and Fitz Hugh signed on as a contributing editor, as reflected in a letter written October 24, 1866, from No. 1 Livingston Place, where Fitz Hugh now lived alone.[4]

My dear Gilmore,
I have only waited in order that I might find Stedman, who has lately moved, & answer you regarding him as well as myself. His health is very delicate & his time occupied in Stocks & the Atlantic, to both of which he is under articles for the year. Nevertheless, he says, put him down among your list of

contributors and he will try & send you a poem occasionally. He has scarcely time & health to write other than already engaged articles of the prose length.

I will send you one article early next week—if possible two, during that week.

In haste but yours truly, Ludlow[5]

Fitz Hugh appeared in the debut of *Northern Lights* in January 1867, with a story entitled "Little Briggs and I." It carried Fitz Hugh's byline, and was copiously illustrated. The magazine itself began with a one page "Salutation":

> Friends! a new name is called, and a new voyage begun. With fluttering pennon our magazine starts upon her trial trip… she will carry pleasant messages from East to West; and what, perhaps, may not be so easy, from North to South.

Early issues of the magazine included a regular feature called "Our Contributors Club," a roundtable discussion which identified contributors by pseudonyms such as St. Leger, the Pythoness, and The Hashish Eater. The contributors were pictured in a drawing seated around a table on which rested a pile of manuscripts. One of the seated characters does resemble the mutton-chopped Fitz Hugh. The feature took the form of dialogue among the characters. Although probably written by Gilmore, a few words about winter sports are attributed to a contributor called "The Hashish Eater," and the style resembles Fitz Hugh's:

> My nose and ears have so often proved favorite subjects for Jack Frost's experiments, that, with all due respect to the creator of the best part of Sherry Cobblers and Sherbet, I much prefer my present quarters to a nearer fellowship with his majesty.

"Little Briggs and I" featured another excursion to the boarding schools of Fitz Hugh's childhood, one he does not characterize as autobiography in which the author remembers only the good things, but as no "ought-to-be-ography" at all. The tale is a courting contest between two boys which continues through young adulthood, but ends when one dies saving the other in battle during the Civil War. The survivor marries the girl, but the couple often think of the fallen friend. Fitz Hugh had lost enough friends [like Fitz James O'Brien and Kappa Alpha brothers Wead and Newbury] to add heartfelt pathos to the story. When the body of the fallen comrade is recovered, a voice says "take it to the next tent…Take *it*. Who was it that had been *he* last night, and was only *it* this morning?" And despite the ending, the story is primarily a humorous one, featuring passages such as, "Mr. Barker was engaged in quarrying a page of Cicero out of some stony boy in whom nature had never made any Latin deposit."

Gilmore was an old friend who had maintained his ties with Fitz Hugh, but others had drifted away. On January 22, 1867, Edwin Booth received the Hamlet Medal from a citizens committee of New York. The committee included Governor John T. Hoffman, George William Curtis, Bayard Taylor, Launt Thompson, Jervis McEntee, and Albert Bierstadt himself, but not Booth's old friend and champion Fitz Hugh. Fitz Hugh seemed forever estranged from the old circle, although Bierstadt and Rosalie had been welcomed back. Some tenuous contact with Stedman is evident from the above letter to Gilmore, but years after Fitz Hugh's death Stedman included an excerpt from *The Hasheesh Eater* in an anthology, and said in the introduction that the tales "seem like a work of imagination rather than an actual happening." Their friendship, sadly, faded with the years.

Northern Lights on January 19 carried an interesting non-fiction sketch by Fitz Hugh, reminiscent of some his *Golden Era* essays, entitled "On the Proper Use of Grandfathers." It shifted into a reformist attitude early on:

> Woman, religion, and the forefathers are all the victims of a false quality of reverence. The world has immorally paid them in the coin of lip-service for the privilege of using their sacredness as a yoke…We pick up the fan of the first, and shoulder her out of her partnership in our serious business of living. We build temples for the second, that she may not gad about among our shops, or trouble the doors of our houses. In the third, we do superstitious homage to a mere accident of time, and feel free to neglect the genial lesson of humanity which is eternal.

Fitz Hugh sought in the article to praise his elders without deifying them, and concluded:

> Their value is that they take the experience of human life, and hold it a sufficient distance from us to be judged in its true proportions…We recognize that unity and all things become possible to us, for thereby even the commonest living is glorified.

In February, Fitz Hugh's immediate family was again the subject of attention from Fitz Hugh's extended family. On February 5, Uncle Samuel wrote to his sister that Helen had described Reverend Henry's heart disease as "a dangerous condition…So who will take him in? We will offer, don't know if he will come."[6] The following week, family physician Dr. Purdy told Samuel he thought Henry's condition "precarious." Fitz Hugh, however, was preoccupied and if anything thought that Henry would pull through as he had in his previous crisis. Cousin Carrie meanwhile wrote to her mother from Washington D.C. that "Mr. Grant tells me he saw Mr. and Mrs. Bierstadt here the other day. She told him they were going to sail for Paris 1st of May."

Northern Lights published another Fitz Hugh short story in February, 1867 entitled "Fleeing to Tarshish." It ran through three issues, but did not carry a byline. Tarshish, and the main character's name Jonas Moddle, come from the biblical book of Jonah. "E Pluribus Unum" had begun by referring to Job's question "Who by searching can find out God?", indicating closer study of the Bible by Fitz Hugh in his post-marital days. The story contains a quote from a text "which has dropped out of the canonical version of his namesake's prophecy," words that ended the book of Jonah with Jonah thanking the Lord exceedingly for the fruit of the gourd "for which thou labored not." This is an interesting sidelight on Fitz Hugh's breadth of learning.

"Tarshish" depicts a struggle of conscience for a young seminary graduate who must decide between a wealthy, cosmopolitan parish and a poor, pastor-less group in western Missouri, a place where one rector "had lost one of his wardens in a knife-fight with a Presbyterian deacon upon the subject of free-will." The wealthy church featured "men [who] do nothing now-a-days but stupefy their souls with business." Moddle becomes disillusioned when he finds through weekly confessions that "so many wives and husbands, who seemed models of conjugal felicity to mankind, in the light of Mr. Moddle's better information became haggard wretches with aching hearts, sitting hard on nature's safety-valves for the sake of society, and tremulously expecting their rust-eaten relation to explode beneath them. So many respectable families contained one irreclaimable drunkard, and some of those drunkards were women." The wife of one of the deacons, who favored a "more splendid ritual" and worked closely with Moddle to implement this reform, scandalously falls in love with the sensitive young minister. The exchange where she declares her love is powerfully erotic in the context of the mood created by Fitz Hugh's style in this story, where he again moves beyond genre restrictions into genuine emotion and drama.

Moddle is injured, falls into a coma which he compares to Jonah's stay in the whale's belly, and then flees to the country. Moddle is now reduced to ministering to a "wretch on his death-bed with delirium tremens, or burying men who had murdered each other in a fight across a cock-pit." At lowest ebb, he feels disgust for a "camp-meeting" that comes to town until his daughter is taken sick. She is cured, he believes, by his repentant prayers acknowledging that all do the Lord's work, no matter the style. This of course is the theme from "The Cruise of the Two Deacons." In camp meeting, the revivalist tells the story of Moddle's daughter's cure through prayer, and suddenly men who wouldn't come near church get interested. But in a step towards realism that Fitz Hugh never took in *Harper's*, Moddle admits that after the revival was "Not the millennium…it is no one-dose remedy which will ever cure the world." As in "The Cruise of the Two Deacons," Fitz Hugh was moved by religious themes to craft a solid story that rose above genre convention.

In the midst of writing this story, Fitz Hugh had left again on a midwestern tour. He wrote in early February from Logansport, Indiana, giving a rare glimpse of his thoughts on the craft of writing:

My Dear Gilmore,

Temporary detention in a small Indiana town waiting for the Great Eastern night express up to Chicago, will I am sure excuse my writing to you on a partially greasy sheet. I may add that the delicate tinge at the upper left hand corner was communicated by sardines—a box of which we have just enjoyed very much, but which possibly may have imparted to this letter, by the time (considering the state of the roads) which it will take it to reach the Center of All Things an ancient & fish-like smell.

I meant to have written to you before I left New York—but just at the last I was called West very unexpectedly and before I went had to do so much preparation for this very trip that I had to leave to Providence all such portions of my correspondence as could possibly be trusted to run itself till I had time to send a series of Parthian missives flying back en route. I knew you had two numbers of "Fleeing to Tarshish" and that if I rest at Chicago a day or two I can probably send you a short sketch or story this week. $60 received from your publishers for "Fleeing from Tarshish"—thank you.

The novel which I wrote & you remind me of is not yet far enough advanced to promise for any number short of an early summer one. I have had great cares & responsibilities laid upon me of late which may narrow the time I can at the best employ for literary effort though I will keep to the original plan I laid down for myself of at least one contribution per fortnight as I can. When I next bring out a book—especially if it be a novel—an arena of such vast competitions for any man to enter!—I desire that it shall have had the very best of my work expended on it as an entirety. I once wrote a serial novelette in some 19 weekly numbers which I reflect with gratitude you have doubtless utterly forgotten—and wrote only as fast as the matter was published. I committed myself early in my plot to a denouement which as the story opened grew gradually more undesirable, and had to introduce an improbability only allowable in broadest burlesque to get myself out of the fire. Even where Dickens has attempted it he has only succeeded by virtue of a genius quite incomparable with any Englishman's but Shakespeare, and he would have succeeded better yet had he mastered his theme & struck all its chords to finis before attempting on it any of those discursive, seductive & entangling little variations which begin with the first published chapter. Sala got into an awful fix by risking himself to keep up with the printer in Alone. The more I look at it the more I feel that I'd like to see my finished work & give it the final touches by which intuition sometimes supplies some exactly needed element of symmetry or takes away some weakening surplusage before I start it out among men.

I only saw three No.'s of the N.L. before leaving New York—but have letters since then saying that every number had improved in beauty of appearance & interest as much as it was continuing to do up to no. 3—A most admirable sketch was that Low Life on the Five Points, a capitally well told story of the Paris sewers. There have been many sewer stories in magazines—but the dog & other elements in this make it the best I ever read.

Write me as usual at New York—whither I hope to return on Thursday. I'll forward more Ms. as soon as I can. I am

Your Friend, Ludlow[7]

This letter reveals two interesting developments. The first of course is Fitz Hugh's announcement of a novel in progress. The other is the trip to Chicago, the purpose of which was to further his acquaintance with a most interesting lady, Maria Owen Milliken, the widow of Judge Milliken, and late of Augusta, Maine. If Rosalie could move on, then so could he.

In March 1867, keeping to the one contribution per fortnight plan, Fitz Hugh returned to *Harper's* with "A Brace of Boys," and he also returned to the genre which had been so lucrative. Although enlivened by wordplay as all his stories are, it is a short-story romance of the most unimaginative type. Clearly, his best work was going to *Northern Lights*. This story makes passing reference to cricket/baseball, and to P. T. Barnum's museum of curiosities as new American pastimes. It also features a first-person narrator who opens the story, proclaiming, "I am a bachelor uncle. That, as a mere fact, might happen to anybody; but I am a bachelor uncle by internal fitness." This is perhaps putting a cheerful public face on his marital failure, somewhat belied by his pursuit of Maria Milliken.

The spring of 1867 found Fitz Hugh's immediate and extended families as active and opinionated as ever. Ellen told Uncle Sam "I think her [Helen] great sorrows and troubles have wonderfully sweetened and enriched her whole nature."[8] However, Carrie on May 19 says of her Reverend Uncle Henry that there is "not the least doubt about his being deranged Gus told me. I pity you having him in the house."[9] Fitz Hugh, however, was still charitable, attempting to do one of the cousins [probably Uncle Samuel's daughter Anna Ludlow] a favor as reflected in a March 28 letter to Beadle & Co. publishers, a house with which he had little known influence or contact.

> Messrs. Beadle & Co.
> My cousin's Ms. received—thanks. I arrive by inspection at the conclusion that three stamps just covers my debt to you for P.O. deficiencies—which please find enclosed and believe me
> Yours truly, Fitz Hugh Ludlow[10]

Also, in June, Cousin Carrie's husband, Colonel Geddings, died, tragically young, after a long illness. Unaware of her extensive disapproving commentary over the years, Fitz

Hugh sent her a book of poems in condolence, with his own poem inscribed:

> Like a fountain's sweet unsealing
> in the opening of thy leaves,
> Waters of repose revealing
> to the shaken heart that grieves.[11]

When she got past her grief, Carrie might have found room in her heart for a little guilt over her hard words said about Fitz Hugh.

Meanwhile, Fitz Hugh's old friend Stedman made an odd passing reference to Fitz Hugh in an April 7 letter to Bayard Taylor concerning Taylor's recent letter on poet and essayist Algernon Swinburne:

> Stoddard and his wife are greatly—immensely—I may say—interested in your Swinburne letter, and think you are quite carried away by his magnetism. I do not think him so great a man—so noble a fellow—as Shelley, though his poems have the same abandon and rhapsody. Your portraiture of his "tricks and manners" is that of a Fitz Hugh Ludlow sublimated by real genius. However, the Stoddards are very happy in their interpretation of your letter, and you could not have pleased Richard so much in any other way, for he is strangely attracted Swinburnewards.[12]

In June, Fitz Hugh was still involved with Gilmore, writing to him on the 24th (from No. 1 Livingston) in what appears to be a drunken scrawl in large letters:

> My dear Gilmore,
> O You rogue! O you two rogues—you & Sykes! To come on God's holy day and pick a man's pocket of his biographies!

Never mind. For the world I wouldn't have had any body do anything in that way about me, but since it is done I can only say it is most kindly & only too complimentary, and remain your friend always, Ludlow

(Turn over)

P.S. I open my envelope because I've just got your note from Boston. Be sure, my dear fellow, that I understand the circumstances exactly—and don't blame Sykes in the least, for, although he did what I would not knowingly have consented to, he at any rate wrote with kindness, appreciation, and enthusiasm.

Tell Messrs. Lee & Shepard please, for me that I today send them a note which by mistake has lain for days while I was visiting down at the Flatbush Lunatic Asylum with my friend, its head, Dr. Chapin.

Always, Dear Gilmore, your friend, Ludlow[13]

Who Sykes was, and what biography is referenced are lost to history, but the visit to Dr. Chapin's asylum was of great moment for Fitz Hugh's future. The visit to an asylum mentioned in the "Lambeth Casual" story was the first hint of a new interest of Fitz Hugh's, which will be discussed in the next chapter.

Old acquaintances were also rolling along. Mark Twain's first book (stories compiled by Charles Henry Webb (Inigo) including the Jumping Frog) was published in May 1867.[14] Twain wrote from New York on June 2 1867 about one of his old friend Bierstadt's paintings:

"The Domes of Yosemite." That is the name of Bierstadt's last picture. The art critics here abused it without stint when its exhibition began, a month ago. They ridiculed it so mercilessly that I thought it surely could not be worth going to see, and so I staid away. I went to-day, however, and I think it is very well worth going to see. It is very beautiful—considerably more beautiful than the original.[15]

On June 22, Bierstadt and Rosalie set sail for Europe for a two-year stay. *Watson's Art Journal* said, "Bierstadt has gone to Europe. It is to be hoped that while there he will learn to reform his style, and be taught that merit consists in quality rather than quantity." The Bierstadts proceeded in their two-year stay to visit all the capitals of western Europe. In Rome they visited Liszt, where the master played for a small group one of his own compositions. In London they gave a dinner for Longfellow, which was attended by Robert Browning and Prime Minister Gladstone. They did not return to the U.S. until the summer of 1869.[16]

As the summer wore on, Fitz Hugh and Maria Milliken began to consider marriage. She was somewhat older than Fitz Hugh, but was charmed by his wit and learning. As widow of a well-to-do man, she had no particular concern for his dubious ability to support a family. And her willingness to consider a long-term relationship with Fitz Hugh certainly hinted at a freer soul than one might expect from a stolid wife of a Maine judge.

In July, Fitz Hugh reached another long-awaited milestone with his first collection of stories, *Little Brother and Other Genre-Pictures*, published by Lee and Shepard. Lee and Shepard was a house that made most of its business from publishing books for young people. Authors Oliver Optic and J. T. Trowbridge were mainstays of the house, with "vigorous, well-told stories; capable, manly heroes; ordinary boys, not marvels."[17] Lee and Shepard became by the end of the decade one of the largest publishers of children's books in the United States. Fitz Hugh was an apt choice for the house. As Frank Carpenter put it, "None but a large-hearted man, one who loved little children, flowers and birds, all things beautiful in Nature, could have written such stories as Little Brother, Little Briggs and I and A Brace of Boys."[18] Fitz Hugh's collection contained "Little Brother" from the 1860 *Harper's*, plus his three most recent stories, "Fleeing to Tarshish" and "Little Briggs and I" from *Northern Lights*, and "A Brace of Boys" from *Harper's*. The dedication read:

> In mind of a courtesy to which three pictures in this cabinet owe their present setting, and a large-heartedness which from the beginning of his career has afforded innumerable helps to their artist, they are inscribed to that wise and generous friend of letters,
> Fletcher Harper, Esq.

Indeed, there could be no one else to whom Fitz Hugh owed as large a debt as Harper. However, it is not clear why he refers to three pictures, when only "Little Brother" and "A Brace of Boys" appeared in *Harper's*. Fitz Hugh might also have reflected by now that Harper had never seen fit to bring out a collection of Fitz Hugh's short works, although surely by now he had amassed enough significant stories to deserve the same attention as others who had published anthologies. Moreover, his current preferred publisher was *Northern Lights* and not *Harper's Monthly*.

At about the same time, "The Proper Use of Grand-fathers" sketch from *Northern Lights* was reprinted in *Stories and Sketches by our Best Authors*, also published by Lee & Shepard, in July 1867. Both anthologies were reviewed in the same review in *The Round Table* on July 20, 1867:

If not absolutely the best, Mr. Ludlow is certainly among the best of our writers of minor fiction, and the four stories contained in his present handsome volume are among his happiest productions. Their only bond of union is indicated by the motto from Juvenal which stands upon the title-page, "Maxima reverentia pueris debetur," although in them all appear the author's rare resources of blended wit, satire, pathos, and robust vitality…we conceive the honor of the best magazine story which has appeared for many a day to be the due of Little Briggs and I—a story which includes in its wide range of scenes so marvelously faithful a sketch of a type of New England boarding-school—now, we trust, nearly extinct—that only the knowledge that he was not prevents our claiming Mr. Ludlow as a schoolmate and fellow-sufferer.

Had he never done so before, Mr. Ludlow gives in the stories of this volume abundant assurance that, if he only would, he could give us the long-looked-for American novel.

Mr. Ludlow also appears in *Stories and Sketches*, the companion volume to his own, and, like it, made up of magazine articles. Unlike the other book, it is extremely unequal in point of merit, opening very poorly but closing very well with a capital account by Mr. Charles D. Shanly of being lost in the sewers of Paris. Of the fourteen writers who contribute to it several are by no means among "Our Best Authors" yet perhaps enough of them may be fairly so ranked to make the volume, on the whole, a pleasant one for half-hour readings by people who want to be amused.

Fitz Hugh must have been gratified by the reviewer's belief that he might write the "long-looked-for American novel." The *New York Times* included a brief notice in its July 3, 1867 issue:

Little Brother and Other Genre Pictures is the title of a volume produced by Messrs. LEE & SHEPARD, Boston, containing four stories by that prolific writer, FITZ HUGH LUDLOW. Besides the tale named in the title the book contains "Fleeing to Tarshish," "Little Briggs and I," and "A Brace of Boys," all of which will be readily recognized by readers of current magazine literature. Mr. LUDLOW inscribes the volume to "that wise and generous friend of letters, FLETCHER HARPER." The same publishers group together in another volume *Stories and Sketches by our Best Authors*. The title of the book would lead one to look for a selection of standard tales, but they prove upon inspection to have been culled from that defunct hebdomedal *Northern Lights*. Although the stories are good enough in their way, it is hardly fair to palm them off upon the public as the production of "our best authors," when at least one half the writers were never heard of save in connection with the periodical named.

Fitz Hugh was encouraged by the publication of the two anthologies to think that book formats might be a lucrative future source of income. He moved to meet the projected demand for product to fill future volumes with two new stories. Unfortunately, *Northern Lights* was indeed already a "defunct hebdomedal." But Lee and Shepard started *Oliver Optic's Magazine for Boys and Girls* the same year, and noted in its opening issue that Optic would "enlist the services of the following eminent ladies and gentlemen: Julia Ward Howe, Edmund Kirke, Fitz Hugh Ludlow" and others.[19] None of the stories subsequently appearing in Optic's magazine were identified as Fitz Hugh's work. Fitz Hugh's two new stories instead would appear in the August and September numbers of *Harper's Monthly*.

"A Reformed Ring-Man" was the tale of a former politician who is proud to have given up that trade to become "an honest mechanic." As a politician, or "Ring-Man," the narrator presents an invoice for services rendered to be paid by special interests, although it "does not include bets on the result of sundry Bills presented during the Session." A woman turns the narrator's morals around, and in the next session he double crosses all his supporters by voting against their special interests. When this happens, "Peghammer, who in former days had bought me at various prices fifty times, looked at me for a moment with a blank countenance, as he might look at a bale of uplands cotton miraculously endowed with power to assert itself, and indignantly demanding to be bought at the price of long-staple."

The story was slight but humorous and cynical, ahead of its time, describing such legislative boondoggles as the Penny Bridge Fluviatile Transportation Co. and the Wire Safe Railroad with its gridiron scheme to lay track through every street in the city. Fitz Hugh also threw another dig at Greeley, "Neither Horace Greeley nor I ran for Assembly in our ward the next time. I don't know which of us would have got the most votes if we had."

"Ring-Man" was followed the next month with "Pairing Off" in the September 1867 Harper's. This was a slightly less humorous sketch, a return to the tried and true romantic formula. The narrator is a minister and the antagonists were co-owners of a mill, Mr. Spotman and Mr. Pratt. Mrs. Pratt was the force in the Pratt family (Mr. Pratt dreamed "mainly about bears, locomotives chasing him, falling off something, or other unsatisfactory themes of the sort"); Spotman was equally a tyrant in his—"The wrong peg on the hat rack, and the moral screw loose, fell under the same Draconian code...the atmosphere of grandeur which hung around Mr. Spotman outside the domestic circle at table spread to the viands, etherealizing every platter." Their children were friendly despite the antagonism of the parents, and had not turned out to be models of behavior. Spotsman's son Disraeli was a drunk at the age of 12 as well as "an ensanguined torturer of cats, a hardened swindler at marbles."

The story shifts gears, "If I should see my pulpit cushion square off some Sunday to thump me back I should scarcely be more stupefied than was Mr. Spotman at the sudden self-assertion of the Pratt family." (This recalls the assertive cotton bale in "Ringman"—perhaps a theme in Fitz Hugh's inner thoughts at this time.) Mrs. Pratt uses Spotman's tobacco addiction to force him to sign a paper signing half the mill over to the Pratts. "Every nerve of his body was hungry for Mrs. Winslow [the same opium syrup referenced in Fitz Hugh's *Cinderella* in 1864], yet every drop of his blood seemed coffee and capsicum." Everything is resolved by the long lost son Jack, who had been off many years traveling to San Francisco, Puget Sound, Rocky Mountains, New York and Brooklyn as well as South America (i.e. Fitz Hugh's western trip and return cruise route.) The unhappy children all got married, were all much improved, but the world was still left waiting for Fitz Hugh's literary maturity.

The Round Table on November 16, 1867 reported "Mr. Fitz Hugh Ludlow is at work upon a novel." But the novel had been further delayed by the deterioration of Fitz Hugh's father Henry. On August 3, Uncle Sam wrote that "HG got letter from Fitz—not awake long enough to read it." On August 9, Samuel reported that HG on his death bed had "abandoned opium altogether—hope F. and Helen for whom we telegraphed yesterday may see him alive...hope to have services in Oswego, F & H permitting, then body to Poughkeepsie." The Reverend Henry Ludlow died on Sunday August 11, 1867, aged seventy years and six months, "at the house of his only brother, as the flock he loved were coming out of their earthly church, he ascended to that heavenly one."[20] The Oswego newspaper carried a sketch of his life:

> Like St. Paul, he loved to be the founder of churches, and went from the cap-stone of one to the corner stone of another.[21]

Another obituary related how Henry risked "prison and death" to convey "into freedom the fleeing wanderers from an unhallowed compact with death and hell, often at the rate of fifty a month—being the Agent of the underground railroad...No man has been more sincerely loved while living—more sorrowed for when he died...we mourn him as men miss a star set to rise on another hemisphere."[22] None of the tributes mentioned his two wives or children. Nevertheless, Helen wrote upon this clipping:

> Keep this. Read it. Read it again.

Fitz Hugh was saddened, but there was little to say. The gulf between them, despite their similarities of strong will and self-righteousness, was never bridged. Fitz Hugh had pleased his father at the end with his courtship of Maria Milliken. Henry saw the woman as a mature match and steadying influence for the still-unpredictable Fitz Hugh. Henry in fact had hoped to officiate at nuptials for the couple until death over-took him. The relations between father and son were too painful, and too intimately bound up to allow a facile tribute or a bitter farewell. Still, one poem entitled "To My Father" (it survives in manuscript, but its date is uncertain) reflects a little of Fitz Hugh's kinder side, though it maintains a certain distance through its formality.

> My Father — loud must be the strife
> Of Earth, if through its jarring tone
> I hear no music from the life
> that gave the keynote to my own.
> There have been those whose deeds and words
> pealed through a broader space and time
> But thine sound with those noble chords that
> make a private life sublime
> The heart that thrilled in chord with Youth
> the hands that touched life's master keys in
> like grand unison thy youth
> and age are full of chords like these!
> They brow though it know not the oil
> that sanctifies the locks of kings, hath
> been anointed by the toil
> of striving for God's noblest things
> A sire to whom an iron right
> was dearer than a golden wrong,
> who brought his own heart to the light
> but veiled a brother's not so strong
> And thou for what thou art to me
> and what thou hast been to thy kind,
> hast more than kingly royalty
> in the escutcheons of my mind.[23]

One direct effect of Henry's passing was that "from that time [Fitz Hugh] took his sister to his own loving care and home."[24] In an October 22 letter, Uncle Samuel mused on Helen and Fitz Hugh, and fears "Helen will spend her life on him, should his life be prolonged. Helen's estate 13,000, interest of 910 annual, of which Fitz is entitled to 280—will be a mere trifle to F & that she will supply the balance."[25]

Fitz Hugh probably needed the money. He had earned perhaps $700 in the first nine months of 1867, but *Northern Lights*, his most promising new editorial home, had already gone out of business. Then, to add to his woes, Fitz Hugh's health failed once again. In November 1867, Cousin Carrie wrote from Livingston Place, where Fitz Hugh now lived, that family physician Dr. Purdy "came to see Fitz who was quite sick last night."[26] A few days later she wrote, "Helen is better than she has been all winter tho' she is thin—still she looks and seems very well—Fitz is not at all well though, and is under Dr. Purdy's care. He has been raising blood from his *throat* (the Dr. says). I have scarcely seen him yet or Maria either." This appears to have been a secondary tuberculosis infection.

A day later,

> Helen went to the Office and told Gus that I probably would not be here this week so I shan't see any of them till I go to see them I suppose and it is so rainy this morning that I think it doubtful whether we go out...Helen is lying on the bed. She sends her love to you all—says to tell you she has found out from Uncle Sam about Thomas Metcalf and the well. She wanted it for a letter from Mr. Halliday of the Five Points Mission. He asked her to write down as many as she could remember of the stories Uncle used to tell the children, as he told them. He wanted them very much and this was one of them.

On November 13, Uncle Samuel wrote to his sister reflecting at length on Henry and his star-crossed family:

> I had heard before your letter came, that Helen was quite unwell, with a severe cold, and that Dr. Purdy after an examination of

her breathing apparatus—had counselled her to take special care of herself—but that there was nothing yet that was alarming. Poor girl! She has what we farmers call a "hard row" in more respects than one. Her ill health—her small income, just discovered to be so—and the dreadful burden which she is compelled to bear, in sustaining that miserable creature, Fitz., which will, I fear, yet exhaust all her means of living, for both of them—demands our warmest & most anxious sympathies—& that is about all, that, in my circumstances, I can bestow on her.

That scene, which you describe, between F. & Gus is truly shocking. His own dreadful temper, inflamed by some one, or all, of his old excitants, hasheesh, whisky, tobacco—make him a very terrible fellow to encounter. I look with "a fearful looking for" for a dreadful termination of his life & pilgrimage—hoping (when I do hope) only against hope. He was, of course, drunk, on that occasion. May the Lord grant Helen, in some way, a good deliverance, in this trying case, before she, herself, becomes wrecked. I have said to her all that I can, to prevent the waste of her entire substance on him.

Surely Mrs. M. cannot be so mad—so given up to believe a lie, touching his reform—as to marry him. If she does, she will, in my estimation of her, be greatly depreciated.[27]

Carrie continued to write her mother from New York, on the 17th: "Helen writes me that she and Mrs. Milliken would like very much for me to come and make them a visit."[28] Again on the 20th: "Helen looks careworn…she must have more than she can bear with F…he's in Elmira now [for a month] *giving up tobacco* she says, poor girl. I hope she does really believe that that is all."[29] In a December 9 letter, Uncle Samuel clarified: "Elmira is water cure. Helen with Mrs. Milliken in NY."[30] Henry's estate actually amounted to only $550 and "this not enough for her and F's needs…if need be she will give every dollar of it to Fitz."

The water cure effected its usual temporary improvement, and on December 23, Fitz Hugh wed Maria Milliken in a small private ceremony. A year and a half of productivity had come to a bittersweet end. Married again, but without his antagonist and role model father, Fitz Hugh faced a new phase of life. He also acquired two step-sons, who were young men in their teens. Mrs. Milliken had her own means of support, and they all moved in to No. 1 Livingston Place in New York.

But Fitz Hugh's new domestic relations were soon overshadowed by a preoccupation which began with Dr. Chapin at the Flatbush Lunatic Asylum, or perhaps with his collapse in Oregon, or perhaps with Mark Twain in San Francisco, or even perhaps with Mr. Anderson the apothecary in Poughkeepsie in Fitz Hugh's long gone youth. Wherever it began, in the summer of 1867, Fitz Hugh rediscovered opium.

1 Justus Richard Pearson, *Story of a Magazine: New York's Galaxy*, New York (n.p.), 1957. Payment as of 1871.
2 Carpenter (1870).
3 Helen Ludlow, 1873-75, p. 6.
4 Howe reported in her journal that "I saw J.R. Gilmour [*sic*] and agreed with him to do editorial service for three months."
5 Fitz Hugh Ludlow to J.R. Gilmore, October 24, 1866, James Roberts Gilmore Papers, Ms. 37, Special Collections, Milton S. Eisenhower Library, The Johns Hopkins University.
6 Samuel B. Ludlow to Caroline Frey, February 5, 1867, NYSHA Library.
7 Fitz Hugh Ludlow to J.R. Gilmore, February 4, 1867, Johns Hopkins University.
8 Ellen Ludlow to Samuel B. Ludlow, May, 1867, NYSHA Library.
9 Carrie Geddings to Caroline Frey, May 19, 1867, NYSHA Library.
10 Fitz Hugh Ludlow to "Messrs. Beadle and Co.," March 28, 1867, The Huntington Library.
11 In Frey papers, NYSHA Library.

12 Stedman and Gould (1910), p. 411.

13 Fitz Hugh Ludlow to J.R. Gilmore, June 24, 1867, Milton S. Eisenhower Library, Johns Hopkins University.

14 The book was printed by John A. Gray and Green, for whom Sam Clemens had set type thirteen years before, and who printed Fitz Hugh's Cinderella adaptation three years earlier. See Franklin Walker and George Dane, *Mark Twain's Travels with Mr. Brown*, New York: A.A. Knopf, 1940.

15 Ibid., p. 249.

16 Hendricks (1973) p. 179-185.

17 Raymond L. Kilgour, *Lee and Shepard, Publishers for the People*, New York: The Shoe String Press, 1965, p. 61.

18 Ibid.

19 Optic was the pen name of a writer whose books had sold over 100,000 copies by that time, rivaled only by Horatio Alger himself. A later review noted "Miss Palfrey's Herman had sold about 12,000 copies, and some of the other novelists, such as Miss Douglas, Ralph Keeler, Miss Cobb, Fitzhugh [sic] Ludlow, J.T. Trowbridge and Edmund Kirke had had some success" in the sales department. Of further interest, in 1871, Lee and Shepard published Carroll's Through the Looking Glass.

20 "A Disciple Whom Jesus Loved," The Evangelist (n.d.).

21 Ibid.

22 Unidentified Obituary, now in Helen Ludlow papers at Hampton University.

23 Manuscript book of poems, now at Schaffer Library, Union College.

24 Helen Ludlow to Leander Hall, June 1, 1876, Schaffer Library.

25 Samuel B. Ludlow to Caroline Frey, October 22, 1867, NYSHA Library.

26 Carrie Geddings to Caroline Frey, November, 1867, NYSHA Library.

27 Samuel Baldwin Ludlow to Caroline Frey, November 13, 1867, NYSHA Library.

28 Carrie Geddings to Caroline Frey, November 17, 1867, NYSHA Library.

29 Carrie Geddings to Caroline Frey, November 20, 1867, NYSHA Library.

30 Samuel B. Ludlow to Caroline Frey, December 9, 1867, NYSHA Library.

XVII.

THE OPIUM HABIT

"WHAT shall they do to be saved?" was the title of an article appearing in the August 1867 issue of *Harper's Monthly*. "They" were opium addicts. Fitz Hugh's visits to Dr. Chapin's asylum had acquainted him with a number of poor unfortunates who had a narcotic addiction to add to their other problems. Moreover, with the Civil War, opium use had become widespread in the U.S. as an anesthetic, without widespread knowledge of its addictive potential. (Unlike hashish, opium use can create a physical addiction. Attempts to stop taking opium result in physical withdrawal symptoms that can be so painful as to deter the addict from making the sustained effort to end its usage.) Opium was more familiar to Europeans after the Opium Wars in India and China between 1840 and 1860, when the Treaty of Tientsin had legalized the opium trade. Fitz Hugh was familiar with this history, as shown by an aside in his story "An International Affair."

Fitz Hugh's article was the first in a major American journal to address the issue, and his reputation as a man of letters as well as a lay interpreter of scientific phenomena underscored the essay. Fitz Hugh had written of opium treatment in his story "John Heathburn's Title" (see Chapter 14) as early as February 1864. His acquaintance with the drug of course dated back to 1856 and Anderson's apothecary, but it may be that his need for it as medicine due to his tubercular infection led him to a more methodical consideration.

The article began with a profile of a successful business-man who began using a preparation known as M'Munn's Elixir. The man had begun taking the Elixir as a medical prescription for an inflamed cornea. He returned to opium "whenever the world went wrong with him," whether the problem was a toothache or insomnia. "There are certain men to whom opium is as fire to tow, and my friend was one of these...The physical power of the drug over him he only realized when attempting its abandonment."The man even-tually moved on to laudanum, which contained opium in a slightly different tincture.

DR. M'MUNN'S ELIXIR OF OPIUM.

Fitz Hugh described the psychological components of addiction with a mixture of literary skill and sensationa-lism. He spoke of his case study in acquiring the drug as going through "subterfuges of a complicated construc-tion and artistic plausibilty which might have puzzled Richelieu." The addiction reduced him "to that automatic condition in which the nervous system issues and enfor-ces only those edicts which are counseled by pure animal self-preservation."

For three months Fitz Hugh tried to treat the man in his own house in New York. He then sent the man to a water cure outside the city to help him deal with the pain of withdrawal, noting (from personal experience) that baths work well as a sedative. Fitz Hugh was unable to watch this man as he would have preferred. When he visited again, the patient had undergone ninety days without opium, but also without sleep. Although the attendants at the baths thought he had been resting, "that which appeared sleep was internally to him only one stupendous succession of horrors which confusedly succeeded each other for apparent eternities of being." This was more horrible than the damage caused by opium use, so that despite his best efforts, Fitz Hugh concluded that the verdict in this case was: "he will have to take opium all his life. Further struggle is suicide."

Fitz Hugh interspersed, throughout his narrative of one man's struggle, more general observations about what had been a major preoccupation for the past six months. He opined on the nature of addiction "which Coleridge felt as he concentrated on that one single cry of his animal nature, and the laudanum which it spoke for, all the faculties of construction and insight which had created the 'Ancient Mariner' and the 'Aids to Reflection.'" In another literary allusion, Fitz Hugh compares liquor to opium as "the clutch of an angry woman to the embrace of Victor Hugo's Pieuvre." And one passage recalled the Chinaman in San Francisco whose agonies Fitz Hugh witnessed after a night's debauch. (See Chapter 13.) Some passages describing opium's effects were reminiscent of Fitz Hugh's hashish dreams:

[H]e had not forgotten the sweet dissolving views at midnight, the great executive achievements at noonday, the heavenly sense of a self-reliance which dare go any where, say any thing, attempt any thing in the world. He had not forgotten the nonchalance under slight, the serenity in pain, the apathy to sorrow, which for one month set him calm as Boodh in the temple-splendors of his darkened room.

And at the other end of the spectrum lay the following quote, which Fitz Hugh attributes to a patient but seems to bear the style of Fitz Hugh:

> God seems to help a man in getting out of every difficulty but opium. There you have to claw your way out over red-hot coals on your hands and knees, and drag yourself by main strength through the burning dungeon-bars.

Fitz Hugh's judgment on such men was not that of moral decay or criminal intent, which was the majority view then much as it is today. For the individuals described above, "such a man is a proper subject, not for reproof, but for medical treatment." The addict is no more responsible for his acts than "the bowels for continuing the peristaltic motion." Fitz Hugh lamented that addicts can't "be properly treated in a special institution of their own."

Fitz Hugh then proceeded to offer elements of his own approach to helping such men. He had made special study of ways to alleviate the physical symptoms of withdrawal. He began this section of the article by describing the progress of withdrawal. Within two days of abstinence came periods of "a feverish condition of the brain, which sometimes amounts to absolute phantasia." Physical pain, in the form of headaches and cramps, followed, with the degree of pain depending on the duration of the addiction, not the cumulative amount consumed. On the third day of abandonment came "profuse and increasingly acrid bilious diarrhea," which Fitz Hugh surmised was ridding the body of internal tissue altered by opium. Medical science now knows that opium paralyzes the intestines and leads to constipation. The diarrhea simply reflected the body's return to normalcy. Nevertheless, many of Fitz Hugh's medical theories were not unreasonable as the product of simple observation.

At this point, Fitz Hugh suggested baths as one form of anesthetic. If the victim were too far gone, Fitz Hugh resorted to the pharmacopeia and gave chloroform, ether, or nitrous oxide. However, the first two "induce death nine cases out of ten." He was still experimenting with nitrous, although it was apparently too powerful to be administered as often as it was needed. Fitz Hugh's conclusion was that no painkiller could be used to alleviate suffering. Also, "There is nothing in the faintest degree resembling a substitute for opium, but from time to time various alleviatives, which can not be discussed in an untechnical article, may be administered with benefit." (These mystery ingredients will be discussed later in this chapter.)

The next symptom described by Fitz Hugh was "self-consciousness in the whole upper part of the digestive canal… chronic gastritis…neuralgic pain spread down the extremities from an apparent centre between the kidneys." After that, the next symptom was hyperaesthesia, or acute sensitivity in all senses. "The totality of the experience is only conceivable by adding this physical torture to a mental anguish which even the Oriental pencil of De Quincey has but feebly painted."

This statement displays a mature confidence compared to Fitz Hugh's humble tribute to De Quincey in the introduction to *The Hasheesh Eater* back in 1857. Further, it may be that had Fitz Hugh written *The Hasheesh Eater* in 1868

rather than 1857, the Victorian confessional tone might have
been replaced with a more objective tone, more fully expli-
cating and perhaps extolling the virtues of the experience,
particularly compared to the real horrors of a true physical
addiction like opium. Such an approach might have contrib-
uted to a different American attitude toward mind-altering
drugs than the neo-Puritanical, zero tolerance view that has
largely held sway since the 19th Century.

It is interesting that Fitz Hugh repeated the custom of
his contemporaries in attributing opium use only to liter-
ary figures who had themselves written about opium. The
actual roster of 19th century "opiumaniacs" includes Keats,
Byron, Dickens, Wilkie Collins, Elizabeth Barrett Brown-
ing, Florence Nightingale, and Louisa May Alcott. Alcott,
author of *Little Women*, used opium in attempts to ease the
effects of mercury poisoning to which she fell victim during
treatment of typhoid fever. In the middle to late 1860s, she
wrote a number of stories revolving around opium use, and
may very well have been a correspondent of Fitz Hugh's.[1]
All of these writers used opium as an anesthetic or soporific,
which underscores the availability of the drug as a medicine.

In the *Harper's* article, the relation of the case study and
Fitz Hugh's failed treatment was followed by a section titled
"What is Opium," giving a physical and scientific description
of opium and the poppy. The article closed with a warning:

> The habit is gaining fearful ground among our professional
> men, the operatives in our mills, our weary serving women,
> our fagged clerks, our disappointed wives, our former liquor-
> drunkards, our very day-laborers, who a generation ago
> took gin; all our classes, from the highest to the lowest, are
> yearly increasing their consumption of the drug. The terrible

demands, especially in this country, made on modern brains by our feverish competitive life, constitute hourly temptations to some form of the sweet, deadly sedative.

This article demonstrated extensive personal experience with a large number of sufferers. It also displayed a considerable knowledge of medical science relative to the level of the profession in the mid-19th century. The article cites the *American Journal of Pharmacy* several times, and also footnotes Mr. Frank Schlitz as having made an analysis of M'Munn's Elixir. Schlitz was a chemist with whom Fitz Hugh had become acquainted during his opium studies. After completing this essay, Fitz Hugh continued his work with opium addicts.

Fitz Hugh had researched and written the opium article in the midst of dealing with the death of his father, the publication of his anthology, and the writing of two short stories for *Harper's*. From September until after his December wedding, Fitz Hugh published nothing, preoccupied with family business and attempting to polish his novel. A letter to Fletcher Harper early in 1868 shows Fitz Hugh again doing a favor for a young writer:

> Let me present to you my friend Mr. Edward T. Mason, son of the late Prof. Cyrus Mason of the University who you doubtless well remember. His highly gifted & versatile-minded father left the gentleman I now introduce numerous valuable mss. some of which, on Politico-Economical subjects he now proposes to publish. By commending him to Mr. Joseph Harper and securing him an early reading you will greatly oblige
> Your Friend Truly, FHL[2]

Cyrus Mason is known to posterity for a biography of Civil War general George McClellan. His Politico-Economical manuscripts remain, alas, unpublished.[3] In March, Cousin Carrie Geddings wrote a letter from New York finding "Helen tired...Fitz too is miserable...Mrs. F and I do like her very much. I wonder more & more tho' how she could marry Fitz."[4] Maria was obviously a woman of quiet strength and not a timid widow. She also was part of a circle of people in Chicago with whom Fitz Hugh became acquainted during his midwestern travels. *The Round Table* magazine reported:

> "A purely literary paper"—whatever that may mean—is to be commenced during this month at Chicago. Its title is to be The Chicagoan, and our only further knowledge of it is that the Rev. Robert Collyer is to have a special department, while Miss Harriet E. Prescott, and Messrs. Fitz Hugh Ludlow, E.P. Whipple, Dr. Tyndall, of London, and other prominent writers have been engaged to contribute. It is about time, in the natural order of things, that Chicago had a journal in which people of refinement and culture can take a pleasure it is impossible for them to derive from the daily journals.[5]

It is not known whether Fitz Hugh ever published anything in that paper, but he did establish literary relations with some midwesterners. A Chicago poet named Peter Fishe Reed published a book entitled *The Voices of the Wind* in 1868. He dedicated it to Fitz Hugh Ludlow:

> because his heart is brimming with the love of all things lovable, and with charity for all that are not.[6]

An April 10 letter from Cousin Carrie showed Helen involved with the Chicago crowd as well, "busy today writing her weekly letter to the Chicagoan. It is a very easy way to earn five dollars."[7] This was Helen's debut as a writer, and the skill stood her in good stead later in life. Carrie also noted "Mrs. Ludlow quite sick with influenza…she has not been up today. I like her really very much & she seems to have taken great fancy to me for some cause or other (perhaps as a fellow widow)."

In April, Fitz Hugh began work on a book for the Harper brothers on the opium habit, to include his *Harper's* article and several other essays, including excerpts from Coleridge and De Quincey. He also began sketching and organizing his ideas on how an addict might successfully abandon opium. "Outlines of the Opium Cure" would eventually be published in the book, but Fitz Hugh's health and continually multiplying obligations prevented him from editing the final product.

In May 1868, Fitz Hugh was back in *Harper's Monthly* with a story called "Uncle George." It is one of the slightest stories he ever wrote. It is mostly notable for its commentary on his travels with his new wife in Maine and Canada. He mentions traveling on the Trunk road between Montreal and Portland in a train car "by some occult figure of speech which may be the Canadian form of facetiousness, denominated 'sleeping'!" Further, "The half day since we crossed Victoria Bridge has divorced Time and Place in our imagination. We can be sure of being nowhere at any given time." When the train is about to reach Island Pond, crossing into America where the "fiscal outhouse" (i.e., customs) awaits, a story is commenced while they wait for customs.

Evidently Fitz Hugh was feeling supernatural, as the word "occult"was sprinkled through the story, and one character was reported "in a metaphysical discussion with the house-maid upon the subject of witchcraft." Virtually the only passage of even passing cleverness related that the narrator:

> sought a Boston Tailor of Largest Ideas, and contracted with him to have ready for me by the evening of the next day but one a suit of wedding raiment on which those largest ideas should be pushed to the verge of possibility. I am not sure that I used those exact words; but he made clothes for Mr. Emerson, and would have understood me if I had.

A letter from Carrie on May 24 notes "Fitz quite sick so did not see him or Maria." Helen later wrote "in the spring of 1868 [Fitz Hugh] was attacked by hemorrhages from the lungs resulting immediately from exposure during a mission of benevolence."[8] Fitz Hugh had begun, as a consequence of "What Shall They Do to Be Saved?", a regular occupation as a consultant to opium addicts. This involved visits to numerous sickbeds, as well as collaboration with physicians and chemists working on the opium problem.

Clearly "Uncle George" was the best literary effort he could manage at the time, but it kept Fitz Hugh afloat long enough to prepare his long-awaited novel for publication. Although he had still not revised the novel to his liking, Fitz Hugh was again in need of "spondulicks," and the Harpers had launched a new magazine, *Harper's Bazar* (later Bazaar), which was in need of a serial story. The magazine had begun publication in November 1867, with Mary L. Booth as the editor. The paper was designed "primarily to cover the fashions of the day, which had up to this time been incidentally treated in the Magazine and Weekly."[9] This was hardly the literary showcase Fitz Hugh desired for his first serious novel. Nevertheless, *The Household Angel* was printed there in thirteen weekly installments between May 30 and August 22, 1868. It carried a byline and full copyright notice.

The novel was set in Kentucky, and Fitz Hugh contrasted the social mores there with the more conservative east. The land itself he described glowingly:

> The glory of and the peace of God welled everywhere—Ear gate, eye-gate—every door of sense was opened to them. It was a day to make the Sybarite forget that any other heaven was promised.

The novel distilled many of Fitz Hugh's travels and experiences. The Negro spiritual that begins the story is drawn from Fitz Hugh's experiences related in his trip "Due South" back in 1860 ("jump in de chariot an' ride ride along, Jesus he come bime-by!") A lynching is included, as he witnessed in 1863 and related in one of his Western articles. The medical studies Fitz Hugh had recently pursued showed in his portrait of the Doctor in the story. Fitz Hugh even worked in opium as a plot device in a tale otherwise about the perils of alcohol abuse. Although a genre story in outline, the story is free of Harper's clichés. The handsome doctor is actually a villain; he tries to steal another man's wife, and she is almost taken in. The ostensible hero of the piece is an incompetent, and is swayed by the villain into becoming a drunkard. More important, the novel's theme of temperance was one to which Fitz Hugh was able to speak better than any contemporary American author.

The story opens with the last days of Old Siebert Kearney, a wealthy old man and drunkard. Kearney was often in "a fearfully acrid state of mind, in which the three kingdoms of Heaven, Earth and Hell seemed to exist only as so many gigantic grudges entertained against this drunken Timon by the universe." On the verge of death,

> Kearney...grew so horribly livid, and such an abject, unutterable terror appealed from his glassy straining eyeballs—from the convulsed chest and clutching, talony fingers of the man, as of one who sees strands untwisting and snapping, a fibre at a time, while he hangs at the rope's end halfway down a slippery steeple.

Cuthbert Kearney's daughter Lily is the Household Angel. When her grandfather dies, she says "'No; he has gone home. It was Jesus came for him. That's why you didn't hear the wheels; his chariot comes without thunder. Hark! I can hear it now!' But to those ears which the world has dulled it sounded only like the wind going in the treetops and over the wall of roses." Fitz Hugh also speaks of Lily's vision, bringing together his intuitive understanding of children and his worldly acquaintance with stimulants:

> if those eyes could only be spared to us for our lifetime, who would ever seek in stimulants the sense of pleasure and well-being? The child is forever in that state of elasticity, ecstasy, and brightness which our potent liquors but feeble imitate—a state of healthy intoxication, to which our feverish adult joys answer only as Anteros to Eros.

Lily cherishes Jesus, and promises "when I get to heaven I'll fall down and kiss you where the cruel nails went in." At times, Fitz Hugh made it virtually impossible to distinguish the line between genre and satire. Cuthbert, at first the anti-hero, is described in ways that mirror Fitz Hugh himself:

his naturally sensitive nature, to which life came ever as to a flayed surface and bare nerve-points, writhed under an anguish of disappointment and despair which nothing but the love of his wife and child kept from becoming suicidal.

Half a dozen years of pedagoguery had put a pallor in his cheek, a stoop in his shoulders, and a precision in his manner which ill consorted with the bluff speech and bearing of the stalwart hunters and graziers among whom he was constantly thrown.

The story is interspersed with observations on substance abuse sharpened by Fitz Hugh's recent ministrations to the opium addict:

Stimulus confers on a nature fresh to, or unjaded by it, a quickness of perception, a masterly promptness and giant facility of execution which enables the man to perform feats looked back on as incredible by his cooler head. If the man could remain for one year, without necessity of advance or danger of retrogression, at the point where he is left by the second glass of whisky, he could conquer the world [a sentiment found in *The Primpenny Family* as well]...he hangs motionless for just an unappreciable instant on the pivot of an earthly omnipotence, and then the scale descends. He drinks again to retain the equilibrium; but that delicate poise is irrecoverable; he swings out of balance the opposite way.

The schoolmaster's speech was more than usually unlocked, and his metaphor or antithesis soared in the firelight, as they discoursed together, into an Oriental fervor beyond the common.

[He had] come out of himself...There was something so heavenly in the escape, that if once knowing the means he had refrained from using them, he would have been a stronger man than any prisoner in the Bastille who had sat motionless in his dungeon, with the master-key to all the barriers in his hand.

Little by little the habit of drinking grew upon him…He was one of the men who can no more hold themselves for years at a certain limit than they can jump off the eaves of a house and say, "I will stop at the third story."

Any expert must have seen in him one of those cases which have lately received from medical science a distinct name for their condition—a case of "Chronic alcoholism"…I meant only to illustrate "Chronic alcoholism" as a form of drinking which is the most insidious of all, because it never disgraces itself.

The last paragraph corresponds to a point made in the case study in "What Shall They Do to be Saved?" Fitz Hugh's observations had led him to conclude presciently that addiction was more a matter of personality than of the power of a particular inebriant.

Derrick, the handsome doctor, drives Cuthbert to drink in order to regain his own birthright, sold by his father. Derrick's motives are internally moral, and Fitz Hugh uses this character to introduce dramatic tension without resorting to the genre staple of a one-dimensional villain. Derrick sought to change Mrs. Kearney's views "upon the subject of such lapses as Cuthbert's to a considerable extent relaxing the severity with which her stern New England Training has all her life taught her to regard them, and making her feel that they were less crimes than offenses against good taste." Cuthbert and Mrs. Kearney (who, although beautiful, is never graced with a first name), are a bickering married couple, another concept foreign to Fitz Hugh's genre writing, if not his life. She accuses Cuthbert repeatedly of drunkenness. "When she accused him she sometimes had the facts on her side; but not content with these, she must supply him motives and draw deductions, which, based on what a woman would have felt, done, or intended under similar circumstances, became erroneous when applied to the man's case."

> At last the terrible rack on which these two poor hearts stretched each other was tacitly folded up and put away—its ropes chopped and its screws burned—two dungeons, far apart and icy cold, with black bread and bitter water, being substituted for the acuter anguish.

At the fulcrum of the story Cuthbert, in a delirium, stumbles upon Derrick kissing his wife and faints. He goes through a period of madness where he considers suicide, but is saved from that by overhearing the prayers of the Household Angel. Cuthbert finds out that Derrick had conspired against him, and finally explodes with a curse that Fitz Hugh may have carried since Rosa and Bierstadt broke his heart. (The book's writing had begun just a few months after the Rosalie-Bierstadt wedding. Probably the Derrick/Cuthbert friendship was modeled on the Bierstadt/Fitz Hugh friendship as well.)

> God wither you, you upas of three lives! God write "Homeless" against your name throughout the universe! May you never have a bed to nestle in where the serpent shall not crawl—may the fiend breathe on every tree under which you seek shadow from the pelting sun or shelter from the scourging hail. May the pure arms of the woman you shall wed drop paralyzed on your marriage-night with the poison of twining round you, or slowly grow leprous with the shame of clasping the brother whom you trust. Or, if God pity her because she is a woman, for my angel Lily's murdered sake, then may she die of merciful swift horror at learning what you are. Where are His lightnings now? How does hell's crust sleep frozen under your feet that you are not cloven where you stand, that the abyss does

not yawn for you, showing me your Judas face and asking me your hypocrite's question? Are you damnation-proof that you come here to see my living corpse, and laugh at the blood oozing afresh from its thousand stains under your self-convicting finger? Where is my wife? She is in perdition! The kisses, still damp on your cheek, are seals on its thousandfold door—not to be broken till the Judgement-day—then to be sealed again for eternity with fire. Where is my wife? He shall ask you that to whom the blood of Abel cried, and compared with the mark which he shall set on you in that day Cain's shall be a bright star of angelic knighthood—a badge of glory and an honorable scar. Seeing it, no man shall kill you—you shall flee howling down eternity over all the deserts of the universe—mad with imperishable thirst for death, the immortal murderer of a soul! Of a soul? No; not one alone! Already those assassin hands of yours smoke with the blood of two. Wretch—villain—fiend! Whatever name they drink your absent health by in the banquet-halls of Satan and pledge to your speedy coming home.

Lily's father, rumored to have killed her, is almost lynched for the crime. This development allows Fitz Hugh some moralizing left over from his Overland journey:

A Lynch trial that ended in any other way would have been regarded as a fraud upon the moral sense of the community, like a church without a sermon, or a Sunday-school book in which all the bad little boys did not go out rowing on the Sabbath and get drowned.

One of the company notes that it is "fine weather for hanging," a quote taken directly from Fitz Hugh's story of the lynching in Kansas.[10] In a darkly humorous note, the Negro servant flees, unable to conceive some other reason for the angry mob coming their way than coming to "roast a live nigger." Lily is revived in time to save her father. Derrick, now exposed, is found to be guilty of even worse crimes, including the sister of one local man "goin' to be a mother without no weddin' ring on her finger." At the last minute, Derrick is also saved by Lily. The mob, after finding no good reason for their anger, is shown by Fitz Hugh to have instinctively shunned the responsibility..."*they* said... *they* were going to hang." Derrick leaves town in disgrace. Cuthbert abjured alcohol forever "from the hour that Cuthbert's angel came back to him," rejoined his wife who loved him more than ever, and Lily to this day "continues to be the Household Angel."

This novel is an unusual effort in its focus. There are no digressive stories within the story, and only Fitz Hugh's favorite pet inclusions in genre stories, such as fondness for strawberries and disdain for preachers, are found in the novel. (The Reverend Mr. Pulpiduster is seen "just managing to keep awake over a sermon which on the next Sunday should even more imperfectly succeed in doing that for his congregation.")

The character of Cuthbert and his descent into alcoholism are developed with a subtlety and depth that Fitz Hugh had never before displayed. The novel treated the institution of marriage as the challenge and the strain that it is, not the fairy tale of the Feminine Fifties. And the lynching, an act of civilized barbarism that affected Fitz Hugh like no other incident from his western travels, was simultaneously the action vehicle for the climax of the serial story and his warning to America of the dark side of the Wild West. Fitz Hugh had written a very good novel, even within the constraints of a *Harper's* magazine, and showed himself capable of writing a great one.

"THROWING HER TENDER ARMS AROUND THE POOR, LIMP NECK, LILY UTTERED. THE PITEOUS CRY, 'OH DEAR, DEAR PAPA!'"

ILLUSTRATION FROM THE HOUSEHOLD ANGEL
SERIALIZED IN HARPER'S BAZAAR.

The Household Angel was not the "long looked for American novel" but neither were any of his contemporaries writing great novels. Post-war literature was "barren," according to critic Van Wyck Brooks. Writers at the end of the 1860s tackled smaller themes compared to earlier writers, partly because the great causes had passed. There was a new, grim, realism in the aftermath of the war. Twain's *The Gilded Age* was the first to come to grips with the movements and events of the post-war years, with its "invasion of the formidable realms of American politics and business, scarcely interpreted hitherto in fiction."[11] Fitz Hugh had in an occasional story dealt with political themes ("A Reformed Ring-Man"), and many of his characters were successful businessmen, or men obsessed by business in a comical way, but such things were not his deepest concern.

Fitz Hugh's interest was human nature, whether idealized or satirized. He was at his most serious in treating the weaknesses of men revealed by substance abuse as in "John Heathburn's Title" or *The Household Angel*, or their peculiar relations with God and their fellow worshippers, as in "The Cruise of the Two Deacons." Indeed, Fitz Hugh's impulses were rapidly turning away from fiction and to dealing directly with the problems of the post-war world. Far from the post-war politics of reconstruction, Fitz Hugh had become a pioneer in the treatment of another of the fallouts of the divisive war, the opium problem. Fitz Hugh also recognized that opium use was a consequence of the industrial revolution, characterizing it as the result of "feverish competitive life." In part, his turn away from fiction was born of frustration. A note in the July 1 issue of *Harper's Bazar* announced "None of the serial stories, originally published in the *Bazar*, have been issued in a separate form. Any desired numbers, or even complete sets of the paper, can still be procured from the publishers, on personal application or by mail." This lack of book publication for *The Household Angel*, and the continued delay of his overland journey tome, further galled Fitz Hugh.

The completion of the novel, combined with his work on a book on opium and travels to keep up his new wife's social contacts, exhausted Fitz Hugh's constitution and brought on further pulmonary spasms. Helen attributed the latest collapse to "hemorrhages from the lungs, resulting immediately from exposure during a mission of benevolence, though no less truly from that life of strain and toil and struggle which seems to be the heritage of genius."[12] Fitz Hugh and his family were forced to seek further rest. In August 1868, Uncle Samuel wrote the following description of Fitz Hugh's recuperation.

Helen & poor Fitz—I should have said Poor Helen, also well, as her case calls, almost as much—perhaps full as much—for our bleeding sympathy as his.

Well, I can't say much in particular about either of them. All that I know is that the whole concern from Livingston Place No. 1—Mr & Mrs. Fitz., her two boys, & Helen are at Glen Haven, for general restoratives, and the *special* recuperation of Fitz, who, of necessity, from his long continued bad habits, is so radically dilapidated, as to demand all sorts of means & appliances to sustain him in life. It must be folly to expect that the wreck can ever be raised & repaired—as I believe. They live & breathe & sleep, as I understand it, in their own little hired cottage, by the sea, but the Water Cure Table feeds them—so that they have no cooking to do. This, of course, must secure to them a great deal of pleasant refreshing & repose—and, in this shape, so far, they appertain to the Water Cure as patients. The cottage, I take it, must be very near the main house of the Invalids, so that they also may have the benefit of such treatment as they may need. They have now been there so long, without the two pairs of sheets, for which Helen now asks, that it may be suspected, if not inferred, that some new phase in Fitz's case—or perhaps only, in Helen's—demands them. It is rather strange that, in her letter to you, she says not a word of Fitz.

This, I should think, she would have done, under almost any circumstances, of course & that she could not forget to do so. But there's a great deal of human nature in mankind—& although I am drawing near, & swiftly, to my octogenarian limit, and have had long experience of men & things, I don't pretend to fathom or comprehend that creature.

Whether they are to prolong & extend their cottage life beyond September 1st, I know not—but, if F. is as well as he was when he went on the Cure, so as to bear transportation, I presume they will, according to their first programme, re-open their boarding house, as this is the means whereby they live.

I have done all that I could or care, to save Helen from the entire sacrifice of her health & estate to what I considered the vain hope of restoring him to health & respectability. I thought that there was a limit, which duty to herself demands, that she should set especially to the outpouring of her estate—which would if not regarded leave her in some destitution in these hard times—but without effect. She seemed determined that all of it should go, in her efforts in his behalf—& if she utterly failed, she would have no self-reproaches on the subject. I resisted, especially, a demand of Fitz for the immediate & exclusive possession of what he called his half of the proceeds of the sale of their Poughkeepsie house, to the principal whereof, neither of them—agreeably to the terms of Mr. Boorman's deed—had any exclusive right to any portion thereof. The grant, you perhaps know, was to Bro., his wife Marie, Fitz & Helen & to the survivors of them—so that when his wife died, the estate belonged to the remaining three and when Br. died, it belonged to F & H jointly—to go, ultimately, (the whole of it) to the one who should outlive the other. Whether she has been governed in this thing by my counsel, I know not; and I don't like to inquire into their affairs—their finances, etc.[13]

Fitz Hugh eased back into the world after the rest home (his eighth such stay in ten years.) One may by this time be struck not so much by Fitz Hugh's physical infirmity as by the mental toughness that allowed him every time to rise from the sickbed and tackle ambitious new projects. On October 21, 1868 he wrote the following to *Bazar* editor Mary Booth:

> My Dear Miss Booth
> If those little wedding verses (which I hardly dare to hope) find sufficient favor in your eyes (from the editorial point of view) to get a place in the Bazar—please keep them back from the compositor till after this day week, as on that date, in far distant Maine, a young friend of my wife's & mine for whom they were written originally is to be married—and I should like to have them appear to her on the handle of the ice pitcher which we send first.
> Truly your friend, FHL[14]

The Opium Habit was published in October 1868, with no editor listed. The book is a collection of essays, with two by Fitz Hugh, one a reprint of the *Harper's Monthly* article. It was partially edited by Fitz Hugh, according to two later letters by Fitz Hugh, but completed by another.[15] The introduction to the reprint of Fitz Hugh's "What Shall They Do to be Saved?" reads as follows:

> Most of the preceding pages were already prepared for the press, when the attention of the compiler was attracted by a very remarkable article in Harper's Magazine for August 1867 entitled What Shall They Do to be Saved. The graphic vividness of the story, as well as the profound insight and wide experience with which it was written, led me to solicit from the unknown author the addition of it to the pages of my own book. It proved to be from the pen of Fitz Hugh Ludlow, already recognized by the public as a writer of eminence, both in science and letters. The permission being freely accorded, I

was still further moved to ask that he would give me a statement of the method pursued by him in dealing with the class to which it refers. The letter following his article was his response to my request...profound conviction upon his mind of the most crying need of the establishment of an institution where opium eaters can be treated specially. In this view of the urgent necessities of the case, the compiler most heartily and earnestly concurs.

The letter referenced in this introduction appeared in the book as a chapter entitled "Outlines of the Opium-Cure," and was dated April 25, 1868, and written at No. 1 Livingston Place.[16] Here, Fitz Hugh may have invented the concept of the halfway house. He gives a plan for the development of an institution necessary because "in his own house a man can not isolate himself from the hourly hearing of matters for which he feels responsible yet to which he can give no adequate attention without his accustomed stimulus." To appropriately remove the institution from the cares of daily life, it would be located on an island. The facilities would include baths, as well as a salon with piano, artwork, fireplaces and library.

Fitz Hugh prescribed a diet as well as a number of prescriptions for the pain of withdrawal which he had learnt since the August 1867 *Harper's* article. These included Fitz Hugh's old friend hashish, to be precise a "cannabis indica extract... as prepared by Hance & Griffith." This is the first western use of cannabis as a medicine since W. B. O'Shaughnessy of the British East India Company recommended it for lockjaw. Further, "my friend Dr. Frank A. Schlitz (a young German chemist of remarkable ability and with a brilliant professional career before him [also mentioned in "What Shall They

Do to be Saved?"])" synthesized what "I have for years been endeavoring to interest some of our great manufacturing pharmaceutists in the attainment of a form—condensed, uniform, and portable—which should stand to cannabis in the same relation which morphia bears to opium." They called it Cannabin, but the recipe is now lost. (Government researchers today are still struggling to perfect synthetic cannabis for medical uses, for which the government cannot bear to allow patients to smoke the weed itself.)

However, cannabis was not a miracle cure. "Like opium it is only secondarily a soporific…the earliest effect will be a cerebral stimulus, sufficient to divert the mind from the body's sufferings during day-light." Chloroform and ether were still being experimented with, but added to the repertoire was the use of belladonna to induce vomiting in overdose victims who had just arrived at the island. Fitz Hugh also tried replacement of opium with codeia before attempting reduction. He even described the use of a galvanic battery to administer electric current to the skin! Fitz Hugh claimed to use it to cure paralysis in patients who had abandoned opium.

Among other ancillary treatments were emetics helpful to restore regularity, a "system of light gymnastics perfected by Dio Lewis [who was often mentioned by Fitz Hugh in his *Harper's* stories], a system combining amusement with improvement to a remarkable degree," and several procedures learned at various water cures, including "the pack," "the dripping sheet," and "hot fomentations" (which were a sort of hot plaster).

The Opium Habit was reviewed in the *New York Times* on October 11, 1868. After noting that the opium habit may be called "the wickedest habit in New York," the review says a lot about the habit and very little about the book. The excerpts by De Quincey and Coleridge are noted but Fitz Hugh is lumped in with "the narratives and experiences of several others." The review closes by saying that "men will always be in the habit of using stimulants of one sort or other. But it is one consolation to think that the great working mass of the people will never take to opium—a thing that draws up the entire manhood, by degrees, into the brain."

The Atlantic Monthly reviewed the book in its November 1868 issue. After summarizing some of the book's overall conclusions, it says:

> This book, where so many dreadful facts are grouped, is to be read with thrilling nerves, and the excitement is not to be allayed even by Mr. Ludlow's "What shall they do to be saved?" though if anything could soothe the reader, that gentleman's gift of making truth appear stronger than fiction would do it. There is very much in his letter, which ends the book, sketching the outlines of an opium-cure to be operated in an opium-eaters's asylum, which must strike every one as very sensible; but every one is not a judge of this part of the business. Inveterate opium-eaters generally cannot be cured; their attempts at reformation end in death, if persevered in beyond the capacity to resume the habit, which if resumed duly kills.

Of course, history has proved Fitz Hugh more correct than this reviewer. *Harper's Monthly* reviewed its own publication in the October edition, curiously professing not to know the editor. This anonymity, as with *The Hasheesh Eater*, reflected the puritanical atmosphere that still pervaded America:

The anonymous author, or rather compiler, of this work has performed a timely labor. Few persons have any conception of the extent to which the use of opium in some of its forms is practiced in this country; and no one except the sufferers, and those physicians who have had occasion to treat such patients, has any idea of the horrors which the victims of the Opium Habit undergo…Then come several suggestive chapters, among which is Fitz Hugh Ludlow's paper entitled, "What shall they do to be saved?" which originally appeared in this Magazine—a paper which we are well assured is absolutely true in every point and particular. The book closes with an ideal sketch of a hospital for opium patients, to which Mr. Ludlow (who by-the-way, is not the author of the book) affixes his name. (Published by Harper and Brothers.)[17]

The book was as influential as Fitz Hugh's original article. Fitz Hugh's friend Frank Carpenter later wrote that the original article "brought him hundreds of letters from all parts of the country." A number of medical and would-be medical men were piqued by the problem. For example, H. James Brown, M.D. in *An Opium Cure*, reprints one of Fitz Hugh's later letters to Harper's and claims to have studied Fitz Hugh's writing in "devising my own system of treatment."[18]

Fitz Hugh's unique perspective on the problem is further attested by Frank Carpenter, describing one night, months after the *Harper's* article in which the two took a long walk and then went to Carpenter's house to sleep:

I went directly to bed, but he was a long time making his preparations, and I at length suspected he was indulging his old craving. For the first time in my life I spoke harshly to him, and characterized his abuse of himself and of the confidence of his friends as shameful. He replied "He saved others, himself he could not save."[19]

Fitz Hugh was not heard from in print between the publication of *The Opium Habit* in October 1868 until the summer of 1869. Depending entirely on his wife, and the income from their boarding house, and suffering from gradually advancing tuberculosis, it is probable that despite the warnings of his own writing, he sought the only available relief from pain.

The Ludlow family continued its orbits around the locus of Fitz Hugh's strong personality. On December 26, 1868, Uncle Sam wrote that since the death of Reverend Henry, "F. & H. understand a little of the meaning of the 'battle of life.'" Cousin Anna Ludlow, whose writing Fitz Hugh had encouraged, had now published stories in *The Evangelist*, *The Christian Union*, and other religious periodicals.[20] Years later, she would publish a book on temperance, entitled *Shall I Marry a Moderate Drinker?* In April, Uncle Samuel wrote to "Elsie," apparently his pet name for Helen, who was now living with Fitz Hugh and family on West 14th St. in Manhattan:

> I have, this morning, your dear letter of the 5th & I notice your business request, to administer for you yr. dear father's estate. To which I make haste to respond…I will…as I am not "next of kin" to yr. dear father. You are—you & Fitz; and so, according to the law of the olden time, when I was in practice, I shall need, for presentation to our Oswego Surrogate, the renunciation of you both of yr. right to administer, in my favor. Ask your good friend, Judge Porter, about this—ask him also to do you the favor to prepare all the needful papers, that my way to the little office which you desire me to take, may be free & clear of all stumbling blocks.
>
> Of Fitz's real upward progress, I am glad to be re-assured by you. Now, let him take severe & special heed to my counsel,

which I have just sent him in the rough—and in haste, and he will be likely to escape relapses—and escaping them he will, I believe, gradatum et ultimatum—and, at no distant day—be able to compete successfully, for the prize, in fact, with the fleetest velocipede of the day. And (Vide John Gilpin) "May I be there to see." He must not fail to cherish a strong will in his purpose to be a sound man again;—marvelous stories are on record, of the power & efficiency of the Strong Will—as a helper & booster, in the up-grade efforts to reach the "summit level" of health.

I am very glad that you are out of The Chicagoan—especially under its new crazy flag. And now you can "spend & be spent" on the Great "Western", "making it"—as yr Mr. Victor once said to you—"as much better than Bonner's Ledger, as you dare."[21]

After a long and painful absence from the literary scene, Fitz Hugh appeared in the June 1869 *Harper's Monthly* with an uncharacteristically melancholy poem entitled "Too Late."

There sat an old man on a rock
And unceasing bewailed him of Fate—
That concern where we all must take stock
Though our vote has no hearing nor weight;
And the old man sang him an old, old song—

Never sang voice so clear and strong
That it could drown the old man's long,
For he sang the song "Too late! Too late!"

When we want, we have for our pains
The promise that if we but wait
Till the want has burned out of our brains
Every means shall be present to sate;
While we send for the napkin the soup gets cold,
While the bonnet is trimming the face grows old,

When we've matched our buttons the pattern is sold,
And everything comes too late—too late!

When strawberries seemed like red heavens—
Terrapin stew a wild dream—
When my brain was at sixes and sevens
If my mother had 'folks' and ice-cream,
Then I gazed with a lickerish hunger
At the restaurant man and fruit-monger—
But oh! how I wished I were younger
When the goodies all came in a stream—in a stream!

I've a splendid blood horse, and a liver
That it jars into torture to trot;
my row-boat's the gem of the river—
Gout makes every knuckle a knot!
I can buy boundless credits on Paris and Rome,
But no palate for menus—no eyes for a dome—
Those belonged to the youth who must tarry at home
When no home but an attic he'd got—he'd got.

How I longed in that lonest of garrets,
Where the tiles baked my brains all July,
For ground to grow two pecks of carrots,
Two pigs of my own in a sty,
A rose-bush—a little thatched cottage—
Two spoons—love—a basin of pottage:
Now in freestone I sit—and my dotage—
With a woman's chair empty close by—close by!

Ah! now, though I sit on a rock,
I have shared one seat with the Great;
I have sat, knowing naught of the clock,
On Love's high throne of state;
But the lips that kissed and the arms that caressed
To a mouth grown stern with delay were pressed,

And circled a breast that their clasp had blessed
Had they only not come too late! too late!

Illness had so affected Fitz Hugh that he could no longer present an optimistic public face.

The last story of Fitz Hugh's ever to appear in *Harper's Monthly* was forebodingly called "Draw Your Conclusions," in August 1869. Inasmuch as it is one of his lightest tales, it is a rather sad coda after "The Household Angel." The plot is nearly nonexistent, and the story rests solely on Fitz Hugh's hypnotic prose, and, fittingly, on a number of typical touches with which Fitz Hugh imbued many of his tales:

1. funny names
   The main character is Belah Buffum.
2. metaphorical humor
   "…having argued several cases clear up to that jumping-off place, that Montauk Point of legal logic, the Court of Appeals."
3. use of the title in the story
   "Are you a villain, Mr. Buffum?" "Draw your conclusions, Master Adolphus."
4. ethnic stereotypes
   "…were both Irishmen; and where could any body get further out of the atmosphere of logic than in such society as that?"
5. ethnocentrism
   Her nose was "our American improvement on the Grecian…our New World feminine nose of character and common-sense."

6. pet peeves
   "crisp pork fried in batter."
7. humorous turns of the phrase
   "Mr. Buffum arose, with his face scarlet, and looked for his hat with as much trepidation as if it were his head he wanted."
8. autobiography
   Old families traveling to Long Branch for the summer.
9. re-use of references from other stories
   There are two references also used in "Fleeing to Tarshish," violets as a symbol of devotion, and a church named St. Simon Stylites.

Despite his illness, Fitz Hugh was not entirely divorced from old friends and family. On November 15, 1869 Uncle Samuel reported that "F. has received a copy of the Apocrypha from a Miss Osborne, Rosalie's sister!"[22] This anecdote is simply inexplicable! Rosa and Bierstadt were back in the country in the fall of 1869, but there is no evidence that they saw Fitz Hugh. The Bierstadts visited Niagara where Bierstadt produced a picture of Fitz Hugh's old inspiration. They went to Boston and visited Aldrich and Longfellow, and sold a painting for $25,000.[23] In October, Cousin Carrie Geddings wrote to her Mother while visiting N.Y. again:

> Gus said he had seen Helen. She and Fitz came into the office a few days ago—and Gus said Fitz was certainly intoxicated either with whiskey or *Opium* & he thought opium, he acted dreadfully, and tho' Helen was with him & the Office full of Gentlemen, he commenced talking & going on like a crazy man, to Gus that he & Lud & him [sic] didn't care for him & treated him so badly, because he was in trouble, & all such

nonsense I can't remember all Gus said. Of course Helen felt terribly & tried to hush him, & poor Gus was mortified to death, poor, poor Helen she must be heartbroken. Oh, if she only had a good brother like either one of mine, I am going to write for her to come & spend a few days with us here.[24]

In December, Uncle Samuel reported that "F. is cheerful but mostly house-bound…heard Beecher on Thanksgiving Day…Helen publishing in Western World, poor H. with F. wrecked physically & morally."[25] The household had moved again, first to West 14th St near Fifth Avenue, and then to 99 Clinton Place. Helen was now Fitz Hugh's primary nurse. Beginning in November, Helen began transcribing a number of Fitz Hugh's early poems, dating from around 1856, his senior year at Union.[26] He wrote a poem of dedication for the book to Helen:

> To the little brown head just up to my shoulder,
> the believing blue eyes that never grew older,
> To her whose dear voice I shall hear at my side,
> a sweet murmuring shell left by childhood's ebb tide.

The manuscript book contained three pages of a new story, beginning with a digression about how most garrets are not garrets—as if he "should pick up a coal scuttle and clap it on my head…I might call it a hat all day if I liked for this is a free country but that wouldn't make it so I suppose!" But Fitz Hugh did not have the strength to go on with the story, and perhaps as well could not sustain a playful attitude. In one poem, he wrote,

> He was not a saint on earth,
> nor wished he in heaven a saint to be

He had lived & loved & lost; that's all,
and the joy which missed him seemed too dear.

And feeling as many around him did that he was slowly
dying, he wrote a somber meditation called "The Poet's Last
Resting Place." It began "Oh bury me not in the dark blue
sea," and concluded

But far from the world where the mountain grey

Heaven's wonder lies at the gates of Day
oh there be my dreamless slumber; there
high on the peak of its hoary crest,
my spirit may mount to the mansions blest,
No touch of the Earth to cumber.

Oh there with the clouds for my winding sheet
and the cast off world beneath my feet
shall ye hear my house of quiet
Where forth from the breast of Heaven's black shroud
the thunder shall peal my requiem loud
And the sweeping blast shall sigh it.

Unexpectedly, Helen's devoted nursing and Fitz Hugh's
reservoir of inner strength led to yet another recovery. For
Christmas, Fitz Hugh sent a copy of "American Leaves" (by
Dr. Osgood) to Maria's mother, Sarah Badger Owen, "in a
box with some other little remembrances to her & Harriet's
family from us here," and the following poem inscribed:

Where the dreary winds complain
    Round the wild inclement shore
When the sheer bleak rocks of Maine
    With the cruel frost are hoar;

When the dreadful sky compels
        Every living soul to fly,
And the tale the weather tells
        Is 'Get in doors or die!'
Then, dear Mother, trim your lamp,
        Wipe your glasses, put them on,
And bid every care decamp
        While this little book you con,
Not a great book, but a pleasant,
        As my mother will discover—
of no value as a present
        Save as showing that I love her.[27]

Fitz Hugh's investigation into the opium question continued whether he was hacking away in New York or traveling in the midwest and Chicago with his wife. He had gathered a large circle of correspondents in the course of his investigations, some attracted by the *Harper's Monthly* article and book, and others hearing of Fitz Hugh's attempts to cure the addiction. (It is instructive that his earlier book on hashish did not bring in scores of letters from cannabis "sufferers," nor did public acclaim call for him to write further on the subject.)

About this time, perhaps in his travels to Chicago, Fitz Hugh became aware of a reputed cure for opium addiction, sold by a Dr. Samuel B. Collins of Laporte, Indiana. Fitz Hugh wrote to Collins on November 24 to inquire about the cure:

Dear Sir
It is possible that you may know me by name and have read some of my published writings upon the subject of the Opium Habit—perhaps have even read the book of that name published by the Messrs. Harpers, in which you will then have

had a good chance to become acquainted with me. I will only here say that I have for many years made this most painful subject a specialty both of study and treatment—have had, perhaps, a larger circle of acquaintance with Opium Eaters than any one else in this country, and have been so happy as to cure a considerable number of the worst cases on record.

None of these cases have, however, I frankly acknowledge, been effected without severe and long protracted suffering... But I have all my life been seeking in vain for some remedy which would act as a substitute and bring the patient out painlessly. Last spring I was almost ready to give the search up in despair—when two of my large circle of Opium correspondents wrote me within a few weeks of each other that you had succeeded in making the discovery—at least that your circulars positively announced the fact, and that several persons who had had recourse to you had found your assertion remarkably corroborated by their experience.

If it does all that I understand to be claimed for it, and is itself no form of extract from the accursed poppy—then you have a right to the thankful praise—the respect—the honorable tributes of every man who loves his race—you have made a discovery, not one whit exceeded in importance by Jenner's discovery of vaccination—one which will quite as justly entitle you to applause, living, and monuments when dead.

I accordingly resolved to write you and make the following proposition, viz. that you supply me with enough of your discovery to make the complete experiment in one case—and if I find it result as my correspondents have said, I will not only give you my personal thanks, but put you in the immediate receipt of many hundred dollars custom.

As I have already said, I am in constant receipt of a larger number of appeals for help from Opium Eaters than any other man in this country—and have a desk-full of applications now which I could hand over to you and which would most gratefully be answered by your Remedy—had I once a chance of satisfying myself of its exact value. Moreover, my position is such in connection with the press and the Medical Profession, that I possess facilities for making you and your Remedy widely known—such as no other man in the country has.

My only desire is to save Opium Eaters—pecuniary advantage is a most subsidiary consideration—but if there is money to be made out of this Remedy at all, it is but right that you should make it. I hope you will be able to patent your secret, so that you may disclose it to the scientific world without pecuniary loss, for if the Remedy does what is claimed for it, it would be one of the greatest of human calamities to have its mode of preparation die with its discoverer. Oblige me by an early answer, and if you think well of my proposition, express as much of the Remedy as may suffice for the experiment.[28]

Collins refused to provide the remedy to Fitz Hugh, although he evidently requested that Fitz Hugh publicize his remedy anyway. Fitz Hugh wrote an indignant letter back to Collins in January, 1870:

I regret your inability to supply me with the means for making such a test of your remedy as would alone justify any conscientious man of any scientific standing in recommending it. You must see, of course, that if such a man has achieved any position where his good word could be of any value to you, that position would be seriously imperilled by his advising patients to take a remedy of which he himself had no practical knowledge.

Moreover, if the experiment proves satisfactory, I possess the power by using my pen in any dozen of the many organs of public information open to me, as a literary man no less than a scientific one, to make your Remedy known and clamored for, from every corner of this country, and eventually of the civilized world.

Three days later, Fitz Hugh sent another letter detailing the specifics of the case of the patient he was proposing for the test, noting "there is the additional motive to select this for an experiment in the fact that the poor woman is indeed almost utterly destitute, and a most worthy object of benevolence in every respect." Several more letters followed. Two weeks later, "When I have time to tell you my proposition (before referred to) you will see that I have a better and much cheaper plan for making your Remedy widely known, than to put into Harper's the advertisement you send—which would cost a dollar a line. If you and I agree, I will publish a letter over my own name in Harper's, calling attention to the fact of a wonderful discovery for the Opium Cure." The months of wrangling finally paid off. On May 10, Fitz Hugh wrote:

> The package of five bottles for which I last wrote, came duly to hand…I am going to take a very important case under my direct charge—the case of a quite distinguished and eminent man, whose cure will be the greatest of triumphs, and who has used Opium very largely for years. I shall probably, as my own health needs rest and recreation after my many long years of hard work, take a voyage to England with him, and stay in London a number of weeks.
>
> …If you will furnish me with all the medicine necessary to treat this case—supplying me with a sufficient stock of bottles (say 10 or 12) when I start, to make sure the case should be interrupted by no delays or accidents, at that long distance of London from La Porte—I will put into both Harper's Weekly and Monthly, over my own name, two letters publishing your Discovery and its value to the several millions who read those periodicals. In no other way, by paying hundreds for advertising, even, could you reach so many people, or so well. Decide and let me know your answer as early as possible.

On June 14, Fitz Hugh wrote one final letter to Collins:

Our mutual friend, Mr. Read, has just been paying me a visit and consulting in regard to some arrangement by which we can work together for the benefit of the Remedy and the Opium Eaters.

I have only to say that I have read the proposition he makes you, over again and again carefully—and fully approve of it. I stand ready to assist him in every way through the press if you and he make the arrangement. Whatever he says, or may hereafter say, on the subject, I agree to. I give notice now, that he represents me in every business arrangement with you in my absence.

I have now put into the Harpers' hands to be published in the very first magazine that there is room for it in, an article recommending your discovery, that every body who has seen it says is one of the finest things I ever wrote. Harper's Magazine is always printed over a month ahead—so it cannot come out in any shorter time—and I rely upon you to believe me, and wait for it, and not come down on Mr. Read for any money for those 12 bottles until you have given it the proper chance and time to be published. If you do come down on him for the money—of course I shall at once learn of it by telegraph, and have the article cancelled and not published at all. But I believe you mean to act square.

Fitz Hugh's first letters to Collins were cautious about testing the remedy, and he even made the point that he needed to be sure the cure was "itself no form of extract from the accursed poppy." However, as his own health continued to deteriorate, the caution was overcome. As noted in one of the above letters, Fitz Hugh and family had decided to travel to Switzerland, then known as a leading center for the treatment of "consumption". Not only was his health precarious, but economic times were bad as well. New York was recovering from a "Black Friday" panic on the gold exchange. Literary markets were not lucrative, and Fitz Hugh was not writing stories or essays.

But amidst his health and business concerns, embers of Fitz Hugh's poetic soul continued to glow. Although he no longer had the strength to write stories, in the May 1870 *Harper's Bazar* there appeared Fitz Hugh's poem "To Florence, On Her Fifteenth Birthday; with a pair of pretty elastic garters, made by hands which had dandled her when a baby." The poem was written in the evening of the day it celebrated.[29]

> Fifteen years have come and gone
> Since this world's extreme surpries
> Broke upon the baby's eyes—
> Since the little startled fawn
>   Oped those soft brown orbs to see
>   What this noisy earth could be!
>
> Then she shut those orbs again,
> And concluded to lie quiet—
> Bustling world! She would not try it!
> Great big women! Great big men!
>   They might run around and shout,
>   Only count the baby out!
>
> But one day the baby peeping
> From her muslin sanctuary,
> Thought, "It don't look awful—very—
> What if I should try it, creeping
>   On the carpet just a tiny
>   Way toward that spot so shiny?"

Sargent, in a rhyming novel,
Published lately, hath not spared
Words to laud "The Woman who Dared"
But in palace or in hovel
  Where is daring, grand and steep,
  Like the baby's earliest creep?

[here appear verses where the baby stands, walks, runs]

The delicious topmost sparkle
Of Life's goblet she is tasting;
Naught she knows of spilling—wasting—
Not a speck i' the nectar darkles—
  Only we, who've reached the dregs—
  Grown up people—lose our legs!

Never mind my sweetest Florry,
Though your walk grows more demure
There is too much grief to cure;
This old world's too sick and sorry,
  For your sunlight to stop glancing
  Where a heart can be set dancing!

All you know of use for members
Then by you unnamed at all
Was to kick them, plump and small,
out, as your mamma remembers,
  At the world where now you fling
  Sunshine from your fifteenth spring.

So—to gird them for their duty,
And to bear their mistress round,
Or to stand a sturdier ground
Where Truth bids them stand, or Beauty—
  I these circlets bring. Ye martyrs Of
  propriety—yes, they're garters!

Love is free, I know, but you
will not grudge it though they bind you,
For I give them to remind you,
By their soft, elastic blue,
    How my love goes every where
    With you, like them and the air.

Also in May, 1870, at long last Fitz Hugh's book on his western journey in 1863, entitled *The Heart of the Continent*, was published by Hurd and Houghton. The book collected articles on the cross-country trip with Bierstadt from the *Atlantic Monthly* (after Fitz Hugh's jealous excisions) plus several previously unpublished chapters adapted from notes and the letters in the *New York Commercial Advertiser* and *The Golden Era*.

The Heart of the Continent contained a frontispiece engraving of a mountain lake by V. Balch "from a painting by A. Bierstadt." Another engraving of Cho-Looke, the Yosemite waterfall, was rendered by an artist named Herley, probably from a Bierstadt painting as well. There were ten other illustrations, some magazine-style, low-quality sketches of prairie dogs and buffalo, and some more-refined sketches of the overland stagecoach in motion, Indians, and prairie settlers. (The book also contains a portrait of Jean Baptiste Moncrevie, the Indian translator who compiled vocabularies of Indian languages, which had been forwarded by Fitz Hugh of the Smithsonian Institution.) These sketches may also have been adapted from Bierstadt, although it must have been a remarkably diplomatic publisher who convinced Fitz Hugh to have any trace of Bierstadt in his book. The book was reviewed in the May 30, 1870 *New York Times*:

We rejoice to see a book of American travel of which we can speak in terms of almost unqualified praise. Mr. Ludlow, while careful and deliberate as to the facts which in such a work are of chief consequence, has not been regardless of the graces of style or of the advantages to be gained through them in the way of influence and circulation. This book is, therefore, not only useful but is thoroughly interesting. We have been read many descriptions of the Yosemite Valley, and when it is said that we have found Mr. Ludlow's as fresh and entertaining as if the subject and locality were altogether novel to us, the reader will understand the sort of merit for which this author deserves credit.

We regret that space will not allow our quoting freely from pages which, whether they treat of the plain or the mountain, of cities or mining camps, of the marvels of nature or the swift products of the enterprise of men, are always graphic, cultivated and absorbing. The occasional picturesqueness of his manner gives great zest to Mr. Ludlow's book, and for this, among many other excellent qualities, he will be indebted for what we are confident will prove an abundant measure of success.

Other reviewers said, "He is one of the few thoroughly good descriptive writers we have," and "the chief merit and the peculiar charm of the 'Heart of the Continent' arises from the fact that the author is a many-sided, versatile man; a close and original thinker, a man of no mean scientific attainments, and, what is better than all, a profound and earnest observer of nature in her every feature."[30]

A review in the July 1870 *Atlantic Monthly* was not so enthusiastic, and in fact was downright hostile. The break that ended Fitz Hugh's publishing career there was still remembered, and the use of material originally published in the *Atlantic* was not to be forgiven:

Since Mr. Ludlow made his explorations, some ten years ago, the Heart of the Continent has been visited by such numbers of travellers that it is well nigh as stale and battered as the heart of a coquette entering upon her fifth or sixth season of flirtations. And shall a man whose passion is ten years old make us listen to his superannuated raptures about buffaloes, and sage-bush, and alkali, and antelopes and parks, and the giant pines and domes of the Yosemite, and Brigham Young's capacity for self-government, and all the rest?

It is rather late for Mr. Ludlow, we must confess, and we think that five hundred and six pages are a good many. Yet Mr. Ludlow is an easy writer, and practised in magazinery so well that he knows how to detect and detain the picturesque and the impressive wherever he finds it, and we readily fancy his book being read through. He is not so fine a hand that there are puzzling subtleties of feeling anywhere in his book; in fact, the savor is somewhat rank at times, and he throws you in whole collops of sentiment whenever he likes.

In some ways he reminds you of travelers of an even remoter antiquity than 1861-62, and chiefly in the matter of being himself the hero of most of the adventures narrated, and the deus ex machina generally. Whilst it is too literary at times, it is yet the most artistically written account of the heart of the continent which we have seen; and the style, where it has not been made too good, is very good indeed,—frank and facile. We always skip scientific knowledge when reading for our own entertainment, and we cannot speak with certainty of the quality of that shown by Mr. Ludlow; but we respect its appearance, and we feel sure that his sketches of the different wild characters, white and red, whose acquaintance he made in his travels, are very pleasant…Of the Indians he does not tell us much that is new,—perhaps there is nothing new to tell,—and he can do little to relieve the national embarrassment concerning those unpleasant brethren, who we all feel that it would be hard to clean and cure of their savagery, and whom we yet do not all seem to see it our duty to kill,—

though this is the self-devoted creed of the plains.

Perhaps the most interesting—certainly the solidest and most thoughtful—part of the book is the Appendix, which is devoted to the consideration of Mormonism.

No mention was made that half the book first appeared in the *Atlantic*, but Fitz Hugh was still listed in the ads for the *Atlantic* as late as 1869 as a contributing author of "Papers on Science and Art." In any case, this is the only largely negative review Fitz Hugh ever received.

To the modern eye, the book remains a remarkably encyclopedic view of the old West. The geological details drag on a bit too long, but the freshness of the scenery to the traveler comes across, and Fitz Hugh's light and leisurely style still entertains. While taking in the reviews, Fitz Hugh sat for a portrait to be painted by his friend Frank Carpenter. Now at Union College, it is a dark and melancholy picture, showing the ravages of chronic disease.

Fitz Hugh made a few last literary efforts, perhaps to raise additional funds for the trip. He published a poem, entitled "To M.S.; with thanks for a paper-knife," which was actually written in 1857 while a teacher at Watertown Academy.[31] It appeared, with byline, in the November 1870 *Appleton's* magazine. In July, *Appleton's* reprinted the poem "A La Dame A La Voile Noire," first published in the *Knickerbocker* way back in 1856, Fitz Hugh's first literary appearance. Fitz Hugh made some minor wording changes, improving the symmetry of construction but not appreciably altering the theme or substance of the poem. It is not known whether the *Appleton's* editor thought he was getting an original poem.

Fitz Hugh and family made their final preparations for the journey to Europe. On June 15, the day after his last letter to Dr. Collins, Fitz Hugh wrote to *Harper's Monthly* a letter subsequently published in the August issue. It was prefaced "Mr. Fitz Hugh Ludlow, well known by the readers of this Magazine, in which many of his most brilliant papers have appeared, sends to the Easy Chair the following letter":

To-day sailing for Europe, an invalid, with all the uncertainties of return which attend such a one, may I ask to say through you a word or two, in parting, to the class of our suffering fellow men and women for whom, as you know, I have spent a large part of my life—all that part, indeed, which is usually the leisure of a laborious profession?

In the book published two years since by the Messrs. Harper, under title of "The Opium Habit," whose earlier chapters were edited by, and the two closing ones original with me, I gave to the public as condensed a statement as my limits made imperative of the course of treatment which many years medical and scientific study, together with an experience among opium-eaters scarcely to be surpassed in extent, had taught me was the safest, quickest, least painful, exit from a hell over whose interior penetralia at least Humanity had for years concurred to write, with a sigh, "Lasciate ogni speranza." There I showed the possibility of a release, and, so far as could be done in such broad touches, sketched the means...I had not then found what I confess was been one of my life's ruling passions—a very agony of seeking to find—any means of bringing the habituated opium-eater out of his horrible bondage, without, or comparatively without, pain.

I ask you, dear Easy Chair, to rejoice with me that, in all probability, that wonderful discovery has now been made.

Were I staying in this country, instead of going abroad as my last chance of life and health, I would joyfully continue to answer the correspondence which floods me on this subject from all parts of the Union, and, at any expense to myself, make known this salvation to the most sorrowful sufferers of this world...The many who can bear me witness how willingly I have responded to all inquiries for help to the opium-eater, by visit or letter, will be glad to know that during my absence such inquirer may apply to my noble-hearted and philanthropic friend, Mr. Henry Read, of Lowell, Massachusetts, who possesses all my information on the subject, and has kindly consented to let me roll off upon his shoulders the loving but heavy burden of answering such questions as might, if I staid here, be addressed to me. By letting me say these parting words from your kindly elevation, my dear Easy Chair, you will bless thousands of sorrowful souls, and send one away to Europe far less sorrowful, because most hopeful, for them. Your friend, FHL

According to *Harper's* editor Curtis, "he was already wasted to a shadow and grievously ill, and his private note [delivered along with the above] clearly shows his premonition that he should not return from the voyage to Europe which he was about to undertake."[32] On July 16, 1870, in Portland, Maine on the eve of the voyage, Fitz Hugh wrote one more letter to his long-time benefactor, Fletcher Harper:

I sent yesterday to Mr. Low's for my letters, being confined in bed by an aggravation of my illness, but although my stepson made particular inquiry he was told that there was no letter for me there from you. Either he did not see the right person or it is possible that you may have handed the letter to Mr. Low. [Mr. Low of Sampson and Low, the English publisher of *The Heart of the Continent.*]

If you will excuse me for troubling you further upon the matter will you have the kindness to give my son who will present this note the letter to Mr. Low for me which you promised on Tuesday, when we met, to give me? You cannot realize how vital it is to me that I should have my financial matters finally arranged, or you would excuse, I am sure, the anxiety I feel and manifest. Mental suffering has done much more than physical to bring me where I am, and in case my continued illness for a day or two should prevent my seeing you personally & I thus fail to get the note to Mr. Low, the thought of being quite without any credentials in my relations to him would be most painful to me. If I should be disappointed as I say in bidding you good-bye, my warmest wishes go with you that you may get the rest & restoration you so much need and receive much more permanent benefit than be hoped for from anything left in this world by

Your friend always, FHL[33]

The Ludlow party, Fitz Hugh and Maria, Maria's son William, and Helen, set sail in July. They arrived in London several weeks later, and stayed there for six weeks. Sampson Low and Son of London had published *The Heart of the Continent*, simultaneously with the Hurd and Houghton edition. This was an arrangement assisted in part by Fletcher Harper as noted in Fitz Hugh's letter above. It was this edition which was reviewed a month before Fitz Hugh's arrival, on June 25, in the London journal *The Saturday Review*.

Heart...is one of those narratives of travel and adventure in the central regions through which the Pacific Railway has at last cut a safe, easy, and uninteresting passage, whereof the public must by this time be pretty nearly tired. Mr. Ludlow is a close observer and an intelligent thinker, and he has something new to say even on so hackneyed a subject. But the chief interest of his book lies in his treatment of another topic even more familiar—Mormonism.

The London Atheneum also gave the book a "very appreciative review."[34] In England, Fitz Hugh was received as something of a celebrity. *Harper's* and the *Atlantic* were both distributed in England.

Ironically, Charles Dickens died on June 9, 1870, just prior to Fitz Hugh's arrival. Dickens in his American travels very likely met Fitz Hugh. Fitz Hugh's friend E. L. Youmans had once dined with Dickens, where Dickens told him Fitz Hugh was his favorite American writer.[35] Dickens' last book, *The Mystery of Edwin Drood* was in part about opium, and may have been influenced by Fitz Hugh's essays. Dickens' friend Wilkie Collins wrote *The Moonstone*, a novel that revolved around opium use. *The Moonstone* appeared in serial form beginning in January, 1868, some four months after Fitz Hugh's "What Shall They Do to be Saved?" *Drood* was being serialized in England (and simultaneously in America by *Appleton's*) in 1870, until Dickens' death left it unfinished.

While Fitz Hugh was in Europe, Dr. Collins attacked his reputation. In July or August 1870 he published a pamphlet entitled *Theriaki; and Their Last Dose.*[36] The pamphlet contained six of the letters Fitz Hugh had written to Collins in the first half of 1870. It also led off with an open letter to Fitz Hugh:

> Mr. Fitz Hugh Ludlow, New York
> I beg leave herewith to submit to your kindly notice this little Pamphlet of mine, containing as you will see, your own Correspondence and a few extracts from the many letters of Mr. Henry Read, bearing upon the subject of my discovery for the cure of the opium habit...The specific discovery to which you referred, or promised to refer, was so carefully concealed that your "noble hearted and philanthropic friend, Mr. Henry Read, of Lowell Massachusetts" to whom in your article you gave such prominence, availed himself of his opportunity to turn an honest penny by representing the article to have been written in behalf of a supposed antidote discovered by a man by the name of Stillman. The wrong which might thus have

been done to thousands of Opium Eaters who rely upon the conscientiousness of your opinion is incalculable.

The pamphlet then profiled Henry Read. Read, according to Collins, had been an opium addict for six years, until he used the Collins antidote and was cured. Read wrote a glowing article in the *Lowell* [Massachusetts] *Courier* in November, which Collins reprinted in *Theriaki*. Collins then printed a series of "extracts...taken from letters written and signed by Mr. Henry Read." The alleged extracts are arranged to make it clear that Read was a swindler who gained Fitz Hugh's trust enough to have Fitz Hugh forward all his correspondence, past and future, to Read. This gave Read essentially the most comprehensive direct-mail-marketing data-base for any opium cure. Read's comments on Ludlow in letters to Collins implied Fitz Hugh's complicity to maximize the business return from the venture.

It seems that Read had actually visited Fitz Hugh in New York after learning from Collins of Fitz Hugh's interest in the Cure. Another Read letter confirmed the delivery of several bottles to Fitz Hugh to treat the case in London. Later letters showed Read turning against Fitz Hugh:

> I will immediately after he (Dr. L.), is gone, make you a good and liberal proposition for a partnership or interest in your Antidote...The fact is, brother Collins, we must please and keep sweet Dr. L.

Once Fitz Hugh was out of the country, Read spent time trying to keep Collins in line:

> ...that you were not referred to by Ludlow in his last letter I

cannot and do not understand. Yet he meant or intended no slight—else why should his first article refer to you and your locality, and as the Originator and Discoverer of this great Remedy?

I will, as soon as I can find time, write all those correspondents of Ludlow's, (that don't happen to see his letter in Harper), and tell them to send for and take the Antidote—Ludlow requested me to do so.

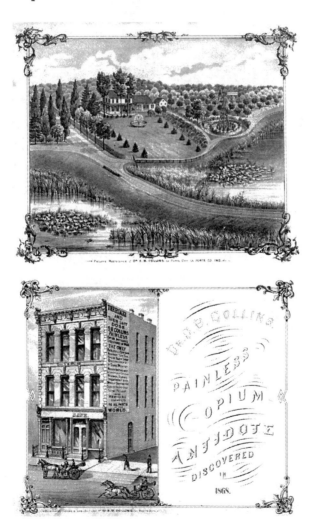

RESIDENCE AND LAB OF S.B. COLLINS IN LA PORTE CITY, INDIANA.
(DAVID RUMSEY HISTORICAL MAP COLLECTION)

He did so, but charged $100 per bottle, while paying Collins only ten dollars per bottle.

Unaware of all this, Fitz Hugh wrote to Frank Carpenter from London, "I am struggling for the sake of my angels in human form to stay a little longer. My sufferings are very bitter, but, oh! what love, what wisdom in them hovers round my bed; and oh! how full of gratitude my soul is. Who am I that such devotion, such unutterable patience and self-abnegation gather round my bed?"[37]

After six weeks in London, Fitz Hugh's health took a turn for the worse and the family headed on to Geneva. After a brief stay in Paris, where he managed to accompany his wife and sister to the Louvre, they arrived in Geneva. There, they stayed briefly at the Hotel de la Paix, but they

> ...soon removed to a more quiet place, on the shore of the lake and overlooking Mount Blanc. He was cared for by an English physician, visited by an English Chaplain and many American friends.

Then, according to Helen:

> We laid our pilgrim in a chamber called "Peace," looking toward the sun-rising. For three weeks he forgot his own sufferings to uphold our courage, looking away from them to Jesus, whose name was ever on his lips and in his heart. His dying message was, "tell all my friends that dear Jesus is all I ever thought him; my only Saviour, my Lord and my God."[38]

Fitz Hugh died at daybreak, September 12, 1870, the day following the thirty-sixth anniversary of his birth, but allowing for difference in time between Switzerland and New York, his birthday.

1 This is the theory of Michael Horowitz and Cynthia Palmer, curators of the Fitz Hugh Ludlow Memorial Library. For a summary of opium use by 19th-century writers, see Virginia Berridge and Griffith Edwards, *Opium and the People*, New Haven: Yale University Press, 1987, p. 55.

2 Fitz Hugh Ludlow to Fletcher Harper, February 11, 1868, Ransom.

3 Edward T. Mason later returned the favor by reprinting excerpts from "Little Briggs and I" and "A Brace of Boys" in an anthology that he edited, *Humorous Masterpieces of American Literature*, New York and London, G. P. Putnam and Sons, 1886.

4 Carrie Geddings to Caroline Frey, March 17, 1868, NYSHA Library.

5 *Round Table*, April 4, 1868.

6 Peter Fishe Reed, *The Voices of the Wind and Other Poems*, Chicago: E. B. Myers and Chandler, 1868.

7 Carrie Geddings to Caroline Frey, April 10, 1868, NYSHA Library.

8 Helen Ludlow, 1873-75.

9 Harper (1912), p. 248.

10 Ludlow (1870), p. 8.

11 Van Wyck Brooks, *The Times of Melville and Whitman*, New York: E. P. Dutton and Company, Inc., 1947, p. 456.

12 Helen Ludlow, 1873-1875.

13 Samuel Baldwin Ludlow to Caroline Frey, August 18, 1868, NYSHA Library.

14 Fitz Hugh Ludlow to Mary Booth, October 21, 1868, UVA.

15 Fitz Hugh Ludlow to Samuel Collins in Samuel Collins, *Theriaki and Their Last Dose*, Chicago: Chicago Evening Journal Print, 1870, p. 32, 42; and *Harper's Monthly*, August, 1870, p. 458. H. James Brown in a book *An Opium Cure* (1872) says the book was "known to have been originated by Parton, and the opening and last two closing chapters contributed by Ludlow — Parton being a layman and Ludlow an amateur physician." And to further muddy the picture, the Library of Congress card catalog lists the book as edited by Horace Day.

16 A footnote refers to "What Shall..." as "hereto prefixed," indicating that Fitz may have originally edited the book, with the introduction appended afterwards by Day. However, the last line of "Outline" thanks the editor "for the courtesy which has afforded so large a space in your book to, Your Friend, Fitz Hugh Ludlow."

17 *Harper's Monthly*, October, 1868, p. 711.

18 H. James Brown, M.D., *An Opium Cure*, New York: Fred M. Brown & Co., 1872, p. 26.

19 Carpenter (1870).

20 According to letters from the Ludlow-Frey papers, Cooperstown, NY.

21 Samuel Baldwin Ludlow to Helen Ludlow, April 8, 1869, NYSHA Library.

22 Samuel B. Ludlow to Caroline Frey, November 15, 1869, NYSHA Library.

23 Hendricks (1973), p. 188.

24 Carrie Geddings to Caroline Frey, October 22, 1869, NYSHA Library.

25 Samuel B. Ludlow to Caroline Frey, December 4, 1869, NYSHA Library.

26 Manuscript book now in Schaffer Library, Union College.

27 Ibid.

28 This letter and other correspondence between Fitz Hugh and Collins were published in Collins (1870).

29 Helen Ludlow, 1873-75.

30 Unidentified reviewer quoted in Helen Ludlow, 1873-1875.

31 See Chapter 8.

32 *Harper's Monthly*, December, 1870, p. 139.

33 Fitz Hugh Ludlow to Mr. Harper, July 16, 1870, Ransom.

34 Helen Ludlow to Leander Hall, June 1, 1876, Schaffer Library.

35 This story was included in a later reminisce by Helen Ludlow. Inspection of a handful of Dickens' biographies failed to turn up any mention of Fitz Hugh.

36 Collins (1870). Theriaki was a name given to "joy pills" introduced in Europe in the 1800s and formulated of datura, opium and cannabis. Ratsch, in Christian Ratsch, ed., *Gateway to Inner Space*, Bridport, Dorset, U.K.: Prism, 1990, dates them back to the Middle Ages as components of the "flying ointment" of witches.

37 Carpenter (1870).

38 Helen Ludlow, 1873-1875.

EPILOGUE

THE family was prevented from returning Fitz Hugh's body to the U.S. by the Franco-German War of 1870. It was not until December of 1871 that his remains were brought to Poughkeepsie and buried in the family plot next to the Reverend Henry. Fitz Hugh died intestate, and Cousin Gus Frey was named administrator of the estate. The estate amounted to less than $100.[1]

A number of periodicals noted Fitz Hugh's passing. *Harper's Bazar* published the following remembrance:

> The Bazar readers will regret to learn of the recent death of the brilliant writer, Fitz Hugh Ludlow, whose pen has so often graced its columns...At an early age, when in college, his insatiable curiosity led him to test upon himself the effect of various poisons, by means of which he fell into habits which undoubtedly undermined his superb constitution, and caused his early death, after years of bitter struggle with diseases thus superinduced. His friends can never cease to lament that his extraordinary experiences, narrated in "The Hasheesh Eater" (published by Harper and Brothers) when he was only twenty years old, "the Opium Habit," and other works and his skill in the treatment of the opium disease—to which many whom he cured can testify—were purchased at such a cost. His "Household Angel," published in the Bazar, stands out as a real work of genius amidst the usually rather vapid temperance literature.[2]

At least one commentator has claimed that Mark Twain

"at the time of Ludlow's death is quoted as having said that Ludlow was America's greatest short-story writer. Twain's remark was a great consolation to Fitz Hugh's family in that last, sad year of his life."[3]

On December 24, 1870, the *New York Evening Mail* printed a more extensive remembrance by Frank Carpenter:

> You asked me to write out for you some recollections of Fitz Hugh Ludlow, together with further particulars of his life and death. I am glad to do this, for justice to one so out of the common mold, or run, as Ludlow was, can hardly be expected from the public at large. He was an exceptional character, and ought not to be judged by the ordinary standards which prevail among men. That he had genius, no one familiar with him or with his writings will deny. That such brilliant powers of mind as he exhibited should have been linked with a morbid and diseased physical organization was his misfortune.
>
> Much as I loved Ludlow, and desire to see justice done him, I cannot deny that in one sense his life is a warning. Let literary and professional men, so liable to the temptation which beset him, take heed of this warning! The forces of an unusually strong constitution were in his case exhausted at the age of thirty-four, and although he died of consumption, the apparent result of a series of hemorrhages from the lungs two years ago, unquestionably his early death was the result of the strain to which his physical organization had been subjected for years. Would to God his voice from the grave might reach and save many who are trifling with tempters; then, indeed, will his life and death not have been in vain!
>
> There may be those who knew Ludlow who will be disposed to scoff at these revelations of an inner experience they never suspected…During the years of my intimacy with Ludlow I never knew him under any circumstances, to shrink from bearing his testimony to the central truth of Christianity.
>
> Another literary friend in a late letter says: "Ludlow was

gifted far above his fellows...I choose to think only of that which was excellent in him—the exalted mind, the tender heart, the exquisite conversational powers, the friendship which so freely went where he thought the object worthy. I think the world did not estimate him at his true value, but whoever loves the choice things of literature will always turn gladly to his pages, and in the hearts of a few who knew him and loved him his memory will be ever green."

Fitz Hugh's poem "Hymn of Forebearance" was appended.[4]

> O living were a bitter thing,
> A riddle without reasons,
> If each sat lonely gathering
> Within his own heart's narrow ring
> The hopes and fears encumbering
> The flight of earthly seasons.
>
> Thank God that in Life's little day,
> Between our dawn and setting,
> We have kind deeds to give away,
> Sad hearts for which our own may pray
> And strength when we are wronged to stay,
> Forgiving and forgetting.
>
> Most like our Lord are they who hear,
> Like him, long with the sinning;
> The music of long suffering prayer
> Brings angels down God's golden stair,
> Like those through Olivet's darkened air,
> Who saw our life beginning.

In December 1870, a eulogy appeared in the *Harper's Monthly* "Easy Chair," probably written by George William Curtis. The poem "Too Late" was also appended. After a recounting of Fitz Hugh's life and career, the Easy Chair grew colder:

> [I]t is evident that his literary reputation did not increase with time, and he had hardly taken the position to which his peculiar literary talent had plainly pointed.
>
> It is a very sorrowful story, not because he died young, for Raphael and Mozart were but little older when they died, but because, with all his brilliant and graceful talent, his career is chiefly a warning to his fellow-laborers in literature. The slight, bright-eyed, alert youth, who came, beaming with hope and confidence, to talk of the literary life, who wrote for this Magazine so many brilliant little sketches, and such touching verses, and who sank under a slow and withering disease, must not be mentioned here as if he were merely a man of sparkling gifts untimely blighted. There are moral distinctions which can not be buried in the grave; and to say that because a man is dead we must forget his faults, and speak him only fair, is to degrade human life and character.
>
> None felt it more than he. In some verses that he wrote, and which were published in this Magazine for June, 1869 ["Too Late"], there is evident, under a light phrase, the most passionate regret and yearning of a soul which has learned that no literary success, nor any external triumph, however brilliant, nor any talent, nor genius, compensates for the lack of moral control of our lives. Of how much tragical consciousness is this poem the expression! This young, sensitive, imaginative soul had a clear, sorrowful glimpse of lost opportunities, of a wasted life. He perceived—who shall say too late?—the immortal consolation of a lofty ideal resolutely cherished, the gay contempt of which only aggravates certain tendencies of the artistic temperament. Those who read this little poem, and who feel the despairing heart beating under the music, will surely think gently and with infinite, tender pity of Fitz Hugh Ludlow.

It is telling that both public eulogies called Fitz Hugh's life "a warning," both seeing the opportunity for making of his life a morality play. Such an interpretation is easy, but superficial. Fitz Hugh overcame many and diverse barriers in his explorations of the unusual and the exotic. He battled chronic illness, a failed marriage, and a civil war occurring in the midst of his prime years as a writer. Through all this, to have written at least one immortal work, and several other major efforts, is a triumph. The life of Fitz Hugh Ludlow could be considered not a warning, but an inspiration. Let the following quote, from one of Fitz Hugh's letters, serve as a more suitable epitaph:

> The man who is maniest-sided will be the man who possesses the most of Heaven.[5]

The extended Ludlow family also paid their respects. Cousin Ellen wrote to Helen, still in Europe, on Christmas, 1870:

> You said you did not doubt that Fitz Hugh was in heaven, but you wanted to see him there...feeling all the gloom and rigor of a Northeast storm and Fitz Hugh's lines came to me with great force this afternoon—
> Oh the mane old city of Livago
> Wherever on earth you may go
> There never was sane, a city so mane
> as the mane old city of Livago.[6]

Ellen mentioned coming across a scrapbook with a picture of a "magnified bed-bug, the work of F's pencil" which was given her just before Fitz Hugh left for Europe:

Can it be that the hand that could draw so many funny things is still?...no doubt Fitz Hugh's merry-making and his hearty laughs, from which every tone of earthly sorrow is gone make many a saint merry in the paradise of God...I remember he never treated me suspiciously...he was often far from rights in his opinions and in his life yet his presence was comforting and warming.

The saga of Dr. Collins, Henry Read and the opium cure played out over the next several years. The November 1870 *Harper's Monthly* column "The Easy Chair," written in October before news of Fitz Hugh's death had reached the U.S., carried a curious notice:

In the August number of this Magazine a letter was published from Mr. Fitz Hugh Ludlow to the Easy Chair, stating that a remedy had been discovered, which seemed to him almost infallible, for the relief of opium-eaters, a subject in which Mr. Ludlow has been, as is well known, long interested. Mr. Ludlow was just sailing for Europe, and referred inquiries to Mr. Henry Read, of Lowell, Massachusetts. Letters which the Easy Chair presently received, from persons evidently painfully anxious upon the subject, stated that a large sum was required to be paid in advance, and that the whole business had a mysterious and suspicious aspect. The Easy Chair, which had printed the letter of Mr. Ludlow as that of an old correspondent of the Magazine, and an authority upon the subject, wrote to Mr. Read, and received from him a long and detailed account of the facts. Mr. Read confirms the statement of our correspondents, that an enormous price is demanded for the antidote; but he claims that he is not responsible, being an agent only, and that neither he nor Mr. Ludlow, who both attest the efficacy of the remedy, has any control of the price.

A second edition of *Theriaki* appeared shortly after Fitz Hugh's death. It contained the same Fitz Hugh letters as the earlier edition, and began with a tribute to Fitz Hugh:

> Missed and mourned he will assuredly be by thousands who have followed with delight his brilliant literary career, there are those who will miss and lament him more: those to whom, in their almost hope-less suffering, he extended an alleviating hand...he was called to new labors in his Father's house: he has found the Fountain of Eternal Youth, for Fitz Hugh Ludlow can never grow old.

Fitz Hugh's letters were also published in a Theriaki journal, published by Collins in 1872. Doctor Collins proceeded to build a fine business for himself, including a new laboratory, over the next ten years. However, gradually fears arose that the antidote actually contained opium itself. It wasn't until 1881, that the truth was published. Dr. Leslie Keeley of Dwight, Illinois, got a bottle of Collins' cure and analyzed it:

> The morphine which this "medicine" contains in such large quantities was so disguised, by quinine as I afterwards learned, that I did not recognize its effects for a considerable length of time, and I honestly thought I had found deliverance from my chains...It is hardly necessary to add that I was not as near being cured when I abandoned the preparation as I was when I began its use...This is the remedy which the brilliant but unfortunate Fitz Hugh Ludlow referred to near the end of his life, as an "antidote" to opium eating. He, in all probability, did not know of what it consisted, but wrote in all honesty; but multitudes of opium consumers have been deceived by the unwarranted use of his name. It is unnecessary to say that a remedy composed of morphine, quinine and glycerine cannot cure the opium habit.[7]

Despite this revelation, Collins was still publishing the *Theriaki* journal in 1886, in which appeared a long rebuttal of the Massachusetts State Board of Health's conclusion that opium cures it had looked at all contained opium. Collins does not contest that they contained opium, but the Board's statement that "the active ingredient was opium." Nevertheless, his gravy train had reached its last stop, and *Theriaki* was seen in the land no more.

Fitz Hugh's letters were still appearing in that 1886 pamphlet, bearing mute testimony to his ultimate ignorance and naïveté. His urge to find a cure, and perhaps a measure of scientific achievement that his literary career never quite attained, led him to abandon his caution. The cure was a cruel hoax, Dr. Collins a snake oil salesman, and Henry Read a common swindler. Fitz Hugh's ill health and essentially trusting nature led his name to be used probably to the detriment of many poor souls.

The life of Fitz Hugh's sister Helen took an interesting turn. She stayed in Florence, Italy the winter after Fitz Hugh's death.[8] After returning to the states, Helen received a letter from an old abolitionist friend of Reverend Henry, General Samuel Chapman Armstrong. Armstrong had decided to found the Hampton Institute for the higher education of freed slaves, and invited her to join him as an instructor in English and other liberal arts:

> Five millions of ex-slaves appeal to you. Will you come? Please telegraph if you can. There's work here and brave souls are needed…We are growing rapidly, there is an inundation of students, and we need more force. We want you as a teacher.

'Shall we whose souls are lighted?' etc. Please sing three verses before you decide and then dip your pen in the rays of the morning light and say to this call, like the gallant old Colonel Newcomb, "Adsum."[9]

Her response was "Is there any answer but one to a call like that?" Chapman's letter back to her read in part:

Yr. decision is cheering. We need you. The increase of students is unprecedented, over 115 admissions. In a few years Yale will be eclipsed by a nigger school and in the hereafter the ruins of N.Y. will be sketched from Brooklyn Heights by a darky.[10]

She began work in 1872. Primarily, Helen taught English at Hampton. But she also acted as writer of promotional materials. She wrote five books about the work and the students of the Hampton Institute. In one book, *Hampton and Its Students* (1875) Helen introduced her section of stories of the students' life stories, and included an apology to her presumably well bred readers for leaving dialect intact. This paternal attitude is reflected in other of her writing, which certainly recall Fitz Hugh's own writings on his "sable brother." In a description of teaching, she says: "the colored student, ordinarily, has had absolutely no surroundings of culture to nourish or stimulate his mind...He has maturity of thought, in some directions, far ahead of the young white collegian. He may have supported himself and others for years before he came here; he is full of practical resource."

Helen published an article on Hampton, with photographs, in *Harper's Monthly* in October 1873 to raise interest in the Hampton Student Singers. This student group was a focal point for fundraising, and Helen's job was to publicize their appearance in N.Y.C., "where we then had many more acquaintances than the school or the General had." Helen was also a chaperone for this group's travels around the U.S., and even wrote lyrics to various melodies for their repertoire. Helen wrote inspirational if somewhat clumsy lyrics to popular airs for the students to sing. One was written for Indian students to sing on "Indian Citizenship Day," and she wrote lyrics to an air by Haydn at the dedication of a library named in honor of Newport News shipbuilder Collis Huntington, a benefactor of the Institute. The Hampton Institute's most famous student, Booker T. Washington gave a memorial address at the dedication of the library. Booker T. Washington graduated Hampton in 1875. He maintained his connection with Chapman and his friendship with Helen Ludlow as he struggled to found the Tuskegee Institute. Washington's letter to James Marshall from Tuskegee in July 1881 includes a message to "Please thank Miss Ludlow for her kindness and tell her that if she has found no one I will try to make out till Miss Davidson comes as the time is so short."[11] Another letter from Marshall to Washington mentions "Miss Ludlow" helping to forward contributions to Washington.[12] A letter from Washington December 30, 1892 to Helen described his trip through the Deep South plantations "to acquaint myself more accurately of the real condition of the masses of the people and their needs." At his suggestion, she published an account of the trip for the *Southern Workman* journal. Helen attended the second commencement exercises of Tuskegee, and eventually wrote in 1884 a book entitled: *Tuskegee Normal and Industrial School for Training Colored Teachers, Its Story and Its Songs.*[13]

She also assisted General Chapman in editing the *Southern Workman*, a journal on the progress of Blacks and native Americans after the Civil War. Among the articles Helen wrote for the *Southern Workman* were "Indians in Normal Classes," "Among the Dakotas," "Negro Miners," "Superior and Inferior Races," "Talks with Socrates about Life," and "The Capture of Geronimo." She also wrote about a dozen poems for the Workman. One of the most interesting pieces she wrote was a review of a new book entitled *Humorous Masterpieces from American Literature*, published in 1886, which happened to contain excerpts from two of Fitz Hugh's stories, "Little Briggs and I" (under the title "Ben Thirlwall's Schooldays") and "A Brace of Boys."

Helen spent the summer of 1884 in the West, especially on Sioux reservations in Dakota—"from which most of our Indian students come." In an article on Indian students she disapprovingly described "young women who…ought to know better…have married in Indian style and gone back to Indian life…[Nevertheless] the Indian problem is likely to disappear in the next century for want of a distinguishable Indian race."[14]

An interesting facet of Helen's life on her own was her lifelong friendship with Martha M. Waldron. Waldron was the school's doctor, who started at Hampton three days before Helen—"Miss Waldron, as we called her in the happy days when she could spend all the Saturdays in a rowboat without the thought of mumps or mill saws." When Helen briefly retired to Brooklyn in 1898-99, she was with Dr. Waldron, writing sketches for Hampton publications. Helen's pamphlet poem "The Rhyme of the Birthday Trees" was dedicated to "MMW, Comrade True." They also lived together in Washington D.C.[15] Another article called Waldron "her chosen companion."[16] Upon Helen's death, she was reported to have lived "at the Magnolia Tree Inn with her life-long friend, Dr. Martha Waldron, who was at her bedside when she died."[17] It seems Dr. Waldron was, as Fitz Hugh had uncannily prophesied in his story "The Battle and Triumph of Dr. Susan" in 1863, "that Twin-Soul which the world that is hath not for her."[18] It had simply not occurred to Fitz Hugh that that twin soul would be a woman. Helen finally retired in 1910, although she remained on the editorial board of *Southern Workman* until 1918. She died in Hampton in 1924 at age of 84.

Fitz Hugh's first love, Rosalie, continued on with Albert Bierstadt, but Bierstadt's fame had peaked. In 1873-74, the couple lived in a studio which had been built by Rosalie's father. In 1877, Bierstadt sold a painting to the Corcoran Gallery only after renaming it "Mount Corcoran," a shameless promotion which he would have been above ten years earlier. Also in 1877, he worked some commissions for an English lord.

Then Rosalie was diagnosed with consumption, possibly contracted from Fitz Hugh. In 1877, Bierstadt began taking Rosalie to Nassau, in the Bahamas, for the winter. In the spring of 1877, Bret Harte was among her visitors. Harte was among several of the friends she had made while married to Fitz Hugh with whom the Bierstadts continued to socialize. When their house, Malkeston, burned to the ground in November 1882 (property including paintings valued at $175,000), Edmund Clarence Stedman wrote to Rosalie "I scarcely need write you to express my sorrow...not that I

suppose you are so wedded to the place itself." The Bier-
stadts traveled to Europe often in the 1880s, because "Albert
had to go where there are rich people to sell his paintings
to."[19] They went to London in 1878, meeting among others
"The Lords [who] were a New York family who had lived
for years in London and whom Mrs. Bierstadt, when she
was Mrs. Fitz Hugh Ludlow, had met in Florida in 1860,
while spending the winter there."[20]

While in Paris, Rosalie found "a new plaything, a small
child, of the people, whom she saw playing in the road. She
bought him a suit of kilts, new boots, a mouchoir, tooth-
brush, big sailor hat."[21] Rosalie never had children with
Bierstadt, and so it seems likely that she and not Fitz Hugh
was responsible for their infertility. Her inability to have chil-
dren made all the glamor and travel seem empty at times, as
shown in a letter she wrote in fall of 1883 to her sister who
was about to have a baby:

> I hope for Father's sake it will be a boy—but I shall love it
> quite as well if it is a girl. Indeed if you should have six of them
> I should not think them too many. Perhaps in such an event
> you would let me have one of them to keep.

Bierstadt went West again in 1881 while Rosalie was in
Nassau. He visited Yellowstone, Mammoth Hot Springs,
Virginia City, and Salt Lake City, painting the country
and recalling the memories of very different younger days.
Rosalie went to Nassau every winter between 1883 and
1893. She died in Nassau on March 1, 1893, at the age of
fifty-two. The funeral was in Waterville. An obituary read,
in part:

Mrs. Bierstadt from childhood was of a sunny and joyous nature, endowed with beauty of person and of mind, and in manner was winning and attractive. She had a rare literary taste and culture, and was a favorite in social life, for which she was especially fitted by her exquisite tact and easy adaptability.[22]

The year after her death, Bierstadt married Mary Hicks Stewart, widow of the millionaire banker David Stewart. After the fire and all the European travel, he still did not have very much money. Bierstadt died in New York in 1902. His reputation dimmed with the advent of modern art, but saw something of a revival beginning in the 1970s. A retrospective at the Smithsonian Institution in 1993 highlighted his contribution to the opening of the West, and his flair for the business management of his artistic product.

Nothing is known of the later years of Maria Milliken Ludlow. She died in Chicago in 1887.

Uncle Samuel and Fitz Hugh's many cousins lived on. The Frey family eventually donated their papers to the New York State Historical Association library in the 1950s.

Fitz Hugh's written work lived on in relative obscurity for a century after his death. In part, Fitz Hugh's reputation was handicapped by publishing policy in the late nineteenth century. The *Little Brother and Other Genre Tales* anthology of four of his short stories was re-published, but only a few other stories were reprinted. Most of his best fiction, *The Household Angel*, "John Heathburn's Title" and "The Cruise of the Two Deacons," and pieces written in a more modern style, like "The Phial of Dread" and the satirical "The Primpenny Family," were never reprinted. Anthologies over the fifty years following his death reprinted only a few charming genre stories, such as "Little Brother," that aged badly in the twentieth century. And of course, *The Hasheesh Eater* came to seem increasingly outré as the nation progressed toward greater puritanism through the next fifty years, culminating in Prohibition.

Nevertheless, his hashish-eating venture was reprinted by S.G. Rains of New York in 1903, with an eerie cover painting and a frontispiece by Aubrey Beardsley. In this edition, it was read and praised by two of the great eccentrics of the early twentieth century, Aleister Crowley and H. P. Lovecraft, but was not otherwise acclaimed.

Fitz Hugh and his best-seller surfaced again in 1937, during the crusade to make marijuana illegal, as mentioned in Chapter 1. But it was the social upheavals of the 1960s that rescued Ludlow from total obscurity. In 1960, the Beatniks discovered Fitz Hugh Ludlow. A one-shot Beat literary review called *The Hasty Papers* was published in New York. *The Hasheesh Eater* was reprinted in its entirety from the 1903 edition, and appeared alongside shorter pieces by Jack Kerouac, Allen Ginsberg, and Jean-Paul Sartre. This would be the touchstone of the Ludlow revival occasioned by the rise of the drug subculture of the 1960s. Excerpts and analyses of *The Hasheesh Eater* appeared in numerous books throughout the decade. *The Berkeley Barb*, dean of the underground newspapers of the 1960s, published extensive excerpts. This appearance spurred the reprinting of *The Hasheesh Eater* by the Gregg Press in 1970. The interest in Fitz Hugh peaked with the founding of the Fitz Hugh Ludlow

Memorial Library in 1970. This library, organized in San Francisco, was devoted to all literature related to drug use and its manifestations, and was named in honor of the first American to publish a full-length work on the subject. In 1975, a Ludlow Library edition of *The Hasheesh Eater* was published by Level Press.

Four years later, a new edition of *The Hasheesh Eater*, a re-presentation of the 1903 edition, was published by Beat Generation pioneer Lawrence Ferlinghetti's City Lights Books. *The Heart of the Continent* also returned to print as one of a series of books of Americana in 1971. A third book, titled *The Opium Habit*, which featured two core essays by Fitz Hugh, was reissued by Arno Press in 1981 as one of its "Addiction in America" series.

The Hashish Eater was re-published most recently in 1989, and was serialized in the magazine "Psychedelic Illuminations" in 1993. A World Wide Web site devoted to Ludlow appeared in 1996, preserving and extending Fitz Hugh Ludlow's legacy into the electronic realm and the twenty-first century.

---

1 According to documents in the Surrogate's Court of the County of New York, admitted probate January 6, 1871.
2 *Harper's Bazar*, (n.d.) p. 723.
3 Peter Vogel, "The Penman and The Painter," (n.p.); from the Fitz Hugh Ludlow Memorial Library. This remark has not been confirmed by any primary source.
4 In the manuscript book at Schaffer Library, Union College, this poem is "dedicated to my father." As a friend of the family, Carpenter may have gotten this poem from Helen, as it was never published.
5 Helen Ludlow, 1873-75, p. 12.
6 Ellen Ludlow to Helen Ludlow, December 25, 1870, Schaffer Library.
7 Leslie Keeley, *The Morphine Eater*, Dwight, IL: C. L. Palmer & Co.,

1881, p. 90. This book also quoted from Fitz Hugh's writings on opium.

8 Helen Ludlow, December 6, 1870.

9 Samuel Chapman Armstrong to Helen Ludlow, September 27, 1872, in *Memories of Old Hampton*, Hampton VA: The Institute Press, 1909, p. 105.

10 Samuel Chapman Armstrong to Helen Ludlow, October 4, 1872, ibid.

11 Booker T. Washington to James Marshall, July 18, 1881, Hampton University Archives.

12 James Marshall to Booker T. Washington, November 12, 1881, Hampton University Archives.

13 James Marshall to Booker T. Washington, November 12, 1881, Hampton University Archives.

14 Helen Ludlow, "Among the Dakotas," *Southern Workman*, (n.d.).

15 H. Frisell to Helen Ludlow, October 28, 1918, Hampton University Archives.

16 *Southern Workman*, April, 1925.

17 Ibid.

18 *Harper's Monthly*, July-August, 1863.

19 Hendricks (1973), p. 260.

20 Ibid.

21 Ibid.

22 Ibid., p. 306.

LETTERS OF FITZ HUGH LUDLOW

Pictographic Letter, 1853

(NEW YORK PUBLIC LIBRARY)

LETTER TO ALICE C. CROSBY, 1855?

My Dear Pet Alice.

Did you ever see anybody at your house with a pair of spectacles on his eyes, whose name sounded like "Cousin Fitz Hugh?" How would you like to have a letter from him? I ask you this because I am Cousin Fitz Hugh, and though I am more than one hundred miles away from your sweet home, I think of you very often and am sitting down now to converse with you on paper. Very often do Mr. Camps and I think about you. I live now in the same house with him and we have the same room. This house is called a College, and there are a great many men living in it and learning lessons every day. They learn a great number of things, such as how to read books with very funny letters and strange hard words, in a language called Greek. It is harder than French but it is the language in which the blessed Bible was written at first by those good men who put on paper the things that the Lord told them. Would you like to see the Greek ABC? Ask Gerty if she does not think it queer. Here it is.

$$\Delta\ \text{B}\ \Gamma\ \Delta\ \text{E}\ \text{Z}\ \text{H}\ \Theta\ \text{I}\ \text{K}\ \Lambda\ \text{M}\ \text{N}\ \Xi$$
$$\text{O}\ \Pi\ \Sigma\ \text{T}\ \Upsilon\ \Phi\ \text{X}\ \Psi\ \Omega$$

A good many of the students, as they call those who study here like Mr. Camps and me, learn more bad than good. They drink rum, and fight, and sometimes tease the teacher very much. Once they took a poor old horse into the house and carried him up stairs and made him look out of the window to make his owner angry. But some are very good men. I like this place very much, although I have to study so hard that I have had no time to write to you before.

I want to see you and Gerty and Lulu very much, but I am afraid it will be several months before I can. You must kiss them both a great many times and give yourself at least a dozen every day for me.

With much love to my darling Alice, her cousin Fitz Hugh bids her a most affectionate

Good Bye.

Letter To Alice C. Crosby, July 7, 1855

My Dear Pet Alice.

Though I live in a place that has that great big hard name that you see above at the top of my letter, I have not grown strange and crooked like that name, but I am the same that I always was, and I love you my little darling, just as much as ever. I think of you very often, and want very much to be out at our dear Woodcliff again, with you on one knee, and Gerty on the other, and Lulu climbing up upon my head while I tell you stories just as fast as the mill inside of my head can make them. If our lives are spared so that we may meet again in about 3 weeks, I will have plenty of very nice things to tell you, and we may hope for many a pleasant hour together.

But while I am talking of so many other things I must not forget to tell my dear little Alice how much I thank her for picking strawberries to send me. They were very beautiful, and so large and fat that I wonder what you give them to eat. The man at whose house I get my meals is very stingy, and has only given us strawberries for tea once this summer, and then they were so small that I guess they must have been the grand-sons of yours if they belonged to the same family at all. One of your strawberries could have taken one of those we had in his arms like a baby just as this picture shows.

(SCHAFFER LIBRARY, UNION COLLEGE)

I thank you very much for thinking of me my dear Alice so much as to pick this pretty present for me, for I have no little girls here to love me, and to know that you care for me when I am far away is a very sweet thought.

You must pray for your precious sisters every day, my dear, so that they with you may make your father and mother as happy as heart can wish, and at the same time please our dear Father who is in Heaven.

Give our darling Gerty and Lulu my heart full of love. Tell them that I often think of them and want to see them very much. Kiss them and the baby for me many times.

And now darling, I must say Good Bye. It is quite late and my bed is crying "come Alice's cousin, come old fellow, or you will be too late for prayers tomorrow morning." So I answer "I'll be there in one minute, Bed, after I have sent a great, great deal of love, and a kiss in this ring [*here there is a circle drawn, within it the words "kiss this for me"*] to Alice from her cousin Fitz Hugh."

Letter To S. Ludlow Frey, July 11, 1855

My Dear Lud,

I must indeed in view of your three letters hitherto unanswered own my conduct uncousinly & unworthy a good correspondent. Since I last saw you I have been through many changes of place & circumstance & after losing my health, trying to find it on a farm & failing, traveling, teaching, entering Princeton, being burned out & losing all my small possessions, I at last find myself in Union, within a year of my graduation. Two weeks from today will find me, if living, a senior, and the roll of a few short succeeding months will bring me to the gate of real life, & thrust me out from these preparatory cloisters forever, into the world, the dusty, mighty, toilsome world. When you pray, ask for me that I may be nerved for struggle with its opposing forces, for might to stand up to its responsibilities.

I have heard & indeed with no small pain, that you are all going to leave your quiet valley with its varying lights & shades, its old memories, its peaceful streams, its wild woods & days that have poured out for you hitherto a mingled cup of joy & sorrow, & turning your back on the rising sun are about to seek a far off home, many a league away in Western woods. I know, dear cousin, what that trial must be, for though I never knew its exact parallel in my own experience, I could tell you many a tale of hopes & memories, dear associations & calm lookings for of future peace, far away from my heart, while I sat dumb stricken in the midst of ruins. But time & my own heart will not let me now tell you these things. When we meet again, be it in the East or West, or far above all earthly points of compass, I may say what I mean, but know that I can sympathize with you in your sorrows, and understand the grief of that hour when all the holy records of the Past, stamped legibly on each familiar field & tree & brookside, on even well-trodden path & green grave, and countenance of living friend, fade into the dim horizon leaving their sad remembrances on the desponding heart. But be you not desponding, dear Lud, Stoutheart be strong! Our earthly migrations are but the exchange of one poor shadow for another; the substance is above. How often do I feel the truth of a sentiment which in a time of deep despondency I embodied for my consolation in a small piece of which this is one stanza—

When these poor temporary tents are folden
    We are not shelterless.
Ours is a city out of sight and golden
    Wherein dwells righteousness;
And though our fallen stars rekindle never
We have a sun whose glowing is forever.

"We look not at the things which are seen but the things which are not seen, for the things which are seen are temporal, but the things which are not seen are eternal." I know you have the Christian's hope dear cousin, therefore be strong. May your home in the west be very happy. I have already in Illinois a family of as dear though humble friends as ever made bright the pathway of my life, if you go there still another tie will bind my heart to the land of the setting sun, and we may hope in God's good Providence to meet again around your fireside. Where you go, remember, Christ goes with you. Blessed be his name neither leagues nor years, nor clouds, nor mountains can make any distance between him & our hearts. "Nothing can separate us from the love of Christ." So cried Paul with his prophetic eye on martyrdom, & Christ was with him in the forum at Rome; so cried Paul & his words have not lost their truth! Though they come sounding over the abyss of eighteen centuries. They are true & they will be true forever.

I should like very much to see you all again before you go. You speak dear Lud of coming to Schenectady to see Mitchell. Why not visit me at the same time? I have no chum, but possess ample room in bed and at board for you, so long as you will gratify me by staying. I have prior claims upon you to Mitchell, though he were the Irish Patriot. May I not hope to see you? Commencement comes two weeks from today. Until then, yes, till the next morning, I shall be here. Will you not come to visit me? My studies are now review & there is so little to do that I can devote almost my whole time to you without the slightest scruple. Write soon & let me know.

Papa & I talk of spending part of August in the Adirondacks, enjoying the wild sports of that solitary region. He needs it very much, having performed most arduous labor in a very precious Revival of God's work in our Church this past winter & spring which I think numbers about 50 converted, & the interest is still unabated. If we do camp out there this summer on our way back, we will if possible come & make you a visit.

Give my heart full of love to darling Aunt Caroline, Carrie who never sends any to me in her letters, to Helen, naughty girl that she is, Gus, Johnnie & your Father if they are at home. Don't pay me in my own coin but write shortly.

Your sincerely affectionate cousin,
F.H. Ludlow

LETTER TO S. LUDLOW FREY, JANUARY 28, 1856

UNION COLLEGE

My Dear Lud,

I was so busy all vacation, reading & writing about 10 hours a day & have been so busy ever since I came back this term that I have not been able to relieve myself of my indebtedness to you for your last letter, nor to Gus thanking him for bringing me my book from Poughkeepsie. I now take the opportunity which a few hours leisure gives me to do both. I have been expecting for months last term & this to see you here on the visit you told me you would make, & my looking for you has kept me from writing. When shall I see you? I have plenty of room for you & shall always be glad to see you, give you good bed & board, so long as you are satisfied with student accommodations, and show the Schenectady lions to you, although they do not roar very loud.

And now I will tell you when under certain conditions you may expect to see me. Uncle John when I was at your house offered me an invitation to lecture at Canojoharie, or told me he would get me one. Was this jocular or will he really keep his word? I may be out on the Western railroad in your direction in a short time to lecture at one or two other places, and if your father would like to have me stop at Canojoharie for the same purpose, I will do so if we arrange upon the day. The lecture I will give, if I do speak there, is "The Peculiarities of Genius." I would like to have you write me very soon even though it be but a few lines, saying whether the good people of your place would like a lecture from me & if so, what time would be best suited to your wishes. I shall then be able to make the arrangements dovetail together.

I should like very much to see you all once more. Uncle John with his quiet pipe enjoying himself by the snug kitchen fire, my dear silver haired Auntie laughing out of her gentle grey eyes at some funny speech of John's. You with your fishing rigging on & Gus sporting the same Mohawk morning costume, Carrie the bouncing roguish girl that used to scratch my eyes & make me swear mildly, when I was about 8 years old & she a baby, John the plump youngster who was running about barefooted last summer but by this time I suppose has acquired an attachment to lamb's wool & kipskin.

I would like once more to take a comfortable smoke with your father & you, to eat four or five tumblers of Aunt Caroline's bread and milk, and to have a good comfortable talk with you about old times.

All these things I hope to have with you soon if all your lecture evenings are not engaged. I know I do not serve a very quick reply from you, but I wish you would do evil for good & let me know how the matter stands pretty quick, in order that may shape some arrangements I am making accordingly.

I suppose you are now like all the United States buried in snow up to your neck. It is said that some people belonging to a church not far from Schenectady have to climb in at the belfry windows on account of a drift which has covered their house of worship but I hardly think this credible as we have yet had no snows near college which reached above the second story windows. A mining company has however been incorporated for the purpose of sinking perpendicular shafts down to a cabbage garden snowed 50 feet under in this vicinity in order to supply sauer-kraut materials to the Dorp Dutchmen, several of whose families have perished from a deprivation of their accustomed food and an indulgence in a new article of diet which they have endeavored to substitute for sauer-kraut called potatoes. The sufferings of the Dutch families around here is beyond conception. One of them in my district whom I called upon as visitor of the poor of Schenectady told me one of the most affecting stories of destitution I have ever heard. He said that during one whole week in the course of the present winter he and his whole family had subsisted upon nothing but beef-steak & bread & for several days had been limited to 20 glasses of lager per diem. They had received no assistance from charity whatever except that on one occasion a benevolent in the neighborhood had sent them in a dish of coleslaw when they did not know where to look for the morrows cabbage-stalk. I gave the man a large red cabbage which he hugged frantically for joy, at the same time bedewing my feet with tears. I put him down in my visitors book for further relief & offered him some temperance tracts which he accepted gratefully saying that they were the very things to light his meerschaum with. Thus the glorious cause of temperance & humanity is flourishing among us, and I hope that the legislature will enact as our society has petitioned, a law for the suppression of vice and immorality against the drinking of tea & coffee & the use of tight boots which people our jails & prisons & send so many victims to an untimely grave.

I hope Aunt Caroline & Uncle & the whole of your are well. When you write let me know. Though I have put a good deal of nonsense in my letter, I'm in earnest about the lecture & would like to have you let me know as soon as you can conveniently.

Much love to all the Palatiniers, & believe me ever your very affectionate cousin,
Fitz Hugh Ludlow

LETTER TO HARPER BROTHERS, JULY 3, 1857

Messr. Harper & Brothers,
Dear Sirs, I enclose to you all my book, paragraphed, chaptered, prefaced & appendixed. It is now ready for the composer.

As an appointment calls me for the next two weeks into Vermont please direct the proof-sheets that are to be corrected within that time thus, Fitz Hugh Ludlow, Arlington, Bennington Co. Vt. They will reach me in one day from New York. When I leave Vt. I will inform you by note from there, giving my next direction.

May I trouble you to mention to Doctor Palmer when he calls at your office, that the enclosed packet directed to him, awaits him with you. You will thus oblige

Yours very Respt'ly,
Fitz Hugh Ludlow

LETTER TO S. LUDLOW FREY, AUGUST 3, 1857

My Dear Lud,

If I have seemed neglectful either of your letter or its very kind invitation, it has been only in seeming. I have been very little at home for the last four months. Either in New York on business or in Vermont & Schenectady for relaxation, I have been as much occupied as any decent man should be. I have had about fifty letters to answer this last week, the first week indeed that I could call my own for a long time. I am sorry now that I have time to be obliged to say that it is physically impossible for me to get to your dear home or to Oswego at all this summer. The combination of proof-sheets for my forthcoming book would keep me near New York even had I the spondulicks to get away, which I am not so imaginative a person as to believe I have, just at present. I have therefore magnanimously put funds into the hands of my family & have said "Go, be happy" at the same time staying at home myself to pass the period of their absence in a sylvan retreat known as Mr. Poorman's place.

But, to put joking aside, my dear boy, I am heartily sorry for my inability to pass the coming few weeks between your home & Wildwood, for although I perhaps abominate Oswego as much as you like it, I would go anywhere short of the Devil, to see you all once more. You are nonetheless in my thoughts for not being written to regularly, if we could I have no doubt have a fine time together, even if we do nothing but talk & keep our pipes alight, that Fate, funds & floods of work will not let me off.

You must come and see me instead. My home from next September until I make my name, fortune, or way in the world, somehow or other will be in New York. Where to find me I will write you particularly and shall claim you as my guest most jealously whenever you will consent to come down to that little village.

My Father, Mother, & Sister by the will of Providence will be at Oswego on Thursday Eve. next. I am desired by my father to acknowledge through you the receipt of Uncle Samuel's letter, & I have no doubt you see him often enough to convey the intelligence of this & the other notable facts of my letter to him.

Give my best love to dear Aunt Caroline, Uncle John, Carrie & the boys & be assured that you cannot be as long not to see me as I am not to see you. I will write more fully when I am not so overhurried & till then believe me your most affectionate cousin,

Fitz Hugh Ludlow

LETTER TO FLETCHER HARPER BROTHERS, JANUARY 2, 1858

(Letterhead of William Curtis Noyes, Tracy, Powers and Tallmadge No. 50 Wall Street, New York)

FLETCHER HARPER, ESQ.

Dear Sir,

Not having by me our contract for the Hasheesh Eater, nor fully remembering its terms, as to time, I ask your kindness to inform me whether I am right sir in thinking that the first payment fell due yesterday Jan 1st. If so, and you find it quite convenient to let me have the note of your house for percentage on the books sold, which I believe is at four months, I shall feel very much obliged to you as, like most young authors I am not superabundantly provided with funds just now. If I mistake the terms of the contract [*he had*] will you have the goodness to let me know it by a line addressed to me here—if I do not, to enclose the note to my order, to the same place, since business at the office will probably prevent my calling personally for a few days to come.

Yours very truly,

Fitz Hugh Ludlow

Letter To Fletcher Harper, January ?, 1859

CLIFTON WATER CURE, ONTARIO CTY, N.Y.
FLETCHER HARPER ESQ.

Very Dear Sir,

I have for weeks been wishing very much to write to you, and this on many accounts, but, for pressing reasons which will now appear, have not done so until now, when I am able at the same time to offer you the congratulations of the New Year.

A few weeks ago I had occasion for sixty dollars. I wrote to our friend Nordhoff to trouble himself with his wonted kindness to ask that an advance to that extent might be made me—and you were so good as to direct that it should be done as I asked. Whereupon the cheque was forwarded.

At the time I wrote Nordhoff, I told him that I should have several articles for him ready by Christmas Day. I as fully expected to fulfill my promise, to the letter. I had hardly made it however, before the nervous ailment, of which I am now, thank God nearly cured, resulted in a congested state of the brain, which had lasted up to a week ago with continual pain and part of the time much danger. I was restricted by my physicians to the very slightest mental effort with which my affairs could be carried on—reduced to the very minimum of letter-writing, even to nearest relatives. Brain fever—or congestion of an active type was apprehended for me, and threats were made both by the Doctors & the disease that I should never be able, very likely, to use my head (all-necessary as it is to me) again, if I used it now.

Let this account to yourself and my friend Nordhoff for the non-fulfilment of my engagement and my silence, heretofore, as to the reasons.

I write so particularly all the facts of the case, because I am peculiarly anxious to have my integrity & good-faith stand well with you as a House—with you as a man. I know no better time of the year than this, when we are all exchanging felicitations with each other, to speak of the light of most sincere friendship and respect in which I regard you. Long before I knew you I had been thrown some- what among enemies of your firm. An especial clique there was (more sectarian than anything else) that never spoke of yourself and your co-partners to me otherwise than with strong hostility, and the consequence was, that until through the kindness of our friend Mr. Curtis I was introduced to you, I had never possessed any opportunity of coming unbiased to my own conclusions in regard to a set of men upon whom it is necessary, for their great prominence in the world of Books & Commerce, to come to some conclusion of one kind or another. Permit me to express to you, my dear Sir, the sincere & very great pleasure with which I have in my own person been disproving every slander which ever came to my ears. As a simple rendition of justice between man and man, let me own to you how growing has been my feeling of warm personal regard to you for all the unusual generosity you have shown in the maintenance of all our relations. Unusual, I say, because it is indeed rare to find any appreciation of each other among men beyond the mere even balance of money-justice. To you, my dear Sir—with pleasure I acknowledge it—I owe almost every encouragement I have received in the progress thus far of a literary career. The debt is far from a heavy one to me. I love to assure you that I am conscious of it. I am but twenty-two years old now—I have had somewhat of illness & of bad habits in stimulus-using to fight on my way up into a more successful and untiring career. The Water Cure and my will has utterly conquered my habits of stimulus—not even tobacco do I touch now—and my health is fast becoming thoroughly resettled. Be assured that when I again return to hard work as an author, I shall recollect (I never forget such things) your kindness to a young writer, and will endeavor to prove more substantially the friendship of

Fitz Hugh Ludlow

My best remembrances to Nordhoff, I hope to send him the Mss. I promised—this month.

LETTER TO MR. HUBBARD, AUGUST 13, 1861

My Dear Mr. Hubbard,
The gentleman referred to as having taken such interest in the Fire
Zoavres is Prosper M. Wetmore. I communicate his name in confi-
dence to yourself and any of the artists it may be necessary to report
the disbursement to under the same obligation as to outsiders, for the
reason that Mr. Wetmore does not like to be brought publicly forward
in connection with certain reforms of a corps somewhat demoralized,
in which he has been prime mover.

He of course is a safe steward for the beneficence of the artists.
Strange also by the way, isn't it? This war has made a general boule-
versement of all our relations. Art always used to be the steward and
bursar of a generous Commerce—Commerce, now in the shape of the
old moneyed man, P.M.W. is (if you like) about to return the favor by
distributing the acquisitions of a generous art.

My wife is now spending a few days at General Morris's. I shall
write to her this afternoon enclosing your kind remembrances. Were
she here she would cordially join in his, your friend,
Fitz Hugh Ludlow.

Letter To Edmund Clarence Stedman, September 5, 1861

(Letterhead: Office of The Evening Post, 41 Nassau Street, Cor, Liberty, New York)

My Beloved Stedman,

You are a man of letters—and love me just as much as if I should write you a thousand apologies for not writing. Me voila! Here is all that is left of Ludlow.

I write this to beg that you will expedite as far as possible in all that relates to his conference with the powers that be—my friend Mr. Hamilton.

He is coming on immediately. You know him already and, as far as convenient, I am sure, will put him in communication with those powers he needs to engage.

I saw your wife one day week before last in going down to Long Branch—she looks well—better than ever before.

Mr. Hamilton will need nothing of course but to introduce himself to you.

Love from Rose (who is now up the river, after Long Branch and Saratoga) and from your companion in bonds and faithful friend, Ludlow

LETTER TO WILLIAM A. COFFIN, 1861

THURSDAY A.M.

My Dear Coffin,
I enclose with pleasure a check for Mrs. Barry Gray and yourself to Linda [Kellogg] on Friday (tomorrow) night. If you wish one for Brooklyn (Sat; Traviata) say so and I will get that too.

I shall send you some more opera gossip, critical & historical, either this P.M. or tomorrow morning—and the biographical notice of Parke Godwin at the same time. I will be much obliged to you (should you see him) if you will tell Henderson so that he may save me a couple of columns

Very truly your friend,
Fitz Hugh Ludlow

```
Ludlow, Fitz-Hugh
   New York, 5 September 1861
   To Edmund Clarence Stedman
   a.l.s.  2p.(with envelope)
```

Office of **The Evening Post,**

41 NASSAU STREET, COR. LIBERTY,

New York, Sept 5th 1861

My Beloved Stedman

You are a man of letters —
and love me just as much as if I
should write you a thousand apolo-
gies for not writing. Me voila! There
is all that
is left of
Ludlow.

I write this to beg that you
will expedite as far as possible
in all that relates to his confer-
ence with the Powers that be —
My friend Mr. Hamilton
He is coming on immedi-
ately. You know him already
and, as far as convenient, I am
sure, will put him in communi-

(COLUMBIA UNIVERSITY)

Letter to Charles Godfrey Leland, November 27, 1861

My Dear Leland,

I have a favor to ask of you. Will you give me the name of the writer of those wonderful sketches of travel through the Cotton States which have appeared in the Knickerbocker? I am pretty sure from internal evidences that you yourself have done a good deal towards cutting the rough diamond of adventure disclosed therein—and the songs are very much more like what C.G.L. knows the negro feels than what that sable brother would be able to say for himself. But Gilmore [publisher of the *Continental Monthly*] told me that the traveller and his adventures are real—and having an extra-cerebral status some-where, I wish to know where that is. Will you do me the kindness to tell me by return mail?

I will tell you in perfect secrecy why I want the information. That man, whoever he is, knows something about the conspiracy to dissolve the Union, which, if ventilated, would put a number of our now white-washed political rascals in their true position before the people. To do this is the duty of every man who loves his country, and especially at this juncture loves New York.

I give you my word that I will not utter the man's name to a living soul without permission. I wish simply to confer with him-not in any sense to operate to his annoyance by extracting facts from him malgré hui.

It is of imperative necessity that I should see this man before our next (Tuesday) election. I beg that you will place in me the confidence which I ask at the very earliest moment possible. I send a duplicate of this letter to Boston—not knowing whether you take your Thanksgiving dinner there or at the paternal house.

Your leaders on the hard war-nut which is to be cracked have given the Knickerbocker a prestige it never had before, and are the admiration of all your friends. You see an issue which is plainly impracticable to the present half-wisdom of the country, but which, as sure as God lives on Earth as well as in the Heavens, will be forced upon the heart of the great people before its prodigally poured blood can congeal into a cement for eternal empire. Your lyrics on the subjects of the war and freedom I consider the best things you ever did. There is the Thor-hammering in them blending into a grand anvil chorus with the sweep of Braga's lute.

Before I close let me say one thing. You have a friend here (soi-disant—I call him sycophant) who is no friend of mine. You and I have always been friends. Let no word of his ever make us other- wise. I mention no names—paper is not a good medium for unpleasant facts. I prefer air—which I will use when we meet. Please reply immediately—and let no one make you dream for a moment that I am other than always your sincere friend,

Fitz Hugh Ludlow

LETTER TO CHARLES GODFREY LELAND, JULY 28, 1862

(Letterhead of the Custom House, Collector's Office)

My dear Leland,

Mr. Beecher this morning asked me if I knew Kirk of the Southern experiences—because he wishes to put him in correspondence with a Baltimore lady who had become very much interested in his book. I said no—but that you did. He then requested me to enclose the within letter to you, begging you to forward it to Kirk and have him answer its inquiries, if he will, to the direction given — then return it to me for Mr. Beecher who wishes to keep it a sample of the good seed which may spring up in thorny places. May I burden you with this good office? It will be such both to H.W.B. & myself as well as the lady. I wish I could write more at length to thank you for your course on the great issues—but am awfully driven—People who think the commerce of the U.S. is going to the bad had better note that we are doing a larger business at the Custom House than has been transacted for six or seven years—and on Saturday (26th) cleared the largest number of vessels to Europe that ever left this port on one day within our history.

Please remember about having Kirk return the letter to me.

Beecher asked that particularly.

I dine with Dick Stoddard this P.M. Lizzie has been very sick but is better now and goes with Dick to spend a week at the [*painter Jervis*] McEntees' farm house in a day or two.

All your friends are well. My wife is out of town (Would I were with her!) or would invite in kind remembrances to Mrs. Leland & God bless you to you with your friend,

Most faithfully,

Fitz Hugh Ludlow

Letter to Frank Carpenter, January 4, 1864

OSWEGO, JAN. 4/64

My Beloved Frank,

Surely I do not deserve to have you love me, so far as external experience can indicate, yet if you have the power of looking into my heart of hearts, you will find that I love you more than ever. And God knows I always loved you dearly!

Before I went off on my journey I was so terribly worked with the preparation to go away leaving all my work done & some ready money for Rose (until I could forward her more from California) that I probably had the appearance of being cold & negligent. Dear boy & brother of my heart, believe one who never was insincere to you—I never was cold & negligent. You can pity a man who has a certain amount of work to do in a given time—and that time very inadequate. The last two months of my stay in New York, after I once resolved to go, were so occupied that if I had not economised every moment's time, I should through sheer desperation have been driven back on those damnable stimulants to support my overtaxed energies. I could not spare an instant from business without running the risk of leaving my Academy Articles for the Post & a dozen other jobs unfinished, and thus going away without giving Rose enough to last her till the work I did for the papers in Cal. (amounting to several hundred dollars in gold) began to pay. So, I made no calls of friendship—and still more, none of ceremony—sure that all my real friends would understand me & how hard I was pressed. Dear Frank: It surely is not necessary for me to tell you that I love you dearly!

When I got back to New York from the Pacific, I was equally driven. I wanted of course to get to my sweet little Rose as quick as I could, yet sheer, mere, unadulterated business kept me in the City, four anxious impatient days, during which I made not a single visit of affection— only sleeping at the Studio or in Booth's house, & passing all my days in business downtown. I got one card from you—your letter says you called three times. I am very, very sorry I did not see you. If I had gone anywhere you should have had my first visit. I have never ceased to love you, & think of you as my heart's dear brother—my companion in the glorious studio of that science of sciences, the Spiritual. One to whom I owe many loving kindnesses, a thousand sweet sympathies in my [turns?] both of sun, shadow & numberless hours of heavenly communion in the matters nearest to both our souls. If for the year past I have been so perpetually occupied that it was with the greatest difficulty I could keep my lovely little wife, father & sister informed of my movements—and if, for months before that I was so tossed & tempest-driven on a sea of work that I could not call my soul my own—still my heart held you dear as ever—and I have always looked forward with more delight than I can express to the time when you should have a home in New York near me, and my affairs should once more yield me some leisure to be spent in those precious seasons of communion where our hearts used to burn while we talked with each other by the way. I am very busy this winter lecturing on my travels—writing three articles of about 10 pages apiece on the subjects connected with the journey which will appear in the April, May & June No.'s of the Atlantic—and preparing the big book of Travels (as large as Livingstone's Africa) which with copious illustrations from Bierstadt, will be about June.

Most of the winter, between Lectures, I shall spend at Clifton for the benefit of Rose's and my own health. I had an attack of typhoid Pneumonia in the most barbarous part of the Oregon Backwoods, where for two whole days my life was despaired of. I had given up all thoughts of seeing home again and given my last directions to my nobly kind Bierstadt. I was at least a hundred miles from any real physician—had no medicine—and through the Mercy of Christ, was only saved at last by B.'s capable nursing & his continual application of cold-water compresses to my chest. Oh my Dear Brother—both then, & several other times, among the frightful Indians of the desert & in storms at sea, have I looked right into the Eternal World since I saw you last—yet, Glory to our dear Savior, I have always found this grace sufficient for me, and the noble view of the spiritual world which we have so often delighted to dwell upon in times of security & health, never once seemed shaken, never once was beclouded by doubt in the presence of imminent death. Let me bear witness my beloved Brother, that the Gospel we profess, & which Christ sent his great Seer, Emmanuel Swedenborg, to declare unto us, in the light of the Eternal World grows only brighter, & clearer & more certain. The great test of a dying bed tries it only to bring forth pure gold.

I hope that after I have finished my book & other literary labors connected with my journey I shall come back to New York a haler & heartier man than I went away—with my little Angel Rose much improved—and my own worldly prospects greatly brightened. I shall now be able to live handsomely by my pen alone—but yet I hope to get a very valuable position before long where my day's work from 10 A.M. to 4 P.M. will amply support me, and leave the rest of my leisure for being a better husband to dear Rose than ever before—and a better friend, with more time for hearts' precious communion, than I have ever been before to you. I will tell you of my plans when we meet.

Your picture of father is greatly admired here. Everybody thinks it one of the best likenesses he ever saw—and I agree with them. Oh how thankful I am to you for perpetuating the lovely benignant face of that precious father, whose whole life, in spite of the warp of Calvinism, has been one long, generous, nurturing self-sacrifice for his children, his friends, the world, and his Savior. This Savior is our common ground. I can talk with father about our love to Christ all day without quarrelling. I have learned studiously to avoid all on theological differences. Surely Christ is enough to agree on!

Please tell me, when you write, if you have received my sister Helen's letter of thanks to you for the noble present of the portrait. She feels very much hurt because you have said nothing about it, and fears that you do not think her gratitude of any value. She is very thankful to you & desires much to know whether you ever received her letter.

Write to me here—care of father. I hope to be in New York a little while this winter, when I shall rush to clasp you in my brotherly arms, you dear, dear boy, you may be sure!

I have not your address by me (I am writing down town)—so I send this to the care of Bierstadt, who will have it delivered. Love to your dear wife, Mother, Florence, the baby—in which Rose, Helen & Father join.

Your most aff. brother Fitz.

Letter to James T. Fields, Undated, Likely Late Summer 1864

PLACE
STUYVESANT SQUARE

My Dear Mr. Fields,
Excuse the great haste which makes me rush at once into business by saying that if you can get along without the "Greatness of New York" Article until November I can furnish you with two more Articles of travel between now and October. One of them will give a running sketch of the entire ride which one may be prophetically seen to take on the Pacific R.R. and furnish some idea of the status which would prevail through the shorter axis of our continent were the enterprise now completed.

Another would treat generally of the Columbia River and its scenery & science.

If these be satisfactory please let me know. I intend to bring my book out during the winter. The engravers and I are hard at work on it now.

In great haste but
Truly Your Friend,
Fitz Hugh Ludlow

LETTER TO EDWARD STANSBURY, NOVEMBER 10, 1864

No. 1 Livingston Place
Stuyvesant Square
Thursday – Nov. 10th/64

My Dear Ed'ard which his other name was Stansbury

I am again in search of you with money! You are a rare & wonderful man. Hundred dollar bills which flee some folk chase you.

You are a male Danae – but an unconscious one. Gold pours in on you but you know it not. I came to see you yesterday – and you were out. It is terrible, My Ed'ard, to be out when the Gods call. Be always at home to Fortune. Tomorrow may I smile on you to the extent of $ 100?

If you will, please be so kind as to send up Joseph for the amt to –

(COURTESY OF THE ALBERT AND SHIRLEY SMALL COLLECTIONS
LIBRARY, UNIVERSITY OF VIRGINIA)

My Dear Ed'ard which his other name was Stansbury,
I am again in search of you with money! You are a rare & wonderful man. Hundred dollar bills which flee some folk chase you.

You are a male Danae—but an unconscious one. Gold pours in on you but you know it not. I came to see you yesterday—and you were out.

It is terrible my Ed'ard, to be out when the Gods call. Be always at home to Fortune—Tomorrow may I smile on you to the extent of $100?

If you will, please be so kind as to send up Joseph for the am't tomorrow about 1 P.M. I would go down today—but Rose is very ill with pneumonia, both the Doctor and I are more alarmed about her than ever before—and I dare not leave her for an instant. I am very anxious indeed. I was up with her almost the entire night. I am pretty well fagged out—but you & I thank God have good con- stitutions and have made them tough for suffering by bearing all the panic & responsibilities possible in this life.

God bless you my dear boy. Love to yours & you from me and mine & believe me one of your best friends,
Ludlow

LETTER TO E. R. PERKINS, NOVEMBER 9, 1864

NO. I LIVINGSTON PLACE
STUYVESANT SQUARE
NOV. 11TH 1864

E. R. PERKINS, ESQ.

Dear Sir,
I should much prefer to lecture for you a little later in the season if I am to go to you on any other night than Dec. 22nd. What do you say to the 29th of Dec.? I wish to stay a little longer in Buffalo, upon busi- ness apart from lectures, than I could if I lectured there and before you on successive nights. If you can make no other arrangement than the 22nd, I will come to you then, but another night, say Dec. 29 or Jan. 6th, would better suit,
   Yours very truly,
   Fitz Hugh Ludlow

LETTER TO JAMES T. FIELDS, NOVEMBER 11, 1864

NOV. 11TH 1864
NO. 1 LIVINGSTON PLACE
STUYVESANT SQUARE

My Dear Mr. Fields,
I have not heard from you since I forwarded the Mss. of the N.Y. article but am sure I should have done so had you not received it. If there be time I wish to make the following addendum in a foot-note on the last page of the article.

In addition to the obligations elsewhere recognized, an acknowledgement is due to the well known archaeologist and statist of New York, Mr. Valentine, who furnished for the purpose of this article the latest edition of his Manual in advance of its general publication, to the much increased convenience of the writer.

Believe me in great haste but very truly yours,
Fitz Hugh Ludlow

P.S. My wife has been so ill with pneumonia ever since the Bryant Festival that she has not been able to put the cap-stone on an excellent review of Emily Chester. My constant press of work & natural anxiety for her have kept me from finishing & publishing it—but I will in a few days.

LETTER TO EDMUND CLARENCE STEDMAN, DECEMBER, 1864

ADDRESS UNTIL 16TH INST.
CARE OF LUDLOW FREY, ESQ.
PALATINE BRIDGE,
MONTGOMERY COUNTY, N.Y.

My Dear Stedman,

If it did not involve a joke (and Christ knows how little I feel like that) I would quote an old saw brought over from abolition times & say "You have acted like a man and a brother."

If you see Stoddard remind him of the fact that I loved his little Millie as no one not his own parent could do...Remind him that when many friends forsook him because of hard feeling they had for things said at his house, I, though I had hard things said to me, stuck by him and Elizabeth—always would have done so—had I not received the final insult a man ever stands from a woman and one for which he would leave ripped up his dearest friend among men had he been hanged for it next day.

Remind him that when I was all alone among the waves of calumny and popular indignation—when my friends like those of Jesus "forsook me & fled"—that I came up to kneel beside my sick wife and take her to my broken heart and there found his wife waiting not only to insult me in my agony but to go down and talk ill of me to one of the few friends who dared to come to me.

Remind him that all my life I have sought to do him and his wife good—acting like an own brother in the criticism of both their works; asking all manner of kindness for even their faults where my influence was of any avail.

Remind him how one of the very best friends he ever had in the world now owes his widowhood & utter desolation in life to—call it a mistake—on the part of Elizabeth—and how the only apology which has ever been made for what to the lowest wretch the world would call cruelty—at least the only apology on the side of the house which the Salic law disinherited, has been the grossest insults and most insane threats ever made by privileged woman to patient, chivalric man.

Remind him that my whole career is proof enough that I neither wish to injure him nor his family and then ask him to come to me not like a second in a duel but an old friend to whom facts may have been represented—or at least to a man ready to do justice to the wife whom he is perfectly right, noble, and honorable in wishing to protect. If he wishes fight—if Barstow wishes it—let either of them say so. I am not in the ordinary sense a duellist—but in extreme cases, where people cannot settle the matter peacefully, I am a fighting man and will gladly accept a challenge from any man who thinks himself aggrieved and will not give me even a chance to know for what I must apologize.

I have written to Dick merely asking him what he wishes me to apologize for. If he will tell me—or if he be unwilling to entrust such a delicate matter to paper, if he will send at our own divided expense a special messenger—you e.g. if you will be so good—to tell me personally; Stedman, do you believe that I am a man of such false pride, so mean, so cowardly, as not to be willing to repair any wrong I may have done in heat ever to the uttermost?

But I cannot—& by the Eternal God I will not, deny words that I do not know— endorse any human beings' character in general terms—or crouch to the twin boy from out of my own mother's womb in humility for our utterly undefined and nameless wrong.

Let not a man whom I have loved—whom I still love (in spite of our latest inter-communication) so much as Stoddard, utterly shut up all door of compromise. I told him—I now tell you (and you have traveled East I believe [here is drawn a triangle with the letter G in it] Stedman, before God I tell you as if I were on my death bed (as I well nigh have been) that I stand ready to do all

"that doth become a man

Who dares do more is none."

Mrs. S. has more grievously insulted me than any male creature ever did—any female since I played "oats pease beans" with choleric little girls in the street—and if I held the extreme code of honor I should seek R.H.S. or W.B. and demand satisfaction of them for the behavior of one for whom they stand responsible. Far enough am I from that. If I were buried under a mountain of frog scum by any woman I would understand too well how little control any man has over any woman's actions to hold her husband, brother, lover accountable.

I stand all alone in the waves. I am however a rock—and assure you "Nec flatu nec fluctu movear." At the same time the littlest naked child may stand on me & be safe.

Tell Stoddard and his wife for me that though they may ruin me by their reports even as one of them (whom I would have defended with my own heart had she not turned on me in my distress) has tried to do to the very friend who offered my weary body an asylum. Tell them that the furthest thing from my wish is to hurt their names, reputations—prospects in any way.

For both their sakes, Rose's, yours and mine, let them not bring a broken hearted and desperate man to bay. Self Defence is the last, the uncontrollable—the automatic principle of human nature. I stand through the result of long unhappiness and public abuse in a place where life is so little dear to me that to hazard it on a cast of my honor's die would be no bravery whatever.

To you I say "I am sick but strong." If you are the man you say—bid the Stoddards act kindly and wisely. For their sake for your sake, for Rose's, for that of all who, false or true, have ever proffered me love & fealty—I will do the same. Until the 16th address me here—after that to Buffalo, N.Y.

Yours, both friend and brother, Ludlow

LETTER TO JOSEPH HENRY, JANUARY 31, 1865

NO. 1 LIVINGSTON PLACE
STUYVESANT SQUARE
JAN 31 1865

Professor Henry,
Dear Sir,
In my Atlantic article on Correlation & Persistence, I wish very much
to obtain your researches in that field that I may give at least a popular
account of them, supposing they be, as I have thought might prove the
case, too highly mathematical for transcription in form.

At a time when all the scientific men of the country are regretting
both your & their own loss in the burning of your papers, I feel hes-
itation in troubling you upon this matter but should think my article
incomplete could you not oblige in this respect,

yours very truly,
Fitz Hugh Ludlow

Letter to William F. Phillips, March 2, 1865

NO. I LIVINGSTON PLACE
STUYVESANT SQUARE
MARCH 2, 1865
WILLIAM F. PHILLIPS ESQ.

Dear Sir,

I have twice past [sic] through Cincinnati since your note of Feb. 14th was written, but not having given orders to forward my mails, only knew of it on my arrival home three days ago.

I shall be happy to address yourself and the "many citizens" whose flattering invitation you proffer, some evening during the last week in this month when I shall again go west via Cincinnati. The "Good Living" lecture I have recast into a magazine article—a form more suitable to its presentation—and am now giving only "Across the Continent"—a running description of the original scenes & people between the Missouri & the Pacific. I need not say it is no rechauffe of matter previously published.

Should this lecture meet your views, I will inform you definitely of the exact time I should like to be with you, as soon as the railroad business on which my movements to a degree depend is arranged beyond peradventure.

Hoping to hear from you as early as convenient I remain,
Truly yours,
Fitz Hugh Ludlow

LETTER TO HIRAM BARNEY, MARCH, 1865

TRINITY BUILDING—MONDAY 10 AM.
CONFIDENTIAL

My Dear Mr. Barney,

I last night came to the conclusion that I would apply to the present administration for a consulate in some one of the Mediterranean ports. My health is failing under the pressure of an amount of work which while necessary to earn my bread will soon put me beyond the need of any. I am now getting letters of recommendation to the President from all my New York and country friends. Will you give me one? If you feel willing to confer this service you may perhaps save me from leaving the world before I have attained the place I am struggling towards among the literary men of my country, dragged back by the terrible double weights of poverty and sickness. I love literature dearly—it is my chosen work—but just now I must have bread, and easier than I now get it.

I don't know how much weight it would have with Mr. Lincoln to tell him that I am a young literary man of some promise (if you think so)—but past administrations have shown a willingness to do the honor to literature of selecting some of their representatives from that class which was quite surprising when we consider how few other creditable things they were willing to do. If you are willing to write for me—it may be best to speak of my literary status—you are the judge of its expediency.

I am a staunch Republican—have been so through defeat and victory. I have the promise of considerable influence among my other friends in the party—but particularly wish yours also—both because I have always felt you were a very kind and warmly interested friend of mine—and because if I either break down or die in my present state my poor wife will be left without a farthing—and every atom of additional influence has a chance of averting that likelihood. Should you feel it is in your heart to give me a recommendatory letter to Mr. Lincoln—please leave it here with one of your clerks and I will call tomorrow noon for it. And with many sincere thanks I shall be as ever,

Your true friend, Fitz Hugh Ludlow

LETTER TO SCHUYLER COLFAX, SEPTEMBER 6, 1865

My Dear Mr. Colfax,

Immediately after I met you last, (on the Erie Road as you will recollect) I went home, and was instantly taken seriously ill. I have never been nearer death than then. Indeed at the time I saw you, nothing but the determination to discharge to the very conclusion a responsibility which in the face of all manner of malignity, slander and opposition I had borne for several months, kept me up long enough to get home and lie down for what I & my few staunch friends supposed was my last illness. That responsibility honorably demitted I should have been very willing to die, for adversity had revealed to me depths of human baseness and ingratitude, yawning right under the supposed solid ground I trod in my sunnier time, which made me shudder at the thought of living any longer on this earth. A wonderful constitution carried me through however, and although I have been too feeble to do anything like the previously accustomed daily work of my life for the last six months, I am now, thanks to noble friends who have (as a strange exception to the general rule) clung all the closer to me when I needed their love, and to the Water cure treatment at this place, getting well rapidly.

I make this statement not because I think it can be of any interest to you to be troubled by the recital of my private affairs but because I wish to rid myself of the imputation of discourtesy and negligence which might otherwise rest upon me in view of my not having complied with your request by sending you that book of Gilpin's. You had set out on your journey before I could lift myself from my bed to a chair and I did not know where to direct to you short of Denver, while I also knew that without trouble or pecuniary loss you could get as many of Gilpin's books at the Territorial library there as you desired. Please accept my apology, for the apparent neglect to obey your wishes has troubled me much ever since I was well enough to think of this world's matters again.

I have a favor to ask of you. My illness has retarded the completion of my book of travels. My publishers are getting very much alarmed because they say that your book will entirely supersede mine. I am sure I should gladly yield the palm to you, but for my publishers' sake, I should be glad to tell them (if it is so) that though our track was the same that the point of view in which we look at the subject is different. I don't suppose we should really interfere. I believe that your book is to be of particular interest to the statesman, statistician, emigrant and commercial man while mine is devoted principally to Scenery with Bierstadt's illustrations, to botany, Geology, Science in general, Adventure, hunting, Anecdote & the usual chatty matter of the tourist.

If I could say to Hurd & Houghton that the interference does not exist it would make it much easier for them & me to cultivate equanimity during the remaining few weeks necessary to get the book to press.

Forgive my troubling you—drop me a line if you will be so kind— tell me how to direct Gilpin's book to you now—and believe me.

Very Truly Yrs.,

Fitz Hugh Ludlow

Letter to James R. Gilmore, October 24, 1866

NO. I LIVINGSTON PLACE
STUYVESANT SQUARE
OCTOBER 24, 1866

My Dear Gilmore,

I have only waited in order that I might find Stedman, who has lately moved, & answer you regarding him as well as myself. His health is very delicate & his time occupied in Stocks & the Atlantic, to both of which he is under articles for the year. Nevertheless, he says, put him down among your list of contributors and he will try & send you a poem occasionally. He has scarcely time & health to write other than already engaged articles of the prose length.

I will send you one article early next week—if possible two, during that week.

In haste but yours truly,
Ludlow

LETTER TO JAMES R. GILMORE, FEBRUARY 4, 1867

LOGANSPORT FEB. 4TH/67

My Dear Gilmore,

Temporary detention in a small Indiana town waiting for the Great Eastern night express up to Chicago, will I am sure excuse my writing to you on a partially greasy sheet. I may add that the delicate tinge at the upper left hand corner was communicated by sardines—a box of which we have just enjoyed very much, but which possibly may have imparted to this letter, by the time (considering the state of the roads) which it will take it to reach the Center of All Things an ancient & fish-like smell.

I meant to have written to you before I left New York—but just at the last I was called West very unexpectedly and before I went had to do so much preparation for this very trip that I had to leave to Providence all such portions of my correspondence as could possibly be trusted to run itself till I had time to send a series of Parthian missives flying back en route. I knew you had two numbers of "Fleeing to Tarshish" and that if I rest at Chicago a day or two I can probably send you a short sketch or story this week. $60 received from your publishers for "Fleeing from Tarshish"—thank you.

The novel which I wrote & you remind me of is not yet far enough advanced to promise for any number short of an early summer one. I have had great cares & responsibilities laid upon me of late which may narrow the time I can at the best employ for literary effort though I will keep to the original plan I laid down for myself of at least one contribution per fortnight as I can. When I next bring out a book—especially if it be a novel—an arena of such vast competitions for any man to enter!—I desire that it shall have had the very best of my work expended on it as an entirety. I once wrote a serial novelette in some 19 weekly numbers which I reflect with gratitude you have doubtless utterly forgotten—and wrote only as fast as the matter was published. I committed myself early in my plot to a denuouement which as the story opened grew gradually more undesirable, and had to introduce an improbability only allowable in broadest burlesque to get myself out of the fire. Even where Dickens has attempted it he has only succeeded by virtue of a genius quite incomparable with any Englishman's but Shakespeare, and he would have succeeded better yet had he mastered his theme & struck all its chords to finis before attempting on it any of those discursive, seductive & entangling little variations which begin with the first published chapter. Sala got into an awful fix by risking himself to keep up with the printer in Alone. The more I look at it the more I feel that I'd like to see my finished work & give it the final touches by which intuition some-times supplies some exactly needed element of symmetry or takes away some weakening surplusage before I start it out among men.

I only saw three No.'s of the N.L. before leaving New York but have letters since then saying that every number had improved in beauty of appearance & interest as much as it was continuing to do up to no. 3. A most admirable sketch was that Low Life on the Five Points, a cap-itally well told story of the Paris sewers. There have been many sewer stories in magazines—but the dog & other elements in this make it the best I ever read.

Write me as usual at New York—whither I hope to return on Thursday. I'll forward more Ms. as soon as I can.

I am Your Friend, Ludlow

LETTER TO MESSRS. BEADLE AND CO., MARCH 28, 1867

NO. I LIVINGSTON PLACE
STUYVESANT SQUARE
MARCH 28/67

Messrs. Beadle & Co.
My cousin's Ms. received—thanks. I arrive by inspection at the conclusion that three stamps just covers my debt to you for P.O. deficiencies—which please find enclosed and believe me.
    Yours truly,
    Fitz Hugh Ludlow

LETTER TO JAMES R. GILMORE, JUNE 24, 1867

NO. I LIVINGSTON PLACE
STUYVESANT SQUARE
JUNE 24TH

My dear Gilmore,
O You rogue! O you two rogues—you & Sykes! To come on God's holy day and pick a man's pocket of his biographies!
    Never mind. For the world I wouldn't have had any body do anything in that way about me, but since it is done I can only say it is most kindly & only too complimentary, and remain your friend always, Ludlow
    ➡ (Turn over)

P.S. I open my envelope because I've just got your note from Boston. Be sure, my dear fellow, that I understand the circumstances exactly—and don't blame Sykes in the least, for, although he did what I would not knowingly have consented to, he at any rate wrote with kindness, appreciation, & enthusiasm.

Tell Messrs. Lee & Shepard please, for me that I today send them a note which by mistake has lain for days while I was visiting down at the Flatbush Lunatic Asylum with my friend, its head, Dr. Chapin.

Always, Dear Gilmore, your friend,

Ludlow

LETTER TO FLETCHER HARPER, FEBRUARY 11, 1868

NO. 1 LIVINGSTON PLACE

STUYVESANT SQUARE

FLETCHER HARPER, ESQ.

My Dear Sir,

Let me present to you my friend Mr. Edward T. Mason, son of the late Prof. Cyrus Mason of the University who you doubtless well remember. His highly gifted & versatile-minded father left the gentleman I now introduce numerous valuable mss. some of which, on Politico-Economical subjects he now proposes to publish. By commending him to Mr. Joseph Harper and securing him an early reading you will greatly oblige

Your Friend Truly,

Fitz Hugh Ludlow

LETTER TO MARY BOOTH, OCTOBER 21, 1868

NO. 1 LIVINGSTON PLACE

STUYVESANT SQUARE

My Dear Miss Booth,

If those little wedding verses (which I hardly dare to hope) find sufficient favor in your eyes (from the editorial point of view) to get a place in the Bazar—please keep them back from the compositor till after this day week, as on that date, in far distant Maine, a young friend of my wife's & mine for whom they were written originally is to be married—and I should like to have them appear to her on the handle of the ice pitcher which we send first.

Truly your friend,
Fitz Hugh Ludlow

Letter to Frank Carpenter, September 26, 1869

NO. 18 WEST 14TH ST.
NEW YORK
SEPT. 26TH, 1869

My Blessed Frank,
Ostensibly I write to enclose a letter which came for you yesterday but in reality that is only the excuse—a sort of nudge to the elbow of my memory, to remind me that I have not written to you nor heard from you save in the most indirect manner since you went away from here. Whenever Florrie has written she has just despatched her business in the most business-like way and concluded as quickly as possible without telling us anything about you or your movements. I have felt so anxious to know about you that I should have written long ago had I not, until a month ago, been as severe a sufferer as I was when you last saw me. Garratt, the Boston Electrician, gave me a little start I think in the right direction during the fortnight or 3 weeks I spent under his daily care, but after I returned home I became very miserable again, & not having the battery to resort to, got at last to a place where my misery made me almost frantic! O my dear brother, what a Valley of the Shadow of Death did I get into! For weeks I was in a state of mind—rather I ought to say of brain, where I was worse than an atheist. I positively hated God and if I had dared would have cursed him to his face. That any being possessed of infinite power could see me in such agony and horrible despair as I was in—hear me cry for mercy day & night and yet vouchsafe me not the slightest relief—not even

an answer—not so much as a comforting, encouraging night vision in which my father or some other blessed angel should be sent to comfort me—seemed so utterly monstrous—so fiendishly cruel—that at last I became wholly possessed of the idea that God—the God of all the Material Universe at least—was a terrible devil—a great, malignant, all powerful force and that if Christ had any power at all at this age of the world it was solely in the spiritual world to which I could only get by dying. How infinite power could be conjoined with infinite love in a being who would sit nonchalantly by and see me suffer what I would cross the wide world to save my worst enemy from—I could not see— it seemed an utter absurdity. Every morning after a perturbed sleep, full of awful dreams, I used to wake up in horror beyond anything I ever before imagined. This would steadily grow worse hour after hour until by 8 or 9 A.M. I would be almost beside myself. For weeks I stopped praying altogether—it seemed like such a superstitious farce to be all the time shrieking aloud into a frozen dome of sky which only mockingly reverberated my agonies. There seemed no God but Echo—and that Echo a devil.

At last I went into the country—went to White Lake, whence I came back two weeks ago tomorrow. This was the first time I had been in high mountain air since I first began to find my health failing, and the change did me good. I staid nearly a month & during that time gained 5 lbs. of flesh. Part of the time, the first 10 days Coo staid with me. When she, dear patient, hard-worked lamb, had to go home because the house must be looked after, sister staid with me and did everything possible to replace my wife's care. My mind became calmer as the strain was gradually lessened from my body and now, everybody says I look better than I have for a year or 18 months. I feel better too—sleeping well—having a tolerable appetite—suffering much less from neuralgia and being able to walk two or three miles at a stretch without undue fatigue or any of that torturing colic which the most trifling exercise, like a walk in the Park, used to bring on when you were here. And sweeter than all, Jesus Christ's dear face shines on me again, and tho' I cannot account for it how an all-powerful being lets me suffer as I have without at least some personal manifestation of himself to tell me his grace is sufficient even while the thorn cannot be removed—though "He moves in a mysterious way"—still I once more stand on this firm rock—he who lived the life and died the death of agony for me which he did must love me perfectly—must be doing the best for me which can be done however impossible it may be for me to understand his dealings. While I can feel the preciousness of Jesus Christ everything is bearable.

I have suffered as much for Coo as I have for myself, for it seemed to me before the present relief came as if she must break down under the burden of being constantly with me—seeing agonies which wrung her soul to its wonderfully tender depths and which she could not relieve—hearing the groans which were forced out of me until she was well nigh as frantic as myself. I was fearfully anxious lest a tendency to dysentery which has troubled her all summer and twice almost got the mastery should finally become uncontrollable and take her away from me. She has had a fearful year of nervous strain. Often I have debated within myself whether it would not really be far better and cost her and Helen less suffering in the end if this weary body of mine should cease its struggle and the tormented soul get its release. I do not think there can be on earth a greater trial of patience—greater wear and tear of nervous system than Coo has undergone in taking care of one with all our household anxieties on her hands besides. Knowing how often she keeps up merely by her wondrous energy of character—her heroic, loving will-power—I have trembled lest at last her overwrought body should sink under the strain, and if she once lay down really sick, her strength would (as I have several times seen illustrated) so rapidly decline that there would be scarcely a chance of her getting up again. And the thought that noble heart ought any day fall a sacrifice to its devotion to a miserable broken-hearted life like mine—that too without her having success in saving me—was too terrible to be borne. If things had not grown better with me I believe indeed she would have been worn out & not survived this winter. To think of my surviving her and knowing that I had killed her! To think of my dragging out the miserable months that might have still been left before my release after she had gone with her two orphaned children forever accusingly before my eyes and my own wretched life bereft of the light which for years has been all that has kept me up & enabled me to hold my course without sinking in the dark waters! Oh! no words can express my gratitude when I think that the Lord has spared me that and seems to mean to preserve to me that infinitely precious life—that love which is my most priceless treasure. I never knew that even in my heart there were such depths of love for any living creature as I feel for that darling Coo! I love her better & better every day, as some new nobility and tenderness—some fresh possibility of self-devotion & self-forgetfulness reveals itself in her character. We have endured together since we first knew each other bitterer, more insulting, cruel, odious wrongs, wickeder revelations of the baseness & ingratitude of human nature, more harassing & protracted sufferings of every kind than I never knew fall to the lot of any two people who loved each other—but I can truly say in spite of all, that my married life has had in it, from our mutual love, more happiness than I knew in all the 10 yrs. before.

(unsigned)

LETTER TO FLETCHER HARPER, JULY 16, 1870

8 WEYMOUTH ST.
PORTLAND, ME

My Dear Mr. Harper,
I sent yesterday to Mr. Low's for my letters, being confined in bed by an aggravation of my illness, but although my stepson made particular inquiry he was told that there was no letter for me there from you. Either he did not see the right person or it is possible that you may have handed the letter to Mr. Low.

If you will excuse me for troubling you further upon the matter will you have the kindness to give my son who will present this note the letter to Mr. Low for me which you promised on Tuesday, when we met, to give me? You cannot realize how vital it is to me that I should have my financial matters finally arranged, or you would excuse, I am sure, the anxiety I feel and manifest. Mental suffering has done much more than physical to bring me where I am, and in case my continued illness for a day or two should prevent my seeing you personally & I thus fail to get the note to Mr. Low, the thought of being quite without any credentials in my relations to him would be most painful to me. If I should be disappointed as I say in bidding you good-bye, my warmest wishes go with you that you may get the rest & restoration you so much need and receive much more permanent benefit than be hoped for from anything left in this world by
Your friend always,
Fitz Hugh Ludlow

THE POETRY OF FITZ HUGH LUDLOW

PART ONE
PUBLISHED, PRINTED OR PRESENTED
DURING HIS LIFETIME

THE VOICE OF THE HOLY SPIRIT

The Voice of the Holy Spirit
How often in the depths of night
When all around is in repose
And e'en the Zephyr quiet lies
Upon the bosom of the rose.

I hear a soft and still small voice
Pouring its accents on my ear
Pleading so softly with my heart
That I cannot but stop & hear

And thus thro' many a silent night
And many a solemn midnight hour
I hear that voice come to my heart
With all its holy gentle power.

TRUTH ON HIS TRAVELS

Truth, tired of lying hidden,
   In volumes old and musty,
To rise from the dust forbidden,
   In the brain of Doctor Rusty;

Determined no longer to lie in check,
   Chained down by an old opinion,
Which for numberless years had galled his neck,
   And made him the sage's minion—

With one strong effort his fetters he broke,
   Determining to rebel;
And with one more vigorous masterly stroke,
   He burst from his dingy cell.

Crying out in exultation—
   "With healing in my wings,
I will visit every nation—
   I'll reveal myself to Kings.

Each mighty potentate on earth,
   Shall feel my power to bless,
And I will hail the heaven-sprung birth
   Of the rule of righteousness."

Thus speaking he wended his airy way,
   To the seven-hilled city of Rome;
For there he heard Dr. Rusty say
   Was the arts' and sciences' home.

So darting down swift as the glance of an axe,
   It chanced that "Willy Nilly"—
He lit in a pack of Italian tracts
   Belonging to Dr. Achilli,

Which were slowly and quietly going along
   On the back of a Roman mule,
To the cadence low of the driver's song,
   Which he hummed in the evening cool.

"Aha," cried Truth, and he gaily laughed
   As he curled himself snugly in,
"I am now in my element, fore and aft,
   In truthfulness up to the chin.

I shall teach to admiring thousands
   These themes that these volumes discuss—
The doctrines of Wickliffe and Luther,
   Of Cramer, Melanchton and Huss."

But without his host did he reckon,
   For the Gend' Armes shook every fibre—
They threw Doctor Achille in prison,
   And Truth and his tracts in the Tiber.

But he scrabbled ashore as well as he could,
   With his wings all draggled and dripping,
And sat sorrowfully down on an old log of wood,
   Like a boy that had got a whipping.

But shaking at length like a Newfoundland dog—
   He managed his pinions to dry,
And taking a leap from the side of the log,
   Soared upward—was lost in the sky.

He went to old England, and called for repeal
   Of the taxes—those terrible bores
Which force men to pay for each pleasure they feel,
   For their sorrows, and sicknesses, and sores;

For their windows, and doors, and each cutlet of veal
   Which take from the widow her last pint of meal;
But John Bull liked his conscience to rest in repose
   So he lifted his toes,
(The ones afflicted by gout, we suppose,)
   And gently kicked Truth out of doors.

Then he crossed the straits of Dover
   To visit sunny France,
And there Right Reason was all over
   The colleague God of Chance;

And he tried to teach the Sans-Culottes
   To serve the King of Kings,
But they stared as if they had been shot,
   At such monarchic things;

And Monsieur Tonson shook his head
   With look of dreadful meaning,
And hinted of the dreamless bed
   That followed Guillotining.

Then Truth exclaimed, "There's no place here
   Where the sole of my foot may rest,
I'll take my flight for the hemisphere
   That lieth away in the west,

Where the setting sun mirrors his blazing front
   On a people true and brave,
As the courser's foot in the forest hunt,
   On Oceans' restless wave,

When he throweth the glare of his burn-eye
   On a nation bold and free,
And looketh down from his home in the skies,
   On a land of liberty.

So with all these magnificent thoughts in his head,
    He landed at half-past nine
In a city not a thousand miles
    From "Mason & Dixon's line."

But the passing throng in the busy street
    Gave no heed to the stranger Truth,
Save some whiskered dandies he chanced to meet,
    Who said it was a pity forsooth,

That a vagrant like him should be strolling about
    Without the policeman's detection,
And declared in full terms that they thought that the lout
    Should be sent to the house of correction.

DONALD P. DULCHINOS

HYMN OF THE SOUL OF MAN
[*Dedicated to Louisa Burritt*]

We are not things of yesterday,
    Our souls' ancestral rivers run
From fountains of Antiquity
    That gushed ere God lit up the sun;
Across the solitudes of time,
    No more by mortal footsteps trod,
There the dead nations sleep sublime,
    Came whispers of our source in God.

The slumber of Humanity
    Is ever vexed by mighty dreams,
She smiles or shudders ceaselessly
    According as the vision seems;
For, ever mingling in her sleep
    Are glorious temples broken down,
And gulfs across whose awful deep
    She grasps at a primeval crown.

And here and there among the years,
    Some giant prophet lifts his hands,
And pours his burdens in her ears
    As Eurus sweeps the oceans sands;
Such was the voice that shook the world
    From out Academia's trees,
And such the lightning that was hurled
    From thy blind eyes, Maconides!

Unconscious prophets though they be,
    Seers meaning more than they have known
And dreaming not that Deity
    Was speaking through them from his throne,
Their words shall like the sea-waves roll,
    Their burning thoughts shall never die

Till beau awakes his sleeping soul
 To know its Immortality.

Arise to deeds of great intent
 Oh beau, and with thy valiant heads
Rear heaven high a monument
 Whose lands;
The glories of a noble strife
 Survive the pulses of endeavor,
The echoes of a mighty life
 Ring through Time's corridors forever!

DONALD P. DULCHINOS

A LA DAME A VOILE NOIRE
(To the Lady of the Night Wind)

As Night the rosy bosomed hills enfolding
Softens their tracery in his weird embrace,
So, more ethereal grew the matchless moulding
Of thy pure, earnest, spiritual face,
Most pensive maid,
Beneath the shade
Of that strange veil of melancholy lace.

Art thou an abbess gliding from the chancel
Where Eloisa poured her soul and prayed,
Unshrouded and revivified to cancel
Some debt of Christian charity unpaid
In years agone,
When the mid-night tone
Of Death's cold angel made thy heart afraid?

Perchance thou'rt but a type of Death's own essence,
Unearthly beauty whose dark borderings
Turn men's hearts chill with horror at his presence,
And make them slaves who timely shall be kings,
But if a heavenly gale
Lifts up the veil,
Straightway they're ravished with death's inner things.

Perhaps thou art a beautiful temptation,
Some mystic bodiment of deadly sin,
Like her who in the veil of consecration,
Mixed with the orisons of the Capuchin,
Him nightly wooing
To his undoing,
Till to his lost soul Satan entered in.

Thou art too beautiful—I'll look no longer
For be thou woman, fantasy, or sprite,
A spell is sinking over me that's stronger
Than silence in the watches of the night,
For good or evil,
From saint or devil,
I dare not lift my eyes to read aright.

THE POET'S LAST RESTING PLACE

He was not a saint on earth,
nor wished he in heaven a saint to be
He had lived & loved & lost; that's all,
and the joy which missed him seemed too dear.

But far from the world where the mountain grey
Heaven's wonder lies at the gates of Day
   oh there be my dreamless slumber;
there high on the peak of its hoary crest,
my spirit may mount to the mansions blest,
   No touch of the Earth to cumber.

Oh there with the clouds for my winding sheet
and the cast off world beneath my feet
   shall ye hear my house of quiet
Where forth from the breast of Heaven's black shroud
the thunder shall peal my requiem loud
   And the sweeping blast shall sigh it.

BENNY HAVENS

There was a jolly fellow, who lived about the town,
He disapproved of toddy, and so—he *put it down*;
He attended public dinners for fun and freedom's sake,
And like a second Polycarp went smiling to the *steak*.

His vests were irreproachable, his trowsers of the kind
Adown whose steep declivities hound rushes after hind;
They were a speaking pattern, all the tailors would agree,
But, O, alas! they were too *tight* to speak coherently.

Up half a dozen pairs of stairs our hero went to bed
With nothing but the angels and the rafters o'er his head,
And so although he loved to be when brandy vapor curled
There never was a man who lived *so much above the world.*

No board of all the roof was known a meeting e'er to hold
And so the room was nothing but a trap for catching cold
There was a door; the carpenter had left the lock behind
It must have slipped him as he had no *Locke* upon the mind.

No dome was there, no window stained with Peter and the keys,
But every winter brought a vast redundancy of *frieze*;
Each empty sash groaned dolefully, as if it felt the *pain*,
By some unearthly grammarye a-coming back again.

Well ceiled were the rooms below, though that's another *story*
But now our hero's fate was sealed and not his dormitory;
When midnight played upon his bones, airs far from operatic,
What wonder that an attic room should make a man rheumatic.

Our hero's uncle used to dye to keep himself alive
He kept a shop in Hempstead Row at number 35
But when as every dyer must he felt his colors fail
Before he kicked the bucket he turned *a little pale.*

He called his nephew to his side & with a mournful mien
Said "I feel blue to leave you (You musn't think it green)
I've not gained much by dying but I leave you all my pelf
It may assist you, if you ever want to dye yourself."

His spirit fled and left the youth to woe and rolling collars
As dolorous as any man who has a heap of dollars
But "oh" said he "let others dye, they're fool enough I trow
For though the colors may be fast, the trade is very slow."

I'll cut the man who cuts my hair & there the thing is plain
That I shall be, beyond a doubt, a lion in the mane;
I'll buy myself a pair of bays as early as I can
For I've often heard my uncle say that life is but a *span*.

But, oh! How vain to try to change the color of his days,
For he could not conceal himself behind his screen of *bays*;
No yarn, of all that he might spin, could hide his uncle's line,
For that worthy was not one of those who dye and give no sign.

And many who had been his uncle's customers of yore
Thought perchance the youth was not behind what he had been before
Daily stopped his gay barouche to promise patronage enough
And thought their fancy fabricated when he muttered "Stuff!"

His dandy friends grew fewer, and, alas! he found between
Their *leaving* and their *falling off*, no summer intervene;
His heart was broken, and at last this fanciest of blades,
Who used to flare in scarlet vests, preferred the *darker shades*.

One morning from a frowning cliff he jumped into the sea,
Crying, "oh! Thou mighty dying vat, behold I come to thee,"
You think him green, and as to that I really cannot tell,
But if he is, it is the kind they call invisible.

DONALD P. DULCHINOS

A LETTER IN VERSE
Union Alumni Monthly, June 1930

When, the last time, the day-god sees
The Earth fanned by the evening breeze,
And glides behind the purple hills
To bathe him in celestial rills;

Who has not felt a sudden dread
As if the gorgeous sun were dead,
A momentary thrill of fear
To see him on his sunset bier?

At such a time, the heart may say,
"What if no more returns the day,
"What if no more upon the earth
"These golden glories shall have birth?"

But the fair sun in his declining
Gives promise of another shining,
And bids the shadows' phantom fingers
Point from the west where still he lingers

Towards the east in prophesy
That there he shall remount the sky;
And every tree and every hill
Obey the summons of his will;

And hoary shadows indicate
His portal of returning state,
Thus, though I mourn the days gone by,
I sigh not with a hopeless sigh.

These thrice delightful College hours
Shall live again by memory's powers;
And when footsore beside the way
I sit me down, too weak to stray,

Dear Henry, will they memory be
Like way side flowers unto me.
Our friendship's sun can never set—
My heart knows not the word "Forget!"

Most affectionately your brother,
    Fitz Hugh Ludlow, K.A.

DONALD P. DULCHINOS

TERRACE SONG

Ye Union boys whose pipes are lit come forth in merry throng,
Upon the terrace let us sit and cheer our hearts with song.
Old Prex may have his easy chair the Czar may have his throne,
Their cushions may get worse for wear but not our seat of stone!

Thou grand old seat of stone, thou jolly old seat of stone;
then here's to thee right merrily thou grand old seat of stone.

Twas here the old alumni sat in the balmy nights of yore,
and many a voice was joined in chat whose music rings no more,
From many a lip the spirals curled and when they rolled away,
the smoker went into the world and came no more for ay!

Thou grand old seat of stone, thou jolly old seat of stone;
the changing year still finds thee here thou grand old seat of stone.

When Captain Jackson sees his plants in bloom a few times more,
Some boys who sport out altered pants will knock at Union's door;
And the Tutes have let them in, Old Terrace, thou shalt see
Them sitting where their dads have been, and singing over thee.

Thou grand old seat of stone, thou jolly old seat of stone;
To thee shall be our legacy, thou grand old seat of stone.

And when we all shall have our "dips" in shining sheets of tin,
Let no one with irreverent lips against thee dare to sin.
A cobbler's bench, a Congress seat, may rest our trotters yet,
But thou, Old Terrace, can't be beat, by any we shall get.

Thou gay old seat of stone, thou jolly old seat of stone;
May smoke and song float o'er thee long, thou grand old seat of stone.

ODE TO UNION

Let the Grecian dream of his sacred stream
and sing of the brave adorning
that Phoebus weaves from his laurel leaves
at the golden gates of morning
But the brook that bounds
through old Union's grounds
gleams bright as the Delphic waters
And a prize as fair as a god may wear
is a "dip" from our alma mater.

Then here's to thee the brave and free old Union smiling o'er us
And for many a day,
as thy walls grow gray,
may they ring with thy children's chorus

Could our praises throng on the waves of song,
Like an Orient fleet, gem-bringing,
We would bear to these the argosy,
And crown thee with pearls of singing;
but thy smile beams down beneath a crown,
whose glory asks no other,
We gather it not from the green sea-grot—
'Tis the love we bear our Mother!

Chorus

Let the joy that falls from thy dear old walls,
Unchanged brave times on-darting,
And our only tear falls once a year
On hands that clasp ere parting;
And when other throngs shall sing thy songs,
And their spell once more hath bound us,
Our faded hours shall revive their flowers,
And the past shall live around us.

Chorus

DONALD P. DULCHINOS

POEM INSCRIBED TO MARY ROOSEVELT
IN A COPY OF HAWTHORNE'S *HOUSE OF THE*
SEVEN GABLES

When the drop-light with its gas sheds
cheer on parlor tables
Till they shine like polished glass
Have I seen the dark-eaved House of the Seven Gables
With her cheek upon her hand
Shadowed from the marble gleams,
Drawn through Hawthornes's mystic land

The young girl seemed half-reading, half in dreams.
The Old Man heard again The stories of his father
Conversations with the men
Who burned witches & drawled psalms with Cotton Mather

The mother dropped a stitch,
From her lap fell down her knitting,
As she burned the page on which
The ruffled ghosts of Pyncheon House were flitting.

The boy pored on dissembling
The fear with which he read.
And then lay all night trembling
While cold fingers plucked the quilt about his head.

And perhaps you are too young
To read of ghostly trial
For the sun of life hath flung
But very little shadow on your dial

Yet take this witchly present
And in reading it remember (Not only on the present
Twenty-fifth day of the chilly month December,
But until Time shall end)

Him, who, little young Miss Mary
Will ever be your friend
Though like the Pyncheons' fortune his may vary.
I've sung my jingle & got to the end
And just left room for the name of your friend

Fitz Hugh Ludlow K A Watertown, N.Y. Dec. 25, 1856

CONTEST IN TRANSLATION
ON THE LETTERHEAD OF THE CUSTOM HOUSE,
NEW YORK, CA. 1862

Italian 1.
Dall uno del mio cuore
   Lorse mia sol prece
Che l'idol mio ammiuri
   Che io l'ammiori, e muoria

    Aldrich 1.
    Out from the depths of my heart
       Has arisen this single cry
    Let me behold my beloved
       Let me behold her & die

    Ludlow 1.
    From the bottom of my heart
       There broke one single cry
    Let me look on my idol
       Look on him & die!

Italian 2.
Alfin, com'alma peccatrice
   Alle porte del ciel io giungo
Nonper entrar cogli eletti
   O! Friammai...soltanto per mouor!

    Aldrich 1.
    At last, like a sinful soul
       At the portals of Heaven & lie
    Never to walk with the blest
       Ah never! Only to die.

    Ludlow 2.
    Then I come to the gates of heaven

A soul all sinful & lonely
Not with the Elect to enter
Ah never! to die! to die only!

I WILL NOT WISH THY LIFE A TINTED BUBBLE

I will not wish thy life a tinted bubble
Floating forever on an unvexed sea
I will not prophesy thee skies whose trouble
Like sun-smit morning clouds shall quickly flee;

Life hath great triumphs in its darkest seasons
For him who bids black heavens shed rains of peace
And he who bears the facts & waits the reasons
Finds dew upon his solitary fleece.

Oh be it thine through life's still varying tissue
To see God's presence like a golden strand
Brighten it ever till the web shall issue
Out of the loom into the Weaver's hand;

May God in kindness grant thee little sorrow
But be earth's changeful seasons what they may,
Look through the gates of the Eternal Morrow
For there awaits thee an unclouded day.

ABEST: SURREXIT
T.S.K.
[Published in Tribute Volume *In Memoriam. Thomas Starr King*, 1864]

I.

OH! vailéd are the clearest eyes
    That ever saw through thrice-vailed Wrong;
The bravest arm unlifted lies,'
    That saved the fainting from the strong.

The purest heart on earth is still—
    No music thrills in our embrace—
God touched the organ, said: "I WILL,
    These stops sound in a larger place."

And we who scarce can see through tears,
    Carve on the arch he would not wait
From heaven to see: "Stand, tell the years
    We lost him—but he saved the State."

II.

A Man who was the whole he seemed;
    And over seeming had excess
Of every gift which could be deemed
    A crown to perfect manliness.

A Brother in whose proffered hand
    Went a whole heart uncalled again;
And yet the lowliest in the land
    Felt it reach to them through their pain.

A wise good Counselor, who wrought
    His hardest counsel: sacrifice
Of Self for Manhood; this he taught,
    Nor of his own life kept the price.

A flame-touched Poet; one who talked
    Of mountains with a speech so rare,
We said in whispers: "He hath walked
    God's mount, and breathed immortal air."

Prophet of God's full triumph; sealed
    Of God upon his forehead pure,
With Sorrow's grateful kisses—yield
    The inmost heavens no seal so sure!

A Noble Soul! a living well
    That knew nor drought, nor ice, nor wall;
Whose healthful waters leapt and fell
    Broadly and brightly over all.

A King indeed! but one who kept
    His people's pleader next the throne;
Nor while the meanest suitor wept,
    Had room for causes of his own.

Who were his people? Ask the Tent,
    The Field, the Hospital—for he
Not only blew "To arms!" but sent
    After the blast his largess free.

Who were his people? Ask the slave
    Now standing up in manhood's day;
Or him who once beside the grave
    Of Asian fathers knelt to pray.

For in the market-place he stood,
    Where Gold was Truth and Self was God,
And cried: "'Love Manhood! God is good!
    Unloose the shackle! break the rod!"

Nor cried he all in vain; for though
   Still toils uncitizened Cathay,
Afric hath broke her bolts; and lo!
   That great pure soul hath half his way.

III.

Hath half! Hath all! for in the light
   Where he hath climbed men wait no more;
But ever through God's open door
   See the full triumph of the Right.

To us the times look evil-starred;
   To him, one glory lights all Time;
Might joins with Right in marriage chime,
   The Holiest Holy is unbarred.

The slow, sad file of suffering Years
   Hath reached its goal. One radiant Now
With its great halo rings his brow
   Unwet by any mist of tears.

The Days have all come home. No more
   Time's poorest prodigal shall say,
"Alas! I am a dreary Day!"
   Not e'en the day when he past o'er.

For each hath laid its burden down
   Before the shining feet of God,
And every weight that seemed a clod
   Turns out a diamond for His crown.

Our brother knew this ere he passed;
   But oh! to see such things as these,
Walking beside the crystal seas
   With him, in vision that shall last!

To sit where he sits—in the throng
    Whom earth's mixed noises vex no more—
Who hear no inarticulate roar
    Confuse God's coronation-song.

To feel what he feels, when the Lyre
    Of his great soul which used to sing
So sweet to our poor fingering,
    Thrills at God's hand of love and fire!

I've lie in darkness at the door
    Which closing caught him out of sight,
And his vast music through the night
    Falls faintly on our stony floor.

IV.

Leaving our Orient Sun he sought its setting,
    Knowing its glory but as Duty's lamp;
Foregoing our embrace but not forgetting,
    In God's far soldier-camp.

He took our best part with him. Times nor places
    For our great love held sentence of divorce;
Our spirits followed like upsurging faces,
    His vessel's foamy course.

He went that God might have a tabernacle
    Between the snow-cliffs and the Western sea,
Where Truth should break divine from grate and shackle,
    And Love's dear voice speak free.

Out of his very heart the fane he builded;
    Himself he laid in each firm shapely stone;
But the glad sun whereby its roof is gilded,
    O God! sees us alone.

No more this threshold greets his coming over;
    Not in this pulpit shall he plead God's cause;
He shall not call on Man's Almighty Lover
    In this great organ's pause.

Not to the earthly throng that gathered round him
    His voice shall ring from carven beam and truss;
God's vergers writing in his closet found him,
    And said: "Come, speak to us!"

We, seeing through a glass, send all our praying
    Back through that glass again; and when we preach,
Before our faces is a veil, delaying
    Still more our stammering speech.

Straightforth his speech for ever! Unencumbered
    By tears, sick dimness, or Man's party walls,
The blessed light through days no night hath numbered,
    On his rapt vision falls!

We hear the word in fragile temples lifted
    With long delay and weary forehead-sweat;
God's breath of hope blows faintly on us, sifted
    Through curtains of regret.

But he hath crossed the sill, and reached the chancel,
    Of the great Temple without hands upbuilt,
Where the first words the Master utters cancel
    All human woe and guilt.

Sing out, thou Organ, o'er our saddest sighing!
    Sun! light our wet eyes through the tinted panes;
Ye who cry after him, hear him replying:
    "Come up, your rest remains!"

V.

He sings above—we mourn below;
　Our tired feet run to and fro;
We miss him everywhere we go—
　This is absence—this is woe.

The whole day long in house and street,
　We feel between us when we meet,
Something lost—yet something sweet.
　Never more return his feet.

When we close our eyelids wary,
　From one grave Sleep doth not vary,
But sits there strewing rosemary,
　Nor to break the silence dare he.

Now we wake, for he doth call:
　"I am not beneath the pall!
Good must be the goal of all;
　How then shall your faint hands fall!"

Brethren, join those hands, for we.
　His executors must be—
Many for one such as he;
　Poor, but oh ! how willingly.

Let our linked hearts beat to make
　Music with old chains that break—
Music for all hearts that ache—
　Birthday music for his sake!

He is born! We only lie
　Till the birth-time draweth nigh;
Waiting our delivery—
　Quick, yet waiting patiently!

DONALD P. DULCHINOS

TOO LATE
"AH! SI LA JEUNESSE SAVAIT—SI LA VIEILLESSE POUVAIT!"

There sat an old man on a rock
    And unceasing bewailed him of Fate—
That concern where we all must take stock
    Though our vote has no hearing nor weight;
        And the old man sang him an old, old song—
        Never sang voice so clear and strong
        That it could drown the old man's long,
            For he sang the song "Too late! Too late!"

"When we want, we have for our pains
    The promise that if we but wait
Till the want has burned out of our brains
    Every means shall be present to sate;
        While we send for the napkin the soup gets cold,
        While the bonnet is trimming the face grows old,
        When we've matched our buttons the pattern is sold,
            And everything comes too late—too late!

"When strawberries seemed like red heavens—
    Terrapin stew a wild dream—
When my brain was at sixes and sevens
    If my mother had 'folks' and ice-cream,
        Then I gazed with a lickerish hunger
        At the restaurant man and fruit-monger—
        But oh! how I wished I were younger
            When the goodies all came in a stream—in a stream!

"I've a splendid blood horse, and a liver
    That it jars into torture to trot;
my row-boat's the gem of the river—
    Gout makes every knuckle a knot!
        I can buy boundless credits on Paris and Rome,
        But no palate for menus—no eyes for a dome—

Those belonged to the youth who must tarry at home
When no home but an attic he'd got—he'd got.

"How I longed in that lonest of garrets,
Where the tiles baked my brains all July,
For ground to grow two pecks of carrots,
Two pigs of my own in a sty,
A rose-bush—a little thatched cottage—
Two spoons—love—a basin of pottage:
Now in freestone I sit—and my dotage—
With a woman's chair empty close by—close by!

Ah! now, though I sit on a rock,
I have shared one seat with the Great;
I have sat, knowing naught of the clock,
On Love's high throne of state;
But the lips that kissed and the arms that caressed
To a mouth grown stern with delay were pressed,
And circled a breast that their clasp had blessed
Had they only not come too late! too late!"

DONALD P. DULCHINOS

TO FLORENCE, ON HER FIFTEENTH BIRTHDAY
"WITH A PAIR OF PRETTY ELASTIC GARTERS, MADE BY HANDS WHICH HAD DANDLED HER WHEN A BABY."

Fifteen years have come and gone
Since this world's extreme surprise
Broke upon the baby's eyes—
Since the little startled fawn
Ope'd those soft brown orbs to see
What this noisy earth could be!

Then she shut those orbs again,
And concluded to lie quiet—
Bustling world! She would not try it!
Great big women! Great big men!
They might run around and shout,
Only count the baby out!

So, for many a bleak spring day,
Many a soft long day of summer,
She—the family's latest comer—
On her mother's bosom lay,
While her little legs grew stout
With no use but kicking out.

This, the baby's chief enjoyment,
Was the only thing she knew
With those cunning legs to do—
Little guessing what employment
In the world for legs is ready-
For all sorts-both frail and steady!

But one day the baby peeping
From her muslin sanctuary,
Thought, "It don't look awful—very—
What if I should try it, creeping

On the carpet just a tiny
Way toward that spot so shiny?"

Sargent, in a rhyming novel,
Published lately, hath not spared
Words to laud "The Woman who Dared"
But in palace or in hovel
Where is daring, grand and steep,
Like the baby's earliest creep?

So, "the girl who dared" began,
On her soft, uncalloused knees,
An advance by slow degrees
Toward her unknown fellow-man—
(Dreaming nothing of a day
When he might approach that way!)

Creep, mouse, creep! A little longer
And the vigorous nature begs
For still sturdier use of legs
As those rosy pins grow stronger.
Joy o'erbrims the mother's cup—
Look! The baby's standing up!

Now—as if while we are talking—
(Ah! Time's legs than ours are faster!)—
She has learned without a master
That neglected Fine Art-walking!
See how proud she draws her breath
Of what bores as half to death!

Not for her the stage—the car—
Her whom only resting tires—
She such help as this desires
No more than a glancing star:
Only stars exalt, and suns,
Like the baby when she runs!

The delicious topmost sparkle
Of Life's goblet she is tasting;
Naught she knows of spilling—wasting—
Not a speck i' the nectar darkles—
Only we, who've reached the dregs—
Grown up people—lose our legs!

Years and years as she grows taller
Are those legs her pride and joy!
Difference 'twixt girl and boy
Ne'er to think on did befall her:
Run she! Jumps she Father Time
Growls not yet "'Tis rude to climb!"

Halcyon morning! All too fleet
Noontide comes and binds her tresses,
Whispering, as she dons long dresses,
"Ladies, dear, have only feet,
And Propriety's utmost rim's
Reached when you lay claim to limbs."

Never mind my sweetest Florry,
Though your walk grows more demure
There is too much grief to cure;
This old world's too sick and sorry,
For your sunlight to stop glancing
Where a heart can be set dancing!

Legs or limbs—whate'er we style them—
They shall bear you here and there,
Gladdening the eyes of Care
With a love that shall beguile them
Of their tears, and make yourself
Glad as when a baby elf.

All you know of use for members
Then by you unnamed at all

Was to kick them, plump and small,
out, as your mamma remembers,
At the world where now you fling
Sunshine from your fifteenth spring.

So—to gird them for their duty,
And to bear their mistress round,
Or to stand a sturdier ground
Where Truth bids them stand, or
Beauty—I these circlets bring. Ye martyrs
Of propriety—yes, they're garters!

Love is free, I know, but you
will not grudge it though they bind you,
For I give them to remind you,
By their soft, elastic blue,
How my love goes every where
With you, like them and the air.

DONALD P. DULCHINOS

TO M.S., WITH THANKS FOR A PAPER KNIFE

Immemorial law of the Muses,
 Decrees that bards may pay
For all they get by playing
 And singing the debt away;

And so, as I look on our present,
 My thanks break forth in verse—
I pray you, take them kindly,
 Be they better or worse!

To the eye of the shallow proser,
 This seems but a paper-knife;
But look with me, and behold it
 A symbol of human life.

How skillfully was it fashioned
 From rainbowed mother-of-pearl!
Its handle how cunningly carven
 In delicate twist and curl!

The hand of a ready workman
 Hath shapen its blade so well,
That we might believe it grew so
 In its primitive sheath of shell.

Its lovingly-burnished surface
 Flashes with changeable sheen,
Like the amaranth dawn of an *alga*
 Through a sea-pool's opaline.

And, where the handle is wedded
 To the curve of the keener part,
It is clasped by a circlet golden,
 From the great mid-montain's heart.

Thus, e'en as a thing of matter,
    What stories it hath to tell
Of the deep earth's unlocked treasure,
    The old sea's briny well!

Yet hark! for its inner spirit
    Discourseth in lower tone,
Lessons of graver meaning,
    That the thoughtful may hear alone.

The union of soul and body
    Is a cunningly-shapen knife,
Daily cutting the pages
    Of the mystical Book of Life.

With well-spun nerve and sinew,
    The body is twisted and curled,
Compactly and roundly fitted
    To bear the weight of the world.

The spirit is bright with lusters
    Of infinite changeableness,
And in lingering rainbows forever
    Her origin doth confess.

And, where body meets with spirit,
    The band of their union seems
To shine with a golden strangeness
    That comes from the mine of dreams.

It is in such suggestions
    That our frame, like the knife, is meant
To have a significance deeper
    Than a mere dumb instrument.

And our gift shall never grow older,
   For there dwelleth an undimmed youth
In every thing daily hallowed
   By teaching an inner truth.

So take my thanks for the token,
   And, when we cut earth's last page,
May we open a book that shall never
   Be spotted by tears or age!

In a manuscript book, M.S. is identified: "To Miss Mary Sessions on her presenting me with the present of a paper knife on New Years day 1867."

INSCRIBED TO SARAH BADGER OWEN
[in a box with some other little remembrances to her & Harriet's
family from us here]

Where the dreary winds complain
　　Round the wild inclement shore
When the sheer bleak rocks of Maine
　　With the cruel frost are hoar;

When the dreadful sky compels
　　Every living soul to fly,
And the tale the weather tells
　　Is 'Get in doors or die!'

Then, dear Mother, trim your lamp,
　　Wipe your glasses, put them on,
And bid every care decamp
　　While this little book you con,

Not a great book, but a pleasant,
　　As my mother will discover—
of no value as a present
　　Save as showing that I love her

DONALD P. DULCHINOS

HYMN OF FOREBEARANCE
[*Dedicated to my Father*]

O living were a bitter thing,
    A riddle without reasons,
If each sat lonely gathering
    Within his own heart's narrow ring
The hopes and fears encumbering
    The flight of earthly seasons.

Thank God that in Life's little day,
    Between our dawn and setting,
We have kind deeds to give away,
    Sad hearts for which our own may pray
And strength when we are wronged to stay,
    Forgiving and forgetting.

Thank God for other feet that be
    By ours in Life's wayfaring—
For blessed Christian charity,
    Believing good she cannot see,
Suffering her friends' infirmity,
    Enduring and forbearing.

We all are travellers, who throng
    A thorny road together,
And if some pilgrim not so strong
    As I, but foot-sore, does me wrong,
I'll make excuse, the road is long,
    And stormy is the weather.

What comfort will it yield the day
    Whose light shall find us dying,
To know that once we had our way
    Against a child of weaker clay,
And bought our triumph in the fray,
    With purchase of his sighing?

Oh, who, when Life to many souls
   So little hath to cheer it,
Will cover up his kindly coals
   In ashes, hoard the slender doles
Which to the shipwrecked on Earth's shoals
   Might still so much endear it?

Most like our Lord are they who hear,
   Like him, long with the sinning;
The music of long suffering prayer
   Brings angels down God's golden stair,
Like those through Olivet's darkened air,
   Who saw our life beginning.

DONALD P. DULCHINOS

THE SCHOOL

Little girl, where do you go to school,
　　And when do you go, little girl?
Over the grass from dawn till dark
　　Your feet are in a whirl;
You and the cat jump here and there,
　　You and the robins sing,
But what do you know in the spelling-book,
　　Have you ever *learned* anything?

Thus the little girl answered—
　　Only stopping to cling
To my finger a minute,
　　As a bird on the wing
Catches a twig of sumac,
　　And stops to twitter and swing,—

When the daisies eyes are a-twinkle,
　　With happy tears of dew,
The swallows waken in the eaves,
　　And the lamb bleats to the ewe;
When the lawns are golden-barred
　　And the kiss of the wind is cool,
And morning's breath blows out the stars—
　　Then do I go to school.

My school-roof is the dappled sky,
　　And the bells that ring for me there
Are all the voices of morning
　　Afloat in the dewy air;
King Nature is the madam
　　And the book whereout I spell
Is dog's eared at the brooks and glens
　　Where I know the lesson well.

Thus the little girl answered
   In her musical out-door tone,
She was up to my pocket,
   I was a man full-grown;
But the next time that she goes to school
   She will not be alone

DONALD P. DULCHINOS

TO THE HOME OF ALL THE LIVING

Garden of the quiet dead,
　　Seed-ground of Eternity,
Many a weary heart and head
　　Longs for silence and for thee.
Here shall sorrow's hand no more
　　Sweep the soul's discordant strings;
And the lyre that oft before
　　Thrilled to love's young carolings,
Voiceless lies from morn till even';
　　But it shall be woke in Heaven.

Island art thou of the Blest,
　　In life's ever-heaving sea;
Here earth's weary ones may rest
　　From the billows' mockery.
Rage ye winds that vex the sky.
　　Chilling summer into death;
But where those sweet sleepers lie
　　Hush your voices to a breath:
Kiss the roses till they yield
　　Perfume from the stilly field.

Heaven's entrance-way thou art
　　From beggar's hut and chair of state;
The throbbings of the dying heart
　　Are only knockings at thy gate.
Other homes may scorn to yield
　　Shelter from the bitter rain,
At thy doors O burial-field,
　　Pilgrim never knocked in vain.
On thy breast we yet may fall,
　　Earth, thou mother of us all!

Lulled to sleep in thine embrace
   Many a weary babe shall lie,
And the chief whose visored face
   Blanched not at the battle-cry.
Here no more the bride shall dream
   Of the rose less fair than she.
And olive-shaded academe
   Shall fade from Plato's memory.
O mysterious place of rest
   Take thy children to thy breast.

NIAGARA

Niagara! I am not one who seeks
   To lift his voice above thine awful hymn;
Mine be it to keep silence where God speaks,
   Nor with my praise to make his glory dim.

Yet unto thee, shape of the stony brow,
   Standing forever in thine unshared place,
The human soul within me yearneth now,
   And I would lay my head beside thy face.

King, from dim ages of God set apart
   To bear the weight of a tremendous crown,
And feel the robes that wrap thy lonely heart
   Deaden its pulses as their folds flow down;

What sublime years are written on the scroll
   Of thine imperial, dread inheritance,
Man shall not read until its lines unroll
   In the great hand that set thy stony trance.

Perchance thy moveless adamantine look
   For its long watch o'er the abyss was bent
Ere the thick gates of primal darkness shook,
   And light broke in upon thy battlement.

And when that sudden glory lit thy crown,
   And God lent thee a rainbow from His throne,
E'en through thy stony breast flashed there not down
   Somewhat of His joy also made thine own?

Who knoweth but He gave thee to rejoice
   Till man's hymn sounded through the time to be,
And when our choral coming hushed thy voice,
   Still left thee something of humanity?

Still seemest thou a priest—still the veil streams
   Before thy reverent eyes, and hides His light,
And thine is as the face of one who dreams
   Of a great glory now no more his right.

Soon shall I pass away; the mighty psalm
   Of thine o'ershadowing waters shall be heard
In memory only; but thy speechless calm
   Hath lessons for me more than many a word,

Teaching the glory of the soul that bears
   Great floods, a veil between him and the sun,
And, standing in the might of Patience dares
   To bide His finishing who hath begun.

THE POETRY OF FITZ HUGH LUDLOW

PART TWO
FROM A NOTEBOOK DONATED TO UNION
COLLEGE BY HELEN LUDLOW

Copies of the Poems and some other writings by my dear brother—
Fitz Hugh Ludlow
And a list taken from his own lips of all his works

Peldi's
The Happy Country
where
A little Brother and sister
lived and played
for
Ten charmed and charming
Years.

by
The Little Brother Grown Up
and known now
as
Fitz Hugh Ludlow

DEDICATION

To the little brown head just up to my shoulder,
The believing blue eyes that never grew older
Little ears that hid in my breast from the thunder.
Little mouth all atremble from terror and wonder.
To the dear little hand in mine clasped securely
While we trod the Child Land where God's light shines so purely;
To the innocent smile and the low mellow ringing
of the laugh that was like happy wood robins' singing;
To the tears that came springing as instantly after
If a sudden boy-grief in my eyes drowned the laughter;
To a heart like the opposite end of a viol
Holding strings stretched from mine and never yearning denial
To a touch that thrilled mine with delight or with trial—
To my sunshine's down shiniest dearest playmate still granted
To come with me not of the kingdom enchanted
By piteous heavens permitted to stay
When the rosy dawn died, and the cold yellow day
With a breath swept the temples and gardens away—
To her whose dear voice I still hear at my side
A sweet murmuring shell left by childhood's ebb tide
That said, "Cheer him with echoes of me! When it kissed her
the last time it sighed up our shores—to my sister
So lovingly little book! Ask her to be
My memory's companion, as she was of me.

DONALD P. DULCHINOS

OVER HIS HEAD THE DAISIES SWIM

Over his head the daisies swim
   In wind—swept eddies of sea—green grass
He hath rest in every limb,
   Nothing can come to pass
Which hath aught in it for him
   To weary or harass.

He was not a saint on earth
   Nor wished he in heaven a saint to be
If a single chair at the father's hearth
   Must go empty for all eternity
"I have been a friend to want and dearth
   without them I will not be saved!" said he.

He had lived and loved and lost; that's all—
   And the joy which missed him seemed so dear
That he could not believe it was under the call
   And the angels say, "He hath found it here."
To the depths of the night he heard them call
   His soul to its Golden Year.

THE POET'S LAST RESTING PLACE

Oh bury me not in the dark blue sea,
Where the moan of the deep my dirge shall be
    And the surge shall be my willow;
Here I gather my limbs for my last long rest,
And lay me not down on the beach's breast,
    With the wave for my hearings pillow.

Lay me not in the house of the dead to sleep,
Where the bat and the owlet their orgies keep,
    And the funeral wove strands o'er me;
Where the pompous marble uprears its head,
And the foot of the passer awakes the dead
    Who have gone to their rest before me.

Oh let me not lie in the forest dark
Where my grave is lit by the glow-worm's spark
    And the cypress boughs o'erlook me;
Where the birds of the night shall scream and wail,
And the leaves of Autumn sure and pale
    Shall whirl in the blasts that rock me.

Oh lay not my head in the grassy hill,
Where the streamlet murmurs on stone and will
    A hush to my quiet sleeping;
And the dew shall fall on my calm cold face.
As nightly it comes to my resting place,
    Its pearls for the poet weeping.

But far from the world where the mountains grey
Heaven's wonder sits at the gates of Day,
    Oh there be my dreamless slumber;
There high on the peak of its hoary crest,
My spirit may amount to the mountains blest,
    The heart of the Earth to cumber.

DONALD P. DULCHINOS

Oh there with the clouds for my winding sheet
And the cast off world beneath my feet
   Shall ye hear my house of quiet,
Where forth from the breast of heaven's black shroud
The thunder shall peel my requiem loud
   And the sweeping blast shall sigh it.

THE DREAMER

Your light is not the Life of thought
Ghosts unwelcome and unsought
      I call Day's defenceless walls,
But when Orion glows in Heaven
Forth the intruder hosts are driven
      And night's portcullis falls.

Through evening's haste and midnight's clamp,
The room lit by Lucretia's lamp
      Has playing ceaselessly;
And thus amid memory's withered leaves
By night my fancy sits and weaves
      mysterious tapestry.

When land and real things depart
With daylight from the aching heart
      How sweet it is to dream!
To breathe with hopes that may not be
The stern cold frost of Destiny
      And stop grief's headlong stream

While midnight's misty moments pass,
As moon beams flit upon the grass
      Or tresses of a maiden;
They scatter on my dreaming eyes
Flowers that glow like sunset skies
      Flowers that breathe of Aidenn.

Oh visionary happiness,
How oft thy weird sweet airiness
      Thy dearest heart hath moved!
From dew-dipped wand of ebony,
Night flung her spell upon the sea,
      I dreamed that I was loved!

Hell might that moment cancel years
When a hot heart dried up the tears
  That sorrow groaned to weep;
I loved—and hope returning, came
Fanning those embers to a flame
  So bright I could not sleep.

Waking I knew I was alone;
No heart throbbed answering to my own
  But in the noiseless night,
I learned a greater grief than Death
As hope was borne upon the breath
  of sighing, from my sight.

Like murmurs of a prophet's tongue,
Or string or flute at random rung,
  Or Ocean's solemn shore.
A voice of matchless melody
For ever saying mournfully,
  Joy shall be thine no more.

EPIGRAM ON A YOUNG LADY WITH RED CURLS

All they curls are winding stairs,
Where my passion nobly dares
To mount higher still and higher
Though the staircase be on fire.

THE VOICES OF A DREARY SOUL

There is many a harp whose strings too early broken
    swing idly in the mind,
Touch them thou skillful hand, but thee, no token
    of days left for behind,
Comes at thy challenge from the waveless deep,
There the forgotten dead of music sleep.

There is a quiet voice which says "Forever,"
    When a star falls from heaven;
And to me know that Earth's quenched torches never
    again light up the even
But when a man is old their brands are shown
In black and heaps where he must die alone.

What is the fairest face that glows like morning?
    A skull with masking on!
Death strips the conquered Knight of his adorning,
    And lo—a skeleton!
The hope is dead that was thy Soul's young bride?
Reck not—though soon shall slumber at her side.

When these poor temporary tents are folden
    We are not shelterless.
Ours is a city out of sight and golden
    Wherein dwells righteousness;
And though our fallen stars rekindle never
We have a sun whose glowing is forever.

DONALD P. DULCHINOS

BATTLE SONG TO THE SOLDIER OF LIFE

Thou whose light is slowly waning
  With no heart to hold thine own,
Know the might of uncomplaining
  Stout endurance all alone!

Up! and be a slave no longer,
  Dare to speak the word "I can!"
Love is strong but souls are stronger
  And the giant will of man.

Up! and fight for day is fleeting,
  He who sleeps and shuns his part,
Lives but in the languid beating
  Of a dull and coward heart.

Though the soul's intensest yearning
  Lash thy bosom like a sea.
Godlike joy shall come in learning
  That thou hast the mastery.

Golden images of Beauty
Lure thee to the dreaming Past,
But though Death march on with Duty,
  Be thy soul's Iconoclast.

From the Heart's enshrining inches,
  From the pomp of gold and gem,
Hurl the statues, though the riches
  of a life go down with them.

Shapes impossible but cherished
  Mighty joys that cannot be
Perish all, as aye have perished
  Those which had reality.

Thus shalt thou lay down thine hammer
    wipe thy brow and rest in peace,
And the trumpet, din and clamor
    of embattled passions cease.

Though the deed that makes thee glorious
    Grim for thee thy burial mound.
E'en thy death shall be victorious,
    And thy head shall slumber crowned.

DONALD P. DULCHINOS

VALENTINE TO MISS FANCY B.

For the sake of the rhyme I'll say ding a ling ding,
And then will begin; it is a very good thing
To have a couple of beaux to your string,
    As well as the strings to your bow;
But according to me it is better by far
To have one good fellow, who sticks like tar
Or words in the throat of a youth at the bar
    Who is striking his maiden blow

Behold such a fellow Miss Fancy am I,
Ready at any moment to die,
(Although no practical dyer am I)
    In defense of Love and Beauty,
I'm an excellent chap to compound lobscouse
Know how long hams must be kept in gouse,
Can get breakfast or dinner as brisk as a mouse,
And "do tea" so that everyone in the house
    Will own I've fulfilled my *do-tea*.

And more I confess I do not care
For what people say a straw or a hair
And even all through the talkative dare
    To cry "*double* minded garcon,"
You have but a single word to say
And I won't be single another day
For our family are famed for having their way,
    And that's—the way to the Parson.

It isn't a very nice thing you may think
To be going without your "vittles and drink,"
Because you are standing upon the brink
    Of the madness which troubled Casso;
Such a heated state makes me apt to catch cold,
But I'd rather catch you and so I can grow bold.

Just over your precious young head to hold
    the matrimonial lasso;
The least little motion and you are mine
There! I've trapped you at last, my Valentine!

DONALD P. DULCHINOS

VALENTINE TO MISS LOUISA B.

Oh, never ever was there swain
In such a doleful case;
The briny tears that token pain
Are running down my face;
The great salt tears as huge as floods
Which whales might swim within;
I eat a cracker for my tea,
And I am growing thin.

The people say I'm getting lean,
And records me they bear,
Though, curious paradox I ween
I have no flesh *too spare*;
I little sleep, and often read
the paper upside down
I sign Louisa in the deed
Where should have been "John Brown"

I plainly see that like a clam
I'm getting in a stew;
How would a dive from off a dam
For divers' reasons do?
But in such vain attempts as that
They only lose their breath,
And it's too awful cold just now
To go and freeze to death.

The doctor says "you need a pill"
And he is a worthy *piller*
of the old therapeutic school
By Hunter Cooke and hiller;
My friends entreat me "Get a horse,"
And make a business steady
Of riding; but my groans have got
Me *hoarse* enough already.

My dear Louisa can you tell
a creature what's the matter?
I think that you perhaps may have
A finger in the batter;
Oh if you have extend it me,
And you shall have a ring.
To hours blest kind Valentine
And still my summoning.

VALENTINE TO JENNIE TAYLOR OF WASHINGTON, D.C.

Lovely little southern charmer
Roguish thief of Cupid's armor
Glance like dart from Cupid's quiver
Mouth like mouth of fairy river
Where the pearls began her tide
Seeking her for Ocean's bride
Sylphids art thou to be kissed
But by me and rosy mist

When nox the blackamoor hath hurled
Darkness over half the world;
(Not the Knox of Reformation
But a colored poor relation).
By the drowsy embers' spark
I sit musing in the dark.
Then thy form comes floating by
Like a thing of witchery!

Then the necromantic Real
Wakes me from my sweet ideal.
Giving reason's hair a twist
And I find thou still art *mist*;
But thy glance so soft and winning
Let's my love-sick brain a spinning;
Spin away, forbid that any
Stop thee. Oh my spinning Jenny!

Who so says thou art not fair
Let him my coup d'oeil beware,
Or he'll get another coup
That will cleave his vizor through;
Ask the Burritts and inquire
If I cannot *strike the liar,*

Should I hit him as I've stated
He nor his slur could be *repated*.

Loveliest of laughing girls,
On thy winding stair of curls
Higher mounts my love and higher
Driven by an inward fire
Ere this swollen heart shall burst
Let oh let me slake my thirst;
In the fountain of the lip
Give my torch of love a dip!

Through my head there runneth not
One sweet dreaming train of thought;
Trains like these must run on sleepers
And I never shut my peepers,
But all night beneath a willow
Groan and wet my grassy pillow,
Hailing loud as Bedford Whaler
Mend my heart, beloved Taylor.

DONALD P. DULCHINOS

TO LAURA N*****

'Tis not Apollo that I love,
This red and hissing wain
May wake the echoes far above
On Heaven's lovely gain;
But though his burning borders blast
The morning's early cool
I reck then not, but turn to bathe
My forehead in the pool.

I love the little stars that shine
When all the world's asleep,
And more than Ocean's wealth of brine
A drop that *you* may weep.
It is the little things of life
That make them sweet to hear
And you my darling Laura are
A little thing and fair.

A fair small wind-kissed chalice swings
Down in the deep old wood;
And the fairy peal the hare-bell rings
Does weary spirits good;
And you are a little and slender thing.
And your height is feet but five,
But Oh your voice is sweet as dreams,
As sure as I'm alive!

There are maidens like the Anakim
And their mien is stern and strong
And their voice is like a Cathedral hymn
Or a mighty dinner gong;
They may stand as stately as Poseidon
Where he frowns on the Grecian sea,
But a lass as tall as that is not
At all the lass for me.

When Cupid shoots from lips so high
He over aims his dart,
But a little woman's gentle sigh
Speaks very near my heart;
Hurrah for a little foot and hand,
And a smile whose witchery
Leaps up into my face like stars
Reflected from the sea!

I love to feel a little hand
Lie softly on my arm,
The Czar himself could not withstand
The spell of such a charm;
But while he felt the pressure soft
Of clinging loveliness,
Would surely grant with all his heart
The freedom of the *press*!

DONALD P. DULCHINOS

ODE TO NIGHT

Oh Lovely Mother Night,
   Thy breath is cool
And on my fevered brow
   I feel it now.
Like angel's hand dipped in Bethesda's pool.

Oh Lovely Mother Night,
   List to my lay;
Thy forehead is more bright
   With gems of light
Than all the splendors of the step-dance Day.

Not with the dust and din
   of feverish strife,
Dost thou, Oh Night draw near;
   Thy voice is dear
Because it whispers of a better life.

Oh Lovely Mother Night,
   Like tired sheep
Within they star watched fold
   The young and old,
The strong and weary shall lie down to sleep.

Wrapt in his senate robes,
   the sage shall dream;
The maiden shall forget
   The river let,
And Plato know no more of Academe.

And Oh how sweet and still
   that rest shall be,
Beneath the shadowy pall,
   that brood o'er all
Expanding into immortality.

[In *The Princeton Poets* anthology, the following verse was added; three other verses were dropped from the version above. *The Princeton Poets* carries no attribution for the poem.]

> The bride whose loved-culled wreath
> Withered anon,
>   More than the jasmine fair,
>   Shall slumber where
> The warrior lies dead with his harness on.

DONALD P. DULCHINOS

GLORY OF FAME
[Dedicated to F.H.L./possibly written by Helen Ludlow?]

In Life's ever hurried marches,
　　Passion going in the can
Leads us under broken arches,
　　Ruins of the hopes of man;

Once where rose the stately column
　　Sculptured fringe of architecture,
Silence reigns alone and solemn
　　O'er the nameless builders' grave.

Shaft of Pyramid external
　　Felt their evanescent art,
But they knew not what eternal
　　Monuments are in the Heart!

Sleep relayed the builders' fingers
　　'Ere the top-stone crowned their name,
And where Desolation lingers
　　Dreamed they in the arms of Fame.

Fame is Glory's shadow falling
　　On a whirlpool of the sea,
From whose waves are voices calling
　　Man to Glory's ecstasy.

Listen to their lying story
　　And thou art in Death's embrace;
Turn thy prow away and Glory
　　As thou goest bathes they face!

Where the trumpet ne'er hath sounded,
　　Where the nations look not on,
By us echoing peaks surrounded,
　　Though may'st win a Marathon!

Though shalt see a glory gleaming
    From the smitten shield of Fate,
Trust to God the outward seaming,
    Only to thyself be great.

He who bears with calm reliance
    tells he knows of God alone,
Throws the gauntlet of defiance
    In thy face Oblivion!

LORD LEVYNN'S LOVE

"The winds and I are all at ease
  "And the ancient clock hath rung
"His peal of twelve on the midnight breeze
  "From his heavy brazen tongue;
"The ghosts and I must walk bright
  "Although it be hand in hand.
"To me there was never a shape of fright
  "That came from the Shadowy Land!"

Thus spake the Lord of Levynn Park
  And the mist bedewed his beard.
And the roof of heaven was fearful dark
  But never the Knight had feared;
So he girt his broad-sword to his side
  And wandered to and fro,
Like the ebb and flow of a restless tide
  Or as midnight spirits go.

He had come from the wars of the Holy Grave,
  Where a sea of spearmen moved
His steel was true and his heart was brave
  But never the Knight had loved;
And now as he passed through the corridors
  By the millions old and dim,
In the castle vaults beneath the floors
  Lay all that had cared for him.

Tramp, tramp, as he strides along
  With a soul that is all unrest,
His heart's heavy pulses beat as strong
  As though they would burst his breast.
And he sharply feels though he knows not why
  And he never hath felt before;
How bitter it is for a man to die
  Alone on his native shore!

He hath been in the thickest of the fray
   When the Saracen's blood hath gushed
Like the Jordan's flood of a stormy day,
   Wherever his Legion rushed;
The suns of Judea leave burned his brow,
   While a hundred passions strove
For the mastery of his soul, but now
   He knows he hath banished love!

His armor clangs in his midnight march
   And he hears its sound alone,
But why does he gaze at yonder arch
   And its buttress of firm grey stone?
"Ha ha, it is not a ghost," cries he
   "But the moon hath cast a gleam
"Through a rent in her cloudy tapestry
   "Athwart yon carven beam.

But the something which he sees draws near,
   And it cannot be the moon,
Does he dream or is it a thing of fear
   That a word shall banish soon?
No moon, nor ghost nor dream is there,
   But a maiden those brow is cool,
With a halo around her golden hair
   And her presence is beautiful.

"Who art thou, lady of lovely mien
   "With thy eyes of grammarye
"And thy circled brow that speaks the queen,
   "I pray thee answer me?"
"Oh knight of the lurid levin crest
   "Of the spotless spear and shield
"I give thee a love that never the breast
   "of woman on earth may yield.

"Thou art walking the night of Life alone
   "As thou hast walked this night.
"I have come to claim thee for my own
   "Lord Levynn, thou art my night!
"No more shalt thou be ill at ease
   "Though the night-maids will not sleep,
"Ere morning aslant shines through the trees,
   "Thy peace with me shall be deep."

His helmet head is on her breast
   Her arms entwine him round,
And he seems to hear as he lies in rest
   Unearthly music sound;
And when the cool arch of the morning heaven
   Hears the reveille clarion,
The pages have found the Lord of Levynn
   Dead with the armor on.

TO MY SISTER ON HER 16TH BIRTHDAY

Sister the morning of thy birth
   Bids we look backward down the years,
To see thee welcomes by the Earth
   Into her many hopes and fears.

Thou wert a little helpless thing
   Brought trembling to the gates of life,
And then laid down unquestioning,
   Unstriving in the midst of strife.

How wert thou watered with our tears,
   Thou bud upon the household tree,
How many smiles for many years
   Shed sunshine on thee lovingly!

She is not here who gave thee birth,
   Her foot grew silent in thy spring,
But if the saints may look on earth
   She watches o'er thy blossoming.

He cannot speak who still are here
   How much our hearts loved thee yearn;
From Death the priceless valuer
   God grant that we may never learn.

He cannot blow away the damps
   That veil thy yet unkindled years,
May he who ligheth up their lamps
   Be better to our hopes than fears.

Much that we look on with delight
   Thy past hath its little arc,
We rest in faith—God weaves aright
   Thy full-orbed circle in the dark.

But if the great All-Father yields
   Room for our hopes around his deed,
Through all Earth's best and sunniest fields,
   Calm vales and heaven-watered weeds.

Forever may thy pathway run,
Until the light of better lands
Breathes on thee from a brighter sun
Where Godlike hopes fill head and hands.

VALENTINE TO M*** M*****
February 14th 1856

Love may be blind as poets say,
    But Oh what grief to me had come
If on the long awaited day
    We were not only blind but dumb!

Yet giving him a childish part
    The ancient rhymers do not err,
For when I try to speak my heart
    I find him but a stammerer.

But if my arms may ever twine
    Around thee on some blissful day
Then shall thy heart pressed close to mine
    Hear what its neighbor has to say.

Sweet Mary M***** when thy glance
    Shot for the first time through my eyes,
No castle of the old romance
    Was e'er so taken by surprise.

I thought my walls impregnable
    Until thine "open sesame"
Unbarred the long shut citadel
    And let thee in to conquer me.

Henceforth thou art the castle's queen,
    And therefore grant this simple prayer,
Thou, whose so long my heart has been,
    Of thy sweet will rest ever there!

I love thee Mary and no more
    has my heart to give thee;
Oh tell me darling I implore,
    Say, canst thou give as much to me?

A TWILIGHT DREAM

Since I was weary of the Day,
   And weary was the day of men,
So o'er the hills it crept away
   We gladly parted company.

The mingled voices of the town
   Like strains of a departing band,
Grew fainter till they trembled down
   Nor came again from slumber-land.

The twilight shadows made me dream
   That I was in the Past again,
Far up the waters of the stream
   That never may flow back for men.

Those arms that ne'er shall clasp me more
   Were known around me tenderly,
And I heard foot falls on the floor
   That may not come again to me.

But sadly did those arms unfold,
   And sadly passed those feet away,
And suddenly my heart grew cold
   Returning to the present day.

Then down I sat with moveless eye,
   Like a wrecked sailor on a rock,
Forever gazing fixedly
   To pierce the cold horizon's lock.

I saw red banners lifted high
   And smitten shields that rang again,
I heard the foot of Fate go by
   To beat the doors of other men;

The voice of all Humanity
   Was tremulous upon my ears,
I heard the sighing of the sea
   That swallows up the dying years.

But sights and voices slipped away
   From the cold channel-ways of sense
For the long shadow of a day
   Gone by, lay o'er me dark and dense.

As thus I sat there seemed to bleed
   With the fixed sadness of my dream,
A face so sweet that it might lead
   More brightness to the morning beam.

With foot more light than music's swell,
   A fair young girl before me stood,
Making the air grow palpable
   With light and love and womanhood.

The smile that lit her eyes of dear
   Fell on me through the mists of sleep.
Like a chance sunbeam shooting through
   The loophole of a ruined keep.

Her very beauty broke my dream,
   I woke and night was in the sky,
But through my heart there flowed a stream
   Of peace that never shall be dry.

For after many days of pain
   I learned at last the only balm
For those whose Past comes not again
   Is present love and trustful calm.

DONALD P. DULCHINOS

TO A YOUNG LADY,
POSSESSOR OF A ONE-EYED DOG

Poor hero with his widowed eye
   Is emblem of your love to me,
True love is blind entirely.
   But that you may the better see
What other nice young men there are,
   You keep one peeper open still,
And when my footsteps are afar
   You look around you at your will.

I want one all-consuming love
   To meet the rapturous flame of mine,
No love that waits for time to prove
   The root of my heart's passion-vine;
The only love that I can bear
   Is that which in abandonment
Finds all in me and naught elsewhere
   And knows not of the word "repent."

She who loves truly throws herself
   Like Sappho headlong to the seas,
Nor sits upon some rock's green shelf
   Dipping her feet in by degrees;
The maiden who is mine indeed
   Must find her world within my arms,
Nor want before she trusts to read
   My face for token of alarms.

If yours is love whose deepest lines
   Finds in my song fair portraiture,
Then by the Zodiacal signs
   My faith to you shall age endure;
Love shall reign empress over lore
   Within the palace of my heart,

Pindar shall be "pinned dar" no more,
   Nor I be drawn off by DeCartes.

No longer shall my lovely life
   Make people say in accents sad,
When asked "why don't he get a wife?"
   "Miss Odd-I-See, and Ill-I-Add,"
For learning bitterly is bought
   With weariness and loss of peace,
And Athens after all is naught
   On Earth except a spot of grease.

So while the twilight shadows lie
   Ere night hath tipped her ink stand o'er
On the fair pages of the sky,
   Steal down where we have met before,
And with your head upon my breast,
   And hands with mine in soft caress,
And lips that Love will not let rest,
   I'll tell you something "Can't you guess?"

DONALD P. DULCHINOS

SERVE GOD WITH THE BEST

God's bounties fill the hand of thrift,
   Yet we with garners stored
Forget the Giver in the gift,
   Nor well requite the Lord;
But we whose strivings he hath blest
Should serve him ever with the best.

When Plenty lets her golden seals
   Where Labor's hand hath been,
When the last harvest-burdened wheels
   Have brought their blessing in,
Let the first fruits of increase won
Be His who gave the rain and sun.

When Morn unlocks her rosy door
   Earth teems with stillness sweet.
Before her paths are printed o'er
   With hurrying humor feet
Give God this opening bud of time
And praise him in the morning's prime.

Give God they manhood's earliest part
   Nor yield him thanklessly
The last sad gleanings of a heart
   Reaped by his enemy;
Shall he behold thee grey in sin
Who dies in youth thy soul to him?

TO MY CLASSMATE E. PHELPS '56

Phelps, if thy life's forever deepening tide
Merge not in billows of the aftertime
Traits which were thrown upon it in thy prime,
Then shalt thou see still floating by thy side,
And keeping pace with thy swift winging sails,
Whichever way thy wave—rushed prow may tend,
The fervent wish of him who was thy friend;
Heaven forever give thee prosperous gales!
The wisher may be passed away but still
Remember that no eye would burn more bright
To see the fortune conquered by thy will
No heart thrill sooner with sincere delight,
Than his, who now so near our last farewell
Breathes this small tribute from his slender shell.

DONALD P. DULCHINOS

SONG WRITTEN FOR THE CONJOINT BIRTHDAY OCCASION OF MY LEAL AND LOVED BRETHREN IN THE BONDS OF KA, SID NORTON AND DAN MANN

[the former of whom became 21 on the 11th, the latter 22 on the 10th of Jan, 1856. We had supper at Slaters', on the night of the 10th and the morning of the 11th, in celebration of the occasion]

> Let the voice of song
> ring glad and long
> And the Stars smile on our meeting
>
> For right good cheer
> befits us here
> In our brotherly birthday greeting;
>
> And may all the sum
> of the years to come
> Be as warm with joy's bright ember,
>
> And as free from care
> to the much loved pair
> Whose birth our songs remember.

SONG WRITTEN FOR THE CONJOINT BIRTHDAY
OF PAT ROBB K.A., AND DAVE POTTER K.A.

[the former 21, the latter 20. The supper was held in my room
at 48 North College on the 17th of March 1856. *To the air of
"Crambambali"*]

All hail the stars whose friendly lustre
    This birthnight of our brethren cheers,
Each heart shall press its ruddiest clustre
    To crown the chalice of their years;

CHORUS   Then fill the bowl and troll the stave,
        Till Father Time is in his grave
        Heaven smile on Pat and Dave
        For aye, for aye.

When future days bring to perfection
    The wreaths that round their brows shall cling,
How fond shall be our recollection
    Of this, the promise of their spring.

Then let this might of choicest greeting
    Be bright with hope and glad with song,
Time has no spell in all his fleeting
    To change the hearts where Love is strong!

DONALD P. DULCHINOS

SONNET WRITTEN IN THE AUTOGRAPH BOOK OF MY BROTHER IN K.A. AND CLASSMATE SID NORTON

[Written March 22nd 1856.]

Sonnet

Like the low music of a wind harp, stealing
Through the mixed murmurs of a breezy noon,
Through sighing boughs, & shrill Cicada's croon,
Its spirit-presence to the soul revealing,
So, far in the time coming we shall hear
Melting through labor's hum and sorrow's moan,
And joy's flute symphonies, in undertone,
The memories of evening air engulphed years,
Noiseless down to the fountain place of tears,
Bridging the chasm of the deep Past all Care
Shall pass so Quiet o'er the viewless piers;
Dear Sidney, in those dreams of memory
How large a place will be bestowed on thee!

DEDICATION TO A BOOK OF POETICAL
EXTRACTS WRITTEN FOR CARRIE Y.

Little book whose spotless pages
      I am now the first to stain,
Chide we not that other ages
      Seem to follow in my train.

I am first to break thy blankness,
      Yet if I could only claim
Place with Earth's least bards, in frankness
      Would I feel I had my aim.

Let these verses be the portals
      Which shall open without din
For the glorious immortals
      of the past to enter in.

Of the Past and of the Present
      For time opes this silent door
To the Poet prince and peasant
      And they live forevermore.

Be thou book a rock rebounding
      Echoes of the Symphony
Which the soul hears ever sounding
      Out of thought's eternal sea.

Like a fountain's sweet unsealing
      Be the opening of thy leaves
Haters of repose revealing
      To the shaken heart that grieves.

In thy shadowy recesses,
      Let the soul that reads thee be
Lifted up from life's distresses,
      Rapt into sublimity.

Be thou a star-dimpled river
    Where the dreaming mind may float,
While the noiseless moonbeams quiver
    On her oarless fairy boat.

Be thy destiny forever
    To give lightness to the wings
Of endurance and endeavor,
    And the hope of better things.

To the over-shadowed spirit
    Pilgrim from the weary Past,
Who sits waiting to inherit
    Glories that shall come at last;

And to every wood discover
    Answers that shall make thee sweet
As the path where lady is lover
    Finds the footprints of her feet.

SONNET FOR THE AUTOGRAPH BOOK OF MY BROTHER IN K.A. PAT ROBB

Thank God, the farewell that I now endeavor
Sadly to speak to thee, the much endeared,
Rings not with echoes of the word "Forever,"
But when some kindlier gale our sky hath cleared,
From the dark clouds of parting, I may see
Not only thy bright mark upon the scroll
Which bears the name of every master soul,
But thy pure face as it was wont to be
In this our golden morning, More delight
Ne'er shed its ecstasy through pilgrims' tears
As after many weary storm-tossed years
His native hills again broke on his sight,
Than I shall feel, when on some blessed day
Again we meet, my brother in K.A.!

DONALD P. DULCHINOS

COMMENCEMENT POEM
UNION COLLEGE—1856

Not on the fiery breast of fight,
Down trampled in an army's flight;
Not where God's vengeful angel stood
O'er the plague smitten multitude;
Not in the thirsty caravan
Where man dies by his brother man,
Did he deliver up his breath
Who first stood face to face with Death
Oh 'tis an easy thing to die
When with the soul's departing sigh
There mingles through the ether wide
The throb of many a heart beside,
And sounds of pulsing spirit-wings
Blend with our own life's rending strings.
Oh who has not prayed fervently
That he might die when others die,
And shrunk with many a bitter groan
From trying the untried alone?
The terrors of that chartless sea
Fade when we voyage in company.
But not to him such boon was given
Who first among the sons of men
Felt Life's colossal columns riven
By pangs undreamed of until then;
Abruptly closed his path of years
Upon a precipice of fears
Whose dizzy wall sank glazed and steep
Into an unimagined deep,
And he beheld himself alone
The pioneer of the Unknown!
Horror unfathomed, undefined
Like a dark midnight atmosphere
Grew solid round his shaken mind

As neither to his intense ear
Came any pulses of a wing
The void beneath him unmoving
Nor quickened by extreme distress
His eye could sound the Visionless.
Pausing upon that dreadful brink
With thoughts which no man else may think,
He sat him down to gather strength
For the inevitable leap,
That leap of mystery and length,
With eyes that saw yet could not weep.
Though they beheld the sundering ties
Of life's most precious sanctities,
Silent the first of dying were
Late self-commencing; breaking then
From the chill bonds of his despair
He poured on the unechoing air
His strong, his last, his bitter prayer.
"My God, thou who of old hast been
the Everlasting, the Unseen,
All Powerful, All surrounding One,
Father to me of life begun,
Our mover of its vanished years,
See how impenetrable fears
Hang on the front of coming Time
(if aught of time to come there be)
And if the Past be all of me
Through what of horror shall I climb
Down to unknown obscurity,
Or shall I leap from Life's excess
At once to voiceless nothingness?
Oh leave me not unanswered, thou
Who hast upheld me until now!
I was, I am, Oh God from thee,
Tell me, is future life for me?"
He ceased, and silence as he stood

Seemed carven in his attitude,
The very air grew still and dense
As it were awed by his suspense,
For he whose eyes Death first made dark
Waited for God's immortal mark!
The sun in sinking glory stood
On the horizon's solitude,
And from his disk a cloud wind-driven
Past up into the deeps of heaven,
Leaving the splendors to beam down,
Unwanted from his burning crown.
Then on the watcher's silent soul
A voice like evening shadow stole:
"Like thee, the sun stands on the verge
Of his extremest monarchy,
As over thee, might vapors surge
Above his parting majesty;
They pass—but lo, behold, thy sign
Is written on his orb divine
Be that which thou from him shalt see
Thy Life's sublimest prophesy.
He looked and from that sinking sphere
A glory glimmered through his fear,
For every osier by the river,
And every rock that stands forever,
And all things that on earth there be
Seemed bathed in dews of prophesy.
Not westward where the sun still lingers
Those prophets point their shadowy fingers,
But backward to the Eastern sky
Made dark by Day's abandonment,
Point all the shadows silently,
As if in calm presentiment
Of glories to again be born
Through that closed portal of the morn.
Then floated that small voice again

Down to the first of dying men,
"God brings again the light, shall He
Uplift the sun forgetting thee?"
Down form the spirit's inner walls
The horror of great darkness falls;
At once the veil of doubt and sense
Glides off, for what he hopes to see
Becomes the real, and for hence
he knows his Immortality!

DONALD P. DULCHINOS

WRITTEN IN SAM NEWBURY'S AUTOGRAPH BOOK JULY 9TH '56—THAT YOUNG MAN BEING MY BROTHER IN KA, A GREAT HISTORIAN AND A PROSPECTIVE ALUMNUS OF '57.

Macaulay's double, David Hume's quintessence
    A grand historic nimbus lights thy brow
Like that which shines from Cleo's queenly presence
    Nor art thou like to us a thing of now;
Thou seemest indeed a very blood relation
    Of men now and the Caryatides
Or some great remnant of the generation
    Who first looked on Athena's Phidian frieze.
Out of the glory which the Past hath scattered
    On plains of prose and mountain peaks of song,
Knowing whose head it was Achilles battered
    And whether Pitt or Fox was in the wrong,
Thou comest with the palm which bye-gone ages
    Throw in to him who taketh all their dates,
And followed by a greater host of pages
    Than tend the dukes of all the German states.
Thou hast the Past, be thine the Future also,
    As musical with deeds of thoughts and truth
As the now Past and that which thou shalt call so
    When frost hath kissed the temples of thy youths
And if amid the chorus of tomorrow
    Thou hearest one small echo of today,
Remember him who loving thee, with sorrow
    Bid farewell unto thee a dear KA.

AUTOGRAPH WRITTEN IN THE BOOK OF STYMP, KA '56, A.I. FELLOW

As travelers in the stage of life,
　　We long have rode inside,
And if the way with dust was rife,
He feared not—ours was not the strife,
　　Soft were the seats and wide

But now our Jehu drops the reigns,
　　And we must take the box;
The laughing girls along the lanes,
The way side flowers, the dewy plains
　　Are ours—so are the knocks.

Drive well dear Stymp—thou hold'st the whip
　　Just right to be a winner;
Unless my coach shall early tip
Oft may we hop upon our trip
　　At the same place for dinner!

DONALD P. DULCHINOS

TO MISS M***** N******

Whom I first met about the time of my graduation.

I met thee first at a rare time—the sun
  Of life's most golden day was at its setting,
And on my soul's sad harp I heard begun
  Strains of a parting that was not forgetting.

So didst thou seem like a new-risen star
  Seen for the first time when the day is going
Over Earth's threshold, and Night's waves afar
  On heaven's strand begin their mystic flowing.

I have not known thee long, and yet thou art
  Among the gentler memories that throng
About the sunniest places of my heart
  Like half-caught strains of a delightful song.

Thou hast the Poet soul—or Nature speaks
  False for the first time from a face like thine,
Though sing'st thyself—else never had thy cheeks
  Harmed answering to a song so rude as mine.

Oh not in vain our meeting will have been
  If from the lute thy modest fear keeps sleeping
My prayer a single sheaf of song shall win
  E'en for thine own heart's unimparted reaping.

Remember me—forget not mine endeavor
  But be my prayer an open sesame
Which shall unlock thy wealth, and as forever
  With its revealing bear rich fruit for me.

So shall I be as one who hath uncovered
  The clear sweet waters of a hidden well
O'er which the wing of sunshine long hath hovered
  Seeking in vain for an awakening spell.

TO MY FATHER

My Father—loud must be the strife
   Of Earth, if through its jarring tone
I hear no music from thy life
   That gave the keynote to my own.

There have been those whose deeds and words
   Pealed through a broader space and time
But thine sound with those noble chords
   That make a private life sublime.

The heart that thrilled in chord with Truth,
   The hands that touched life's master keys
In like grand unison—thy youth
   And age are full of chords like these!

Thy brow, though it know not the oil
   That sanctifies the locks of kings,
Hath been anointed by the toil
   Of striving for God's noblest things.

And when my sons in future time
   Shall ask me what we have of birth
To glorify the poet's rhyme
   Or deck the heraldry of Earth.

I will not point to blazonments
   Brought mouldering from an age forgot,
Shields grim with old chivalric dents
   And banners given up to rot;

But knowing (Oh to know like thee!)
   The worth of honor over fame,
Shall I reply, Our heraldry
   Shines with my father's spotless name;

A sire to whom an iron right
   Was dearer than a golden wrong,
Who brought his own heart to the light
   But veiled a brother's not so strong

Who unto noble deeds gave birth
   As silent as his own pure thought,
Shaming the purchased love of Earth
   With priceless love, yet love unbought.

And thou for what thou art to me,
   And what thou hast been to thy kind,
Hast more than kingly royalty
   In the escutcheon of my mind.

A FRAGMENT

The Present hath an amaranthine glory
    Whose orb its fear its great alone may wear,
The Past is like a dream-enchanted story
    Of shapes seen Kingly through a rosy air;
And if we have not here our crowns by climbing
    Time's golden shadow wraps us as we wait,
For the knell of all the Dead blends with the chiming
    Of Today's bells of triumph for her great.
The Dead are one—their Past a mount of wonder
    Whose less and loftier peaks grand height make one
And they all echo with one deathless thunder,
    And all drink glory from one quenchless sun;
There is an awful grandeur in the solemn
    Reality of having passed away
From Earth, God knoweth whither, that the column
    Of Present Triumph giveth not to clay,
"Tis well we thus are made—That God hath folden
    The Past to us in sublime sanctity,
Teaching us in the Present that the olden
    Time is but what we owe our selves shall be,
And if a bye-gone soul hath worth so golden
    How dread a trust its living stewardry!

DONALD P. DULCHINOS

MY GENTLER MEMORIES (TO THE BURRITT'S)

It is not the great deeds that cover
    A life with their memories
As the earth at evening is covered
    By the sunset shadow of trees.

The deeds that are set to a trumpet
    May ring from the Alps of Time
While the heart in its vales beneath them
    Thrills to a shepherd's rhyme.

Better some still sweet gladness
    With hearts that our joy may bless
Than to climb above their Communion
    And be great in loneliness.

Thus did I speak in my musing
    As I thought of a time gone by
When the whole of Earth seemed poorer
    Than a finger's breadth of sky.

But I learned that our threads of sunshine
    By mingling in Life's great loom
With strands from Earth's dew-wet distaff
    Weave roses of best perfume.

Among the loveliest figures
    That loom ever wove for me
Is one of a parlor hallowed
    By household sympathy.

It is the room of a household
    But it hath such a blessed art
That its door seems an unaware entrance
    To some tender and loving heart.

The odorous spirit of flowers
  Floats ever upon the air
Like the benediction of angels
  With heaven-dews in their hair;

And the thought of their fragrant blessing
  In absence comes to me
Making an Indian summer
  In the fields of memory.

And like a clear sweet well-spring
  From a shadowy dell upsent
Come fragrant gushes of music
  From a rich toned instrument,

Sometimes a single murmur
  That might lull a child to sleep,
Sometimes a symphony mystic
  As its birth in the soul was deep.

How echoes of Old time spirits
  Who thrilled on the heights of song,
How ballads sung by a mother
  When the road through life looked long.

And another music is lurking
  In all that pastor's nooks
For one who can hear the voices
  Of noble and genial books.

And the place is glad with the presence
  Of gentle sisters three—
Earth had many friends beside them
  But not such as they are to me.

DONALD P. DULCHINOS

We have been together in shadow
   We have been together in sun
And we will forget each other
   When the Past shall be undone.

The curtains that robe that parlor
   Are richer than webs of state,
For their shadows fold memories dearer
   Than to know that I were great.

TO WARNER CRAIG KA ON HIS DEPARTURE
FOR KENTUCKY

Again in this good old College
   I sit as in days of old,
When I shook the tree of knowledge
   Till it rattled down pippins of gold.

And though I coined none of those pippins
   To the shape of a Phi Beta Key,
Yet their fragrance is now the poorer
   In the hoards of memory.

In the mystic summer twilight
   I seem to sit once more
And shadowy forms come round me
   Out of the days of lore.

They sit them down beside me
   The longed for yet vainly sought,
And we draw from our pipes together
   The ethereal milk of thought.

When I think of the love and vanished
   And am on the terrace alone,
"Oh world," I say, "be as gentle
   To them as this seat of stone."

The grass that died with this summer
   In the spring shall be green as then
But we who were here together
   Shall be never together again.

At home beneath a Linden
   I sit in my tipped-back chair
And smoke my lovely meerschaum
   With a put-on College air;

And in a land of strangers
  As mid blue-jays hoots an owl,
I try to revive the language
  Of bolt and fizzle and rowl.

Again I cross the Campus
  With a dinnerish look in my eye,
And Stymp's old Continental
  Bobs up and down close by.

Again from four till chapel
  I sit drowsy and limber-necked
At the biographical notice
  Of the fleas of intellect.

I see the delightful memoirs
  Of lever and screw and wedge
Thrown down for an old forehander
  And Sam cries "Privilege!"

Again the bell for chapel
  Through the morn-mist sounding din
Lull me to longer slumbers
  Like a mother's gentle hymn.

Cradle song of my Alma Mater
  How often waking at home,
Has my sleep been spoiled for the morning,
  When thy cadence did not come.

Ah Craig, how frail the tenure
  By which we hold all these things!
But they would not be birds of beauty
  If they lead not well-planned wings.

If we put them in our cages
  They die as we slide the bolt,

And the best of our memories only
   Are birds who have stopped to moult.

Oh long have we wandered together
   Through these calm uncrowded wats
And thou shalt not be forgotten
   Choice friend of my choicer days!

But next we at the fire-side
   When I have one of my own
Shall a set be ready for thee
   That shall hold thee like a throne.

Many a hill and valley
   Shall stretch between us soon,
But we are no more divided
   Than the Ocean and moon.

And with invisible tendrils
   Whose root is in the past
We still should be bound together
   Were the distance twice as vast!

Light ever shine on thy spirit
   God speed thee in thy aims
Until "qui nunc ad astra"
   be written o'er both our names.

WRITTEN IN THE AUTOGRAPH BOOK OF E.O. BARTLETT KA

We knew each other in the days of old
　　Nor shall we to each other be unknown
Until the ashes of the Past grow cold
　　Upon the silent ground that hides our own,
And as the hours of our mornings grew
　　Into the fullness of clear manhood's day
Life's sun ascending in his orbit threw
　　On our twin bud the same unfolding ray.
And now a little in advance I go
　　Forth on a path which you must tread ere long,
Out of sweet dreams which ever ebb and flow
　　To strive where hands must tire yet hearts be strong.
Yet oft shall I in intervals of din
　　Going apart as priest of memory
Slide back her temple-doors and enter in
　　To chant some low sweet song in thought of thee:
We have been friends together in our prime
　　Nor shall the love of our maturer day
Shame the remembrance of that holy time
　　For I await thee on life's rugged way;
And long may we here after travel on
　　Sharing together the same cloud and light
Until the last step of the road is won
　　And we leave off our harness with the night
Emerging, as all dark things break away,
　　To peace unshadowed, Brother in KA!

WRITTEN IN DAN HILLARD'S (KA) AUTOGRAPH BOOK

You are there yet my old-time friend
    In those cloisters dear and grey;
I have read the book and got to the end,
And into a world where they buy and read
Where the strong must mount and the weak must bend
    Heigh ho! I am pushing my way.

The world's broad and the din is loud
    And our hands work in the dark
Yet I ply my loom away the crowd
And weave my web beset with cloud
My robe of victory or my shroud
    Who knoweth? God save the mark!

The moon shall grow a few time o'er
    From hollow into round;
Where we would together in days of lore
Your prints shall be swept off the floor,
And through the sad gates of nevermore
    Shall you come to our fighting ground.

I welcome you out into the fight
    Our hearts shall be knit and warm
As when together we whiled the might
In hymns of strength and bodings bright
And called each other to see the light
    Through life's yet lingering storm.

On! On! there is work to do
    And our cheeks will not be paled;
Brave vanguard souls are shouting "Through!"
And side by side I will strike with you,
Let us be calm and let us be true
    And the fortress shall be sealed!

And if there be time on the march to sing
 A song for strength and cheer,
With old time echoes its strain shall ring
And out of the Past our souls shall bring
Memories rich to nerve the wing
 Of Hope through the laggard year.

There is triumph ahead in the days to come
 For those who will be great;
Yet never those memories shall grow dumb
Although we may climb above the hum
Of the world's great wheels, and her rattling drum
 Call not to the fields of fate!

For our old-time love through the days away die
 Shall be an immortal thing,
And the robes of peace that our toil shall buy
Shall be laced together by many a tie
Which was spun beneath an earlier sky
 Too strong for sundering!

HYMN TO OUR INTERCESSOR
[Written at Watertown]

Not from thine incommunicable glory
    Wherein, Oh God, thou sat'ist in might eternal
Years numberless before the mountains hoary,
    Shineth the lesson our weak souls may learn;
Like snow we melt away in our ongazing
    The weak and stained before the Strong and Good,
And the faint voice of our presumptuous praising
    Dieth away in Thine Infinitude.

Our hymns and tears by earthly winds updriven
    Float back from viewless barriers in the sky
Nor are the battlements celestial riven
    To let in unto thee our earnest cry;
Through Christ Thy on our earnest souls came only
    And stand untrembling in the might of trust,
At the dear gates where in abide the lonely
    Glory unsullied though enshrined in dust.

Here, meekly here, our deep unworthy confessing
    Even to touch the walls thou dwellest in,
He having nought of thee the All-possessing
    Ask for that wealth thy poverty did win,
Ask for the rest thy brow of thorns did gain us
    Without a pillow for its weariness,
Ask for that wishing from the spots that stain us
    Which thy sore wounds found not in their distress.

Thou who hast felt the pains of Godhead rending
    Thy fleshy tent on midnight mountains bleak
Knowest; above our sleep-locked eyelids bending,
    The spirit willing though the flesh be weak;
Breathe thy might into us, make our souls earnest
    Whether it be to labor or to weep

Till noiseless at the sundown thou returnest
And gently givest thy beloved sleep.

I DID NOT ASK THAT I MIGHT HAVE A NAME

I did not ask that I might have a name
　To sound forever like a wind-lashed sea,
I sought no glory bursting like a flame
　Upon Humanity.

In days gone by the shadow of a crown
　Hung over me and wooed me to be great—
I sought the sunshine that I might lay down
　Its visionary weight.

I bent my forehead coldly from the kiss
　Of fair cajoling Fortune, braving out
Her threat of shrouded destiny and bliss
　Wrecked if she turned about

My God, thou knowest it was not with these
　I spent my labor or laid up my trust
Nor ever stretched my eager hands to seize
　Their heaps of withered dust!

No! All I asked was somewhere in the world
　To love and be repaid with love; as deep
Ere out of life's small daylight I was hurled
　Into forgotten sleep.

Ah, few men with a burden like my own
　Have ever vexed their prayers through nights untold
Deeming it little to be loved alone
　While Life hath pomp and gold!

Was it that I implored so small a boon
    That my prayer floated back as clouds of even
Drift from the icy barriers of the moon
    Too light to enter heaven?

Or did I in my daring ask a thing
    So mighty that it challenged God to mark
Me as one thenceforth doomed to wandering
    Forever in the dark?

I am not answered. It were better so;
    He who without a lamp sits though the night
Seeth no better that his soul doth know
    Wherefore he hath no light.

Oh how in yearning I have spent my time,
    Wasting into the socket heart and strength
While the years rounded like a shallow rhyme
    Their slow unfruitful length.

I stand as one who from a dungeon dream
    Of open air and the free arch of stars
Waking to things that be from things that seem
    Beats madly on the bars

I am not yet quite used to be aware
    That all my labor and my hope had birth
Only to freeze me with the coffined stars
    Of void and soulless earth.

Yet soon I shall be vexed with no more thought;
    If all of good for which I wished can burst
Like a chilled bubble, I too may be nought
    And I have known the worst.

TO MISS ELLIE SESSIONS

[on her presenting me with an ivory memorandum-book on the same day as Mary Sessions presented a paper-knife, the subject of *To M.S.*, *with thanks for a paper-knife.*]

It hath a pleasant look
    As I hold it in my grasp
With its polished silver clasp
    A fair and tiny book;
It hath leaves of spotless ivory
And it was my little friend who gave it to me.

It is made to bear the token
    Of that which each day bringeth
    And on my shoulders flingeth
What is to be done and what is to be spoken;
Ah me! It will hold many a varied mark
Some shining and some dark!

Kind offices to do and mild reproving
    Hard labors to be undergone
Pleasant prospects that grow nearer like the dawn
    And all that doth pertain
    In bust heart and brain
To the work of suffering and loving;
Tomorrow's cloud of trial, and the sun
Of victory that breatheth thereupon.

Where the wayside fountain bubbles
    Oft shall I turn aside
    From life's pathway hot and wide
And rest me from my troubles
    A little while until I write
    Upon these tablets white
Some notes of pilgrimage
    While a loving tree

Sheddeth over me
The shadow of the leaves that crown its old age.

And when I am like a spring,
    That hath naught to do
    But to leap toward the blue
Heaven which it reflecteth and to sing,
    Then my wayward phantasy
    Shall record itself in thee
            Little Book,

And thou shalt hold for mine own look
    The rejoicing of a merry mood
    Which hearing itself and thee
            Where'er we be
    Knoweth us solitude.

    Now thou art near
Yet soon thou shalt be to me like a brother
    Since with each other
    We shall have so much to do;
Never may a single leaf
Of all thy tablets broken be
    Since when I know thee well
    That would be a grief
    As unbearable
    As losing an outer part of memory.

Little book go with me then
    In my path through things and men,
And when I leave no other friend to whom
    I can speak my gladness or my gloom,
    Then do thou be near
To take the tone complexion
Of the moments' joy or disaffection
    To hold the record of a smile or tear;

So shalt thou laugh with me in my folly
And be my comforter in melancholy.

Many thanks my little friend,
    Who gave this book to me
    For the pleasant sympathy
That it shall yield me to the end;
    And when the prayer to remember
And to feel kindness answering back to kindness
    Goeth out in the final blindness
    Like a chilled and wasted ember,
Then, when I am asleep
    Take back this little book to thee
    As the poet's legacy
If the thought of the old time will not make thee weep.

ON THE DEATH OF CHARLES BARTLETT

In the high-places, Death!
For not a higher height throweth shadows down
On that sun visited hill-crown
 Where thou didst yield my breath.

In the high places, Night!
For thou, with those pure beams which good deeds are
Didst shine, a high advance star—
 And we have lost thy light.

Not with the hireling woe
Of sable housings, heavy pall and plume,
Here thou put from us to the gloom
 Whither our changes flow.

Ah no! The deep distress
Of thine own smitten house blent with the tears
Which thou hadst stayed for many years—
 Widows and Fatherless!

Gone from among us—gone—
No longer making sunshine at the door
Where hoe's cold shadow lay before—
 The shadow stays alone!

The councils of the good
Wait sadly for thy voice to waft the True,
Nor feel thy Godward impulse thrilling through
 The channels of their blood.

Ah Grief! how many a chair
Is empty, where of old he sat beloved;
How many a heart whose fountains he hath moved
 Looks for him everywhere.

Gone! yet we know not why—
So vital to the life of such a host
Bereaved most when him they needed most
    Called, out of time, to die.

Not so—though Sense rebels.
The hand that chills over wondrous stream of Being
Is only leading it beyond our seeing
    To flow from purer wells.

Great need was ours of him
Whom God hath taken; yet it well may be
That Heaven had nobler work for him than we
    Whose sight for tears is dim.

Some mission lacked a heart
Perchance as brave as his to bear it through,
And now, he doeth more than he could do
    For God, by earthly Art.

He will not murmur. He
Who hath our Dead in his more lovely spheres
Can shed his memory through our helpless tears
    With light of Prophecy.

Lead us, O Good and Great
Up through the road which our beloved hath trod
Through goodness unto God,
    Till we pass through the gate!

THE BOYS OF OLD UNION!
A UNION COLLEGE SONG TO THE AIR
"WHEN FIRST I SAW SWEET PEGGY"

You may talk of big-wigged Oxford
    In her long-tailed sable gown,
I'll sing you a stave, my comrades brave,
    That'll take that lingo down;
She is welcome to her glory
    Of caps that darken the sun,
But she's far behind if I speak my mind
    In the fellows who put them on!

Chorus:
        For the sons that Old Union bare
        Are the boys beyond compare
                With song and with glee
                And spirits as free
        As their pipe-wreaths in the air.

There's Yale with all her Tutors
    In the land of notions and sass,
And I do declare, 'twould make you stare
    To see her elms and grass;
But greener are the pumpkins
    Who from their Freshman year
Are trundled about in Class and out
    By their hawk-jawed Profs. austere.

Cho. But the sons—

Once in two years Yale bores them
    With pangs no man can speak,
That L.L.D.'s may try like cheese
    The flavor of their Greek;
By-any-awl that's handy

Blunt Prof. or sharper Yute
They bore away, and thus, they say
Bi-enni-al got its root.

Cho. But the sons—

There's Princeton in the Jersey's
And Dartmouth at the poles,
And in Hamilton College their pap of knowledge
Is fed to infant souls;
The University of New York
Is Gotham's sacred den
But its Universe is mighty "skurce"
For it holds but twenty men!

Cho. Oh the sons—

Then here's to all who love us
Both here and everywhere,
If now they rove in Union's grove
Or fight the World and Care;
Sub-Graduates or Alumni,
We may wander where we will
Yet find on earth no place whose worth
Compares with this old Hill.

Cho. Oh the sons—

"HE IS NOT HERE—HE IS RISEN!"
[Included in a biographical sketch by Helen Ludlow]

"He is not here—he is risen!"
Thus spake the angels of our conquering Lord;
Christ and His brethren by the self-same word
    Are called to break their prison.

"Great need was ours of him
Whom God hath taken, yet it well may be
That heaven hath nobler work for him than we
    Whose sight for tears is dim.

"Some mission lacked a heart
Perchance, as brave as his to bear it through,
And now he doeth more than he could do
    For God by earthly art.

"We will not murmur, He
Who hath our Dead in His more holy spheres
Can shed his memory through our helpless tears
    With light of prophecy."

DONALD P. DULCHINOS

SOCRATES SNOOKS

Mister Socrates Snooks, a lord of creation,
The second time entered the married relation:
Xantippe Caloric accepted his hand,
And they thought him the happiest man in the land.

But scarce had the honeymoon passed o'er his head,
When one morning to Xantippe Socrates said:
"I think, for a man of my standing in life,
This house is too small, as I now have a wife;

So, as early as possible, carpenter Carey
Shall be sent for to widen my house and my dairy."
"Now, Socrates, dearest," Xantippe replied,
"I hate to hear everything vulgarly my'd;

Now, whenever you speak of your chattels again,
Say, our cowhouse, our barnyard, our pigpen."
"By your leave, Mrs. Snooks, I will say what I please
Of my houses, my lands, my gardens, my trees."

"Say our," Xantippe exclaimed in a rage.
"I won't, Mrs. Snooks, though you ask it an age!"
Oh, woman! though only a part of man's rib,
If the story in Genesis don't tell a fib,

Should your naughty companion e'er quarrel with you,
You are certain to prove the best man of the two.
In the following case this was certainly true;
For the lovely Xantippe just pulled off her shoe,

And laying about her, all sides at random,
The adage was verified—"Nil desperandum."
Mister Socrates Snooks, after trying in vain,
To ward off the blows which descended like rain—

Concluding that valor's best part was discretion—
Crept under the bed like a terrified Hessian;
But the dauntless Xantippe, not one whit afraid,
Converted the siege into a blockade.

At last, after reasoning the thing in his pate,
He concluded 'twas useless to strive against fate:
And, so, like a tortoise protruding his head,
Said, "My dear, may we come out from under our bed?"

"Ha! ha!" she exclaimed, "Mr. Socrates Snooks,
I perceive you agree to my terms by your looks;
Now, Socrates—hear me—from this happy hour,
If you'll only obey me, I'll never look sour."

'Tis said the next Sabbath, ere going to church,
He chanced for a clean pair of trousers to search;
Having found them, he asked, with a few nervous twitches,
"My dear, may we put on our new Sunday breeches?"

APPENDIX I

The Hasheesh Eater Covers

FITZ HUGH Ludlow's vivid descriptions of his visions under the influence of hashish inspired some baroque cover art.

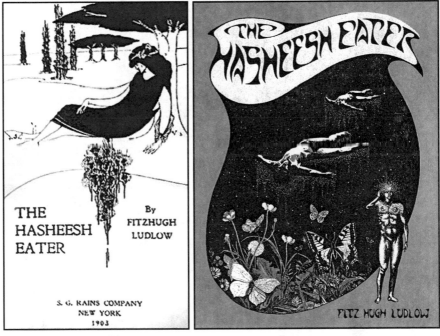

S. G. RAINS COMPANY 1903,
DESIGN BY AUBREY BEARDSLEY.

LEVEL PRESS, 1975.

ILLUSTRATION FROM THE LEVEL PRESS EDITION.

CITY LIGHTS 1979, DESIGN
BY AUBREY BEARDSLEY.

FITZ HUGH LUDLOW MEMORIAL
LIBRARY, ILLUSTRATION BY
WILFRIED SÄTTY 1975.

H.P. LOVECRAFT'S COPY OF *THE HASHEESH EATER.*

RUTGERS UNIVERSITY PRESS,
EDITED BY STEPHEN RACHMAN
2006.

INDEPENDENT EDITION 2015,
COVER TAKEN FROM "A NEW VICE:
OPIUM DENS IN FRANCE,"
AN ILLUSTRATION FROM LE
PETIT JOURNAL, 5 JULY 1903.

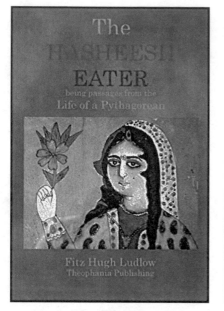

THEOPHANIA PUBLISHING 2011.   PORTRAIT BY KATT.

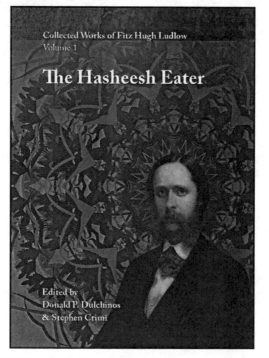

LOGOSOPHIA BOOKS COVER BY JACK E. TAYLOR 2017.

APPENDIX II

Newspaper Clippings

A collection of newspaper clippings having to do with the life and work of Fitz Hugh Ludlow.

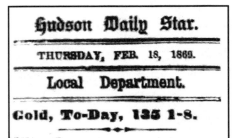

Hudson Daily Star.

THURSDAY, FEB. 18, 1869.

Local Department.

Gold, To-Day, 135 1-8.

THE MONSTROUS DOCTRINE OF FREE LOVE.

The doctor alleges that his wife had no cause whatever for deserting him, save her monstrous doctrine of free love—setting aside all legal restraint and the conservative usages of society, and demanding free intercourse with any one to whom she might feel attracted, or for whom she might have any "affinity."

SCANDALOUS REVELATION.

She was a consort of people holding such doctrines, and was before marriage, and ever continued thereafter, an intimate friend and acquaintance of Mrs. Fitz Hugh Ludlow, who left her husband, obtained a divorce, and is now the wife of the artist Bierstadt, living abroad; and also of Mrs. McFarland, who ran away from her husband with one Alfred D. Richardson, and is now, as deponent is informed and believes, living with him somewhere out West, seeking a divorce from her husband, and with others of like character.

HOW THE LOVERS MANAGED TO MEET.

From September, 1865, to April, 1866, Hennessey was on intimate terms with Mrs. Ward, and she with him. He regularly spent Monday, Wednesday, and Saturday, and frequently other evenings, at her house, at her request, and she would always put off other engagements for those evenings, or else have him go along in company. She would always send for him whenever they were going out to the park or to any place of amusement. Mrs. Ward's mother objected to these frequent visits.

A *HUDSON DAILY STAR* 18 FEBRUARY 1869 REPORT HEADLINED: "REMARKABLE DIVORCE TRIAL IN HIGH LIFE—CONJUGAL TRIBULATIONS OF A PHYSICIAN AND HIS WIFE—A SCANDAL IN THE ARTISTIC WORLD—THE LADY A FORMER HUDSONIAN," CITES MRS. WARD'S ASSOCIATION WITH PURPORTED "MONSTROUS FREE LOVE" ADVOCATES ROSALIE OSBORNE (LATER LUDLOW AND AFTER THAT BIERSTADT) AND ABBY RICHARDSON (WHOSE EX-HUSBAND DANIEL MCFARLAND WOULD NINE MONTHS LATER KILL HER HUSBAND TWO DAYS AFTER THEY WERE MARRIED BY REV. HENRY WARD BEECHER).

TRANSCRIPT OF LUDLOW'S TESTIMONY IN THE DANIEL
MCFARLAND MURDER TRIAL FROM THE *NEWARK COURIER*.
MCFARLAND WAS ACQUITTED ON MAY 11, 1870.

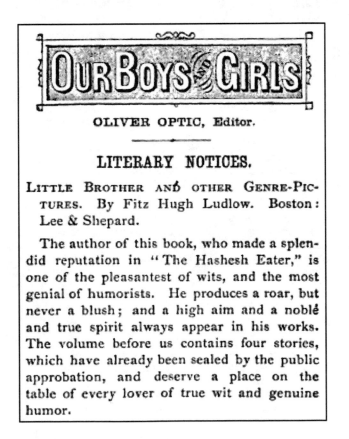

PERSONAL.

Bierstadt, the artist, and Fitz Hugh Ludlow, the author, returned home last evening from their extended tour in California and Oregon. Mr. Ludlow has prepared a series of four lectures, giving an account of his whole tour, with more especial reference to the overland journey, the Mormons, the great Yo-Semite Valley, and the mountains of the Pacific coast. Each of these may be delivered independently. We will add, for the information of lecture committees and others, that Mr. Ludlow's address, for the next three weeks, will be at Oswego, New York; and after that, to the care of the EVENING POST. Bierstadt's portfolio is filled with a large number of studies of the scenery and incidents met with in those regions. His oil studies fill by far the largest part of his portfolio, and among these the views of the great Yo-Semite Valley, Mount Shasta and Mount Hood, are the most striking successes he has ever accomplished.

LUDLOW'S LECTURE TOUR ADVERTISED IN
THE *GENEVA EVENING POST*, 17 DECEMBER, 1863.

OUR BOYS AND GIRLS

OLIVER OPTIC, Editor.

LITERARY NOTICES.

LITTLE BROTHER AND OTHER GENRE-PICTURES. By Fitz Hugh Ludlow. Boston: Lee & Shepard.

The author of this book, who made a splendid reputation in "The Hashesh Eater," is one of the pleasantest of wits, and the most genial of humorists. He produces a roar, but never a blush; and a high aim and a noble and true spirit always appear in his works. The volume before us contains four stories, which have already been sealed by the public approbation, and deserve a place on the table of every lover of true wit and genuine humor.

REVIEW OF *LITTLE BROTHER AND OTHER GENRE-PICTURES* IN
OUR BOYS AND GIRLS VI-2, 1867. (HATHITRUST DIGITAL LIBRARY)

Fitz Hugh Ludlow has lately visited the Elmyra Water Cure, where he has been making arrangements to test his plan for curing those who are addicted to the use of opium.

VISIT TO THE ELMYRA WATER CURE.

FITZ HUGH LUDLOW'S LECTURE.—Notwithstanding the severity of the weather, Dodworth Hall was tolerably well filled on Saturday night, to hear Fitz Hugh Ludlow's lecture on "The Overland Route" to the Pacific coast. The lecture bore indications of having been carefully prepared. It was long, sometimes witty, and, in the graphic passages, always eloquent. To speak well of it, this is all that can be said. It literally contained no novelty. Opening with the description of an event (i. e. the hanging of a bushwhacker at a town on the Upper Missouri) which we have seen better described by fifty newspaper correspondents during the war, Mr. Ludlow lingered long among the buffaloes, antelopes and red skins of the plains, in terms which have long been rendered trite by the numerous books which were born of the California gold excitement, and by any number of letters and sketches since. The lecturer would have been more successful with Utah and the Mormons had not Artemus Ward so recently preceded him. As it was, some of his descriptions of mountain scenery, more especially that of California, were vigorous and poetical—recalling, in their color and sweep, some of those glorious passages of the Hasheesh Eater's rhapsodies. The drift of Mr. Ludlow's remarks was a noble one—an argument in favor of the Pacific Railroad. He paid a glowing tribute to the State of California. In his opinion, her boundless vegetable and mineral resources would abundantly enable her to take care of herself as a separate nationality, and therefore no pains should be spared by the Atlantic States to strengthen the link—attenuated by the vast interval of wilderness—which binds her to the Union.

REVIEW OF A LUDLOW LECTURE.

DONALD P. DULCHINOS

TWO VISITORS.

A gentleman of nature's creation, among whatever class of society found, differs as much from an upstart counterfeit, as the pure gold differs from the bogus counterfeit of a Gift Book Lottery. The former, instinctively a gentleman, always a gentleman, needs no foreign aid to make him pass for what he is; the latter is the creation of accident—to-day made, to-morrow again in the dust, but, wherever found, always grovelling—never as what he assumes, and never can be, for as instinctively as the one is great and noble the other is base, bogus, a counterfeit. They are formed, fashioned alike; but in these alone is the resemblance—they come no nearer. In everything of soul they are the very antipodes of each other; they are beings of another species; the one is the light of life, the other is the darkness of death; the one is the embodiment of truth and honor, the other is a conglomeration of falsehood and perjury; the one is a blessing to society, the other is its curse; the one is an angel of peace, the other is a demon of discord; the one is born to reflect honor on humanity, the other is born to disgrace it—such is the difference between the true and the false in life.

When we laid the slip of paper before us on which these reflections are traced, we had no intention of usurping the province of the teacher and moralist, we purposed only to notice some public "gentlemen" who have honored Utah with a passing visit, and who have, since their "return to civilization," regaled the other world with the delectable stories of their fevered brains: the paragraph, however, is written and we let it go with the rest, and come to our text.

Two weeks ago, we gave our views on the charge of unsociability against the Saints and stated there freely, in substance, that the world abounded in corrupt men, and it required some time to discover the honorable from the dishonorable. We stated mildly what we had to say—for that is our style; but had we said bluntly what was in our mind we would just have said that the world in which we live is most wofully corrupt, and few men can be trusted in any society without close watching; and we have seen so much of that kind of thing, where least expected, that we prefer to hasten slowly, and to submit to the charge of unsociability, rather than to throw open the doors of our habitations to every scape grace in the name of a gentleman that comes among us burthened with claims to attentions from the other world of mankind. Our kindness has been so often abused, and our liberality and courtesy so frequently serving only to bring our traducers better before the public, and to clothe them with something like the authority of an arceté of inner life, that we really are not particularly partial to the friendship of brief acquaintence; but we did not then think that we would so soon have fresh grounds for the exercise of this caution.

Less than a year ago, a party of literary "gentlemen" and artists passed through here from the east to the Pacific. One of the company, a professional writer, an author, was particularly solicitious to be introduced here and there, and through the influence of friends to whom he came recommended, he was made welcome. Every place was open, every attention he could desire was extended to him. He was but a few days in the city but was long enough, when sober, to call upon some of our principal citizens and have the free intercourse of gentlemen. He came to the city inebriated, was unable to walk unassisted to his hotel, was probably sober the greater part of the 3d of July, and may have been sober some other hours of his sojourn here; but he was literally a perfect sot, or in the language of more than one who saw him; "He was drunk when he came, he was terribly drunk when he left, and was beastly drunk while he stayed." Yet this same Christian writer regales the reading public with the vilest abuse of the people of Utah that a certain Gentile merchant establishment in Whisky street could stuff him with, and what the pens of profligate Federal officers from the days of Brocchus to Harding and op-states could furnish him—all of which, of course, he deals out to the greedy crowd as precious morsels of his own collating. On the Atlantic seaboard, he serves his purposes through the *Atlantic Monthly* and the Lecture Halls; on the Pacific, through the columns of the *Golden Era*, a paper owned and edited by a gentleman who really professes friendship for the people of Utah.

That Fitz Hugh Ludlow has personally any grudge against the Latter Day Saints, that he seeks in this way to gratify, we think very questionable; but it is popular with some to abuse the Mormons. If writers told the truth they would have but little to say, and have few readers, and as pelf must be made by the professional, he must make it as the public taste demands. Had it been a better paying concern to "write us up," he would have done so. He did not know enough to make truth interesting and his bibulous propensity overcoming him at the hour he should have labored by observation to discover the truth, he had to draw on the sources we have named, and rushing impetuously from falsehood to falsehood he wove his web.

But a daub of another class and of a more recent date presents himself in the person of E. P. Hingston, the business agent of Artemus Ward, a contributor to "wild cat literature," the author of Folly Petticoat or "the Hangman's daughter." We shall, till we have reason for doing otherwise, regard Artemus, as he professed to be, a gentleman. The go-a-her exhibited the lustincts of a gentleman, however he may use them; but Hingston carried with him the undisguised graces of a refined prince of the purlieus of London. As a manager, he was no doubt huge in the profession, and, as he claimed, was to Artemus "the power behind the throne." While here, both were treated with much kindness, and the language and actions of Artemus, from first to last, as far as we have learned, were noways contrary to his profession. We hope we shall have no occasion to change our good opinion of him personally; but of his agent, we hope never to be again afflicted with the sight of him. He has written for the New York *Atlas* an account of his visit to the Theatre of Salt Lake, during the lecture of Artemus, professing, of course, no relationship with the lecturer, which is such a picture of misrepresentation, and so overlaid and interwoven with fabrications, that we believe the very lowest class of our gentiles are ashamed of it. That he should seek to keep Artemus before the public, and feed it with "great expectations" of an interesting lecture after his return from "Mormondom" is all professional, and only such as might be expected, and to which no reasonable exception can be taken; but, low in deed must be the standard of that man's morality, who would accept the courtesies of a people, and the moment that he was away from their firesides, present them before the public as the greatest conglomeration of ignorance, booryism and mental degradation, without brains, led by the wave of a handkerchief to smile, to cheer and to applaud what the capricious taste of another might indicate, and to carry throughout his story the greatest misrepresentation of facts that his mind could conceive. With us individually it has been a matter of question whether the letter in the *Atlas* was written before or after the lecture. We can hardly credit, that a public man, however habituated to lying, could be so far indifferent to the opinion of even his own kin as to write with such a reckless pen, and tell as many lies in so brief a space. It may be flattering to Mr Hingston to have a reputation, a compliment from one of his most intimate acquaintances here: he is told, on the authority alluded to, to be "the greatest liar in America."

For ourselves, we are indifferent to what representation is made of us, we care nothing; but while we occupy this anomalous position assigned to us, of being in the heart of the world, yet out of it to the rest of mankind, thinking, the dispassionate, will probably find in the article we have penned the philosophy of our situation, and the application of our first paragraph.

MORMON'S *DESERET NEWS* REBUTTAL TO LUDLOW'S
REPORTS OF HIS EXPERIENCES OF THEM.

CLEVELAND LEADER.

PUBLISHED

Daily, Tri-Weekly and Weekly,

BY THE

LEADER PRINTING COMPANY.

OFFICIAL PAPER OF THE CITY.

SATURDAY, NOVEMBER 14, 1868.

LITERARY.

New Books.

THE OPIUM HABIT. New York: Harper & Brothers.

If the habit of opium eating is as prevalent throughout this country and England as hospital reports and the opinions of noted physicians would have us believe, the volume before us is destined to be the vehicle of much good to a class of unfortunates who certainly deserves a warm place in the world's sympathy. Beyond the hasheesh stories of eastern travelers, little was definitely known concerning the nature and extent of the opium passion, until 1821, when the famous "Confessions" of De Quincey revealed to the astonished British public, that not only among the swarthy Indians and the lower ranks of English society did the baleful drug find its victims, but that one of England's finest minds was wrestling madly but vainly with the silent enemy. Mr. Joseph Cottle followed in the *London Magazine* with the story of Coleridge's helpless slavery to opium, and from that time the "Opium Habit" has been a recognized theme among essayists. All the eloquence and pathos of some of the best writers in the language have been thrown into the scale, and those writings have found, as might be supposed, a wide and eager circle of readers. Still, ghastly as the subject has been painted, it is doubtful whether any of these essays has gone far toward curing or preventing the habit. The thrilling descriptions of De Quincey of an experience possible only to minds like his, have drawn many a dreamy idler into the vortex over which his genius has thrown so fatal a glamour. At all events, the practice has steadily increased, and given rise to many of the puzzling and abnormal derangements that prove so perplexing to physicians. The present book contains an admirable collection of the best literature which the subject has evoked. Although not wholly a compilation it includes De Quincey's "Confessions;" Mr. Cottle's account of Coleridge's opium-eating; an article from *Lippincott's Magazine*, entitled "A Morphine Habit Overcome;" one from *Harper's Magazine*, entitled "What Shall They Do to be Saved!" "Outlines of the Opium Cure," a contribution by Fitz Hugh Ludlow, who also wrote the *Harper* article, and some individual experiences. The anonymous compiler prefaces these selections with a minute and exceedingly interesting account of "A Successful Attempt to Abandon Opium." Altogether the book presents the "learning" on the subject treated thoroughly, almost exhaustively and practically. It has been prepared especially for opium-eaters, and will be of the greatest service to those who have not yet realized the depth of the miseries into which the use of opium is leading them, or who, having experienced these miseries, feel unable to shake off the habit.

For sale by Cobb, Andrews & Co.

CLEVELAND LEADER REVIEW OF *THE OPIUM HABIT*, 14 NOVEMBER, 1868.

DEATH OF FITZ HUGH LUDLOW, THE HASHEESH-EATER.

From the N. Y. World.

A letter from Geneva, in Switzerland, brings tidings of the death at that city of Fitz Hugh Ludlow, who is very well known to all cultivators of our lighter literature as having been one of the most vivacious and successful contributors to American periodicals. He was the son of the Rev. H. G. Ludlow, a Congregationalist clergyman, settled for many years at Poughkeepsie, and subsequently at Oswego, where he died six or seven years ago. The first essays of young Ludlow were published about 1855, in New York newspapers. He contributed voluminously to the *Evening Post*, and in a more fitful way to other journals. These contributions were of course anonymous, but they were recognizable by a certain random quickness of fancy and felicity of phrase, which showed him to be a leading disciple of that school of writing which Poe founded, and in which Curtis and Winthrop are the best known names.

The first literary venture to which his name was attached was the "Hasheesh Eater," published about 1857. As its title indicates he had fallen into the habit of narcotizing himself with that potent and pernicious drug, and the book is an attempt to portray poetically both the pleasures and the pains induced by it. Such a book could hardly escape a comparison with De Quincey's "Opium Eater," which, indeed, it resembles, and the main fault of which—weakness of construction—it shares with many of its merits of vivid description, though of course, in a lesser degree. A series of stories appeared soon afterwards in *Harper's Magazine*, of which, though all were extravagant, the best are very pleasant reading. Those best are in a humorous vein. Those which aim at serious impressiveness are equally extravagant, but by no means so successful. In the same manner as the stories of Poe, they attain only a faint reminder of his malign power. They show a morbid fancy, quickened and distorted by the nervous taxation to which the writer had subjected himself at first in the form of hasheesh, and afterwards in that of opium. The stories were afterwards collected under the title of "Little Brother."

Soon after the publication of these he took a journey across the Plains in company with Mr. Bierstadt, the artist. The fruits of this expedition, so far as he was concerned, appeared in a series of entertaining papers in the *Atlantic Monthly*. His statements about the Mormons, made in those papers, were flatly denied, and his conclusions fiercely resented by the representatives of that sect. Upon his return to New York he wrote in a desultory way, and mostly anonymously, for many journals and periodicals, and prepared two books. The first of these, "Across the Continent," was a collection of the magazine papers and lectures he had devised from his trip. The second, "The Opium Habit," was a recital of his experience with opium, which attempted a much more scientific and less romantic treatment than he had given to hasheesh. No constitution could stand the draughts made upon it by two forms of mental and bodily dissipation so wasteful, and for some years his health has been utterly shattered, and the catastrophe which has now ended his career has been evidently imminent. His last public appearance was as a witness at the trial of MacFarland, where he was engaged in an altercation with the prosecuting counsel.

Mr. Ludlow was married about ten years ago; but the union was not fortunate, and after some years, his wife obtained a divorce from him, and was subsequently married to a distinguished artist.

Mr. Ludlow had many fine gifts, which would have made him a deserved distinction if he had had the steadiness of character necessary to make the best of them. His death, at so early an age as 33, put a period to a life of which the actual results are very evidently and sadly short of the promises and possibilities.

EULOGY IN THE *NEW YORK WORLD*, PRINTED IN THE BUFFALO *EVENING COURIER & REPUBLIC*, 7 OCTOBER, 1870.

A FITZ HUGH LUDLOW BIBLIOGRAPHY

"Truth on His Travels," *College Hill Mercury*, December, 1850.

"Ode to Old Union," 1856.

"Union Terrace Song," 1856.

"The Hymn of the Soul of Man," *The New Era*, 1856.

"A La Dame A Voile Noire," *Knickerbocker*, October, 1856.

"The Apocalypse of Hasheesh," *Putnam's Monthly*, December, 1856.

The Hasheesh Eater, New York: Harper Brothers, 1857.

The Hasheesh Eater, London: Sampson Low and Son, 1857.

"The New Soul of John Markham," *Harper's Weekly*, December 5, 1857.

"The Rector's Cross," *Harper's Weekly*, January 9, 1858.

"Little Good for Nothing," *Harper's Weekly*, August 7, 1858.

"Our Queer Papa; A Case of Organic Affection," *Harper's Monthly*, November, 1858.

"The Loan of a Lyre," *Harper's Monthly*, December, 1858.

The Hasheesh Eater, 2nd Edition, New York: Harper Brothers, 1858.

"The Phial of Dread: By An Analytic Chemist," *Harper's Monthly*, November, 1859.

"Regular Habits," *Harper's Monthly*, December, 1859.

The New Partner in Clingham & Co., Bankers, *Harper's Weekly*, January-April, 1860.

"Little Brother," *Harper's Monthly*, February-April, 1860.

"The Ransom of a Heritage," *Waterville Times*, February-March, 1860.

The Hasheesh Eater, 3rd Edition, New York: Harper Brothers, 1860.

"The Century Plant," *Harper's Monthly*, June, 1860.

"The Cruise of the Two Deacons," *Harper's Monthly*, July-September, 1860.

"My Velvet Shoes," *Harper's Monthly*, October, 1860.

"Due South Sketches," *New York Commercial Advertiser*, October 19, 1860-January 22, 1861. (24 installments)

The Primpenny Family, Vanity Fair, January–April, 1861.

"The Taxidermist," *The Knickerbocker,* January, 1861.

"Evenings at the Club," *New York Commercial Advertiser,* February 23, 1861–March 25, 1861.

"The Taxidermist," in *Tales of the Time,* John T. Irving, ed., New York: H. Dexter & Co., 1861.

"Thrown Together," *Harper's Monthly,* June, 1861.

"The Music Essence," *New York Commercial Advertiser,* December 31, 1861.

The Hasheesh Eater, 4th Edition, New York: Harper Brothers, 1861 or 1862(?).

"D'all uno del mio cuore," unpublished, with T.B. Aldrich, ms. in Houghton Library.

"A Drawn Game," *Harper's Monthly,* February, 1862.

"A Strange Acquaintance of Mine," *New York Leader,* March, 1862.

"Masks and Music," *The Home Journal,* October 11, 1862–February 14, 1863. (weekly column)

"Biographical Sketch of John Nelson Pattison," New York, 1863?

"Letters from Sundown: The Artists' Western Expedition," *New York Evening Post,* May 26, 1863.

"Letters From Sundown, No. II," *New York Evening Post,* June 5, 1863.

"Letters From Sundown, No. III. The Wonders of Colorado," *New York Evening Post,* July 24–5, 1863.

"Letters From Sundown, No. IV. The Colorado Gold Mines," *New York Evening Post,* July 30, 1863.

"The Battle and Triumph of Dr. Susan," *Harper's Monthly,* July–August, 1863.

"Letters from Sundown," *The Golden Era,* August 2, 1863 (reprint from the *New York Evening Post*).

"Letter on Theatre in Denver," *New York Evening Post,* September, 1863.

"On Good Living," *The Golden Era,* September 13, 1863.

"On Marrying Men," *The Golden Era,* September 20, 1863.

"On 'Care' That 'Killed the Cat'," *The Golden Era,* November 1, 1863.

"Plain Talks—No. 1. How It Strikes One," *The Golden Era,* November 8, 1863.

"I will not wish thy life a tinted bubble," November 16, 1863. (ms. in autograph book of Charles Warren Stoddard, now in Huntington Library.)

"P.P.C.—Goodbye Article," *The Golden Era,* November 22, 1863.

"Plain Talks No. 2," *The Golden Era,* December 20, 1863.

"Reminiscences of an Overlander: From the Missouri to the Rocky Mountains," *The Golden Era*, January 31, 1864, February 21, 1864.

"Reminiscences of an Overlander: Denver to Salt Lake Inclusive," *The Golden Era*, February 28, March 6, 20, 27, 1864.

"John Heathburn's Title," *Harper's Monthly*, February-March, 1864.

"Reminiscences of an Overlander: Salt Lake to San Francisco," *The Golden Era*, April 17, 1864.

"Among the Mormons," *Atlantic Monthly*, April, 1864.

Cinderella, New York: J.A. Gray and Green, 1864.

Ed., *In Memoriam, Thomas Starr King*, New York Sanitary Fair, New York, 1864.

"Abest: Surrexit," in *In Memoriam, Thomas Starr King*, New York, 1864.

"Finding A Sensible Tongue in Trees," *The Californian*, May 28, 1864. (Reprinted from *New Nation*, date unknown.)

"Seven Weeks in the Great Yo-Semite," *Atlantic Monthly*, June, 1864.

"The Prisoners of Portland: An Historical Novel of the Present, Past and Future," *The Golden Era*, June 12, 1864.

"The Prisoners of Portland: Book Second, and Last," *The Golden Era*, June 19, 1864.

"On Horseback Into Oregon," *Atlantic Monthly*, July, 1864.

"Through Tickets to San Francisco," *Atlantic Monthly*, November, 1864.

"On the Columbia River," *Atlantic Monthly*, December, 1864.

"The American Metropolis," *Atlantic Monthly*, January, 1865.

"Harriet Hosmer's Zenobia," *Atlantic Monthly*, February, 1865.

"If Massa Put Guns Into Our Han's," *Atlantic Monthly*, April, 1865.

"The Loan of a Lyre," in *The Treasure Trove Series*, New York, 1865.

"An International Affair," *Harper's Monthly*, January-February, 1866.

"The Gray Jockey: A Rocky Mountain Camp-Fire Story," *Harper's Monthly*, March, 1866.

"A Result of 'The Lambeth Casual'," *Harper's Monthly*, September, 1866.

"E Pluribus Unum," *Galaxy*, November, 1866.

"Little Briggs and I," *Northern Lights*, January, 1867.

"Fleeing to Tarshish," *Northern Lights*, February, 1867.

"The Proper Use of Grandfathers," *Northern Lights*, March, 1867.

"A Brace of Boys," *Harper's Monthly*, March, 1867.

"A Reformed Ring-Man," *Harper's Monthly*, August, 1867.

"What Shall They Do To Be Saved," *Harper's Monthly,* August, 1867.

"Pairing Off," *Harper's Monthly,* September, 1867.

Little Brother and Other Genre Tales, Boston: Lee & Shepard, 1867.

"The Proper Use of Grandfathers," in *Stories and Sketches by our Best Authors,* Boston: Lee & Shepard, 1867.

"Uncle George," *Harper's Monthly,* May, 1868.

The Household Angel, Harper's Bazaar, May-August, 1868.

Ed., with Horace Day, *The Opium Habit,* New York: Harper Brothers, 1868.

"What Shall They Do to Be Saved" and "Outlines of the Opium Cure," in *The Opium Habit,* New York: Harper Brothers, 1868.

"Too Late," *Harper's Monthly,* June, 1869.

"Draw Your Conclusions," *Harper's Monthly,* August, 1869.

The Heart of the Continent, Boston: Hurd and Houghton, 1870.

The Heart of the Continent, Sampson Low and Son, 1870.

"To Florence, On Her Fifteenth Birthday," *Harper's Bazar,* May 1870.

"A La Dame A La Voile Noire," *Appleton's Magazine,* July, 1870.

Letters in *Theriaki and Their Last Dose,* Chicago: Evening Journal Print, 1870.

"Hymn of Forbearance," *New York Commercial Advertiser,* December 24, 1870. (Published along with eulogy by Frank B. Carpenter).

"To M.S., with thanks for a paper-knife," *Appleton's Magazine,* November, 1870.

"Oh how in yearning have I spent my time," ms., date unknown (From collection of Schaefer Library, Union College.

"Where the dreary winds complain," ms. poem, private collection, 1870.

"The School," *Child Life; A Collection of Poems,* Ed. by John Greenleaf Whittier, J. R. Osgood Company, 1871.

"Too Late," *A New Library of Poetry and Song,* Ed. by William Cullen Bryant, New York: J. B. Ford and Co., 1876.

"Niagara," "A La Dame a Voile Noire," "To the Home of All the Living," "Ode to Night," "To a Red Headed Girl," "The Jolly Fellow," in *The Princeton Poets,* Ed. by S. Miller Hageman, Princeton: Princeton University Press, 1879.

"Ben Thirlwall's Schooldays," and "Selections from A Brace of Boys," *Humorous Masterpieces from American Literature,* Ed. by Edward T. Mason, New York and London, G. P. Putnam's Sons, 1886. (Excerpt from "Little Briggs and I".)

"The Yosemite Valley," *Half Hours with the Best American Authors,* Selected and Arranged by Charles Morris, Philadelphia: J. B. Lippincott Co., 1887. (Excerpt from *Heart of the Continent.*)

"The Hour and the Power of Darkness," *Library of American Literature*, Ed. by Edmund C. Stedman & Ellen Hutchinson, 1888. (excerpt from *The Hasheesh Eater*.)

Augustus Jones, Jr., Boston: Lee and Shepard, the Good Company Series, 1891. (Reprint of *Little Brother and Other Genre Tales*.)

"Little Briggs and I," *Little Classics, Volume 11: Heroism,* Ed. by Rossiter Johnson, Boston and New York: Houghton, Mifflin, and Company, 1900.

"Too Late," *Little Classics, Volume 16: Minor Poems,* Ed. by Rossiter Johnson, Boston and New York: Houghton Mifflin and Co., 1900.

"A Brace of Boys," *Little Classics, Volume 17: Humanity,* Ed. by Rossiter Johnson, Boston and New York: Houghton, Mifflin and Co., 1900.

"Loan of a Lyre," *Bancroft Library of the World's Best Short Masterpieces*, New York: A. Sanderson-Whitten Co., 1901 (reprint of the Treasure Trove Series, 1865).

The Hasheesh Eater, New York: S. G. Rains, 1903.

"A Brace of Boys" (selections), *Little Masterpieces of American Wit and Humor,* Ed. by Thomas L. Masson, New York: Doubleday, Page and Company, 1903.

"A Brace of Boys," *Short Story Classics,* Vol. 1, Ed. by William Patten, New York: Collier and Son, 1905.

The Hasheesh Eater (excerpts), *The Equinox. A Journal of Scientific Illuminism,* London: September, 1910.

"Socrates Snooks," in *The Best Loved Poems of the American People*, Hazel Felleman, Editor, Garden City Publishing; New York: Doubleday, 1936.

The Hasheesh Eater (excerpts), in Robert Walton, *Marihuana: America's New Drug Problem,* Philadelphia: Lippincott, 1938.

The Hasheesh Eater (excerpts), in *Drugs and the Mind,* Ed. by Robert S. DeRopp, New York: Grove Press, 1957.

The Hasheesh Eater, in *The Hasty Papers. A One Shot Review,* Ed. by Alfred Leslie, New York, 1960.

The Hasheesh Eater (excerpts), in *The Drug Experience,* Ed. by David Ebin, New York: Grove Press, 1961.

The Hasheesh Eater (excerpts), *The Marijuana Papers,* Ed. by David Solomon, Indianapolis: Bobbs-Merrill, 1966.

The Hasheesh Eater, Louisville: Lost Cause Press, 1969.

The Hasheesh Eater, Upper Saddle River, NJ: Gregg Press, 1970.

The Hasheesh Eater (excerpts), *Berkeley Barb,* September 11, 1970-September 18, 1970.

The Heart of the Continent, New York: AMS Press, 1971.

The Hasheesh Eater (excerpts), in *Drugs and the Other Self,* New York: Harper & Row, 1971.

The Hasheesh Eater, San Francisco, Level Press, Fitz Hugh Ludlow Memorial Library edition, 1975.

The Hasheesh Eater, San Francisco: City Lights Books, 1979.

The Opium Habit, New York: Arno Press, Addiction in America Series, 1981.

The Hasheesh Eater, Portland: Subterranean Press: A City Lights Book, 1989.

The Hasheesh Eater, (excerpts), in *Psychedelic Illuminations,* 1993.

The Hasheesh Eater, Edited and with an Introduction by Stephen Rachman, Rutgers University Press; New Brunswick, New Jersey, 2006.

ACKNOWLEDGMENTS

The editors benefited from the attention and kindnesses of Fitz Hugh Ludlow's alma mater, Union College. Thanks to Jill Murphy, Assistant Professor of English & American Literature, for her arrangement of our lecture on campus, a classroom workshop, and general encouragement for the project. Thanks also to Ethan Pearce, K.A. in C.C., for his introduction to Professor Murphy.

Thanks India Spartz, Head of Special Collections & Archives, for approving access to the collections and even babysitting one of our transcription assistants. Thanks Annette LeClair, Director of Collection and Technical Services, who gave us the key introduction to the HathiTrust project.

The HathiTrust Digital Library is a national treasure. This project would have taken five years without it. Thanks also to the University of Michigan, our partner institution for access.

While not used directly on this project for digital versions, the Atlantic Monthly and Harper's magazines are to be commended for having so much of their historically important archives available in digital forms; these archives were very helpful in research and organization for this project. The New York Public Library was also important for similar reasons. We also thank the University of Virginia's Albert and Shirley Small Special Collections Library for permission to print an image from Ludlow's letter to Edward Stansbury.

Despite the advances of digital archiving, there were still hundreds of pages of documents that had to be manually transcribed, despite occasionally poor source copies. Thanks to Teddy Dulchinos for the excellent job on the *Masks and Music* broadsheets, to David Olio for the work on the Helen Ludlow manuscript book of poems, and Krystina Crimi and Diana Fowler for their intrepid work on the sadly deteriorated *Due South* diaries.

As every editor knows, a good proofreader is worth his or her weight in bitcoin, and while digital scanning introduces peculiar typos of its own, our readers also had to contend with Ludlow's idiosyncratic and often archaic spelling and punctuation; exotic place names that had not yet achieved a consensus spelling; and his Twain-esque attempts to depict various American dialects and immigrant accents. The latter engendered several nightmares in which single quotation marks loomed menacingly. Thanks to our proofreaders Mindi Meltz, Becky Shipkosky and Krystina Crimi.

And special thanks to Jack Emery Taylor for the beautiful cover art and Susan Yost for her skillful and gorgeous layout, cover design and illustration work.

Rather than update all of Ludlow's spellings into contemporary American English, our method was to keep the older spellings as much as possible to keep the 'flavor' of his writing, and only change place names that were not clear, and update alternate spellings that 'look' like typos, to keep the reader's distractions to a minimum. Obviously in a project of this scope there will be cracks, but the editors can only hope that that will be how the light gets in.

ABOUT THE EDITORS

DONALD P. DULCHINOS is the author of *Pioneer of Inner Space: The Life of Fitz Hugh Ludlow, Forbidden Sacraments: The Survival of Shamanism in Western Civilization and Neurosphere: The Convergence of Evolution, Group Mind, and the Internet.* He has found time between these projects for a career in the information and telecommunications technology industry.

STEPHEN CRIMI is the author of *Katabatic Wind: Good Craic Fueled by Fumes from the Abyss*; the editor of two collections of talks by biodynamic pioneer Alan Chadwick, *Performance in the Garden*, and *Reverence, Obedience and the Invisible in the Garden*; and the publisher of Logosophia Books. He lives with his wife Krys in Asheville NC, where he continues to mid-wife literature amidst the splendor of her gardens.

Dulchinos and Crimi graduated three years apart from Union College in Schenectady, NY, where they followed Fitz Hugh Ludlow as members of the Kappa Alpha Literary Society, and walked the same campus where Ludlow had his visions more than a century earlier.

Designer's Note on Font Selection

THIS SERIES OF COLLECTED WORKS by Fitz Hugh Ludlow is set in Adobe Caslon Pro to capture the spirit of Ludlow's era.

The Caslon font was originally cut by William Caslon (1692–1766) circa 1722 in London, and was used prolifically throughout the American colonies and England in eighteenth century printing. Early versions of the American Constitution and Declaration of Independence were set in Caslon, and it was a favorite of Benjamin Franklin who applied it in his own print shops.

Of the many modern variants, the Adobe version, created by American designer Carol Twombly from 1990-1992, is one of the few that remain truest to the original design.

Caslon is considered an English Baroque typeface, apparent in its elegant swashes and ligatures. Robert Bringhurst in his book *Elements of Typographic Style* describes it as "rich with activity and takes delight in the restless and dramatic play of contradictory forms."

An interesting characteristic of the original cut is that it did not contain a bold style. Instead, a larger size, italic, small or large cap was used for emphasis.

CPSIA information can be obtained
at www.ICGtesting.com
Printed in the USA
LVOW10*1759270618
582079LV00005B/90/P